C. S. Lewis

& Philosophy
as a Way of Life

A
Comprehensive
Historical
Examination
of His
Philosophical
Thoughts

Adam Barkman

C.S. Lewis & Philosophy as a Way of Life
Copyright © 2009 Adam James Barkman
Allentown, PA

Zossima Press titles may be purchased for business or promotional use or special sales.

Book design by Robert Trexler

10-9-8-7-6-5-4-3-2-1

Zossima
Press

ISBN 0-9723221-6-7
ISBN-13 978-9-7223221-6-4

This book is dedicated to

My Teacher, Mr. B

and

My Students, Dan, Gord, Tony, Sam and Heather

Acknowledgements

To begin with, I would like to thank my wife, Ashley, for reading and editing the manuscript of this book countless times: although Lewis said that the sign of a good book is that it will be reread, I'm sure he wasn't thinking about those who reread for the sake of editing!

I would also like to thank my editor, Bob Trexler, for his enthusiasm for this project and for accommodating my many requests: it is a rare thing for an author to have such freedom when it comes to publication.

Thanks to Heidi Truty at the Marion E. Wade Center for being such a gracious hostess and for sending me copies of many of Lewis's unpublished manuscripts (even when I was above the photocopy limit!).

Likewise, I would like to thank Libby and Kasia, librarians at the University of North Carolina at Chapel Hill, for giving me complete access to their C. S. Lewis Collection and for letting me take photographs of many of the books.

I would also like to thank Don King and *Christian Scholar's Review* for allowing me to republish herein part of my essay "'We Must Go Back to Our Bibles': A Response to Mary Stewart Van Leeuwen." *Christian Scholar's Review* 36, no. 4 (Summer 2007): 445-54.

I am grateful to Rachel Churchill and the C. S. Lewis Ltd. for giving me permission to make copies of many of the unpublished material that I used herein.

Thanks also to my students in the EIC for helping me index this book.

I must also acknowledge the support and constructive criticism I received from David Clark, David Baggett, Jim Como, René Wouldenberg and Bob Sweetman: truly as "iron sharpens iron," or, perhaps better: "as, you, the blacksmiths, sharpened the iron of my book..."

Two influential Christians mentioned in these pages who are worthy of tribute died while this book was in production: Fr. Richard Neuhaus and Cardinal Avery Dulles. Their lives are good examples of what I mean by philosophy as a way of life.

Finally, it would be unjust not to mention the blessings I have received from both my mentor, Mr. B, who introduced me to the work of C. S. Lewis, and my former students at Prairie Bible College, particularly Tony, Dan, Sam, Gord and Heather: it is to all of you – you lovers of Truth – to whom this book is warmly dedicated.

Table of Contents

Introduction

C. S. Lewis and Philosophy?

A. J. Ayer, one of the leaders of logical positivism in Britain, recounts an exchange he once had with C. S. Lewis:

> While the analytic movement, in one form or another, took increasing control of the English philosophical scene, there were some pockets of resistance to it. One of those who fought a rearguard action against it in Oxford was the English scholar C. S. Lewis, who had once had the ambition to become a tutor in philosophy and still took a lively interest in the subject. He presided over the Socratic Club, which then drew a large audience to meetings at which the principal speakers usually struck a religious note. At one of these meetings, not long after my return to Oxford, I undertook a reply to a paper by Michael Foster, who had spent part of the war as an officer in Northern Ireland and had come back strengthened in his Puritanism. I dealt with his paper rather harshly, and when he made little effort to defend it, C. S. Lewis took over from him. Lewis and I then engaged in a flashy debate, which entertained the audience but did neither of us much credit, while Foster sat by, suffering in silence.[1]

This passage is interesting because it shows C. S. Lewis, a man generally perceived as a literary critic, fantasy writer and / or lay theologian, engaged in a philosophical debate with one of the twentieth century's most influential philosophers. And this was not just a one-time occurrence: over the course of his life, Lewis crossed paths with many great philosophers such as Gilbert

---

1   A. J. Ayer, *Part of My Life: Memoirs of a Philosopher* (London: Harcourt Brace Jovanovich, 977), 296-7.

Ryle,[2] Antony Flew,[3] C. E. M. Joad,[4] Fredrick Copleston,[5] Basil Mitchell,[6] and George Grant.[7] If one thinks about it for a moment, these philosophical debates point to a dimension of Lewis – a philosophical dimension – which has been greatly overshadowed by his theological and literary accomplishments.

This brings me to the purpose of this book. By and large it seems as though friends and critics alike have been content with reducing any discussion of Lewis and philosophy, if they mention it at all, to his apologetics. I find this lack of attention given to all of Lewis's philosophical interests both saddening because it robs "Lewis of the philosophic insights that constitute the very texture of his apologetic,"[8] and surprising given the vast outpouring of publications about Lewis every year. It is lamentable that, for instance, during the Christmas 2005 holiday season alone, more than twenty books were written about *The Lion, the Witch and the Wardrobe*, none of which told us anything new about Lewis ("a shelf-full of mediocrity,"[9] as one critic put it). Of course there have been a few attempts at drawing attention to Lewis and philosophy, notably: the recently released collection of essays on Lewis's understanding of Truth, Beauty and Goodness (which is wonderfully

---

2   John Mabbott, *Oxford Memories* (Oxford: Thornton's, 1986), 77-8.
3   "The Socratic Club was a lively forum for debates between atheists and Christians, and I was a regular participant at its meetings. Its redoubtable president from 1942 to 1954 was the famous Christian writer C. S. Lewis." Antony Flew, *There is a God: How the World's Most Notorious Atheist Changed His Mind* (New York: HarperOne, 2007), 22-3. Cf. Antony Flew and Gary Habermas, "My Pilgrimage from Atheism to Theism: A Discussion between Antony Flew and Gary Habermas," *Philosophia Christi* 6, no. 2 (2004): 200. Cf. Antony Flew and Gary Habermas, "From Atheism to Deism: A Conversation between Antony Flew and Gary Habermas," in *C. S. Lewis as Philosopher: Truth, Goodness, and Beauty*, ed. David Baggett, Gary Habermas and Jerry Walls, 37-52 (Downers Grove, IL: InterVarsity Press, 2008).
4   Christopher W. Mitchell, "University Battles: C. S. Lewis and the Oxford University Socratic Club," in *C. S. Lewis: Lightbearer in the Shadowlands; The Evangelistic Vision of C. S. Lewis*, ed. Angus J. L. Menuge, 329-52 (Wheaton: Crossway Books, 1997), 329.
5   Walter Hooper, "Oxford's Bonny Fighter," in *C. S. Lewis at the Breakfast Table and Other Reminiscences*, ed. James Como, 137-85 (San Diego: Harcourt Brace & Company, 1992), 180.
6   Basil Mitchell and Andrew Walker, "Reflections on C. S. Lewis, Apologetics, and the Moral Tradition," in *Rumours of Heaven: Essays in Celebration of C. S. Lewis*, ed. Andrew Walker and James Patrick, 7-26 (London: Eagle, 1998), 7. Basil Mitchell, "C. S. Lewis on *The Abolition of Man*," in *C. S. Lewis Remembered*, ed. Harry Lee Poe and Rebecca Whitten Poe, 174-83 (Grand Rapids, MI: Zondervan, 2006), 174. 0
7   Ron Dart, "C. S. Lewis and George Grant: A Tale of Two Anglican Tories," *Pilgrimage: The Toronto C. S. Lewis Society Bulletin* 9, no. 2 (April 2002): 1.
8   James Patrick, *The Magdalen Metaphysicals: Idealism and Orthodoxy at Oxford 1901-1945* (N.p.: Mercer University Press, 1985), 164.
9   Laura Miller, "Return to Narnia," *The Los Angeles Times*, December 4, 2005.

titled *C. S. Lewis as Philosopher*),[10] another recently released collection of essays on *The Chronicles of Narnia* and philosophy,[11] Erik Wielenberg's book which discusses the views of Lewis, Russell and Hume largely on natural theology,[12] French philosopher Iréne Fernandez's book on Lewis's theory of reason and myth,[13] the third volume of Bruce Edward's *C. S. Lewis: Life, Works, and Legacy*,[14] Owen Barfield's and Lionel Adey's insights into Lewis's "Great War" with Owen Barfield,[15] Peter Kreeft's selected essays on Lewis's argument from desire and Natural Law,[16] Victor Reppert's books and essays on Lewis's argument from reason,[17] Richard Purtill's philosophical insights into Lewis's theological project,[18] Peter Schakel's discussion about reason

10 David Baggett, Gary Habermas and Jerry Walls, eds., *C. S. Lewis as Philosopher: Truth, Goodness, and Beauty* (Downers Grove, IL: InterVarsity Press, 2008). Let me extend my gratitude to David Baggett, who graciously provided me with all the chapters to this book before it was published.
11 Gregory Bassham and Jerry L. Walls, eds., *The Chronicles of Narnia and Philosophy: The Lion, the Witch, and the Worldview* (Chicago: Open Court, 2005).
12 Erik Wielenberg, *God and the Reach of Reason: C.S. Lewis, David Hume, and Bertrand Russell* (Cambridge: Cambridge University Press, 2008). Also see Adam Barkman, review of *God and the Reach of Reason: C.S. Lewis, David Hume, and Bertrand Russell*, by Erik Wielenberg, *Christian Scholar's Review* 38, no. 2 (Fall 2008): 160-3.
13 Iréne Fernandez, *C. S. Lewis – Mythe, Raison Ardente: Imagination et Réalité Selon C. S. Lewis* (Geneva: Ad Solem, 2005).
14 Bruce Edwards, ed., *Apologist, Philosopher, & Theologian*, vol. 3, *C. S. Lewis: Life, Works, and Legacy* (West Point, CT: Greenwood, 2007).
15 Owen Barfield, *Owen Barfield on C. S. Lewis*, ed. G. B. Tennyson (Middletown, CT: Wesleyan University Press, 1989). Lionel Adey, *C. S. Lewis's 'Great War' with Owen Barfield* (Victoria, BC: University of Victoria Press, 1978).
16 Peter Kreeft, "C. S. Lewis' Argument from Desire," appendix A in *Heaven: The Heart's Deepest Longing*, 201-32 (San Francisco: Ignatius Press, 1989). Peter Kreeft, *C. S. Lewis for the Third Millennium: Six Essays on The Abolition of Man* (San Francisco: Ignatius Press, 1994).
17 Victor Reppert, *C. S. Lewis's Dangerous Idea: In Defence of the Argument from Reason* (Downers Grove, IL: Intervarsity Press, 2003). Victor Reppert, "The Green Witch and the Great Debate: Freeing Narnia from the Spell of the Lewis-Anscombe Legend," in *The Chronicles of Narnia and Philosophy: The Lion, the Witch and the Wardrobe*, ed. Gregory Bassham and Jerry Walls, 260-72 (Chicago: Open Court, 2005). Victor Reppert, "*Miracles*: C. S. Lewis's Critique of Naturalism," in *Apologist, Philosopher, & Theologian*, vol. 3, *C. S. Lewis: Life, Works, and Legacy*, ed. Bruce Edwards, 153-82 (Westport, CT: Praeger, 2007). Victor Reppert, "Defending the Dangerous Idea: An Update on Lewis's Argument from Reason," in *C. S. Lewis as Philosopher: Truth, Goodness, and Beauty*, ed. David Baggett, Gary Habermas and Jerry Walls, 53-67 (Downers Grove, IL: InterVarsity Press, 2008). Also see Adam Barkman, review of *C. S. Lewis's Dangerous Idea: A Philosophical Defense of Lewis's Argument from Reason*, by Victor Reppert, *Pilgrimage* 12, no. 1 (January 2005): 8.
18 Richard Purtill, *C. S. Lewis's Case for the Christian Faith* (San Francisco: Harper & Row, 1985). Richard Purtill, *Lord of the Elves and Eldils: Fantasy and Philosophy in C. S.*

and the imagination,[19] James Patrick's essays on Lewis and idealism,[20] Basil Mitchell's papers about Lewis and ethics,[21] Christopher Mitchell's essay on Lewis and the Socratic Club,[22] John Beversluis's attack on Lewis's rational religion,[23] and selected essays by prominent Catholic theologians like Avery Cardinal Dulles, who said Lewis was "competent in philosophy,"[24] and Joseph Ratzinger (now Pope Benedict XVI), who spoke of Lewis as "the English author and philosopher."[25] Nevertheless, while all of these books and essays touch on various aspects of Lewis's philosophical thought, none of them have done justice to Lewis's insistence that "a complete philosophy must get in *all* the facts,"[26] for none of them have provided (1) a clear and complete historical account of Lewis's understanding of the purpose of philosophy (hence the constant misunderstanding of the "Anscombe Legend"), (2) a complete historical and historiographical account of Lewis's philosophical

Lewis and J. R. R. Tolkien (Grand Rapids, MI: Zondervan, 1974).

19 Peter Schakel, *Reason and Imagination in C. S. Lewis: A Study of Till We Have Faces* (Grand Rapids, MI: Eerdmans, 1984).

20 Patrick, *The Magdalen Metaphysicals*, 109-34. James Patrick, "C. S. Lewis and Idealism," in *Rumours of Heaven: Essays in Celebration of C. S. Lewis*, ed. Andrew Walker and James Patrick, 156-73 (London: Eagle, 1998).

21 Mitchell, "Reflections on C. S. Lewis, Apologetics, and the Moral Tradition," 7-26. Mitchell, "C. S. Lewis on *The Abolition of Man*," 174-83.

22 Mitchell, "University Battles: C. S. Lewis and the Oxford University Socratic Club," 329-52.

23 John Beversluis, *C. S. Lewis and the Search for Rational Religion* (Grand Rapids, MI: Eerdmans, 1985). It should be noted that while a second, revised edition of this book was released in 2007, I have not made use of it since all of the basic arguments – with their respective theses and conclusions – are basically unchanged.

24 Avery Cardinal Dulles, "C. S. Lewis: The Case for Apologetics," *CSL: The Bulletin of the New York C. S. Lewis Society* 36, no. 1 (January-February 2005): 1-9.

25 Joseph Ratzinger, "Consumer Materialism and Christian Hope," http://www.catholic-ew.org.uk/resource/totf/ratzinger.html (accessed August 4, 2005). Cf. "I think one of the most illuminating comments I have ever heard about Lewis was from someone who hadn't met him but who could understand human motivation very well and who also was a writer, and that was the Pope. I met him in 1984, and as I understand it the meeting was at his suggestion because he was the one who wanted to talk about Lewis. John Paul had been reading the works of Lewis at least since the fifties. Anyway, it was a great moment for me when I had the talk with him and he began by asking me, 'Do you still love your old friend C. S. Lewis?' I said, 'Yes, Holy Father, both *storge* and *philia*,' and he said, 'Ah, you knew I liked *The Four Loves*!' But at the end of the interview he then made a comment about Lewis. He said, 'C. S. Lewis *knew* what his apostolate was.' There was a long pause, then he said, 'And he *did* it!'" Walter Hooper, "Tolkien and C. S. Lewis: An Interview with Walter Hooper," in *Tolkein: A Celebration*, ed. Joseph Pearce, 190-8 (San Francisco: Ignatius Press, 2001), 194.

26 C. S. Lewis, *Miracles*, in *C. S. Lewis: Selected Books* [Long Edition] (London: HarperCollins, 1999), 1131.

journey, (3) an examination of Lewis's unpublished philosophical material and marginalia in his editions of the philosophers, nor (4) a unified look (I do not say *systematic*, for such I believe to be impossible with Lewis) at how Lewis saw all the branches of philosophy. My purpose, consequently, is to rectify this situation by attempting a complete exploration of the history of Lewis's philosophical thought; however, I should add for those critics who expect to find in this book detailed discussions of Lewis's philosophical arguments that because many of Lewis's philosophical arguments, particularly those in natural theology, have been suitably dealt with elsewhere (e.g. in Reppert, Wielenberg, Baggett et al.), my book will mostly focus on explaining the *historical* aspect of Lewis and philosophy.

So what was the Oxford don's philosophy? In regard to philosophical labels, Lewis's mature thought reveals him to have been an eclectic thinker who, if one had to put him in a box, is best described as a proponent of Neoplatonic Christianity, a philosophy which attempts to synchronize, as well as it can, the best of Plato, Aristotle, the Stoics and pagan religion with Christianity. In regard to the purpose of philosophy, Lewis insisted that philosophy is the transformation of life and not merely an academic exercise. In this respect he is in agreement with the philosophers of antiquity, starting with Socrates, who understood philosophy to be "a method of spiritual progress which demanded a radical conversion and transformation of the individual's way of being."[27] Moreover, Lewis agreed with such philosophers that the truly philosophical life will utilize not only reason, but also the imagination and other faculties of the soul to probe physical, metaphysical and mythological reality for answers as to how one ought to live.

Hence, it is my view that if one understands philosophy in the classical sense, as a way of life or a process by which one seeks after knowledge and then attempts to live by its dictates, Lewis may be justly considered a philosopher. Vector Reppert, although he formulates it differently than I, agrees:

> Lewis was a thinker with what I believe to be outstanding philosophical instincts. . . . It is sometimes presupposed by those who are familiar with the technical side of a discipline like philosophy that no one who is not similarly a 'professional' has anything serious to say. But of course 'professionalism' in philosophy is a rather recent development: the majority of those who have made significant contributions to philosophy over the past twenty-five centuries would not qualify as 'professional' philosophers in the contemporary sense.[28]

27 Pierre Hadot, *Philosophy as a Way of Life: Spiritual Exercises from Socrates to Foucault*, ed. Arnold I. Davidson, trans. Michael Chase (Oxford: Blackwell, 1995), 265.
28 Reppert, *C. S. Lewis's Dangerous Idea*, 12, 15. Cf. "Technically, [Lewis] was throughout

Nevertheless, while I will be arguing throughout this book that Lewis is a philosopher in the ancient sense of the word (and one who has much to say to contemporary philosophers[29]), let me strongly emphasize that I have no intention of turning a blind eye (as so many Lewis scholars do) to Lewis's philosophical shortcomings, nor do I intend to prove in any way that Lewis is a "serious" or "professional" philosopher if by this we mean, as Pierre Hadot does when he speaks of the modern understanding of the philosopher, someone who strives "to invent . . . a new construction, systematic and abstract, intended somehow or other to explain the universe, or at the least . . . elaborate a new discourse about language."[30] It would be odd indeed if after lamenting the poor state of Lewis scholarship, I would then proceed to commit the most common of all mistakes in regard to Lewis scholarship – to oversimplify him and then hail him as infallible.

Methodologically, I will be using a combination of a problem-centered approach (how do we solve this apparent inconsistency?) and a genealogical approach (what came before this?) to reconstruct Lewis's philosophy. And while these two approaches can provide a fairly accurate picture of what is going on, historical-philosophic reconstruction is no straightforward matter as the meaning of terms and concepts change from philosopher to

---

most of his adult life a professor of literature. But really, he was a philosopher. Philosophy is the love of wisdom, along with an unending desire to find it, understand it, put it into action, and pass it on to others. Lewis brought a philosophical caste of mind to everything he did." Tom Morris, "Foreword," in *C. S. Lewis as Philosopher: Truth, Goodness, and Beauty*, ed. David Baggett, Gary Habermas and Jerry Walls, 9-10 (Downers Grove, IL: InterVarsity Press, 2008), 10. Cf. Paul Vincent, "C. S. Lewis as Amateur Philosopher," *The New York C. S. Lewis Society Bulletin* no. 9 (July 1970): 1-3. Cf. "The popular literature on C. S. Lewis, from the first, has tended to run to excessive adulation; yet his Christian apologetics have usually been dismissed out of hand by serious philosophers and theologians. Neither attitude, as it seems to me, properly takes Lewis's measure." Hugo Meynell, "An Attack on C. S. Lewis," *Faith and Philosophy* 8, no. 3 (July 1991): 305.

29   Thus, I agree with Erik Wielenberg when he writes, "Whatever the reason for the relative neglect of Lewis in contemporary philosophy, I believe that it is a mistake, and one of my aims in this book is to show that Lewis's philosophical work is worthy of serious attention. . . . [Drawing attention to weaknesses in naturalism] is among Lewis's most important contributions to contemporary philosophy." Wielenberg, *God and the Reach of Reason: C. S. Lewis, David Hume and Bertrand Russell*, 4, 104.

30   Pierre Hadot, *What is Ancient Philosophy?* trans. Michael Chase (Cambridge, MA: The Belknap Press of Harvard University Press, 2004), 2. Hence, I agree with Scott Burson and Jerry Walls when they write, "So the first thing we should realize is that when we come to Lewis . . . we should not come expecting the philosophical rigor of a Plantinga or Swinburne. Those who come with such expectations are sure to be disappointed." Scott Burson and Jerry Walls, *C. S. Lewis & Francis Schaeffer: Lessons for a New Century from the Most Influential Apologists of Our Time* (Downers Grove, IL: InterVarsity Press, 1998), 240.

philosopher. And even this would not be so difficult were Lewis not so well-read and eclectic, for the huge diversity of philosophical positions that he took over the years, culminating in Neoplatonic Christianity, make getting at the meaning of such apparently simple words as "idealism," "reason" or "imagination" extremely difficult. Additionally, while it is philosophically and literarily tricky to look to works of fiction for insight into an author's philosophy, I believe that in many cases we can do this with Lewis, for as James Como has pointed out, "From annotation to notebook, from notebook to essay or address, from address to one sort of book, from one sort of book to another – from one way of knowing to another – Lewis and his world of discourse form a coherent whole, a tapestry of meaning."[31] Nevertheless, the reader must keep in mind that all of this requires a lot of finesse and gap-filling, an activity which Lewis himself was somewhat skeptical of despite being an eminent student of history and the evolution of ideas; as he said, "I wonder how much *Quellenforschung* in our studies of older literature seems solid only because those who knew the facts are dead and cannot contradict it?"[32]

As for the structure of this book, I have divided it into two main parts. In the first part, which I have divided into five chapters, I discuss Lewis's *definition of philosophy* and his *philosophical journey*, which, I argue, culminates in the Oxford don's *identity as a philosopher*. Thus, the first chapter focuses on the historical definition of philosophy as way of life. The second chapter begins to relate this understanding of philosophy to Lewis, particularly in regard to the roles that rational analysis and training had in his philosophical journey. The third chapter develops this further by shifting focus to the crucial affect in Lewis's philosophical journey: heavenly desire. The fourth chapter further refines Lewis's philosophical journey by discussing the centrality of one object of heavenly desire, Myth. And the fifth chapter completes the sketch of Lewis's philosophical journey by examining the role of culture in the Oxford don's philosophy. In the second part of this book, I narrow the discussion of Lewis and philosophy by investigating the *particulars* of the Oxford don's philosophy. Subsequently, chapter six focuses on metaphysics and some aspects of natural theology. Chapter seven explores Lewis's psychology, logic and epistemology. Chapter eight has to do with Lewis's ethics. Chapter nine examines Lewis's socio-political philosophy,

---

31   James Como, *Branches to Heaven: The Geniuses of C. S. Lewis* (Dallas: Spense Publishing, 1998), 141.

32   C. S. Lewis, *The Collected Letters of C. S. Lewis: Volume III; Narnia, Cambridge, and Joy 1950-1963*, ed. Walter Hooper (San Francisco: HarperSanFrancisco, 2007), 992 [November 28, 1958].

including issues such as family, politics and education. And chapter ten deals with the Oxford don's aesthetics. Finally, I conclude with an assessment of Lewis's philosophical project as a whole.

Part I

Philosophical Definition, Journey & Identity

Chapter One

Definition

Lewis's definition of philosophy "as a way of life" was not his own; rather, as I mentioned in the introduction, it belonged to antiquity. Consequently, before Lewis's philosophy can even be discussed, it is crucial that we first examine some of the most important philosophies of antiquity in order to get a clearer idea of this definition. Furthermore, since I have taken the phrase "philosophy as a way of life" from Pierre Hadot, I propose to start by laying out his criteria for philosophy as a way of life and then proceed to investigate the primary sources of antiquity themselves to defend my two-part claim – to be dealt with in this chapter and the next – that ancient philosophy was considered a complete way of life and that Lewis accepted this definition as his own.

I: Ancient Philosophy as a Way of Life

In his 1987 book, *Philosophy as a Way of Life*, Pierre Hadot defined ancient philosophy as "a method of spiritual progress which demanded radical conversion and transformation of the individual's way of being."[1] Years later, in his 1995 book, *What is Ancient Philosophy?* Hadot refined his definition, claiming that ancient philosophy, at least since the time of Socrates, began as "a choice of life and an existential option" attained in "a complex interrelation with critical reaction to other existential attitudes, with global vision of a certain way of living and of seeing the world, and with voluntary decision itself;"[2] furthermore, Hadot insisted, the ancient philosopher, desiring to live a certain way, joined a philosophical "school," which subsequently helped him, through *askēsis* – disciplined training or the practice of spiritual exercises, such as fasting, meditating, reading, etc. – change his entire way of being as he was expected to live in accordance with the school's philosophy or "vision

---

1   Hadot, *Philosophy as a Way of Life*, 265.
2   Hadot, *What is Ancient Philosophy?* 3.

of the world," which had been revealed by rational, theoretical discourse.[3] Combining these two definitions, Hadot appears to have understood ancient philosophy to be (1) a choice (2) made in a cultural context (3) to follow a certain group of people who (4) had a certain take on life which (5) demanded training – be it "physical," "discursive" or "intuitive"[4] – which (6) was, importantly, the result of rational discourse, and which (7) would ultimately lead to a fully converted life.

While I think this definition of ancient philosophy is excellent, it is possible that Hadot overemphasized the importance of (3) and (4) since Socrates, for instance, does not appear to have belonged to a philosophical "school" like that of the Pythagoreans, Platonists, Aristotelians or Stoics. Furthermore, when we come to Lewis, we shall see that although the Oxford don clearly subscribed to (1), (2), (5), (6) and (7) and although there is a strong case for his having admitted (3) and (4), particularly when he was under the guidance of Kirkpatrick, Lewis, like Socrates, was as much a lone thinker as he was a member of a particular school.

However, this later comment is peripheral, and I would now like to test Hadot's definition of ancient philosophy in order to demonstrate its relative accuracy.

II: Plato

Although philosophy began before Socrates and Plato, it was Plato, and not Pythagoras, who is remembered for defining philosophy or *philo-sophia* as "the love of wisdom."[5] According to Plato, the philosopher is a lover who is attracted by, and drawn to, the Beauty that is present in speculative wisdom and Truth.[6] It is only by pursuing the glimmers of wisdom and Truth that one comes to understand one's place in the cosmos and how one is then to live. What such wisdom partially reveals is that one is made to contemplate "what lies outside the heavens,"[7] the eternal, immaterial Ideas or Forms, for the soul, which is physical[8] but immortal, fell from the heavens, where it

---

3 Ibid.
4 Ibid., 6.
5 Plato *Symposium* 204d.
6 Ibid., 200e. Plato *Phaedrus* 230.
7 Ibid., 247.
8 Not all agree that the Platonic soul is physical (as opposed to immaterial). George Karamanolis, for instance, points out the difficulty in interpreting Plato in this regard, for Karamanolis believes that Plotinus was largely in agreement with Plato when Plotinus rejected the Stoic doctrine of the physicality of the soul and accepted the Aristotelian doctrine of the immateriality of the soul: "Plotinus is more concerned

had previously enjoyed the purely intellectual activity of thinking about the perfect, unchangeable Forms. The soul's fall from its pure vision of the Forms was caused by a turn toward the even-more-physical, mortal, ever-changing world.[9] Hence, the return to happiness, the return to heavenly contemplation, is accomplished by following the knowledge roadmap that the immortal soul has innate within.[10] By remembering or recollecting through the use of dialectic its true home and by following what it learns, the soul can eventually return home.

Thus, while purely theoretical knowledge, contemplation and speculative wisdom may be understood as the highest form of happiness in itself, purely theoretical knowledge is not good enough in this world of flux: the soul must recover its true self through the exercise of both practical wisdom and dietary, meditative and discursive *askēsis*.[11] The result of this exercise is the development of virtue, which in turn leads to eminently rational actions in this life.[12] Hence, Hadot rightly tells us that "for Plato, knowledge is never purely theoretical. It is the transformation of our being; it is virtue."[13]

In short, good men are wise men and it is they and they alone who can eventually escape from the horrible cycle of reincarnation that plagues all "fallen" souls; thus, "the philosopher's soul is ahead of all the rest."[14]

III: Aristotle

After Plato came Aristotle and the peripatetics. While it must be admitted at the onset that they certainly differ from Plato in emphasis, they nevertheless agree with Plato and his Academy by insisting that the truly happy man must not only be a lover of speculative wisdom, but also that speculative wisdom via practical wisdom must produce fruit in the individual. This concept is often easy to overlook because Aristotle is far more systematic than Plato and he is often accused of living in an ivory tower of theoretical knowledge. Yet

---

with the Stoics than with Aristotle, because he finds the Stoic doctrine that the soul is corporeal more mistaken than that of Aristotle, that is, more at odds with and more distortive of Plato's own belief. From the Platonist point of view, Aristotle fared better because he at least did not deny the immaterial status of the soul." George Karamanolis, *Plato and Aristotle in Agreement? Platonists on Aristotle from Antiochus to Porphyry* (Oxford: Oxford University Press, 2006), 219-20.

9   Plato *Phaedrus* 248.
10 Plato *Phaedo* 72b.
11 Plato *Laws* 673-4, 728.
12 Plato *Protagoras* 323d. Plato *Gorgias* 507c.
13 Hadot, *What is Ancient Philosophy?* 70.
14 Plato *Phaedo* 65c.

as we have seen with Plato, it is not impossible to maintain the superiority of the contemplative life, theoretical knowledge and speculative wisdom over and against the practical life and practical wisdom and knowledge *if* one remembers that Aristotle, as much as Plato, thinks that when action is called for – and it is always called for in one form or another since that is what life is – it must be done in virtue, from wisdom. Aristotle himself explains:

> If we are right in our view, and happiness is assumed to be acting well, the active life will be the best, both for every city collectively, and for individuals. Not that a life of action must necessarily have relation to others, as some persons think, nor are those ideas only to be regarded as practical which are pursued for the sake of practical results, but much more the thoughts and contemplations which are independent and complete in themselves; since acting well, and therefore a certain kind of action, is an end, and even in the case of external actions the directing mind is most truly said to act.[15]

Thus, while Aristotle certainly emphasizes theoretical knowledge, recommending, for instance, the philosopher restrict his job to advising political leaders as opposed to Plato's recommendation that the philosopher become a political leader, Aristotle agrees with Plato that philosophy is a way of life and not a *purely* contemplative affair, for the pursuit of wisdom – firstly speculative and secondly practical – and the following of its dictates (i.e. developing virtues) is the key to happiness, which is the goal of life.[16]

IV: Cynicism, Skepticism, Epicureanism and Stoicism

Cynicism, founded by Antisthenes and continued by Diogenes the Cynic, followed on the heels of Platonism and Aristotelianism. Antisthenes was a follower of Socrates who strongly emphasized that virtue is sufficient for happiness. His follower Diogenes the Cynic was called "Socrates gone mad" by Plato, for Diogenes denounced the life of argument and teaching for the life genuinely lived in accordance with nature, which for him meant that which was minimally required for human life.[17] The Cynics would have agreed that philosophy is a way of life, for while their philosophy does not emphasize teaching others, it does emphasize the life lived in accordance with their philosophy and as such is achieved only through *askēsis* or the practice of spiritual exercises such as walking barefoot in the snow or eating whatever can be found, which are, of course, concrete ways of reinforcing

---

15   Aristotle *Politics* 1325b15-20.
16   Aristotle *Ethics* 1097b20-1098a22.
17   Diogenes Laertius *Lives of the Philosophers* 6.54.

that the happy life is the simple life.

Pyrrho of Elis, the founder of Pyrrhonism, and Sextus Empiricus, the one who developed Pyrrhonism into Skepticism, would also have accepted the definition of philosophy as a way of life. According to them, the philosopher develops arguments to set up opposition between all beliefs to demonstrate that all judgments (the cause of much fear and pain) must be suspended, the result of which is relative freedom from anxiety, which is the closest thing[18] Skeptics have to happiness: "Skepticism is an ability to set up an opposition of appearances and thoughts, in any way at all, an ability from which we come, through the equal force of the opposing statements and states of affairs, first into suspension and after that into freedom from disturbance."[19]

Epicurus founded the school of Epicureanism, which teaches that the goal of life is pleasure. At first glance it might seem that they are an exception to our definition of philosophy, but it is not so; for the Epicureans, philosophy is to be lived just as much as it is for all the other schools we have looked at. Everything, therefore, seems to turn on what the Epicureans call "pleasure." According to them, pleasure is chiefly found in freedom from fear – fear of death, the gods, etc: "We do what we do to avoid suffering and fear."[20] Epicurus demonstrates how philosophy is a way of life by insisting that through the use of reason one can come to understand that the soul is mortal and that the gods are made of material atoms (like all of the cosmos) and are perfectly good (i.e. unconcerned with judging us). Philosophy, therefore, is therapeutic; it is a life that trains the philosopher not to desire or pursue things that are either unnecessary but natural (e.g. sex) or unnecessary and unnatural (e.g. fame and power).[21] The pursuit of things that can only cause more anxiety and pain are bad, for pleasure is found in peace and harmony.[22]

Perhaps the least controversial when it comes to understanding philosophy as a way of life is Stoicism, founded by Zeno of Citium. Zeno was hugely influenced by the ethics (but not the metaphysics and epistemology) of Socrates and Plato. In particular, the Stoics agree that all men desire the

---

18   Martha Nussbaum, *The Therapy of Desire: Theory and Practice in Hellenistic Ethics* (Princeton: Princeton University Press, 1996), 301.
19   Sextus Empiricus *Outlines of Pyrrhonism* 1.8.
20   Epicurus *Letter to Menoecus* §128.
21   Ibid.
22   After Lewis became a Christian, he charged the Epicureans with loving comfort more than truth; if so, this would problematize the Epicurean stance. Nevertheless, there is nothing in Epicurus himself, at least, that suggests he was disingenuous in claiming comfort was the result of the love of truth (i.e. rational inquiry) and not vice versa.

good, and that the good is happiness. Happiness and the good, which are to be identified with tranquility and self-sufficiency, are achieved by living in accordance with reason, which is to say that it consists in right action and the development of virtue. The philosopher's duty is to transform souls through reason and *askēsis*, not to waste time *solely* with logical puzzles. As Seneca tells us: "There is no time for playing around. . . . You have promised to bring help to the shipwrecked, the imprisoned, the sick, the needy, to those whose heads are under the poised axe. Where are you deflecting your attention? What are you doing?"[23]

V: Neoplatonism and Early Christianity

Neoplatonism is the accumulation of classical philosophy, and although no Neoplatonist identified himself as anything other than a Platonist (Plotinus, for instance, was adamant about his orthodox Platonism[24]), the Neoplatonic "school" is clearly a syncretism of Platonism (early and Middle), Aristotelianism, Stoicism and pagan *religion*. Now while many modern philosophers are uncomfortable with an intimate relationship between philosophy and religion, it was not always so in the ancient world. The spiritual exercises practiced in the Pythagorean school, for instance, owed a lot to Orphism and Egyptian religion, and although Socrates was accused of corrupting the youth – using philosophy to critique the traditional understanding of the Olympian gods – he, nevertheless, spoke reverently about the gods, claiming that philosophy helped him be more pious.[25] However, while ancient philosophy often borrowed from religion, and while most of the ancient philosophers generally thought that discursive reason was able to critique or at least exegete religious revelation, the relationship between philosophy, which makes rational inquiry primary, and religion, which makes non-rational, supra-rational or mythical revelation primary,[26] in regard to Neoplatonism has often been contested.

On the one hand, Neoplatonism – particularly Plotinus's Neoplatonism – appears to have been more of a philosophy than a religion since (1)

---

23 Seneca *Letters to Lucilius* 48.8.
24 Plotinus *Enneads* 5.1.8. Moreover, as Karamanolis points out, to have called Neoplatonists anything but Platonists – indeed, even to have called them "eclectics or syncretists" – would have been "largely pejorative." Karamanolis, *Plato and Aristotle in Agreement? Platonists on Aristotle from Antiochus to Porphyry*, 24.
25 Plato *Phaedrus* 279.
26 I have attempted to give a basic definition of religion, particularly as it is distinct from philosophy, although I agree with Peterson et al. that such a task is a "notoriously difficult" one since any definition is "subject to counterexamples." Michael Peterson et al., *Reason & Religious Belief*, 3rd ed. (New York: Oxford University Press, 2003), 6.

Neoplatonists like Plotinus always identified themselves as philosophers, indeed, as Platonists; (2) Plotinus's *Enneads*, for instance, generally emphasizes philosophical matters;[27] and (3) Neoplatonism in general was in complete agreement with the ancient understanding of philosophy as a transformative method by which the soul, through reason, spiritual exercises and virtuous living, can move upward through the Great Chain of Being and eventually attain happiness.[28] On the other hand, Neoplatonism could also be viewed as a philosophical religion since on top of its interest in religious rituals and theurgy, it insists that mystical union with the One, and *not* the soul contemplating the Forms, is the highest good.

In my opinion, I think Neoplatonism – at least that of Plotinus – should be considered a philosophy with heavy religious influences since (1) much of Plotinus's, and therefore Neoplatonism's, emphasis on the mystical nature of the One comes, importantly, from philosophical sources such as Plato's *Parmenides* and *Republic*, and (2) Plotinus's insistence on the value of discursive reason at preliminary stages throughout the soul's assent toward the One implies that it is discursive reason itself that informs the soul about the value of mystical experience. Consequently, I do not see the Neoplatonic emphasis on the mystical union with the One as something strongly distinct from philosophy but rather as something that is affirmed on the basis of rational consideration. Discursive reason, in other words, just as much for the Neoplatonists as for the other ancient philosophers, is the judge of religious revelation and mystical practices, but it judges in a way that often points to its own inadequacies and so endorses the rationality of accepting the mystical and religious.[29]

However, if the border between philosophy and religion in Neoplatonism is difficult to discern, it is more so with Christianity. On the one hand, Christianity was sometimes seen as a non-rational, or even irrational, religion which made claims, such as the triune nature of God, which *prima facie* seemed absurd (as many Manicheans and Platonists, such as Celsus and Porphyry, pointed out). On the other hand, Christianity was not, as was usually the case with pagan religion, something that was incredible for the rational man to accept without allegory or other literary devices; Jesus's

---

27   A. H. Armstrong, "Plotinus," in *The Cambridge History of Later Greek and Early Medieval Philosophy*, ed. A. H. Armstrong, 195-210 (Cambridge: Cambridge University Press, 2005), 195.

28   "Plotinus, [being] devoted to himself, was never relaxed, except during sleep; but he was prevented from sleeping because he ate so little (often he did not even eat bread) and because he constantly oriented his thought toward spirit." Porphyry *Life of Plotinus* 8.20.

29   A. C. Lloyd, *The Anatomy of Neoplatonism* (Oxford: Clarendon Press, 2005), 166.

miracles, for instance, were not primarily understood as allegories for some deeper spiritual truth, but rather were thought to be literal *evidence* of His divinity; moreover, despite Paul's warning to the Colossians to be careful of "hollow and deceptive philosophers,"[30] he himself argued like a philosopher both with Jewish religious leaders about *evidence* for Jesus in the Bible and with Greek philosophers about the "Unknown God."

Nevertheless, while acknowledging the historical tension between Christianity's revealed and philosophical aspects, it is important to realize that the majority of early church leaders and thinkers soon came to endorse a basic compatibility between rationality and Christianity in one of two ways: they saw Christianity as either (1) a philosophical religion, which has (unwarranted) faith as primary and reason employed in defense of doctrines that flow from it; or, (2) a philosophy, which has reason as primary and reason accepting the mysteries of faith.[31] St. Augustine, for instance, favored the former understanding of Christianity[32] despite saying ambiguously, "Now if wisdom is identical with God, by whom all things were made, as we are assured by divine authority and divine truth, then the true philosopher is the lover of God,"[33] whereas Justin Martyr favored the latter understanding of Christianity, calling Christianity "the definitive philosophy"[34] and insisting that "Reason directs those who are truly pious and [directs] true philosophers to honour and love only what is true, to decline to follow traditional opinions, if these be worthless."[35] Thus, Hadot speaks too imprecisely in regard to (1) or (2) when he says, "From its very beginnings – that is, from the second century AD on – Christianity had presented itself as a philosophy: the Christian way of life;"[36] nevertheless, I believe that quite a few early Christian thinkers – type (2) Christians – can justly be seen as *philosophers* in the ancient sense of the word since, firstly, they accepted Christianity based on its truth-value and, secondly, were subsequently schooled in Christianity in churches, which demanded not only that they practice various spiritual exercises, such as penance and prayer, to strengthen their faith but also that their actions flow from their knowledge and faith to form a fully converted life.

---

30   Colossians 2:8.
31   Of course I am guilty of committing an anachronism here by pitting faith against reason (terminology from the seventeenth century onward); however, I believe that this helps clarify the general situation for readers.
32   Augustine *On The Trinity* 4.4.21.
33   Augustine *City of God* 7.1.
34   Justin Martyr *Apology* 1.46.
35   Ibid., 2.1.
36   Hadot, *Philosophy as a Way of Life*, 269.

VI: The Decline of Philosophy as a Way of Life

The idea of Christianity as a *philosophy* continued, in some small measure, on through the centuries to the point where the seventeenth-century Anglican priest Thomas Traherne (whose *Centuries of Meditations* was a very important book to Lewis) could arguably still be seen as an advocate of such an idea: "Philosophers are not those that speak but do great things. . . . Every man therefore according to his degree, so far as he is a Christian, is a Philosopher."[37] Nonetheless, generally the understanding of philosophy as a way of life – (1) a choice (2) made in a cultural context (3) to follow wholeheartedly a certain group of people who (4) had a certain take on life which (5) demanded training which (6) was the result of rational discourse, and which (7) would ultimately lead to a fully converted life – slowly began to fade in the Middle Ages.

As the majority of Christians began more and more to rely on dogma (which admittedly may have been rationally accepted at one point in time), free rational inquiry became more difficult. Moreover, over time the emphasis on intense spiritual exercises became more the activity of mendicant orders and less something that all Christians practiced. On top of this, while the medieval university could be seen as parallel to the philosophical schools of antiquity and while the theologian could be seen as parallel to the ancient philosopher, the professional theologian, who usually taught philosophy, was often accused of spending too much time on theory and not enough time on practice: "If we disregard, for the moment, the monastic usage of the word *philosophia*, we can say that philosophy in the Middle Ages had become a purely theoretical and abstract activity."[38] While this accusation is, admittedly, flawed since many professional theologians in the Middle

---

37   Thomas Traherne, *Centuries of Meditation*, ed. Bertram Dobell (London: Robert Stockwell, 1950), 229, 232 [4.2, 4.5]. Another of Lewis's favorite authors, St. Francis de Sales, a seventeenth-century Catholic bishop, wrote: "The philosophers of old gave out that they were philosophers, in order that they might be left to lead a philosophic life, and we should give out that we aim at leading a devout life, in order that we may be permitted to lead a devout life." Francis de Sales, *Philothea, or An Introduction to the Devout Life* (1608 reprint; Rockford, IL: Tan Books, 1994), 317 [5.18]. Very likely because of men like Traherne and de Sales, Lewis had Screwtape the devil remark, "It sounds as if you supposed that *argument* was the way to keep [your patient] out of the Enemy's clutches. That might have been so if he had lived a few centuries earlier. At that time the humans still knew pretty well when a thing was proved and when it was not; and if it was proved they really believed it. They still connected thinking with doing and were prepared to alter their way of life as the result of a chain of reasoning." C. S. Lewis, *The Screwtape Letters*, in *C. S. Lewis: Selected Books* [Long Edition] (1942 reprint; London: HarperCollins, 1999), 741.

38   Hadot, *Philosophy as a Way of Life*, 270.

Ages belonged to mendicant orders and so would have been expected to act in accordance with their theories,[39] nevertheless, as philosophy largely came to be viewed as a tool of theology and as the university became both more institutionalized and more secularized, philosophy gradually became less a total way of life (except in some monastic orders) and more a mere philosophical discourse:

> One of the characteristics of the university is that it is made up of professors who train professors, or professionals training professionals. Education was thus no longer directed toward people who were to be educated with a view to becoming fully developed human beings, but to specialists, in order that they might learn how to train other specialists. This is the danger of 'Scholasticism,' that philosophical tendency which began to be sketched at the end of antiquity, developed in the Middle Ages, and whose presence is still recognizable in philosophy today.[40]

Indeed, one could even say that someone like René Descartes, whose method of doubt can reasonably be seen as a spiritual exercise which largely constituted his entire way of life,[41] probably escaped much of the bad habit of separating theory from practice precisely because he was *not* a philosophy professor. But then, I only claim to speak generally, for my point in this chapter has been simply to show that classical philosophy was largely seen as a way of life, whereas medieval philosophy and onward was largely seen as a tool or discourse. Since I think this has been sufficiently shown, I now turn to C. S. Lewis's philosophical journey in order to prove, vis-à-vis an examination of his philosophical growth, that he understood philosophy in the classical sense of the word.

---

39 Depending on the time and university, the proportion of secular masters (who, of course, were still Christians and could teach not just in the law and medicine departments, but also in the theology department) as opposed to masters from mendicant orders varied. However, it is important that "by 1254 the secular masters at Paris had no more than three out of fifteen chairs in the theology faculty." John Marenbon, *Later Medieval Philosophy (1150-1350)* (London: Routledge, 2003), 16.

40 Ibid.

41 That Descartes held to the classical understanding philosophy is somewhat apparent in a quotation like this – "But I admit that long exercise is needed as well as frequently repeated meditation, in order to become accustomed to looking at everything from this point of view" – or this: "I had met with such extreme contentment since the time I had begun to make use of this method." René Descartes, *Discourse on Method*, trans. Donald Cress (Indianapolis: Hackett Publishing, 1998), 15 [3.26-27].

Chapter Two

Rational Discourse and Training

Whenever Lewis was asked to write about his conversion to Christianity, he always pointed out that his, like Justin Martyr's,[1] was "almost [a] purely philosophical [conversion]" which came about as the result of a *philosophical journey*;[2] thus, to one inquirer, he wrote, "My own history was so mixed up with technical philosophy as to be useless to the general [public],"[3] and to another, "The details of my own conversion were so technically philosophical on one side, and so intimate on the other that they can't be used in the way you suggest."[4] However, despite the central role philosophy played in Lewis's conversion (and beyond, as we shall see), the Oxford don felt he had to downplay it in his conversion narrative *Surprised by Joy* for the sake of his audience. This is extremely unfortunate since most people – Lewis scholars included – now have a very poor understanding of Lewis's definition of philosophy, which informed, and was informed by, his philosophical journey.

Nevertheless, those interested in Lewis's philosophical journey have a small concession, for prior to both *Surprised by Joy* and the inquiries about his conversion, Lewis had written a semi-autobiography,[5] *The Pilgrim's Regress*,

---

1   Justin always wore a philosopher's robe and passed from the peripatetic school to the Pythagorean, Stoic and Platonic schools before eventually finding Truth in Christ and the prophets of the Old Testament.

2   "I gave up Christianity at about fourteen. Came back to it when getting on for thirty. Not an emotional conversion: almost purely philosophical." C. S. Lewis, "Autobiographical Note," prepared by the Macmillian Company in 1946 (The Marion E. Wade Center, Wheaton College), 1.

3   C. S. Lewis, *The Collected Letters of C. S. Lewis: Volume II; Books, Broadcasts, and the War 1931-1949*, ed. Walter Hooper (San Francisco: HarperSanFrancisco, 2004), 568 [April 12, 1943].

4   Ibid., 575 [May 20, 1943].

5   "In this preface the autobiographical element in John has had to be stressed because the source of the obscurities lay there. But you must not assume that everything in the book is autobiographical. I was attempting to generalise, not to tell people about my life." C.

in the preface to the third edition of which he gave us a synopsis of his philosophical journey and conversion: "On the intellectual side my own progress had been from 'popular realism' to Philosophical Idealism; from Idealism to Pantheism; from Pantheism to Theism; and from Theism to Christianity."[6] While it must be admitted that Lewis's outline in *The Pilgrim's Regress* was intended as a non-technical sketch, I still think that it is useful for a more technical exploration of the Oxford don's all-important philosophical journey. Moreover, while a sympathetic reading of any author is necessary in order to understand his or her ideas, a historian, in particular, a historian of philosophy, must be able to separate himself from his subject in order to see things that the author / subject may not have been able to see. Thus, in the case of Lewis, I have found at least six things that need to be added to his outline and subsequently addressed in the body of this chapter.

First, it needs to be pointed out that Lewis's outline omits the fact that he was baptized at birth and lived the first eleven years of his life as a Christian; while he may not have thought of this as "on the intellectual side" of his philosophical growth, this must be mentioned – even if only here – in order to give context to his return to Christianity.

Second, "popular realism" will need to be clarified. This word itself is not used by professional philosophers; however, given the great battle at Oxford in the first half of the twentieth century between what philosophers like F. H. Bradley and A. J. Ayer called "realism and idealism,"[7] we may assume that Lewis's "popular realism" was actually "metaphysical realism," which maintains the existence of real, spatiotemporal objects that exist separately of people's knowledge of them and which have properties and enter into relations independently of the concepts with which people understand them. Moreover, in another outline, Lewis's "popular realism" is simply referred to as metaphysical *materialism*: "I went from *materialism* to idealism, idealism to pantheism, from pantheism to theism, and from theism to Christianity."[8] Thus, throughout this and subsequent chapters, we must be careful with Lewis's language because while Lewis the metaphysical materialist / metaphysical realist was also an epistemological realist, Lewis the Christian still remained an epistemological realist.

S. Lewis, the preface to the third edition of *The Pilgrim's Regress*, in *C. S. Lewis: Selected Books* [Short Edition] (1933 reprint; London: HarperCollins, 2002), 12.

6   Ibid., 5.

7   F. H. Bradley, *Appearance and Reality: A Metaphysical Essay* (N.p.: Elibron Classics, 2005), 547. A. J. Ayer, *Language, Truth and Logic* (1936 reprint; London: Penguin, 2001), 150.

8   Lewis, *The Collected Letters of C. S. Lewis: Volume II*, 145 [October 25, 1934].

Third, I will need to address a metaphysical dualist phase that Lewis underwent in 1918, but which he failed to mention in his outline.

Fourth, I will need to distinguish between two different materialist positions Lewis held: Lucretian materialism (1909-1917) and Stoical materialism (1920-1923).

Fifth, I will need to clarify Lewis's understanding of idealism and pantheism, for not only did the Oxford don, at different times, subscribe to two different types of idealism (subjective idealism and absolute idealism), but he also seemed to have equated one of these idealisms (absolute idealism) with pantheism.

And sixth, it must also be pointed out that Lewis's outline gives us no indication of his *repeated* repositioning – a pendulum-like movement of probably two swings back and forth – between absolute idealism (1923-1924 and 1927-1929) and subjective idealism (1924-1926 and possibly 1929), all of which occurred in the space of about six years.

Nevertheless, even though Lewis was not always clear about the details of his own philosophical journey and conversion, he did provide us – as we shall see – with an example of a man who slowly came to understand philosophy in the ancient sense of the word: as a way of life, or (1) a choice (2) made in a cultural context (3) to follow wholeheartedly a certain group of people who (4) had a certain take on life which (5) demanded training which (6) was the result of rational discourse, and which (7) would ultimately lead to a fully converted life. Of course, since the task of mapping out Lewis's philosophical journey is too complex for just one chapter, what begins in this chapter – Lewis's philosophical journey *qua* rational discourse and training – will continue through to the end of chapter five. Moreover, it should also be noted that in this chapter readers should not expect me to go into any great detail pertaining to particular issues in philosophy, such as Lewis's understanding of essence, time or the universal moral law, for these topics are properly discussed in the chapters which make up the second half of this book.

I: Lucretian Materialism

In 1911, when C. S. Lewis was 13 years old, he started reading some of the classics at Cherbourg School, which he called "Chartres" in *Surprised by Joy*.[9] He was sent there by his father, who was an "intelligent man" but

---

9   C. S. Lewis, *Surprised by Joy*, in *C. S. Lewis: Selected Books* [Long Edition] (1955 reprint; London: HarperCollins, 1999), 1276. The name "Chartres" is a reference to

one who "cared . . . little for metaphysics."[10] This separated the elder Lewis from the younger Lewis, for even at that early age, Lewis had read some of the classical philosophers and had digested them to a respectable degree. For instance, in his 1913 essay "Are Athletes Better Than Scholars?" Lewis wrote things like, "No philosopher, however learned, has ever discovered what we exactly mean by the word 'good'" and "But while allowing that the pursuit of athletics is a wholesale – nay, a necessary pastime – one cannot lose sight of the mistakes and wrong ideas arising from an exaggerated estimation of their value."[11] Moreover, a few months after having written "Are Athletes Better Than Scholars," Lewis gained a Classical Entrance Scholarship to Malvern College ("Wyvern"), where we are told explicitly that he had to read at least one dialogue by Plato.[12]

Yet whatever Plato's influence may have been on the early teenage Lewis, we do know that even before Lewis wrote "Are Athletes Better Than Scholars?" – by 1909 or 1910 – he had read, and shortly after largely accepted, the philosophy of Lucretius, the author of *On the Nature of Things*. Indeed, Lucretius's Epicurean materialism had been one of the important factors that predisposed Lewis for his loss of faith in Christianity: an event which occurred in 1911.[13]

Lewis's attraction to Lucretius's Epicureanism was the comfort that it offered in the form of dispelling the fear of God. Prior to his loss of faith, Lewis told us that he came to perceive God wholly in terms of judgment and damnation due to his earliest years living and studying in England under a severe Anglo-Catholicism: "if in my books I have spoken too much of Hell, and if critics want a historical explanation of the fact, they must seek

the alleged early medieval School of Chartres, which focused on reconciling, through literary techniques, Platonism and scripture. Lewis was quite fond of this school and he made use of many of their ideas. For instance, in *Out of the Silent Planet*, Lewis mentioned "*Oyarses*," which he read about in Bernardus Silvestris's *Cosmographia*, and in *Perelandra*, there is an allusion to Jean de Hanville's *Architrenius*.

10   Ibid., 1247.
11   C. S. Lewis, "Are Athletes Better Than Scholars?" *Cherbourg School Magazine*, no. 2 (1913), found in *The Lewis Papers: Memoirs of the Lewis Family; 1850-1930*, ed. Warren Lewis, vol. 3 (The Marion E. Wade Center, Wheaton College), 318-9.
12   "At Malvern he [C. S. Lewis] had to read whatever they were doing in his form. The Greek was hardly suitable – a dialogue of Plato and the *Bacchae* of Euripides." W. T. Kirkpatrick, "Letter: October 2, 1914," in the preface of *Spirits in Bondage: A Cycle of Lyrics*, by C. S. Lewis, ed. Walter Hooper (1919 reprint; San Diego: Harcourt Brace & Company, 1984), xvii. Cf. C. S. Lewis, *The Collected Letters of C. S. Lewis: Volume I; Family Letters 1905-1931*, ed. Walter Hooper (London: HarperCollins, 2000), 26 [July 6 1913].
13   Lewis, *Surprised by Joy*, 1281.

it not in the supposed Puritanism of my Ulster childhood but in the Anglo-Catholicism of the church at Belsen."[14] This fear of God is reflected by John of *The Pilgrim's Regress*, a resident of "Puritania" who lives in fear of the "Landlord" who makes all the rules and who "was quite extraordinarily kind and good to his tenants, and would certainly torture most of them to death the moment he had the slightest pretext."[15] As an Epicurean, Lucretius believed that through the use of reason a person could find peace by realizing that creation could never have occurred – for "nothing ever springs miraculously out of nothing"[16] – and so while the gods do exist, they are completely made up of atoms like the rest of the cosmos and are not at all concerned with judgment and rules. Hence, partly inspired by Lucretius's reduction of the gods, and partly by the pseudo-Darwinian philosophy that abounded in the early twentieth century, Lewis began to identify himself as an atheist – though he probably should have called himself an agnostic[17] – who endorsed what he called "The Argument from Undesign" ("Had God designed the world, it would not be a world so frail and faulty as we see"[18]).

Now while it would be far from wrong to call Lewis an Epicurean materialist, perhaps it would be better to call him a *Lucretian* materialist since Lewis – probably misunderstanding Lucretius's therapeutic purpose in working through the rage of the passions in *On the Nature of Things*[19] – likely came to identify his own bitter pessimism and promethean anger towards God[20] with the cathartic rage poetry of Lucretius and not the tranquil maxims of Epicurus.[21] Consequently, while it is fair to say Lewis's adolescent

---

14   Ibid., 1262.

15   Lewis, *The Pilgrim's Regress*, 21.

16   Lucretius *On the Nature of Things* 1.150.

17   Lewis claimed he "became an atheist at the age of fourteen." Lewis, *The Collected Letters of C. S. Lewis: Volume III*, 1551 [June 9, 1944]. However, he is best understood as an agnostic, for in a 1916 letter, we read: "Of course, mind you, I am not laying down as a certainty that there is nothing outside the material world: considering the discoveries that are always being made, this would be foolish. Anything MAY exist: but until we know that it does, we can't make any assumptions. The universe is an absolute mystery." Lewis, *The Collected Letters of C. S. Lewis: Volume I*, 231 [October 12, 1916].

18   Lewis, *Surprised by Joy*, 1281.

19   Nussbaum, *The Therapy of Desire*, 240. Also see the appendix of this book.

20   "I was at this time living, like so many Atheists or Antitheists, in a whirl of contradictions. I maintained that God did not exist. I was also very angry with God for not existing. I was equally angry with him for creating a world." Lewis, *Surprised by Joy*, 1310. I will examine this pessimism and anger more in chapter three, but suffice to say these are very evident in Lewis's 1912-1913 poem, *Loki Bound*, which was inspired by Lucretius's *On the Nature of Things*, Aeschylus's *Prometheus Bound* and Norse mythology.

21   The only place that Lewis talked directly about Epicurus himself is in *The Pilgrim's Regress*, where Lewis had Drudge, the caretaker of Mr. Sensible's house, say of Epicurus:

acceptance of Lucretian materialism was more an "emotional need" than a well-reasoned philosophical conclusion[22] – witness Dymer's passionate escape from the Platonic Republic-like school in Lewis's canto one of *Dymer* – it would be wrong to overlook the philosophizing that occurred, for long after Lewis converted to Christianity, he still found the argument from design unconvincing, preferring Percy Shelley's diatribe against God for not existing over William Paley's clockmaker argument: "There is something holier about the atheism of a Shelley than about the theism of Paley."[23] Furthermore, when Lewis spoke of atheism as "boy[']s philosophy,"[24] he was not trying to make a straw man, but rather spoke of it as such because for him, atheism, or rather agnosticism, was the philosophy that he accepted when he was a boy and as such was fairly simplistic.

Lewis's materialism, however, did not begin and end with Lucretius. For another ten years, he developed his agnostic philosophy through a variety of sources. Yet before I mention these, it is important to remind ourselves of two things. First, from his earliest days onward, Lewis was deeply steeped in the classics: they were his main academic pursuit from secondary school through to university. Second, Lewis felt an internal struggle between his agnosticism on the one hand and his romantic longings and attraction to mythology on the other. This latter point I will discuss more in chapter four, but for now I want to keep the former point, Lewis's continual classical training, in mind as we examine his Lucretian materialism.

After what *may* have been an early attempt at honest agnosticism, Lewis's embryonic philosophical integrity seems to have been compromised a bit. He tells us that at Malvern College he started to become an intellectual prig or highbrow due to his increasing pride,[25] which, he confessed, was his besetting sin for more than half his life.[26]

"'Mr Epicurus was the first [to live in the house]. Mental case he was, poor gentleman: he had a chronic fear of the black hole [i.e. Hell]. Something dreadful. I never had a better employer, though. Nice, kind, quiet-spoken sort of man.'" Lewis, *The Pilgrim's Regress*, 101.

22 Long after his conversion, Lewis said he held onto popular realism "partly [because it] satisfied an emotional need." Lewis, *Surprised by Joy*, 1365.

23 C. S. Lewis, *"De Futilitate,"* in *C. S. Lewis: Essay Collection & Other Short Works*, ed. Lesley Walmsley (London: HarperCollins, 2000), 680. Cf. C. S. Lewis, "To Roy Campbell," in *Poems*, by C. S. Lewis, ed. Walter Hooper (San Diego: Harcourt Brace Jovanovich, 1964), 66.

24 C. S. Lewis, *Mere Christianity*, in *C. S. Lewis: Selected Books* [Long Edition] (1952 reprint; London: HarperCollins, 1999), 346.

25 Lewis, *Surprised by Joy*, 1301.

26 Lewis, *The Collected Letters of C. S. Lewis: Volume I*, 878 [January 30, 1930], 882 [February 10, 1930].

Nevertheless, while this intellectual snobbery stayed with Lewis for some time, it slowly (the key word here) began to weaken in 1914, when he went to Great Bookham to be tutored by W. T. Kirkpatrick, "an Atheist . . . [and] 'Rationalist' of the old, high and dry nineteenth-century type."[27] Lewis started to regain his interest in philosophy because he was so impressed by Kirkpatrick's great emphasis on dialectic and the Socratic dictum of only saying what you mean; indeed, Lewis remarked, "Yet though I could never have been a scientist, I had scientific as well as imaginative impulses, and I loved ratiocination. Kirk excited and satisfied one side of me."[28] Moreover, while Kirkpatrick should probably be understood as a typical proponent of philosophy as mere rational discourse and not as a way of life ("if ever a man came near to being a purely logical entity, that man was Kirk. Born a little later, he would have been a Logical Positivist"[29]), Kirkpatrick, who Lewis called "an honest clear-headed sceptic like J. S. Mill,"[30] had at least one virtue of the ancient philosophers: intellectual integrity and an unswerving fidelity to reason. The evidence for this is found in two places.

First, in *That Hideous Strength*, the third book in Lewis's Cosmic Trilogy, Lewis makes it clear that he modeled the character of MacPhee on Kirkpatrick: both are skeptics and both are utterly devoted to logic.[31] For instance, Lewis tells us a story in *Surprised by Joy* where Kirkpatrick is talking to a certain individual who tells him that they differ in opinion, to which Kirkpatrick replied, "'Good heavens! I have no *opinions* on any subject whatsoever.'"[32] And in *That Hideous Strength*, MacPhee tells Jane Studdock the same thing: "'Mrs. Studdock, I have *no* opinions – on any subject in the world. I state the facts and exhibit the implications. If everyone indulged in fewer opinions . . . there'd be less silly talking and printing in the world.'"[33] This connection between Kirkpatrick and MacPhee is important because despite being a skeptic, MacPhee is ultimately on the right side in the battle between good and evil. Ransom, the leader of St. Anne's (modeled on the

---

27   Lewis, *Surprised by Joy*, 1324.
28   Ibid., 1322-3.
29   Ibid., 1322.
30   Lewis, *The Collected Letters of C. S. Lewis: Volume II*, 657 [May 28, 1945].
31   It is also possible to see the professor in *The Lion, the Witch and the Wardrobe* as modelled on Kirkpatrick, although my own feeling is that the professor is based on Lewis himself. Whatever the case, the professor does love logical thinking: "'Logic!' said the Professor half to himself. 'Why don't they teach logic at these schools?'" C. S. Lewis, *The Lion, the Witch and the Wardrobe* (1950 reprint; London: Fontana, 1985), 47.
32   Lewis, *Surprised by Joy*, 1323.
33   C. S. Lewis, *That Hideous Strength*, in *The Cosmic Trilogy*, by C. S. Lewis (1945 reprint; London: Pan Books, 1990), 520.

early Christian community and Augustine's City of God[34]), clearly shows his support[35] for MacPhee when he tells Jane: "'He is our sceptic; a very important office. . . . I want you to like him if you can. He's one of my oldest friends. And he'll be about our best man if we're going to be defeated. You couldn't have a better man at your side in a losing battle.'"[36]

Second, Lewis said explicitly that because of Kirkpatrick's insistence on intellectual consistency, he himself started to become more self-aware:

> The materialist universe had one great, negative attraction to offer me. It had no other. And this had to be accepted; one had to look out on a meaningless dance of atoms (remember, I was reading Lucretius), to realize that all the apparent beauty was a subjective phosphorescence, and to relegate everything one valued to the world of mirage. That price I tried loyally to pay. For I had learned something from Kirk about the honour of the intellect and the shame of voluntary inconsistency.[37]

Thus under the honest skepticism of Kirkpatrick, Lewis's dialectical abilities greatly increased; indeed, upon hearing the news that Lewis had been accepted into Oxford, Kirkpatrick told Lewis's father: "As a dialectician, an intellectual disputant, I shall miss him, and he will have no successor. Clive [C. S. Lewis] can hold his own in any discussion, and the higher the range of the conversation, the more he feels himself at home."[38] Lewis himself even went so far as to tell us that the time he spent at Kirkpatrick's – reading, walking and philosophizing – were some of the best years of his life: "Such is my ideal, and such then (almost) was the reality, of 'settled, calm, Epicurean life.'"[39] During that time, Lewis read for pleasure works by Francis Bacon,[40] whose *Essays*, years later, Lewis said "is a book for adolescents,"[41] Jean-Jacques

---

34   Charles Moorman, *The Precincts of Felicity: The Augustinian City of the Oxford Christians* (Gainesville, FL: University of Florida Press, 1966), 78.

35   This support, however, is not totally unqualified, and though MacPhee is part of the group, he is clearly seen, to put it in Pauline language (1 Corinthians 3:1), as a spiritual infant: "'It is no good, MacPhee,' said the Director, 'you can't go. For one thing you don't know the language. And for another – it's time for frankness – you have never put yourself under the protection of Maledil [God]. . . . I will not send you. It would be like sending a three-year old child to fight a tank.'" Lewis, *That Hideous Strength*, 584.

36   Ibid., 539.

37   Lewis, *Surprised by Joy*, 1343.

38   W. T. Kirkpatrick, "Letter: 1916," in *The Lewis Papers: Memoirs of the Lewis Family; 1850-1930*, ed. Warren Lewis, vol. 5 (The Marion E. Wade Center, Wheaton College), 165.

39   Lewis, *Surprised by Joy*, 1326.

40   Lewis, *The Collected Letters of C. S. Lewis: Volume I*, 121 [May 13, 1915].

41   C. S. Lewis, *Poetry and Prose in the Sixteenth Century*, vol. 4, *The Oxford History of English Literature* (1954 reprint; Oxford: Clarendon Press, 1997), 537.

Rousseau,[42] and Kirkpatrick's favorite, Arthur Schopenhauer,[43] whose pessimism added fuel to Lewis's anger at God for not existing.[44] However, it is imperative to keep in mind that Lewis was not formally studying skepticism and materialist philosophy, but was largely submerged in the classics in preparation for Oxford. In another letter to Lewis's father, Kirkpatrick wrote: "Since Clive came, our reading has been almost exclusively Classical. The ancient Classics are no drudgery to him. On the contrary, they are a source of entertainment and delight. He is one of the rare exceptions among boys, who ought to be learning the Classics."[45]

Of the important classics that Lewis, who was then beginning "to think in Greek,"[46] read in regard to his philosophical development were Aristotle's *Ethics* (1917) and Plato's *Phaedrus* (1915),[47] *Phaedo* (1915),[48] *Meno* (probably 1915),[49] and *Republic* (which he had read before 1916, for that is the year in which he started his epic poem *Dymer*,[50] which he confessed was in many ways a reaction to the education system in Plato's masterpiece: "The Platonic and totalitarian state from which Dymer escapes in Canto I was a natural invention for one who detested the state in Plato's *Republic* as much as he

42 Lewis, *Surprised by Joy*, 1351.

43 "I have also been reading in library copies, Schopenhauer's 'Will and Idea' [*The World as Will and Idea*]. . . . Schopenhauer is abstruse and depressing, but has some very interesting remarks on the theory of music and poetry. . . . Kirk, I need hardly say, is strong on him, and will talk on the subject for hours." Lewis, *The Collected Letters of C. S. Lewis: Volume I*, 151 [November 15, 1915]. Cf. Lewis, *Surprised by Joy*, 1324.

44 Lewis, *Surprised by Joy*, 1362.

45 Kirkpatrick, "Letter: October 2, 1914," xvii.

46 Lewis, *Surprised by Joy*, 1325.

47 Lewis, *The Collected Letters of C. S. Lewis: Volume I*, 130 [June 18, 1915].

48 W. T. Kirkpatrick, "Letter: August 17, 1915," in *The Collected Letters of C. S. Lewis: Volume I*, 141. Lewis, *The Collected Letters of C. Lewis: Volume I*, 145 [October 12, 1915].

49 The exact date of when Lewis read Plato's *Meno* is not clear; however, because Lewis read Plato's *Republic* sometime before 1916 (see the following footnote) and since there is an annotation in Lewis's edition of *Republic* which mentions *Meno* ("Cf. Meno"), it is very possible that Lewis made this annotation when he first read *Republic* and it is likely that when he did so he had already read *Meno*. Hence, it is very possible that Lewis read *Meno* in 1915 or 1916. C. S. Lewis, marginalia in his edition of *RES PVBLICA*, by Plato, ed. Ioannes Burnet (Oxonii: E Typographeo Clarendoniano, n.d.; The Rare Book Collection, The University of North Carolina at Chapel Hill), 506c.

50 "I can see my way clear to the end of 'Dymer' now and will let you have an instalment next Sunday: three more will finish him." Lewis, *The Collected Letters of C. S. Lewis: Volume I*, 269 [January 28, 1917]. Nevertheless, it must be noted that while Lewis started the poem in 1916, he did not publish it until 1926, meaning that it is possible that he could have completely changed some of the themes of the poem, including his tirade against Plato's educational system. But this scenario, at least concerning the first canto, I find unlikely.

liked everything else in Plato"[51]). Nevertheless, although none of these works by Plato and Aristotle had yet to bear fruit in Lewis's hungry mind – "I . . . believe[d] in nothing but atoms and evolution"[52] – the seeds were planted.

II: Pseudo-Manichean Dualism

Lewis's Lucretian materialism, which upon reflection he said was founded on "a glib and shallow 'rationalism,'"[53] continued past his time with Kirkpatrick and into WWI, when Lucretius was still "among [his] serious books" and Schopenhauerian pessimism continued to haunt him.[54] Yet, he soon became exposed to new philosophy, and it was during the year that he fought in WWI that his love affair with metaphysics, aesthetics, and ethics really seized him . . . and like all love affairs, his was turbulent, exciting and emotional.

The books that shook Lewis up during that time were Plato's books that touched on aesthetics (namely, *Phaedrus, Phaedo* and *Republic*), George Berkeley's *Three Dialogues between Hylas and Philonous*, Henri Bergson's *Creative Evolution*, and a book about William Morris (*William Morris: His Work and Influence*). Of course Lewis was reading other philosophy during WWI, notably Schopenhauer (who Lewis thought "is not really a philosopher at all in the technical sense"[55]), John Locke,[56] and David Hume,[57] but Plato, Berkeley, Bergson and the Morris book were the important ones.

Even though Lewis the Lucretian materialist had rejected many aspects of Plato's philosophy, we can see that his interest in Platonic aesthetics grew

---

51   C. S. Lewis, preface to the 1950 edition of *Dymer*, in *Narrative Poems*, by C. S. Lewis, ed. Walter Hooper (1926 poem reprint; London: HarperCollins, 1994), 3.

52   Lewis, *Surprised by Joy*, 1344.

53   Ibid., 1342.

54   Lewis, preface to the 1950 edition of *Dymer*, 5.

55   Lewis, *The Collected Letters of C. S. Lewis: Volume I*, 406 [October 13, 1918].

56   Walter Hooper, preface to *Spirits in Bondage*, by C. S. Lewis (San Diego: Harcourt Brace & Company, 1984), xxxi-ii. When I asked Hooper about his source for his claim that Lewis read Locke during this time – for I could find nothing in Lewis's own words that indicated that he had done so – Hooper told me the following: "I don't find any evidence that Lewis was reading John Locke's *Essay* as far back as 1918. Why did I mention it in the Preface to *Spirits in Bondage*? That was written some years ago, but I don't think I'd have said what I did without good reason. I *think* it may have been because it is clear from some of Lewis's war-time letters, and certainly from his diary (*All My Road Before Me*) that he was keen to read in advance all the texts mentioned in the Oxford syllabus for Honour Moderations and Greats. And Locke's *Essay* was part of the required reading." Walter Hooper, "Private Letter to Adam Barkman: May 31, 2007."

57   Lewis, *The Collected Letters of C. S. Lewis: Volume I*, 389 [June 3, 1918].

over time. Thus, during WWI, he endlessly debated the nature of Beauty,[58] and appears to have followed Plato – though with some help from other sources, as we shall see – in asserting not only that Beauty is objective, but also that Beauty should be associated with the immaterial and not the material. This latter assertion, of course, indicates an enormous change in Lewis's metaphysics; however, this change was not so much the doing of Plato as it was of other sources.

Berkeley, the eighteenth-century founder of subjective idealism (or "immaterialism" as he called it), is possibly the most underrated philosophical influence on Lewis. Nevertheless, during WWI what Lewis gained from Berkeley was not a specific doctrine, such as *"Esse est percipi,"*[59] but rather he acquired a general interest in metaphysical questions:

> This week I have been reading the works of Bishop Berkeley, an eighteenth century country man of ours, & philosopher. Published under the title of 'Principles of Human Knowledge etc' in the Everyman. The part I have been reading is 3 dialogues written to prove the existence of God – which he does by disproving the existence of matter. The reasoning is very subtle but not difficult. Look here, oh my Galahad, philosophy is a subject I am just arriving at, so why shouldn't we start abreast & read it side by side. What do you say? Expend 1/- on Berkeley and have a go on those 3 Dialogues![60]

And a few months later he added:

> But philosophy or metaphysics is my great find at present: all other questions really seem irrelevant till its ones are solved. I think you should take it up – its probing would at least save you from the intellectual stagnation that usually awaits a man who has found complete satisfaction in some traditional religious system.[61]

Berkeley's idealist metaphysics provided the materialist Lewis with an important challenge: how can we know that matter has existence independent of mind? Moved by the force of Berkeley's arguments against matter (which we will examine later), Lewis started to see that his simplistic materialism was flawed and was in need of the spiritual; years later, in *The Pilgrim's*

---

58 Lewis, *Surprised by Joy*, 1354.

59 George Berkeley, *Three Dialogues between Hylas and Philonous*, in *Philosophical Works including the Works on Vision*, ed. Michael Ayers (London: Everyman, 1975), 162 [1.172]. Lewis entitled the third chapter of book four of *The Pilgrim's Regress* "Esse est Percipi," demonstrating, as we will see shortly, Berkeley's impact on Lewis.

60 Lewis, *The Collected Letters of C. S. Lewis: Volume I*, 330-1 [July 24, 1917].

61 Ibid., 342 [November 4, 1917].

Regress, Lewis said that the problem he had had with Lucretian / Epicurean materialism was that because its arguments against the spiritual fail, it really is – mark this well – more concerned with comfort than Truth. Mr. Sensible, who served John "the bread, the salt, and the apples [that] had been left by Epicurus," says,

> 'Sense is easy, Reason is hard. Sense knows where to stop with gracious inconsistency, while Reason slavishly follows an abstract logic whither she knows not. The one seeks comfort and finds it, the other seeks truth and is still seeking. . . . Philosophy should be our mistress, not our master. . . . We go to the Porch [Aristotle's school] and the Academy to be spectators, not partisans.'[62]

Nevertheless, even though Lewis felt rationally compelled to give up his simplistic Lucretian materialism, he did not immediately convert to idealism, for he had another important metaphysical encounter: Bergson.

Lewis credited Bergson with three things: (1) teaching him (later on, in 1920) that "the materiality is the intelligibility,"[63] (2) dispelling his pessimism about life due to a sense that he got from *Creative Evolution* that life is necessary[64] (odd as it may sound[65]), and (3) giving him a new appreciation for the beauty and vitality of life.[66] This latter point especially is important as it is in many ways a metaphysical counterpart to romanticism and mythology, which Lewis was drawn to at the time (and which we will talk about more in chapters three and four).[67]

---

62   Lewis, *The Pilgrim's Regress*, 98, 96-7.

63   C. S. Lewis, *All My Road Before Me: The Diary of C. S. Lewis; 1922-1927*, ed. Walter Hooper (San Diego: Harcourt Brace & Company, 1991), n279.

64   Lewis, *Surprised by Joy*, 1362.

65   "Oddly" because Bergson emphasized the divergent directions and "willed" aspect of the *élan vital* over and against the mechanism of pure Darwinism. Henri Bergson, *Creative Evolution*, trans. Arthur Mitchell (1911 reprint; Lanham, MD: University Press of America, 1983), 231.

66   "The other momentous experience [during WWI] was that of reading Bergson in a Convalescent Camp on Salisbury Plain. Intellectually this taught me to avoid the snares that lurk about the word *Nothing*. But it also had a revolutionary effect on my emotional outlook. Hitherto my whole bent had been towards things pale, remote, and evanescent; the water-colour world of Morris, the leafy recesses of Malory, the twilight of Yeats. The word 'life' had for me pretty much the same associations it had for Shelley in *The Triumph of Life*. I would not have understood what Goethe meant by *des Lebens goldens Baun*. Bergson showed me. He did not abolish my old loves, but he gave me a new one. From him I first learned to relish energy, fertility, and urgency; the resource, the triumphs, and even the insolence, of things that grow." Lewis, *Surprised by Joy*, 1358-9.

67   During WWI, Lewis's romanticism, which had dualistic tendencies stretching back

Yet, what is significant is that Lewis combined his romantic tendencies with his experiences as a solider, Plato's aesthetics, Berkeley's language of Spirit and Bergson's quasi-dualism[68] of the biological and the "spiritual" *élan vital* (that mysterious element which, by guiding biological evolution, impels life to overcome the downward entropic drift of matter[69]). The result of this romantic, violent, incoherent combination is a kind of Manicheanism or Gnostic dualism wherein "nature is wholly diabolical & malevolent and God, if he exists, is outside of and in opposition to the cosmic arrangements;"[70] as Lewis explained further:

> You will be surprised and I expect, not a little amused to hear that my views at present are getting almost monastic about all the lusts of the flesh. They seem to me to extend the dominion of matter over us: and, out here, where I see spirit continually dodging matter (shells, bullets, animal fears, animal pains) I have formulated my equation Matter=Nature=Satan. And on the other side Beauty, the only spiritual & not-natural thing that I have yet found. . . . You see the conviction is gaining ground on me that after all Spirit does exist; and that we come in contact with the spiritual element by means of these 'thrills' [i.e. the mysterious connection between an individual and an object of beauty, like a tree]. I fancy that there is Something right outside time & place, which did not create matter, as the Christians say, but is matter's great enemy: and that Beauty is the call of the spirit in that something to the spirit in us. You see how frankly I admit my views have changed.[71]

---

to Gnosticism, reached new heights of influence on Lewis's mental development. For Gnosticism's influence on romanticism, see Richard Smith, "Afterward: The Modern Relevance of Gnosticism," in *The Nag Hammadi Library*, ed. Richard Smith, 532-49 (San Francisco: HarperSanFrancisco, 1990), 536.

68 Many, like James Patrick, believe Bergson is a monist. Patrick, "C. S. Lewis and Idealism," 164. But it is unclear to me, as it was for Lewis, whether Bergson was a dualist or a monist; as Lewis wrote: "If Evolution is an abstract H.C.F. ["Highest Common Factor"] of all biological chances (as *sphericity* of all spherical objects) of course it is not an entity in addition to particular organisms. That is the view I'd take. My point was that Butler, Bergson, Shaw, D. H. Lawrence etc. keep on talking as if it *were* a thing (a Platonic εἶδος ["Form"] or daemon)! They call it *Life*. But *life* (H.C.F.) can't be alive any more than *speed* can move quickly!" Lewis, *The Collected Letters of C. S. Lewis: Volume III*, 1269 [May 21, 1961]. Cf. Ibid., 628 [July 4, 1955].

69 Bergson, *Creative Evolution*, 239.

70 Lewis, *The Collected Letters of C. S. Lewis: Volume I*, 397 [September 12, 1918].

71 Ibid., 371 [May 23, 1918], 374 [May 29, 1918]. Lewis's poem "Satan Speaks" also demonstrates this philosophy: "I am Nature, the Mighty Mother, / I am the law: ye have none other. / I am the flower and the dewdrop fresh, / I am the lust in your itching flesh." Lewis, *Spirits in Bondage*, 3 [1.1]. Years later, Lewis pointed out that "*Contemptus mundi* is dangerous and may lead to Manicheanism." Lewis, *The Collected Letters of C. S. Lewis: Volume II*, 392 [April 16, 1940].

While Lewis's metaphysical and aesthetic views were shifting due to Plato, Berkeley, Bergson and the Romantics, his ethical theory (more on this in chapter eight) was also developing, for during WWI Lewis read *William Morris: His Work and Influence*, which, though not strictly a philosophical book, was important for his understanding of morality:

> Hitherto I had always thought there were only two possible views of morals: either, if you believed in a religion, that they were a god-imposed law; or, if you did not, that they were merely rules for convenience – 'The rules of our prison-house' as Blake called them. This man [William Morris] gives a third possibility which is very interesting – regarding them as a kind of art, an object to be pursued for its own beauty.[72]

Lewis went on to say that the book was neither exciting nor original (remember he had probably read, or was in the stages of reading, Aristotle's *Ethics*), yet he credited it with changing his view of morality. And this book, along with a few moral friends,[73] likely provided Lewis with "his first explicitly moral experience,"[74] which he allegorically represented by the character Virtue in *The Pilgrim's Regress* (a figure likely derived from Martianus Capella's *The Marriage of Philology and Mercury*[75]); thus, as John of *The Pilgrim's Regress* was far from Christianity when Virtue first joined him, so too was Lewis the pseudo-Manichean dualist far from Christianity when he strove to be more virtuous. And this moral resolve, as was consistent with a growing desire to live his philosophy, was further strengthened when Lewis amazingly kept his promise to his friend Paddy Moore to take care of Paddy's mother, Mrs. Moore, if Paddy died in the war.[76]

III: Stoical Materialism

Lewis's dualism, which apparently he thought was still "materialism" if we

---

72   Lewis, *The Collected Letters of C. S. Lewis: Volume I*, 343 [November 4, 1917].

73   Lewis, *Surprised by Joy*, 1360.

74   Lewis, *The Pilgrim's Regress*, 39.

75   Lewis would have read *The Marriage of Philology and Mercury* before he wrote *The Pilgrim's Regress*, for Lewis began researching *The Allegory of Love*, in which *The Marriage* is mentioned, in 1928, four years before he began to write *The Pilgrim's Regress*. In *The Marriage of Philology and Mercury*, Lewis would have read about how Mercury sets out to find a bride, yet cannot make progress in his journey without Virtue accompanying him: "Then, as usual, he [Mercury] gave his caduceus to Virtue, so that she could penetrate the secret parts of the world with him, and with equal swiftness could break into the more remote quarters of heaven." Martianus Capella *The Marriage of Philology and Mercury* 1.9.

76   George Sayer, *Jack: A Life of C. S. Lewis* (Wheaton, IL: Crossway Books, 1988), 135.

follow his own description of his philosophical journey, continued into his first year at Oxford, where he began reading for a degree in Classical Honour Moderations ("Honours Mods"), "the most searching examination in Latin and Greek in any university in the world."[77]

It was at this time that Lewis took on what he called his "New Look," which in essence was a complete rejection of pessimism (thanks to Bergson) and supernaturalism / romanticism (thanks to the new psychology, of which we will speak more of in chapter four).[78] The philosophy of his "New Look," which Lewis claimed to have held from about 1919-1923 and which was, no doubt, encouraged by his realist philosophy tutor, E. F. Carritt, was "a sort of Stoical Monism," which he identified with the universe and not God.[79] However, if Lewis's self-confessed monism (meaning that there is really only one metaphysical substance) was identified with the universe, then what happened to Lewis's previous dualism of Spirit and Nature and his enthusiasm for Spirit? It is possible to say that Lewis reduced the apparent dual substances of Spirit and Nature into the single substance "universe" in manner similar to those who interpret Bergson's *élan vital* as the highest common factor of the biological (material monism) and not as a totally different substance (dualism). The problem with this view, however, is that exactly during this time, in 1920,[80] Lewis postulated the existence of a "Spirit" or "God":

> You will be interested to hear that in the course of my philosophy – on the existence of matter – I have had to postulate some sort of God as the least objectionable theory: but of course we know nothing. At any rate we don't know what the real Good is, and consequently I have stopped defying heaven: it can't know less than I, so perhaps things really are alright.[81]

There seems to be only two ways to understand this: either (1) Lewis thought "God" was likely but did not think His existence mattered metaphysically

77   Robert Currie, "The Arts and Social Studies, 1914-1939," in *The History of the University of Oxford: Volume VIII; The Twentieth Century*, ed. Brian Harrison, 109-38 (Oxford: Clarendon Press, 1994), 111.
78   Lewis, *Surprised by Joy*, 1362.
79   Ibid.
80   In *Surprised by Joy*, Lewis said his "New Look" began when he entered Oxford, which was in 1919, and seems to have lasted (1) at least until Owen Barfield became an Anthroposophist, which we know from Lewis's diary occurred in 1923, and (2) until he became an idealist, which occurred during Lewis's Great War with Owen Barfield, which again did not begin until late 1922 or 1923. Ibid., 1363. Lewis, *All My Road Before Me*, 254 [July 7, 1923].
81   Lewis, *The Collected Letters of C. S. Lewis: Volume I*, 509 [September 25, 1920].

at all; hence, for all intents and purposes, he considered himself an agnostic materialist; or, (2) this reference to God is the dregs of Lewis's dualism, which we would then have to say ended in 1920, thus marking the monistic, material universe as the starting of Lewis's "New Look," which subsequently began in late 1920 or early 1921. In either case, we know that by 1921 Lewis was once again a materialist.[82]

As to the nature of Lewis's Stoical (materialist) monism, we know that it caused him to assume a position of neither pessimism nor optimism.[83] He called his attitude "Stoical Monism" because he felt, like the Stoics and the Bertrand Russell of "A Free Man's Worship,"[84] that everything is necessary and all the real philosopher – the man who lives according to his beliefs[85] – can do is staunchly will what he wants, even though what he wants is necessary; or, as Russell put it:

> The Stoic freedom in which wisdom consists is found in the submission of our desires but not of our thoughts. From the submission of our desires springs the virtue of resignation; from the freedom of our thoughts springs the whole world of art and philosophy, and the vision of beauty by which, at last, we half reconquer the reluctant world.[86]

This outlook was so much the ethos of Lewis's "New Look," that in 1921 he won the Chancellor's English Essay Prize for a paper he wrote called "Optimism," which, though lost, seems to have reflected the philosophy of his "New Look":

82   In a letter dated June 17, 1921, Lewis wrote that he "already regret[s] one or two things in *Spirits in Bondage*" (his collection of poems written during his pseudo-Manichean dualist phase). Lewis, *The Collected Letters of C. S. Lewis: Volume I*, 551 [June 17, 1921]. Likely what he regretted was his flirtation with the spiritual. Indeed, Owen Barfield seems to confirm this, for he said that during his Great War with Lewis, which started in 1922 or 1923, "[Lewis] was philosophically a materialist. He didn't believe that any access to the spiritual or supernatural world was possible for the human mind." Owen Barfield, "C. S. Lewis as Christian and Scholar," in *C. S. Lewis Remembered*, ed. Harry Lee Poe and Rebecca Whitten Poe, 25-35 (Grand Rapids, MI: Zondervan, 2006), 24-5.

83   Lewis, *Surprised by Joy*, 1362.

84   Ibid.

85   In a debate with a philosopher friend, Lewis expressed frustration that his friend did not even attempt to align his beliefs with his actions: "Fasnacht was once more proof how little purely intellectual powers avail to make a big man. I thought that he had not *lived* a single one of this theories: he had worked them with his brain but not with his blood." Lewis, *All My Road Before Me*, 150 [December 5, 1922].

86   Bertrand Russell, "A Free Man's Worship," in *Why I Am Not a Christian and Other Essays on Religion and Related Subjects*, ed. Paul Edwards (New York: A Touchstone Book, 1957), 110.

Some of the insolent passages may amuse you: I hope you will like the way I dealt with the difficulty of 'God or no God.' To admit that person's existence would have upset my whole applecart: to deny it seemed inadvisable, on the off chance of there being a Christian among my examiners. I therefore adopted the more Kirkian alternative of proving – at any rate to my own satisfaction – that it 'really made no difference whatsoever' whether there was such a person or no. The second part of my essay you may use as a mild test whether you are ever likely to come to metaphysics or not.[87]

To Lewis's credit, he did admit later on that the philosophy of his "New Look" was somewhat inconsistent, pointing out that his metaphysical materialism (i.e. "popular realism") could in no way account for the immaterial phenomenon of reason: "We [Owen Barfield and Lewis] had been, in the technical sense of the term, 'realists'; that is, we accepted as rock-bottom reality the universe revealed by the senses. But at the same time we continued to make for certain phenomena of consciousness all the claims that really went with a theistic or idealistic view."[88] This said, I get ahead of myself since Lewis's awareness of his inconsistency only came when he became an idealist. And before I can discuss Lewis's idealism, two things need to be addressed.

First, in 1920, Lewis took a First in Honours Mods and began a two year degree in *Literae Humaniores* ("Greats"), which is a combination of classics, history and philosophy, and "is the oldest and is admitted on all hands the premier School in dignity and importance. It includes the greatest proportion of the ablest students, it covers the widest area of studies, it makes probably the severest demands, both on examiner and candidate, and it carries the most coveted distinction."[89] Since "Greats" focused more on its philosophical component than anything else,[90] it was Lewis's intention to pursue a career

87 Lewis, *The Collected Letters of C. S. Lewis: Volume I*, 557 [July 1, 1921]. Upon reading Matthew Arnold's *Empedocles on Etna*, Lewis said Empedocles's first speech to Pausanias was "a very full expression of what I almost begin to call my own philosophy." The lines he was referring to are "The Gods laugh in their sleeve / To watch man doubt and fear, / Who knows not what to believe / Since he sees nothing clear, / And dares stamp nothing false where he finds nothing sure." Lewis, *All My Road Before Me*, 159 [December 25, 1922].

88 Lewis, *Surprised by Joy*, 1364.

89 Currie, "The Arts and Social Studies, 1914-1939," 111. In his review of Hastings Rashdall's *Ideas and Ideals*, T. S. Eliot commented: "His philosophy is Greats philosophy. Of such was the salt of Oxford." T. S. Eliot, review of *Ideas and Ideals*, by Hastings Rashdall, *Criterion* 8 (1928-1929): 757.

90 Lewis, *The Collected Letters of C. S. Lewis: Volume I*, 438 [February 28, 1919].

as a philosophy professor upon graduation.[91] Yet, it must be added that "Greats" was not like a degree in philosophy as we understand it today; it was concerned with preparing its future philosophers to be "generalists rather than specialists"[92] – a point well worth remembering when assessing the pros and cons of Lewis's philosophical project.

Second, during his "Honours Mods" and "Greats" years, Lewis read a lot of philosophy: Benedetto Croce's *Philosophy of the Practical: Economic and Ethic* and *Essence of Aesthetic*, Descartes' *Discourse on Method*, David Hume's *Treatise of Human Nature*, Horace Joseph's *An Introduction to Logic*, John Locke's *Some Thoughts Concerning Education*, Plato's *Republic*, Immanuel Kant's *Metaphysics of Morality*, Aristotle's *Ethics* and *Politics*, William James's *Varieties of Religious Experience*, Cicero's *De Finibus*, Thomas Hobbes's *Leviathan*, Bernard Bosanquet's *The Philosophical Theory of the State*, F. H. Bradley's *Ethical Studies* and *Appearance and Reality*, etc. While the seeds of Plato and Aristotle, whose *Republic* and *Ethics* were "the left and right lung of Oxford humanization,"[93] were still far from sprouting – indeed, Lewis was known during these years as the man "who seem[ed] to think that Plato is always wrong"[94] – the most influential philosophers Lewis was reading were Bosanquet and Bradley, the two most important British Idealists, both of whom, ironically, were greatly influenced by Plato.

IV: Subjective Idealism

After taking another First, this time in "Greats" (with an "A" in philosophy, an "AB" in ancient history, a "B" in other histories and a "B" in classics[95]), Lewis decided to pursue a third degree, in English language and literature, in hopes of bolstering his chances of getting a fellowship at Oxford when he graduated in 1923. Nevertheless, it must be stressed that all along he still hoped to become a philosophy professor due to his excellent showing in "Greats" and his ever-growing interest in philosophical discourse (even though one of his professors felt, not totally unjustified if one understands philosophy to be strictly a philosophical discourse, that Lewis was "not a real philosopher, but quite brilliant"[96]).

---

91   Lewis turned down a classical lectureship at University College, Reading, because he not only wanted to do philosophy, but also was not interested in doing only classics: "As well, pure classics is not my line." Ibid., 595 [July 20, 1922].
92   Currie, "The Arts and Social Studies, 1914-1939," 116.
93   C. S. Lewis, "Interim Report," in *C. S. Lewis: Essay Collection & Other Short Pieces*, ed. Lesley Walmsley (1956 essay reprint; London: HarperCollins, 2000), 639.
94   Lewis, *All My Road Before Me*, 53 [June 21, 1922].
95   Ibid., 83 [August 8, 1922].
96   Ibid.

Near the end of his time in the English School, Lewis's relationship with Owen Barfield, whom he had met back in 1919, began to evolve into an all-out philosophical bout, which Lewis called "The Great War." This Great War spanned from 1922 or 1923 until 1931, when Lewis became a Christian.[97] The immediate cause of The Great War was Lewis the materialist's horror at Barfield's (and his friend, Cecil Harwood's) conversion to Anthroposophy, the philosophy founded by Rudolf Steiner, which emphasizes occult-science and, especially in the case of Barfield (a Coleridgian), the centrality of the imagination.[98]

Lewis's attack on Anthroposophy was connected to his growing interest in psychoanalyzing spiritual and romantic experiences: "That's what the Great War is about," writes Barfield, "whether imagination is a vehicle for truth or whether it is simply a highly desirable and pleasurable experience of the human soul."[99] Since Lewis thought that romanticism and the imagination were the latter, Barfield was, according to him, like the dwarfs in *The Last Battle*, "being taken in" by man-made delusions and fantasies.[100] But behind this interest in psychology is something far more important for our immediate concern: Lewis rejected the solace of Anthroposophy, much like the security of Epicureanism, because he thought they were false; he wrote, "The comfort [Barfield and Harwood] got from [Steiner] (apart from the sugar plum of promised immortality, which is really the bait with which he caught Harwood) seemed something I could get much better without him"[101] – sentiments echoed by Vertue in *The Pilgrim's Regress*, who, we recall, represented Lewis's ethical integrity: "'I meant to choose things because I chose to choose them – not because I was paid for it. Do you think I am a child to be scared with rods and baited with sugar plums?'"[102] Of course as we will discuss later on, desiring heaven (and its "sugar plums") is far from being mere wish-fulfillment, yet what is important for now is that once again Lewis demonstrated his constantly maturing view of philosophy as a way of life.

---

97 Lewis was often unclear about his dates. That is, although he said in one place that the Great War began in the summer of 1922, when he finished "Greats," he said in another that it began when Barfield converted to Anthroposophy, which happened in 1923. Since the "War" was largely the result of the disagreement between Lewis and Barfield concerning Anthroposophy, it seems likely that it began in 1923. Lewis, *Surprised by Joy*, 1367.

98 Ibid., 1364.

99 Barfield, *Owen Barfield on C. S. Lewis*, 138.

100 C. S. Lewis, *The Last Battle* (1956 reprint; London: Fontana, 1985), 141.

101 Lewis, *All My Road Before Me*, 254 [July 7, 1923].

102 Lewis, *The Pilgrim's Regress*, 140.

However, before we continue with our discussion about The Great War, I want to direct our focus to two factors which occurred during The Great War and which, combined with The Great War, helped Lewis move from materialism to idealism.

The first is the books Lewis was reading while he was studying English. At that time, Lewis became familiar with many important classical-medieval Christian writers, who may have softened him toward the spiritual. The most important of these writers was Boethius, who Lewis likely read in or before 1922,[103] and whose *Consolation of Philosophy* is listed as one of the top ten influences on Lewis's "vocational attitude and . . . philosophy of life."[104] Although the importance of *The Consolation of Philosophy* was minimal at this point, it is important to remember that this book (along with works of Plato and Aristotle) was probably simmering in the back of Lewis's mind during The Great War.

The second is that in January 1924, about half a year after Lewis took another First, this time in English, he began to research the seventeenth-century Cambridge Platonist Henry More with the thought of doing a D.Phil. in philosophy.[105] Although Walter Hooper thinks Lewis chose More as his research topic because of Lewis's interest in ethics, this does not seem correct. It is true that Lewis was deeply interested in ethics at the time: witness his paper "The Promethean Fallacy in Ethics," which he read to the Philosophical Society in March 1924,[106] and the two sets of lectures he gave half a year later, the first entitled "The Good – Its Place Among the Values," which was a historical account of the Good, examining the theories of Locke, Hume, Gottfried Leibniz, Kant and Berkeley (beginning on October 14, 1924),[107] and the second entitled "The Moral Good – Its Place Among Values," likely focusing on the ethical theories of Baruch Spinoza, Leibniz, Hume, Kant

<hr/>

103 Lewis, *All My Road Before Me*, 134 [November 9, 1922].
104 C. S. Lewis, "Interview," *Christian Century* 79 (June 6, 1962).
105 Lewis, *All My Road Before Me*, n280. Ultimately Lewis gave up on the D.Phil. idea because it was "a fool's errand," meaning that he thought it would only cause his classics and philosophy (oddly, considering More was a philosopher) to rot. Ibid., n297. Wheaton College still has the notes Lewis took when he was contemplating doing his D. Phil on More. See C. S. Lewis, "Henry More" (Unpublished notes [1924]; The Marion E. Wade Center, Wheaton College).
106 Lewis, *All My Road Before Me*, 283 [January 9, 1924]. Lewis's interest in ethics is also apparent in his essay "Hegemony of Moral Values," which he tried to publish in the reputed philosophy journal *Mind*. Ibid., 298 [March 6, 1924].
107 Ibid., 348. Prior to these lectures, Lewis read Nietzsche's *Beyond Good and Evil* (April 11, 1924), Leibniz's *Monadology* and *New System* (May 6, 1924), Berkeley's *Principles of Human Knowledge* (June 12-13, 1924) and Hume's *A Treatise of Human Nature* (August 16, 1924).

and Mill (beginning on January 11, 1925).[108] Yet despite this, the notes that
Lewis made as he was reading through More do not reveal any interest in
ethics; rather, they suggest an interest in More's Platonic metaphysics, to
which Lewis was increasingly drawn.[109] Indeed, without getting ahead of
myself, it seems likely that around the time of his research on More, Lewis
was, if not an already an idealist, at least very near to becoming one.

Now as for The Great War proper, Barfield's interest in the imagination
and epistemology, along with Samuel Alexander's distinction between
"Enjoyment" and "Contemplation" (which we will return to in chapter
four),[110] helped Lewis the philosopher develop in two ways.

First, Barfield's (and later, Lewis's friend Nevill Coghill's[111]) love of the
past and all its spiritual peculiarities helped rid Lewis of his chronological
snobbery, the attitude that uses "the names of earlier periods as terms of
abuse,"[112] which, of course, entails the idea that because something was
written in the past, it must be useless or of no worth. Incidentally, it is
interesting to compare Lewis's first reaction to Barfield's occult-sciences
("'Why – damn it – it's *medieval*'"[113]) to Lewis's much later self-identification
as an "Old Western Man" (we will return to this in chapter five).

Second, Barfield pointed out that Lewis's assumptions in logic, morality
and aesthetics required some kind of spiritual metaphysics since Lewis could
not properly maintain his belief in the objectivity of reason, morality and
art with his combination of Stoical materialism and epistemological realism.
As a result of both Barfield's comments and Lewis's previous readings in
Berkeley, Bradley and Bosanquet, we are told by Lewis:

---

108 Ibid., n348. Probably in preparation for these lectures, Lewis read T. H. Green's
Prolegomena to Ethics (December 1924), Kant's *The Metaphysics of Morals* and *Critique
of Practical Reason* (February 6-7, 1925), Mill's *Utilitarianism, Liberty and Representative
Government* and *Principle of Political Economy with Some of Their Applications to Social
Philosophy,* (February 9, 1925), Hume's *An Enquiry Concerning the Principle of Morals
in Enquiries* (February 9, 1925), Lebniz's *Monadology* and *New System* (February 11,
1925), Russell's *Problems of Philosophy* (February 17, 1925), Spinoza's *Ethics* (February
17, 1925) and G. E. Moore's *Philosophical Studies* (February 18-20, 1925). On top of
these, Lewis was reading a lot of logic in 1925, for instance, Bradley's *The Principles of
Logic* and Mill's *A System of Logic, Ratiocinative and Inductive.*
109 Lewis was also re-reading Plato's *Phaedrus,* and discussing his *Philebus,* at the time.
Ibid., 284 [January 17-20, 1924], 293 [February 29, 1924].
110 Lewis, *Surprised by Joy,* 1370.
111 Ibid., 1367.
112 Ibid., 1363.
113 Ibid.

I was therefore compelled to give up realism. I had been trying to defend it ever since I began reading philosophy. Partly, no doubt, this was mere 'cussedness.' Idealism was then the dominant philosophy at Oxford and I was by nature 'against Government.' But partly, too, realism satisfied an emotional need. I wanted Nature to be quite independent of our observation; something other, indifferent, self-existing. . . . But now, it seemed to me, I had to give that up. Unless I were to accept an unbelievable alternative, I must admit that mind was no late-come epiphenomenona; that the whole universe was, in the last resort, mental; that our logic was participation in a cosmic *Logos*.[114]

This marked Lewis's conversion to idealism, which, broadly-speaking, is the philosophical doctrine that says reality is mind-coordinated or that the objects constituting the "external world" are not independent of minds, but exist only correlatively to mental operations. However, there is a problem here: although the evidence, *pace* James Patrick,[115] suggests that Lewis became an idealist around late 1923 to early 1924 (based on his critique of Russell and some comments – which will be mentioned shortly – concerning Berkeley[116]), it is unclear what *kind* of idealism Lewis had in mind when he converted.[117] I suggest the following.

For about a year into his conversion to idealism (from 1923 or 1924 to about 1924 or 1925), Lewis was a confused supporter of the absolute idealism of the British Idealists (Green, Bradley and Bosanquet) as evidenced by his confession of his "watered down Hegelianism."[118] His attraction to this kind of idealism, which claims that the Absolute or Reality *is* the sum total of all Appearances or experiences,[119] had to do with the quasi-religious feeling he got when reading about the hidden glory of Reality behind the veil of all Appearances; or, as Bradley rather Platonically put it:

It may come from a failure in my metaphysics, or from a weakness of the flesh which continues to blind me, but the notion that existence could be the same as understanding strikes as cold and ghost-like as the dreariest materialism. That the glory of this world in the end is

---

114 Ibid., 1364-5.

115 Patrick thinks that Lewis became an idealist in 1922. This seems unlikely because the best evidence shows that during The Great War, which likely only began in 1923, Lewis became an idealist. Patrick, *The Magdalen Metaphysicals*, 115.

116 Lewis, *Surprised by Joy*, 1373.

117 "[Lewis] gave no name to the idealism that influenced him when he came to Magdalen in 1925." Patrick, *The Magdalen Metaphysicals*, xxix.

118 Lewis, *Surprised by Joy*, 1373.

119 Bradley, *Appearance and Reality*, 455.

appearance leaves the world more glorious, if we feel it is a show of some fuller splendour; but the sensuous curtain is a deception and cheat, if it hides some colourless movement of atoms, some spectral woof of impalpable abstractions, or unearthly ballet of bloodless categories.[120]

This great sense of the hidden glory of things, Lewis wrote, "had much of the quality of Heaven," and so was an experience that he "should be very sorry not to have passed through."[121] Indeed, it was a fundamental building block in his philosophical journey, for it taught him that "it is more important that Heaven should exist than that any of us should reach it."[122]

But Lewis did not initially dwell long in the tents of the British Idealists because their doctrine, Lewis originally felt, was confusing; for example, in 1922, just before Lewis became an idealist, we read: "After lunch I read Bradley's *Appearance and Reality* – the chapter on Reality. It is most difficult: he seems to do the very thing he protests against, namely, pass from the necessary consistency of the Absolute for *thought* to its harmony for *feeling*, using the word 'inharmonious' in an ambiguous sense. But probably I do not understand him;"[123] and in 1924, just after Lewis became an idealist, we read again: "Went into town shopping in the morning and sat for a long time in the Union reading Bosanquet's *Suggestions in Ethics* wh[ich] I brought out for the sake of the beautiful passage about the Absolute eating out of your hand. Bosanquet has apparently the right point of view about most things . . . but a little bit woolly."[124]

As a result of this confusion, Lewis turned to the more lucid subjective idealism of Berkeley, which claims (1) "there is no other substance than *spirit*"[125] because there is nothing behind spirit / mind and its perceptions,[126] and (2) since "God" is the perfect Spirit, He must perceive all.[127] What resurrected Lewis's interest in Berkeley – what reminded him of the Bishop's clarity – is an extremely important episode in itself.

120 F. H. Bradley, *The Principles of Logic*, vol. 2 (Oxford: Oxford University Press, 1922), 591.
121 Lewis, *Surprised by Joy*, 1363.
122 Ibid.
123 Lewis, *All My Road Before Me*, 74 [July 23, 1922].
124 Ibid., 323 [May 15, 1924].
125 George Berkeley, *Principles of Human Knowledge*, in *Philosophical Works including the Works on Vision*, ed. Michael Ayers (London: Everyman, 1996), 91 [1.7].
126 Ibid., 90 [1.3].
127 Berkeley, *Three Dialogues between Hylas and Philonous*, 203 [2.213].

During the academic year of 1924-1925, Lewis got his first professorship, a temporary position teaching philosophy (his life long ambition) at University College, Oxford, and in the following year, in 1925-1926, he got his second professorship, a fellowship teaching English at Magdalen College, Oxford.[128] Of this important change, Lewis wrote at length to his father:

> As to the other change – from Philosophy to English . . . I am rather glad of the change. I have come to think that if I had the mind, I have not the brain and nerves for a life of pure philosophy. A continued search among the abstract roots of things, a perpetual questioning of all that plain men take for granted, a chewing the cud for fifty years over inevitable ignorance and a constant frontier watch on the little tidy lighted conventional world of science and daily life – is this the best life for temperaments such as ours? Is it the way of health or even of sanity? There is a certain type of man, bull necked and self satisfied in his 'pot bellied equanimity' who urgently needs that bleak and questioning atmosphere. But what is a tonic to the Saxon may be a debauch to us Celts. And it certainly is to the Hindoos. . . . I am not condemning philosophy. Indeed in turning from it to literary history and criticism, I am conscious of a descent: and if the air on the heights did not suit me, still I have brought back something of value. It will be a comfort to me all my life to know that the scientist and the materialist have not the last word: that Darwin and [Herbert] Spencer undermining ancestral beliefs stand themselves on a foundation of sand; of gigantic assumptions and irreconcilable contradictions an inch below the surface. It leaves the whole thing rich in possibilities: and if it dashes the shallow optimisms it does the same for the shallow pessimisms. But having once seen all this 'darkness,' a darkness full of promise, it is perhaps best to shut the trap door and come back to ordinary life: unless you are one of the really great who can get into it a little way – and I was not. . . . At any rate I escape with joy from one definite drawback of philosophy – its solitude. I was beginning to feel that your first year carries you out of the reach of all save other professionals. No one sympathises with your adventures in that subject because no one understands them: and if you struck treasure trove no one would be able to use it. But perhaps this is enough on the subject.[129]

While Lewis was happy on the whole with his move to English, it must be emphasized that this neither marked the end of his philosophical interests – for, we must remember, Lewis did not think of philosophy chiefly as a discourse and profession – nor did it even mark the end of his philosophy

---

128 Lewis, *Surprised by Joy*, 1369.
129 Lewis, *The Collected Letters of C. S. Lewis: Volume I*, 648-9 [August 14, 1925].

teaching since part of the reason that Magdalen College gave Lewis the fellowship was because he could teach English *and* philosophy: "Lewis had to be always ready to 'fill in' with a philosophy tutorial or lecture if required. Of the sixteen pupils Lewis had in 1926 only five were reading English."[130]

To relate this, then, to Lewis's renewed interest in Berkeley, we know that when he was teaching at University College, he lectured on the modern philosophers, one of whom was Berkeley, but on top of this, at both University College and Magdalen College, Lewis gave weekly tutorials to philosophy students, which meant, according to him, that he "needed a [philosophical] position of [his] own as a basis from which to criticise [his] pupils' essays."[131] As a result, the philosophical position that Lewis assumed in 1924 or 1925 was Berkeleyan subjective idealism (with a twist[132]):

> I was now teaching philosophy (I suspect very badly) as well as English. And my watered down Hegelianism wouldn't serve for tutorial purposes. A tutor must make things clear. Now the Absolute cannot be made clear. Do you mean Nobody-knows-what, or do you mean a superhuman mind and therefore (as we may as well admit) a Person? After all, did Hegel and Bradley and all the rest of them ever do more than add mystifications to the simple, workable, theistic idealism of Berkeley? I thought not. And didn't Berkeley's 'God' do all the same work as the Absolute, with the added advantage that we had at least some notion of what we meant by Him. I thought he did. So I was driven back into something like Berkeleyianism; but Berkeleyianism with a few top-dressings of my own. I distinguished this philosophical 'God' very sharply (or so I said) from 'the God of popular religion.' There was, I explained, no possibility of being in a personal relation with Him. For I thought He projected us as a dramatist projects his characters, and I could no more 'meet' Him, than Hamlet could meet Shakespeare. I didn't call Him 'God' either; I called Him 'Spirit.' One fights for remaining comforts.[133]

---

130 Roger Lancelyn Green and Walter Hooper, *C. S. Lewis: A Biography*, revised ed. (London: HarperCollins, 2003), 76.

131 Lewis, *Surprised by Joy*, 1373.

132 In many ways, Lewis was like philosopher R. G. Collingwood, who was teaching philosophy at Magdalen College, Oxford, at the time: "[There was] no ready-made class into which you could put a philosopher who, after a thorough training in 'realism' had revolted against it and arrived at conclusions of his own quite unlike anything of the school of Green [the idealist] had taught." R. G. Collingwood, *An Autobiography* (Oxford: Clarendon Press, 1939), 99.

133 Lewis, *Surprised by Joy*, 1373.

V: Absolute Idealism

Nevertheless, Lewis's subjective idealism did not last long. His move from absolute idealism to subjective idealism was a pendulum that swung back and forth, for Lewis revisited both positions in turn under the names "pantheism" and "theism" over the next few years.

For instance, in a 1928 Great War letter, Lewis spoke of the danger of "[r]elapse into extreme subjective idealism."[134] Since Lewis's subjective idealism came after his initial hiatus with absolute idealism, the implication is that Lewis was a pantheist at this time as pantheism follows idealism in *The Pilgrim's Regress* outline; and the "pantheism" that Lewis referred to in his outline and which he subscribed to in 1928 (and earlier, as we will see), moreover, appears to be none other than the absolute idealism of the British Idealists, whom Lewis had rejected earlier on. As evidence for this, we need to recall that the philosophy of the British Idealists – or more accurately, that of Bradley, with whom Lewis was the most acquainted (and whose nephew Lewis tutored in philosophy![135]) – teaches that there is one all-encompassing Absolute Reality that in some sense forms a coherent and all-inclusive system (of every experience or Appearance); in other words, save for emphasis (for which we may once again chastise Lewis for his imprecise use of language), Bradley's absolute idealism, which focuses on the conditions for an intelligible world, is really no different than pantheism, which focuses on religion, since both doctrines would agree that everything is God. And this should come as no surprise because while Bradley rejected many things from the absolute idealism of G. W. F. Hegel, it is likely that he borrowed Hegel's pantheistic doctrine that the totality of all beings is God.[136] Indeed, because Lewis later identified the absolute idealism of Hegel with pantheism,[137] and since there is a strong link between Hegel and Bradley (Lewis called him a "British Hegelian"[138]), I would say that while Lewis specifically *called* the British Idealists "Idealists,"[139] he actually *meant* that they, and in particular, Bradley, represented the pantheism mentioned in his outline in *The Pilgrim's Regress*.

---

134 Lewis, *The Collected Letters of C. S. Lewis: Volume III*, 1636 [January 1928, "The Great War Letters" Series I, Letter 8].

135 Lewis, *All My Road Before Me*, 350 [February 10, 1925].

136 Richard Wollheim, introduction to *Ethical Studies*, by F. H. Bradley, 2nd ed. (Oxford: Oxford University Press, 1988), xvi.

137 Lewis, *The Pilgrim's Regress*, 151.

138 Lewis, *Surprised by Joy*, 1365.

139 Lewis saw a nominal difference between British Idealism and pantheism, referring to his conversion from idealism to pantheism on the same page as he mentioned the British Idealists: "Idealism itself went out of fashion. The dynasty of Green, Bradley, and Bosanquet fell." Lewis, preface to the third edition of *The Pilgrim's Regress*, 5.

Nonetheless, while it is clear that Lewis moved from subjective idealism (i.e. "Idealism") to absolute idealism (i.e. "Pantheism"), it remains to be determined when this transition happened and what motivated it.

Since Lewis converted to idealism in either 1923 or 1924 and seems to have maintained this doctrine while he was teaching philosophy at Oxford (which was for about three years in total, including his year as a full-time adjunct), the most reasonable date for Lewis's move back to absolute idealism is around 1926-1927. But while we can date this conversion fairly accurately, it is harder to say why Lewis rejected "the simple, workable, theistic idealism of Berkeley" in favour of absolute idealism, for Lewis himself mentioned that one of the reasons why he chose Berkeleyanism as his philosophy of choice when giving tutorials was because it was better than his "watered down Hegelianism" – i.e. absolute idealism or pantheism.

I believe that as Lewis began to develop as an idealist, he started to make more sense of Bradley and the others, and consequently found their answer to the problem of how we can know other finite spirits more convincing than Berkeley's pseudo-solipsism (more on this in chapter six). Most likely what helped Lewis better understand the absolute idealist position is the many discussions he had had not only with Barfield, but also with the members of the "Philosopher's Tea" or "Wee Teas" (an exclusive philosophy club of only six members, including the celebrated philosopher Gilbert Ryle)[140] and

140 "Our seniors had an institution called 'The Philosopher's Teas.' They met on Thursdays at 4 o'clock. Anyone present could raise a point for discussion. We juniors were invited to join and we found the occasions friendly and unstuffy (again the genuine democracy of the faculty could be clearly felt). But, as a forum for discussion, they were not a success. . . . Tea-time is not a philosophic hour: and, by the time the crumpets had gone round, it would be 4.15 or 4.30. We juniors were under such tutorial pressure that we had to teach daily from 5 to 7 o'clock, so we had to leave at 4.50 to get back to our Colleges. . . . We juniors established a group built on our experience of the 'Teas.' We agreed that evening is the time for thought. . . . Membership should be limited to the number ideal for a discussion, which we agreed to be six. To avoid competitive luxury, dinners were to be three-course, and with beer not wine. (This was not pedantically maintained). Our original membership was: Gilbert Ryle, Henry Price, Frank Hardie, C. S. Lewis, T. D. Weldon and myself. C. S. Lewis soon seceded from philosophy to English literature, popular theology and science fiction; but not before he had assisted in a happy contribution to our proceedings. . . . [I]t was understood that opening remarks need not be finished papers but rather flying kites (even in note form if desired). We knew each other so well that our basic methods and interests could be taken for granted, and our growing points exposed straightway to lively, frank and friendly scrutiny. . . . I am sure that everything any of us published would have been considerably less well-argued but for running this gauntlet. . . . Quite apart from its value to our philosophy, I count my membership as, apart from my marriage, the happiest and most refreshing experience of my life." John Mabbott, *Oxford Memories* (Oxford: Thornton's, 1986),

the members of the Oxford Philosophical Society, which, importantly, was largely made up of absolute idealists:

> Oxford Philosophy, as we found it, was completely inbred. It had practically no contacts with Cambridge, or the Continent, or America. The traditional doctrine was Hegelian idealism, filtered through the great Scottish prophets, [Edward] Caird, [Andrew Seth] Pringle-Pattison, [Andrew] Seth, [David George] Ritchie and [William] Wallace, and our own T. H. Green, [Bernard] Bosanquet and [F. H.] Bradley.[141]

Moreover, when Lewis went to Magdalen College in 1925, he spent a lot of time walking, breakfasting and "drift[ing] into philosophical conversation" with two important resident absolute idealists,[142] Clement Charles Julian Webb and John Alexander Smith,[143] to whom Lewis acknowledged his intellectual debts:[144] "The philosophy shared by Webb, Lewis [and] Smith . . . would without hesitation have been identified by their university contemporaries as [absolute] idealism."[145]

VI: Theism

As we have seen throughout all of Lewis's philosophical phases, conversion is not a straightforward procedure; for example in 1927, when Lewis was "officially" an absolute idealist, he wrote:

> Was thinking about imagination and intellect and the unholy muddle I am in about them at present: undigested scraps of anthroposophy and psychoanalysis jostling with orthodox idealism over a background of

---

77-8.
141 Ibid., 73.
142 Lewis, *The Collected Letters of C. S. Lewis: Volume I*, 899 [June 1, 1930].
143 Adam Fox, also a fellow at Magdalen College at the time of Lewis, recounted Lewis's relationship with Smith: "But Lewis was a philosopher as well as a man of letters, and as such able to bring out J. A. much better and make him show his paces. He asked him enticing questions and chaffed him not a little in an affectionate way." Adam Fox, "At the Breakfast Table," in *C. S. Lewis at the Breakfast Table and Other Reminiscences*, ed. James Como, 89-95 (San Diego: Harcourt Brace & Company, 1992), 92.
144 "The worst is that I must leave undescribed many men whom I love and to whom I am deeply in debt: G. H. Stevenson and E. F. Carritt, my tutors, the Fark (but who could paint him anyway?), and five great Magdalen men who enlarged my very idea of what a learned life should be – P. V. M. Benecke, C. C. J. Webb, J. A. Smith, F. E. Brightman, and C. T. Onions. Except for Oldie, I have always been blessed both in my official and my unofficial teachers." Lewis, *Surprised by Joy*, 1369.
145 Patrick, *The Magdalen Metaphysicals*, xv. "Smith, an almost slavish follower of Croce, called his own philosophy absolute idealism." Ibid., xxiii.

good old Kirkian rationalism. Lord what a mess! And all the time (with me) there's the danger of falling back into most childish superstitions, or of running into dogmatic materialism to escape them.[146]

Therefore, it should come as no surprise that Lewis's move from absolute idealism to theism was not a clear-cut issue.

From about 1928-1929, for instance, Lewis slowly began to phase out the pantheistic word "Absolute" and replace it, once again, with the more Berkeleyan – though also to a lesser extent, Bradleyan or Crocean – term, "Spirit," which in turn was interchanged with "God" for a time before becoming simply "God."[147] Although it might be confusing why Lewis began to revert back to more Berkeleyan terms after he had abandoned them for pantheistic ones only a few years earlier, the answer is quite simple: Lewis started to use "Spirit" instead of "Absolute" because Berkeley's idealism, subjective idealism, was also known as *theistic* idealism, and so it made sense for Lewis, who was on the road to theism, returning to the belief in the separateness of finite sprits and Spirit, to once again use the term "Spirit."[148] In fact, the theism of Berkeley was likely important in acting as a bridge between idealism and more Platonic, dualistic theism, for when he was asked what ultimately brought him back to Christianity, the first thing Lewis mentioned was "philosophy" and then added, "I still think Berkeley is unanswerable."[149] We are in great danger of misunderstanding Lewis if the impact of Berkeley's theistic idealism is overlooked.

However, while this linguistic consideration shows *that* Lewis was returning to theism, it does not say *why* he was doing so. What began to convince Lewis of the truth of theism was in large part the books he was reading and lecturing on at the time. That is, while Lewis was teaching philosophy and English, he became intimately aware of, and increasingly drawn to, the greatest philosophers (and poets) of antiquity and the Middle Ages: Plato, Aristotle, Boethius, Richard Hooker[150] et al., all of whom Lewis

---

146 Lewis, *All My Road Before Me*, 431-2 [January 18, 1927].

147 Lewis, *Surprised by Joy*, 1381. Of course, this transition was far from a black and white thing. For example in a letter dated December 26, 1929, Lewis, then technically a theist, referred to the Creator as "the Absolute." Lewis, *The Collected Letters of C. S. Lewis: Volume I*, 845 [December 26, 1929].

148 Moreover, in many of the later Great War documents, such as *De Bono et Malo*, Lewis made constant reference to the "Christian myth" to make philosophical points. C. S. Lewis, *De Bono et Malo* (Unpublished "Great War" document [1929?]; The Marion E. Wade Center, Wheaton College), 2.

149 Lewis, *The Collected Letters of C. S. Lewis: Volume II*, 703 [February 15, 1946].

150 Although I would consider Hooker a man of the late Middle Ages, some would say that he properly belongs to the Renaissance. For my part, I am inclined to agree with Lewis

interpreted as either dualists with theistic leanings (Plato and Aristotle)[151] or theists proper (Boethius and Hooker). For instance, when Lewis taught philosophy at University College (1924-1925), his interest in Plato's ethics, especially as presented in *Philebus* and *Republic*,[152] was apparent; indeed, it is not unimportant that Lewis's take on the moral law as presented in "Hegemony of Moral Value," written in 1922 and revised in 1924, probably approximated to his take on the universal moral law as found in *The Abolition of Man*, written ten years after he became a Christian. Furthermore, when Lewis taught both philosophy and English at Magdalen College (1924-1927), he read, taught and enjoyed the *Theaetetus*,[153] *Statesman*,[154] and *Erastae* of Plato,[155] the *Ethics* and *Politics* of Aristotle,[156] *Of the Laws of Ecclesiastical Polity* by Hooker (who Lewis called "a great man"[157]) and *The Consolation of Philosophy* by Boethius.[158] Finally, when Lewis taught English at Magdalen College (1928), he said he was "deep in medieval things,"[159] not only because he was teaching a great deal of medieval literature but also because he chose, as his first academic book, to write about medieval allegory, which would later become *The Allegory of Love*, a book overflowing with Neoplatonic, theistic philosophy. Hence, because of Lewis's increasing focus on classical-medieval philosophy and literature, the seeds of a Neoplatonic, theistic worldview – which had long been planted, beginning with Plato and Aristotle – slowly began to choke out the weeds (or lesser plants, at least[160]) of absolute idealism:

---

that the division between the Middle Ages and Renaissance is vague at best (see chapter five).

151 Strictly speaking, it is simply wrong to call Plato and Aristotle theists. Plato's "Good," which is "beyond being," cannot literally be spoken of and so it is not clear whether "the Good" is "God" or not, nor is Plato's "Demiurge," the lesser god who created the world, enough like God to justify calling Plato a theist. Furthermore, although Aristotle's "Unmoved Mover" is often thought of as "God," a careful reading of Aristotle reveals that he thought there were many such "Intelligences." Hence, Plato and Aristotle should probably be understood more as polytheists and dualists than theists. Lewis himself was unclear as to what he thought of Plato and Aristotle, yet he did rightly, though anachronistically, speak of "the almost miraculous avoidance of the Pantheistic swamp by Plato and (still more) by Aristotle." Lewis, *The Collected Letters of C. S. Lewis: Volume II*, 771 [April 15, 1947].

152 Patrick, *The Magdalen Metaphysicals*, 127.

153 Lewis, *All My Road Before Me*, 453 [February 17, 1927].

154 Ibid., 449 [February 8, 1927].

155 Ibid., 456 [February 27, 1927].

156 Ibid., 383 [May 1, 1926], 384 [May 2, 1926], 385 [May 3, 1926], 397 [May 17, 1926], 434 [January 22, 1927].

157 Ibid., 406 [June 4, 1926].

158 Lewis, *The Collected Letters of C. S. Lewis: Volume I*, 740 [December 12, 1927].

159 Ibid., 754 [April 24, 1928].

160 Lewis always acknowledged his philosophical debt to idealism, and so it would be

"The fox had been dislodged from Hegelian Wood and was now running in the open, 'with all the wo in the world,' bedraggled and weary, hounds barely a field behind. And nearly everyone now (one way or another) in pack; Plato, Dante . . . Everyone and everything had joined the other side."[161]

However, what finally pushed Lewis from idealism to theism is a factor much more important than books: livability. Perhaps due to the ultimate breakdown between the categories of good and evil in absolute idealism,[162] Lewis realized that "[Absolute] Idealism can be talked, and even felt; it cannot be lived."[163] Yet the Oxford don did not simply drop idealism and remain in a vacuum, for through a deep appreciation for classical and medieval philosophy and literature, he came to see that theism *could* be lived; as he would later say in *The Abolition of Man*: "For the wise men of old the cardinal problem had been how to conform the soul to reality, and the solution had been knowledge, self-discipline, and virtue."[164]

Indeed, these events coincided with another event which finally forced Lewis to define philosophy as it ought to be defined:

> Once, when [Dom Bede Griffiths] and Barfield were lunching in my room, I happened to refer to philosophy as 'a subject.' 'It wasn't a *subject* to Plato,' said Barfield, 'it was a *way*.' The quiet but fervent agreement

---

wrong to consider it a totally false philosophy. Moreover, idealism owed much to older sources, such as Plato, Aristotle and Christianity. In *The Pilgrim's Regress*, Lewis said of Bosanquet: "Another of the family [Mr. Wisdom's family], Bernard by name, was in radiant health. John had seen him drinking Mother Kirk's [the Church's] wine with great relish and refreshment by moonlight: but the waking Bernard maintained that Mother Kirk's wine was merely a bad, early attempt at the admirable barley-water which his father sometimes brought out on birthdays and great occasions; and 'to this barley-water,' he said, 'I owe my health.'" Lewis, *The Pilgrim's Regress*, 145.

161 Lewis, *Surprised by Joy*, 1374.

162 Even back in 1926, Lewis was aware of the moral difficulty of absolute idealism. Writing to a friend, he asked, "Again, in your pantheistic conclusion, should you not show that you are aware of some of the moral difficulties? I mean, if the spirit grows in the grass etc, and in the cancer and the murderer, if it does everything, must it not be simply the neutral background of good and evil?" Lewis, *The Collected Letters of C. S. Lewis: Volume III*, 1500 [1926].

163 Lewis, *Surprised by Joy*, 1375. Because Lewis converted from idealism to theism (and then Christianity) and because idealism was not livable, Leanne Payne is only partially right when she says, "It was, in fact, the experience of the 'living presence' of God that eventually brought Lewis from a form of philosophical idealism . . . to a supernatural knowledge of a personal God." Leanne Payne, *Real Presence: The Christian Worldview of C. S. Lewis as Incarnational Reality* (Westchester, IL: Crossway Books, 1988), 14.

164 C. S. Lewis, *The Abolition of Man; or, Reflections on Education with Special Reference to the Teaching of English in the Upper Forms of Schools*, in *C. S. Lewis: Selected Books* [Short Edition] (1943 reprint; London: HarperCollins, 2002), 427.

of Griffiths, and the quick glance of understanding between these two, revealed to me my own frivolity. Enough had been thought, and said, and felt, and imagined. It was about time that something should be done.[165]

The significance of both Lewis's move toward theism because of livability and his conviction that philosophy is not merely an academic discourse cannot be understated. More than either his philosophical training or his stint as a philosophy professor at Oxford, the aforementioned events demonstrate Lewis's understanding of philosophy as a way of life; indeed, shortly after these events, Lewis admitted that living according to reason required him both to make "an attempt at complete virtue"[166] and practice spiritual exercises, among which he humorously included "Calvinistic exercises,"[167] and quite seriously, though odd for a non-theist, *prayer*; in fact, Lewis's situation was in many ways reflected in Orual's in *Till We Have Faces* when she says, "But if I

---

165 Lewis, *Surprised by Joy*, 1374. Barfield's account of this story is even more illuminating as it reminds us that the understanding of philosophy as a way of life was not a new concept to Lewis even at that time: "What enabled him to have patience with my ignorant blunderings was the fact I have alluded to that he himself was constitutionally incapable of treating philosophy as a merely academic exercise. Oddly enough, on page 212 of the English edition of *Surprised by Joy* he accuses himself of that very failing, that is, of treating philosophy as an academic exercise. Referring to an occasion when a man named Griffiths and I were lunching with him, he says 'I happened to refer to philosophy as a 'subject.' 'It was not a *subject* to Plato,' said Barfield, 'it was a way.' The quiet but fervent agreement of Griffiths and the quick glance of understanding between these two revealed to me my own frivolity.' Well, flattering as that passage may be to my self-esteem, I am bound to say, and I am rather glad to have this opportunity of saying it, that it is, as far as my recollection goes, pure applesauce, unless of course Lewis is using the word *frivolity* in a highly specialized and limited sense. . . . Lewis could not help trying to live by what he thought. 'Idealism,' he says in the same book, 'can be talked and even felt. It cannot be lived.' And that was why he gave it up." Barfield, *Owen Barfield on C. S. Lewis*, 10.

166 Lewis, *Surprised by Joy*, 1374.

167 As we know, Lewis was raised in Protestant Ireland, and as such was surrounded by Calvinists and Puritans. Thus, it is of little surprise that Lewis had many inside jokes about such people, particularly in regard to their severity. For instance, Lewis once joked with his father, saying: "As I have probably told you before, every group of Awarders consists of one Oxford and one Cambridge man, and they shift them about from year to year. This time I have lost my Cambridge colleague with whom I have worked very pleasantly for the last four years, and getting instead a man whom everyone has warned me against. . . . He has quarrelled with every previous colleague he has had and it remains to see whether I shall fare better. He is old too, which makes the matter worse: it is easier to stand ones rights to contemporaries without the appearance of insolence. Can you suggest any spiritual exercises – perhaps our old friend 'Calvinistic exercises' would do – suitable as a prophylactic against loss of temper in trying circumstances?" Lewis, *The Collected Letters of C. S. Lewis: Volume I*, 799-800 [July 7, 1929].

practiced true philosophy, as Socrates meant it, I should change my ugly soul into a fair one. And this, the gods helping me, I would do."[168] Consequently, what Lewis found when he started living his philosophy – when he started praying and "the gods" started helping him – was that "idealism turned out, when you took it seriously, to be disguised Theism."[169] And so being "allowed to play at philosophy no longer,"[170] Lewis, in the Trinity Term of 1929, finally admitted "that God was God" and became a theist.[171]

VII: Neoplatonic Christianity

The final move in Lewis's philosophical journey is from theism to Christianity (concerning which Lewis once remarked, "[I]n our Western civilization we are obligated both morally and intellectually to come to grips with Jesus Christ; if we refuse to do so we are guilty of being bad philosophers and bad thinkers"[172]). Now at this point, some may protest about my terminology, maintaining that since the destination is a religion and not a philosophy, I should now speak of Lewis's *religious* journey or "journey to faith."[173] Perhaps so, but since, as we shall see, Lewis only endorsed Christianity because he thought it *true* – or, in other words, since Lewis came to Christianity out of obedience to *reason* (from which faith later followed) – I would maintain that Lewis was on a philosophical journey from theism to Christianity, and as such he (much like Justin Martyr) explicitly or implicitly understood Christianity to be a *philosophy*.[174] Moreover, although Lewis's conversion to Christianity was the most important conversion of his life, much of what needs to be said about Christianity will be deferred until later chapters due to its intimate connection with two key concepts: heavenly desire and Myth. For my immediate purpose, I want to draw attention to the more "purely" philosophical or rational factors that led to Lewis's conversion.

---

168 C. S. Lewis, *Till We Have Faces*, in *C. S. Lewis: Selected Books* [Long Edition] (1956 reprint; London: HarperCollins, 1999), 1006.

169 C. S. Lewis, "Is Theology Poetry?" in *C. S. Lewis: Essay Collection & Other Short Pieces*, ed. Lesley Walmsley (1945 essay reprint; London: HarperCollins, 2000), 20.

170 Lewis, *Surprised by Joy*, 1375.

171 Ibid., 1376.

172 C. S. Lewis, "Cross-Examination," in *C. S. Lewis: Essay Collection & Other Short Pieces*, ed. Lesley Walmsley (1963 essay reprint; London: HarperCollins, 2000), 557.

173 David Downing, *The Most Reluctant Convert: C. S. Lewis's Journey to Faith* (Downer's Grove, IL: InterVarsity, 2002).

174 What Lewis said of Paul Elmer More could well be applied to the Oxford don himself: "He talked for truth not victory." Lewis, *The Collected Letters of C. S. Lewis: Volume III*, 1543 [August 3, 1941].

In 1926, when Lewis was undergoing his second transition between subjective idealism and absolute idealism, he read the hugely influential *Everlasting Man* by G. K. Chesterton (who was praised by the great Neoscholastic philosopher Etienne Gilson as "one of the deepest thinkers who ever existed," and who, like Lewis though to a lesser degree, may be considered a philosopher in the more ancient sense of the word[175]). Although *The Everlasting Man* did not, like so many books in Lewis's philosophical journey, have an immediate impact on him, when Lewis became a theist, Chesterton's account of Christianity started to look increasingly more plausible.

And this plausibility was enormously enhanced by "increasing knowledge of medieval literature," for, Lewis insisted, "It became harder & harder to think that all those great poets & philosophers were wrong."[176] And of the medieval philosophers or philosophical-poets Lewis had in mind, Augustine, Boethius and Dante Alighieri were the most prominent.

Augustine's impact on Lewis in his early years as a theist is difficult to gauge, but his later influence on Lewis is nearly impossible to overstate; indeed, save for a few minor criticisms,[177] it is possible to see Augustine as Lewis's pre-eminent philosopher during Lewis's Christian phase, not only because the Saint's golden touch is evident on nearly every branch of Lewis's thought, but also because Lewis himself confessed his debt to the Bishop of Hippo, describing himself as one "who loved Balder before Christ and Plato before St. Augustine."[178] Although we do not know exactly when Lewis read

---

175 Michael Aeschliman gives us good reasons for why Chesterton, in many ways like Lewis, ought to be considered a philosopher in the broad sense of the word: "Chesterton was, in the words of the great twentieth-century French Thomist philosopher and historian Etienne Gilson, 'one of the deepest thinkers who ever existed,' despite the fact that he was neither a scholar, nor a systematic philosopher, nor even what we now call an 'intellectual.' He was instead like the early Swift and Johnson, a journalist, and even, in a sense, a hack writer; but he was a metaphysical journalist, a hack writer who 'saw life steadily and saw it whole.' In the tradition of Arnold, he tried to get what he believed was every person's right and duty to get, what he called the 'vision of life in light of a general philosophy.' In an age of specialists, he was a generalist; in an age of philosophy professors, he was a philosopher." Michael Aeschliman, *The Restitution of Man: C. S. Lewis and the Case Against Scientism* (Grand Rapids, MI: Eerdmans, 1983), 38-9.

176 Lewis, *The Collected Letters of C. S. Lewis: Volume II*, 703 [February 15, 1946].

177 The only two criticisms Lewis had of Augustine are the Saint's view that it is better not to love things too much in this life because they hurt you too much when they die, and the explicitly devotional aspects of *Confessions*. Lewis, *The Four Loves*, 76. Lewis, *The Collected Letters of C. S. Lewis: Volume II*, 190 [April 34, 1936].

178 C. S. Lewis, "Religion without Dogma?" in *C. S. Lewis: Essay Collection & Other Short Pieces*, ed. Lesley Walmsley (1946 essay reprint; London: HarperCollins, 2000), 165. Cf. Sara McLaughlin, "*The City of God* Revisited: C. S. Lewis's Debt to Saint Augustine,"

Augustine, he must have read *Confessions* sometime before 1932, for in that year Lewis wrote *The Pilgrim's Regress*, in which *Confessions* is mentioned. Since it is likely that Lewis, searching for philosophical influences on the English writers he was researching during the late 1920s,[179] read Augustine when he was still a theist, it is probable that the Saint's philosophical journey, his Neoplatonic Christianity and his love of Truth appealed to Lewis, who shared many of the same experiences and values; in fact, in the final book of *Surprised by Joy*, which deals with Lewis's conversion from theism to Christianity, Lewis quoted Augustine approvingly in regard to philosophy as a way of life: "For it is one thing to see the land of peace from a wooded ridge . . . and another to tread the road that leads up to it."[180]

Boethius I have spoken of before and I need only add that his Neoplatonic Christianity and his blend of reason and poetry, primarily as found in *The Consolation of Philosophy*, was perfectly suited to Lewis the poet-philosopher; in fact, Lewis even went so far as to claim that Boethius's account of time and eternity is even clearer than Plato's,[181] and as we shall see in subsequent chapters, Lewis's metaphysics, epistemology, ethics and literary style all owe something to the Last of the Romans.

Finally, Dante, whom Lewis had read with little benefit back in his Lucretian materialist days at Great Bookham, had a wonderful effect on Lewis the theist, who, in 1930, was making "an attempt at religion."[182] On rereading Dante's *Paradiso* (in Italian, of course), Lewis said, "[It] really opened a new world to me. . . . I should describe it as feeling more *important* than any poetry I have ever read . . . wheel within wheel, but wheels of glory, and the One radiated through the Many."[183] Indeed, the impact of Dante was so strongly felt that Lewis recommended his friend Arthur Greeves read *The Divine Comedy* – note this well – almost as a *spiritual exercise*:

CSL: *The Bulletin of the New York C. S. Lewis Society* 23, no. 6 (April 1992): 1-9.
179 "I myself was first led into reading the Christian classics, almost accidentally, as a result of my English studies. Some, such as Hooker, Herbert, Traherne, Taylor and Bunyan, I read because they are themselves great English writers; others, such as Boethius, St. Augustine, Thomas Aquinas and Dante, because they were 'influences.'" C. S. Lewis, "On the Reading of Old Books," in *C. S. Lewis: Essay Collection & Other Short Pieces*, ed. Lesley Walmsley (1944 essay reprint; London: HarperCollins, 2000), 440.
180 Augustine *Confessions*, 8.21. Lewis, *Surprised by Joy*, 1377.
181 Concerning the doctrine of God's timelessness and eternity, Lewis wrote: "I have so ruthlessly condensed an argument of such importance, both historical and intrinsic, that the wise reader will go for it to the original. I cannot help thinking that Boethius has here expounded a Platonic conception more luminously than Plato ever did himself." Lewis, *The Discarded Image*, 89-90.
182 Lewis, *The Collected Letters of C. S. Lewis: Volume I*, 857 [January 2, 1930].
183 Ibid.

> Read a small daily portion, in rather a liturgical manner, letting the
> *images* and the purely intellectual conceptions sink well into the mind.
> I.e. I think what is important (or most important) here is to remember
> [to] say 'The figures stand in these positions, coloured thus, and he
> is explaining about free will' – rather as if one was remembering
> a philosophical ceremony. It is not really like any of the things we
> know.[184]

Moreover, Dante's philosophical, deeply religious poetry later greatly
influenced Lewis's own, for on one occasion, when a future biographer
expressed his opinion that *Perelandra* owed much to John Milton's *Paradise
Lost*, Lewis replied, "Milton I think you possibly over-rate: it is difficult to
distinguish him from Dante & St. Augustine."[185]

But books were not Lewis's only impetus to Christianity. *Askēsis*, the
practice of spiritual exercises, was a crucial part of Lewis's lived philosophy.
In fact, the extent to which Lewis the theist made "an attempt at religion"
is a true testimony to his classical- medieval philosophical heritage: he was
in constant prayer (as John in *The Pilgrim's Regress* was when "Philosophy
. . . turn[ed] into Religion"[186]), and he even started going to chapel every
morning: "I have started going to morning Chapel at 8. . . . My moral history
of late has been deplorable. More and more clearly one sees how much of
one's philosophy & religion is mere talk: the boldest hope is that concealed
somewhere within it is some seed however small of the real thing."[187]
Lewis found that the more he really tried to live out his theism, the more
difficult, but illuminating, things became:

> I think the trouble with me is *lack of faith*. I have no *rational* ground
> for going back on the arguments that convinced me of God's existence:
> but the irrational deadweight of my old skeptical habits, and the spirit
> of this age, and the cares of the day, steal away all my lively feeling of
> the truth, and often when I pray I wonder if I am not posting letters
> to a non-existent address. Mind you I don't *think* so – the whole of
> my reasonable mind is convinced: but I often *feel* so. However, there is
> nothing to do but to peg away. . . . How well I *talk* about it: how little
> else I do. I wonder would it be better not to speak to one another of

---

184 Ibid., 876 [January 30, 1930].
185 Lewis, *The Collected Letters of C. S. Lewis: Volume II*, 630 [October 29, 1944].
186 Lewis, *The Pilgrim's Regress*, 156. The more Lewis practiced true philosophy, the more
personal God started to become: "Terrible things are happening to me. The 'Spirit' or
'Real I' is showing an alarming tendency to become much more personal and is taking
the offensive, and behaving just like God. . . . You'd better come on Monday at the
latest or I may have entered a monastery." Lewis, *The Collected Letters of C. S. Lewis:
Volume I*, 882 [February 3, 1930].
187 Ibid., 942 [October 29, 1930].

these things at all? Is the talking a substitute for the doing?[188]

Like the ancient and medieval philosophers (not to mention a whole host of others), Lewis found that his emotions were constantly threatening his better judgment. Yet he held on. And as he did, he began to formulate his theism in a new way: perhaps, he thought, it is not so much man's choice of God that matters, so much as God's choice of man:

> On my side there are changes perhaps bigger: you will be surprised to hear that my outlook is now definitely religious. It is not precisely Christianity, tho' it may turn out that way in the end. I can't express the change better than by saying that whereas once I would have said 'Shall I adopt Christianity,' I now wait to see whether it will adopt me: i.e. I now know there is another Party in the affair – that I'm playing Poker, not Patience, as I once supposed.[189]

Nonetheless, although Lewis was then close to God, he still felt far from Christ. As a lover of reason, Lewis simply refused to abandon her dictates when it came to making sense of Christ: "In spite of my recent changes of view, I am still inclined to think that you can only get what *you* call 'Christ' out of the Gospels by picking & choosing, & slurring over a good deal."[190] What finally convinced him of the truth of Christianity was, as we shall see more clearly in chapter four, J. R. R. Tolkien's explanation of Christ as the "True Myth" or the ultimate fulfillment of both pagan mythologies and Jewish prophecies. Subsequently, Lewis felt that Christianity was the most probable philosophy ("I recommended Christianity because I thought its affirmation to be objectively *true*"[191]), and so recalling the words of Augustine

---

188 Ibid., 944-5 [December 24, 1930].
189 Ibid., 887 [March 21, 1930].
190 Ibid., 862 [January 9, 1930].
191 C. S. Lewis, "Modern Man and His Categories of Thought," in *C. S. Lewis: Essay Collection & Other Short Pieces*, ed. Lesley Walmsley (London: HarperCollins, 2000), 619. Cf. "We want the Faith wh[ich] is true not a Faith wh[ich] will historically survive. They are not <u>necessarily</u> the same ('When the Son of Man cometh, shall He find faith on the earth!')." C. S. Lewis, marginalia in his edition of *An Interpretation of Christian Ethics*, by Reinhold Niebuhr (London: Student Christian Movement Press, 1937; The Rare Book Collection, The University of North Carolina at Chapel Hill), 44. Cf. "If Christianity is untrue, then no honest man will want to believe it, however helpful it might be: if it is true, every honest man will want to believe it, even if it gives him no help at all." C. S. Lewis, "Man or Rabbit?" in *C. S. Lewis: Essay Collection & Other Short Pieces*, ed. Lesley Walmsley (1946 essay reprint; London: HarperCollins, 2000), 352. Cf. "What you say about [T. S.] Eliot's 'collapse into Anglo-Catholicism' instead of 'newer and stranger things' . . . is profoundly disquieting. You don't seem even to consider the hypothesis that he might have embraced this belief because he thought it *true* – that he might be looking for the truth, not the 'new and strange' (of course

("*Securus te projice*"[192]) and putting into practice the important spiritual lesson he learned about diving (the rational act of trust[193]), he became a Christian in 1931, and consequently said with conviction: "I believe in Christianity as I believe that the Sun has risen not only because I see it but because by it I see everything else."[194]

Yet Lewis's philosophical journey did not end there. Because the Oxford don came to Christianity because he thought it true, he never lost his interest in reason and philosophy. For instance, over the years Lewis went on to write numerous apologetic works, which, though overly simplistic for professional philosophers, were written with the sole purpose of playing the mid-wife for the philosophical and theological development of laymen (for whom he was consciously writing, it must be added). Furthermore, he also became the founding president of the Socratic Club, a philosophical club designed to examine the truth of Christianity, and remained in that position for twelve years (1942-1954): "Socrates had exhorted men to 'follow the argument wherever it led them': the Club came into existence to apply this principle to one particular subject-matter – the *pros* and *cons* of the Christian Religion."[195] Lewis's time in the Club (not to mention with another club, the Inklings, where "Platonic discussion[s]" sometimes took place[196]) was invaluable in helping the Oxford don exercise his reason and use it to show others the rationality of Christian belief.

Nevertheless, there is one philosophical event in Lewis's life that is constantly brought up among Lewis scholars as evidence that Lewis lost interest in philosophy, and as such demands some commentary. The event, of course, is the so-called "Anscombe Legend,"[197] which occurred at the Socratic Club on February 2, 1948.[198] One year prior to this, Lewis had

the two might turn out to coincide, but we've no right to assume that *a priori*, and the seeking of the former is a quite different activity from seeking the latter)." Lewis, *The Collected Letters of C. S. Lewis: Volume II*, 443 [September 12, 1940].

192 "Throw yourself away." Lewis, *The Pilgrim's Regress*, 187.
193 Concerning a time he went swimming with Barfield, Lewis wrote: "Here I learned to dive wh[ich] is a great change in my life & has important (religious) connections." Lewis, *The Collected Letters of C. S. Lewis: Volume I*, 915 [July 8, 1930].
194 Lewis, "Is Theology Poetry?" 21.
195 C. S. Lewis, "The Founding of the Oxford Socratic Club," in *C. S. Lewis: Essay Collection & Other Short Pieces*, ed. Lesley Walmsley (1942 essay reprint; London: HarperCollins, 2000), 591.
196 C. S. Lewis, "Preface," in *Essays Presented to Charles Williams*, ed. C. S. Lewis (London: Oxford University Press, 1947), viii.
197 This term is used by J. R. Lucas, "The Restoration of Man" (A Lecture Given in Durham on Thursday, October 22, 1992 http://users.ox.ac.uk/~jlucas/lewis.html).
198 Hooper, "Oxford's Bonny Fighter," 181.

written *Miracles*, in which he argued that philosophical naturalism is self-refuting. His argument, based in some measure on Arthur Balfour's *Theism and Humanism* (especially Appendix A[199]), was a *reductio ad absurdum*, claiming that if everything came about as a matter of blind chance, then even our rational thoughts must be the by-product of blind chance, in which case there is no reason, quite literally, to think our thoughts are in anyway valid or can give us objective knowledge:

> Thus, a strict materialism refutes itself for the reason given long ago by Professor Haldane: 'If my mental processes are determined wholly by the motions of atoms in my brain, I have no reason to suppose that my beliefs are true. . . . And hence I have no reason for supposing my brain to be composed of atoms (*Possible Worlds*, p. 209). . . . But Naturalism, even if it is not purely materialistic, seems to me to involve the same difficulty, though in a less obvious form. It discredits our processes of reasoning or at least reduces their credit to such a humble level that it can no longer support Naturalism itself.[200]

G. E. M. Anscombe, a Catholic philosophy professor, disagreed with Lewis because Lewis had carelessly claimed that according to naturalism, Nature is the product of an irrational cause, whereas naturalism actually claims that Nature is the result of a non-rational cause; moreover, Anscombe thought the naturalist could evade Lewis's critique by pointing to the deficiency of Lewis's terminology, namely, Lewis's failed attempt to distinguish the *ground* of a conclusion, which is based on rationality (i.e. *reasons*, whether good or bad), and the *cause* of a conclusion, which need not be based on rationality (e.g. *a physical cause* like a brain tumour etc.).[201]

While readers interested in the details of this argument should read both Victor Reppert's *C. S. Lewis's Dangerous Idea* and Erik Wielenberg's *God and the Reach of Reason*, the important thing for our purpose here is that the result of Lewis's debate with Anscombe has, until very recently, been extremely ambiguous: some arguing that Anscombe won (though not with

---

199 "Reason: *Traditional*: The universe is the creation of Reason, and all things work together towards a reasonable end. *Naturalism*: So far as we can tell, reason is to be found neither in the beginning of things nor in their end; and though everything is predetermined, nothing is fore-ordained." Arthur J. Balfour, *Theism and Humanism*, ed. Michael Perry (Seattle: Inkling Books, 2000), 163.
200 Lewis, *Miracles*, 1110.
201 G. E. M. Anscombe, *Metaphysics and the Philosophy of Mind*, vol. 2, *The Collected Papers of G. E. M. Anscombe* (Minneapolis: University of Minnesota Press, 1981), 224-5.

any devastating finality if she did[202]), and some that Lewis won[203] (even if he did not necessarily feel he had been able to counter all of Anscombe's attacks[204]). This is to say, of course, that there have been so many claims on both sides of the debate as to who won (and who *felt* they won), that the question has been nearly impossible to answer. Scholars like Carpenter,[205] Wilson,[206] and Beversluis,[207] who are largely hostile towards Lewis (in particular, towards his apologetics), have often been completely dismissed by defenders of Lewis, who insist that Lewis could do no wrong. But thanks to the third volume of *The Collected Letters of C. S. Lewis*, published in 2007, we now know that at least the *sources* of the claim that Lewis lost the Anscombe debate – the testimony of Anscombe, Antony Flew,[208] and three of Lewis's students: Sayer, Griffiths and Brewer (none of whom actually attended the debate, it should be added in defence of those who questioned the credibility of the sources against Lewis[209]) – agree with Lewis's opinion of the matter,

---

202 Ibid., 10.

203 "Lewis told me he did not lose the argument. A few years later when I met Miss Anscombe in the common room of Somerville College and asked what she remembered of the meeting, she removed her cigar from her mouth only long enough to say, 'I won.'" Hooper, "Oxford's Bonny Fighter," 163.

204 George Sayer, a former student of Lewis, wrote: "[Lewis] told me that he had been proved wrong, that his argument for the existence of God had been demolished. . . . When told years later of the effect of the discussion on Jack, Professor Anscombe was surprised and upset. 'Oh dear! I had no idea that he took it so seriously. As a matter of fact I don't think I agree that I won.'" Sayer, *Jack*, 307. This agrees with what another former student, Dom Bede Griffiths, wrote: "I remember Lewis saying to me that [Anscombe] had completely demolished his argument." Dom Bede Griffiths, "The Adventure of Faith," in *C. S. Lewis at the Breakfast Table and Other Reminiscences*, ed. James Como, 11-30 (San Diego: Harcourt Brace & Company, 1992), 21.

205 Humphrey Carpenter, *The Inklings: C. S. Lewis, J. R. R. Tolkien, Charles Williams and Their Friends* (London: HarperCollins, 1997), 216-7.

206 A. N. Wilson, *C. S. Lewis: A Biography* (New York: W. W. Norton & Company, 1990), 213-4.

207 Beversluis, *C. S. Lewis and the Search for Rational Religion*, 66-7.

208 Flew does not say that Lewis, whom he calls "the greatest Christian apologist of the last century," lost the debate. Flew, *There is a God*, 4. However, Flew seems to indicate that Lewis thought he lost the debate: "Many of the leading atheists at Oxford locked horns with Lewis and his fellow Christians. By far the best-known encounter was the celebrated February 1948 debate between Lewis and Elizabeth Anscombe, which led Lewis to revise the third chapter of his book *Miracles*. I still remember being a member of a small group of friends returning together from that great debate, walking directly behind Elizabeth Anscombe and her party. She was exultant, and her friends were equally exultant. Immediately in front of this party, C. S. Lewis trod alone, walking as rapidly as he could to refuge in his rooms in Magdalen College, just off the bridge we were all crossing." Ibid., 23.

209 Derek Brewer wrote in his diary: "None of us were at first very cheerful. Lewis was obviously deeply disturbed by his encounter last Monday with Miss Anscombe, who

for in 1950 Lewis said of Anscombe, "Having *obliterated me as an Apologist* ought she not to *succeed* me?"[210] Consequently, there is a clear lesson here for Lewis scholars: in our love for the man, we must not exercise blind devotion, but ought to follow Truth even if it appears to differ with our heroes, for such was Lewis's own approach to philosophy. Indeed, the very fact that Lewis confessed defeat at the hands of Anscombe precisely *disproves* subsequent arguments by Carpenter, Wilson and Beversluis (who argue that Lewis realized Christianity was no longer rational and so became a fideist and retreated into the world of fiction[211]), for Lewis was a *philosopher*, a lover of Truth, and so was willing to admit Truth when he saw it; moreover, Lewis's self-confessed defeat did not imply, as Wilson has argued, that "Lewis had been shown to have no competence to debate with a professional philosopher on her own terms,"[212] for just two years before the debate, on October 14, 1946,[213] Lewis had sparred with a philosopher of no lesser stature than A. J. Ayer, and, according to Ayer's own testimony, Lewis had kept pace with him;[214] furthermore, in 1950, when Lewis was asked for his recommendation concerning who should speak at the Socratic Club during the Michaelmas Term, he fearlessly recommended Ryle, Ayer and even Anscombe herself[215] despite the fact that he freely admitted that philosophers like these often "wipe the floor with us."[216] Consequently, I wholeheartedly agree with Victor

---

had disproved some of the central theory of his philosophy about Christianity. I felt quite painfully for him. Dyson said – very well – that now he had lost everything and was come to the foot of the Cross – spoken with great sympathy." Brewer added that the imagery Lewis used in describing the debate "was all of the fog of war, the retreat of infantry thrown back under heavy attack," although Brewer himself (like Lewis's other students George Sayer and Dom Bede Griffiths) admitted, "I missed Miss Anscombe's evening." Derek Brewer, "The Tutor: A Portrait," in *C. S. Lewis at the Breakfast Table and Other Reminiscences*, ed. James Como, 41-67 (San Diego: Harcourt Brace & Company, 1992), 59.

210 Lewis, *The Collected Letters of C. S. Lewis: Volume III*, 35 [June 12, 1950] (emphasis mine).

211 Richard Purtill has answered some of these charges well. See Richard Purtill, "Did C. S. Lewis Lose His Faith?" in *Rumours of Heaven: Essays in Celebration of C. S. Lewis*, ed. Andrew Walker and James Patrick, 27-62 (London: Eagle, 1998).

212 Wilson, *C. S. Lewis: A Biography*, 214. Basil Mitchell, incidentally, agrees with Wilson's assessment: "I can't remember the debate at all clearly. I don't have the sense that anything decisive happened at that moment, although it is the case, as you say, that from that point onwards Lewis obviously concluded that he wasn't equipped to cope with the professional philosophers." Mitchell and Walker, "Reflections on C. S. Lewis, Apologetics, and the Moral Tradition," 8-9.

213 Hooper, "Oxford's Bonny Fighter," 179.

214 Ayer, *Part of My Life*, 296-7.

215 Lewis, *The Collected Letters of C. S. Lewis: Volume III*, 33-5 [June 12, 1950].

216 Ibid., 462 [April 22, 1954].

Reppert, who calls for the end of the Anscombe Legend: the false tale of Lewis's retreat from philosophy as a result of his encounter with Anscombe.[217]

Yet, if it is false that Lewis was afraid of philosophical debates after his Anscombe encounter, it is true that as he got older, he began to feel both that he had said nearly all that he wanted in regard to apologetics *per se* and that his argumentative abilities were waning: "like the fangless snake in *The Jungle Book*," he wrote in 1951, "I've largely lost my dialectical power."[218] Indeed, after the Anscombe debate, Lewis apparently told Sayer that he could "never write another book" like *Miracles*,[219] and subsequently, in 1954, Lewis resigned his post as the president of the Socratic Club, hoping they would find "a better and more active man as [his] successor."[220] Thus, while Lewis's interest in apologetics *per se* declined along with his years, it is erroneous to say, as Austin Farrer does, that Lewis's "philosophical experience belonged to the time of his conversion,"[221] or that Lewis lost the belief that Christianity is rational, for to say these things is to misunderstand Lewis's entire approach to life itself; that is, as I have argued throughout, Lewis understood philosophy to be a way of life and as such believed in Christianity because he thought it is *true*. There is absolutely no evidence to suggest Lewis thought otherwise, only the fallacy of the argument from silence, which points to Lewis's lack of philosophical work after 1948 and the increase in his imaginative work thereafter. Yet even here, if one were to entertain a fallacy, one would find the spirit of a philosopher, for Lewis not only continued to write letters of an apologetic nature throughout his life, but he also infused his philosophy

---

217 "It is my contention that the Anscombe Legend is a pernicious falsehood about C. S. Lewis that richly deserves to be put to rest completely and permanently." Victor Reppert, "The Ecumenical Apologist: Understanding C. S. Lewis's Defense of Christianity," in *Apologist, Philosopher, & Theologian*, vol. 3, *C. S. Lewis: Life, Works, & Legacy*, ed. Bruce Edwards, 1-28 (Westport, CT: Praeger, 2007), 6. Michael Ward is another critic who agrees with Reppert, although Ward argues that Lewis's philosophy became more implicit as it was embodied in his fiction. Michael Ward, *Planet Narnia: The Seven Heavens in the Imagination of C. S. Lewis* (Oxford: Oxford University Press, 2008), 215-19.

218 Lewis, *The Collected Letters of C. S. Lewis: Volume III*, 129 [July 10, 1951].

219 Sayer, *Jack*, 308. Cf. "I wish your project heartily well but can't write you articles. My thought and talent (such as they are) now flow in different, though I think not less Christian, channels, and I do not think I am at all likely to write more *directly* theological pieces. The last work of that sort which I attempted had to be abandoned. If I am now good for anything it is for catching the reader unawares – thro[ugh] fiction and symbol. I have done what I could in the way of frontal attacks, but I now feel quite sure those days are over." Lewis, *The Collected Letters of C. S. Lewis: Volume III*, 651 [September 28, 1955].

220 Ibid., 400 [January 1, 1954].

221 Austin Farrer, "The Christian Apologist," in *Light on C. S. Lewis*, ed. Jocelyn Gibb, 23-43 (London: Geoffrey Bles, 1965), 31.

into his imaginative work – for instance, he transplanted the ontological argument into his fifth Narnian book, *The Silver Chair* – and he even, as a testimony to his love of Truth and as vindication of Hooper's claim that Lewis did not lose the debate with Anscombe, rewrote a section of *Miracles* in 1960, just three years before he died. And indeed, Lewis even died like a philosopher, for Socrates had said that true philosophy is "practicing death" or learning how to die well,[222] and this Lewis did, for on his death bed in 1963, he is reported to have said, "I have done all I wanted to do, and I'm ready to go."[223]

As for the question as to what *kind* of philosophy Lewis held from his conversion until his death, this is one of the central foci of this book and as such will be explored throughout. For the time being, suffice to say Lewis was familiar with many radically different types of philosophies, one of the results of which is that his philosophy always remained rather eclectic. Like the Schoolmen, who tried to reconcile Aristotle and Christianity, or Kant, who tried to reconcile empiricism and rationalism, Lewis drew on, and tried to reconcile (because of his love of internal consistency), many different philosophical streams of thought in order to make what we may call "C. S. Lewis's philosophy." Nevertheless, while Lewis was neither fully able to escape Berkeley's argument against matter nor banish the language Bradley used when he spoke of the "glory" hidden behind Appearances, Mary Carman Rose is certainly not far off when she labels Lewis's eclectic philosophy "Christian Platonism."[224] For my part, I would call Lewis's philosophy Neoplatonic Christianity because not only was he first a Christian (though he understood such to be above all a lover of *Truth*), and second a Platonist,[225] but also, similar to Neoplatonic Christians such as Augustine and Boethius,

---

222 Plato *Phaedo* 80b. In his edition of *Phaedo*, Lewis summarized Plato thus: "Readiness to die thus becomes the test of the genuinely philosophical character." C. S. Lewis, marginalia in his edition of *Phaedo*, by Plato, in *PLATONIS OPERA TOMVS I*, ed. Ioannes Burnet (Oxonii: E Typograheol Clarendoniano, 1899; The Rare Book Collection, The University of North Carolina at Chapel Hill), 67e. Cf. "The doctrine of death which I describe is not peculiar to Christianity. . . . The Greek philosopher tells us that the life of wisdom is 'a practice of death.'" C. S. Lewis, *The Problem of Pain*, in *C. S. Lewis: Selected Books* [Long Edition] (1940 reprint; London: HarperCollins, 1999), 524.

223 Lewis, *The Collected Letters of C. S. Lewis: Volume III*, 1484 [November 21, 1963].

224 Mary Carman Rose, "The Christian Platonism of C. S. Lewis, J. R. R. Tolkien, and Charles Williams," in *NeoPlatonism and Christian Thought*, ed. Dominic J. O'Meara, 203-12 (Norfold, VA: International Society for NeoPlatonic Studies, 1982), 203.

225 "Although I am an Anglican, the two writers who helped me most to Christianity were a Presbyterian (George Macdonald) and a Papist (G. K. Chesterton) – I might add a third and a pagan, Plato." Lewis, "Autobiographical Note," 1.

Lewis was interested in reconciling the metaphysics and dialectic of Plato, the psychology, ethics and literary theory of Aristotle, the ethics of the Stoics (via Kant) and the myths of the pagans with Christianity, the True Philosophy. In this way, Lewis's major philosophers were Plato, Aristotle, Augustine and Boethius, all of whom fit under the broad, though admittedly imprecise and problematic, umbrella that is "Neoplatonism." Of course, many of the disciples of Plato, Aristotle, Augustine and Boethius were also influences on Lewis, yet the Oxford don tended to go back to original sources for much of his philosophizing since – we do well to remember – he read the classics long before he became a medievalist; thus, for example, where some have seen Thomas Aquinas in Lewis's theology, it turned out to be Aquinas's Master: "As I perhaps said before, a great many people think I'm being Thomistic where I'm really being Aristotelian. He's a top form boy, and I a bottom form boy, in the same school: what we share we get from the Teacher. I am certainly not anti-Thomist. He is one of the great philosophers."[226] And while it is true Lewis was ignorant of some of the finer points of disagreement between the philosophers – "On points at issue between Christian Platonism and Christian Aristotelianism I have not got a clear line"[227] – he was able to appreciate many of their differences;[228] indeed, "'The very seas would lose their shores' was a quotation from Ovid he was fond of, and . . . '*Distinguo*' was a favorite word of warning."[229] Subsequently, whether through ignorance or awareness, Lewis, like the Neoplatonic philosophers he loved, preferred ligature to rupture, desiring to see how differing philosophies could be

226 Lewis, *The Collected Letters of C. S. Lewis: Volume III*, 995 [December 10, 1958].
227 Ibid.
228 "Such unambiguous statements of the neo-Platonic creed are not, however, very common. The men of that age were such inveterate syncretists, so much more anxious to reconcile authorities than to draw out their differences, that the Aristotelian and neo-Platonic views are not clearly opposed and compared, but are rather contaminated by each other and by many more influences as well. Aristotle himself was sometimes misinterpreted in a sense which brought him very close to Plotinus. Thus Fracastorius (1483-1553) in his *Naugerius* explains that while other writers give us the naked fact (*rem*), the poet gives us the form (*ideam*) clothed in all its beauties . . . 'which Aristotle calleth the vniuersal.' These 'beauties' however are not very relevant to Aristotle's immanent universal – the general character in situations of a given kind, the 'sort of thing that might happen;' they have come in because Fracastorius is really thinking of a Platonic and transcendent form, a reality prior to, and exalted above, Nature. And Aristotle himself had unwittingly invited such a confusion when he allowed, in contexts which had nothing to do with poetry, that Nature often tends to or aims at . . . a greater perfection than the indeterminacy of matter allows her to achieve (*De. Gen. Anim.* 778a; *Polit.* 1255b)." Lewis, *Poetry and Prose in the Sixteenth Century*, 321.
229 George Watson, "The Art of Disagreement: C. S. Lewis (1898-1963)," in *C. S. Lewis Remembered*, ed. Harry Lee Poe and Rebecca Whitten Poe, 77-88 (Grand Rapids, MI: Zondervan, 2006), 78.

unified under Christian truth.

Thus, with Lewis's definition of philosophy clear and his philosophical journey *qua* rational discourse and training in place, I now turn to the affect that helped *move* Lewis to think rationally about life and subsequently convert: heavenly desire.

Chapter Three

Heavenly Desire

In the previous chapter, I examined "the merely argued dialectic of [Lewis's] philosophical progress;"[1] that is, I was mainly concerned with Lewis's philosophical journey *qua* rational discourse and training. Needless to say, such is only part of Lewis's philosophical journey, for the truly philosophical quest does not neglect the non-rational and supra-rational, and every true philosopher is also a poet. Hence, in the next two chapters, I am going to discuss the non-rational and supra-rational part of Lewis's philosophical formation, which have to do with two key concepts: heavenly desire and Myth. Since my focus in the first part of this book is on Lewis's philosophical definition, journey and identity more than on his complete thought, I will restrict my discussion at the moment – though I will return to these issues again in chapter seven – to how Lewis the philosopher was both led by heavenly desire (that urgent element in the soul that moves the philosopher homeward) and beckoned by Myth (that mysterious thing that touches Beauty, Truth and Happiness yet is best understood as Reality itself, That Thing "*about which* truth is"[2]).

As for the structure of this chapter, I propose to work through the various concepts Lewis used in regard to heavenly desire to give us an appreciation for not only the Oxford don's eclecticism in regard to this concept, but also the value he put on the role of affect in his philosophy. The various concepts that make up, or at least are broadly related to, heavenly desire will be looked at in *roughly* chronological order in regard to Lewis's encounter with, or mention of, them, starting with Platonic *eros,* which is the original concept, and then moving on to "Romanticism," the *numinous, Sehnsucht,* "Joy," and hope. Finally, I will conclude with a discussion about how these concepts tied into what Lewis called "the dialectic of desire."

---

1   Lewis, preface to the third edition of *The Pilgrim's Regress,* 9.
2   C. S. Lewis, "Myth Became Fact," in *C. S. Lewis: Essay Collection & Other Short Pieces,* ed. Lesley Walmsley (1944 essay reprint; London: HarperCollins, 2000), 141.

I: Platonic *Eros*

The first concept I want to examine in regard to heavenly desire is Platonic *eros*, or, as Lewis called it, "Eros Religion"[3] or "spiritual *eros*."[4] My reason for beginning with this term is twofold. First, Plato was the first to give a *philosophical* description of heavenly desire.[5] And second, despite the fact that Lewis's first *feeling* of heavenly desire was when he was less than ten years old (when he saw his brother's toy garden, an event we will talk more about in the next chapter),[6] Lewis's first *intellectual* encounter with heavenly desire was in Plato's dialogues, which, we recall from chapter two, he started reading back in 1913 at the age of fifteen. Indeed, the best example of Platonic *eros* is found in Plato's *Phaedrus*, which Lewis read in 1915 and reread many times over the course of his life, including during the time he was writing his first

---

3   Lewis mentioned this term in regard to Spenser's *Faerie Queene*: "Arthur is an embodiment of what Professor Nygren calls 'Eros Religion,' the thirst of the soul for the Perfection beyond the created universe. . . . It is in that very nature of the Platonic quest and the Eros religion that the soul cannot know her true aim till she has achieved it. The seeker must advance, with the possibility at each step of error, beyond the false Florimells to the true, and beyond the true Florimell to the Glory. Only such an interpretation will explain the deep seriousness and the explicitly religious language of Arthur's subsequent soliloquy (55-60)." Lewis, *Poetry and Prose in the Sixteenth Century*, 383.

4   Lewis used this term when he again spoke about *The Faerie Queene*: "This leads us on to the Platonic aspect of the poem. Platonically considered, Arthur is the purged philosophical soul, smitten with a spiritual *eros* for the One, the First Fair, and trying like Plotinus to make the flight alone into the alone. When at III, iv, 54, he wishes that Florimell were his Faerie Queen . . . Arthur is therefore not entirely on the wrong track. Indeed, he comes very near to voicing a prayer that sums up the whole tradition of affirmative theology; except that here the prayer 'This also is Thou, neither is this Thou' passes into 'O that this were Thou, o that Thou were this.' Unless Arthur only means 'O that I were now really finding Thee,' it is a dangerous sentiment. . . . But there is something like it in Plotinus: 'Those to whom the divine *eros* is unknown may guess at it by the passions of earth, if they remember how great a joy the possession of a beloved person is, and also remember that these earthly beloveds are mortal and harmful and that our love of them is a wooing of images' (Enneads VI, ix, 9)." C. S. Lewis, *Spenser's Images of Life*, ed. Alastair Fowler (Cambridge: Cambridge University Press, 1967), 133-4.

5   Following his claim that "Poets have said more about [heavenly desire] than philosophers," Lewis asserted that "[Heavenly desire] is there in bits of the Odyssey, in Pindar, in some of the choruses of Euripides, in Lucretius' bit about the home of the gods, in the Anglo-Saxon *Seafarer*." Lewis, *The Collected Letters of C. S. Lewis: Volume III*, 995-6 [December 10, 1958]. Nevertheless, no poet writing before the time of Plato worked out a theory of heavenly desire, and so Plato is properly seen as the originator of this idea.

6   Lewis, *Surprised by Joy*, 1247.

major works: *The Quest of Bleheris*[7] and *Dymer*.[8] And it is from *Phaedrus* that we read the following mythical account of Platonic *eros*.

Once, long ago, the soul dwelt in the upper heavens with the gods and together they were enraptured in the beatific vision: the contemplation of true Beauty and Reality – i.e. the eternal Forms. But one day the soul looked away from the world of the Forms due to its rational faculty exercising imperfect control over its passionate faculty. Consequently, when the soul looked away, it plunged further into the physical world, resulting in distorted knowledge and the loss of true happiness. Forgetfulness of its true home set in when the soul was incarnate; however, it was not total amnesia. The soul had the ability to remember its true home if it would only direct its attention to the knowledge innate within itself which would, in turn, point to its origin, the eternal Forms, the object the soul truly desired; or to put it another way, the soul needed to be possessed by a god, whose maddening love or *eros* for knowledge would propel the soul heavenward:

> This then is the fourth type of madness, which befalls when a man, reminded by the sight of beauty on earth of the true beauty, grows his wings and endeavours to fly upward, but in vain, exposing himself to the reproach of insanity because like a bird he fixes his gaze on the heights to the neglect of things below; and the conclusion to which our whole discourse points is that in itself and in its origin that is the best of all forms of divine possession, both for the subject himself and for his associate, and it is when he is touched with this madness that

---

7   In his 1916 novel *The Quest of Bleheris*, Lewis described how the hero of the novel, Bleheris, had a perfect life and yet still longed for something more: "'What ails me now? Is it an evil thing that I shall wed with the love of my desire and all men have me in envy? Or shall a man long for drink, and then thrust away a cup that one giveth him?' And he <u>cursed himself</u>, for the joy that would not grow in his heart. . . . [H]e too had his dreams, and thought <u>that surely he should do great things in the world, and fight and love as mightily as the heroes of old song</u>. But now it seemed that his life was but a short space, [of] little worth: that he should marry and live at ease and beget sons to live also at ease, as others did before him, and at the latter end to [grow] old and die, with all his dreams yet hidden a soft jerkin that none might know him from another." C. S. Lewis, *The Quest of Bleheris* (Unpublished novel [1916?]; The Marion E. Wade Center, Wheaton College), 10, 11.

8   In a rough draft of *Dymer*, Lewis wrote the following: "Because of this land only did we love / The horizon, when in earth. Our sweet disease / Of longing. Our huge hope we fabled of / Our Apple-islands and Hesperian trees / Were but the faint stir of the laden breeze / Soft blowing from this coast, and for one breath / Of that breeze men went mad and longed to death." C. S. Lewis, "*Dymer* Rough Draft," in "Henry More and Dymer, MS-170" (Unpublished draft [1924?]; The Marion E. Wade Center, Wheaton College), 160. Cf. Michael Slack, "Sehnsucht and the Platonic Eros in *Dymer*," *CSL: The Bulletin of the New York C. S. Lewis Society* 11 (August 1980): 3-7.

the man whose love is aroused by beauty in others is called a lover. As I have said, every human soul by its very nature has beheld true being – otherwise it would not have entered into the creature we call man – but it is not every soul that finds it easy to use its present experience as a means of recollecting the world of reality.[9]

From this myth in *Phaedrus*, along with another myth in *Symposium* (a book Lewis said "to die without having read . . . would be ridiculous"[10]), we may draw the following conclusions. First, Platonic *eros* is the innate desire or appetite for Beauty (since love must always have an object[11]). Second, since Platonic *eros* or love is always for something it knows about but lacks, the soul has some knowledge of true Beauty but lacks complete knowledge of it; hence, Platonic *eros* is the son of Poverty (a mortal who is always wanting) and Contrivance (an immortal god who, in virtue of his immortality, lacks nothing, including knowledge).[12] Third, since "wisdom is one of the most beautiful things, and Love is love of Beauty, it follows that Love must be a lover of wisdom;"[13] that is, Platonic *eros* is a love of Truth because it loves the Beauty in Truth; indeed, it is from this that we get the concept of the philosopher, who is a lover of Truth. Fourth, since what is good is the same as what is beautiful, the soul, lacking the Good, also desires it.[14] Fifth, because without the Good, the soul cannot be happy, the soul, by desiring Goodness (and Beauty and Truth), also desires happiness: "'And what will have been gained by the man who is in possession of the good?' 'I find that an easier question to answer; he will be happy.'"[15] Sixth, since the soul's home – its goodness and happiness – consists in the soul contemplating Beauty (and Truth), the soul, by desiring after Beauty, Truth, Goodness and happiness, also desires after its true home. And seventh, while all people desire after Beauty, Goodness, happiness and their true home, most fail to find these because they mistake images or copies of these Forms for the Forms themselves; indeed, instead of using the images or copies of the Forms in this world of flux as signposts that point beyond themselves to the Real World, most settle for loving the imperfect images. Only the true philosopher sees objects of beauty in the lower physical world as markers that help the soul remember true Beauty.

---

9   Plato *Phaedrus* 249-50.
10   William Griffin, *C. S. Lewis: The Authentic Voice* (Trig: Lion Publishing, 1988), 264.
11   Plato *Symposium* 199e.
12   Ibid., 202a, 203b.
13   Ibid., 204d.
14   Ibid., 200e.
15   Ibid., 204d.

Now Lewis was familiar with all of this from very early on, but his knowledge of it grew considerably around 1922, when he, though still an atheist, first read Boethius's *Consolation of Philosophy*, which presented Platonic *eros* proper in a Neoplatonic Christian form. Mythical elements aside, Boethius's understanding of Platonic *eros* and its relation to Beauty, Truth, Goodness, happiness and home was virtually the same as Plato's. However, there were two important differences: (1) Boethius accepted Plotinus's assessment that "the soul in its nature loves the One and longs to be one with Him;"[16] that is, Boethius agreed with the Father of Neoplatonism that the *eros* in the soul is a desire not simply for knowledge of the One (Plato), but also union with the One (Plotinus); however, (2) while Plotinus's doctrine of the soul's mystical union with the One carried with it connotations that Christians were often uncomfortable with, Boethius knew that Jesus himself spoke in similar terms (e.g. the union of the Father, Son and believers), and so, following Augustine (and perhaps others), argued that the *eros* in the soul is a desire for Perfect Happiness or Happiness That Never Fails, which also happens to be Perfect Goodness, and since "nothing better than God can be conceived of," Boethius equated God with Perfect Goodness which in turn he equated with Perfect Happiness and the true Home of the soul.[17] And of course since the Christian loves God, the Christian is also the true philosopher for he is a lover of wisdom or Truth, which is Beauty itself and therefore God *qua* the Good.

Nevertheless, as Lewis himself confessed: even when he read Boethius's Christian account of Platonic *eros*, he, like Boethius's "drunken man [who] cannot find by what path he may return home,"[18] did not immediately associate his own longings (which we will talk about shortly) with Platonic *eros* and the desire for God. In fact, these explicit connections only occurred when Lewis wrote *The Pilgrim's Regress*, in which he quoted approvingly from both Plato's *Phaedo* and Boethius's *Consolation of Philosophy* in regard to what the Oxford don then called "Romanticism."

II: "Romanticism"

In *Surprised by Joy*, Lewis said that throughout his childhood, and indeed, throughout his entire life, neither of his parents "ever listened for the horns

---

16   Plotinus *Enneads* 6.9.9.
17   Boethius *The Consolation of Philosophy* 3.10.25-35.
18   Ibid., 3.55. Cf. C. S. Lewis, *The Discarded Image: An Introduction to Medieval and Renaissance Literature* (1964 reprint; Cambridge: Cambridge University Press, 1998), 84.

of elfland"[19] – a phrase which he borrowed from Alfred Lord Tennyson's poem *The Princess* and one which both he and J. R. R. Tolkien[20] thought captured an important aspect of the best sort of romanticism: not of "'[t]itanic characters,'" the macabre, revolution, dangerous adventures, egoism nor Nature, but of the preternatural:

> The marvelous is 'romantic,' provided it does not make part of the believed religion. Thus magicians, ghosts, fairies, witches, dragons, nymphs, and dwarfs are 'romantic;' angels, less so. Greek gods are 'romantic' in Mr James Stephens or Mr Maurice Hewlett; not so in Homer and Sophocles. In this sense Malory, Boiardo, Ariosto, Spenser, Tasso, Mrs Radcliffe, Shelley, Coleridge, William Morris, and Mr E. R. Eddison are 'romantic' authors.[21]

Nevertheless, while this is the kind of romantic *literature* Lewis liked best (both when he was young and old), it was not what he meant when he wrote a subscript under *The Pilgrim's Regress*, which reads: "An allegorical apology for Christianity, Reason and *Romanticism*."

What Lewis meant by "Romanticism" back in 1932, when he had just become a Christian and wrote *The Pilgrim's Regress*, "was a particular recurrent experience which dominated [his] childhood and adolescence and which [he] hastily called 'Romantic' because inanimate nature and marvelous literature were among the things that evoked it."[22] This "recurrent experience," Lewis said, is one of "intense longing,"[23] "immortal longings,"[24] or "strenuous longing."[25] And while it is easy to see Romanticism as simply a synonym for Platonic *eros*, I believe that this is not completely correct. Certainly the two concepts are related in that both are desires that lead the soul past false homes on to its true Home or "the Island;"[26] however, they are also autonomous

---

19   Lewis, *Surprised by Joy*, 1246.
20   Lewis, *The Collected Letters of C. S. Lewis: Volume II*, 103 [March 25, 1933].
21   Lewis, preface to the third edition of *The Pilgrim's Regress*, 6.
22   Ibid., 7.
23   Ibid.
24   Lewis, *Surprised by Joy*, 1341.
25   "Hope died – rose again – quivered, and increased in us / The strenuous longing. We re-embarked to find / That genuine and utter West." C. S. Lewis, "The Landing," in *Poems*, by C. S. Lewis, ed. Walter Hooper (1948 poem reprint; San Diego: Harcourt Brace Jovanovich, 1964), 27-28 [lines 33-5]. The "utter West" will be examined further in chapter five.
26   Lewis, *The Pilgrim's Regress*, 22. Compare this to *The Last Battle*, in which Jewel the unicorn says upon arriving in the New Narnia, "'I have come home at last! This is my real country! I belong here. This is the land I have been looking for all my life, though I never knew it till now. The reason why we loved the old Narnia is that it sometimes looked like this.'" Lewis, *The Last Battle*, 162. Also, in *The Boy and his Horse*, Shasta

concepts since while Platonic *eros* is the desire for Beauty, Romanticism was never explicitly linked to it. That is, while some beautiful objects, copies of true Beauty, ignited desire in Lewis, not all beautiful objects did; indeed, it seems that only objects that Lewis specifically identified as romantic (e.g. "the noise of falling waves" or "the title of *The Well at the World's End*"[27]) and not other beautiful objects (e.g. a new car) stirred the Oxford don. It is clear, then, that while Lewis's Romanticism was in large part inspired by Platonic *eros*, it was also the product of both his own personal experiences and, it can hardly be denied, the larger Romantic Movement (since he mentioned "the Blue Flower," Samuel Taylor Coleridge's "Kubla Khan" and other related sources in this regard[28]). Yet as I have already said, both Platonic *eros* and Romanticism should be seen as pieces in the larger set which I have simply called heavenly desire. And it is to a third piece in this set I now turn.

III: The *Numinous*

In 1936, three years after Lewis first used the term "Romanticism" in regard to heavenly desire, he read Rudolf Otto's *The Idea of the Holy: An Inquiry into the Non-Rational Factor in the Idea of the Divine and its Relation to the Rational*,[29] one of the ten books that most influenced Lewis's philosophy of life. In Otto's work, Lewis read about "the *Numen*" or "the Holy," which is a technical word Otto used to describe the Sacred *minus* any moral or rational aspects.[30] From the word *Numen*, Otto derived the word "*numinous*," from which he then spoke of a *numinous* category of value which is always present when an individual is in a *numinous* state of mind. "This mental state," Otto wrote, "is perfectly *sui generis* and irreducible to any other; and therefore, like every absolutely primary and elementary datum, while it admits of being discussed, it cannot be strictly defined."[31] Nevertheless, despite Otto's initial insistence that the *numinous* is absolutely basic and unique, later on not only did he concede that the *numinous* is intimately related to Kant's Sublime, but

expresses this same sentiment: "'Oh hurrah!' said Shasta. 'Then we'll go North [to Narnia]. I've been longing to go to the North all my life.' 'Of course, you have,' said the Horse. 'That's because of the blood that's in you.'" C. S. Lewis, *The Horse and His Boy* (1954 reprint; London: Fontana, 1985), 20.

27 Lewis, preface to the third edition of *The Pilgrim's Regress*, 9.
28 Ibid., 8-9.
29 "Congratulations to the 'local printer' on giving us a translation of Otto's *Das Heilige* at 3/6 – very nice." Lewis, *The Collected Letters of C. S. Lewis: Volume II*, 203 [August 20, 1936].
30 Rudolf Otto, *The Idea of the Holy: An Inquiry into the Non-rational Factor in the Idea of the Divine and its Relation to the Rational*, trans. John W. Harvey (Oxford: Oxford University Press, 1958), 6.
31 Ibid., 7.

also that it is, though he did not say so in so many words, broadly related to heavenly desire. However, before any of these connections can be made, it is important to be clear about the nature of the *numinous*.

According to Otto, the *numinous* is the feeling that overcomes the mind when the individual "is submerged and overwhelmed by its own nothingness."[32] This feeling, in turn, is always accompanied by a sense of complete dependence on the Divine.[33] However, this feeling of dependence is not merely a natural feeling of dependence, such as insufficiency resulting from a difficult circumstance; rather, it is a mystical sense of dependence, like the dependence Abraham felt when he pled with God for the men of Sodom: "Behold now, I, who am but dust and ash, have taken upon me to speak unto the Lord."[34] Otto called this kind of dependency the "creature-feeling"[35] and following him, Lewis spoke of it as "the shame of being mortal."[36] Nevertheless, while the *numinous* is broadly identified with "creature-feeling" (or "shame"), Otto claimed that this can be divided into two key elements: (1) the feeling of *mysterium tremendum*, and (2) fascination. For the sake of systemization, I will begin with *mysterium tremendum*, and then move onto fascination.

When an individual experiences *mysterium tremendum*, he feels he is in the presence of something which is at once awful, august, majestic, overpowering, living, urgent, wholly different, pulsating and uncanny.[37] The feeling of *mysterium tremendum* may "burst in sudden eruption up from the depths of the soul with spasms and convulsions, or lead to the strangest excitements, to intoxicated frenzy, to transport, and to ecstasy;" in itself, this feeling may be either demonic or angelic, something wild and grisly or beautiful and pure.[38] Yet in whatever mode this feeling takes, it always makes the mind shutter and the individual think of himself as less than nothing

---

32   Ibid., 10.

33   Ibid., 25.

34   Genesis 28:27.

35   Otto, *The Idea of the Holy*, 8.

36   When Psyche met Cupid for the first time, she said, "'When I saw the Westwind I was neither glad nor afraid (at first). I felt ashamed . . . Ashamed of looking like a mortal; ashamed of being a mortal. . . . This shame . . . It's the being mortal; being, how shall I say it? . . . insufficient." Lewis, *Till We Have Faces*, 910, 911. Also consider one of Lewis's favorite quotations from Thomas Browne which reads: "I am not so much afraid of death as ashamed thereof." Thomas Browne, *Religio Medici*, in *The Harvard Classics*, ed. Charles W. Elliot (New York: P. F. Collier & Sons, 1937), 291 [1.40]. Cf. Lewis, *The Collected Letters of C. S. Lewis: Volume II*, 763 [February 12, 1947].

37   Otto, *The Idea of the Holy*, 13-30.

38   Ibid., 12-3.

since he feels himself to be in the presence of something that is non-natural, wholly other and yet pulsating with an energy and life more real than his own.

Lewis himself – as is evident by an underlining in his edition of *The Idea of the Holy* (not to mention by his 1952 essay "Is Theism Important?"[39]) – was particularly interested in Otto's idea that the feeling of *mysterium tremendum* can be "awful" and yet "<u>wholly distinct from that of being afraid</u>."[40] In fact, Lewis's interest in this topic was not merely an academic interest, not only because he never thought of philosophy as such, but also because the Oxford don, some six years before reading Otto, had actually experienced this awfulness firsthand upon reading the mystic Jacob Boehme:

> In the evening I started to read the Everyman volume of Jacob Boehme . . . the Signatura Rerum. . . . I saw, alas, that it was hopelessly beyond me: yet tantalising for I could just grasp enough to be quite sure that he was talking about something tremendously real, and not merely mystifying you. . . . I had two quite distinct experiences in reading it. (a) Certain sentences moved and excited me although I couldn't understand them . . . 'That the nothing is become an eternal life and has found itself, which cannot be, in the Stillness.' – 'The wrath extinguishes and the turning orb stands still, and instead of the turning a sound is caused in the essence.' (b) At certain points a feeling of distress, and even of horror. I had always assumed, in my way, that if I could reach the things Boehme is here talking about, I should *like* them! . . . I wish to record that it has been about the biggest shaking up I've got from a book, since I first read *Phantastes* [by George MacDonald].[41]

This passage is important not only because it depicts Lewis's experience with the awfulness of *mysterium tremendum*, but also because it shows his experience with the other part of *mysterium tremendum*: its eeriness.

Now the eeriness or uncanny nature of *mysterium tremendum* is a vital part of this concept since it points to the unlimited, non-natural and indeterminate nature of the *numinous*. Otto himself compared this element of the *numinous* to Kant's Sublime, for while neither are concerned with Beauty,

---

39 C. S. Lewis, "Is Theism Important?" in *C. S. Lewis: Essay Collection & Other Short Pieces*, ed. Lesley Walmsley (1952 essay reprint; London: HarperCollins, 2000), 56.

40 C. S. Lewis, underlining in his edition of *The Idea of the Holy: An Inquiry in to the Non-Rational Factor in the Idea of the Divine and its Relation to the Rational*, by Rudolf Otto, trans. John W. Harvey (Oxford: Oxford University Press, 1936; The Rare Book Collection, The University of North Carolina at Chapel Hill), 13.

41 Lewis, *The Collected Letters of C. S. Lewis: Volume I*, 858-9 [January 5, 1930].

both are concerned with the mysterious, the maddening, the daunting, the unformed and the boundless[42] (although, of course, Kant's Sublime has to do with aesthetics, whereas Otto's *numinous* has to do with religion; hence, Otto said Kant's Sublime is "a pale reflexion of" the *numinous*[43]). And these common elements in the *numinous* and the Sublime are also shared with Lewis's Romanticism, for as we recall, Romanticism is not, as with Platonic *eros*, concerned with Beauty as such, but with the wonderful, the marvellous, the elusive and the haunting.[44] Hence, both the *numinous* and Romanticism can be incited by things like romantic literature, fairy stories and myths; as Otto wrote: "But the fairy-story proper only comes into being with the element of the 'wonderful,' with miracle and miraculous events and consequences, i.e. by means of an infusion of the *numinous*. And the same holds good in an increased degree of *myth*."[45] While we will talk more about myth and fairy stories in the next chapter, one quotation from *The Lion, the Witch and the Wardrobe* is worth mentioning now as it shows the union of the *numinous* and Romanticism in Lewis's thought; thus, consider the various sensations the four Pevensie children experience upon hearing the name "Aslan," who, as we know, is Christ, the very *Numen* Himself:

> And now a very curious thing happened. None of the children knew who Aslan was . . . but the moment the Beaver had spoken these words everyone felt quite different. Perhaps it has sometimes happened to you in a dream that someone says something which you don't understand but in the dream it feels as if it had some enormous meaning – either a terrifying one which turns the whole dream into a nightmare or else a lovely meaning too lovely to put into words, which makes the dream so beautiful that you remember it all your life and are always wishing you could get into that dream again. It was like that now. At the name of Aslan each one of the children felt something jump

---

42 For Kant, emotion is irrelevant to Beauty, but not to the Sublime. Moreover, while Beauty has to do with quality, the formed, the finite and the natural, the Sublime has to do with quantity, the unformed, the infinite and the non-rational. Immanuel Kant, *Critique of Judgement*, trans. J. H. Bernard (1790 reprint; New York: Hafner, 1961) [2.23]. It should be noted that the division between the Sublime and the Beautiful did not originate with Kant, for Kant himself derived this idea from Edmund Burke's *On the Sublime and Beautiful* (not Longinus' *On the Sublime*). However, since Otto dealt with Kant and not Burke, I have restricted my comments to Kant. Cf. Edmund Burke, *On the Sublime and Beautiful* (1756 reprint; New York, P. F. Collier & Son, 1937), 101 [3.27].

43 Otto, *The Idea of the Holy*, 40.

44 Lewis's poem "Sweet Desire" gives an excellent description of men "long-haunted" by Romanticism and the *numinous*. C. S. Lewis, "Sweet Desire," in *Poems*, by C. S. Lewis, ed. Walter Hooper, 114-5 (San Diego: Harcourt Brace Jovanovich, 1964), 115 [18].

45 Otto, *The Idea of the Holy*, 122.

in its inside. Edmund felt a sensation of mysterious horror. Peter felt
suddenly brave and adventurous. Susan felt as if some delicious smell
or some delightful strain of music had just floated by her. And Lucy
got the feeling you have when you wake up in the morning and realize
that it is the beginning of the holidays or the beginning of summer.[46]

The second and final element in the *numinous* is fascination. This
sensation occurs in the individual as a result of his experiencing the mysterious
and unknown. Awe, it is true, brings the individual to his knees, but desire
to see and understand the mystery – indeed, fascination and "love" for the
mystery[47] – causes him to raise his eyes. And what he sees when he raises
his eyes causes him to be overcome with a kind of madness, but it is the
madness of the finite looking into the infinite,[48] and in this sense, it bears
some resemblance to Platonic *eros*, which speaks of the need for the soul to
be possessed by divine *eros* in order to ascend into the heavens. Consequently,
the individual who experiences the *numinous* feels at once terrified of, and
attracted to, the haunting mystery. He sees it, as the Priest in *Till We Have
Faces* does of the perfect sacrifice, as "both the best and the worst."[49]

Now as we have seen, the *numinous* is neither synonymous with Platonic
eros, since it has little to do with Beauty, Truth, the Good, Happiness nor
Home,[50] nor is it synonymous with Romanticism, since the *numinous* places
much greater emphasis on the "creature-feeling." However, all three concepts
are united under the broad banner of heavenly desire in at least two ways:
first, the individual is aware of his poor state in comparison to the Divine,
and second, the individual subsequently becomes fascinated with, or desirous
of, the Divine.

46 Lewis, *The Lion, the Witch and the Wardrobe*, 65. This passage is in many ways similar
    to one that Lewis wrote in his 1916 unpublished romance, *The Quest of Bleheris*, in
    which he wrote, "'In God's name,' said Bleheris, 'speak to me plain, and riddle not.'
    So the churl, looking yet once again at the dark stairway, put his haggard face close
    to the youth, and whispered so low that it was scarely to be heard, 'Bethrelladoom.'
    At the sound of that word, Bleheris felt on a sudden strange terror come upon him:
    yet not in truth an honest fear, as he had felt towards the Lumpher of the Sunken
    Wood, but rather a shrinking awe as a savage might feel towards the frightful god of his
    imaginings." Lewis, *The Quest of Bleheris*, 29. In addition to being the *Numen*, Christ
    is also Goodness itself; hence, "Goodness is either the great safety or the great danger
    – according to the way you react to it." Lewis, *Mere Christianity*, 340.
47 Otto, *The Idea of the Holy*, 41.
48 Ibid., 29.
49 Lewis, *Till We Have Faces*, 875.
50 Otto said that *Numen* or "the Holy" is analogous to, but not synonymous with, Beauty
    and the Good. Otto, *The Idea of the Holy*, 51.

IV: *Sehnsucht*

The fourth word Lewis used to describe heavenly desire is the German word *Sehnsucht*. The origin of this word has been lost to time, but we know that it was a word that was in vogue in the eighteenth and nineteenth centuries especially with the great Austrian and German composers, such as Wolfgang Amadeus Mozart, Ludwig van Beethoven and Franz Schubert, and the early and late German Romantic writers, such as Johann Wolfgang von Goethe, Friedrich von Schiller and Novalis. Now Lewis had read, or had tried to read, Goethe and Novalis in German while studying with Kirkpatrick between 1914-1917; however, given Lewis's poor proficiency in German and relative neglect of the language throughout his life, it is just as likely as not that his appropriation of the word *Sehnsucht* came from sources other than the German romantics.[51] For instance, we know Lewis encountered this word in William James's *Varieties of Religious Experience*, which he read in 1922,[52] and it is very possible that Lewis's first appropriation of this word came after a deeper study of English Romantics like William Wordsworth or Coleridge (who were heavily influenced by Goethe) or George MacDonald (who was heavily influenced by Novalis). Whatever the case may be, Lewis strongly believed that "poets have said more about it than philosophers."[53]

Nevertheless, since Lewis himself did not begin to use the word (in print at least) until the 1940s (indeed, he did not use it at all in regard to Romanticism in the 1930s),[54] it is clear that *Sehnsucht*, despite having become the title of the newest peer-reviewed journal dedicated solely to Lewis studies,[55] was not

---

51   "I . . . read a good deal in an English translation of Goethe's *Dichtung und Wahrheit* – wh[ich] I began to read in the original with Kirk a long time ago." Lewis, *All My Road Before Me*, 307 [March 28, 1924]. "I have again begun my German and do half an hour every morning before beginning my other work. I am still at Novalis – you will wonder how I have not finished it long ago, and even to myself I seem to have been reading it almost all my life. . . . Novalis is perhaps the greatest single influence on MacDonald." Lewis, *The Collected Letters of C. S. Lewis: Volume I*, 922 [August 13, 1930].

52   "Called at the Union . . . to take out W[illiam] James's *Varieties of Religious Experience*. I have been reading this most of the afternoon, a capital book." Lewis, *All My Road Before Me*, 48 [June 11, 1922]. "An excellent old German lady, who had done some traveling in her day, used to describe to me her *Sehnsucht* that she might yet visit 'Philadelphia,' whose wondrous name had always haunted her imagination." William James, *The Varieties of Religious Experience: A Study in Human Nature*, ed. Martin Marty (1902 reprint; Toronto: Penguin, 1982), 383.

53   Lewis, *The Collected Letters of C. S. Lewis: Volume III*, 995-6 [December 10, 1958].

54   C. S. Lewis, "Christianity and Culture," in *C. S. Lewis: Essay Collection & Other Short Pieces*, ed. Lesley Walmsley (1940 essay reprint; London: HarperCollins, 2000), 80.

55   *Sehnsucht* is a peer-reviewed journal started in 2007 by the Arizona C. S. Lewis Society.

the Oxford don's preference when discussing heavenly desire.

Now as with Lewis's Romanticism or Otto's *numinous*, the precise definition of *Sehnsucht* is unclear. It has connotations of "seeing the sublimity of nature," "longing for the unattainable" and "dreaming of fantasy worlds," all of which it picked up from its association with "the Blue Flower" motif as found in the medieval Scandinavian ballads *Längtans Blåa Blomma*[56] and German literature, especially Novalis's *Heinrich von Ofterdingen*,[57] but it also has connotations of remembering the happy past, and so is generally translated as "nostalgia." And while it is possible to see a connection between Platonic *eros* and *Sehnsucht*, any strong correlation would be hasty. Plato, for instance, understood *eros* in terms of the desire resulting from the soul's pre-existent state in which the immortal soul contemplated Beauty and thus experienced a happiness it no longer possesses. But this was not likely the case for the Germans, who probably understood *Sehnsucht* in terms of either a remembered past in *this life* or something like Otto's "fascination" in regard to the *numinious*.

As for Lewis himself, he spoke of *Sehnsucht* in many different ways, for instance, he talked about "*Sehnsucht*, awakened by the past, the remote, or the (imagined) supernatural,"[58] and mentioned that a picture of an American landscape "raise[d] extreme *Sehnsucht*."[59] However, usually the Oxford don referred to *Sehnsucht* in terms of "our lifelong nostalgia;"[60] furthermore, the evidence seems to suggest he thought of this nostalgia more in terms of the metaphysics of a Christianized Platonic *eros* and less in terms of merely remembering the past in this life: "Now, if we are made for heaven, the desire for our proper place *will be already in us*."[61]

Nonetheless, I hasten to add that despite being close friends with Barfield, a Christian Anthroposophist who believed in reincarnation and past lives, Lewis thought reincarnation incompatible with Christianity. Therefore, the Oxford don looked to orthodox Christians like Augustine and Boethius, who offered Christian interpretations of the Platonic theory of the innate knowledge of Happiness by associating Happiness with God and substituting

---

56   Corbin Scott Carnell, *Bright Shadow of Reality: Spiritual Longing in C. S. Lewis* (Grand Rapids, MI: Eerdmans, 1999), 22.

57   Novalis, *Heinrich von Ofterdingen*, in *The Collected Works of Novalis*, ed. Hans-Joachim Mähl, vol. 1 (Munich: Hanser, 1978), 237-413.

58   Lewis, "Christianity and Culture," 80.

59   Lewis, *The Collected Letters of C. S. Lewis: Volume III*, 199 [June 10, 1952].

60   C. S. Lewis, "The Weight of Glory," in *C. S. Lewis: Essay Collection & Other Short Pieces*, ed. Lesley Walmsley (1941 essay reprint; London: HarperCollins, 2000), 104.

61   Ibid., 98.

God-given knowledge for reincarnation. For example, Lewis underlined the
following in his edition of Augustine's *Confessions*:

> If except in my memory I find you, I am unmindful of you. . . . How,
> then, do I seek Thee, O Lord? For when I seek Thee, my God, I seek
> a happy life. . . . But I ask whether the happy life be in the memory?
> For did we not know it, we should not love it. We hear the name, and
> we all acknowledge that we desire the thing; for we are not delighted
> with the sound only. For when a Greek hears it spoken in Latin, he
> does not feel delight, for he knows not what is spoken; but we are
> delighted, as he too would be if he heard it in Greek; because the thing
> itself is neither Greek nor Latin, which Greeks and Latins, and men
> of all other tongues, long so earnestly to obtain. It is then known to
> all, and could they with one voice be asked whether they wished to be
> happy, without a doubt they would all answer that they would. And
> this could not be unless the thing itself, of which it is the name, were
> retained in their memory.[62]

Lewis agreed with Augustine that people can find knowledge of God *qua*
Happiness in their memories (and hence they can desire Him); however,
despite John Randolph Willis's insistence that Augustine's desire for God (i.e.
"Our hearts are restless until they rest in Thee") rested on the same principles
as Lewis's *Sehnsucht*,[63] this is not always clear, for while Lewis definitely
resembled the younger Augustine[64] in regard to our natural knowledge of
Happiness and God, Lewis – taking a less severe approach to the Fall – did
not agree with the older Augustine that our *knowledge* of Happiness and God
is purely the act of God's grace.[65]

---

62   C. S. Lewis, underlining in his edition of *Confessions*, by Augustine, trans. William
     Watts, 2 vols. (London: William Heinemann, MCMXXXI; The Rare Book Collection,
     The University of North Carolina at Chapel Hill) 10.17, 20.

63   John Randolph Willis, *Pleasures Forevermore: The Theology of C. S. Lewis* (Chicago:
     Loyola University Press, 1983), 38.

64   The younger Augustine was more Platonic in regard to free will and man's natural
     desire for happiness. For instance, in Augustine's first Catholic text, *The Happy Life*,
     the reference to, and subsequent argument surrounding, the phrase *"flagrante caritate"*
     or the "blazing love" the good man has for God was not *merely* Pauline but also owed
     a lot to Plato. John Rist, *Augustine: Ancient Thought Baptized* (Cambridge: Cambridge
     University Press, 2003), 150-1. Incidentally, Peter Brown gives an interesting argument
     for why Augustine could be considered a precursor to the Romantics, which would
     make a comparison between Lewis and Augustine even more compelling. See Peter
     Brown, *Augustine of Hippo: A Biography*, new ed. (Berkeley: University of California
     Press, 2000), 150.

65   Augustine *Confessions* 10.27.38.

Thus, we may say that while *Sehnsucht* emphasizes remembering more than the other members of heavenly desire, it, nevertheless, agrees with Platonic *eros*, Romanticism and the *numinous* in affirming at least the minimal requirements for heavenly desire, which are, once again, a feeling of loss or lack on the part of the individual in regard to something Distant and Profound, which, consequently, leads to longing for that Object.

V: "Joy"

The fifth term Lewis used in regard to heavenly desire is "Joy," which he used in his 1924 poem "Joy"[66] and then employed again in his 1955 autobiography, *Surprised by Joy*, which in turn got its name from the poem "Surprised by Joy" by the romantic poet Wordsworth.[67] Like Platonic *eros*, Romanticism, the *numinous* and *Sehnsucht*, Joy expresses the duality of loss (which results in pain) and desire: "It is that of an unsatisfied desire which is itself more desirable than any other satisfaction. I call it Joy, which is here a technical term and must be sharply distinguished from both Happiness and Pleasure. Joy (in my sense) has indeed one characteristic, and one only, in common with them; the fact that anyone who has experienced it will want it again."[68]

In this description of Joy, on top of seeing the basic *positive* similarities between Joy and the other concepts of heavenly desire, we can also see some of the *negative* similarities, which I have not yet mentioned. That is, already back in *The Pilgrim's Regress*, Lewis was aware that Romanticism has a dark side (e.g. attraction to magic, the occult, etc.) and in a 1940 essay, "Christianity and Culture," Lewis said frankly, "The dangers of romantic *sehnsucht* are very great."[69] Thus, it is hardly new that in *Surprised by Joy*, Lewis also spoke of the addictive nature of Joy in a way that mirrored his earlier discussion of Turkish Delight in *The Lion, the Witch and the Wardrobe*:

---

66 C. S. Lewis, "Joy," *The Beacon* 3 (May 1924): 444-51. Cf. "The speed [of the motorbike], the sunlight, and the sense of coming home put me into an unusually prolonged fit of 'joy.'" Lewis, *All My Road Before Me*, 317 [April 26, 1924].

67 Lewis, *Surprised by Joy*, 1253.

68 Ibid. During his absolute idealist phase, Lewis understood Joy to be the painful pleasure that arises as a result of at once desiring unity with Spirit and then realizing that such a unity can never take place since an Appearance must forever remain either an Appearance *qua* Spirit (and thus be separated from Spirit, which is Spirit *qua* the totality of all Appearances) or be dissolved into Spirit (and thus loose any individuality). C. S. Lewis, *Clivi Hamiltonis Summae Metaphysices Contra Anthroposophos Libri II* (November 1928 Unpublished "Great War" document; The Marion E. Wade Center, Wheaton College), 51.

69 Lewis, "Christianity and Culture," 80.

At last the Turkish Delight was all finished and Edmund was looking very hard at the empty box and wishing that she would ask him whether he would like some more. Probably the Queen knew quite well what he was thinking; for she knew, though Edmund did not, that this was enchanted Turkish Delight and that anyone who had once tasted it would want more and more of it, and would even, if they were allowed, go on eating it till they killed themselves.[70]

Nevertheless, it is crucial to see that Lewis stressed the danger of Joy and heavenly desire, not because they are bad, but because they are not ends in themselves. As we shall see in subsequent chapters, the Oxford don felt that Joy (to be specific now) is valuable only insofar as it leads us to its proper object, which is God *qua* Happiness; indeed, it is for this reason that Lewis clearly distinguished between Joy and Happiness, for the former leads to the latter.

Now the connection between heavenly desire and Happiness is something which Joy shares with Platonic *eros*. No doubt the desire for Happiness is in some way related to Romanticism and *Sehnsucht*, but it is more so with Joy, for the name is no accident in either Wordsworth's poem or Lewis's autobiography. Thus, Lewis had Joy or Platonic *eros* in mind when he spoke of people not having been given "an appetite for beatitude"[71] "in vain,"[72] and having been "made for infinite happiness."[73] Indeed, Happiness is so much the central focus of life that according to Lewis, God Himself, far from being in essence a lover of duty for duty's sake, is "a hedonist at heart."[74] Moreover, we see this emphasis on Happiness increasing in Lewis's later works, such as

70 Lewis, *The Lion, the Witch and the Wardrobe*, 38
71 Lewis, *The Discarded Image*, 94.
72 "I mean the pursuit of knowledge and beauty, in a sense, for their own sake, but in a sense which does not exclude their being for God's sake. An appetite for these things exists in the human mind, and God makes no appetite in vain. . . . This is the teleological argument that the existence of the impulse and the faculty prove that they must have a proper function in God's scheme – the argument by which Thomas Aquinas proves that sexuality would have existed even without the Fall." C. S. Lewis, "Learning in Wartime," in *C. S. Lewis: Essay Collection & Other Short Pieces*, ed. Lesley Walmsley (1939 essay reprint; London: HarperCollins, 2000), 583.
73 C. S. Lewis, *The Great Divorce*, in *C. S. Lewis: Selected Books* [Long Edition] (1946 reprint; London: HarperCollins, 1999), 1057. Cf. "The process of being turned from a creature into a son would not have been difficult or painful if the human race had not turned away from God centuries ago. They were able to do this because He gave them free will: He gave them free will because a world of mere automata could never love and therefore know infinite happiness. The difficult part is this. All Christians are agreed that there is, in the full and original sense, only one 'Son of God.'" Lewis, *Mere Christianity*, 438.
74 Lewis, *The Screwtape Letters*, 794.

in *Till We Have Faces*, where we read:

> 'I have always – at least, ever since I can remember – had a kind of longing for death.'
>
> 'Ah, Psyche,' I said, 'have I made you so little happy as that?'
>
> 'No, no, no,' she said. 'You don't understand. Not that kind of longing. It was when I was happiest that I longed most. It was on happy days when we were up there on the hills, the three of us, with the wind and the sunshine . . . where you couldn't see Glome or the palace. Do you remember? The colour and the smell, and looking across at the Grey Mountain in the distance? And because it was so beautiful, it set me longing, always longing. Somewhere else there must be more of it. Everything seemed to be saying, Psyche come! But I couldn't (not yet) come and I didn't know where I was to come to. It almost hurt me. I felt like a bird in a cage when the other birds of its kind are flying home.'
>
> . . .
>
> '– my country, the place where I ought to have been born. Do you think it all meant nothing, all the longing? The longing for home? For indeed it now feels not like going, but like going back. All my life the god of the Mountain has been wooing me.'[75]

Now Joy has roots both in the eudaimonian ethics of the Greek philosophers and the teachings of the Bible: both Plato and Jesus give us incentives for doing what is right – one says be virtuous because this is the way the soul can return to its heavenly home and the other says do as I, the Standard of Right and Wrong, command and you will be with Me in Paradise. Needless to say, Joy and happiness forced Lewis to reject the deontological ethics of Kant, which maintains that doing a moral deed for the sake of happiness always compromises ethical integrity: "If there lurks in most modern minds the notion that to desire our own good and earnestly to hope for the enjoyment of it is a bad thing, I submit that this notion has crept in from Kant and the Stoics and is no part of the Christian faith."[76]

---

75 Lewis, *Till We Have Faces*, 888-9. Cf. "Of that breeze men went mad and longed to death." Lewis, "*Dymer* Rough Draft," 160.

76 Lewis, "The Weight of Glory," 96. Lewis owned a copy of the Stoic philosopher Seneca's *Moral Essays,* and he likely knew the following passage from it: "There is a great difference between the Stoics and the other schools of philosophy as there is between males and females. . . . Other philosophers, using gentle and persuasive measures, are like the intimate family physician, who, commonly, tries to cure his patients, not by the best and quickest method, but as he is allowed. The Stoics, having adopted the heroic course, are not so much concerned in making it attractive to us who enter upon it, as

Of course, here we are speaking of Lewis the Neoplatonic Christian, not Lewis of any other philosophical phase, for the Oxford don's thoughts on the relation between duty and Joy shifted a lot over the years. For instance, in *The Pilgrim's Regress*, which broadly parallels the chronology of Lewis's philosophical journey, we see the character "Vertue" enter the story (i.e. after a few chapters) around the same time Lewis entered into his first moral experience (i.e. 1917). Moreover, just as Lewis was schooled in Aristotle's *Ethics* from an early age, so too was Vertue "brought up on Aristotle,"[77] and just as Lewis passed from the eudemonism of the Greeks to the deontology of Stoical materialism (1919-1923), so too did Vertue pass on to become a Kantian or Stoic.[78] Furthermore, both Lewis the Stoical materialist and Vertue the Stoic / Kantian shared the same admirable devotion to duty ("I know that the rule is to be obeyed because it is a rule and not because it appeals to my feelings at the moment"[79]), yet both of them saw this devotion to duty in opposition to Joy. Lewis psychoanalyzed, and subsequently discarded, all romantic and supernatural feelings, and then agreed with Kant when the German said that willingly obeying the imperative commands of the moral law simply because it is objective and absolute is the supreme good, better, even, than the desire for happiness;[80] in fact, in his edition of Kant's *Critique of Practical Reason*, Lewis called the aforementioned argument a "Teleological Argument" because "practical reason is a bad means to happiness. Therefore it must be means to something else."[81] Vertue the Stoic believed something similar, for he said:

> 'Then there is the life I have been leading myself – marching on I don't know where. I can't see that there is any other good in it except the mere fact of imposing my will on my inclinations. And that seems to be good *training*, but training for what? Suppose after all it was training for battle? Is it so absurd to think that that might be the

---

in having it rescue us as soon as possible and guide us to that lofty summit which rises so far beyond the reach of any missile as to tower high above all fortune." Seneca *The Dialogues of Lucius Annaeus Seneca: Book II; To Serenus on the Firmness of the Wise Man* 1.1.

77   Lewis, *The Pilgrim's Regress*, 96.

78   In the last part of *The Pilgrim's Regress*, we read: "'I am cured of playing the Stoic,' said Vertue." Ibid., 218.

79   Ibid., 109.

80   Immanuel Kant, *Critique of Practical Reason*, in *The Cambridge Edition of the Works of Immanuel Kant: Practical Philosophy*, trans. and ed. Mary J. Gregor (Cambridge: Cambridge University Press, 1999), 165 [1.1.7].

81   C. S. Lewis, marginalia in his edition of *Critique of Practical Reason and Other Works on the Theory of Ethics*, by Immanuel Kant, trans. Thomas Kingsmill Abbott (London: Longmans, Green & Co., 1923; The Marion E. Wade Center, Wheaton College), 12.

thing we were born for? A fight in a narrow place, life or death; – that must be the final act of will – the conquest of the deepest inclination of all.'

'I think my heart will break,' said John after he had gone many paces in silence. 'I came to find my Island. I am not high-minded like you, Vertue: it was never anything but sweet desire that led me.'

Vertue sat down as one not noticing that he did it.

'Don't you see?' he said. 'Suppose there is anything East and West. How can that give me a motive for going on? Because there is something pleasant ahead? That is a bribe. Because there is something dreadful behind? That is a threat. I meant to be a free man.'

'Vertue,' said John, 'give in. For once yield to desire. Have done with your choosing. *Want* something.'[82]

As we can gather from chapter two, eventually Vertue, like Lewis, began to "want something," thus reflecting Lewis's Christian attitude that "if God were a Kantian, who would not have us till we came to Him from the purest and best motives, who could be saved?"[83] Consequently, Lewis the Neoplatonic Christian found a way to reconcile Joy and duty when he declared: "A *perfect* man w[oul]d never act from sense of duty; he'd always *want* the right more than the wrong."[84]

While I could go into much greater detail in regard to Joy and duty, I will defer further discussion until chapter eight. What is important for the moment is that on top of sharing special emphasis on happiness with Platonic *eros*, Joy properly belongs in the conglomerate heavenly desire, for it bespeaks deep spiritual emptiness and profound longing for the divine.

VI: Hope

The sixth and final word that Lewis used in conjunction with heavenly desire was hope, which shares an awareness of loss or lack and an orientation toward divine fulfillment with the five other members of heavenly desire. However, according to Lewis, *one* of the things that sets hope apart from all the rest (there is more than one thing, of course) is that while Platonic *eros* and Joy are *natural* desires for happiness (and, derivatively, God), hope is a *supernatural* desire for God – it is one of the three theological virtues – and as such is only given by *grace*:

---

82 Lewis, *The Pilgrim's Regress*, 123-4.
83 Lewis, *The Problem of Pain*, 521.
84 Lewis, *The Collected Letters of C. S. Lewis: Volume III*, 872 [July 18, 1957].

Hope is one of the Theological virtues. This means that a continual looking forward to the eternal world is not (as some modern people think) a form of escapism or wishful thinking, but one of the things a Christian is meant to do. It does not mean that we are to leave the present world as it is. If you read history you will find that the Christians who did most for the present world were just those who thought most of the next. . . . I must make it the main object of life to press on to that other country and to help others to do the same.[85]

Thus, it seems that Lewis, perhaps following the lead of other Christian philosophers and theologians like Thomas Aquinas,[86] envisioned hope to be a God-given honing or amplification of Platonic *eros*, *Sehnsucht* or Joy.[87]

---

85   Lewis, *Mere Christianity*, 406, 408. Cf. "Nothing is more likely to destroy a species or a nation than a determination to survive at all costs. Those who care for something else more than civilization are the only people by whom civilization is at all likely to be preserved. Those who want Heaven most have served Earth best. Those who love Man less than God do most for Man." C. S. Lewis, "On Living in an Atomic Age," in *C. S. Lewis: Essay Collection & Other Short Pieces*, ed. Lesley Walmsley (1948 essay reprint; London: HarperCollins, 2000), 365-6.

86   For further discussion, see Simo Knuuttlia, *Emotions in Ancient and Medieval Philosophy* (Oxford: Oxford University Press, 2006), 246.

87   Lewis, *Mere Christianity*, 369, 406. Moreover, while it is only a suggestion, it is also possible to see in Lewis's poem "No Beauty We Could Desire" hope, which is not typically understood as an aesthetic affect, recognizing True Beauty in a form that natural Platonic *eros*, which is an aesthetic affect, cannot perceive; in this poem, Lewis seemed to be saying that God's leading, guiding and gifting – which includes the gifting of hope – is vital to the success of man's natural desire and quest for God; as we read:

> Yes, you are always everywhere. But I,
> Hunting in such immeasurable forests,
> Could never bring the noble Hart to bay.
>
> The scent was too perplexing for my hounds;
> Nowhere sometimes, then again everywhere.
> Other scents, too, seemed to them almost the same.
>
> Therefore I turn my back on the unapproachable
> Stars and horizons and all musical sounds,
> Poetry itself, and the winding stair of thought.
>
> Leaving the forests where you are pursued in vain
> – Often a mere white gleam – I turn instead
> To the appointed place where you pursue.
>
> Not in Nature, not even in Man, but in one
> Particular Man, with a date, so tall, weighing
> So much, talking Aramaic, having learned a trade;
>
> Not in all food, not in all bread and wine
> (Not, I mean, as my littleness requires)
> But this wine, this bread . . . no beauty we could desire.

VII: The Dialectic of Desire

Drawing on insights from Platonic *eros*, "Romanticism," the *numinous*, *Sehnsucht*, Joy and hope, Lewis gave the twentieth century a fresh taste of an old philosophical truth in his numerous writings about heavenly desire, particularly when formulated as an argument for the existence of Heaven (and thus God). While the accolade for these writings has not always been universal (philosopher John Beversluis says "The pursuit of Joy is a childish thing"[88]), many have been impressed by it; indeed, philosopher Alvin Plantinga praised "C. S. Lewis's Argument from Nostalgia"[89] and philosopher Peter Kreeft, calling the same argument "C. S. Lewis' Argument from Desire,"[90] thinks, after Anselm's ontological argument, that it is "the single most intriguing argument in the history of human thought."[91] Yet, while it can hardly be denied that Lewis, bringing together so many threads of meaning, made an important philosophical contribution to the doctrine of heavenly desire, he can hardly be said to have created a new doctrine; in fact, much like the medieval philosophers, he always denied that he was trying to be original.[92] Nevertheless, Kreeft's comment about Lewis's argument from desire being the second most intriguing argument in the history of human thought behind Anselm's ontological argument raises an interesting question, not about the differences between these two arguments (though there are differences), but about their similarities. Thus, what I would like to do is to spend some time discussing Lewis's take on these arguments, and then I would like to evaluate the philosophical worth of the argument from desire.

Anselm's ontological argument, best known to Lewis through Descartes[93] (and Boethius![94]), is the argument that proceeds from the idea of God to

C. S. Lewis, "No Beauty We Could Desire," in *Poems*, by C. S. Lewis, ed. Walter Hooper, 124-5 (San Diego: Harcourt Brace Jovanovich, 1964), 124-5 [1-18].

88 Beversluis, *C. S. Lewis and the Search for Rational Religion*, 30.

89 Alvin Plantinga, "Two Dozen (or so) Theistic Arguments," in *Alvin Plantinga*, ed. Deane-Peter Baker, Contemporary Philosophy in Focus (Cambridge: Cambridge University Press, 2007), 227.

90 Kreeft, "C. S. Lewis' Argument from Desire," 201.

91 Ibid., 210.

92 "If any real theologian reads these pages he will very easily see that they are the work of a layman and an amateur. . . . I have believed myself to be restating ancient and orthodox doctrines. If any parts of the book are 'original,' in the sense of being novel or unorthodox, they are so against my will." Lewis, *The Problem of Pain*, 471.

93 Lewis, *The Collected Letters of C. S. Lewis: Volume II*, 7 [October 24, 1931].

94 Lewis also felt that there was an "Ontological Proof" in Boethius's *Consolation of Philosophy*. C. S. Lewis, marginalia in his edition of *King Alfred's Old English Version of Boethius's De Consolatione Philosophiae*, ed. Walter John Sedegefield (Oxford: Clarendon Press, 1899; The Rare Book Collection, The University of North Carolina at Chapel

God as a reality or existent being. It can be put in the form of a categorical syllogism: (1) God is that-which-no-greater-can-be-thought (i.e. I have an idea of a perfect, necessary being); (2) That-which-no-greater-can-be-thought must exist, not only mentally as an idea, but also extra-mentally in reality (i.e. because existence is a perfection, I could not say I have an idea of a perfect, necessary being unless a perfect, necessary being really exists); (3) Therefore, God exists, not only mentally as an idea, but also extra-mentally in reality (i.e. it is impossible for a perfect, necessary being to be merely possible; He must necessarily be existent).[95] During Lewis's idealist phases (as found in his 1924 essay "The Whole"[96] and his 1928 Great War letters), Lewis believed the ontological argument was a failure because he thought the question of essence is utterly separate from the question of existence:

> We cannot (strictly speaking) be agreed about a whatness. We can *share* a whatness by sense or imagination, and can then agree or disagree as to whether this whatness is realised in such and such an actual or no. For you will observe that whatness does *not* contain actuality: the bringing before the mind *what* X is, is preliminary to the question *whether* X exists. You cannot get the *that* into the what as an element: it was the mistake of Descartes to suppose that you could. (I take it this may be what Plato means when he says that good is ἐπέχεινα τῆς οὐσίας on the far side of being).[97]

However, shortly after becoming a Christian (1931), Lewis showed signs of softening toward the argument despite still being inclined to reject it based on the meaning of the words used:

Hill), 83 [4.2].

95   Anselm *Proslogion* 2. René Descartes, *Meditations on First Philosophy*, vol. 2, *The Philosophical Writings of Descartes*, trans. John Cottingham, Robert Stoothoff and Dugald Murdoch (Cambridge: Cambridge University Press, 1999), 31 [3.45].

96   In March 1924, Lewis started a paper called "The Whole," in which he explored the problem of potentiality and actuality, existence and essence: "I also started tentatively an essay on the "Whole" which I thought might be a more systematic exposition of my theory of potentiality." Lewis, *All My Road Before Me*, 301 [March 10, 1924]. "I spent most of the morning at my essay on the Whole, trying to tackle the question of *essentia* and *exisentia*." Ibid., 304 [March 14, 1924]. While I was examining Lewis's notes on Henry More, I came across an incomplete version of this essay (which was not mentioned in the Marion E. Wade Center's list of the unpublished works by Lewis that they have). Although I will discuss this essay later, it basically deals with Lewis's account of how there can be non-existent essences. See C. S. Lewis, "The Whole," in "Henry More and Dymer, MS-170," 105-14 (Unpublished essay [March 1924]; The Marion E. Wade Center, Wheaton College).

97   Lewis, *The Collected Letters of C. S. Lewis: Volume III*, 1633-4 [January 1928, "The Great War Letters" Series I, Letter 8].

The particular one you quote ('I have an idea of a perfect being') seems to me to be valid or invalid according to the meaning you give the words 'have an idea of.' I used to work it out by the analogy of a machine. If I have an idea of a machine which I, being unmechanical, couldn't have invented on my own, does this prove that I have received the idea from some really mechanical source – e.g. a talk with the real inventor? To which I answer 'Yes, if you mean a really detailed idea': but of course there is another sense in which e.g. a lady novelist 'has an idea of' a new airship invented by her hero – in the sense that she attached *some* vague meaning to her words, which proves nothing of the sort. So that if anyone asks me whether the idea of God in human minds proves His existence, I can only ask 'Whose idea?'[98]

This is to say that Lewis was unconvinced people have a clear idea of a perfect being in their minds; as a result, he thought the ontological argument fails as universal proof for God's existence.

Nevertheless, the Oxford don *did* think that people have an idea of God *qua* Goodness, Beauty and / or Happiness because in order for heavenly desire to pursue things like Goodness and Beauty, it must have at least some *idea* of what they are like; that is, there must be some deep metaphysical bond between heavenly desire, the copies it is attracted to, and the Originals it really desires;[99] indeed, in one place, Lewis said plainly, "The form of the desired is in the desire,"[100] and in another,

[I]t is arguable that the 'idea of God' in *some* minds does contain, not a mere abstract definition, but a real imaginative perception of goodness and beauty, beyond their own resources: and this not only in minds which already believe in God. It certainly seems to me that the 'vague something' which has been suggested to ones mind as desirable, all ones life, in experience of nature and music and poetry, even in such ostensibly irreligious forms as 'The Land East of the Sun and West of the Moon' in Morris, and which rouses desires that no finite object pretends to satisfy, can be argued *not* to be any product of our own minds. Of course I am not suggesting that these vague ideas of something we want and haven't got, wh[ich] occur in the Pagan period of individuals and of races (hence mythology), are anything more than the first and most rudimentary forms of the 'idea of God.'[101]

---

98 Lewis, *The Collected Letters of C. S. Lewis: Volume II*, 7 [October 24, 1931].
99 "In other words, whether, while I was right in seeing that a copy must be different from an original, I ought to have remembered that it must also be *like* it – else how w[oul]d it be a copy?" Lewis, *The Collected Letters of C. S. Lewis: Volume I*, 914 [July 8, 1930].
100 Lewis, *Surprised by Joy*, 1371.
101 Lewis, *The Collected Letters of C. S. Lewis: Volume II*, 7 [October 24, 1931].

Relating this to his own conversion about ten years later (1943), Lewis said, in a Pseudo-Dionysian fashion, that heavenly desire, if followed correctly, would lead to a recognition in philosophy after philosophy, copy after copy, that while these *really* point to, and participate in, Truth and the Original (the Way of Affirmation), they themselves – as *incomplete* philosophies and copies – are not the ultimate object of our longing, for we long for perfection (the Way of Negation); and this, for Lewis, who we remember believed philosophy is a way of life, constituted a kind of *lived* ontological proof:

> I knew only too well how easily the longing accepts false objects and through what dark ways the pursuit of them leads us: but I also saw that the Desire itself contains the corrective of all these errors. The only fatal error was to pretend that you had passed from desire to fruition, when, in reality, you had found either nothing, or desire itself, or the satisfaction of some different desire. The dialectic of Desire, faithfully followed, would retrieve all mistakes, head you off from all false paths, and force you not to propound, but to live through, a sort of ontological proof.[102]

The dialectical process of this ontological proof, which we will examine in greater detail in a moment, reflects Lewis's Neoplatonic absorption of Aristotelian logic or dialectic, which Lewis summarized in his edition of Aristotle's *Ethics* as following:

> In Philosophy, if we know how to see the difficulty in two contradictory *endoxa* [opinions or philosophies] . . . we shall more easily detect the truth, falsehood in each. It is also useful for the first positions of any science: these clearly cannot be approached. . . . [W]e must therefore

---

102 Lewis, preface to the third edition of *The Pilgrim's Regress*, 9. *The Pilgrim's Regress* is not the only place Lewis talked about the dialectic of desire; in a book review about William Morris, Lewis wrote: "His [Morris'] real theme is very difficult to describe, but it is 'actual' enough. Morris himself does not state it philosophically. We may say, if we will, that it becomes explicit in 'The House of the Wolfings' when the hero has to choose between immortality and mortal life with 'The Glittering Plain' where we reach the land of the ever-living only to long for our escape from it. But in so far as these stories pose a question and give an answer they are not typical. . . . We recognize (it is no other poet's theme) the endless hithering and thithering of natural desire, the irrepressible thirst for immortality, and its inevitable recoil to the familiar – the sweet familiar whose very sweetness must once more reawake the rebel passion. Morris may build a world in some ways happier than the real one, but happiness puts as stern a question as misery. It is this dialectic of desire presented with no solution, no lies, no panacea, which gives him his peculiar bittersweet quality, and also his solidity. He has faced the facts." C. S. Lewis, "The Sagas and Modern Life: Morris, Mr Yeats and the Originals," a review of *The Works of Morris and of Yeats in Relation to Early Saga Literature*, by Dorothy M. Hoare, *The Times Literary Supplement* (May 29, 1937): 409.

deal with them by going through the relevant *endoxa*. This is . . . the dialectic method.[103]

It was by going from *endoxa* to *endoxa*, finding the truth and flaw in each, saying "this also is Thou; neither is this Thou,"[104] that Lewis eventually came to declare himself "an empirical Theist," claiming, "I have arrived at God by induction."[105]

On top of this, we have good reason to think Lewis never changed his views on this dialectic of desire. In a letter just one month before he died (1963), Lewis told a mother who appreciated his sixth Narnian book, *The Silver Chair*, "I suppose your philosopher son – what a family you have been privileged to bring into the world! – means the chapter in which Puddleglum puts out the fire with his foot. He must thank Anslem and Descartes for it, not me. I have simply put the 'Ontological Proof' in a form suitable for children."[106] The passage the mother was talking about is a variation of Lewis's argument from desire, which Lewis apparently thought akin to the ontological argument. The context for the argument is Puddleglum and his friends are held captive by an evil witch in a subterranean world, and she is trying to convince them that there is neither an over-world nor an Aslan, to which Puddleglum replies:

> 'One word, Ma'am,' he said, coming back from the fire; limping, because of the pain. 'One word. All you've been saying is quite right, I shouldn't wonder. I'm a chap who always liked to know the worst and then put the best face I can on it. So I won't deny any of what you said. But there's one thing more to be said, even so. Suppose we *have* only dreamed, or made up, all those things – trees and grass and sun and moon and stars and Aslan himself. Suppose we have. Then all I can say is that, in that case, the made-up things *seem a good deal more important* than the real ones. Suppose this black pit of a kingdom of yours *is* the only world. Well, it strikes me as a pretty poor one. And that's a funny thing, when you come to think of it. We're just babies making up a game, if you're right. But four babies playing a game can make a play-world which licks your real world hollow. That's why I'm

103 C. S. Lewis, marginalia in the back of his edition of *The Ethics of Aristotle*, by Aristotle, ed. John Burnet. (London: Methuen & Co., 1900; The Rare Book Collection, The University of North Carolina at Chapel Hill).

104 Charles Williams, *He Came Down from Heaven* (London: Heinemann, 1938), 25. Lewis loved this line from Williams's book (a line which likely had roots in Pseudo-Dionysius). Lewis, *The Collected Letters of C. S. Lewis: Volume II*, 228 [June 7, 1938].

105 C. S. Lewis, quoted in *C. S. Lewis: A Biography*, by Roger Lancelyn Green and Walter Hooper, 111.

106 Lewis, *The Collected Letters of C. S. Lewis: Volume III*, 1472 [October 26, 1963].

going to stand by the play-world. I'm on Aslan's side even if there isn't any Aslan to lead it. I'm going to live as like a Narnian as I can even if there isn't any Narnia.'[107]

Since Lewis's argument from desire in *The Silver Chair* is not especially clear, it is worth looking at the argument's basic premises as laid out by Kreeft: (1) Every natural and innate desire in us bespeaks a corresponding real object that can satisfy the desire (note: this is based on Lewis's Aristotelian belief that "nature does nothing in vain,"[108] and on his Platonic belief that every desire has an object); (2) There exists in us a desire which nothing in time, nothing on earth, no creature, can satisfy; (3) Therefore, there exists[109] something outside of time, earth, and creatures which *can* satisfy this desire.[110]

Now as with any philosophical argument, the argument from desire has had its share of defenders, critics and counter-critics; consequently, for the sake of demonstrating the importance of, and controversy surrounding, Lewis's most notable contribution to natural theology (there are others, however, as we shall see), I have tried to distill all that has been said about

107 C. S. Lewis, *The Silver Chair* (1953 reprint; London: Fontana, 1985), 156-7 (emphasis mine).

108 Lewis, preface to the third edition of *The Pilgrim's Regress*, 9.

109 Although I believe that Kreeft's rendition of Lewis's argument is accurate, it is important to notice something about Lewis's original language, particularly in regard to the strength of the claim. Kreeft's third premise has an implied "necessarily" when he says, "Therefore, there (*necessarily*) exists something outside of time, earth, and creatures which *can* satisfy this desire." However, not *all* Lewis's formulations of this argument express necessity. For instance, in his 1941 essay "The Weight of Glory," Lewis wrote: "In the same way, though I do not believe (I wish I did) that my desire for Paradise proves that I shall enjoy it, I think it a *pretty good indication* that such a thing exists and that some men will." Lewis, "The Weight of Glory," 99 (emphasis mine). And again in his 1942 BBC talks on "Christian Behaviour," Lewis said: "The Christian says, 'Creatures are not born with desires unless satisfaction for those desires exists. A baby feels hunger: well, there is such a thing as food. A duckling wants to swim: well, there is such a thing as water. Men feel sexual desire: well, there is such a thing as sex. If I find in myself a desire which no experience in this world can satisfy, the most *probable* explanation is that I was made for another world.'" Lewis, *Mere Christianity*, 407 (emphasis mine). Nevertheless, what justifies Kreeft's rendition of Lewis's argument is that in the Oxford don's 1943 preface to *The Pilgrim's Regress*, Lewis contended: "It appeared to me therefore that if a man diligently followed this desire, pursuing the false objects until their falsity appeared and then resolutely abandoning them, he must come out at last into the clear knowledge that the human soul was made to enjoy some object that is never fully given – nay, cannot even be imagined as given – in our present mode of subjective and spatio-temporal experience. This Desire was, in the soul, as the Siege Perilous in Arthur's castle – the chair in which only one could sit. And if nature makes nothing in vain, the One who can sit in this chair *must* exist." Lewis, preface to the third edition of *The Pilgrim's Regress*, 9 (emphasis mine).

110 Kreeft, "C. S. Lewis' Argument from Desire," 201-2.

this argument into eight points of contention.

The first point of contention is *what* the argument is about. Peter Kreeft,[111] John Beversluis,[112] Hugo Meynell,[113] Douglas Hyatt,[114] and Erik Wielenberg[115] think that the argument is a proof for the existence of *God*,[116] whereas Edward Cook thinks that it is an argument for the existence of *Heaven*.[117] Cook thinks his objection is significant because he does not want to ascribe to Lewis what the Oxford don did not (precisely) believe: i.e. that heavenly desire is a desire for God. This objection might have some force if Cook divided heavenly desire into its different concepts and then argued that some of these concepts do not have God as their object in either an immediate or easily derived way (e.g. the *numinous*); however, since the majority of the concepts in heavenly desire *do* have God as their immediate, or approximate, object – not to mention the fact that Lewis partly associated his argument from desire with the ontological argument, which is a proof for *God's* existence – Kreeft, Beversluis, Meynell, Hyatt and Wielenberg are surely right that the argument from desire is an argument for the existence of God.

The second point of contention is Beversluis's claim that just because something does not *ultimately* satisfy us, it does not mean that we did not really want it in the first place. Beversluis attempts to prove that (2) is flawed by arguing that just as a man's returning hunger does not prove that he did not want food before,[118] so a man's dissatisfaction with a finite thing does not prove that he did not want that thing originally. Nevertheless, it is apparent that Beversluis's objection is based on a false analogy, for (2) does not claim that goal of *every* desire is ultimate satisfaction; it only claims that ultimate satisfaction (if this is even the right phrase) is the goal of a *specific* desire: heavenly desire.

111 Ibid., 201.
112 Beversluis, *C. S. Lewis and the Search for Rational Religion*, 15.
113 Meynell, "An Attack on C. S. Lewis," 313.
114 Douglas Hyatt, "Joy, the Call of God in Man: A Critical Appraisal of Lewis's Argument from Desire," in *C. S. Lewis: Lightbearers in the Shadowlands; the Evangelistic Vision of C. S. Lewis*, ed. Angus Menuge, 305-28 (Wheaton, IL: Crossway Books, 1997), 305.
115 Wielenberg, *God and the Reach of Reason: C. S. Lewis, David Hume and Bertrand Russell*, 109.
116 Beversluis, *C. S. Lewis and the Search for Rational Religion*, 15.
117 Edward Cook, "Does Joy Lead to God? Lewis, Beversluis, and the Argument from Desire," http://homepage.mac.com/edcook/lewis-desire.html (accessed on February 12, 2005), 1.
118 Beversluis, *C. S. Lewis and the Search for Rational Religion*, 16.

The third point of contention is similar to the second in that it simply denies the existence of heavenly desire. Kreeft voices this possible objection, but then he turns around and says that people who deny the existence of heavenly desire are guilty of playing the "stupidest wager in the world" and their words verge "on culpable dishonesty."[119] Lewis himself was generally more tolerant than Kreeft; indeed, instead of calling a man like John Stuart Mill "one of the shallowest minds in the history of human thought," as Kreeft does,[120] Lewis called Mill, as we recall from chapter two, "an honest skeptic." Moreover, in his incomplete 1960 essay, "The Language of Religion," Lewis gave a Socratic "likely story" or myth – based on Barfield's theory of "ancient semantic unity," which we will discuss later – explaining that the ontological argument *fails* because it requires a degree of clarity that some *honest* people do not have. Nevertheless, while Lewis went so far as to concede that the ontological argument fails on account of some honest people lacking a *clear* concept of a perfect being, he thought the argument from desire succeeds (and thus agrees with Kreeft) since it only requires a *vague* desire, which all people have whether they are aware of it or not:

> Something like this may be happening. You remember Well's *Country of the Blind*. Now its inhabitants, being men, must have descended from ancestors who could see. During centuries a gradual atrophy of sight must have spread through the whole race; but at no given moment, till it was complete, would it (probably) have been equally advanced in all individuals. During this intermediate period a very interesting linguistic situation would have arisen. They would have inherited from their unblind ancestors all the visual vocabulary – the names of the colours, words like 'see' and 'look' and 'dark' and 'light.' There would be some who still used them in the same sense as ourselves: archaic types who saw the green grass and perceived the light coming at dawn. There would be others who had faint vestiges of sight, and who used these words, with increasing vagueness, to describe sensations so evanescent as to be incapable of clear discrimination. . . . And there would be a third class who had achieved full blindness, to whom *see* was merely a synonym for *understand* and *dark* for *difficult*. And these would be the vanguard, and the future would be with them, and a very little cross-examination of the archaic type that still saw would convince them at its attempt to give some other meaning to the old visual words was merely a tissue of vague, emotive uses and category mistake. . . . [In this way] I sometimes wonder whether the Ontological Argument did not itself arise as a partially unsuccessful

translation of an experience without concept or words. I don't think we can initially argue from the *concept* of Perfect Being to its existence. But did they really, inside, argue from the experienced glory that it could not be generated subjectively?[121]

The fourth point of contention is from Beversluis and Wielenberg. Beversluis's assertion is that Lewis confused grammar with, and so read grammar back into, reality: "All desires must have *grammatical* objects but they need not have *real* ones."[122] Although Kreeft exaggerates when he calls this "a typical Logical Positivist objection," he makes a good point when he argues thus: "Lewis' argument does not begin with a purely grammatical observation but with a metaphysical observation: that real desires really do have real objects. But he does not say that *all* desires do, only that all natural, innate, instinctive desires do. Desires for imaginary things, like Oz, are not innate. Desire for God is."[123] While Wielenberg disagrees with Kreeft that all natural and innate desires can be satisfied,[124] I think that the truth of Kreeft's statement is fairly apparent.

The fifth point of contention comes from Beversluis (again), who asks, "How could Lewis have known that every natural desire has a real object *before* knowing that Joy has one?"[125] Beversluis's challenge is directed against the truth of (1), for he maintains that (1) can only be established by a posteriori knowledge and enumerative induction (i.e. knowing *every* example of a given category, including the example given in the conclusion). This kind of objection – the objection of a radical empiricist who discounts deduction and rejects a priori knowledge – is one that is more or less irresolvable. Of course, a radical empiricist *could* withhold judgment concerning the truth of (1) until he has done the impossible task of cataloging every example of natural desire; however, I agree with rationalists like Aristotle, Boethius, Kreeft and indeed Lewis himself that through abstraction and deduction we can recognize universal truths. Hence, I would rule in favor of (1).

---

121 C. S. Lewis, "The Language of Religion," in *C. S. Lewis: Essay Collection & Other Short Pieces*, ed. Lesley Walmsley (1960 essay reprint; London: HarperCollins, 2000), 265-6. Cf. "I have known some who were completely convinced by Descartes' Ontological Proof: that is, they received Faith-A [a settled intellectual assent] from Descartes first and then went on to seek, and to find, Faith-B. . . . Of course Faith-A usually involves a degree of subjective certitude which goes beyond the logical certainty." Lewis, "Is Theism Important?" 55.

122 Beversluis, *C. S. Lewis and the Search for Rational Religion*, 16.

123 Kreeft, "C. S. Lewis' Argument from Desire," 229. Cf. Lewis, *Mere Christianity*, 407.

124 Wielenberg, *God and the Reach of Reason: C. S. Lewis, David Hume and Bertrand Russell*, 111.

125 Beversluis, *C. S. Lewis and the Search for Rational Religion*, 19.

The sixth point of contention is, yet again, from Beversluis, who again attacks the truth of (1) by simply denying that a natural desire proves that there is a natural object to satisfy it:

> The phenomenon of hunger simply does not prove that man inhibits a world in which food exists. One might just as well claim that the fear that grips us when we walk through a dark graveyard proves that we have something to be afraid of. What proves that we inhabit a world in which food exists is the discovery that certain things are in fact 'eatable' and that they nourish and repair our bodies. The discovery of the existence of food comes not by way of an *inference* based on the inner state of hunger; it is, rather, an empirical discovery. . . . The desire in and of itself proves nothing, points to nothing.[126]

Of all Beversluis's objections to the argument from desire, this one certainly has the most force in contemporary society, which is dominated by a worldview dictated by Darwinianism. Yet as with Beversluis's previous objections, there is nothing that can force a person to accept, or reject, his claim. Thus, whereas Meynell gives "very little weight to the principle that 'nature does nothing in vain,'"[127] Kreeft thinks that to deny this principle is not only to reject the lessons of Nature, but also the authority of the Bible itself: "Only words are signs, things are not, to the Empiricist. In other words, the world is not full of the grandeur of God, and Paul must have been philosophically wrong . . . in saying, in effect, that the world is a sign and that we should be able to read it, that 'the invisible things of God are known *through* the things that are made.'"[128] While admittedly a person can problematize the idea that "nature does nothing in vain" by pointing out examples of defects and mutations, I am inclined to agree with Kreeft (and Lewis, and Aristotle et al.) not simply that "nature does nothing in vain" but also that all defects are rightly called thus since a defect always presupposes a standard and set nature which dictate the proper function of the natural thing in question. Of course, many nowadays would bite the bullet and counter by saying that there are no such things as defects and mutations since there is no such thing as a set or fixed nature; thus, while I think a *reductio ad absurdum* can be used to show the preference for things having fixed natures as opposed to open natures, on this mark, there is nothing that can *absolutely* move the argument in one way or the other.

---

126 Ibid., 189.
127 Meynell, "An Attack on C. S. Lewis," 313.
128 Kreeft, "C. S. Lewis' Argument from Desire," 230.

The seventh point of contention centers around an apparent inconsistency, not in the argument from desire as such, but in the apparent contradictory way Lewis spoke about his own conversion to theism. That is, Beversluis thinks Lewis's dialectic of desire is flawed because Lewis at once spoke of being attracted to God via heavenly desire and yet shrinking away from Him when he, "the most dejected and reluctant convert in all England,"[129] actually encountered Him; Beversluis writes: "Either God is the ultimate Object of desire or he is not. If he is, then it makes no sense to talk about shrinking from him the moment he is found. If he is not, then we will not find our heart's desire by following Joy any more than mice will find theirs by pursuing the cat."[130] The obvious fallacy in this argument is not, as Beversluis tries to anticipate, that people lose interest in the thing they were pursuing once they obtain it;[131] rather, the fallacy is that people can at once desire something for one reason and in one way, and yet also feel frightened of it for another reason and in another way. Hence, a young girl may be excited to see her daddy after he has been away for awhile, and yet she may also feel shy when she actually sees him; or a young man may be excited about seeing his new wife on his wedding night, and yet he may feel terrified of what she will think of him.

The eighth and final point of contention is one that sees Beversluis and Hyatt arguing that an unfallen heavenly desire is incompatible with man's sinful nature, on the one hand, and Kreeft and Meynall arguing against this, on the other.

The problem Beversluis and Hyatt see is that the Bible seems to speak of man's desires as totally fallen; thus, they argue that heavenly desire – as a natural desire – can neither point us to, nor lead us toward, God (Ephesians 2:3, Romans 1:24-32 and Galatians 5:17). Moreover, Hyatt uses both Augustine and Pascal to draw attention to the alleged hamartiological weakness of Lewis's dialectic of desire,[132] and Beversluis believes that heavenly desire (and thus the dialectic of desire) has its origin in Greek philosophy and not Christianity, and so it should be rejected in the context of this argument; hence, he says Lewis's theory of attraction to, and fear of, God is "a philosophical hybrid, a conceptual mongrel that lacks the authentic pedigree of either parent."[133] Ultimately, their conclusion – though only Beversluis has the courage to say

---

129 Lewis, *Surprised by Joy*, 1376.
130 Beversluis, *C. S. Lewis and the Search for Rational Religion*, 21.
131 Ibid.
132 Hyatt, "Joy, the Call of God in Man: A Critical Appraisal of Lewis's Argument from Desire," 321.
133 Beversluis, *C. S. Lewis and the Search for Rational Religion*, 22.

it – is that Lewis was either lying or mistaken about the precise workings of
his philosophical journey, for the Oxford don was convinced that heavenly
desire played an important part in his own conversion.

Kreeft and Meynell reply to these charges in more or less the same way.
They both assume that Platonism (at least) can be made compatible with
Christianity: Kreeft, for instance, says, "Plato is eminently convertible,
Christianizeable;"[134] and Meynell insists, "The conviction that Platonism is in
many respects closely allied to Christianity, for all its opposition to the tenets
of classical Protestantism, has so much prevailed, among the enemies as well
as the friends of Christianity, that it cannot easily be dismissed."[135] However,
more importantly, both men believe that there is evidence in scripture to
support the idea of an unfallen heavenly desire: Kreeft quotes approvingly
from Ecclesiastes 3:11 ("You have made everything fitting for its time, but
you have also put eternity into man's heart"),[136] and Meynell argues, "If the
idea of God as the ultimate satisfaction of human longing were alleged all the
same to be unscriptural, one might allude to several references in the Psalms
to God's beauty or desirableness; or for that matter to St. Paul's remark that
'our troubles are light and short-lived; and their outcome an eternal glory
which outweighs them far.'"[137]

While I agree with Kreeft and Meynell that heavenly desire is compatible
with the fallen nature of man, I think they should have tried to explain *why*
Lewis thought heavenly desire is compatible with a belief in man's fallen
state. They should have pointed out that Lewis understood heavenly desire
(at least *qua* Platonic *eros* and Joy) to be something like the *rational desire* in
the will,[138] whose task is similar to Aquinas's will *qua* "intellectual appetite"
in that it is *necessarily* inclined toward the Good and Happiness as a *general*
end;[139] indeed, Kreeft and Meynell should have explained that Lewis thought
that while reason and the will *qua* heavenly desire are *incomplete*,[140] the non-

---

134 Kreeft, "C. S. Lewis' Argument from Desire," 214.
135 Meynell, "An Attack on C. S. Lewis," 314.
136 Kreeft, "C. S. Lewis' Argument from Desire," 213.
137 Meynell, "An Attack on C. S. Lewis," 314.
138 Lewis, *The Collected Letters of C. S. Lewis: Volume III*, 628 [July 4, 1955].
139 Thomas Aquinas *Summa Theologica* 1-11 q. 3, a. 4.
140 "As regards the Fall, I submit that the general tenor of scripture does not encourage
   us to believe that our knowledge of the Law has been depraved in the same degree
   as our power to fulfill it. . . . In that very chapter (Romans 7) where [Paul] asserts
   most strongly our inability to keep the moral law he also asserts most confidently that
   we perceive the Law's goodness and rejoice in it according to the inward man. . . .
   A theology which goes about to represent our practical reason as radically unsound
   is heading for disaster." C. S. Lewis, "The Poison of Subjectivism," in *C. S. Lewis:*

rational desires (i.e. those mentioned by Paul) and the will *qua* the inclination to a particular way of accomplishing the general end are *fallen*.

Nevertheless, while I do not want to go into this in more detail here (since I discuss most of this in greater detail later), it is important to concede to Lewis's critics that the Oxford don did not always speak clearly about these matters.[141] Furthermore, it should be noted that Lewis was not, as some might fear, a triumphant Pelagian, for he was aware of both the seriousness of sin and the corruption of our particular inclinations toward goodness. On top of this, the Oxford don did not neglect God's role in man coming to the point of confession, for he believed that God is constantly active in the world and aids man's heavenly desire and reason in many ways.

In conclusion, we have seen throughout that Lewis used many different concepts in regard to the affect which I have simply called "heavenly desire." Each of these concepts – Platonic *eros*, "Romanticism," the *numinous*, *Sehnsucht*, "Joy" and hope – have unique characteristics and foci, yet they also share a sense of loss, lack or alienation, which in turn causes the individual to feel desire or fascination for the Great Thing – Beauty, Happiness, the Good, Home, the Mysterious Other, God, etc. – which can ultimately satisfy him. Consequently, with the nature and importance of this concept (suitably) clear, I can now turn to investigate arguably the most important object of heavenly desire: the Mysterious Other or God *qua* Myth, for without Myth, Lewis's philosophical journey would have taken him to theism, but no further.

Essay Collection & Other Short Pieces, ed. Lesley Walmsley (1943 essay reprint; London: HarperCollins, 2000), 663.
141 Lewis, *Surprised by Joy*, 1374.

Chapter Four

Myth

So far, we have seen that Lewis understood philosophy to be a way of life. This means that he chose to follow reason and subsequently conformed his entire life, through training and other activities, to Truth. However, while reason was primary for Lewis throughout his philosophical journey, he believed that it needed motivation, and this, as we discussed in the previous chapter, was heavenly desire. Yet as we saw, heavenly desire has many objects, some of which do not specifically point to Christianity; thus, in order to explain how Lewis's philosophical journey culminated in Christianity, we now need to investigate one particular object of heavenly desire – Myth or God *qua* the Mysterious Other – for Myth is the key to understanding Lewis's most profound beliefs.

However, in order to discuss Myth properly, five important points need to be made at the outset.

First, we must distinguish Myth from myth. On the one hand, Myth with a capital "M" is part of Reality itself; it is a true aspect of God's concrete nature which, while rationally understood by God Himself (i.e. it is "supra-rational"[1]), is "opaque to the [human] intellect,"[2] meaning that natural reason could never come to it by its own power; thus, for instance, God *qua* the dying-and-rising-god is Myth. On the other hand, myth with a lowercase

---

1 C. S. Lewis, "Priestesses in the Church?" in *C. S. Lewis: Essay Collection & Other Short Pieces*, ed. Lesley Walmsley (1948 essay reprint; London: HarperCollins, 2000), 401.

2 C. S. Lewis, *Prayer: Letters to Malcolm*, in *C. S. Lewis: Selected Books* [Short Edition] (1964 reprint; London: HarperCollins, 2002), 289. Because of the opaqueness of Myth, Mark Freshwater has compared the experience of Myth to that which a Zen Buddhist experiences when he creates a *koan* or paradoxical puzzle. Mark Freshwater, *C. S. Lewis and the Truth of Myth* (Lanham, MD: University Press of America, 1988), 39. If this connection is taken loosely it is okay; however, strictly speaking, the Buddhist's *koan* is supposed to point to the ultimate *unintelligibility* of reality, whereas Lewis's myth is supposed to point to the supra-rationality of Ultimate Reality. Huston Smith, *The Religions of Man* (New York: Harper & Row, 1989), 198.

"m" flows from Myth as an imperfect copy does from the perfect original; hence, a myth is a particular story or a series of stories (mythology) which prophets and poets capture in their imaginations and embody in literature and revelatory works. Both the first few chapters of Genesis and *The Epic of Gilgamesh* are myths in that they are both imperfect works which come from, and point to, some larger Myth; however, the difference between the mythical elements[3] in scripture and the mythical elements in other stories is that scripture is a more accurate representation of the Myth being communicated since God Himself works in a more intimate way with the prophet than with the pagan poet. Nevertheless, the supra-rational, mythical elements in all religions and religious writings are what cause the Priest in *Till We Have Faces* to say truly, "Holy places are dark places."[4]

Second, Myths should neither be confused with Jungian, Neokantian structuralist archetypes that exist solely in the mind,[5] nor should they be identified with Platonic Forms. While the former claim probably requires little explanation (i.e. Myths exist essentially in God, not man), the latter claim is more complicated; indeed, it is so much so that I have yet to see any Lewis scholar make this distinction, no doubt because very few appreciate the degree to which the Oxford don was influenced by absolute idealism, in particular, the concept, or at least the language, of concrete universality.[6] Now in order to distinguish Platonic Forms from Myths, we need to understand what they both are. On the one hand, Platonic Forms can only be understood by people as universals abstracted from particular exemplifications of that universal; for instance, the Platonic Form "Horseness" is an idea in the mind of God, out of which God creates concrete particular horses, from which people abstract the universal "horse," which corresponds to the Platonic Form "Horseness" in the mind of God. On the other hand, Myths can only be understood by people as particulars that express universality

---

3   Not everything in scripture is mythical. Indeed, the majority of the Bible is non-mythical.

4   Lewis, *Till We Have Faces*, 875.

5   C. G. Jung, "The Role of the Unconscious [1918]," in *Civilization in Transition*, vol. 4, *The Collected Works of C. G. Jung*, 2nd ed., ed. H. Read et al., 3-28 (Princeton, NJ: Princeton University Press, 1970), 10.

6   Dabney Hart is a typical (misguided) Lewis scholar in this regard: "Lewis's concept of the mythic form or *Idea* was Platonic, with emphasis on the universality of the form or *Logos*." Dabney Hart, *Through the Open Door: A New Look at C. S. Lewis* (N.p.: The University of Alabama Press, 1986), 18. Cf. "This Platonic view of myth being equal to Reality or Truth is worked out further in a Socratic exchange on appearance and reality between Ransom and the Oyarsa of Mars." Marius Buning, "*Perelandra* in the Light of Modern Allegorical Theory," in *Word and Story in C. S. Lewis*, ed. Peter Schakel and Charles Huttar, 277-98 (Columbia, MO: University of Missouri Press, 1991), 288.

without abstraction; for instance, Myth is a mysterious aspect of God's wider nature and not merely an idea, like the Platonic Forms, in the mind of God; subsequently, God *qua* Myth unveils Himself to the prophet and the poet, in whose imaginations Myth is processed as a myth or a concrete universal, which has the quality of all universals yet in order for it to remain myth and not merely a universal, it must remain incarnate in a complex particular form (e.g. a story, a painting, etc.); thus, myths and concrete universals are reflections of the concrete, "heavier-than-matter" Reality of God's fuller self. Now this may sound odd and Myth *qua* "God's fuller self" and "wider nature" may appear to be no different than Platonic Forms which *are* God (Who *is* the ultimate Mind and Spirit); nevertheless, I believe the distinction between Myth and Platonic Forms should be seen as an attempt to express – using the language of idealism – an important metaphysical insight into unbounded, mysterious, infinite nature of God, which is best expressed in the mysterious concrete universal Myth, Christ.

Third, Myth has no direct connection to mysticism. Myth is a mysterious, supra-rational aspect of God, whereas mysticism has to do with individuals who have immediate experiences of the Divine. While a mystic could have an experience of the Divine *qua* Myth (e.g. Moses was mystically inspired with the story of the creation of the world), this is not necessary (e.g. Julian of Norwich's mystical revelations are more words of encouragement than visions of Myth). Thus, while the mythical refers to the mysterious content in the imagination, the mystical refers to the mysterious way certain content – mythical or otherwise – enters the imagination.

Fourth, while Myth is a proper object of heavenly desire *qua* Romanticism, the *numinous*, *Sehnsucht* and Joy, it is not, strictly speaking, the proper object of heavenly desire *qua* Platonic *eros* since Romanticism, the *numinous*, *Sehnsucht* and Joy all have an element of desire for the Mysterious, whereas Platonic *eros* desires Beauty. Thus, while in many cases we are justified in speaking of heavenly desire in a general sense, in this chapter, I will use it in a sense that purposely excludes Platonic *eros* unless I say otherwise. Some may object and point out that Plato himself loved myth, but, as I will discuss herein, the Platonic and Neoplatonic interest in myth is either in creating new myths to explain some philosophical theory (Plato) or in allegorizing pagan myths to reveal rational truths behind the myth (Neoplatonists) instead of seeing myth as pointing to some larger, irreducible Myth (Lewis).

Fifth, since Myth is only one of the objects of heavenly desire, it is crucial that the boundaries of investigation in this chapter be set as firmly as possible in order to distinguish Myth as much as possible from things like Beauty, which are properly investigated in other chapters. Thus, while it is impossible to discuss Myth without reference to the imagination and psychology (chapter seven), divine attributes and metaphysics (chapter six) and aesthetics (chapter ten), my intention is to focus on Myth and not these other factors. Nevertheless, because Lewis's philosophical journey shows that he needed myths in order to understand Myth – just as Plato needed beautiful objects to follow in pursuit of Beauty itself – a large portion of this chapter will deal with literary matters. But this, it must be emphasized is accidental, for myths, romances and fairy tales are *not* ends in themselves, but are merely indicators of the larger Reality. Thus, this chapter is not intended as literary analysis so much as a chronological, philosophical investigation into Lewis's understanding of Myth, which in turn should illuminate the Oxford don's philosophical journey and ultimately his philosophical identity.

I: Myth during the Lucretian Materialist Phase

As I mentioned in the previous chapter, Lewis first experienced heavenly desire when he, a Christian boy of about ten years, saw a toy garden his brother had made. Importantly, that garden filled the young Lewis with a deep sense of the *mythical*, for he said that the garden carried with it the idea of Paradise, one of the most basic mythical concepts: "As long as I live my imagination of Paradise will retain something of my brother's toy garden."[7]

Shortly after this, Lewis's love of myth *qua* the ancient and mysterious began to deepen as he "developed a great taste for all the fiction [he] could get about the ancient world."[8] However, at the same time, he also began attending Cherbourg School, where his childhood Christian faith was badly damaged not only by Lucretius (as I mentioned in chapter two), but also by the school matron, who opened Lewis's eyes to the fact that people really believe in myths and religions other than Christianity:

> Now it so happened that Miss C., who seemed old to me, was still in her spiritual immaturity, still hunting, with the eagerness of a soul that had a touch of angelic quality in it, for a truth and a way of life. . . . She was (as I should now put it) floundering in the mazes of Theosophy, Rosicrucianism, Spiritualism; the whole Anglo-American Occultist tradition. Nothing was further from her intention to destroy my faith; she could not tell that the room into which she brought this candle was full of gunpowder. I had never heard of such things before; never, except in a nightmare or a fairy tale, conceived of spirits other than God and men. I had loved to read of strange sights and other

7   Lewis, *Surprised by Joy*, 1247.
8   Ibid., 1263.

worlds and unknown modes of being, but never with the slightest belief.[9]

Probably about one year after this, in 1911, Lewis first read Norse mythology and was profoundly moved by Henry Longfellow's translation of Isaias Tenger's *Drapa*, which began "I heard a voice that cried, / Balder the beautiful / Is dead, is dead":

> We are taught in the Prayer Book to 'give thanks to God for His great glory,' as if we owed Him more thanks for being what He necessarily is than for any particular benefit He confers upon us; and so indeed we do and to know God is to know this. But I had been far from any such experience; I came far nearer to feeling this about the Norse gods whom I disbelieved in than I had ever done about the true God while I believed.[10]

More than any other mythology that of the Vikings moved Lewis, not to mention his oldest friend, Arthur Greeves, toward Myth: "I passed on from Wagner to everything else I could get hold of about Norse mythology, *Myths of the Norsemen*, *Myths and Legends of the Teutonic Race*, Mallet's *Northern Antiquities*. I became knowledgeable. From these books again and again I received the stab of Joy."[11]

Indeed, Norse mythology was such an important influence on the young Lewis that in 1912, he began to write his first poem, entitled *Loki Bound*, which combined Norse content with the structure, and some of the themes, of Greek drama. Although Lewis did not say it himself, *Loki Bound* derived its name from two sources: (1) Loki, the clever but evil giant of Norse mythology who always plots against the gods; and (2) *Prometheus Bound*, Aeschylus's poem that depicts the usurping tyrant-god Zeus punishing Prometheus, the god who became the hero of men because he gave them intelligence and fire.[12] Lewis's interest in Loki and Prometheus is very significant but in contrary ways. On the one hand, this interest was positive since it shows that Lewis was deeply infatuated with myth, which, if correctly understood, would eventually lead to Myth and thence, Christianity. On the other hand, this interest was negative since Lewis's emotional attachment to Loki and Prometheus, coupled with his budding Lucretian materialism, caused him

---

9   Ibid., 1279-80.
10 Ibid., 1288. Years later, Lewis would speak of the Absolute in these terms and then finally the Christian God. Cf. "Appreciative love says: 'We give thanks to thee for thy great glory.'" Lewis, *The Four Loves*, 15. Cf. Lewis, *Prayer: Letters to Malcolm*, 279.
11 Lewis, *Surprised by Joy*, 1289.
12 Aeschylus *Prometheus Bound* 444-500.

to ignore the teaching of true philosophy (e.g. his Christian upbringing and, perhaps, Plato's dialogues); in fact, the future don's identification with Loki and Prometheus,[13] especially when he started school, hardened him into a proud and arrogant outsider who romantically imagined himself to be superior to his vulgar, athletic schoolmates, the "Bloods."[14]

And during this time, two more important events occurred.

The first event was the *confirmation* of Lewis's rejection of Christianity (which had been largely instigated by Lucretius and Lewis's school matron). This oddly came about vis-à-vis Lewis's teachers' rejection of *pagan* mythology. That is, when Lewis began reading classics in school, he, perhaps remembering his school matron, found it difficult to understand why his teachers had no trouble dismissing pagan mythology as ridiculous, while at the same time finding Christian mythology perfectly believable:

> Here, especially in Virgil, one was presented with a mass of religious ideas; and all teachers and editors took it for granted from the outset that these religious ideas were sheer illusion. No one ever attempted to show in what sense Christianity fulfilled Paganism or Paganism prefigured Christianity. The accepted position seemed to be that religions were normally a mere farrago of nonsense, though our own [Christianity], by a fortunate exception, was exactly true. The other religions were not even explained, in the earlier Christian fashion, as the work of the devils. That I might, conceivably, have been brought to believe. But the impression I got was that religion in general, though utterly false, was a natural growth, a kind of endemic nonsense into which humanity tended to blunder. In the midst of a thousand such religions stood our own, the thousand and first, labelled True. But on what grounds could I believe in this exception? It obviously was in some general sense the same kind of thing as all the rest. Why was it so differently treated? Need I, at any rate, continue to treat it differently?[15]

The second event, which occurred in 1914, was Lewis the materialist's dangerous attraction to the mythical poems of William Butler Yeats, who, Lewis told his friend Greeves, "[is] an author exactly after my own heart. . . . He writes plays and poems of rare spirit and beauty about our old Irish mythology."[16] That is, despite writing beautiful mythical poetry, Yeats,

---

13   "Loki was a projection of myself." Lewis, *Surprised by Joy*, 1310.
14   Ibid., 1292.
15   Ibid., 1279-80.
16   Lewis, *The Collected Letters of C. S. Lewis: Volume I*, 58 [June 5, 1914]. "Among all the poets whom I was reading at this time . . . there was one who stood apart from the rest.

whom many years later Lewis met and discovered was a real magician,[17] was another factor that, while not allying itself with Lewis's philosophical materialism, further propelled Lewis's love of myth *away from* Myth and down toward the perverse mythology and magic of his school matron. And this is crucial to keep in mind since Lewis's philosophical journey was not simply an unemotional journey away from false propositions to true ones, but was also a journey from the attractions of the occult to the mysteries of Christianity.

A few years after these events, Lewis began to study under the skeptic Kirkpatrick. At that time, he was exposed to James Frazer's anthropological masterpiece, *The Golden Bough*, which was a favourite of Kirkpatrick, and which systematically put all mythologies, including Christianity, on a level playing field.[18] The result of Kirkpatrick's teaching was an increased bifurcation of Lewis's personality. On the one hand, he was a Lucretian materialist who thought that all mythologies were equally false and no gods were worthy of worship. On the other hand, he was a passionate romantic who not only loved to read myths (e.g. Edmund Spenser's *Faerie Queene*, William Morris's *Well at the World's End* and Apuleius's *The Golden Ass*), but also loved to write them (e.g. *The Quest of Bleheris* and *Dymer*[19]). Now as one can imagine, this bifurcation of Lewis's personality had a few negative results.

To begin with, Lewis became emotionally addicted to mythology since he thought that by reading of lot of mythology, he would be able to recover

---

Yeats was this poet." Lewis, *Surprised by Joy*, 1344.

17   Lewis met Yeats in 1921. Lewis, *The Collected Letters of C. S. Lewis: Volume I*, 525 [March 14, 1921]. In *Dymer*, published five years later, Lewis based his Magician on the Irish poet.

18   Lewis, *Surprised by Joy*, 1324. Colin Duriez is certainly right that *The Golden Bough* did a lot of damage to Christianity simply by failing to ask whether any one myth mentioned in its thirteen volumes is *truer* than any other. Colin Duriez, "C. S. Lewis's Theology of Fantasy," in *Behind the Veil of Familiarity: C. S. Lewis (1898-1998)*, ed. Margarita Carretero González and Encarnación Hidalgo Tenorio, 301-26 (Bern: Peter Lang, 2001), 317. Nevertheless, it seems to me that Frazer's book was designed more as an anthropological encyclopaedia than as a critical work, and hence it probably does not deserve the scorn that many Christians have directed at it. Indeed, I would recommend Christians, and particularly Lewis scholars, read chapters 1, 2, 7, 12, 13, 24, 26, 33, 38, 42, 47, 50, 58 and 61.

19   *The Quest of Bleheris* is an unfinished romance and it is in my opinion the best thing that Lewis wrote before he became a Christian (indeed, Lewis the Lucretian materialist's use of Christian imagery in this novel is remarkably good and surprisingly free of priggery). *Dymer* is a finished poem that was published ten years later, in 1926. Lewis, *The Collected Letters of C. S. Lewis: Volume I*, 216 [July 18, 1916].

the "thrill" that he once felt when he saw his brother's garden and read Norse mythology; in retrospect and in form true to the language of philosophy as a way of life, Lewis spoke of this attempt as "a perverse *askēsis*," for he recognized that he had been training himself to attain heavenly desire itself (the mean), and not Myth (the end).[20]

Furthermore, Lewis likely felt a bit like a temple-desecrater or blasphemer since he used his "glib and shallow 'rationalism'" to break any connection between myth and Truth:

> All religions, that is, all mythologies to give them their proper name are merely man's own invention – Christ as much as Loki. Primitive man found himself surrounded by all sorts of terrible things he didn't understand – thunder, pestilence, snakes etc: what more natural than to suppose that these were animated evil spirits trying to torture him. These he kept off by cringing to them, singing songs and making sacrifices etc. Gradually from being mere nature-spirits these supposed being[s] were elevated into more elaborate ideas, such as the old gods: and when man became more refined he pretended that these spirits were good as well as powerful. . . . Thus religion, that is to say, mythology, grew up . . . and so Christianity came into being – one mythology among many, but the one that we happen to have been brought up in.[21]

Nevertheless, in the middle of all this corruption (the occult) and / or destruction (Lucretian materialism) of myth, one myth, brightly reflective of true Myth, made an impression on Lewis: George MacDonald's *Phantastes*. This romance was another of the top ten books Lewis listed as influencing his philosophy of life and it was the one myth which, according to him, had the taste of "Holiness."[22] As Lewis wrote:

> I had already been waist-deep in Romanticism; and likely enough, at any moment, to flounder into its darker and more evil forms, slithering down the steep descent that leads from the love of strangeness to that of eccentricity and thence to that of perversity. Now *Phantastes* was romantic enough in all conscience; but there was a difference. . . . I was only aware that if this new world was strange, it was also homely and humble. . . . What it actually did to me was to convert, even to baptize . . . my imagination. It did nothing to my intellect nor (at that time) to my conscience. Their turn came far later and with the help of many other books and men.[23]

20 Lewis, *Surprised by Joy*, 1341.
21 Lewis, *The Collected Letters of C. S. Lewis: Volume I*, 230-1 [October 12, 1916].
22 Lewis, *Surprised by Joy*, 1347.
23 C. S. Lewis, preface to *George MacDonald: An Anthology*, by George MacDonald, ed.

Moreover, one of the ways by which *Phantastes* "baptized" Lewis's imagination was through its mythical and holy tone, which, Lewis said, "sounded like the voice of my mother or . . . nurse."[24] And this statement is important for us to keep in mind, for years later, the Christian Lewis insisted that one of the key means by which the mythical enters the imagination is through the instruction of honest, simple people like nurses, mothers and "old wives;" indeed, Narnia and Drum bear witness to this.[25]

II: Myth during the Pseudo-Manichean Dualist Phase

While *Phantastes* may have baptized Lewis's imagination, it was the baptism of a parent forcing a child to submerge rather than an adult choosing to do it himself. In other words, like Lewis's early readings in Plato, Aristotle and Boethius, *Phantastes* was a seed planted in Lewis's mind that took years to develop. Thus, we must remember that when Lewis finally left Kirkpatrick's to go to Oxford and then to fight in WWI, he went as one torn between myth (and the occult), on the one hand, and Lucretian materialism, on the other.

Now during the war, the future don read little in the way of myth, preferring, as we recall from chapter two, to read books on philosophy instead. However, while one might think that this increased attention on

---

C. S. Lewis (1947 reprint; New York: Simon & Schuster, 1996), xxxiii. Cf. Lewis, *Surprised by Joy*, 1348.

24 Lewis, *Surprised by Joy*, 1347.

25 The nurse in *Prince Caspian* is the person who Caspian loved best and who told him many wonderful stories about Old Narnia. C. S. Lewis, *Prince Caspian: The Return to Narnia* (1951 reprint; London: Fontana, 1984), 42-4. And the Archbishop tells the Queen of Drum, "Hence, if you ask me of the way / Yonder, what can I do but say / Over again (as God's own Son / Seems principally to have done) / The lessons of your nurse and mother?" C. S. Lewis, *The Queen of Drum*, in *Narrative Poems*, by C. S. Lewis, ed. Walter Hooper (London: HarperCollins, 1994), 151 [3.1.174-8]. Cf. Lewis, *The Pilgrim's Regress*, 87. Cf. C. S. Lewis, "On Ethics," in *C. S. Lewis: Essay Collection & Other Short Pieces*, ed. Lesley Walmsley (1998 essay reprint; London: HarperCollins, 2000), 307. Moreover, along with the figure of the nurse is the "old wife," whose tales are usually dismissed as superstitious nonsense, but are in fact usually very close to the truth of the matter. For instance, concerning John Bunyan, Lewis wrote: "My own guess is that the scheme of a journey with adventures suddenly reunited two things in Bunyan's mind which had hitherto lain far apart. One was his present and lifelong preoccupation with the spiritual life. The other, further way and longer ago, left behind (he had supposed) in childhood, was his delight in old wives' tales and such last remnants of chivalric romance as he had found in chap-books. The one fit the other like a glove. Now, as never before, the whole man was engaged." C. S. Lewis, "The Vision of John Bunyan," in *Selected Literary Essays*, by C. S. Lewis, ed. Walter Hooper (1962 essay reprint; Cambridge: Cambridge University Press, 1969), 147. Cf. Lewis, *The Magician's Nephew*, 25.

philosophy would have finally swayed Lewis's divided mind in favour of materialist philosophy (against myth), this was not at all the case as is evident in his 1919 poem "The Philosopher," which reveals the desire for a philosophy that can be reconciled to myth.[26] Indeed, we should probably see Lewis's love of myth as allied with his new interest in non-materialist philosophies in a struggle against his former materialism, the ultimate result of which was the formation of Lewis's new philosophy, pseudo-Manichean dualism. As evidence for the importance of myth in Lewis's pseudo-Manichean dualism, consider the following.

First, I believe that Lewis's association of Satan with (material) Nature and Beauty with Spirit came not only from the anti-materialist philosophies he was reading (e.g. Plato and Berkeley) and his own wartime experience of seeing the carnage of physical Nature, but also from Norse mythology. My reason for thinking this is that in the Norse myths, the *world* (i.e. Nature) was created from the flesh of the *evil* frost giant Ymir[27] (i.e. Satan), against whose children the heroic gods' struggled (i.e. the beautiful Spirit struggled). In this way, the theomachy of Norse mythology would have provided Lewis with a concept of cosmic warfare complementary to that of Manicheanism and his own real-life experience of warfare.

Second, Satan is a mythical figure on his own right and his existence in Lewis's philosophy is a clear meshing of the mythical and the philosophical.

Third, Lewis's mention of "Beauty" is significant. Although I mentioned at the beginning of this chapter that Myth is not to be confused with Beauty, it would be wrong to say that there is no overlap between them, for while the desire for Beauty (Platonic *eros*) and the desire for Myth (the *numinous*, *Sehnsucht*, etc.) are different, they are still both *desires*, and all desires are for things that are attractive in *some* way (indeed, one could say that the fascination for the Terrible that comes from one aspect of the *numinous* is an attraction to the Terrible). Thus, I believe that when Lewis pitted Satan and Nature against Beauty and Spirit, he was using these pairs (in addition to other things) as metaphors for his own inner struggle between his Lucreatian materialism (bad) and his love of myth (good).[28]

26   Don King, *C. S. Lewis, Poet: The Legacy of His Poetic Impulse* (Kent, OH: Kent State University Press, 2001), 88-9.

27   Snorri Sturluson *Glyfaginning* 1.5-8.

28   Of course, given the brutal conditions of WWI, the opposition between Satan / Nature and Beauty / Spirit *might* also have been a metaphor for Germany vs. Britain. However, I seriously doubt this since Lewis was rarely political and never saw himself as anti-German *qua* the men or culture. Thus, I see Lewis's pseudo-Manichean dualism as a philosophy grounded in rational inquiry (mostly concerning the war between

III: Myth during the Stoical Materialist Phase

Nevertheless, when Lewis returned to Oxford, his materialism struck back against his dualism and love of myth, causing him to make the radical separation between reason and imagination which was fundamental to the Stoical materialism of his "New Look." While Lewis himself gave us four reasons why he assumed his New Look and demoted the mythical, I would add a fifth.

First, Lewis met "an old, dirty, gabbling, tragic, Irish parson who had long since lost his faith but retained his living."[29] This parson, upon whom Lewis later modelled the character Straik in *That Hideous Strength*, was interested in neither the Beatific Vision nor any other mythical or beautiful notion associated with religion or the spiritual; nevertheless, he was still obsessed with finding "assurance that something he would call 'himself' would, on almost any terms, last longer than his bodily life."[30] As a result of this experience, Lewis said "the whole question of immortality," including any mythical hope that such is possible, "became rather disgusting to me."[31]

Second, on top of the mad parson, Lewis had firsthand experience of a doctor friend going mad as a result, or so Lewis believed at the time, of flirting with occult sciences. Subsequently, when the tormented doctor died, Lewis took this to be a warning that no good can come from taking the mythical too seriously.[32]

Third, Bergson gave Lewis the reassuring sense of the necessity of existence over and against both "the old haunting idea, Schopenhauer's idea, that the world 'might not have existed'"[33] and the frightening vagueness of the mythical. And this I find very interesting because combined with both Lewis's disgust with the Irish parson and the horror he felt during the doctor's madness, it shows that on the one hand, Lewis was becoming more consistent philosophically – i.e. his materialism was properly demoting myth – but on the other hand, it shows that Lewis's *motivations* for doing so were not fully consistent with philosophy as a way of life, for at times it does not seem as though reason was directing Lewis to reject myth, so much as uncontrolled emotion. This is important to note since when we actually arrive at Lewis's conversion to Christianity, we see him converting *despite* his emotions;

---

materialism and myth) and bolstered by mythical, and then to a lesser extent, real-war, imagery.

29 Lewis, *Surprised by Joy*, 1360.
30 Ibid.
31 Ibid.
32 Ibid., 1361.
33 Ibid., 1362.

indeed, converting simply because he thought the mythical elements (not to mention the other elements) of Christianity true.

Fourth, Lewis was deeply interested in the "new Psychology" of Sigmund Freud and Carl Jung at the time,[34] having read or skimmed six books on psychology in less than six weeks at one point: Freud's *Introductory Lectures* (June 3, 1922), James's *Varieties of Religious Experience* (June 11, 1922), H. Crichten Miller's *The New Psychology and the Teacher* (July 3, 1922), Jung's *Analytical Psychology* (July 4, 1922), W. H. R. River's *Instinct and the Subconscious* (July 5, 1922) and R. H. Hingley's *Psychoanalysis* (July 16, 1922). Lewis's interest in modern psychology is important, for once he became convinced that any serious belief in magic and the occult was a danger to his well-being (remember, Lewis had also just met Yeats, the mythmaker and magician, at this time), he needed a way to explain myth and its corresponding desire, heavenly desire. Accordingly, heavenly desire was identified as (simply) a valuable "aesthetic experience,"[35] and any talk of taking myth seriously, resulted in myths being labelled "Christiana Dreams"[36] or the product of "wishful thinking": "No more Avalon, no more Hesperides. I had (this was very precisely the opposite of the truth) 'seen through' them. And I was never going to be taken in again."[37]

Fifth, as we can see from Lewis's account of how his New Look took shape, his disgust, fear and in some measure, reason, forced a separation between the future don's materialist philosophy, on the one hand, and his love of myth, on the other. However, what Lewis did not mention is that during this time, he also found strong arguments from aesthetic philosophers as to why myth should simply be seen as art and not as art pointing to Myth, for instance. Thus, from Benedetto Croce, Lewis learned that art, which includes myth

---

34   Ibid., 1360-2. Annotations in Lewis's edition of Aristotle's *Ethica Nicomachea* indicate that he was familiar with Freud already as far back as 1917. C. S. Lewis, marginalia in his edition of *Ethica Nicomachea*, by Aristotelis, ed. I. Bywater (Oxonii: E Typographeo Calredoniano, n.d.; The Rare Book Collection, The University of North Carolina at Chapel Hill), back of the book.

35   Lewis, *Surprised by Joy*, 1362.

36   This is the name which Lewis and others referred to concerning their romantic wishfulness and it is an epithet associated with Samuel Butler's character Christiana Pontifex in *The Way of All Flesh*. Lewis, preface to the 1950 edition of *Dymer*, 4.

37   Lewis, *Surprised by Joy*, 1362. Phrases like "seen through" and "be taken in" are very common in Lewis's corpus and are reflective of his attitude during his "New Look." These phrases are used by both the prisoners of Sigismund Enlightenment in *The Pilgrim's Regress* and the dwarfs in *The Last Battle*. For instance, "'It is one more wish-fulfilment dream it is one more wish-fulfilment dream. Don't be taken in again.'" Lewis, *The Pilgrim's Regress*, 73. And, "'We haven't let anyone take us in. The Dwarfs are for the Dwarfs.'" Lewis, *The Last Battle*, 141.

or "the purely fantastic,"[38] is a "lyrical intuition" that can never be assessed by the intellect,[39] meaning, of course, that no myth can be truer than any other myth; from George Santayana, Lewis discovered that "art is action which transcending the body makes the world a more congenial stimulus to the soul,"[40] and while this sounded nice to Lewis at the time, it said nothing about myth reflecting transcendental Reality and giving us knowledge of the Divine; and from E. F. Carritt, Lewis's philosophy supervisor and tutor, the future don was fed generous portions of both aforementioned philosophers, in particular, Croce, about whom Carritt, in his influential book *The Theory of Beauty*,[41] wrote: "I believe that a greater amount of truth is contained in Croce's *Estetica* than in any other philosophy of beauty that I have read."[42] The ultimate result of Lewis's Stoical materialism was a reduction of myth from a type of art that is supposed to act as a signpost pointing toward supra-rational knowledge of Myth to a type of art that is supposed to inspire people, through non-rational means, to become well-rounded individuals on humanistic terms.

IV: Myth during the Idealist Phases

Lewis's "New Look," we recall, was damaged and eventually destroyed by conversations the Oxford don had with Owen Barfield. These conversations, known as "The Great War," were chiefly about whether or not the imagination is a vehicle for Truth, which, for Lewis and Barfield, entailed the important

---

38 Benedetto Croce, *Philosophy of the Practical: Economic and Ethic*, trans. Douglas Ainslie (London: MacMillian and Co., 1913), 267 [1.2.6].

39 "Again, with the definition of art as intuition, we deny that it has the character of *conceptual knowledge*. Conceptual knowledge, in its true form, which is the philosophical, is always realistic, aiming at establishing reality against unreality, or at reducing unreality by including it in reality as a subordinate moment of reality itself. But intuition means, precisely, indistinction of reality and unreality, the image with its value as mere image, the pure ideality of the image; and opposing the intuitive or sensible knowledge to the conceptual or intelligible, the aesthetic to the noetic, it aims at claiming the autonomy of this more simple and elementary form of knowledge, which has been compared to the dream (the dream, and not the sleep) of the theoretic life, in respect to which philosophy would be the waking. . . . Artistic intuition, then, is always *lyrical* intuition." Benedetto Croce, *The Essence of Aesthetic*, trans. Douglas Ainslie (London: William Heinemann, 1921), 16-7, 32. Lewis, *All My Road Before Me*, 36 [May 17, 1922], 39 [May 23, 1922].

40 George Santayana, *Reason in Art*, vol. 4, *The Life of Reason* (1905 reprint; London: Dover, 1982), 15. Lewis, *All My Road Before Me*, 182 [January 19, 1923], 224 [March 26, 1923], 281 [January 6, 1924].

41 Carritt actually published two well-received books about the philosophy of art: *The Theory of Beauty* and *Philosophies of Beauty*.

42 E. F. Carritt, *The Theory of Beauty* (1914 reprint; London: Methuen & Co., 1949), 281.

question of whether or not the imagination gives us the ability to know mythical beings and spirits. Lewis, starting out as a Stoical materialist steeped in Aristotle, Freud and Croce, said "no" on both accounts, but Barfield, as an Anthroposophist and follower of romantic poet Coleridge, said "yes." Needless to say, the question of the imagination was central to Lewis's understanding of myth, and so The Great War was an extremely important phase in Lewis's intellectual life. However, because The Great War occurred over a long stretch of time (1923-1931), both thinkers, but especially Lewis, underwent many changes throughout.

The first important change for Lewis (if we pass over his valuable re-reading of Euripides's *Hippolytus*[43]) happened on March 8, 1924, when he read Samuel Alexander's *Space, Time and Deity*, another book which the Oxford don listed as one of his top ten philosophical influences.[44] *Space, Time and Deity*, or more specifically, the introduction to *Space, Time and Deity*, helped Lewis overcome some of the extreme reservations he had toward myth and heavenly desire as a result of his New Look.

In Alexander's book (though ultimately from G. E. Moore's essay "The Refutation of Idealism"[45]), Lewis read about the distinction between "Enjoyment" and "Contemplation" (or, as Lewis himself would call it later, "looking along" / *connaître* or "looking at" / *savoir*[46]), the former consisting

---

43   Lewis, *Surprised by Joy*, 1370-1.

44   Lewis, *All My Road Before Me*, 301 [March 8, 1924]. As I mentioned in chapter two, Lewis's chronology is not always perfect. For instance, in *Surprised by Joy*, he said that he had started working in the English department at Magdalen College in 1925, yet he mentioned this *after* his "New Look" was destroyed, for which he gave Alexander some credit. This cannot be completely accurate because Lewis's journal and letters indicate that Alexander had already made an impact on him when he first read him in 1924. I think the only way around this is to say, as we said before, that Lewis's letters and journal are a more accurate account of the *particulars* of his life than *Surprised by Joy*. Of course, we could also say that while Lewis's first reading of Alexander was extremely important, it simply took a year for it to sink in, and this would be perfectly consistent with the pattern of the books Lewis read and the philosophical phase that developed out of them; that is, it usually took about two years for the impact of a powerful book or books to stimulate Lewis's change.

45   Norbert Feinendegen, "Contemplating C. S. Lewis's Epistemology: Reflections on C. S. Lewis's Argument with Owen Barfield about the Distinction between Enjoyment and Contemplation during the 'Great War,'" *VII: An Anglo-American Literary Review* 24 (2007): 30.

46   "We must, on pain of idiocy, deny from the very outset the idea that looking *at* is, by its own nature, intrinsically truer or better than looking *along*. One must look both *along* and *at* everything. In particular cases we shall find reason for regarding the one or the other vision as inferior." C. S. Lewis, "Meditation in a Toolshed," in *C. S. Lewis: Essay Collection & Other Short Pieces*, ed. Lesley Walmsley (1945 essay reprint; London: HarperCollins, 2000), 609. Cf. "We can get no further than this in knowledge about

in "the act of mind," a singular event, and the latter consisting in "the object," a dual event;[47] for example, "When you see a table you 'enjoy' the act of seeing and 'contemplate' the table. Later, if you took up Optics and thought about Seeing itself, you would be contemplating seeing and enjoying the thought."[48] The value of Alexander's distinction lay in the fact that Lewis realized he could not Contemplate heavenly desire and Enjoy its object, myth, simultaneously: "You cannot hope and also think about hoping at the same time; for in hope we look to hope's object and we interrupt this by (so to speak) turning round to look at the hope itself."[49] As a result of this, Lewis stopped thinking about heavenly desire and how he could recapture the "thrill" that it presented,[50] understanding that it was not heavenly desire

---

(*savoir*) God: but we are vouchsafed some knowledge-by-acquaintance (*connaître*) of Him in our devotional and sacramental life." Lewis, *The Collected Letters of C. S. Lewis: Volume III*, 1173 [July 19, 1960].

47   Samuel Alexander, *Space, Time and Deity: The Gifford Lectures at Glasgow, 1916-1918*, vol. 1 (New York: Dover Publications, 1966), 12.

48   Lewis, *Surprised by Joy*, 1370.

49   Ibid. Already back in 1924, Lewis employed Alexander's distinction to help make sense of the philosophical problems he was dealing with: "There is this truth in Berkeley: that when I try to find what is in my mind when thinking of a universal I always get either a picture or the words of a definition. I know, however, that neither of these is what I am really thinking of. (Is it that there is something wrong about this kind of test? For to ask 'what is in my mind while I am thinking' usually means to stop the real thinking and then 'introspect': and then I naturally find only the irrelevant pictures or words which, as a matter of psychological fact, do accompany the thinking. Perhaps the thinking, being an act, cannot be introspected – only the παθήματα – [in the] same way will cannot be introspected. Does all introspection always leave out all the important things?)." C. S. Lewis, "The Moral Good – Its Place Among the Values" (Lecture Notes, The Marion E. Wade Center, Wheaton College), 31. It should be noted that although Wheaton College has labelled this document – or rather, these lecture notes – "The Moral Good – Its Place Among the Values" it should be labelled "The Good – Its Place Among the Values." There are two reasons for this. First, the lecture notes that Wheaton has labelled "The Moral Good" are dated "1924," but as Walter Hooper has indicated, the lectures that Lewis delivered in 1924 were "The Good" not "The Moral Good." Second, the content of the lectures at Wheaton are not primarily concerned with ethics; hence, it is unlikely that they would be called "The Moral Good." While it is fairly apparent, then, that Wheaton has mislabelled its set of lecture notes, I will follow Wheaton's labelling system even though it should be clear that when I cite "The Moral Good – Its Place Among the Values," I am talking about "The Good – Its Place Among the Values."

50   "For resorting to the same object again, in the hope of repeating the same experience, they learn by disappointment that no object has by its mere nature the infallible power of evoking spiritual experience." Lewis, *Clivi Hamiltonis Summae Metaphysices Contra Anthroposophos Libri II*, 55. Years later, in his Christian science-fiction novel *Out of the Silent Planet*, Lewis emphasized the danger of trying to repeat pleasures. C. S. Lewis, *Out of the Silent Planet*, in *The Cosmic Trilogy*, by C. S. Lewis (1938 reprint; London:

that was important, but the object toward which it was pointing – though, of course, Lewis did not yet understand this object to be God.

The second important change for Lewis during The Great War was that he became an idealist (the differences between subjective and absolute idealism are not important here). Lewis's conversion to idealism impacted his theory of myth in many ways, but two are worth mentioning in this immediate context.

First of all, Lewis began to see how his desire for myth – i.e. heavenly desire – could be seen as an aesthetic experience with a quasi-spiritual twist, for according to Bradley, all people are subjective fragments or Appearances who – note the word – have "transcendent *longings*" for unity with *Reality* or the Absolute.[51] Thus, Lewis wrote:

> I saw that Joy, as I now understood it, would fit in. We mortals, seen as the sciences see us and as we commonly see one another, are mere 'appearances.' But appearances of the Absolute. In so far as we really are at all (which isn't saying much) we have so to speak, a root in the Absolute, which is the utter reality. And that is why we experience Joy: we yearn, rightly, for that unity which we can never reach except by ceasing to be the separate phenomenal beings called 'we.' Joy was not a deception. Its visitations were rather the moments of clearest consciousness we had, when we became aware of our fragmentary and phantasmal nature and ached for that impossible reunion which would annihilate us or that self-contradictory waking which would reveal, not that we had had, but that we *were*, a dream. . . . This new dovetailing of my desire-life with my philosophy foreshadowed the day, now fast approaching, when I should be forced to take my 'philosophy' more seriously than I ever intended.[52]

Second of all, long after Lewis stopped being an absolute idealist, he still valued the emphasis idealism, and in particular, Bradley, put on the hidden glory of *Reality* behind all Appearances. Norse mythology had prepared Lewis for the sense of veiled, mythical glory, but it was Bradley who solidified this sense in him, for while Lewis had not believed in the Norse gods, he did believe in the Absolute.[53] And I pause long enough here to suggest the Bradleyan sense of Reality (minus the pantheism) was perhaps *one* element Lewis had in mind when he, as a Christian, later referred to Myth as "Reality": "What flows into you from the myth is not truth but

Pan Books, 1990), 63.
51   F. H. Bradley, *Ethical Studies*, 2nd ed. (Oxford: Oxford University Press, 1988), 85.
52   Lewis, *Surprised by Joy*, 1372.
53   Ibid., 1366.

reality (truth is always *about* something, but reality is that *about which* truth is), and, therefore every myth becomes the father of innumerable truths on the abstract level."[54]

The third important change for Lewis during The Great War was his actual dispute with Barfield concerning the imagination and subsequently the mythical and supernatural. Although the debate had been running for many years, it really began to heat up in 1926. At that time, Lewis the absolute idealist believed the following things about myth and the imagination: (1) in the tradition of Bradley,[55] he thought "reason is utterly inadequate to the richness and spirituality of real things: indeed this is itself a deliverance of reason"[56] – this, of course, potentially left room for a supra-rational Reality (which Myth would later help fill); (2) he, importantly, acknowledged that the imagination was capable of receiving super-intelligible symbols, but he rejected any *theory* about how these symbols could enter the imagination (e.g. Christian theories about the Holy Spirit inspiring prophets, demonology, etc.); (3) his definition of myth, though not yet as his Christian self would understand it, was becoming more and more refined: "A *myth* is a description or a story introducing supernatural personages or things, determined not, or not only, by motives arising from events within the story, but by the supposedly immutable relations of the personages or things; possessing unity: and not, save accidentally, connected with any given place or time;"[57] and (4) Lewis adamantly *denied* that the imagination was capable of both knowing Truth and communing with mythical beings or spirits (hence, the imagination *can* have moments of revelation or inspiration, but it cannot account for *how* it got this revelation, and the truth-value of any revelation must be judged by reason, not the imagination). Lewis summarized all of these points well in a letter to Harwood:

> Nor do I doubt the presence, even in us, of faculties embryonic or atrophied, that lie in an indefinite margin around the little finite bit of focus which is intelligence – faculties anticipating or remembering the possession of huge tracts of reality that slip through the meshes of the intellect. And, to be sure, I believe that the symbols presented by

54 Lewis, "Myth Became Fact," 141.
55 "Fully to realize the existence of the Absolute is for finite beings impossible." Bradley, *Appearance and Reality*, 159. Cf. "Agreed (by you and me, also by Kant, Coleridge, Bradley etc) that discursive reason always fails to apprehend reality, because it never grasps more than an abstract relational framework." Lewis, *The Collected Letters of C. S. Lewis: Volume III*, 1600 [1927, "The Great War Letters" Series I, Letter 1].
56 Lewis, *The Collected Letters of C. S. Lewis: Volume I*, 670 [October 28, 1926].
57 Lewis, *The Collected Letters of C. S. Lewis: Volume III*, 1619 [1927? "The Great War Letters" Series I, Letter 4]. Cf. Adey, *C. S. Lewis's 'Great War' with Owen Barfield*, 55.

imagination at its height are the workings of that fringe and present to us as much of the super-intelligible reality as we can get while we retain our present form of consciousness. *My skepticism begins when people offer me explicit accounts of the super-intelligible and in so doing use all the categories of the intellect.* If the higher worlds have to be represented in terms of number, subject-and-attribute, time, space, causation etc (and thus they nearly always are represented by occultists and illuminati), the fact that knowledge of them had to come through the fringe remains inexplicable. It is more natural to suppose in such cases that the illuminati have done what all of us are tempted to do: – allowed their intellect to fasten on those hints that come from the fringe, and squeezing them, has made a hint (that was full of truth) into a mere false hard statement. Seeking to know (in the only way we can know) more, we know less. *I, at any rate, am at present inclined to believe that we must be content to feel the highest truths 'in our bones': if we try to make them explicit, we really make them untruth.* At all events if more knowledge is to come, it must be the wordless & thoughtless knowledge of the mystic: not the celestial statistics of Swedenborg, the Lemurian history of Steiner, or the demonology of the Platonists. *All this seems to me merely an attempt to know the super-intelligible as if it were a new slice of the intelligible*: as though man with a bad cold tried to get back smells with a microscope. Unless I greatly misunderstand you, you are (in my way) more rationalist than I, for you would reject as mere ideology my 'truths felt in the bones.'[58]

Despite the certainty of Lewis's tone in this letter, three months after writing it, the Oxford don said he was in "an unholy muddle" about reason and the imagination and was becoming increasingly more concerned about the Anthroposophist's understanding of the imagination as a medium for communing with spirits and thereby gaining knowledge of Myth or "super-intelligible" reality. As a result, he took comfort in two things: (1) Wordsworth's *Prelude*, which was another book Lewis listed in his top ten philosophical influences, and which tended to focus on Nature and not Supernature,[59] hence giving Lewis the impression that reality was free of "bogies;"[60] and (2) Bergson's doctrine of the necessity of existence (again), which, note the anti-MacDonaldian language, helped Lewis get "all the '*nurse* and grandma from my soul.'"[61]

---

58   Lewis, *The Collected Letters of C. S. Lewis: Volume I*, 670-1 [October 28, 1926] (emphasis mine).

59   William Wordsworth, *The Prelude*, in *William Wordsworth: The Major Works* (Oxford: Oxford University Press, 2000), 565 [11.251-7].

60   Lewis, *The Collected Letters of C. S. Lewis: Volume I*, 440 [January 26, 1927].

61   Ibid. (emphasis mine).

But mere comfort was not enough for Lewis, who, we must always remind ourselves, really was trying, though not always with perfect success as we saw, to live his philosophy: "I suddenly found myself thinking 'What I won't give up is the doctrine that what we get in the imagination at its highest is real in some way, tho[ugh], at this stage one can't say how': and then my intellectual conscience smote me for having got to that last pitch of sentiment – asserting what 'I won't do' when I ought to be enquiring what I can know."[62] Consequently, Lewis "decided to work up the whole doctrine of Imagination in Coleridge,"[63] no doubt due to the recommendation of Barfield, whose theory of the imagination was part Anthroposophistic and part Coleridgean.[64]

Now Coleridge understood the imagination to be twofold, consisting of a primary and a secondary imagination: the primary imagination is "the living power and prime agent of all human perception, and as a repetition in the finite mind of the external act of creation in the infinite I AM," while the secondary imagination is a mere "echo" of the primary imagination and as such is "identical with the primary in the kind of its operation;" and both types of imagination are distinguished from fancy, which is "a mode of memory" that "has no other counter to play but fixities and definites."[65] Moreover, the imagination had such a prized place in Coleridge's psychology that the romantic poet even went so far as to declare that it transcends reason in dignity and importance.

While impressed by much of what Coleridge and Barfield said about the imagination, Lewis, as one raised on the classics and as was typical of one growing increasingly more attracted to Neoplatonic ways of thinking, was a strong advocate of Aristotle's *De Anima*;[66] indeed, Lewis was the one who

---

62 Lewis, *All My Road Before Me*, 432 [January 19, 1927].

63 Ibid.

64 Although Barfield did not know Kant very well or make as much use of him as Lewis did (see chapter eight), R. J. Reilly speaks of Barfield's "Steiner-Kant-Coleridge epistemology." R. J. Reilly, *Romantic Religion: A Study of Owen Barfield, C. S. Lewis, Charles Williams and J. R. R. Tolkien* (Great Barrington, MA: Lindisfarne Books, 2006), 46.

65 Samuel Taylor Coleridge, *Biographia Literaria; or, Biographical Sketches of My Literary Life and Opinions*, vol. 7, *The Collected Works of Samuel Taylor Coleridge*, ed. James Engell and W. Jackson Bate (Princeton: Princeton University Press, 1983), 304-5.

66 For the importance of Aristotle's *De Anima* on Neoplatonism see A. C. Lloyd, "The Later Neoplatonists," in *The Cambridge History of Later Greek and Early Medieval Philosophy*, ed. A. H. Armstrong, 272-322 (Cambridge: Cambridge University Press, 2005), 302. For the influence of *De Anima* on Lewis's thought consider the following: "I have also got the poetic and the other mind settled now. It all comes in Aristotle *De Anima* III v.2. There are two elements the *nous poietikos* ["the poetic mind"] and the

introduced Barfield to *De Anima*, a quotation from which was eventually placed at the front of Barfield's *Poetic Diction* (the book that in many ways was the key document in The Great War[67]). Thus, in principle, but not always in practice, Lewis tended to follow the Aristotelian or scholastic threefold division of imagination, which consists of (1) the sensitive imagination, which is common to both animals and men and whose function is merely to receive the *simple image* of a sensible thing when it is perceived (this is like Coleridge's "fancy"), (2) what Albert the Great called "the phantasy," which is also common to both animals and men and whose function is to connect or join simple images in the sensitive imagination to make more *complex images*, the result of which is the image of a thing with a determinate size and shape, and as belonging to a particular time (this is like Coleridge's "secondary imagination"),[68] and (3) the deliberative imagination or, in more Lewisian terms, "the poetic imagination,"[69] which is unique to rational creatures, and whose function is to work with the active intellect or "poetic" mind (the only faculty of the soul that actually *makes* anything[70]) in the creation of art and other things (this is like Coleridge's "primary imagination).[71] This latter type of imagination came to Lewis largely from Aristotle, yet because the Oxford don had also been influenced by the Romantics' exaltation of the imagination, not to mention Bergson's concept of *homo faber*,[72] the Oxford

---

nous pathetikos ["the pathetic mind"]. 'And one mind [the pathetic mind] corresponds in becoming everything; the other mind [the poetic mind] corresponds in making everything. The latter alone is immortal and ageless. But we do not remember because this is without emotion. The pathetic mind dies.'" Lewis, *The Collected Letters of C. S. Lewis: Volume III*, 1507-8 [February 2, 1927].

67 Adey, *C. S. Lewis's 'Great War' with Owen Barfield*, 13.

68 Albert the Great maintained that there are four grades of abstraction in the mind, the first being common sense, which allows us to be aware of our external sense, the second being the imagination, which retains the images of sensible things when they are no longer present, the third being phantasy, which is the sense power that allows us to play with things that in no way exist outside the mind, and the fourth being the (primary or active) intellect, which abstracts the universal from the particular phantasm. Albert the Great *De Anima* 2.3.1. Lewis actually touched on Albert the Great's psychology in *The Discarded Image*, the book based on his popular lectures introducing the medieval worldview: "The distinction between Phantasy and Imagination – (*vis*) *phantastica* and (*vis*) *imaginative* – is not so simple. Phantasy is the higher of the two; here Coleridge has once more turned the nomenclature upside down. . . . According to Albertus, Imagination merely retains what has been perceived, and Phantasy deals with this *componendo et dividendo*, separating and uniting." Lewis, *The Discarded Image*, 162-3.

69 Lewis, *The Collected Letters of C. S. Lewis: Volume III*, 1605 [1927, "The Great War Letters" Series I, Letter 2].

70 Aristotle *Metaphysics* 1049a1-35.

71 Aristotle *De Anima* 434a5.

72 "Man the toolmaker." Lewis, *The Collected Letters of C. S. Lewis: Volume III*, 683-4

don's language was often imprecise. For example, he often slurred over the difference between phantasy and deliberative imagination, for while both of these faculties, strictly speaking, create meaning, this was not always apparent in Lewis's writings: "B[arfield] and L[ewis] *agree* that there is a valuable activity called imagination – wh[ich] is not the same as *imaginatio, phantasia,* the image making faculty – the exercise of which is necessary for the conaissance of meaning."[73] Or again, while Lewis was usually quite good at separating the sensitive imagination and the other two types of imagination, it is not always clear – no doubt partly due to his trying to incorporate Aristotelian psychology into absolute idealism – what type of imagination he was speaking of. For instance, consider the following passage: "For human poets produce scenery by one kind of imagination, and characters by another. The characters the poet makes out of himself: The scenery out of images retained by memory from the surrounding world. The kind of imagination which thus constructs a raw material of memory images, I call Phantasy."[74] While likely the distinction here is between the sensitive imagination, which makes "scenery," and phantasy / the deliberative imagination, which makes "characters," this is not perfectly lucid, for strictly speaking, "scenery," being a complex image, should be created by phantasy, and "characters," being a purely rational construct, should be created by the deliberative imagination. Many years later, Lewis demonstrated how often his earlier *language* – though not his *concepts* – differed from that of Aristotle and his commentators: "To the best of my knowledge no medieval author mentions either faculty [the sensitive imagination or phantasy] as a characteristic of poets."[75]

However, while Lewis's philosophical inconsistencies must be noted, it cannot be stressed enough that the Oxford don strongly diverged from both Coleridge and Barfield in regard to the emphasis they placed on the primary imagination "half perceive[ing] . . . half create[ing]" the world,[76] for to give so much prestige to the primary, or, in Aristotelian terms, deliberate, imagination is to make it a judge unto itself, which was totally unacceptable for Lewis since he insisted that reason, on account of its very nature, is the sole judge of the products of the imaginations, such as myth. Moreover, following Aristotle and others, Lewis thought that because both phantasy and deliberative imagination are concerned with rearranging simple images,

---

[December 14, 1955].

73   Ibid., 1620 [1927? "The Great War Letters" Series I, Letter 5].

74   Lewis, *Clivi Hamiltonis Summae Metaphysices Contra Anthroposophos Libri II*, 33.

75   Lewis, *The Discarded Image*, 162.

76   Owen Barfield, *Poetic Diction: A Study in Meaning* (1927 reprint; London: Wesleyan University Press, 1984), 27.

these faculties, importantly, are capable of error, and therefore need to be ruled by reason or the faculty of judgment:

> The relation between meaning and Truth seems to be this. A thing can't be true or false unless it means something: but to find out what it means is not to find out whether it is true or false. Poetry can bring out the *quality* or *whatness* of the content of a hypothesis: but the truth of the hypothesis is known not by its content but by its connection with other concepts – by linking it with what is outside itself.[77]

Using Alexander's distinction between "Contemplation" and "Enjoyment," Lewis insisted that even though the imaginations often produce true images, the imaginations can never *know* they did so, for once the imaginations have finished Enjoying their images, it is not the imaginations that Contemplate or judge the images, but reason. Thus, "the truth of a proposition is not vouched for by the fact that it springs from imaginative experience."[78]

Yet despite reason's ability to judge the imaginations, Lewis believed, *pace* the most influential anthropologists of his day, Max Müller and James Frazer,[79] that the abstract language associated with reason and logical thought – prosaic language – is inferior to poetic language, for while prosaic language can only express that-which-truth-is-about in a universal, abstract way, poetic language – Lewis said, using the language of absolute idealism – can express that-which-truth-is-about in both a universal *and* concrete way through the employment of things like metaphors: "Poetry, in its task of revivifying 'counters' – of establishing a gold currency – has to use every device . . . to bring the thing home to your business and bosom. In fact, it has to be more accurate and concrete (less 'in the air') than prose."[80] Hence, Lewis approved of Barfield's statement that Plato's language, for example, is

---

77   Lewis, *The Collected Letters of C. S. Lewis: Volume III*, 1622 [1927? "The Great War Letters" Series I, Letter 6].

78   Ibid., 1610 [1927, "The Great War Letters" Series I, Letter 2].

79   Max Müller (1823-1900), who is generally regarded as the founder of comparative mythology, and James Frazer (1854-1941), who I mentioned earlier, both delighted in world mythology, yet both saw it as a primitive stage in the development of human history. Eric Csapo, *Theories of Mythology* (Oxford: Blackwell, 2005), 26, 38. Indeed, Müller saw poetic language as the natural expression of the simple mind and mythology as the "disease of language," while Frazer, perhaps partially influenced by Auguste Comte (more on him in the next chapter), saw human development in terms of three ages: the Age of Magic, the Age of Religion and the Age of Science, where the Ages of Magic and Religion use poetic language and the Age of Science uses prosaic language.

80   Lewis, *The Collected Letters of C. S. Lewis: Volume III*, 1624 [1927? "The Great War Letters" Series I, Letter 6].

better than Aristotle's,[81] as the former is more metaphorical, and therefore, richer in meaning, than the latter: "In other words," wrote Lewis, "when you think of 'The Lord' as my 'shepherd' you get at once something of the real flavour of care and protection – a little bit of the whatness wh[ich] was merely symbolized in 'benevolent superintendence.'"[82]

Lewis's theory of poetic language and the concrete universality of metaphors was intimately related to his theory of *myth*, but before this can be discussed, it must be seen, as with his theory of imagination, in comparison with Barfield's theory of myth, which rested on the premise that there is an "ancient semantic unity"[83] in our minds, in which old words such as *pneuma* ("breath," "spirit" AND "wind") point past themselves to a time when there was *real* communion between mythical spirits and men, a time when concrete Myth as "a living Figure" walked the Earth:

> It is these 'footsteps of nature' [ie. old words like *pneuma*] whose noise we hear alike in primitive language and in the finest metaphors of poets. Men do not invent those mysterious relations between separate external objects [i.e. "spirit" "breath"], and between objects of feelings or ideas, which it is the function of poetry to reveal. These revelations exist independently, not indeed of Thought, but of any individual thinker. And according to whether the footsteps are echoed in primitive language or, later on, in the made metaphors of poets, we hear after a different fashion and for different reasons. The language of primitive men reports them as direct perceptual experience. The speaker has observed a unity, and is not therefore himself conscious of *relation*. But we, in the development of consciousness, have lost the power to see this one as one. Our sophistication, like Odin's, has cost us an eye; and now it is the language of poets, in so far as they create true metaphors, which must *restore* this unity conceptually, after it has been lost from perception. Thus, the 'before-unapprehended' relationships of which Shelley spoke, are in a sense 'forgotten' relationships. For though they were never yet apprehended, they were at one time seen. And imagination can see them again.[84]

Even though Lewis the idealist agreed with Barfield that the higher imaginations have the power to create meaning (i.e. signification), which in turn can be expressed in metaphors, which in turn are used in myths, the Oxford don insisted that none of the imaginations can, or could, in any way

---

81   Barfield, *Poetic Diction*, 61.
82   Lewis, *The Collected Letters of C. S. Lewis: Volume III*, 1623 [1927? "The Great War Letters" Series I, Letter 6].
83   Ibid., 1509 [1928].
84   Barfield, *Poetic Diction*, 86-7.

commune with spirits or mythical creatures, who *point to their source*, Myth, and whose existence is necessary in order for Barfield's "ancient semantic unity" to be probable or true.

The reason why Lewis rejected Barfield's belief that we can commune with mythical beings and spirits lies in both the Oxford don's Aristotelian psychology and his "vague and tentative idealism."[85] That is, Lewis believed that in order for something to be known to the (sensitive) imagination, it has to be something that is *material* (though of course as an idealist, Lewis believed that the entire material world is a thought imagined by Spirit; more on this in chapter six).[86] The material world provides boundaries, which, of course, mark distinctions, and so only material creatures can leave images or phantasms in the sensitive imagination – immaterial spirits can leave no image and thus we cannot commune with them, even though, take note, it is "very probable" that they exist.[87] Thus, when Barfield asserted that his imagination can perceive the supernatural or, in the words of Kant,[88] the supersensible, he was mistaken, for it was simply a matter of either his deliberative imagination or phantasy operating without an image derived from *hylē* or matter, the result of which is the production of empty fantasies or "Pseudo object[s]."[89] If souls could perceive spiritual beings, then it would imply that neither of them are restricted by matter, and so they would simply cease to be the distinction that is 'soul' and 'spiritual being' and the two of them would "relapse into Spirit" (the totality of all Appearances or individuals);[90] Lewis's idealist argument is that souls do not Enjoy each other in the Alexandrian sense, but rather "a soul contemplated is exactly what we mean by a body,"[91] for to Enjoy another soul, an active subject, would be to treat my soul and the other soul as a singularity, as one *subject* – i.e. Spirit

85   Lewis, *The Collected Letters of C. S. Lewis: Volume III*, 1645 [1928? "The Great War Letters" Series II, Letter 2].

86   Lewis, *Clivi Hamiltonis Summae Metaphysices Contra Anthroposophos Libri II*, 2.

87   Ibid., 15.

88   Both Lewis and Barfield knew the major works of Kant, and while Aristotle's influence is far greater on Lewis, the Oxford don made use of some Kantian concepts (more on this in chapter eight) and it is at times difficult to decide whether Lewis is thinking of Aristotle or Kant when he said that we cannot have knowledge of the supernatural, for both Aristotle and Kant would have said that we cannot have knowledge of anything that we do not first sense. For more on Kant, see Immanuel Kant, *Critique of Pure Reason*, trans. and ed. Paul Guyer and Allen Wood. (Cambridge: Cambridge University Press, 2006), 117 [BXXX].

89   Lewis, *The Collected Letters of C. S. Lewis: Volume III*, 1601 [1927, "The Great War Letters" Series I, Letter 1].

90   Lewis, *Clivi Hamiltonis Summae Metaphysices Contra Anthroposophos Libri II*, 9.

91   Ibid.

– whereas to Contemplate the other soul via its body, a passive object, is to treat myself and its bodies as a duality, as subject and object; thus,

> let us suppose that my soul and my neighbour's were deprived of the material world. Then either his soul will continue to appear to me or not. If not we are no longer compresent and I lose the representation 'his soul': and also, since I have no correlative 'other,' I lose the representation 'myself.' Souls therefore disappear altogether and I am pure Spirit.[92]

For this reason, we should not look outward for spiritualist contact with mythical beings and the like, nor should we, like the mystics, "contemplate our own souls" – i.e. treat a subject as if it were an object – hoping we have some occult power to communicate with mythical beings, but we should "enjoy Spirit: which we do by contemplating the world, in art, philosophy, history or imagination," for souls

> who seek Spirit in their own souls are in danger of great reactions (the dark night of the soul), great folly (fantastic ascetic practices often verging on perversion) and great wickedness (antinomianism). Plotinus stands almost alone among the mystics in having escaped these dangers: but Plotinus was a philosopher. . . . It is therefore the touchstone of every seemingly spiritual activity to ask whether it looks outward, and hastens, like Spirit, to embody itself in matter.[93]

Consequently, Lewis thought that mythical visions are neither true nor false, for lacking a material form and hence a distinct image to impress on the sensitive imagination, myths cannot be empirically verified (as true or

---

92 Ibid., 10. Concerning the time when he published *Dymer*, Lewis wrote: "I was an idealist, and for an idealist all supernaturalisms were equally illusions, all 'spirits' merely symbols of 'Spirit' in the metaphysical sense, futile and dangerous if mistaken for facts." Lewis, preface to the 1950 edition of *Dymer*, 5.

93 Lewis, *Clivi Hamiltonis Summae Metaphysices Contra Anthroposophos Libri II*, 53-4. Evidently, Lewis was aware of Christian mystic St. John of the Cross and his doctrine of "the Dark Night of the Soul," which Lewis likely read about in William James. James, *Varieties of Religious Experience*, 408. Be that as it may, Lewis almost certainly was familiar with the origin of St. John of the Cross's "Dark Night of the Soul," which is found in Pseudo-Dionysius (which in turn was taken from Plotinus, Plato and the Book of Job). According to Pseudo-Dionysius, those who pursue the *via negativa*, or the Way of Negation, as an approach to God ultimately come to realize, after seeing that every created thing is imperfect, that God is "Super-Essential Darkness" because He is so holy and, paradoxically, bright: "Existing beings do not know it [the Supreme Cause] as it actually is and it does not know them as they are. There is no speaking of it, nor name nor knowledge of it. Darkness and light, error and truth – it is none of these." Pseudo-Dionysius *The Mystical Theology* 1048a-b.

false).[94] The only way for myths to be true is if spirits or mythical creatures manifest themselves materially; however, if they were to do so, their existence could be empirically verified and the resulting myth could be said to be true or false accordingly: "Occultism keeps [spirits] worldly but reduces them to regions within our world. Whether such regions exist becomes therefore purely a question of *empirical* evidence."[95]

Nevertheless, even though Lewis neither believed that the existence of mythical creatures could be verified nor took myths to be true, the Oxford don still cherished myths for their aesthetic value.[96] Indeed, we can see that under the varying influences of Croce, Santayana, Bradley and Barfield, Lewis gave art and myth a high place in his philosophy, calling it "an image of the spiritual life,"[97] which is to say that the concrete universality of metaphors and myths were deemed by Lewis to give people an impression or a visual image of what Reality is like (for more on the "spiritual life" and the supreme importance of the imagination, see chapter eight). And this is very significant, for it reveals an important step that Lewis took in the development of his Christian theory of myth, for myth as "an image of the spiritual life" is very similar to myth as a signpost pointing toward Myth.

Consequently, while Lewis borrowed some of Barfield's ideas about the concrete universality of metaphors and myths, he strongly rejected any attempt to rationalize, Contemplate, or reduce myth *qua* image of the spiritual life. For instance, he not only criticized Barfield by insisting that "if all mythology were proven true, 'the poets would throw it away and invent a new one, warranted untrue,'"[98] but he also prepared the way for his rejection

---

94   "I still think Sidney may have been right when he said that the poet never lied because he alone never asserted." Lewis, *The Collected Letters of C. S. Lewis: Volume III*, 1611 [1927? "The Great War Letters" Series I, Letter 1]. Cf. Philip Sidney, *The Defence of Poesy*, in *Sir Philip Sidney*, ed. Katherine Duncan-Jones, The Oxford Authors (Oxford: Oxford University Press, 1989), 235 [930].

95   Lewis, *Clivi Hamiltonis Summae Metaphysices Contra Anthroposophos Libri II*, 25.

96   "I can see no case, prima facie, for erecting Truth into the sole good." Lewis, *The Collected Letters of C. S. Lewis: Volume III*, 1613[1927? "The Great War Letters" Series I, Letter 1].

97   Lewis, *Clivi Hamiltonis Summae Metaphysices Contra Anthroposophos Libri II*, 45.

98   Ibid., 66. This idea can again be found in Lewis's edition of Samuel Butler's *God the Known and God the Unknown*, where Butler wrote, "It is only natural that we should be asked how such an idea has remained in the mind of so many . . . for so long a time if it was without foundation and a piece of dreamy mysticism only" – whereupon Lewis commented, "This man is a fool – mysticism points to a reality not yet real." C. S. Lewis, marginalia in his edition of *God the Known and God the Unknown*, by Samuel Butler (London: A. C. Fields, 1909; The Marion E. Wade Center, Wheaton College), 49.

of any Neoplatonic attempt to "get behind" myths to discover hidden, secondary meanings:

> [I] read the myth from [Plato's] *Politicus* in Jowett's crib, wh[ich] worried me by being so anthroposophical, till it occurred to me that of course Steiner must have read Plato. A pest on all this nonsense which has half spoiled so much beauty and wonder for me, degraded pure imagination into pretentious lying, and truths of the spirit into mere matters of *fact*, slimed everything over with the trail of its infernal mumbo-jumbo! How I w[oul]d have enjoyed this myth once: now behind Plato's delightful *civilised* imagination I always have the picture of dark old traditions picked up from mumbling medicine-men, professing to be 'private information' about facts. [99]

Obviously, then, Lewis believed that by denying the truth-value of myth – by "disenchanting" myth, as Santayana would have it[100] – he was not abusing myth, but rather was allowing it to be "re-enchanted," which is to say that when a myth is known to be simply a beautiful story (disenchanted), it can then have the power to communicate inspiring Beauty to us and which will neither enslave us nor cause us to idolize it (re-enchanted). Hence, Lewis (as a Santayanian) insisted that Christians, for instance, were idolaters because they argue about the *truth* of a beautiful story, which is to fail to focus on the proper function of myth and art, which is to act as a beautiful aid to the spiritual life:

> But the idolater having determined to treat an empirical value as a spiritual and refusing to despise that object as a worldly object, that is, refusing the disenchantment, is very far from the re-enchantment. For we must cease to live, or fear, or reverence any object empirically before we begin to apprehend it spiritually. Therefore, even the debauchee is nearer to the spiritual life than the idolater: for satiety or disease or age must sooner or later disenchant the objects which he loves, and it will then be possible that he may proceed to the spiritual point of view.[101]

Thus, we can say that Lewis's theory of myth during his idealist phases progressed a lot and played an increasingly important role in the Oxford don's philosophical journey, particularly in regard to the idea that myths are concrete universal stories that are images of the spiritual life. Nevertheless,

---

99 Lewis, *All My Road Before Me*, 449 [February 8, 1927].
100 Lewis, *Clivi Hamiltonis Summae Metaphysices Contra Anthroposophos Libri II*, 57.
101 Ibid. Cf. "For neither in the history of art nor in a rational estimate of its value can the aesthetic function of things be divorced from the practical and moral." Santayana, *Reason in Art*, 16.

Lewis's interest in "the science of the nature of myths" or "mythologics"[102] was still largely that of a man who understood myth to be imaginative fiction "unconsciously" (as opposed to symbolism, which is "consciously") created by people who enjoy "imaginative vision of they-know-not-what."[103]

V: Myth during the Theist Phase

During the latter part of The Great War, from 1928 to 1930, Lewis gave many of his anti-Barfieldian treatises medieval names, such as *Clivi Hamiltonis Summae Metaphysics Contra Anthroposophos Libri II*, *Commentarium in Tractatum De Toto et Parte* and *De Bono et Malo*. Of course, the reason for this is the Oxford don was deeply immersed in medieval literature, in particular, medieval allegory, at the time. Indeed, he was giving weekly lectures and tutorials on the classics of the Middle Ages,[104] and doing research for *The Allegory of Love*, which he began in 1928, when he was an absolute idealist, and eventually published in 1936, five years after he became a Christian.

And this, of course, ought to remind us of the important role the medieval philosophers and poets had in Lewis's conversion to both theism (1929) and Christianity (1931), and it should also cause us to ask what, if any, was the influence of the medieval philosophers and poets on Lewis's theistic theory of *myth*? While many Lewis scholars would likely say, "a lot," this, surprisingly, would be incorrect, for even though Lewis both learned a lot about *allegory* from medieval writers, and appropriated and later used a lot of medieval *facts* in his Christian writings, the Oxford don's theory of myth was largely unchanged by the medieval writers. In order to make this clear, we first need to see how these writers, who were mostly Neoplatonists of one kind or another, understood myth.

Both pagan Neoplatonists of late antiquity and the Christian Neoplatonists of the early Middle Ages developed their theories of myth

---

102 Lewis, *The Collected Letters of C. S. Lewis: Volume I*, 765 [June 8, 1928] (emphasis mine).

103 Lewis, *Clivi Hamiltonis Summae Metaphysices Contra Anthroposophos Libri II*, 60, 64. "In myth and symbolism then we enjoy imaginative experience together with the ignorance 'of what.'" Ibid., 64.

104 During the Michaelmas Term 1926, Lewis gave a set of lectures entitled "Some Thinkers of the Renaissance (Elyot, Ascham, Hooker, Bacon)." Lewis repeated these lectures again in 1929 and 1930. But in-between these lectures, during the Michaelmas Term 1928, Lewis lectured on "The Romance of the Rose and its Successors," and after this, in 1932, Lewis began his most important lectures, "Prolegomena to Medieval Poetry," which would be repeated every year through to 1954 and would subsequently become the manuscript for *The Discarded Image*. Walter Hooper, *C. S. Lewis: Companion & Guide* (San Francisco: HarperSanFrancisco, 1996), 524.

from two chief sources: Plato and the Stoics.[105] Plato had said that because mythmakers and poets tell many lies about the gods,[106] the divine-lover, the philosopher, is behooved to rationally dissect the myths that have been handed down in order to discover the truths latent in them (ironically when Socrates did this, he was killed for, among other things, "disbelieving in the gods"[107]); in addition, when Plato himself created myths, such as those found in *Phaedrus* and *Symposium*, it is clear that he was far more concerned about the rational truth behind the myth than he was about Enjoying the concrete universality of the myth itself. As for the Stoics, they were the ones who popularized the practice of *hyponoia* or the unveiling of hidden meanings in myths; indeed, it was largely with them that this practice became known as *allegoriai* or allegorizing,[108] which is when an individual discards the surface meaning of a text, for instance, "Ulysses' ship," for a deeper, spiritual meaning, such as "the human soul;" as Cicero said of the Stoics: "A great deal of . . . trouble was taken by Zeno [the Stoic], then Cleanthes and lastly by Chrysippus, to rationalize these purely fanciful myths and explain the reasons for the names by which the various deities are called."[109] Subsequently, combining insights from Plato and the Stoics, the ancient and medieval Neoplatonists developed sophisticated theories about myth and its place in philosophy. For the purpose of comparing these Neoplatonic theories of myth with Lewis's, I want to focus our attention on two theories of myth that Lewis would have been exposed to during his theist phase: (1) the theory belonging to the pagan Neoplatonist Macrobius,[110] and (2) the theory belonging to the Christian Neoplatonic School of Chartres.

In his most famous work, *Commentary on the Dream of Scipio*, Macrobius set out to write a Neoplatonic commentary on a section of Cicero's *Republic*. The first part of *Commentary* largely revolves around the question of what kind

---

105 To this the Christians might also add St. Paul.

106 "'And we'll deny the truth of the stories that [Achilles] dragged Hector around Patroclus' tomb and slaughtered prisoners on his funeral pyre. And we won't allow our citizens to believe that Achilles – the child of a goddess and of Peleus (who was himself a model of self-discipline and a grandson of Zeus) and tutored by the sage Cheiron – was so full of turmoil that he suffered from the two conflicting diseases of mean-spirited avarice and disdain for gods and men.'" Plato *Republic* 391b-c.

107 Plato *Apology* 22e-24a.

108 Plutarch *Moralia* 19e-f.

109 Cicero *On the Nature of the Gods* 3.24.63.

110 C. S. Lewis, *The Allegory of Love: A Study in the Medieval Tradition* (1936 reprint; Oxford: Oxford University Press, 1969), 46. Although *The Discarded Image*, which dedicates ten pages to Macrobius, was published in 1964, its content was based on Lewis's lectures on medieval literature that he gave when he was at Oxford.

of story is acceptable in philosophizing. Macrobius, following Porphyry,[111] began by claiming that only the story with a didactic function should be used; this, interestingly, apparently eliminates Apuleius's *Golden Ass*,[112] a favorite of Lewis's and the source of *Till We Have Faces*. Nevertheless, it is not just the story with a didactic purpose that is used in philosophy, but the story that "rests on a solid foundation of truth, which is treated in a fictitious style;"[113] this kind of story is called a *narratio fabulosa* to distinguish it from ordinary, fictitious *fabulae* or fables like Aesop's. Now *narrationes fabulosae* are concerned with communicating certain dimensions of the spiritual life (namely, those having to do with the World Soul, spirits and gods) to people in the form of sacred rituals and, importantly, ancient myths. However, while all myths apparently have *some* foundation in Truth, not all of them are fit or appropriate for philosophy, for some of the myths – and here we catch a glimpse of Plato in the *Republic* – tell lies about the gods and show them doing immoral or base things, such as Cronos cutting off Uranus's privy parts. Hence, the myths acceptable to philosophy are those that are the truest, those that show the gods doing moral things in a dignified manner, and these, Lewis would have read, were myths with some grounding in Truth and, importantly, hidden behind "a modest veil of allegory."[114] Finally, no story or myth is appropriate for a philosophical discussion of the two highest hypostases in the Neoplatonic Trinity, the One and *Nous*, for these in no way touch the world of imperfection (our world and the world of the gods) and so these hypostases shun both the imagination, which is a lesser faculty than speech and reason;[115] consequently, the One and *Nous* can only be spoken of

---

111 Pierre Hadot, *The Veil of Isis: An Essay on the History of the Idea of Nature*, trans. Michael Chase (Cambridge, MA: Belknap Press, 2006), 51.

112 "Fables – the very word acknowledges their falsity – serve two purposes: either merely to gratify the ear or to encourage the reader to good works. They delight the ear as do the comedies of Menander and his imitators, or the narratives replete with imaginary doings of lovers in which Petronius Arbiter so freely indulged and with which *Apuleius*, astonishingly, sometimes amused himself." Macrobius *Commentary on the Dream of Scipio* 1.2.7-8 (emphasis mine). Commenting on this passage, William Stahl wrote: "The reference is undoubtedly to Apuleius's great work, the *Golden Ass*, which abounds in romance and adventure. It is not surprising to find Macrobius expressing astonishment over such literary extravagances of Apuleius, for the latter was an eminent Platonist."

113 Ibid., 1.2.9.

114 Ibid., 1.2.11.

115 When the Platonic soul fell from its original abode, the first tunic or covering it took on was the imagination, which is, of course, the image-making faculty of the person. The farther the soul fell from its original home, the more coverings it took on until it finally was completely covered with a physical body. In Platonic thought, there is a strong connection between the imagination, the material world and clothing on the one hand, and reason, the immaterial world and nakedness on the other.

analogically or metaphorically as Plato did when he spoke of the "Good" as the "Sun" (and even then it seems impossible, for if the "Good" is "beyond Being" then how can we say *anything* of it?).

The new humanism of Neoplatonic Christians,[116] in particular, those of the School of Chartres, went even further than the pagan philosophers in rejecting the literal or historical interpretation of the pagan myths. While two of the key figures in the School of Chartres, William of Conches and Thierry of Chartres, were largely unknown to Lewis,[117] the Oxford don was well acquainted with the ideas of Bernardus Silvestris and, to a lesser extent, Alain de Lille and Jean de Hanville (indeed, Lewis used ideas from both the former and the latter in *Out of the Silent Planet*[118]); moreover, Lewis's very interest in writing *The Allegory of Love, The Romance of the Rose,* was co-written by a man, Jean de Meun, who was deeply influenced by Chartrian approaches to myth and allegory. While it is always a danger to speak in generalizations, it may be fair to speak broadly of a Chartrian approach to myth and allegory, for all of those associated with the School believed in the following things. First, a *fabula* or fable was more or less a synonym for "myth;" this was not so much due to the pagan Macrobius, who still revered the ancient gods, as to the Christian Augustine, who either disbelieved the pagan myths or thought they were true stories about real demons.[119] Second, fables were often spoken of as *integumentum, involucrum* and / or *allegoria*,[120] which are myths with particular emphasis on their hidden or inner meanings;[121] in other words, they, and quite literally in the case of *involucrum*, show that the myth is a "covering" or "wrapping" for a deeper, more philosophical *significatio* or meaning.[122] Third, since all myths are fables and as such are not meant to be taken as literally true, the Chartrians had no trouble rejecting Macrobius's restrictions on only using dignified myths for philosophy, for the Christian Chartrians thought all pagan myths were equally false if taken literally, and equally true if taken metaphorically;[123] in this way, even a story like Cronos cutting off his father's privy parts can be interpreted allegorically to the benefit of the reader.[124]

116 Winthrop Wetherbee, *Platonism and Poetry in the Twelfth Century: The Literary Influence of the School of Chartres* (Princeton: Princeton University Press, 1972), 13.
117 Indeed, Lewis even mistakenly called Thierry of Chartres "Thierry of Conches." Lewis, *The Allegory of Love*, 88.
118 Lewis, *The Collected Letters of C. S. Lewis: Volume II*, 451 [October 24, 1940].
119 Augustine *The City of God* 6.6.
120 Peter Dronke, *Fabula: Explorations into the Uses of Myth in Medieval Platonism* (Leiden: E. J. Brill, 1974), 5, 45.
121 Wetherbee, *Platonism and Poetry in the Twelfth Century*, 42. Dronke, *Fabula*, 119.
122 Bernardus Silvestris *Commentum Super Sex Libros Eneidos Virgilii* 11.18-20.
123 Wetherbee, *Platonism and Poetry in the Twelfth Century*, 46.
124 Dronke, *Fabula*, 28.

After having examined a few different theories of myth which Lewis would have been exposed to during his theist phase, we can see that although the Oxford don's love and understanding of *allegory* was clearly enriched by his interaction with philosophers like Macrobius and Bernardus Silvestris, his theory of myth was not. That is, where the Neoplatonists said, for instance, that Sibyl's discourse with the gods in Virgil's *Aeneid*, (another book that Lewis listed in his top ten philosophical influences) was a matter of *obscures vera involvens* – "wrapping truth in dark sayings" – the Oxford don denied that the "dark sayings" of Sibyl, not to mention all of the pagan and Christian myths, could be known to be *true* since in order for something to be known to be *true*, it has to be verifiable and myths can never be verified; indeed, this is why Lewis considered himself a *theist* at the time and *not* a Christian (i.e. God's existence could be verified or argued for, but the specifically mythical elements in Christianity could not be). Consequently, Lionel Adey misunderstands Lewis the theist when he says the Oxford don "approached Christianity via a Platonism tinged with Stoicism, tolerating popular mythology like an eighteenth-century aristocratic deist,"[125] for Lewis had at once a far *more* generous, and far *less* generous, attitude toward mythology than either the Stoics or the deists – far less generous because he thought that poetry should not be diminished by rational interpretation (via allegory), and far more generous because while poetry can be *judged* by reason, it cannot be *interpreted* in a meaningful way by reason. In sum, then, Lewis the theist agreed with Chesterton (whom, we recall, the Oxford don had read during the latter part of The Great War) when the journalist said bluntly: "Myths are not allegories."[126]

VI: Myth during the Neoplatonic Christian Phase

When Lewis the absolute idealist was simultaneously engaged in The Great War with Barfield and teaching medieval approaches to myth at Oxford, one of the most important events of his life happened: he met J. R. R. Tolkien, a fellow colleague and English professor at Oxford and a great lover of both George MacDonald (who we remember helped "baptize" Lewis's imagination) and Norse mythology. Beginning in 1926 or 1927, Lewis started attending the Kólbitar, a club dedicated to reading Norse literature, at the invitation of Tolkien, who founded the club and whose interest in Norse mythology would later bare fruit in the form of *The Hobbit*, *The Lord of the Rings* and *The Silmarillion*.[127]

125 Adey, *C. S. Lewis's 'Great War' with Owen Barfield*, 66.
126 Chesterton, *The Everlasting Man*, 104.
127 Lewis, *All My Road Before Me*, 392-3 [May 11, 1926]. Lewis, *The Collected Letters of C. S. Lewis: Volume I*, 701 [June 26, 1927].

On top of encouraging Lewis's pre-existing love of Norse mythology, Tolkien did far more than this, for it was he, along with their mutual friend Hugo Dyson, who eventually convinced Lewis, who had just become a theist, that *all* mythologies, far from being beautiful stories disengaged from Truth or "lies breathed in silver" are actually examples of "*praeparatio evangelica*"[128] or copies which prepare people for the True Myth, Christ:

> Now what Dyson and Tolkien showed me was this: that if I met the idea of sacrifice in a Pagan story I didn't mind it at all: again, that if I met the idea of a god sacrificing himself to himself . . . I liked it very much and was mysteriously moved by it: again, that the idea of the dying and reviving god (Balder, Adonis, Bacchus) similarly moved me provided that I met it anywhere *except* in the Gospels. The reason was that in Pagan stories I was prepared to feel the myth as profound and suggestive of meanings beyond my grasp even tho[ugh] I could not say in cold prose 'what it meant.'

> Now the story of Christ is simply a true myth: a myth working on us in the same way as the others, but with this tremendous difference that *it really happened*: and one must be content to accept it in the same way, remembering that it is God's myth where the others are men's myths: i.e. the Pagan stories are God expressing Himself through the minds of poets, using such images as he found there, while Christianity is God expressing Himself through what we call 'real things.' Therefore it is *true*, not in the sense of being a 'description' of God (that no finite mind could take in) but in the sense of being the way in which God chooses to (or can) appear to our faculties. The 'doctrines' we get *out of* the true myth are of course *less* true: they are translations into our *concepts* and *ideas* of that wh[ich] God has already expressed in a language more adequate, namely the actual incarnation, crucifixion, and resurrection.[129]

Tolkien's theory of myth, then, was crucial to Lewis's *rational* conversion to Christianity, for it provided the Oxford don with intellectually satisfying reasons for becoming a Christian; indeed, the explanation of Christ as the True Myth satisfied not only Lewis's Kirkian mind but also his imaginations and heavenly desire since reason, imagination and desire are all complete in Christ: "This is not 'a religion,' nor 'a philosophy.' It is the summing up and actuality of them all."[130] Indeed, as two of Lewis's mentors – G. K.

128 Lewis, *The Collected Letters of C. S. Lewis: Volume II*, 453 [November 4, 1940].
129 Lewis, *The Collected Letters of C. S. Lewis: Volume I*, 996-7 [October 18, 1931]. Cf. "Our mythology is based on a solider reality than we dream." C. S. Lewis, *Perelandra*, in *The Cosmic Trilogy*, by C. S. Lewis (1943 reprint; London: Pan Books, 1990), 328.
130 Lewis, *Surprised by Joy*, 1380.

Chesterton and Henry More – had said even earlier, "The Catholic faith is the reconciliation because it is the realization both of mythology and philosophy,"[131] and, "Christianity fulfils not only the law of Moses but all that was good in Paganism."[132]

However, Lewis's understanding of myth did not end with his conversion. In *The Pilgrim's Regress*, for instance, Lewis developed Tolkien's theory of myth by arguing that "the Landlord" (God) gave "the Shepherd people" (the Jews) "Rules" and the "Pagans" "Pictures" in order to keep them on the "Road" (to Heaven).[133] According to Lewis, the pagan "Pictures" or myths, contain a "divine call" that brings light if rightly understood and followed:

> The resemblance between these myths and the Christian truth is no more accidental than the resemblance between the sun and the sun's reflection in a pond, or that between a historical fact and the somewhat garbled version of it which lives in popular report, or between the trees and hills of the real world and the trees and hills in our dreams. . . . [W]hen I meditate on the Passion while reading Plato's picture of the Righteous One, or on the Resurrection while reading about Adonis or Balder . . . [t]here is a real connection between what Plato and the myth-makers most deeply were and meant and what I believe to be the truth. I know that connection and they do not. But it is really there. It is not an arbitrary fancy of my own thrust upon the old words. One can, without any absurdity, imagine Plato or the myth-makers if they learned the truth, saying, 'I see . . . so that was what I was really talking about. Of course. That is what my words really meant, and I never knew it.'[134]

Furthermore, these pagan myths are comparable to parts of the Old Testament as they both are types of revelation from God, and both are ultimately superseded or fulfilled by Christ, the Original Myth.

One of the implications of all this is that Lewis believed, much to the vexation of fundamentalists, the Old Testament, and indeed, the entire Bible, contains elements that are mythical and non-historical: "Of course I believe the composition, presentation and selection for inclusion in the Bible, of all the books to have been guided by the Holy Ghost. But I think He means us

---

131 Chesterton, *The Everlasting Man*, 246.
132 Lewis, "Henry More," 96.
133 Lewis, *The Pilgrim's Regress*, 168-9, 190.
134 C. S. Lewis, *Reflections on the Psalms*, in *C. S. Lewis: Selected Books* [Short Edition] (1958 reprint; London: HarperCollins, 2002), 367. And Mother Kirk asks John, "'Have you not heard among the Pagans the story of Semele? Or was there any age in any land when men did not know that corn and wine were the blood and body of a dying and yet living God?'" Lewis, *The Pilgrim's Regress*, 190.

to have sacred myth & sacred fiction as well as sacred history."[135] On top of this, Lewis asserted that just as pagan mythology can be in error, so also can the Bible,[136] for scripture is the joint creation of fallible, human prophets and an infallible God. In this way, the Oxford don rejected both "The Dictation Theory," which states that God literally dictated every word in the Bible to His prophets, and "The Plenary Verbal Inspiration Theory," which states that God's inspiration extends completely to every historical detail and every word the prophets chose.[137] Nevertheless, granted there are trivial errors in Holy Writ, Lewis strongly felt the Bible was the most unique expression of God's revelation to us and if a person reads it with the right heart, looking for God's intended meaning, it usually can be found. Michael Christensen explains:

> Lewis would admonish us to receive the message of Scripture in the same way that we catch 'the sacred Fish.' The net required is 'love' – an affirmative attitude toward the Word of God in Scripture. The mesh needed is 'a man's whole heart' – a baptized literary embrace of the biblical images which allows us to taste reality and be transformed. . . . An affirmative literary embrace of the message of Scripture would not negate, in Lewis's opinion, Paul's teaching on the submission of a wife to her husband, for example. An honest reading of Scripture would attempt to get behind Paul's culturally conditioned language to the divine principle of submission being conveyed. To reject Paul's hierarchical view in principle as culturally relative and accept egalitarian feminism is not to embrace with loving affirmation the intended message of the Bible. It is one thing to look beyond the words of Scripture to its embodied message, yet quite another to dismiss its intended meaning.[138]

Therefore, if Lewis's approach to scripture must be given a label, his would be "The Limited Inspiration Theory," which admits the presence of human

---

135 Lewis, *The Collected Letters of C. S. Lewis: Volume III*, 653 [October 5, 1955]. Cf. Ibid., 246 [November 8, 1952].

136 In his early years, Lewis was influenced by higher critics like Ernest Renan, who attempted to reduce the Bible to a mere work of literature. Lewis, *The Collected Letters of C. S. Lewis: Volume I*, 309 [May 27, 1917]. Some of this influence – for better or for worse – remained with Lewis throughout his life.

137 Bill T. Arnold and Bryan E. Beyer, *Encountering the Old Testament: A Christian Survey* (Grand Rapids, MI: Baker Books, 1999), 24-5.

138 Michael J. Christensen, *C. S. Lewis on Scripture: His Thoughts on the Nature of Biblical Inspiration, the Role of Revelation and the Question of Inerrancy* (London: Hodder and Stoughton, 1979), 93. Cf. Lewis, *The Collected Letters of C. S. Lewis: Volume III*, 1045-7 [May 7, 1959] and 960-1 [July 19, 1958].

errors, but insists on God's inspiration permeating every book.[139]

While I myself happen to agree with something like the aforementioned theory, a person could seriously press Lewis – and not enough people have – as to whether he was too uncritical in his belief that pagan myths are compatible, even if in a very limited way, with Christianity; indeed, it is hard not to feel he went too far when he said of his trip to Greece: "At Daphni it was hard not to pray to Apollo the Healer. But somehow one didn't feel it w[oul]d have been very wrong – w[oul]d have only been addressing Christ *sub specie Apollinis*."[140] Lewis's extreme sympathy with paganism, of course, is due to his classical upbringing and identity with Old Western Culture, which ultimately provoked his claim that he was "a converted Pagan"[141] (more on this in the next chapter); nevertheless, Lewis's attitude toward paganism is in stark contrast with Elijah's, for instance, who seemed *utterly* opposed to the prophets of Baal on Mt. Carmel;[142] moreover, while we tolerate (and even enjoy, in my case) Disney's *Hercules*, it is hard to imagine a Christian parent taking his children to see a cartoon version of *The Baal Cycle*. Thus, while I do not feel that Lewis is completely wrong to value paganism as he did – after all his cultural context was different than Elijah's – I think that we have to remember that Lewis, like any man, needs to be scrutinized as, of course, Lewis the philosopher would have us do.

Moving on from this, we see that along with his new understanding of myth *qua* revelation, Lewis needed to give a fuller account of how myth fits into his theory of the imaginations. Thus, he wrote:

> I think we have to distinguish (1.) The mere image-making faculty of the 'mind's eye' (also its nose, ear etc.) wh[ich] ought to be called imagination if we literary meddlers hadn't spoiled the word for its plain sense. (2.) The uses (or abuses) of this (a) By the Holy Ghost in visions *proprement dites* ["as such"]. (b) By the body and the unconscious to produce dreams (c) By our (waking) starved wishes or suppressed fears to produce reverie in wish-fulfillment or fear-fulfillment. (d) By pathological agencies to produce hallucinations. (e) By I-don't-know-

---

139 Arnold, *Encountering the Old Testament*, 25. Cf. "Lewis was the most effective Christian apologist for certainly the latter part of the twentieth century. When the BBC recently asked if I had absolutely refuted Lewis's Christian apologetic, I replied: 'No. I just didn't believe there was sufficient reason for believing it. But of course when I later came to think about theological things, it seemed to me that the case for the Christian revelation is a very strong one, if you believe in any revelation at all.'" Flew, *There is a God*, 24.

140 Lewis, *The Collected Letters of C. S. Lewis: Volume III*, 1154 [May 23, 1960].

141 Lewis, *Surprised by Joy*, 1283.

142 1 Kings 18:16-46.

what, call it Muse, to produce (with or without our conscious volition) figments ('I *thought* of Mr. Pickwick').

Now distinct from all these we have the plastic, inventive, or constructive power, *homo faber*. This wants to make things out of any plastic material, whether within the mind or without; stone, metals, clay, wood, cloth, memory, & imagination. It will take from imagination *any* of the materials I've enumerated.[143]

Though this summary of the imaginations is a popular, and not a philosophical, one, the only major difference between Lewis's Great War theory of the imaginations and his Christian one is the additional belief that the imaginations *can*, though not necessarily *will*, have real communion with mythical beings and spirits.[144] Hence, in regard to the relationship between myth *qua* revelation and the imaginations, Lewis believed that first the Holy Spirit mystically (a problematic word in Lewis's vocabulary[145]) inspires (another difficult word[146]) the imagination, and then the human author, using his deliberative imagination, writes down what he has been inspired with. And this, of course, requires a certain kind of language.

Now the language of scripture and religion, like the language of pagan mythology, is largely poetic language, the power of which is "[to] communicate

---

143 Lewis, *The Collected Letters of C. S. Lewis: Volume III*, 683-4 [December 14, 1955].

144 "I am glad you never read my *Summa* [i.e. *Clivi Hamiltonis Summae Metaphysics Contra Anthroposophos Libri II*], for all that is dead mutton to me now: and the points chiefly at issue between the Anthroposophists and me then were *precisely* the points on which anthroposophy is certainly right – i.e. the claim that it is possible for man, here and now, in the phenomenal world, to have commerce with the world beyond – which is what I was denying." Lewis, *The Collected Letters of C. S. Lewis: Volume II*, 107 [March 28,1933]. Cf. Robert Holyer, "C. S. Lewis on the Epistemic Significance of the Imagination," *Soundings* 74, no. 1 and 2 (1991): 217-18.

145 "I have not made up my mind about Mysticism. Two things give me pause. 1. That the similarity between Christian and non-Christian mysticism is strong I by no means conclude from this that it is un-Christian in the sense of being incompatible with Christianity: but I am inclined to think that it is not *specifically* Christian. . . . 2. I am struck by the absence of much mysticism from the New Testament." Lewis, *The Collected Letters of C. S. Lewis: Volume II*, 201 [July 28, 1936]. On account of Lewis's skeptical or hesitant approach to mysticism, I found David Downing's book *Into the Region of Awe: Mysticism in C. S. Lewis* unconvincing, for Downing is searching for "the overlooked Lewis," who is, in my opinion, a phantom. David Downing, *Into the Region of Awe: Mysticism in C. S. Lewis* (Downers Grove, IL: InterVarsity Press, 2005), 11.

146 Concerning Bunyan's *Pilgrim's Progress*, Lewis wrote: "'For having now my Method by the end; Still as I pull'd, it came.' *It came.* I doubt if we shall ever know more of the process called 'inspiration' than those two monosyllables tell us." Lewis, "The Vision of John Bunyan," 147.

more Reality to us"[147] or "to convey to us the quality of experiences which we have not had, or perhaps can never have, to use factors within our experience so that they become pointers to something outside our experience – as two or more roads on a map show us where a town that is off the map must lie."[148] That is, religion uses poetic language because, as we saw earlier, such language is the most metaphorical and therefore the most meaningful as it can convey a sense of concrete universality:

> But open your Plato, and you will find yourself among the great creators of metaphor, and therefore among the masters of meaning. If we turn to Theology – or rather to the literature of religion – the result will be more surprising still; for unless our whole argument is wrong, we shall have to admit that a man who says *heaven* and thinks of the visible sky is pretty sure to mean more than a man who tells us that heaven is a state of mind. . . . It will have escaped no one that in such a scale of writers the poets will take the highest place; and among the poets those who have at once the tenderest care for old words and the surest instinct for the creation of new metaphors.[149]

Of course, this approach to religious language, meaning and metaphor, as I said, did not entail Lewis creating a radically new theory of the imagination. Thus, even though the Oxford don did concede that the deliberative imagination has a "kind of psycho-physical parallelism in the universe"[150] – i.e. a certain sensitivity to the mysterious connection between things, which in turn accounts for the creation of metaphors[151] – Lewis still firmly believed

---

147 "Mythologies and religions are products of imagination in the sense that their content is *imaginative*. The more *imaginative* ones are 'nearer the mark' in the sense that they communicate more Reality to us. Poetry 'creates life' in the sense that its products are something more than fictions occurring in human minds, mere psychological phenomena, and can therefore be described as inhabiting a 'spiritual world.' Poets 'proclaim the mystery' in the sense that they somehow convey to us an inkling of supersensual and super-intellectual Reality: which is a Mystery in the sense of *mysterium tremendum*, something not merely wh[ich] we happen not to know but which transcends our common modes of perception. They produce the illusion of penetrating it in the sense that they make us feel we have *understood* when we have really been refreshed by contact of quite a different kind with Reality. Poetry is a great power in the sense of actually enriching our deepest life by such contacts." Lewis, *The Collected Letters of C. S. Lewis: Volume II*, 445 [September 24, 1940].
148 Lewis, "The Language of Religion," 259.
149 C. S. Lewis, "Bluspels and Flalansferes," in *Selected Literary Essays*, by C. S. Lewis, ed. Walter Hooper (Cambridge: Cambridge University Press, 1969), 265.
150 Ibid.
151 As Lyle Smith Jr. has pointed out, to expect a detailed theory from Lewis of how metaphors are made is unreasonable: "When [Lewis] does talk about metaphor, he is concerned with what it does, rather than with how it works. If we read Lewis for

that neither type of imagination could know Truth since only *reason* could do so: "I am a rationalist," he wrote, "for me, reason is the natural organ of truth; but imagination is the organ of meaning. Imagination, producing new metaphors or revivifying old, is not the cause of truth, but its condition."[152] While I need to mention that by "rationalism" Lewis meant "the determined practice of reason" and not "the name given in the nineteenth century to the school of thought which denied the supernatural,"[153] I must insist that Lewis, as one who believed philosophy is a way of life, was firmly convinced – for his *entire* Christian life, as I will argue in greater detail in chapter seven – that it is the job of reason to scrutinize every proposition, including those pertaining to myth, for it is reason, dwelling "on the soul's acropolis,"[154] that distinguishes the man-made lies in mythology ("The Pictures alone are dangerous"[155]) from the god-inspired elements; as Lewis had learned from Henry More, "take away Reason and all Religions are alike true."[156] However, this leads to the next point.

In keeping with his dual insistence that the prosaic language of philosophy is *inferior* to the poetic language of myth and that the faculty of reason is *superior* to the imaginations, Lewis maintained that as with Neoplatonic allegorical interpretations of pagan myths, abstract theological interpretations of biblical myths are often dangerous; indeed, he believed that "there is some death" in such attempts.[157] Thus, he thought that people were better off simply Enjoying a myth, "simply swallowing the story," rather than Contemplating the myth and "trying to find an allegorical, separable

a clearly articulated theory of metaphor, such as those of I. A. Richards, Max Black, Monroe Beardsley, Douglas Berggren, Marcus Hester, Philip Wheelwright or Paul Ricoeur, we shall not find it. It would be surprising if we did, for Lewis was . . . not a linguist or a rhetorician." Lyle Smith Jr, "C. S. Lewis and the Making of Metaphor," in *Word and Story in C. S. Lewis*, ed. Peter Schakel and Charles Huttar, 11-28 (Columbia, MO: University of Missouri Press, 1991), 11.

152 Lewis, "Bluspels and Flalansferes," 265. Cf. "The Romantics make huge claims for the Imagination as an organ of truth; but they never have the courage either to withdraw those claims or to support them quite seriously and face their implications." C. S. Lewis, "Who Gaf Me Drink?" a review of *Romanticism Comes of Age*, by Owen Barfield, *Spectator* (9 March 1945): 224.

153 C. S. Lewis, "C. S. Lewis on Rationalism: (Unpublished Notes)," *VII: An Anglo-American Literary Review* 9 (1988), 88.

154 C. S. Lewis, "Reason," in *Poems*, by C. S. Lewis, ed. Walter Hooper (San Diego: Harcourt Brace Jovanovich, 1964), 81 [1].

155 Lewis, *The Pilgrim's Regress*, 168.

156 Lewis, "Henry More," 5. Cf. "Reason must never be forsaken for inspiration, wh[ich] may not come, and if it did, w[oul]d be according to reason." Ibid., 26.

157 Lewis, "The Language of Religion," 262.

significatio."[158] Consequently, Lewis had little sympathy with modernist interpretations of scripture – "Stoic allegorisations of the myths standing to the original cult rather as Modernism to Christianity"[159] – because he insisted that by totally Contemplating or allegorizing myths, something inexplicable and mysterious is actually lost,[160] for while *all* myths *can* be interpreted allegorically – where you are given, at least according to Lewis's narrow view of allegory,[161] "one thing in terms of another"[162] – myths, at their best, resist being put in strict "conceptual terms"[163]: "But it remains true that wherever the symbols are best, the key is least adequate. For when allegory is at its best, it approaches myth, which must be grasped with the imagination, not with the intellect. . . . It is the sort of thing you cannot

---

158 Lewis, *The Collected Letters of C. S. Lewis: Volume II*, 441 [August 23, 1940].

159 Lewis, *The Collected Letters of C. S. Lewis: Volume III*, 830 [February 10, 1957]. Also consider the fact that in *Till We Have Faces*, Lewis made the Fox a person who represents Stoicism: "The Fox expresses *neither* Anthroposophy *nor* my views, but Stoicism." Ibid., 1419 [March 26, 1963]. And then later Lewis said the Stoic Fox is an embodiment of a "shallow 'enlightenment,'" much like modernist demythologizing of the Bible. Ibid., 1382 [November 1962].

160 C. S. Lewis, *An Experiment in Criticism* (1961 reprint; Cambridge: Cambridge University Press, 1999), 45.

161 "There is enough evidence to suggest that Lewis entertained a narrow view of allegory. He is mainly concerned with 'naïve' and 'continuous' allegory in which the relation between the two levels is predetermined and overly systematized, with little or no freedom for the reader to make up his or her own mind. This is the case, for instance, in Prudentius' *Psychomachia*, which Lewis takes to be the archetype of all allegories, and in his own *The Pilgrim's Regress*. . . . Of the latter work it can only be said that it epitomizes naïve, frigid, inferior allegory, with its tedious abstractions and bloodless personifications." Buning, *"Perelandra* in the Light of Modern Allegorical Theory,"* 281. Buning is not alone in finding Lewis's one-to-one correspondence theory of allegory overly simplistic. Paul Piehler, for instance, calls *The Allegory of Love* a "leaky vessel" because of its inadequate treatment of allegory. Paul Piehler, "Visions and Revisions: C. S. Lewis's Contributions to the Theory of Allegory," in *The Taste of the Pineapple: Essays on C. S. Lewis as Reader, Critic, and Imaginative Writer*, ed. Bruce Edwards, 79-91 (Bowling Green, OH: Bowling Green State University Popular Press, 1988), 90. While I certainly agree with both Buning and Piehler that Lewis's theory of allegory is inadequate, we must remember that the Oxford don was not at all interested in the different shades of allegory in myth, but was mainly concerned about the essential features that differentiated them.

162 Lewis, "The Vision of John Bunyan," 148. In this same essay Lewis went on to explain how an allegory should be used: "We ought to be thinking 'This green valley, where the shepherd boy is singing, represents humility;' we ought to be discovering, as we read, that humility is like that green valley. That way, moving always into the book, not out of it, from the concept to the image, enriches the concept. And that is what allegory is for." Ibid., 149.

163 Lewis, *The Collected Letters of C. S. Lewis: Volume II*, 438 [August 18, 1940].

learn from definition: you must rather get to know it;"[164] this is to say that myth points to an essentially non-abstract, supra-rational thing: "In poetry the words are the body and the 'theme' or 'content' is the soul. But in myth the imagined events are the body and something *inexpressible* is the soul."[165] As a result of their elusive, supra-rational nature, myths, like "manna" (which "is to each man a different dish and to each the dish he needs"),[166] are often opened to a variety of readings, whereas allegories are not: "A good myth (i.e. a story out of which ever varying meanings will grow for different readers and in different ages) is a higher thing than an allegory (into which *one* meaning has been put). In an allegory a man can put only what he already knows: in a myth he puts what he does not yet know and c[oul]d not come to know in any other way."[167]

Hence, Lewis came to believe that far from being simply a didactic allegory, myth as Myth "does not essentially exist in *words* at all;"[168] indeed, it is "extra-literary."[169] And so owing much to Barfield's "ancient semantic unity," which, we recall, stressed the real presence of mythical beings that the ancients experienced first hand (i.e. the Myth of the gods dwelling among us – God walking with Adam in the Garden, etc.), and Bradley's Hegelian

---

164 Lewis, preface to the third edition of *The Pilgrim's Regress*, 12. Cf. "The mere fact that you *can* allegorise the work before you is of itself no proof that it is an allegory. Of course you can allegorise it. You can allegorise anything, whether in art or real life." C. S. Lewis, "On Criticism," in *C. S. Lewis: Essay Collection & Other Short Pieces*, ed. Lesley Walmsley (London: HarperCollins, 2000), 550. This is an incomplete essay that appears to have been written fairly late in Lewis's life.

165 Lewis, "The Language of Religion," 262 (emphasis mine). Cf. "A really fine work of folk-lore, like *The Golden Bough*, will leave too many readers with the idea, for instance, that this or that story of a giant's or wizard's heart in a casket or a cave only 'means' some stupid and static superstition called 'the external soul.' But we do not know what these things mean, simply because we do not know what we ourselves mean when we are moved by them." Chesterton, *The Everlasting Man*, 105.

166 C. S. Lewis, "Shelley, Dryden and Mr. Eliot," in *Selected Literary Essays*, by C. S. Lewis, ed. Walter Hooper (Cambridge: Cambridge University Press, 1969), 205. This idea may owe something to Santayana, who wrote: "The poet who creates a symbol must do so without knowing what significance it may eventually acquire, and conscious at best only of the emotional background from which it emerged." Santayana, *Reason in Art*, 90-1.

167 Lewis, *The Collected Letters of C. S. Lewis: Volume III*, 789-90 [September 22, 1956]. Cf. "'Rough male taste' is, of course, a metaphor. It still seems to me the right one – but of course all metaphors are touch-and-go and don't appeal equally to all imaginations." Ibid., 146 [December 1, 1951]. Moreover, the interpretive freedom in regard to myth is apparent when one considers the various Chartrian interpretations of the Vulcan, Venus and Mars myth, for instance. Wetherbee, *Platonism and Poetry in the Twelfth Century*, 118.

168 Lewis, *George MacDonald: An Anthology*, xxvii.

169 Lewis, *An Experiment in Criticism*, 43.

doctrine of the "concrete universal,"[170] which we have already discussed in
relation to metaphor, Lewis insisted that the experience of Myth is to "taste
a universal principle," "to see," as he said of symbolism, "the archetype in the
copy,"[171] or to enjoy or experience in a concrete way a profound reality that
cannot be fully explained:

> In the enjoying of a great myth we come nearest to experiencing as
> a concrete what can otherwise be understood only as an abstraction.
> At this moment, for example, I am trying to understand something
> very abstract indeed – the fading, vanishing of tasted reality as we try
> to grasp it with the discursive reason. . . . If I remind you, instead, of
> Orpheus and Eurydice, how he was suffered to lead her by the hand
> but, when he turned round to look at her, she disappeared, what was
> merely a principle becomes imaginable. You may reply that you never
> till this moment attached that 'meaning' to that myth. Of course
> not. You are not looking for an abstract 'meaning' at all. . . . You
> were not knowing, but tasting; but what you were tasting turns out
> to be a universal principle. The moment we *state* this principle, we are
> admittedly back in the world of abstraction. It is only while receiving
> the myth as a story that you experience the principle concretely. When
> we translate we get abstraction – or rather, dozens of abstractions.
> What flows into you from the myth is not truth but reality (truth
> is always *about* something, but reality is that *about which* truth is),
> and, therefore, every myth becomes the father of innumerable truths
> on the abstract level. Myth is the mountain whence all the different
> streams arise which become truths down here in the valley. . . . Or,
> if you prefer, myth is the isthmus which connects the peninsular
> world of thought with the vast continent we really belong to. It is
> not, like truth, abstract; nor is it, like direct experience, bound to the
> particular.[172]

Thus, as I said before, if myth cannot be completely reduced to allegory,
then the mythical elements in the Bible, as a reflection of Myth, ought not
to be completely demythologized, for to explain away mythical elements like

170 Bradley, *Ethical Studies*, 176.
171 Lewis, *The Allegory of Love*, 45. However, it must be added that Lewis thought Myth
is more than a Jungian archetype: "I have no answer to the question Jung has raised. I
can only say – indulging once more in the same primordial image – that the mystery
of primordial images is deeper, their origin more remote, their cave more hid, their
fountain less accessible than those suspect who have yet dug deepest, sounded with the
longest cord, or journeyed farthest in the wilderness." C. S. Lewis, "Psycho-Analysis
and Literary Criticism," in *Selected Literary Essays*, by C. S. Lewis, ed. Walter Hooper
(1942 essay reprint; Cambridge: Cambridge University Press, 1969), 300.
172 Lewis, "Myth Became Fact," 140-1.

the Fatherliness of God, the Atonement, the divinity of the heavens or the Sonship of Christ is to reduce the Bible, shockingly, and to modern minds, paradoxically, to a mere *human* construct.[173] That is, the theologian's analogy or the philosopher's metaphor must not, at all costs, explain the image of God as Father, for instance, as *simply* meaning that God is authoritative (and worse, by adding that this is merely a product of a patriarchal culture): it is true that God's Fatherliness represents his authority, but it does not *only* mean that, for women, nowadays, can be in positions of authority, and yet it would be fundamentally wrong, according to Lewis, to say that God, therefore, could be represented *equally* as Mother:

> Suppose the reformer stops saying that a good woman may be like God and begins saying that God is like a good woman. Suppose he says that we might just as well pray to 'Our Mother which art in Heaven' as to 'Our Father.' Suppose he suggests that the Incarnation might just as well have taken a female as a male form, and the Second Person of the Trinity be as well called the Daughter as the Son. Suppose, finally, that the mystical marriage were reversed, that the Church were the Bridegroom and Christ the Bride.

> Now it is surely the case that if all these supposals were ever carried into effect we should be embarked on a different religion. Goddesses have, of course, been worshipped: many religions have had priestesses. But they are religions quite different in character from Christianity. Common sense, disregarding the discomfort, or even the horror, which the idea of turning all our theological language into the feminine gender arouses in most Christians, will ask 'Why not?'

> Since God is in fact not a biological being and has no sex, what can it matter whether we say *He* or *She, Father* or *Mother, Son* or *Daughter?*'

> But Christians think that God Himself has taught us how to speak of Him. To say that it does not matter is to say either that all the masculine imagery is not inspired, is merely human in origin, or else that, though inspired, it is quite arbitrary and unessential. And this is surely intolerable: or, if tolerable, it is an argument not in favor of Christian priestesses but against Christianity. It is also surely based on

---

173 Thus, when James Patrick says Lewis thought the Incarnation is the "'allegory of allegories,'" Patrick gets it completely wrong, for an allegory is a less real thing – it is a copy or a shadow of something higher – while a Myth is something transcendent and real. Patrick, "C. S. Lewis and Idealism," 170. Indeed, "Grammatically, the things we say of Him are 'metaphorical': but in a deeper sense it is our physical and psychic energies that are mere 'metaphors' of the real Life which is God." Lewis, *Miracles*, 1168

a shallow view of imagery.[174]

Furthermore, while it is not wrong for theologians to try to explain the Atonement, Lewis agreed with George Macdonald[175] that such theologians are always on dangerous ground because *how* Christ's death takes away sin is not so important as *that* it does; it is for this reason that while most who read *The Lion, the Witch and the Wardrobe* probably get the impression Lewis is being perfectly Anselmian in regard to Aslan's sacrifice for Edmund, these same people are often surprised when they read Lewis's letters and discover that he wavered unconcernedly between the Anselmian model and the Christus Victor model,[176] the Oxford don regulating the *how* of Christ's death, which is the theological question, as subordinate to the *that* – "the Deep Magic," the mythical, transcendent fact.[177] Similarly, in *The Voyage of the Dawn Treader* when Eustace says a star "is a huge ball of flaming gas," he plays the demythologizing theologian, for he (unlike Schiller of "The Gods of Greece"[178]) fails to understand the mythical nature of a star: "'Even in

174 Lewis, "Priestesses in the Church?" 400-1.

175 "'The sum of all this is that you do not believe in the atonement?' I believe in Jesus Christ. Nowhere am I requested to believe in any thing, or in any statement, but everywhere to believe in God and Jesus Christ." George MacDonald, *Unspoken Sermons: Series I, II, III* (Boston, MA: IndyPublish, n.d.), 304 [3.7].

176 Lewis insisted that Gustaf Aulén's classic work on the Atonement, *Christus Victor*, was something he "liked, but c[oul]d make no use of." Lewis, *The Collected Letters of C. S. Lewis: Volume III*, 980 [October 13, 1958]. Nevertheless, it seems possible that Lewis's lack of enthusiasm for the Anselmian account of the Atonement was in some measure due to Aulén, who wrote: "My work on the history of Christian doctrine has led me to an ever-deepening conviction that the traditional account of the history of the idea of the Atonement [the Anselmian account] is in need of thorough revision." Gustaf Aulén, *Christus Victor: An Historical Study of the Three Main Types of the Idea of Atonement*, trans. A. G. Herbert (1931 reprint; Eugene, OR: Wipf & Stock, 2003), 1. Thus, while in a 1942 letter, Lewis recommended Robert Moberley's *Atonement and Personality*, which defends the Anselmian account, Lewis added that this book "sh[oul]d be corrected by Aulén['s] *Christus Victor* [which] giv[es] a different kind of theory." Lewis, *The Collected Letters of C. S. Lewis: Volume II*, 529 [August 19, 1942]. For more on Lewis's leaning toward the Christus Victor account of the Atonement, see Charles Taliaferro and Rachel Traughber, "The Atonement in Narnia," in *The Chronicles of Narnia and Philosophy: The Lion, the Witch and the Wardrobe*, ed. Gregory Bassham and Jerry L. Walls, 245-59 (Chicago: Open Court, 2005).

177 Lewis, *The Lion, the Witch and the Wardrobe*, 148. Cf. Lewis, *The Collected Letters of C. S. Lewis: Volume II*, 502 [December 21, 1941].

178 In his poem "The Gods of Greece," the romantic philosopher-poet Schiller blamed Christianity for allowing modern science to develop, which in turn reduced the sun to simply a fiery globe instead of something more: "Where lifeless – fixed afar, / A flaming ball to our dull sense is given, / Phoebus Apollo, in his golden car, / In silent glory swept the fields of heaven!" Friedrich von Schiller, "The Gods of Greece," in *The Poems of Schiller* (New York: Dodo Press, 2007), 3.1-4.

your world, my son, that is not what a star is but only what it is made of.'"[179] Finally, when Jesus is called the *Son* of God, this word, according to Lewis, was chosen not so much for anthropomorphic reasons but because it depicts a reality that cannot be better described with any other word: "The theologian will describe it as 'analogical,' drawing our minds at once away from the subtle and sensitive exploitations of imagination and emotion with which poetry works to the clear-cut but clumsy analogies of the lecture-room."[180]

Naturally, none of what has been said is to deny the truth in Negative Theology, which states that all creatures or copies *as* creatures or copies are imperfect and therefore cannot fully grasp Perfection (God), for Lewis was too familiar with Edwyn Bevan's *Symbolism and Belief* and Martin Buber's *I and Thou* to deny the danger in anthropomorphism – the danger of idolatry, making God in our image;[181] as Lewis said in his poem "Footnote to all Prayers":

> He whom I bow to only knows to whom I bow
> When I attempt the ineffable Name, murmuring *Thou*,
> And dream of Pheidian fancies and embrace in heart
> Symbols (I know) which cannot be the thing Thou art.
> . . .
> Worshipping with frail images a folk-lore dream,
> . . .
> And all men are idolators, crying unheard
> To a deaf idol, if Thou take them at their word.
> . . .
> Take not, oh Lord, our literal sense. Lord, in Thy great,
> Unbroken speech our limping metaphor translate.[182]

Nevertheless, Lewis's theory of myth suggests he felt anthropomorphism was far less a danger than agnosticism, which often results from continual abstraction and allegorization: "What a bugbear 'anthropomorphism' used to be! How long it repelled me from the truth! Yet now that one has submitted to it how easy is the burden, how light the yoke. Odd too, that the very things we thought proofs of our humility while we were philosophers, now

---

179 C. S. Lewis, *The Voyage of the Dawn Treader* (1952 reprint; London: Fontana, 1984), 159.

180 Lewis, "The Language of Religion," 262.

181 See Edwyn Bevan, *Symbolism and Belief* (1938 reprint; Boston: Beacon Press, 1957), 313-5. Despite being a book that Lewis recommended to people, *Symbolism and Belief* is in many ways opposed to Lewis's approach to myth, for Bevan believed that prosaic or scientific language is superior to poetic or metaphorical language.

182 C. S. Lewis, "Footnote to all Prayers," in *Poems*, by C. S. Lewis, ed. Walter Hooper (1933 poem reprint; San Diego: Harcout Brace Jovanovich, 1964), 129 [1-4, 6, 11-14].

turn out to be forms of pride."[183]

In many ways, then, myth *qua* an irreducible, profoundly meaningful, concrete universal has much in common with other supra-rational phenomena such as *glossolalia* ("speaking in tongues") or the sacraments, for Myth-*bearing* myth along with tongues and the sacraments are all examples of "transposition," or "the adaptation from a richer to a poorer medium."[184] That is, just as Myth as transposition indicates the mythical reality of God Himself descending into our imaginations, so too does sacrament as transposition point to the Real Presence of God descending in a special way into ordinary human experience. Since this connection between transposition, sacrament and Myth-*bearing* myth is so strong, it should not surprised us that Lewis, despite a lot of imprecision in his vocabulary, came extremely close to speaking of Myth-*bearing* myth as sacramental.[185] Indeed, in one of his last books *Prayer: Letters to Malcolm*, Lewis even called the Holy Communion "magic" and defined it as "'objective efficacy which cannot be further analysed.'"[186] The magical element in the sacrament, like the magical element in myth, is an essential feature and *differentia* of Christianity, and as such serves a unique and important purpose:

> Now the value, for me, of the magical element in Christianity is this. It is a permanent witness that the heavenly realm, certainly no less than the natural universe and perhaps very much more, is a realm of objective facts – hard, determinate facts, not to be constructed *a priori*, and not to be dissolved into maxims, ideals, values, and the like. One cannot conceive a more completely 'given,' or, if you like, a more 'magical,' fact than the existence of God as *causa sui*.[187]

183 Lewis, *The Collected Letters of C. S. Lewis: Volume II*, 189 [April 24, 1936].
184 C. S. Lewis, "Transposition," in *C. S. Lewis: Essay Collection & Other Short Pieces*, ed. Lesley Walmsley (1962 essay reprint; London: HarperCollins, 2000), 271. Cf. "'Transposition' amounts in my view to a theory of imagination, in which imagination is not mentioned." Barfield, *Owen Barfield on C. S. Lewis*, 103.
185 In *The Allegory of Love*, published in 1936, Lewis equated "sacramentalism or symbolism" over and against allegory and he defined the former as "to see the archetype in the copy." Lewis, *The Allegory of Love*, 45. He then went on to give Plato's metaphor of the Sun as a copy of the Good as an example of this. Yet later on, Lewis tightened up his understanding of sacrament and Myth and so discontinued using symbolism as equivalent to sacrament; indeed, in his 1962 essay "Transposition," Lewis explicitly said that sacrament is something *more* than symbolism: speaking about the mythical quality that transcends conventional signs, the Oxford don wrote: "If I had to name the relation I should call it not symbolical but sacramental." Lewis, "Transposition," 272. Cf. Lewis, *The Collected Letters of C. S. Lewis: Volume II*, 438 [August 18, 1940].
186 Lewis, *Prayer: Letters to Malcolm*, 290.
187 Ibid.

Therefore, just as the Neoplatonists go too far in reducing all myths to allegories, and modernists go too far in eliminating gendered and politicized language for God, so too do many misguided theologians attempt to dispense with the "magical" elements in Christianity; however, in doing so, in attempting to be wise, they become fools, for they underestimate the supra-rational:

> Enlightened people want to get rid of this magical element in favour of what they would call the 'spiritual' element. But the spiritual, conceived as something thus antithetical to 'magical,' seems to become merely the psychological or ethical. And neither that by itself, nor the magical by itself, is a religion. I am not going to lay down rules as to the share – quantitatively considered – which the magical should have in anyone's religious life. Individual differences may be permissible. What I insist on is that it can never be reduced to zero. If it is, what remains is only morality, or culture, or philosophy.[188]

In our discussion of Lewis's Christian theory of myth, we have seen that there is a descent of Myth from the mysterious aspect of God Himself, to the Incarnation and finally to revelation and, to a lesser extent, pagan mythology. Yet there is still one aspect of myth left to discuss: myth as non-revelatory literature, as popular romance or epic, and even though this might appear to be more properly discussed in chapter ten, I believe that for the sake of completion and the light it shines on Lewis's philosophical journey, it is better dealt with here.

And so, as we already know from Lewis's idealist days, his approach to myth and literature was "a neo-Aristotelian theory of literature . . . which *inter alia* . . . re-affirm[s] the romantic doctrine of the imagination as a truth-bearing faculty, though not quite as the romantics understood it."[189] Moreover, Lewis's Neoaristotelian theory of the imagination was also "a 'Realistic' theory . . . in the sense of Plato not of Zola."[190] This, of course, is not to say that myth and literature are bad things because they are copies of Reality, but rather that they, like everything else, are good things because they are "designed" and "significant."[191] In addition to the Aristotelian and Platonic elements in Lewis's theory of myth *qua* non-revelatory literature, the

---

188 Ibid.

189 Lewis, *The Collected Letters of C. S. Lewis: Volume III*, 1523 [June 2, 1931].

190 Lewis, *The Collected Letters of C. S. Lewis: Volume II*, 157 [April 5, 1935]. Cf. Carritt, *The Theory of Beauty*, 75.

191 C. S. Lewis and E. M. W. Tillyard, *The Personal Heresy* (1939 reprint; London: Oxford University Press, 1965), 21. Sections of this book were previously published in *Essays and Studies* (1934, 1935, 1936).

Oxford don's theory could also be called Tolkienian, for Lewis – no doubt softened by his Aristotelian understanding of the deliberative imagination and Bergsonian understanding of *homo faber* – largely endorsed Tolkien's belief that the poet or myth-maker is a "sub-creator" to God's "Creator;" the divine image in man, in other words, is not just man's intellect, reason and free will, but also his deliberative imagination; as Tolkien said, "We make in our measure and in our derivative mode, because we are made: and not only made, but made in the image and likeness of a maker."[192] Yet despite all these influences, one should probably just call Lewis's theory of myth *qua* non-revelatory literature Neoplatonic Christian not only because his Aristotelian psychology and approach to invention was absorbed by the Neoplatonists, but also because Tolkien's doctrine of a "sub-creator" was not a new one; indeed, it went back to the Neoplatonists themselves: "[Sidney's] central doctrine, that the poet is a second Creator producing a second Nature, is taken from Scalinger . . . [and] [b]ehind Scalinger, as we have seen, lies Plotinus."[193]

Subsequently, Lewis the Neoplatonic "sub-creator" said there are six essential elements to keep in mind when writing myth: (1) Myth is "extra-literary" – this is the most important aspect as we already know;[194] (2) myth does not depend "on such usual narrative attractions as suspense or surprise;"[195] (3) myth does not elicit the projection of the self into the story[196] (hence it cannot be reduced to Freud's "fantasy"[197]); (4) myth usually deals with the "fantastic"[198] – something which Lewis had always believed (and which he found himself at odds with his friend Charles Williams about, for Williams was interested in romance and myth *qua* ladies, whereas Lewis was interested in myth *qua* gods[199]); (5) myth is usually "grave"[200] (which is why Lewis hated T. H. White's *The Sword in the Stone*[201] and loved *Paradise*

---

192 J. R. R. Tolkien, "On Fairy-Stories," in *The Tolkien Reader* (New York: Ballantine Books, 1975), 55.
193 Lewis, *Poetry and Prose in the Sixteenth Century*, 343.
194 Lewis, *An Experiment in Criticism*, 43.
195 Ibid.
196 Ibid., 44.
197 "But [Freud] makes it clear that we enjoy [art] as a fantasy – that reading, as well as writing, is wish-fulfillment. Indeed it is obvious that he believes all imagining or day-dreaming to be of a single kind – that in which the dreamer pretends that he is a famous man, or a millionaire, or an irresistible lady-killer, while in reality he is no such thing." Lewis, "Psycho-Analysis and Literary Criticism," 287.
198 Lewis, *An Experiment in Criticism*, 44.
199 Lewis, *The Collected Letters of C. S. Lewis: Volume II*, 185 [March 23, 1936].
200 Lewis, *An Experiment in Criticism*, 44.
201 Lewis, *The Collected Letters of C. S. Lewis: Volume II*, 456 [December 11, 1940].

Lost[202]); and (6) myth is "awe-inspiring" as it has to do heavenly desire, in particular, the *numinous*.[203]

In this way, it is not hard to see that most of Lewis's fiction would fall into the category of myth. For example, concerning his *Cosmic Trilogy*, Lewis said that he "like[d] the whole interplanetary idea as a *mythology*."[204] Moreover, the Oxford don explicitly denied that *The Chronicles of Narnia* is an allegory, preferring to label it a "supposition,"[205] which is a mythical story that is full of "truth" but should not be dissected in the search "for a 'point'"[206]: it is a story that says "*suppose* that there were a land like Narnia and that the Son of God, as He became a Man in our world, became a Lion there."[207] And finally, Lewis adamantly maintained that *Till We Have Faces* "isn't allegory," for, he insisted, "I was [just] trying to tell a story;"[208] and indeed the story that Lewis was trying to tell was, interestingly, a reinterpretation of the Psyche and Cupid *myth*.

In addition to all this, we ought to keep in mind that Lewis's theory of mythical literature was heavily influenced by Tolkien's essay "On Fairy-Stories," in which Tolkien listed three key elements in the Christian construction of myth and fantasy: (1) Recovery, which has to do with recovering "a clear view" of creation, (2) Escape, which has to do with escaping *from* the prison of worldly concepts *to* a place which portrays the world as it ought to be, and (3) Consolation, which has to do with happy endings on account of the Real Happy Ending being secured by the victory of the True Myth, Christ.[209] Lewis, of course, agreed with Tolkien's list, and indeed took Tolkien's idea of recovering a clear view of creation in myth-making to a new level when he

202 C. S. Lewis, *A Preface to Paradise Lost* (1942 reprint; Oxford: Oxford University Press, 1969), 17.
203 Lewis, *An Experiment in Criticism*, 44.
204 Lewis, *The Collected Letters of C. S. Lewis: Volume II*, 236 [December 28, 1938]. Cf. Lewis, *The Collected Letters of C. S. Lewis: Volume III*, 87 [January 14, 1951]. Also, in the introduction to *Perelandra*, Lewis wrote: "This story can be read by itself but is also a sequel to *Out of the Silent Planet* in which some account was given of Ransom's adventures on Mars – or, as its inhabitants call it, *Malacandra*. All the human characters in this book are purely fictitious and *none of them is allegorical*."
205 Speaking of Narnia and *Perelandra*, Lewis said: "This is not an allegory at all. . . . This also works out a *supposition*. . . . Allegory and such supposals differ because they mix the real and the unreal in different ways." Lewis, *The Collected Letters of C. S. Lewis: Volume III*, 1004 [December 29, 1958].
206 Ibid., 388 [December 18, 1953].
207 C. S. Lewis, *Letters to Children*, by C. S. Lewis, ed. Lyle W. Dorsett and Marjorie Lamp Mead (New York: Simon & Schuster, 1995), 45 [May 29, 1954]. Cf. Lewis, *The Collected Letters of C. S. Lewis: Volume III*, 1113 [December 24, 1959].
208 Lewis, *The Collected Letters of C. S. Lewis: Volume III*, 1090 [September 24, 1959].
209 Tolkien, "On Fairy-Stories," 55-70.

claimed that such an activity is a philosophical *askēsis*. Concerning a boy who reads fairy-tales, Lewis wrote:

> Does anyone suppose that he really and prosaically longs for all the dangers and discomforts of a fairy tale? – really wants dragons in contemporary England? It is not so. It would be much truer to say that fairy land arouses a longing for he knows not what. It stirs and troubles him (to his life-long enrichment) with the dim sense of something beyond his reach and, far from dulling or emptying the actual world, gives it a new dimension of depth. He does not despise real woods because he has read of enchanted woods: this reading makes all real woods a little enchanted. . . . [Now] there are two kinds of longing. The one is an *askēsis*, a spiritual exercise, and the other is a disease [Freudian wish-fulfillment].[210]

Thus, Tolkien's "Recovery," which Lewis the absolute idealist called "the highest form of the spiritual life"[211] and Lewis the Christian called "The Beatrician Experience" (in honor of Charles Williams and Dante[212]), is a

210 Lewis, "On Three Ways of Writing for Children," 511. Cf. "The true exercise of the imagination, in my view, is (a) To help us to understand other people (b) To respond to, and, some of us, to produce, art. But it has also a bad use: to provide for us, in a shadowy form, a substitute for virtues, successes, distinctions etc. which ought to be sought *outside* in the real world – e.g. picturing all I'd do if I were rich instead of earning and saving. Masturbation involves this abuse of imagination in erotic matters." Lewis, *The Collected Letters of C. S. Lewis: Volume III*, 759 [June 3, 1956].

211 Concerning the highest form of the spiritual life (which we will discuss in chapter eight), Lewis the absolute idealist wrote: "Others feel that what seemed dead things are charged with life, and people the hills and trees with vague personality: nor are they wrong, for we share the life of the Spirit which knows itself alive beneath all its vesture. But all alike know that such moments are our highest life. For their continuation would be the redemption of the world. . . . This highest form of the spiritual life I call imagination." Lewis, *Clivi Hamiltonis Summae Metaphysices Contra Anthroposophos Libri II*, 51.

212 "The Beatrician experience may be defined as the recovery (in respect to one human being) of that vision of reality which would have been common to all men in respect to all things if Man had never fallen. . . . The lover sees the Lady as the Adam saw all things before they foolishly chose to experience good as evil. . . . [In] the Beatrician experience . . . the glory is temporary. . . . But a transitory vision is not necessarily a vision of the transitory. . . . It has in fact been a glimpse of what is eternally real. The phenomenal Beatrice – Beatrice as she is in this fallen world – has for an instant been identical with the real Beatrice – Beatrice as she (and all things) will be seen to be, and always to have been, when we reach the throne-room at Byzantium. The precise moment at which the phenomenal Beatrice loses her identity with the real one is a repetition of the Fall, as Palomides discovers in a later poem when 'division stretched between / The Queen's identity and the Queen.'" C. S. Lewis, *The Arthurian Torso: Containing the Posthumous Fragment of 'The Figure of Arthur' by Charles Williams and a Commentary on the Arthurian Poems of Charles Williams* (1948 reprint; London: Oxford

spiritual exercise that fosters heavenly desire in individuals when they meditate on Myth through myth and mythmaking. The result of this meditation is that individuals – indeed, philosophers, *pace* Richard Dawkins[213] – bring a bit of Heaven to Earth, which in turn transforms the Earth and helps the individuals to see it as it is, as a place alive with spiritual energy and divine concern:

> 'But why,' (some ask), 'why, if you have a serious comment to make on the real life of men, must you do it by talking about a phantasmagoric never-never land of your own?' Because, I take it, one of the main things the author wants to say is that the real life of men is of that mythical and heroic quality. . . . Imagined beings have their insides on the outside; they are visible souls. And Man as whole, Man pitted against the universe, have we seen him at all till we see that he is like a hero in a fairy tale? In the book Eomer rashly contrasts 'the green earth' with 'legends.' Aragorn replies that the green earth itself is 'a mighty matter of legend.' . . . The value of myth is that it takes all the things we know and restores to them the rich significance which has been hidden by 'the veil of familiarity.' The child enjoys his cold meat (otherwise dull to him) by pretending it is buffalo, just killed with his own bow and arrow. And the child is wise. The real meat comes back to him more savoury for having been dipped in a story; you might say that only then it is the real meat. If you are tired of the landscape, look at it in a mirror. By putting bread, gold, horse, apple, or the very roads into a myth, we do not retreat from reality: we rediscover it.[214]

What, therefore, would Lewis and Tolkien say to the charge of escapism? How would they answer modernist intellectuals and Freudian "Jailors," who say lovers of myth are "escapists" or "wishful-fillers?"[215] How did John

---

University Press, 1952), 116-7.

213 Richard Dawkins begins *The God Delusion* by saying: "Isn't it enough to see that a garden is beautiful without having to believe that there are fairies at the bottom of it too?" Richard Dawkins, *The God Delusion* (New York: Houghton Mifflin, 2006). While Lewis may or may not have believed in fairies, he certainly thought that because belief in the supernatural is the most rational belief, the inability to see, or attempt to see through the imagination, the supernatural was an impoverishment.

214 C. S. Lewis, "Tolkien's *The Lord of the Rings*," in *C. S. Lewis: Essay Collection & Other Short Pieces*, ed. Lesley Walmsley (1954 and 1955 essay reprint; London: HarperCollins, 2000), 524-5.

215 "Our Jailor (well he may) prefers / Our thoughts should keep a narrower range. / 'The proper study of prisoners / Is prison,' he tells us. Is it strange? / And if old freedom in our glance / Betrays itself, he calls it names / 'Dope' – 'Wishful thinking' – or 'Romance,' / Till tireless propaganda tames. / All but the strong whose hearts they break, / All but the few whose faith is whole. / Stone walls cannot a prison make / Half so secure as rigmarole." C. S. Lewis, "The Prudent Jailor," in *Poems*, by C. S. Lewis, ed.

answer Mr. Humanist, who annoyingly asked, "'Do you take me for an escapist?'"[216] The answer is simple: it is not a question of escape being good or bad in itself, so much as what a person escapes *to*, for if people were made for Heaven and if myths are true copies of heavenly Myths,[217] which beckon people through heavenly desire, then the sanest man in the world, indeed, the true philosopher, is he who practices "thoughtful wishing"[218]:

> Finally, what shall we say about the stigma of 'escapism'? . . . Now there is a sense in which all reading whatever is an escape. . . . All such escape is *from* the same thing; immediate, concrete actuality. The important question is what we escape *to*. . . . Escape, then, is common to many good and bad kinds of reading. By adding *–ism* to it, we suggest, I suppose, a confirmed habit of escaping too often, or for too long, or into the wrong things, or using escape as a substitute for action where action is appropriate, and thus neglecting real opportunities and evading real obligations. If so, we must judge each case on its merits. Escape is not necessarily joined to escapism. The authors who lead us furthest into impossible regions – Sidney, Spenser, and Morris – were men active and stirring in the real world. The Renaissance and our own nineteenth century, periods prolific in literary fantasy, were periods of great energy. . . . Since the charge of escapism against a very unrealistic work is sometimes varied or reinforced with that of childishness. . . . Two points need to be made. . . . Most of the

Walter Hooper (1947 poem reprint; San Diego: Harcourt Brace Jovanovich, 1964), 77 [13-24]. Cf. "That is perhaps why people are so ready with the charge of 'escape.' I never fully understood it till my friend Professor Tolkien asked me the very simple question, 'What class of men would you expect to be preoccupied with, and most hostile to, the idea of escape?' and gave the obvious answer: jailers. The charge of Fascism is, to be sure, mere mud-slinging. Fascists, as well as Communists, are jailers; both would assure us that the proper study of prisoners is prison." C. S. Lewis, "On Science Fiction," in *C. S. Lewis: Essay Collection & Other Short Pieces*, ed. Lesley Walmsley (1955 essay reprint; London: HarperCollins, 2000), 456.

216 Lewis, *The Pilgrim's Regress*, 113.

217 It probably goes without saying that Lewis really believed that even in sub-created myths, the image of Myth is still present. In this way, he is like St. Basil, who said "honour rendered to the image passes to the prototype," for Lewis said that Mark in *That Hideous Strength* refused to trample on, and insult, a large crucifix because "to insult even a carved image of such agony seemed an abominable act." Lewis, *That Hideous Strength*, 701. Basil *Concerning the Holy Spirit* 18.45.

218 Lewis, preface to the 1950 edition of *Dymer*, 4. Cf. "I wonder do we blame T.V. and the Comics too much? Was not a certain sort of boy in a certain sort of home wasting his time just as badly in other ways before they were invented? It annoys me when parents who read nothing but the newspapers themselves – i.e. nothing but lies, libels, poppycock, propaganda, and pornography – complain of their children reading Comics! Upon my soul I think the children's diet is healthier than their parents." Lewis, *The Collected Letters of C. S. Lewis: Volume III*, 1178 [August 18, 1960].

great fantasies and fairy-tales were not addressed to children at all, but to everyone. . . . Secondly, if we are to use the words *childish* or *infantile* as terms of disapproval, we must make sure that they refer only to those characteristics of childhood which we become better and happier by outgrowing; not to those which every sane man would keep if he could and which some are fortunate for keeping.[219]

As we have seen throughout this chapter, myths – "gleams of celestial strength and beauty"[220] – played an extremely important role in Lewis's philosophical journey. Initially, as we know, Lewis the narrow rationalist reduced all myths to fun, but ultimately, valueless, stories. However, over time, Lewis's rationalism widened, allowing him to see that certain myths reflect, and subsequently give our minds special knowledge or revelation about, God's wider nature; nevertheless, Lewis was no mystic, for he insisted that reason is able to declare some myths false insofar as they contradict other aspects about God, such as His moral nature, and is able to declare other myths as being potentially true reflections of God on account of various factors; thus, while the majority of mythical images are supra-rational to the human mind (meaning that they cannot be reduced to other concepts), they are perfectly rational to Logos Himself.

In addition to this, we have also seen that Lewis viewed myth-making as an important spiritual exercise; indeed, one that the true philosopher ought not to neglect. Consequently, having examined the rational, affective and supra-rational aspects of Lewis's philosophical journey, all that remains to be discussed in regard to the Oxford don's philosophical journey, and subsequent identity as a philosopher, is his cultural identity, for we recall that philosophy as a way of life assumes that every philosophical discourse takes place in some cultural context.

---

219 Lewis, *An Experiment in Criticism*, 68, 69, 70, 71. Cf. "We have had enough, once and for all, of Hedonism – the gloomy philosophy which says that Pleasure is the only good. But we have hardly yet begun what may be called *Hedonics*, the science or philosophy of Pleasure. . . . [The realist jailor] accuses all myth and fantasy and romance or wishful thinking: the way to silence him is to be more realist than he – to lay our ears closer to the murmur of life as it actually flows through us at every moment and to discover there all that quivering and wonder and (in a sense) infinity which the literature that he calls realistic omits. For the story which gives us the experiences most like the experiences of living is not necessarily the story whose events are most like those in a biography or a newspaper." C. S. Lewis, "Hedonics," in *C. S. Lewis: Essay Collection & Other Short Pieces*, ed. Lesley Walmsley (1945 essay reprint; London: HarperCollins, 2000), 688.
220 Lewis, *Perelandra*, 328.

Chapter Five

Culture

Over the course of the past four chapters, we have seen that throughout his philosophical journey, Lewis was a man who became increasingly more devoted to Truth. Indeed, it was because of the Oxford don's love of Truth that he came to see that heavenly desire was more than an aesthetic experience and that mythical instances point to supra-rational Reality. Moreover, Lewis's rational beliefs were not merely theoretical, for out of them flowed a number of different spiritual exercises, such as prayer, chapel attendance and myth-making, all of which were set in place for the explicit purpose of putting into practice what he believed. The result of this, then, was a life that was remarkably holistic; indeed, as we have seen, Lewis's life is best understood as a modern representation of the ancient understanding of philosophy: philosophy as a way of life.

Nevertheless, there is one element in philosophy-as-a-way-of-life which I have thus far neglected: culture. As we saw in chapter one, every choice to follow reason and a given philosophy is a choice made in a particular cultural context. Of course to say this is not to nullify the power of reason to critique culture; in fact, the true philosopher is precisely the man whose mind is so awake that he, following the Oracle's edict to "know thyself," can turn his rational gaze onto his own particular context. Nonetheless, one cannot deny that culture is an important factor in philosophy, for it provides the philosopher with – for better or for worse – a unique experience-set with which he has to grapple.

And Lewis was no different. He was a straight, white, middle-class, Irish, Anglican, Oxford don, who was unmarried for most of his life, traveled little, had almost no interest in public policy and shunned technological advances. However, to Lewis's credit as a philosopher, he was remarkably self-aware; indeed, it is for this reason that after more than fifty years of self, and cultural, analysis, he came to identify himself as "an Old Western

Man."[1] Consequently, I believe that by engaging with this concept of an Old Western Man, we will find the final component needed to complete our overview of Lewis's philosophical journey and identity.

However, in order to even begin to engage this concept, two things must be established. First, I need to demonstrate that despite the Oxford don's romanticizing tendencies, which some people might think is at the root of his self-identification as an Old Western Man, he was historically-sensitive and valued cultural particulars. Second, I need to show why Lewis thought generalizations, such as that of an Old Western Man, were justified in even being used at all. Once these preliminary issues have been dealt with, then I will be in a position to discuss Lewis's cultural identity – that of an Old Western Man – vis-à-vis a combination of the Oxford don's own writings and a study of the cultural movements of his day.

I: Concerning Particulars

For many with an appreciation for history, the first thing that comes to mind when they hear Lewis refer to himself as an Old Western Man is that he was a deluded, romantic prisoner to the past, for how, they ask, could the Oxford don be so historically irresponsible by speaking in such broad cultural generalizations? Indeed, they insist, it is hard enough to say what an American or a Canadian is, much less a person who presumably spans a period of two thousand years dwelling in over twenty countries and speaking even more languages.

Yet while there is some truth in this reaction, it is largely unwarranted, and indeed, dispelled by the facts.

First of all, we must remember that it was not Lewis the Christian who was insensitive to the particulars of time, but rather Lewis the Stoical materialist, for it was he, like many fashionable academics in the 1920s, who exercised "chronological snobbery" towards the Middle Ages, believing that philosophy jumped from antiquity to the Enlightenment, skipping a thousand years of medieval philosophy in between; indeed, Lewis's "Greats" philosophy, which was largely the product of First Humanism,[2] emphasized

---

1   C. S. Lewis, *"De Descriptione Temporum,"* in *Selected Literary Essays*, by C. S. Lewis, ed. Walter Hooper (1955 essay reprint; Cambridge: Cambridge University Press, 1969), 14. Also see Adam Barkman, "C. S. Lewis and the Concept of an 'Old Western Man,'" *Inklings-Jahrbuch für Literatur und Ästhetik* 25 (2007): 253-68.

2   Although it is debatable, many believe that there are three distinct humanisms which developed over the years: First Humanism, which is what Lewis understood by Humanism, began with Erasmus during the Renaissance; Second Humanism began with Goethe in the eighteenth century; and Third Humanism began with Werner

just this:

> At this time the name of St. Thomas was scarcely known in Oxford. His philosophy was not studied in any of the schools and he had no place in the curriculum. Even the *Metaphysics* of Aristotle was scarcely known to the ordinary student. In Greats the *Ethics* was studied but not the *Metaphysics* and as a result the whole of the system of philosophy which had been the foundation of the studies of medieval Oxford was practically unknown. We were still living by the light of that Renaissance humanism, to which Cicero was of more importance than St. Thomas and Descartes of more value than St. Augustine.[3]

Yet as we recall, Barfield showed Lewis the value of all time periods, and another friend, Alfred Jenkin, taught the Oxford don to relish the "quiddity of each thing."[4]

Second of all, as a trained historian and renowned medieval scholar, not to mention a lover of dialectic and a man whose favorite word was "*distinguo*," Lewis constantly stressed the importance of cultural and historical particulars. For instance, in *The Discarded Image*, he criticized the "astonishing failure or refusal" of medieval man "to distinguish – in practice, though not always in theory – between books of different sorts;"[5] and in *Poetry and Prose in the Sixteenth Century*, he reminded us that "the ancients were not ancient, nor the men of the Middle Ages middle, from their point of view;"[6] and finally, in an unpublished essay entitled "On Bolshevism," he reinforced the significance of *differentia*, writing:

> A Pagan contemporary of S[t]. Paul or of S[t]. Augustine must have been surprised when he first looked into Christian writings and the

---

Jaeger in the nineteenth century.

3   Dom Bede Griffiths, *The Golden String: An Autobiography* (1954 reprint; London: Fount Paperbacks, 1979), 62.

4   Lewis, *Surprised by Joy*, 1359. When Lewis became a subjective idealist, he was certainly aware that Berkeley denied the existence of universals: "The greatest source of error," wrote Lewis, summarizing Berkeley, "is the belief that the mind 'hath a power of framing abstract ideas or notions of things.' I find I have no such power. I can have no idea of colour, only of particular colours: no idea of Man, only of particular men." Lewis, "The Moral Good – Its Place Among the Values," 31. Nevertheless, as we shall see, the best evidence suggests that Lewis the subjective idealist still rejected Berkeley's nominalism.

5   Lewis, *The Discarded Image*, 31.

6   Lewis, *Poetry and Prose in the Sixteenth Century*, 55. Cf. "The central fact: medieval man did not care about being medieval." C. S. Lewis, underlining in his edition of *St. Thomas Aquinas*, by G. K. Chesterton (N.p.: n.p., 1933; The Marion E. Wade Center, Wheaton College), 129.

extent to which these authors are pre-occupied with polemics, not against Paganism, but against other sects of Christianity. He would have learned with amazement that a group of cognate movements which he had hitherto classed together was involved in violent internal dissension. He would have realized, for the first time, the eagerness of the orthodox teachers not only to establish their doctrine as against prevalent philosophies of ancient civilisation but also to distinguish it and disentangle it as clearly as possible from all those other doctrines which bore a superficial resemblance to it. . . . It is natural for a movement to wish to be itself and no difference is too small for men who believe that vital principles are involved.[7]

Thus, as a lover of dissimilarity, Lewis went on famously to claim that the Renaissance – that great historical generalization – for instance, never even occurred, saying in one place, "My hope is to kill some popular mythology about that fabulous monster called 'the Renaissance,'"[8] and in another, "My line is to *define* the Renaissance as 'an imaginary entity responsible for anything a modern writer happens to approve in the Fifteenth or Sixteenth Century.'"[9] Of course, while this claim was fairly radical for its time, it was not something wholly original, for in his edition of Chesterton's *St. Thomas Aquinas*, Lewis underlined the following: "the Renaissance might be called the Relapse."[10]

As a result of all this, it ought to be apparent that Lewis felt all cultural and historical generalizations falsify to some degree. Consequently, he recommended that people "clean the lens and remove the stain" from their

7   C. S. Lewis, "On Bolshevism," in "The Moral Good – Its Place Among the Values" (Lecture notes [1920-1925?]; The Marion E. Wade Center, Wheaton College), 66, 67. For some reason, "On Bolshevism" is found, preceded by a considerable amount of poetry, at the back of the manuscript containing Lewis's "The Moral Good – Its Place Among the Values." While we do not know when this essay was written, it could have been written somewhere around 1924-1925 since that is when the other documents in the folio were composed. We know that as late as 1939 Lewis taught his political science students about Lenin, who this essay is about; however, internal evidence suggests that this essay was written by a neophyte, which, if this is the case, would mean that it was likely written by Lewis when he was a student in "Greats" – thus, somewhere between 1920-1922. Cf. "I studied history at Magdalen from 1935 to 1938. Lewis taught, not only the students of English, but also the historians, students of political science – Aristotle to Lenin, more or less all the way." W. R. Fryer, "Disappointment at Cambridge?" in *In Search of C. S. Lewis*, ed. Stephen Schofield, 29-35 (South Plainfield, NJ: Bridge, 1983), 29.

8   Lewis, *The Collected Letters of C. S. Lewis: Volume III*, 158 [January 10, 1952].

9   Lewis, *The Collected Letters of C. S. Lewis: Volume II*, 475 [March 28, 1941]. Cf. Lewis, *Poetry and Prose in the Sixteenth Century*, 55.

10   Lewis, underlining in his edition of *St. Thomas Aquinas*, 41.

modern perspectives "so that the real past can be seen better."[11] Naturally,
the result of this *spiritual exercise* is that people can see that the real past
is not something that they create – though of course it is impossible for
them to completely put themselves in the shoes of their fathers[12] – rather, the
past is a mixture of things people are comfortable with and things they are
uncomfortable with, things people like and things they dislike, things people
value and things they disvalue. For this reason, while Lewis praised many
particular qualities of the past, claiming, for instance, "I like the *Bacchae*
because it's exciting, not because it is – loathsome word! – 'cultured,'"[13] he
was also not afraid of critiquing the past. For instance, he said that Plato's
"tittering" about homosexuality was a blindness that belonged to the Greeks,
and Aristotle's concept of magnanimity was nothing more than pride;[14]
he believed that John Calvin emphasized the Fall too much,[15] and Hooker
did not emphasize it enough;[16] he thought Dante was inclined to hatred,
William Shakespeare to "the ethical tomfoolery of honour and revenge," and
Homer to barbarity;[17] he insisted that the medieval model of the universe was
false in its totality, and pagan mythology was not identical with Christian
revelation.[18] In other words, if one looks close enough, one finds not only

11   C. S. Lewis, "*De Audiendis Poetis*," in *Studies in Medieval and Renaissance Literature*, by
     C. S. Lewis, ed. Walter Hooper (1966 essay reprint; Cambridge: Cambridge University
     Press, 1998), 2.
12   Ibid.
13   Lewis, *The Collected Letters of C. S. Lewis: Volume III*, 721 [March 20, 1956].
14   "Those loved authors, so civilised, tolerant, humane, and enlightened, every now and
     then reveal that they are divided from us by a gulf. Hence the eternal, roguish tittering
     about pederasty in Plato or the hard pride that makes Aristotle's *Ethics* in places almost
     comic." C. S. Lewis, "The Psalms," in *C. S. Lewis: Essay Collection & Other Short
     Pieces*, ed. Lesley Walmsley (1958 essay reprint; London: HarperCollins, 2000), 220.
     Cf. "Self-renunciation is thought to be, and indeed is, very near the core of Christian
     ethics. When Aristotle writes in praise of a certain kind of self-love, we may feel, despite
     the careful distinctions which he draws between the legitimate and the illegitimate
     Philautia, that here we strike something essentially sub-Christian [*N.E.* bk 9, ch. 8]."
     C. S. Lewis, "Two Ways with the Self," in *C. S. Lewis: Essay Collection & Other Short
     Pieces*, ed. Lesley Walmsley (1940 essay reprint; London: HarperCollins, 2000), 297.
15   C. S. Lewis, "The Poison of Subjectivism," in *C. S. Lewis: Essay Collection & Other Short
     Pieces*, ed. Lesley Walmsley (1943 essay reprint; London: HarperCollins, 2000), 663.
16   "In reading Hooker we are reminded sometimes of Tyndale, often of Traherne's
     Centuries. Sometimes a suspicion crosses our mind that the doctrine of the Fall did
     not loom quite large enough in his universe." Lewis, *Poetry and Prose in the Sixteenth
     Century*, 461.
17   Concerning the flaws of Spenser, Lewis wrote: "But they must be set beside the
     barbarity of Homer, the hatreds of Dante, the pride of Milton – and perhaps we may
     add, Shakespeare's apparently contented acquiescence in the ethical tomfoolery of
     honour and revenge." Lewis, *The Allegory of Love*, 357.
18   Lewis, *The Discarded Image*, 216.

that Lewis could "Enjoy" the past and delight in its quiddity, but he could also "Contemplate" it and critique its flaws.

Nevertheless, one might still claim that Lewis was culturally and historically insensitive by pointing out that the Oxford don's writings (not to mention his readings) bespeak a romanticizing tendency to pave over cultural and historical *differentia*, a tendency which indicates a retreat into the past – possible as a result of his alleged defeat at the hands of Anscombe. In reply, I suggest we need to keep two things in mind.

First, Lewis never denied he was influenced by, nay, he spoke approvingly of, the medievalism and romanticized classicism of men like Morris, Spenser and Tolkien. But unlike most historians, Lewis was also a philosopher; consequently, as we discussed in the previous chapter, he was more than willing to provide rational justification for his interest in medievalism and romanticized classicism.

That is, Lewis said that history is valuable not only for its assistance in avoiding the mistakes of the past and contextualizing the Spirit of the Age,[19] but also, indeed, more so, for its *latent mythical qualities*, which need to be abstracted by the intellect and then transformed by the deliberative imagination into myths and stories that point to a Reality greater than history; indeed, this process of abstraction and creation ties directly into the spiritual exercise of myth-making which we discussed in chapter four. Moreover, it also reinforces the Neoaristotelian elements in Lewis's literary theory, for it shows that Lewis agreed with Aristotle that poetry, which exhibits universals, is superior to history, which merely demonstrates particulars (though Lewis would add that the universals exhibited in poetry are *concrete* universals, as we have already discussed).[20] The medievalism and classicism found in myth, therefore, are not antithetical to the real history of the Middle Ages and antiquity, but rather are the mythical dust in these time periods, which only the poet can see;[21] consequently, to desire the abolition of medievalism

---

19   Lewis, "*De Descriptione Temporum*," 12.

20   Aristotle *Poetics* 1451b.5-7. Cf. Lewis, *Poetry and Prose in the Sixteenth Century*, 319-20.

21   Concerning William Morris, Lewis wrote: "Still less does he understand the Christian and sacramental view of such things [love]. He is the most irreligious of all our poets – *anima naturaliter pagana*. . . . To see this is, of course, to see that his medievalism is a kind of accident. The real interests of the Middle Ages – Christian mysticism, Aristotelian philosophy, Courtly Love – mean nothing to him. . . . Morris chose to build up his imaginary world on hints furnished by the Middle and Dark Ages as these existed in the imagination of his own time and his own circle in particular. With that circle he doubtless shared many historical errors. But his choice was poetically right simply because that misconception of the Middle Ages (for reasons which go far back

or romanticized classicism is, in some small measure, to revile Reality itself. Speaking of his early childhood readings of Homer and making reference to the Tolkienian theory of myth, which we examined in the previous chapter, Lewis said,

> Of course my appreciation was very romanticized – the appreciation of a boy soaked in William Morris. But this slight error saved me from that far deeper error of 'classicism' with which the Humanists have hoodwinked half the world. I cannot therefore deeply regret the days when I called Circe a 'wise-wife' and every marriage a 'high-tide.' That has all burned itself out and left no snuff, and I can now enjoy the *Odyssey* in a maturer way. The wanderings mean as much as ever they did; the great moment of 'eucatastrophe' (as Professor Tolkien would call it) when Odysseus strips off his rags and bends the bow, means more.[22]

Hence, it is clear Lewis had little sympathy for either "pure" historians, who, to use a contemporary example, dislike *Braveheart* because the Battle of Stirling was fought on a field instead of on a bridge, or Humanists, whose classicism and love for antiquity resulted in both a hatred of anything medieval – be it historical or imaginative – and a false equivocation (à la Mr. Humanist[23]) between heavenly desire and the desire for the halcyon days of yore: "I am," wrote Lewis, "solidly anti-Humanist: i.e. tho[ugh] I love the classics I loathe classicism."[24] This, of course, explains Lewis's often-questioned hostility towards "the Humanist prison"[25] of men like Desiderius Erasmus, who "would forbid a young prince to read 'Arthurs and Lancelots,'"[26] and T. S. Eliot, whose "constant profession of humanism and his claim to be a 'classicist' may not be consciously insincere, but they are erroneous. . . . He shows no love of any disciplined and magnanimous writer save Dante. Of Homer, Sophocles, Virgil . . . he has nothing to say."[27] Nevertheless, none of what has been said is to affirm that medievalism and romanticized classicism are history *qua* fact: they are not; and it is the duty of every historian, Lewis

into the time of Percy and the Wartons) already existed, and existed poetically, in the public imagination. It was, and to some extent still is, part of our mythology." C. S. Lewis, "William Morris," in *Selected Literary Essays*, by C. S. Lewis, ed. Walter Hooper (1937 essay reprint; Cambridge: Cambridge University Press, 1969), 223.

22 Lewis, *Surprised by Joy*, 1327.

23 Lewis, *The Pilgrim's Regress*, 9, 109-14.

24 Lewis, *The Collected Letters of C. S. Lewis: Volume III*, 498 [July 30, 1954].

25 C. S. Lewis, "Addison," in *Selected Literary Essays*, by C. S. Lewis, ed. Walter Hooper (1945 essay reprint; Cambridge: Cambridge University Press, 1969), 164.

26 Lewis, *Poetry and Prose in the Sixteenth Century*, 29.

27 Lewis, *The Collected Letters of C. S. Lewis: Volume II*, 163 [May 23, 1935].

himself insisted, to point this out: "The real temper of those ages was not romantic. The Arthurian stories represent, perhaps, a truancy or escape from habitual concerns. . . . Characteristically, medieval man was not a dreamer nor a spiritual adventurer; he was an organizer, a codifer, a man of system."[28]

Second, apart from the spiritual exercise inherent in medievalism and romanticized classicism, it is unconvincing to say Lewis had an unhealthy attachment to the past – that he saw the past as a place of comfort and escape *from* the harsh reality of analytic philosophy that had, for a time, un-sworded him. As a man who understood philosophy to be a way of life, Lewis – at least the mature Lewis – was no such coward, for he believed that heavenly desire is a desire for *God* and self-realization, not for the earthly past. Indeed, as a careful reader of Dante, Lewis knew that in the *Inferno* it is the lost souls, not the saved ones, who are constantly looking to the past.[29] Lewis himself took this to be a profound theological and psychological truth and made it one of the themes in *The Great Divorce*, wherein we read of a theologian who preferred to search the past for answers about God instead of embracing His present Reality in Heaven, and a husband who preferred his life on Earth with his wife to the prospect of loving God first in Heaven.[30] In other words, Lewis thought that when heavenly desire is transformed by the theological virtue of hope, the Christian becomes the ultimate lover of the *future* who, at the same time, still finds great value in the past in order to transform the *present*.

Thus, it ought to be clear that Lewis not only appreciated the particularities of culture and history but also was far from being an escapist in the negative sense of the word when reading and writing romanticized history. Nonetheless, it remains to be demonstrated that Lewis was justified in speaking of cultural and historical generalizations.

II: Concerning Generalizations

Although Lewis the subjective idealist ought to have followed Berkeley in denying the existence of universals, the Oxford don did not do so. Indeed, in his 1924 "Provisional Critique of Berkeley," the Oxford don expressed his

---

28   C. S. Lewis, "Imagination and Thought in the Middle Ages," in *Studies in Medieval and Renaissance Literature*, by C. S. Lewis, ed. Walter Hooper (Cambridge: Cambridge University Press, 1998), 44. Cf. "The real musician is similarly troublesome to a man who wishes to indulge in untaught 'musical appreciation;' the real historian is similarly a nuisance when we want to romance about 'the olden days' or 'the ancient Greeks and Romans.'" Lewis, *Miracles*, 1161-2.

29   Lewis, *The Collected Letters of C. S. Lewis: Volume III*, 1274 [June 5, 1961].

30   Lewis, *The Great Divorce*, 1047, 1084.

doubts about Berkeley's nominalism, saying,

> According to Berkeley a particular idea becomes general by being made
> to stand for all others 'of the same sort.' Now if we know that it stands
> not for any ideas whatsoever but for ideas 'of the same sort,' we must
> admit that there are ideas of the same sort and that we know which
> they are. This implies that we can perceive the (relevant) similarities
> between them: which must mean some common quality = a universal.
> Berkeley says that in geometry we have only the idea of 'this Δ' and we
> make it universal by using in the proof nothing which is <u>peculiar</u> to 'this
> Δ.' But, in order to do so, we must know that there <u>are</u> some properties
> of this Δ which we may use in the proof and others which we may not:
> that is, we must know that there are some properties peculiar to this
> Δ, and some others common to all Δs. But these common qualities are
> just the universal. Berkeley's difficulty depends on his contention that
> we have no 'idea' of a Δ which is not particular: and by idea he means
> 'picture.' And it is certainly true that we have no 'picture' of Colour,
> Humanity or Triangularity. But, whether we can explain it or not, we
> must have <u>concepts</u> of them, for, as a matter of fact, we use them.[31]

From this critique, we can see that Lewis was convinced not only that
universals are absolutely necessary for the explanation of such obvious
universal objects as numbers and logical truths, but also for nearly[32]
everything else since similarity is actually identity, and identity presupposes
universals, which, according to him, are those things which have existence in,
and also independent of, their particular exemplifications: "Nothing except
a universal can be common to different particulars. . . . We could not attend
to such common elements or universals if they were not there."[33] That is, the

---

31 "The Provisional Critique of Berkeley" is part of Lewis, "The Moral Good – Its Place
Among the Values," 37.

32 Despite having been written when Lewis just converted to idealism, Lewis's essay
"The Whole" indicates that the Oxford don was willing to admit that nominalism
can explain a few things: "Now the problem which essence is introduced to answer
is the problem of hypothetical judgment. Some of the uses of essence are otiose and
may be disregarded. Thus for the centaur, whom I mentioned a minute or two ago, a
nominalistic explanation will suffice." Lewis, "The Whole," 110.

33 Lewis, "The Moral Good – Its Place Among the Values," 37. 26. It should be noted that
Lewis's realist argument for universals is primarily directed against the nominalism
of Berkeley and not against any other formulation, such as William of Ockham's or
Jean Buridan's (despite being well-read in medieval literature, Lewis was poorly read in
medieval scholastic philosophy). Berkeley's nominalism is grounded in his anti-realist
epistemology, which maintains that since God presents everyone with direct perceptions
of particular things, there is no reason to postulate universals in terms of *real* things
– i.e. not merely terms or concepts – independent of particular exemplifications. Lewis's
argument is that even if anti-realist epistemology is true, people still need universals to

Oxford don believed that when we speak of metaphysical participation or unity-in-likeness, it follows that this unity must be a real, ontological unity and not merely a linguistic or conceptual one; for example, while Peter and Paul are two particular men – each with their own quiddity (i.e. Peter-ness and Paul-ness) – they are also identical, and not merely similar, to each other *qua* their natures as men[34]: if this were not the case, Lewis the Platonist felt,[35] then we would not be able to recognize the nature of each man as a man (and hence be "left with a chaos of absolutely unrelateable ideas"[36]). Furthermore, the Oxford don believed that any similarity we can think, or speak, of, be it metaphor or, *pace* Aquinas, analogy, must have some univocity (i.e. actual identity), or else it would be impossible to speak of similarity; in other words, in order for Plato to say that the Good is *like* the Sun, Plato presupposes that he already has an idea of the Good, or else it would be meaningless for him to say that the Good is like anything at all (hence it seems inconsistent for Plato to speak of the Good as "beyond Being").

Now how this relates to the question of Lewis's justification in speaking of cultural and historical generalizations should be obvious. On the one hand, Lewis felt that all generalizations – i.e. collections of things at once

---

make sense of real (not merely conceptual or linguistic) similarity, for real similarity is in fact real identity, and real identity demands a real universal. While Lewis's argument could be directed against other forms of nominalism, it would have to address objections other than those Berkeley raised. For instance, Ockham's nominalism is grounded in the belief that universals are not only *unnecessary* in accounting for facts (as Berkeley believed) but also *internally contradictory*. That is, Ockham believed that it is contradictory to say that a given substance is at once the same (really participates in a given universal) and not the same (is not totally that universal); hence, Ockham would have said that Peter and Paul do not *really* share in the same *nature qua* Man. Although we can only speculate about what Lewis would have said to Ockham, it is likely that on top of maintaining the necessity of universals, the Oxford don would have followed a line of argument similar to that of Marilyn McCord Adams, who denies Ockhams's claim that belief in real universals are contradictory. Marilyn McCord Adams, *William Ockham*, vol. 1, 2nd revised ed. (Notre Dame, IN: University of Notre Dame Press, 1989), 31-3.

34 That is, Lewis the Christian believed both that there are transcendental or Platonic universals (i.e. the Ideas in the mind of God) and immanent or Aristotelian universals (e.g. the universal shared by the particular men Peter and Paul); however, Lewis did think that it is difficult to explain *how* immanent universals can exist in two different people: "It would certain[ly] be 'convenient' to say that universals etc *subsist* if one c[oul]d attach any clear meaning to the word *subsist*? Can one?" Lewis, *The Collected Letters of C. S. Lewis: Volume III*, 1351 [June 15, 1962].

35 "I will indeed confess that some desultory investigation of the problem of the Universal has left me with a certain respect for the solution . . . which Plato inclined to in the dialogues of his middle period." Lewis, *The Personal Heresy*, 51.

36 Lewis, "The Moral Good – Its Place Among the Values," 59.

different and identical to each other – falsify insofar as they speak of different objects;[37] thus, Lewis wrote: "Is there a homogeneous 'West'? I doubt it."[38] On the other hand, Lewis believed that insofar as generalizations speak of identical things, they point to a legitimate unity: "A real transfusion of spirit involves intangibles: to study it is to study things that can only be known by long and sympathetic reading of originals."[39] Thus, Lewis maintained that cultural and historical generalizations are necessary,[40] and indeed are more necessary than people might think: "<u>I think critics have a far too acute eye for differences, and are far too insensitive to substantial unities</u>."[41]

As for examples of generalizations in Lewis's corpus, his most famous is, without a doubt, his use of Richard Baxter's "Mere Christianity" – a generality that, even today, has cachet with many Christian philosophers and theologians, including Alvin Plantinga, Peter Van Inwagen and J. P. Moreland.[42] Yet, setting aside the difficult task of explaining this "plain, central Christianity,"[43] this "belief that has been common to nearly all Christians at all times," I turn to the even more difficult task of elucidating Lewis's boldest generalization – that of an Old Western Man.

III: Old Western Man

In 1898, Lewis was born in Belfast, the largest city in "Ulster" or Northern Ireland. Ulster had been under English rule since it had been defeated by Elizabeth I at the end of the Nine Years War in 1603. As a result of the war,

---

37 "'To generalize is to be an idiot,' said Blake. Perhaps he went too far. But to generalize is to be a finite mind. Generalities are the lenses with which our intellects have to manage." Lewis, *Prayer: Letters to Malcolm*, 259. Cf. "I looked into G. K. Chesterton's *Browning* – a thoroughly bad book, full of silly generalizations." Lewis, *All My Road Before Me*, 297.

38 C. S. Lewis, "Revival or Decay?" in *C. S. Lewis: Essay Collection & Other Short Pieces*, ed. Lesley Walmsley (1958 essay reprint; London: HarperCollins, 2000), 740.

39 C. S. Lewis, "The Idea of an 'English School,'" in *Rehabilitations: And Other Essays*, by C. S. Lewis (London: Oxford University Press, 1939), 71.

40 "But though 'periods' are a mischievous conception they are a methodological necessity. The mass of literature which I attempt to study in this book must be divided up somehow." Lewis, *Poetry and Prose in the Sixteenth Century*, 64. Cf. "Generalisations are legitimate only when we are dealing with matters to which our faculties are adequate." Lewis, *The Collected Letters of C. S. Lewis: Volume III*, 355 [August 3, 1953].

41 C. S. Lewis, underlining in his edition of *The Philosophy of the Good Life*, by Charles Gore (London: J. M. Dent, 1938; The Marion E. Wade Center, Wheaton College), 262.

42 Alvin Plantinga, "Ad Hick," *Faith and Philosophy* 14, no. 3 (July 1997): 295. Peter Van Inwagen, "A Reply to Professor Hick," *Faith and Philosophy* 14, no. 3 (July 1997): 300. J. P. Moreland, *Kingdom Triangle* (Grand Rapids, MI: Zondervan, 2007), 14, 29, 32.

43 Lewis, "On the Reading of Old Books," 439.

the English settled many Englishmen, Scots and Welshmen – most of whom were Protestant – in Ulster. Yet the native Ultonians, most of whom were Catholic, resented these new Protestant settlers, and so slaughtered thousands of them in revolt (an event, it must be noted, that remained strong in Ulster Protestant folk-memory even in Lewis's day). Ethno-religious wars ensued and strongly divided many communities in Northern Ireland, but with the ascendancy of William of Orange, British and Protestant supremacy was secure in Ireland; however, even though Scottish Presbyterians became the majority in Ulster, they did not share the same political rights as Anglican Protestants, most of whom descended from English settlers. Consequently, Ulster was torn by a twofold tension between an alliance of Catholic and Presbyterian republicans against Anglican loyalists, on the one hand, and between Catholics and Protestants, in particular, those who belonged to the Church of Ireland (Irish Anglican), on the other. The tension between the Presbyterian republicans and Anglican loyalists largely dissipated in 1801, when the Act of Union, which abolished official religious discrimination, was passed, but the tension between Catholics and Protestants (who had by then formed the Orange Order) largely remained. Indeed, in the nineteenth century, sectarian divisions hardened into the political categories of "unionist," who were (mainly Protestant) supporters of union with Britain, and "nationalists," who were (mostly Catholic) supporters of Irish self-government and Home Rule (though of course some unionists and some British politicians, such as the liberal Prime Minister William Gladstone, supported Irish Home Rule). During WWI, the Irish were initially exempt from fighting; however, in the midst of the war in Europe, Irish nationalists staged the Easter Rising (1916), which ultimately culminated in the Anglo-Irish War (1919-1921).[44] The fighting largely ceased with the signing of the 1921 Anglo-Irish Treaty, which ended in the partition of the Irish Free States (which in 1949 became the Republic of Ireland) and Northern Ireland or six of Ulster's nine counties, including Lewis's Belfast and County Down.

Albert Lewis, C. S. Lewis's father, was a Church of Ireland man, a lawyer greatly interested in politics, and a unionist,[45] and so would have been a supporter of the Ulster Volunteer Force (UVF), who were opposed to the Irish Republican Army (IRA). In all likelihood, Albert's unionism is what eventually softened him to the idea of sending his two young sons, Warren and Clive (C. S. Lewis), to boarding schools in England.

---

44   Arthur Marwick, *A History of the Modern British Isles, 1914-1999: Circumstances, Events and Outcomes* (Oxford: Blackwell, 2000), 15-6.

45   Lewis, *Surprised by Joy*, 1247.

As for C. S. Lewis, he supported Home Rule (like his grandmother Hamilton[46]), and probably never became a unionist like his father.[47] Indeed, the younger Lewis never spoke well of British colonialism, for he loved the quiddity of each particular nation – in this case, Ireland – so much. Yet despite Lewis's Irish identity, he was not patriotic when that meant mixing religion and politics as the Orange Order did: "We have learned from the political sphere that committees of public safety, witch-hunters, Ku Klux Klans, Orangemen, Macarthyites *et hoc genus omne* can become dangers as great as those they were formed to combat."[48] Furthermore, although Lewis's affection for Ulster never ceased, he spent most of his life in England, first as a student and later as a professor, and so became deeply attached to the English way of life, particularly as was found in the university towns of Oxford and Cambridge: "Hitherto there has always been something not so much in the landscape as in every single visual impression (say a cloud, a robin, or a ditch) in Ireland, which I lacked in England: something for which homeliness is an inadequate word. This something I find I am now getting in England – the feeling of connectedness, of being part of it."[49] I suggest that these loyalties and loves formed in Lewis a dual identity, which is certainly what caused him to define Heaven as "Oxford lifted and placed in the middle of the County Down."[50] Given this, it is small wonder that Lewis's Irish identity is so little-known among his readers; indeed, many share the sentiments of the Irish Nobel Prize Winner Seamus Heaney when he said he thinks of Lewis as "unlocalized."[51] Thus, although far from being a complete explanation of the Oxford don's practice of speaking broadly about western culture, it seems likely that the national ecumenism of Lewis's later years had at least a small part to play in his subsequent belief that there is a general unity called Old Western Culture:

> Here I must indulge my love of preaching by warning you [Arthur Greeves] not to get too much bound up in a cult. Between your other penchant . . . and the Irish school you might get into a sort of little by-way of the intellectual world, off the main track and lose yourself there. Remember that the great minds, Milton, Scott, Mozart and so on, are always sane before all and keep in the broad highway of thought and

---

46 Ronald Bresland, *The Backward Glance: C. S. Lewis and Ireland* (Belfast: The Institute of Irish Studies, 1999), 15-6.
47 Lewis, *The Collected Letters of C. S. Lewis: Volume I*, 330 [July 24, 1917].
48 Lewis, *An Experiment in Criticism*, 127.
49 Lewis, *The Collected Letters of C. S. Lewis: Volume I*, 943 [December 24, 1930].
50 David Bleakley, *C. S. Lewis – at Home in Ireland* (Eason, Ireland: Strandtown Press, 1998), 53.
51 Seamus Heaney in Bleakley, *C. S. Lewis – at Home in Ireland*, 22.

feel what can be felt by all men, not only a few. . . . It is partly through this feeling that I have not begun by sending my M. S. [of *Spirits in Bondage*] to Maunsels [i.e. an Irish publisher].[52]

Now using "*De Descriptione Temporum*" and "Modern Man and His Categories of Thought" as a very rough guide, I have assembled eight elements which partly constitute Lewis's understanding of an Old Western Man: (1) an Old Western Man identifies with western culture, which is to say that he is a person who relates to the conglomerate that is Judaic, European pagan, Christian thought, though, of course, Judaic thought obviously has its roots in Asia and even European paganism has been influenced by Egypt and the Middle East; (2) an Old Western Man is either a pre-Christian or a Christian, but not a post-Christian; (3) it follows, then, that an Old Western Man, though called "old," does not suggest only dead Europeans; rather, it indicates the person described in (1) of any time period – past, present or future – who happens to identify with the culture we are now defining; (4) an Old Western Man is one who respects tradition and history; (5) consequently, an Old Western Man, while he may believe in teleology and even biological evolution, rejects the grand evolutionary myth of progress in the form of such theories as Hegelian historicism or Darwinianism; (6) one of the key elements in tradition and history that an Old Western Man endorses is a hierarchical, not an egalitarian, conception of existence in some form or another (politically, ecclesiastically and / or socially); (7) an Old Western Man, as a lover of Nature, does not overvalue or worship technology and machinery; and (8) yet, an Old Western Man neither doubts the power of reason to apprehend objective Truth nor is skeptical of objective values in ethics and aesthetics.

Subsequently, with Lewis's general understanding of an Old Western Man in place, I now turn to investigate each particular component of this generalization. However, it should be remembered that my intention herein is *not* exhaustively to examine and critique Lewis's views on all the issues that arise (we will examine most of these in subsequent chapters); rather, it is to provide the reader with a basic understanding of the Oxford don's cultural identity vis-à-vis his writings and the culture of his day.

***

According to Lewis – the Irish Oxonian – an Old Western Man is a man or woman of western, not eastern, culture. Lewis seemed to identify this largely with European culture (be it in Ireland, England etc.), which is in many ways

52 Lewis, *The Collected Letters of C. S. Lewis: Volume I*, 394 [August 31, 1918].

the product of religious thought: it is a European pagan-Christian synthesis wherein the paganism, as we discussed in the previous chapter, prefigured, or anticipated à la Plato or Virgil, the advent of Christianity. This, of course, is not to deny that the same phenomena happened in Africa or the East when Christianity replaced paganism in many countries such as Kenya or Korea, but only to say that this was a phenomenon especially close to Europe. Nevertheless, it must be added that European culture is fairly opaque since it has been greatly influenced by the culture of the Middle East (e.g. Judaic and Egyptian religion, Babylonian astronomy, Arabic numbers and philosophical commentaries etc.). Now, precisely because Lewis *chose* to identify himself with European culture, which has often been slow to recognize the influence of other continents and races, some critics have wondered whether or not he was (1) a racist and (2) a reviler of non-European culture.

As for (1) – whether or not Lewis was a racist – Philip Pullman, the author of *His Dark Materials* trilogy, thinks Lewis is "blatantly racist,"[53] Michael White claims that some aspects of *The Chronicles of Narnia* are "appalling," including Lewis's description of the dark-skinned Calormenes,[54] and Wesley Kort believes that "racism appears in [Lewis's] work. The most troubling instance is his depiction of the evil Calormenes in *The Last Battle* in terms consistent with the longstanding English disdain toward darker-skinned Mediterranean peoples. Lewis seems unaware of his racism, and it is particularly troubling that it appears in one of the Narnia Chronicles."[55] While Pullman, White and Kort's assertion is clearly representative of the first impression of many casual readers of Lewis, it is both unscholarly and erroneous.

That is, the Calormenes in *The Chronicles of Narnia* are always contrasted with the Narnians, *not* because of their skin colour, but because of their religion: skin colour, in other words, is *accidental* to physical location wherein there is a specific religion. The medievalish Calormenes are the symbolic enemies of the true faith, which is represented by the medievalish Narnians; hence, for Lewis, a medieval scholar (and one who lived during the re-conquest of the Holy Land[56]), the parallel would have been between

---

53   Philip Pullman, quoted in "Narnia Books Attacked as Racist and Sexist," by John Ezard. *Guardian*, June 3, 2002. http://www.guardian.co.uk/uk_news/story/0,3604,726739,00. html (accessed February 3, 2005): 1.

54   Michael White, *C. S. Lewis: The Boy Who Chronicled Narnia* (London: Abacus, 2005), 224.

55   Wesley Kort, *C. S. Lewis: Then and Now* (Oxford: Oxford University Press, 2001), 11.

56   On November 5, 1914, the British declared war on the Ottoman Empire as the result of the Ottoman Turks siding with the Germans in WWI. The Turks responded to the British declaration of war by declaring a military jihad. On December 11, 1917, General

the European Christians (there were hardly any Christians elsewhere in the Middle Ages[57]) and the Middle Eastern Muslims (this also explains the title of chapter nine in *That Hideous Strength*, "The Saracen's Head");[58] indeed, Islam was always seen as the perfect anti-Christian symbol, not only because Muslims attacked Christian lands, but mostly because they, perhaps more than anyone else, denied the central teaching of Christianity: the divinity of Christ. Lewis's comments on Charles Williams's Arthurian poems drive this home:

> Islam was for Williams the symbol (as it is certainly the greatest historical expression) of something which is eternally the opposite of Sarras and Carbonek. Islam denies the Incarnation. . . . It stands for all religions that are afraid of matter and afraid of mystery, for all misplaced reverences and misplaced purities that repudiate the body and shrink back from the glowing materialism of the Grail.[59]

Nevertheless, even in regard to the Crusades, which we will take up again in chapter nine, Lewis spoke of them in a mixed voice, blaming *both* the Turks and the Norman barbarians for destroying Byzantium.[60] Moreover, since Aslan's Land or Paradise is actually located in the East,[61] not the West, and Narnia herself is in the North, not the West (though this direction is also important to Lewis due to the *Sehnsucht* of "Northernness" he felt on reading the Norse myths in his youth), these locations were surely intentional for the symbolically-minded Oxford don, no doubt because he was precisely trying to avoid the false representation of the West as perfectly good and the East (which contains the Holy Land) and elsewhere as perfectly bad.[62] On

---

Edmund Allenby conquered Jerusalem and most of the Holy Land.

57 I am aware that until about the end of the Second Crusade, there was a significant number of European (Orthodox) Christians in the Levant and there were pockets of Nestorian (heretical) Christians throughout the Middle East, North Africa and even into the more western parts of Asia.

58 That the Calormenes represent Islam in a very general sense is seen not only by comments about their unbelief, their skin colour and their historical hatred of Narnia, but also by their poetry, for just as Europeans have been taken with romance, Middle Easterners have been taken with short maxims and proverbs; as the servant of the Calormene Tisroc says in *The Horse and His Boy*: "For the gods have withheld from the barbarians the light of discretion, as that their poetry is not, like ours, full of choice apophthegms and useful maxims, but is all of love and war." Lewis, *The Horse and His Boy*, 101.

59 Lewis, *The Arthurian Torso*, 124-5.

60 Lewis, *The Collected Letters of C. S. Lewis: Volume III*, 803 [October 31, 1956]. Needless to say, Lewis's commentary on William's poem should be taken as pointing to a general truth and not as making a universal statement, for the mystical literature of Sufism often speaks mysteriously about the unity of material creation and God.

61 Lewis, *The Voyage of the Dawn Treader*, 189.

62 Of course, one could argue that the symbolic importance of the East is precisely an

top of this, it is clear that race was not the issue in Narnia since it is in *The Last Battle*, the very book that Kort calls racist, in which Lewis, flexing his inclusivist theology, actually has a Calormene who *denied* Aslan enter the New Narnia because the Calormene, Emeth, which is Hebrew for "truth," was faithful and true to the only god he knew and such faithfulness and devotion could only be offered to the source of all Faithfulness and Truth, Aslan.[63] Thus, the dark-skinned Calormene is saved despite rejecting Aslan *per se*, which clearly shows not only that the Oxford don was far from being a clear-cut proponent of the "demonisation of Islam," as one critic put,[64] but also he was not being racist in *The Chronicles of Narnia*. And if this is not enough, we know from Lewis's letters that he hated Nazi race theory and was actually invited by philosopher John Orth Riedl to attend the Nürnberg trials to help the High Commission in its reorientation work.[65] Moreover, he expressed outrage toward the racism a certain Chinese woman faced in the United States, saying: "I'm shocked to find that a shop wouldn't serve a Chinese. But I have long known that the talk about Brotherhood, wherever it occurs, in America or here, is hypocrisy. Or rather, the man who talks it means 'I have no superiors': he does *not* mean 'I have no inferiors.' How loathsome it all is!"[66] Finally, had Pullman and Kort done their homework, they would have come across Lewis's point-blank rejection of racism, where he wrote, "I am very glad they should get over the colour bar."[67]

Yet, if Lewis was not a racist, was he not, some may press, (2) a reviler of non-European culture, in particular, the East? This is a more complicated question than the question of racism. Chronologically speaking, while Lewis was *always* opposed to colonialism, it seems undeniable that if the early Lewis did not dislike the East, he, as a typical early twentieth-century Oxonian,[68] had few good things to say about. In *Surprised by Joy*, Lewis

---

intrinsic part of Western ethnocentrism, and so Lewis was not really being fair-minded in placing Aslan's Land in the East; however, I am not sure why we cannot say that the recognition of the Holy Land in the East (or the Center, as they would have said) is precisely a western recognition of the good inherent in the East.

63 Lewis, *The Last Battle*, 153-7.
64 Although Lewis believed Islam to be the perfect anti-Christian *symbol*, he was far from rejecting any positive value in Islam, much less exercising total "demonisation of Islam," as Andrew Blake believes the Oxford don did. Andrew Blake, "Of More Than Academic Interest: C. S. Lewis and the Golden Age," in *Behind the Veil of Familiarity: C. S. Lewis (1898-1998)*, ed. Margarita Carretero González and Encarnación Hidalgo Tenorio, 47-60 (Bern: Peter Lang, 2001), 51.
65 Lewis, *The Collected Letters of C. S. Lewis: Volume II*, 854 [May 22, 1948].
66 Lewis, *The Collected Letters of C. S. Lewis: Volume III*, 618 [June 7, 1955].
67 Lewis, *The Collected Letters of C. S. Lewis: Volume II*, 328 [January 21, 1940].
68 A sense ranging from mere discomfort with "the other" to blatant racism dominated

said that "Oriental imagery and style largely repelled me,"[69] and on his Scholarship Examination to enter Malvern College, Lewis chose, out of three possible topics, to write on "West is West, and East is East, and never the twain shall meet;"[70] indeed, not only did eastern things not suit Lewis, as is demonstrated by his comments about Buddhism upon reading *The Gospel of Buddha According to the Old Records* (i.e. in 1921, the atheistic Lewis spoke of atheistic Buddhism's "inferiority to Christianity"[71]), but Lewis, even as a Christian, entertained the idea that the East was more severely fallen than the West:

> I have played with the idea that Christianity was never intended for Asia – even that Buddha is the form in which Christ appears to the Eastern mind. But I don't think this will really work. When I have tried to rule out all my prejudices I still can't help thinking that the Christian world is (partially) 'saved' in a sense in which the East is not. We may be hypocrites, but there is a sort of unashamed and *reigning* iniquity of temple prostitution and infanticide and torture and political corruption and obscene imagination in the East, which really does suggest that they are off the rails – that some necessary part of the human machine, restored to us, is still missing with them.[72]

Of course, this need not necessitate a strong distaste for eastern culture so much as an assertion of the inadequacy of their *religions*; indeed, Buddhism's Nirvana, which is the absence of individuality and therefore of all desires, is precisely the opposite of Christianity's Heaven, wherein a person attains real individuality and the overflowing of Joy; this difference, Lewis believed,

---

Oxford and Lewis's own college, Magdalen, in the early nineteenth century: "College harmony was threatened by nationality as well as by social status. Between the wars 6 per cent of junior members came from the Commonwealth and 5 per cent from elsewhere overseas. Some colleges rejected Indians or wanted them assigned a college of their own. . . . President Gordon in 1934, warding off the possibility of an Indian applicant to Magdalen, told a Harrow schoolmaster in confidence that 'the College is very English in its atmosphere, and, with the best will in the world, seems unable to absorb anything quite so foreign.'" Brian Harrison, "College Life, 1918-1939," in *The History of the University of Oxford: Volume VIII; The Twentieth Century*, ed. Brian Harrison, 81-108 (Oxford: Oxford University Press, 1994), 97.

69   Lewis, *Surprised by Joy*, 1343.
70   Colin Duriez, *The C. S. Lewis Chronicles: The Indispensible Biography of the Creator of Narnia Full of Little-Known Facts, Events and Miscellany* (New York: BlueBridge, 2005), 46.
71   Lewis, *The Collected Letters of C. S. Lewis: Volume I*, 567 [July 1921]. And even in 1962, Lewis repeated the same basic idea: "Zen is, so far, utterly opaque to me." Lewis, *The Collected Letters of C. S. Lewis: Volume III*, 1378 [October 28, 1962].
72   Lewis, *The Collected Letters of C. S. Lewis: Volume II*, 70 [April 8, 1932].

was "at the bottom irreconcilable."[73] Moreover, Hinduism, as Lewis understood it from his friend Dom Bede Griffiths, the *Bhaghavad Gita*,[74] and other sources, is like Buddhism in that it is not so much sub-Christian, as traditional European paganism was (which Lewis was fond of), so much as a purely natural religion: "i.e. it displays the natural trend of the speculative intellect *sibi relictus* ['left to itself'] – the line it will always follow when it escapes savagery and does not receive Grace. Hence such parallel systems as Stoicism, Hegelianism."[75] Furthermore, as a purely natural religion, Lewis thought Hinduism is "*far further* from the true Faith than the semi-barbarous pagan religions" of Europe,[76] not only because it is far harder for a Hindu to convert to Christianity than a European pagan, but also because the relationship between God and man in Hinduism[77] is precisely the *opposite* of the relationship between God and man in Christianity:

> I even feel that the kind of union (with God) wh[ich] [the Hindus] are seeking is precisely the opposite to that which He intends for us. We all once existed potentially in Him and in that sense were not other than He. And even now inorganic matter has a sort of unity with Him that we lack. To what end was creation except to separate us in order that we may be reunited to Him in that unity of love wh[ich] is utterly different from mere numerical unity and indeed presupposes that lover & beloved be distinct? . . . Thus the whole Indian aim seems to me to be *backward* towards a sort of unity wh[ich] God deliberately rejected and not onward to the true one. If mere unity (as to union) is the aim all Creation seems otiose.[78]

73 "The gulf between the Christian ideal of love, and the ideals of Buddha, Schopenhauer and Tolstoi, which means the destruction of the individual, is at the bottom irreconcilable." C. S. Lewis, underlining in his edition of *Studies of Political Thought from Gerson to Grotius 1414-1625*, by John Neville Figgis (Cambridge: Cambridge University Press, 1923; The Marion E. Wade Center, Wheaton College), 81.

74 Although we do not know if Lewis read any Hindu scriptures, he favorably alluded to one in his Great War documents: "No doubt a man may make both yielding and repentance too easy by reflecting that his action will in any case 'produce good.' But this comes from a false moral philosophy which placed the value of right action not in the form of right willing itself but in the consequences. The true doctrine can be studied in Kant and the Baghavat-Gita (on the fruits of action)." Lewis, *De Bono et Malo*, 18.

75 Lewis, *The Collected Letters of C. S. Lewis: Volume II*, 771 [April 15, 1947].

76 Ibid., 770 [April 15, 1947].

77 "For my own part, I have sometimes told my audience that the only two things really worth considering are Christianity and Hinduism. (Islam is only the greatest of the Christian heresies, Buddhism only the greatest of the Hindu heresies. Real Paganism is dead. All that was best in Judaism and Platonism survives in Christianity)." C. S. Lewis, "Christian Apologetics," in *C. S. Lewis: Essay Collection & Other Short Pieces* (1945 essay reprint; London: HarperCollins, 2000), 158. Cf. Lewis, *The Collected Letters of C. S. Lewis: Volume II*, 225 [April 29, 1938], 770 [April 15, 1947].

78 Lewis, *The Collected Letters of C. S. Lewis: Volume II*, 880 [September 27, 1948].

Eastern religions, then, were understood by Lewis to be something largely (though not completely) incompatible with Christianity.

As one who teaches Asian philosophies and religions in the Far East, I find Lewis's comments about eastern religions a bit thin; indeed, it seems to me indisputable that Lewis demonstrated a prejudice for the West that degraded the East, for the West and its religions were not totally free of the atrocities he attributed to the East, and it is hard to imagine how Lewis failed to appreciate the introspection of Hinduism or the ethics of Buddhism, both of which are surely pre-Christian in at least some sense.

However, I suspect that *part* of the reason why he spoke so strongly against eastern religions is not only because his friend Dom Bede Griffiths was greatly attracted to Hinduism and Lewis wanted to keep his friend on the correct path, but also because Lewis himself had come through pantheism *qua* absolute idealism and was particularly aware of its flaws; indeed, one of Lewis's favorite idealists, Bradley, had been influenced by Hinduism and it is possible to see this influence transferred to Lewis's fiction, for the worldly, appearances-minded Orual in *Till We Have Faces*, who is also called "Maia," is likely a representation of the Hindu "Maya" or "Appearances."[79]

Thus, while Lewis certainly deserves some chastisement in regard to his view of eastern *religions*, it must be pointed out that he actually valued some eastern *philosophies*, in particular *The Analects* of Confucius and certain elements of Taoism (not to mention some of the proverbs and allegorized myths of Egypt and Mesopotamia[80]); indeed, already back in 1940, Lewis read about the similarity between the Tao and the Stoical / Pauline Natural Law in Charles Gore's *The Philosophy of the Good Life*:

> Thus the traditional wisdom of China finds at the basis of all things a divine principle or law – Tao [the Way] – closely akin to what the Stoics described as Nature, to which all things in heaven and earth must conform, and to which human nature is akin; so that for man the highest knowledge is to know the Tao and the highest wisdom is to live by it. In the Chinese Classics the Rites, religious and social, of the Chinese tradition are regarded as the will of 'Heaven,' which

---

79   Lewis, *Till We Have Faces*, 888. Lewis also encountered the idea of "Maya" in William James. See James, *The Varieties of Religious Experience*, 386.

80   There are quite a few ancient Egyptian and Babylonian proverbs mentioned in the appendix of *The Abolition of Man*, and, as I alluded to in the previous chapter, due largely to Frazer's *Golden Bough*, Chesterton's *Everlasting Man*, Apuleius's *Golden Ass*, Martianus Capella's *Marriage of Mercury and Philology* and Andrew Lang's *Myth, Ritual and Religion*, Lewis was acquainted with Egyptian mythology, in particular, the idea of Osiris as a pagan-Christ.

is the name for the Supreme Power ruling the affairs of men as an omnipotent and omniscient righteousness.[81]

Shortly after reading Gore's book, Lewis used the word "Tao" instead of "Natural Law" in *The Abolition of Man*,[82] no doubt, to demonstrate that Goodness and Truth do not belong exclusively to the West. In like manner, Lewis also felt that the true essence of China – for as we shall see in chapters six and nine, he believed all nations have *essences* – is the "Kingdom of Heaven," which is China's better self, just as "Logres" is England's better self.[83] Finally, due largely to his semi-interest in China and her philosophy, Lewis became sensitive towards some differences within the East: "Of course we must beware of thinking of 'the East' as if it were homogeneous. I suppose the Indian and the Chinese *ethos* are as alien to each other as either is to us."[84]

What, then, should one conclude about Lewis's attitude towards the East? Did his identity as an Old Western Man imply a hatred of the East? I believe that in his early days, this, at least implicitly, was the case. Yet, as he got older, I believe he came to see that patriotism is a mixed bag:

> I turn now to the love of one's country. Here there is no need to labour M. de Rougemont's maxim; we all know now that this love becomes a demon when it becomes a god. Some begin to suspect that it is never anything but a demon. But then they have to reject half the high poetry and half the heroic action our race has achieved. We cannot keep even Christ's lament over Jerusalem. He too exhibits love for His country.[85]

That is, as a mature Christian, Lewis believed that patriotism is a virtue and as such, for instance, men of the West ought to "reverence the ancient Greeks;"[86] nevertheless, this patriotism is a dangerous thing and can easily turn universal truths into provincial lies. Hence, in Lewis's early writings,

81 Charles Gore, *The Philosophy of the Good Life* (London: J. M. Dent, 1954), 87.

82 Thus, John West Jr. is only partly correct when he says that Lewis was "speaking within the western natural law tradition." John West Jr., "C. S. Lewis and Materialism," *Religion and Liberty* 6, no. 6 (November and December 1996): 1-6 http://www.acton.org/publicat/randl/article.php?id=211 (accessed February 3, 2005), 3.

83 See C. S. Lewis, "Edmund Spenser 1552-99," in *Studies in Medieval and Renaissance Literature*, by C. S. Lewis, ed. Walter Hooper (1954 essay reprint; Cambridge: Cambridge University Press, 1998), 145; Lewis, *Reflection on the Psalms*, 341.

84 Lewis, *The Collected Letters of C. S. Lewis: Volume III*, 408 [January 16, 1954]. Cf. Lewis, *The Collected Letters of C. S. Lewis: Volume II*, 842 [March 25, 1948].

85 C. S. Lewis, *The Four Loves*, in *C. S. Lewis: Selected Books* [Long Edition] (1960 reprint; London: HarperCollins, 1999), 18.

86 Lewis, *The Collected Letters of C. S. Lewis: Volume III*, 119 [May 25, 1951].

such as *The Pilgrim's Regress* and "The Landing," Lewis longed for the West (and also the North), but in his later writings, such as *The Voyage of the Dawn Treader*, he longed for the East; moreover, it is with this sensitivity towards the abuse of patriotism in mind that Lewis repeatedly emphasized an admiration for the true believer of all religions, convinced that *integrity* was a universal loved by God:

> I believe that, in the present divided state of Christendom, those who are at the heart of each division are all closer to one another than those who are at the fringes. I would even carry this beyond the borders of Christianity: how much more one has in common with a *real* Jew or Muslim than with a wretched liberalizing, occidentalised specimen of the same categories: it is perhaps the only form of 'work for re-union' which never does anything but good.[87]

Nevertheless, Lewis believed that pagans of both the East *and* West are "poor dears" who need Christian revelation,[88] which, subsequently, he believed was available to all: "Christianity is for all men, not simply for modern Western Europeans."[89]

***

As for the second part of Lewis's understanding of an Old Western Man – that such a person will be either a pre-Christian or Christian but not a post-Christian – most of this has already been discussed. For instance, we know Lewis felt the pagans (with their "Pictures") and the Jews (with their "Rules") were like "virgins" who had the right elements needed for an easy conversion to "married" life, Christianity.[90] However, what has not yet been discussed is (1) what Lewis thought of Christians who reverted to paganism or Judaism (or any other religion for that matter) and (2) what he meant by

---

87   Ibid., 249 [November 10, 1952].
88   Ibid., 776 [August 3, 1956].
89   Lewis, *The Collected Letters of C. S. Lewis: Volume II*, 393 [April 18, 1940].
90   Lewis, *The Collected Letters of C. S. Lewis: Volume III*, 365 [September 15, 1953]. Lewis thought that Boethius's *Consolation of Philosophy* is a wonderful example of pre-Christian thought *qua* natural theology, while Boethius's *Concerning the Faith* is a wonderful example of Christian thought *per se*: "[*The Consolation of Philosophy's*] philosophy is a profoundly religious philosophy. It might be described as prolegomena to any of the great religions; it teaches the insufficiency of the world and points on the Eternal – after that the various religions can have their say as to the nature of the Eternal and the means of approaching it. We need not doubt that Boethius passed through this philosophy preliminary and reached that particular religion described in his *De Fide*." C. S. Lewis, review of *Boethius: Some Aspects of His Times and Works*, by Helen Barrett, *Medium Aevum* 10, no. 1 (February 1941): 33.

a "post-Christian."

In the late nineteenth and early twentieth century, alternative forms of religion began springing up around Europe due to the weakening of Christianity (as we will discuss shortly). In the 1850s, there was renewed interest in Emanuel Swedenborg (1688-1772) and spiritualism, which is the practice of communicating with the dead. At the same time, occultism, in particular the Theosophical Society, headed by Madame Blavatsky (1831-1891), the Hermetic Order of the Golden Dawn, the London branch of which was founded by A. E. Waite (1857-1942), and the Anthroposophical Society, which started as an off-shoot of Theosophy by Rudolf Steiner (1862-1925), were attracting many prominent artists and writers, such as William Butler Yeats, Ezra Pound, Charles Williams and Owen Barfield. Since some of these pagans later became orthodox Christians (e.g. Charles Williams[91]) and others remained at a fairly high-level of noble paganism (e.g. Yeats and Barfield), not to mention the fact that one of Lewis's own stepsons reverted to Judaism (David Gresham[92]), Lewis generally thought that even Christians who became pagans or Jews were in a better place than those who rejected all forms of the supernatural. Hence, he did not distinguish between pre-Christians (i.e. those before Christianity was known) and sub-Christians in general (i.e. those before Christianity was known and those who knew of Christianity and rejected it for paganism or some other religion). I think that Lewis's failure to make this distinction is culturally telling, for although the Bible clearly condemns all manner of magic, witchcraft and false religion, Lewis, as a man of the early twentieth century, believed that Christianity was faced with threats far more sinister than occultism and spiritualism: modernity.

Thus, if the pre-Christians – pagans and Jews (and presumably Christians who reverted back to paganism, Judaism etc.) – are like virgins, and Christians

---

91   When Williams, Lewis's best friend, left the Hermetic Order of the Golden Dawn, he founded a society of Christians called "The Companions of the Co-inherence," whose members were "enjoined to orient their lives towards their functions as members of one another; to draw together in prayer and recollections; and to live as members of the co-inherent Body of Christ." Glen Cavaliero sees the foundation of this society as a sign of Williams's "ultimate rejection of the exclusiveness of gnosticism and magic." Glen Cavaliero, *Charles Williams: Poet of Theology* (Grand Rapids, MI: Eerdmans, 1983), 5.

92   David Gresham had always been interested in Judaism, but he only converted to the religion after his mother, a Christian Jewess, died. Lewis, *The Collected Letters of C. S. Lewis: Volume III*, 1323 [March 20, 1962]. Cf. "To us Christians the unconverted Jew (I mean no offence) must appear as a Christian *manqué*; someone very carefully prepared for a certain destiny and then missing it." C. S. Lewis, "Foreword," in *Smoke on the Mountain: An Interpretation of the Ten Commandments*, by Joy Davidman (Philadelphia: Westminster Press, 1953), 8.

are like married women, then the post-Christians are like "widows,"[93] "divorcees,"[94] or "adulteresses"[95] – those who have completely forsaken the good *qua* supernaturalism and Christianity. The post-Christian, in other words, is the modernist who hates, at least insofar as they make a claim on him, pre-Christian or Christian elements.[96] In and around Lewis's time, the predominant post-Christians would have been philosophers like Karl Marx and Fredrick Engels, whose *Communist Manifesto* (1847) maintained that religion is merely a tool the bourgeoisie use to exercise economic control over people; scientists like Charles Darwin, whose *Origin of Species* (1859) gave atheism a scientific foundation; higher critics like Ernest Renan, whose *Life of Jesus* (1861) presented Jesus completely in human terms; and psychoanalysts like Sigmund Freud, whose *Interpreting Dreams* (1899) reduced religion to merely childhood neurosis.

Now if we combine the fact that we are living in a post-Christian era with Lewis's comment to Nathan Starr that "it is a terrible thing to live in a post-civilized world,"[97] then we get the conclusion not only that Lewis believed we are living in the most godless age in history, but also that the Oxford don's identification with Old Western Culture is an identification with the days when pagan mythology and philosophy were treated with respect and assimilated into the greater revelation, Christianity; subsequently, Lewis's Old Western Man is in many ways like a typical medieval man, who

> find[s] it hard to believe that anything an old *auctour* has said is simply untrue. And [he] inherit[s] a very heterogeneous collection of books; Judaic, Pagan, Platonic, Aristotelian, Stoical, Primitive Christian, Patristic. . . . Obviously [his] *auctours* will contradict one another. . . . [Yet] all the apparent contradictions must be harmonized.[98]

This Old Western syncretism, I suggest, has a symbiotic relationship with Lewis's Neoplatonism – with his comment that "to lose what I owe to Plato and Aristotle would be like the amputation of a limb"[99] or his disagreement that there is a large gap between Plato and Aristotle[100] – because of all the

93   Lewis, *The Collected Letters of C. S. Lewis: Volume III*, 307 [March 17, 1953].
94   Lewis, *"De Descriptione Temporum,"* 10.
95   Lewis, *The Collected Letters of C. S. Lewis: Volume III*, 365 [September 15, 1953].
96   "Would it not be equally true to say, more shortly, 'Moderns of every kind have one characteristic in common: they *hate*?' The matter deserves, perhaps, more attention than it has received." Ibid., 1539 [November 1940].
97   Ibid., 121 [May 29, 1951].
98   Lewis, *The Discarded Image*, 11.
99   Lewis, "The Idea of an 'English School,'" 64.
100   In *Poetic Diction*, Barfield wrote: "Thus the old, instinctive consciousness of single meanings, which comes down to us as the Greek myths, is already fighting for its life

philosophies the western world has known, it is Neoplatonic Christianity, according to Lewis, that has been able to assimilate the best elements of the pre-Christians with a unified Christian philosophy. This, however, is not to argue that Lewis believed such a philosophy is always coherent or consistent: it is only to say that he thought it the best way of philosophizing:

> The last, and neo-Platonic, wave of Paganism which had gathered up into itself much from the preceding waves, Aristotelian, Platonic, Stoic, and what not, came far inland and made brackish lakes which have, perhaps, never been drained. Not all Christians at all times have detected them or admitted their existence: and among those who have done so there have always been two attitudes. There was then, and is still, a Christian 'left,' eager to detect and anxious to banish every Pagan element; but also a Christian 'right' who, like St. Augustine, could find the doctrine of the Trinity foreshadowed in the *Platonici*, or could claim triumphantly, like Justin Martyr, 'Whatever things have been well said by all men belong to us Christians.'[101]

Inevitably, this way of thinking has elicited a lot of comparison between Lewis's approach to history, philosophy and Christianity and that of the Neoscholastics, who beckoned people to return to the medieval, syncretistic philosophy and theology of Aquinas, for "St. Thomas," wrote Pope Pius IX, the major figure in the revival of Neoscholasticism, "has refuted by himself the errors of preceding times, and has provided invincible weapons for the refutation of errors that were to be ever springing up in days to come."[102] Yet surprisingly Lewis did not like Neoscholasticism ("there is no section of religious opinion with which I feel less sympathy"[103]), questioning the Catholic Church's official endorsement of it,[104] considering it too

---

by Plato's time as the doctrine of Platonic Ideas (not 'abstract,' though this word is often erroneously used in English translations); Aristotle's logic and his Categories, *as interpreted by his followers*, then tend to concentrate attention exclusively on the *abstract* universals, and so to destroy the balance." Barfield, *Poetic Diction*, 95. To this Lewis replied: "Of course I disagree with your account of Plato and Aristotle and may have to explode it in a footnote some day." Lewis, *The Collected Letters of C. S. Lewis: Volume III*, 1498 [January 24, 1926].

101 Lewis, *The Discarded Image*, 48-9.
102 Pius IX, "Letter," *Acta Sanctae Sedis in Compendium Opportune Redacta* 12:97.
103 Lewis, *The Collected Letters of C. S. Lewis: Volume II*, 134 [April 4, 1934]. In *The Pilgrim's Regress*, the character "Neo-Angular" is a Neoscholastic figure based on T. S. Eliot and Jacques Maritain. Lewis, preface to the third edition of *The Pilgrim's Regress*, 9.
104 Lewis, *The Collected Letters of C. S. Lewis: Volume II*, 179 [February 20, 1936].

"antagonistic to Idealism,"[105] and viewing it as a "fad"[106] or "fashion"[107] amongst intellectuals. While it is easy to understand both Lewis's Anglican distrust of papal recommendations and, given his philosophical journey, his anger toward Neoscholastic anti-idealism,[108] it is difficult to see why Lewis thought Neoscholasticism was a fad, for while it is true that such philosophy was foreign to Oxford and "Greats" philosophy, Neoscholasticism is simply the syncretism of the past with an eye toward present-day application; indeed, when Lewis said he rejected the *philosophia perennis* of Thomism, it is hard not to see him contradicting his own approach to philosophy vis-à-vis Neoplatonic Christianity. The one difference, I suppose, is that while Lewis felt his Neoplatonic Christianity can be mistaken, he doubted whether the Neoscholastics would confess to error, especially if they were sanctioned by the Pope:

> About Scholastics, I must have expressed myself very badly if you thought I held that one system of philosophy was as good as another or that pure reason was mutable. All I meant was that no philosophy is perfect: nor can be, since, whatever is true of Reason herself, in the human process of reasoning there is always error and even what is right, in solving one problem, always poses another. I therefore reject the idea of any real *philosophia perennis*.[109]

Lewis, of course, was mistaken in thinking that Catholics view the *philosophia perennis* of Neoscholasticism as infallible; nevertheless, what is important is something that is quite easy to miss: Lewis's humble regard for the limits of philosophy, for against the confident Neoscholastic Dom Bede Griffiths, Lewis, a great lover of reason, asserted: "We have no abiding city even in

---

105 Ibid., 134 [April 4, 1934].
106 Ibid.
107 Ibid., 176 [January 8, 1936].
108 Neoscholasticism's anti-idealism dates back to the early part of the nineteenth century, when Joseph Kleutgen came to Scholastic philosophy: "Strongly opposed to all forms of idealism, [Kleutgen] wrote a defence of traditional theology against it. . . . For Kleutgen, what matters most is a defence of objectivity in knowledge against idealism, and the first half of [*Die Philosophie der Vorzeit vertheidigt*] is entirely concerned with epistemology. His preoccupations made him see the scholastic revival in a way that many would see it after him: a rejection of idealism, a rational vindication of elements in religious beliefs, a call to return to a neglected but enduring heritage." F. J. Fitzpatrick, "Neoscholasticism," in *The Cambridge History of Later Medieval Philosophy: From the Rediscovery of Aristotle to the Disintegration of Scholasticism 1100-1600*, ed. Norman Kretzmann, Anthony Kenny and Jan Pinborg, 838-52 (Cambridge: Cambridge University Press, 2003), 842.
109 Lewis, *The Collected Letters of C. S. Lewis: Volume II*, 188 [April 24, 1936].

philosophy: all passes, except the Word."[110]

***

The third constituent in Lewis's understanding of an Old Western Man states that such a man need not be one who only lived in the past. What this means is that while an Old Western Man is not a *modernist*, he could be a *modern*. In "*De Descriptione Temporum*," for instance, Lewis spoke of Old Western Culture as "that whole thing, from its Greek or pre-Greek beginnings down to *the day before yesterday*,"[111] which explains how Lewis *qua* a modern can claim to belong to this culture: "I myself belong far more to that Old Western order than to yours."[112] Consequently, although Lewis was influenced by many modern thinkers, such as Bradley and Freud, the elements that he took from these thinkers into his Old Western worldview were not elements that he thought incompatible with the concept; hence, Bradley's understanding of freedom and Freud's unconscious, for instance, represent, for Lewis, a proper development or growth of Old Western Culture.

While this certainly helps us understand Lewis as a philosopher better, some may question whether or not Lewis's identification with the past hindered his objectivity toward the culture he was describing. Hopefully I have already demonstrated to such critics' satisfaction that Lewis was not afraid of "Contemplating," or critiquing, the past. And while Lewis certainly can be criticized for his lack of knowledge about contemporary affairs (he hated newspapers) and modern literature ("You have no idea how many books written this century are unknown to me"[113]), which may, incidentally, have been partly pathological ("I am conscious of a partly pathological hostility to what is fashionable, of which I think I could give the causes if it were necessary"[114]), what I have not shown or discussed is Lewis's firm belief that "Enjoying," or being part of, Old Western Culture is actually an *aid* to understanding it.

That is, love knows what love is because by Enjoying its object, love gains a knowledge that it could not gain by only Contemplating it; likewise, Lewis felt not only that he, as a self-proclaimed "dinosaur,"[115] could be studied

110 Ibid., 176 [January 8, 1936].
111 Lewis, "*De Descriptione Temporum*," 12 (emphasis mine).
112 Ibid., 13.
113 Lewis, *The Collected Letters of C. S. Lewis: Volume III*, 1985 [September 6, 1959]. Cf. "You pay a wholly undeserved compliment to my erudition by supposing that my debts to modern theologians might be too complicated to sort out! There are hardly any such debts at all; I am not sufficiently well read." Ibid., 878 [October 13, 1958].
114 Lewis, *The Collected Letters of C. S. Lewis: Volume II*, 372 [March 26, 1940].
115 Lewis, "*De Descriptione Temporum*," 13.

as a specimen of Old Western Culture, but also that he, as a genuine (Old Western) *Christian*, could help his readers understand, for example, Milton's (Old Western) *Christian* epic *Paradise Lost* better:

> In order to take no unfair advantage I should warn the reader that I am a Christian, and that some (by no means all) of the things which the atheist reader must 'try to feel as if he believed' I actually, in cold prose, do believe. But for the student of Milton my Christianity is an advantage. What would you not give to have a real, live Epicurean at your elbow while reading Lucretius?[116]

***

The fourth part of Lewis's understanding of an Old Western Man has to do with respect for history and tradition. This, too, has already been touched on, yet it is important to emphasize it, for as an Anglican (who were the majority at Oxford in first part of the twentieth century[117]), Lewis believed that all our knowledge is the result of reason, experience and authority,[118] the former having no content without the latter two, and the latter, authority, being nearly synonymous with "tradition;" consequently, without authority or tradition, we would lack an enormous amount of knowledge and be inclined not only to repeat the mistakes of the past but also to neglect the wisdom inherent in the historical process (as History tells us in *The Pilgrim's Regress*[119]). For example, to have no knowledge of antiquity is most certainly

---

116 Lewis, *A Preface to Paradise Lost*, 65. Cf. "It has been assumed without discussion that if you want the true account of religion you must go, not to religious people, but to anthropologists; that if you want the true account of sexual love you must go, not to lovers, but to psychologists; that if you want to understand some 'ideology' (such as medieval chivalry or the nineteenth-century idea of a 'gentleman'), you must not listen to those who lived inside it, but to sociologists. . . . The people who look *at* things have had it all their own way; the people who look *along* things have simply been browbeaten. It has even come to be taken for granted that the external account of a thing somehow refutes or 'debunks' the account given from inside. . . . That, in fact, is the whole basis of the specifically 'modern' type of thought. . . . We must, on pain of idiocy, deny from the very outset the idea that looking *at* is, by its own nature, intrinsically truer or better than looking *along*. One must look both *along* and *at* everything." Lewis, "Meditation in a Toolshed," 608, 609.

117 During Lewis's time at Oxford, the university's formal links to the Church of England were very strong as seventeen of the sixty-nine heads of the colleges were ordained Anglican ministers. Harrison, "College Life, 1918-1939," 82.

118 C.S. Lewis, "Religion: Reality or Substitute?" in *C. S. Lewis: Essay Collection & Other Short Pieces*, ed. Lesley Walmsley (1943 essay reprint; London: HarperCollins, 2000), 137-8.

119 Lewis, *The Pilgrim's Regress*, 164-71.

to misunderstand the Middle Ages,[120] and to misunderstand the Middle Ages is to misunderstand Descartes and the Enlightenment, and so on: "If you join at eleven o'clock a conversation which began at eight you will often not see the real bearing of what is said."[121]

It is for these reasons that Lewis made two telling comments about tradition and its relation to books. First, he rejected the idea of compiling a list of "Best Books" which would be read outside of their particular traditions:

> I rather doubt whether a list of masterpieces picked from all over the world – mostly, I presume to be read in translations? – is a v[ery] useful thing.
>
> I would rather see young men beginning from where they are and being lead on from one thing to another: e.g. that Milton sh[oul]d lead them *either* to Virgil and Homer (and therefore to a really serious study of Latin and Greek) *or* to Dante (and therefore to a whole course of Medieval and Italian studies). That, after all, is how every educated person's development has actually come about.
>
> The sort of culture one can get from the 100 or 1000 Best Books read in isolation from the societies and literature that begot them seems to me like the sort of knowledge of Europe I sh[oul]d get from staying at big hotels in Paris, Berlin, Rome, etc. It w[oul]d be far better to know intimately one little district, going from village to village, getting to know the local politics, jokes, wines, and cheeses. Or so it seems to me.[122]

Second, the Oxford don advised that "after reading a new book, never . . . allow yourself another new one till you have read an old one in between;"[123]

---

120 "You will observe that I begin with classical authors. This is a point I would press on anyone dealing with the Middle Ages, that the first essential is to read the relevant classics over and over: the key to everything – allegory, courtly love etc – is there." Lewis, *The Collected Letters of C. S. Lewis: Volume II*, 141 [June 7, 1934].

121 Lewis, "On the Reading of Old Books," 439.

122 Lewis, *The Collected Letters of C. S. Lewis: Volume III*, 1082-3 [August 25, 1959]. Compare this to what Lewis wrote when he was a younger man: "I have not yet exhausted the horrors of the place: I was glad to see a book case in the lounge. All the books were uniformly bound, and I was surprised to see such unlikely tidbits as the Ethics of Aristotle and the works of the Persian epic poet Firdausi. I solved the mystery by finding out that they were a uniform series of Lubbock's HUNDRED BEST BOOKS!!! How I abominate such culture for the many, such tastes ready made, such standardization of the brain. To substitute for the infinite wandering of the true reader thro[ugh] the byways of the country he discovers, a char-a-banc tour." Lewis, *The Collected Letters of C. S. Lewis: Volume I*, 581 [August 7, 1921].

123 Lewis, "On the Reading of Old Books," 439.

in other words, Lewis believed that the *spiritual exercise* of reading old books (along with talking to wise men, traveling, partaking in rituals etc.) is one of the most useful correctives for historical ignorance and the loss of tradition:

> Every age has its own outlook. It is specially good at seeing certain truths and specially liable to make certain mistakes. We all, therefore, need the books that will correct the characteristic mistakes of our own period. And that means the old books. All contemporary writers share to some extent the contemporary outlook – even those, like myself, who seem most opposed to it.[124]

Of course, being a lover of history, tradition and old books (in context) does not mean that an Old Western Man cannot critique these; on the contrary, he is one of a few who can, for he is one of a few who understands his subject matter enough to comment on it: "To study the past does indeed liberate us from the present, from the idols of our own market-place. But I think it liberates us from the past too. I think no class of men are less enslaved to the past than historians. The unhistorical are usually, without knowing it, enslaved to a fairly recent past."[125]

Now in Lewis's day, despite "progress" being the Spirit of the Age, there were many calls to return to tradition – be it literary, religious etc. Werner Jaeger's Third Humanism (*Der Dritte Humanismus*),[126] Catholic *Ressourcement*,[127] Protestant interest in the Patristics (characterized by the

---

124 Ibid.

125 Lewis, "*De Descriptione Temporum*," 12.

126 Werner Jaeger (1888-1961), the founder of what is sometimes known as Third Humanism, was almost an exact contemporary of Lewis (1898-1963). Jaeger was a German classicist who helped develop what is known as the Nazi reading of Plato (i.e. Plato chiefly as a political philosopher). Yet despite Hitler's attraction to some of Jaeger's classical theories, Jaeger fled to American out of concern for his (second) wife, a Jewess (interestingly, Lewis's wife was also Jewish). Jaeger's humanism, which started in the 1920s, centered around the belief that a renewed interest in classical languages, education and culture (*paideia*) would restore a decadent early twentieth-century Europe to the values of its Hellenic origins. Werner Jaeger, *Paideia: The Ideals of Greek Culture*, vol. 1, 2nd ed., trans. Gilbert Highet (New York: Oxford University Press, 1963), xxv, xxviii.

127 The Second Vatican Council (1962-1965) has been understood in two differing, but not necessarily contradictory, ways. The first way has been to see Catholicism in need of *Aggiornamento* or "updating," which conveys the need for the Church to adjust itself to historical change and to make evangelization more effective by understanding the needs of the modern world. The second way has been to see Catholicism in need of *Ressourcement* or "a return to the sources," which sees Catholic reform in terms of recovering the earliest roots of the Faith by judging later developments by the criterion of authoritative early teachings, in particular, the Bible.

founding of the International Conference on Patristic Studies at Oxford),[128] and the Ecumenical Movement[129] are all examples of twentieth-century conservatism. However, Lewis himself did not fit snugly into any of these. On the one hand, he would have agreed with Jaeger in emphasizing the importance of the classics, with the Catholic *Ressourcement*'s desire to return to the Bible and earlier sources, with Protestant interest in Patristics, and with the Ecumenical Movement's focus on Christian unity. On the other hand, the Oxford don would not have been sympathetic with Jaeger's insistence on the contemporary value of Greek political totalitarianism (which often characterized Third Humanism and sometimes linked it to Nazism), nor did he have any real interest in any of the non-Latin Fathers, nor, in spite of being called a "proto-ecumenist"[130] and even having written an article for the Ecumenical Movement,[131] did he wholehearted support such meetings.[132] And so while Lewis would have seen all of these movements as part of Old Western Culture, he would have seen them as strands different from his own.

And this is important to keep in mind, for although Lewis often spoke about tradition and its importance to Old Western Culture, he himself did not clarify how his own tradition fit into this larger Culture. For instance, he did not say that *his* tradition in terms of classicism was that of a Renaissance humanism (e.g. *Literae Humaniores*) which was modified by medieval literature and romanticism; nor did he make great efforts to emphasize that *his* Christianity was an Anglicanism which, much like the Oxford Movement

---

128 The International Conferences on Patristic Studies, which are the most important conferences having to do with Patristic revival, started to meet at four-year intervals at Oxford beginning in 1951, when Lewis was at the height of his popularity. Sadly, we have no evidence to suggest Lewis ever attended these conferences.

129 The Ecumenical Movement has a long history, but it culminated in the formation of the World Council of Churches in Amsterdam in 1948. Both the Ecumenical Movement and the World Council of Churches focus on the movement in the Church towards the *recovery* of the unity of all believers in Christ, transcending differences of creed, ritual and polity.

130 "Lewis was an ecumenist (in effect) long before the word, or even the idea, became fashionable." Christopher Derrick, *C. S. Lewis and the Church of Rome: A Study in Proto-Ecumenism* (San Francisco: Ignatius Press, 1981), 15.

131 C. S. Lewis, "Modern Man and His Categories of Thought," in *C. S. Lewis: Essay Collection & Other Short Pieces*, ed. Lesley Walmsley (London: HarperCollins, 2000). This essay, written in 1946, was prepared for the first meeting of the World Council of Churches in 1948.

132 "I feel some of the same qualms as you about the Ecumenical Movement." Lewis, *The Collected Letters of C. S. Lewis: Volume III*, 432 [February 22, 1954]. Although we do not know what "qualms" Lewis had about the Movement, it is possible that he feared it would water-down Christianity in an effort to accommodate all denominations.

of the early part of the nineteenth century,[133] made every effort to connect itself to the historical, orthodox Church.

And this, incidentally, is one of the reasons why Lewis the Anglican (*pace* Joseph Pierce,[134] Christopher Derrick,[135] and Walter Hooper[136]) did

---

133 The Oxford Movement was a movement in the Church of England, originating at Oxford University in 1833, which sought to link the Anglican Church more closely to the Roman Catholic Church. The Movement wished to do so because it wanted to defend the Church of England as a divine institution against the threats of liberal theology and government interference. Ultimately, the Movement culminated in the formation of Anglo-Catholicism or, as it had historically been called, "High" Anglicanism, as opposed to "Low" (more Protestant) or "Broad" (more liberal) Anglicanism. Although Lewis shared in the Anglo-Catholic love of ritual, its wariness of liberal theology and its respect for tradition, not to mention the fact that the Oxford don was a regular contributor to the High Anglican newspaper *The Guardian*, Lewis said that he was "not especially 'high' nor especially 'low' [church]." Lewis, *Mere Christianity*, 313.

134 Pierce is the harshest of Lewis's Catholic critics, for not only does he think Lewis, as an Anglican, is out of line with tradition, but he also strongly denounces Lewis's mere Christianity as "deficient," claiming it is "*less* Christian than the Church" etc. Joseph Pierce, *C. S. Lewis and the Church of Rome* (San Francisco: Ignatius Press, 2003), 168.

135 While Derrick would agree with Pierce that Lewis's Anglicanism is out of line with Catholic, and therefore correct, tradition, Derrick was a friend of Lewis's and preferred to critique Lewis in a more generous way: "'Why didn't [Lewis] become a Roman Catholic?' Lewis intensely disliked any raising of that question, or of any similarly 'denominational' question; and having known him well, I have no doubt at all that during his lifetime, he would have disapproved most strongly of this present book." Derrick, *C. S. Lewis and the Church of Rome*, 15-6.

136 Like Derrick, Hooper was a personal friend of, and has an enormous respect for, Lewis; nevertheless, I believe Hooper's own conversion from Anglicanism to Catholicism caused him to misstep when he said he thought that were Lewis alive today, he would convert to Catholicism: "One of the last papers that [Lewis] wrote was to Anglican seminarians in Cambridge. And in that well-known paper – called *Fern-seed and Elephants* – he points out that, if they continue to talk that sort of liberalism that they were then talking – and increasingly more now – he said that their readers and hearers would leave the Anglican church and become either atheists or Roman Catholics. I think he would probably have had to include himself in that group." Walter Hooper, "Interview," *Crisis* (July-August 1994). Hooper's argument fails (and I say with the utmost respect for the man) not only because Lewis did not include himself among the liberal Anglicans he was addressing (and hence would not have been forced into a false dilemma between atheism and Catholicism), but also Lewis, though he did not like to talk about it, had a distrust of the dogmatism of Rome (among other things), which accounted for his fear that his brother would convert to Catholicism when he was being treated for alcoholism by some admittedly "charming nuns." Lewis, *The Collected Letters of C. S. Lewis: Volume II*, 790 [July 6, 1947]. And if this were not enough, Lewis himself explicitly denied having any inclination towards Rome; thus, he told a certain lady: "I believe we are very near to one another, but not because I am at all on the Rome-ward frontier of my own communion." Lewis, *The Collected Letters of C. S. Lewis: Volume III*, 249 [November 10, 1952].

not convert to Catholicism: he believed that Catholic doctrines like the infallibility of the papal office and the Immaculate Conception represented a disunity with Christian tradition and orthodoxy (particularly as understood by Anglicans): "By the time I had really explained my objection to certain doctrines which differentiate you [a Catholic] from us [Protestants] (and also in my opinion from the Apostolic and even the Medieval Church), you would like me less."[137] That is, while Lewis felt that Protestants, including his own Anglicans, were inclined to distort tradition by stripping away whatever appears superfluous – usually meaning ritual and tradition – he felt Catholics tend to distort tradition by adding too much to it: "You see in Protestantism the Faith dying out in a desert: we see in Rome the Faith smothered in a jungle."[138] In other words, both Protestants and Catholics can pervert the Christian tradition, but they do so in different ways. For this reason, Lewis believed that an Old Western Man needs to attain a deep respect for the past, but not, of course, one that denies his inner philosopher a healthy critique of historical development and his own cultural milieu.

***

The fifth part of Lewis's description of an Old Western Man states that an Old Western Man puts no faith in historicism as understood by the grand myth of evolutionary development.

Pointing to Lewis's essay "Historicism," Barfield claimed that Lewis failed to appreciate historical development and the idea of progressive revelation, the result of which, Barfield contested, is that Lewis overemphasized the transcendence of God to the detriment of God's immanence.[139] While it is easy to see how Barfield, an Anthroposophist who believed in progressive revelation and developmentalism, could feel that Lewis did not do these areas enough justice, I think Barfield gets Lewis wrong since Lewis wrote

137 Ibid., 106 [March 1951]. This also should answer Peter Milward, who thinks that Lewis's neglect of the Virgin Mary is a sign that he was outside of the *real* Christian tradition. Peter Milward, *A Challenge to C. S. Lewis* (London: Associated University Presses, 1995), 62-3.
138 C. S. Lewis "Christian Reunion: An Anglican Speaks to Roman Catholics," in *C. S. Lewis: Essay Collection & Other Short Pieces*, ed. Lesley Walmsley (London: HarperCollins, 2000), 396. This essay was probably written around 1944. Cf. "When Catholicism goes bad it becomes the world-old, world-wide *religio* of amulets and holy places and priestcraft: Protestantism, in its corresponding decay, becomes a vague mist of ethical platitudes. Catholicism is accused of being much too like all the other religions; Protestantism of being insufficiently like a religion at all. Hence Plato, with his transcendent Forms, is the doctor of Protestants; Aristotle, with his immanent Forms, the doctor of Catholics." Lewis, *The Allegory of Love*, 323.
139 Barfield, *Owen Barfield on C. S. Lewis*, 78.

some of his most admirable essays and literature – *The Chronicles of Narnia* not the least of which – precisely about God's immanence and His purpose in Creation (think Aslan); moreover, Lewis clearly had an idea of what development should be like as we can see when he wrote the following about fairy tales:

> The modern view seems to involve a false conception of growth. They accuse us of arrested development because we have not lost a taste we had in childhood. But surely arrested development consists not in refusing to lose old things but in failing to add new things? I now like hock, which I am sure I should not have liked as a child. But I still like lemon-squash. I call this growth or development because I have been enriched: where I formerly had only one pleasure, I now have two. But if I had to lose the taste for lemon-squash before I acquired the taste for hock that would not be growth but simple change. I now enjoy Tolstoy and Jane Austen and Trollope as well as fairy tales and I call that growth: if I had to lose the fairy tales in order to acquire the novelists, I would not say that I have grown but only that I had changed. A tree grows because it adds rings: a train doesn't grow by leaving one station behind and puffing on to the next.[140]

Thus, when Lewis denied Historicism – "the belief that men can, by the use of their natural powers, discover an inner meaning in the historical process"[141] – he was simply denying that we can *know* the meaning of all historical events, not that there is no purpose to the events or genuine development within history (we must remember Lewis loved Chesterton's *Everlasting Man*, a book about the history of Christianity *qua* the history of the World). In this, Lewis agreed with Boethius, who thought that while everything looks like Fortune from man's perspective, from God's perspective, everything is Providence.[142]

Moreover, according to Lewis *qua* Old Western Man, just because creation and history have a purpose, it does not follow that they are "growing" – as opposed to merely "changing;" indeed, the history of creation – *contra* Hegelians, Marxists and Darwinians – seems to be more a matter of "New Learning and New Ignorance" than anything else,[143] for while Lewis believed that the twentieth century "grew" in regard to technology and "more social conscience than there has ever been before," he thought it merely "changed"

---

140 Lewis, "On Three Ways of Writing for Children," 508.
141 C. S. Lewis, "Historicism," in *C. S. Lewis: Essay Collection & Other Short Pieces*, ed. Lesley Walmsley (1950 essay reprint; London: HarperCollins, 2000), 621.
142 Boethius *The Consolation of Philosophy* 4.4-5.
143 This is the title of the introduction to Lewis's *Poetry and Prose in the Sixteenth Century*.

in regard to morality, rationality, art etc.[144]

Thus, even though Lewis conceded that biological life *may* be evolving, he did not think that this meant that things are getting better, for "things" are not merely biological, but are also spiritual and spiritual matters entail freedom of choice, which in turn entails good and bad results; therefore, the Oxford don believed that an Old Western Man is a person who is aware of Darwin's confession of spiritual and metaphysical ignorance – "My power to follow along a purely abstract train of thought is very limited; and therefore I could never have succeeded with metaphysics or mathematics"[145] – and he resists importing a biological theory which may be true, and therefore compatible with Old Western Culture, into the spiritual or metaphysical realm: "Again, for the scientist Evolution is a purely biological theorem. It takes over organic life on this planet as a going concern and tries to explain certain changes within that field. It makes no cosmic statements, no metaphysical statements, no eschatological statements."[146]

Moreover, Lewis thought that political structures, *contra* Hegel and Marx, in no way demonstrate inevitable development or improvement, for such are largely made by people: creatures of mixed spiritual motives. Accordingly, while Lewis believed that an Old Western Man need not agree with the medieval philosophy of history – "The nearest we get to a widespread 'philosophy of history' in the Middle Ages is . . . the frequent assertion that things were once better than they are now"[147] – Lewis thought that he should be neither a pessimist nor an optimist in regard to history, for while such a man (in his Christian form) knows that ultimately Christ will return and save the day (hence Tolkien's "Eucatastrophe" or mythical happy ending),

---

144 Lewis, "Modern Man and His Categories of Thought," 620. Cf. "Progress means not just changing, but changing for the better. . . . We all want progress. But progress means getting nearer to the place where you want to be. And if you have taken a wrong turning, then to go forward does not get you any nearer. If you are on the wrong road, progress means doing an about-turn and walking back to the right road; and in that case the man who turns back soonest is the most progressive man." Lewis, *Mere Christianity*, 329, 338. Cf. "I do not think that all who choose wrong roads perish; but their rescue consists in being put back on the right road. A sum can be put right: but only by going back till you find the error and working it afresh from that point, never by simply *going on*." Lewis, *The Great Divorce*, 1025.
145 C. S. Lewis, underlining in his edition of *Autobiography*, by Charles Darwin, ed. Francis Darwin (London: Watts and Co., 1929; The Marion E. Wade Center, Wheaton College), 75.
146 C. S. Lewis, "The Funeral of a Great Myth," in *C. S. Lewis: Essay Collection & Other Short Pieces*, ed. Lesley Walmsley (London: HarperCollins, 2000), 25. Cf. Lewis, "Modern Man and His Categories," 618.
147 Lewis, *The Discarded Image*, 184.

until then, the world remains a varied place. As Lewis told Tolkien, "All my philosophy of history hangs upon a sentence of your own 'Deeds were done which were not *wholly* in vain.'"[148]

***

The sixth component in Lewis's portrayal of an Old Western Man is that he (or she), must acknowledge that the universe is ultimately hierarchical. From Moses to St. Paul, from Plotinus to Bernardus Silvestris, from Milton to Johnson, Old Western Men have always believed that all of existence is a "Chain of Being."[149] This means that *everything* has its proper place in an absolute ontological hierarchy, entailing, of course, that Aristotle is right when he said, "Justice means equality for equals, and inequality for unequals;"[150] moreover, belief in a Great Chain of Being involves the conviction that when an individual acts justly – i.e. according to his nature and place in the hierarchy – then he will be happy:

> According to this conception degrees of value are objectively present in the universe. Everything except God has some natural superior; everything except unformed matter has some natural inferior. The goodness, happiness, and dignity of every being consists in obeying its natural superior and ruling its natural inferior. When it fails in either part of this twofold task we have disease or monstrosity in the scheme of things until the peccant being is either destroyed or corrected.[151]

Critics of Old Western Culture will very naturally ask if this metaphysical hierarchy entails political, social and ecclesiastical hierarchy – if democracy, feminism and anti-clericalism, in other words, are incompatible with Old Western Culture. Since I will return to most of these issues in chapters six and nine, I will try to be brief for the time being.

First, Lewis agreed with Robert Filmer that if Adam and Eve had not fallen, then "patriarchal monarchy would be the sole lawful government."[152] Democracy, as a result, would have been incompatible with Old Western Culture were people not fallen, but since people are fallen, democracy is the best political structure they have, for it minimizes the abuse that comes from absolute rulers:

148 Lewis, *The Collected Letters of C. S. Lewis: Volume III*, 1396 [December 24, 1962]. Cf. Ibid., 971 [September 11, 1958].
149 Lewis, "Christianity and Culture," 77.
150 Aristotle *Politics* 12801a10-10-15. Cf. Lewis, *A Preface to Paradise Lost*, 74.
151 Lewis, *A Preface to Paradise Lost*, 73-4.
152 C. S. Lewis, "Membership," in *C. S. Lewis: Essay Collection & Other Short Pieces*, ed. Lesley Walmsley (1945 essay reprint; London: HarperCollins, 2000), 337.

I believe in political equality. But there are two opposite reasons for being a democrat. You may think all men so good that they deserve a share in the government of the commonwealth, and so wise that the commonwealth needs their advice. That is, in my opinion, the false, romantic doctrine of democracy. On the other hand, you may believe fallen men to be so wicked that not one of them can be trusted with any irresponsible power over his fellows.[153]

Hierarchy in politics, therefore, is a danger according to Lewis, yet two things should be kept in mind. Firstly, Lewis believed that the politicians of his day, in particular those belonging to the Labour Party[154] and its Welfare State,[155] were concerned with *"Govertisement"* or *"government by advertisement,"*[156] which was largely possible thanks to the rise of public radio, television and cheap daily newspapers in the twentieth century.[157] The Oxford don thought

153 Ibid., 336-7.
154 On July 22, 1901, the Taff Vale Railway Company successfully sued the trade union Amalgamated Society of Railway Servants for the costs of industrial action taken by its members. The Labour Representative Committee, which was a socialist federation formed in 1900, convinced the trade unions that the political representation of labour was now necessary. This organization later became the Labour Party. About thirty years later, on May 30, 1929, the Labour Party won its first general election. The party went on to win three more general elections during Lewis's lifetime. Duncan Tanner, "Electing the Governors / the Governance of the Elect," in *The British Isles: 1901-1951*, ed. Keith Robbins, 43-72 (Oxford: Oxford University Press, 2006), 47, 50, 67-71. Of the Labour Party's 1950 government, Lewis said to his American friend Warfield Firor: "Have you any parallel to their imbecility? All rulers lie: but did you ever meet such bad liars?" Lewis, *The Collected Letters of C. S. Lewis: Volume III*, 67 [December 6, 1950].
155 In November 1942, Sir William Beveridge's report *Social Security and National Insurance* gave a summary of principles aimed at banishing poverty from Britain, including a system of social security that would be operated by the government, and would come into effect at the end of WWII. Beveridge argued that the war gave Britain a unique opportunity to make revolutionary changes. Berveridge's recommendations for the creation of a Welfare State, including the creation of the National Health Service, were implemented by Labour Prime Minster Clement Attlee after the war. Marwick, *A History of the Modern British Isles, 1914-1999*, 178-84. In a 1944 letter to The Society for the Prevention of Progress, Lewis humorously wrote: "While feeling I was *born* a member of your Society, I am nevertheless honoured to receive the outward seal of membership. I shall hope by continued orthodoxy and unremitting practice of Reaction, Obstruction, and Stagnation to give you no reason for repenting your favour." Lewis went on to say at the bottom of the letter: "Beverages not Beveridges (my motto)." Lewis, *The Collected Letters of C. S. Lewis: Volume II*, 613-4 [May 1944]. Later, in 1958, Lewis wrote an essay called "Willing Slaves of the Welfare State," in which he critiqued Beveridge's handiwork, even though he approved of the National Health Service. Lewis, *The Collected Letters of C. S. Lewis: Volume III*, 914 [January 14, 1958], 1064 [July 7, 1959], 1429 [June 10, 1963].
156 Lewis, *"De Descriptione Temporum,"* 8.
157 *The Daily Herald*, for instance, was founded on May 13, 1912, and the British

that political elections were more about political charisma and keenness (indicated by "appeals," "drives" and "campaigns") than they were about justice.[158] Naturally, Lewis thought this is contrary to Old Western Culture, for while politicians of all ages have been corrupt, the majority of those in the past (and some in the present, we must remember) were not as concerned about image, for in the past they did not fear the popular vote as much. Secondly, even in a democracy, Lewis believed that a nation such as England should not completely eliminate its symbolical monarchy, for the concept of the King is full of deep spiritual and mythical significance as it communicates to people the hierarchical nature of Reality:

> We Britons should rejoice that we have contrived to reach much legal democracy (we still need more of the economic) without losing our ceremonial Monarchy. For there, right in the midst of our lives, is that which satisfies the craving for inequality, and acts as a permanent reminder that medicine is not good. Hence a man's reaction to Monarchy is a kind of test. Monarchy can easily be 'debunked,' but watch the faces, and mark well the accents, of the debunkers. These are the men whose tap-root in Eden has been cut: whom no rumour of the polyphony, the dance, can reach – men to whom pebbles laid in a row are more beautiful than an arch.[159]

Second, even in a fallen world, Lewis did not believe that feminism, the doctrine that states the sexes are equal, is true or compatible with Old Western Culture except insofar as women ought to have equal political rights in the democracies of a fallen world (hence, such rights are "legal fiction"[160] or "egalitarian fiction"[161]). Lewis thought that scripture's insistence on the subordination of wives to husbands was neither a fallen teaching nor merely the product of a patriarchal culture; rather, he believed that familial hierarchy, as with ceremonial monarchy, is a *mythical* representation of Reality itself. While we will explore this debate further in chapter nine, we ought to keep in mind that although Lewis's reasons for granting women political rights were different than those of the prominent feminists of his

---

Broadcasting Corporation (BBC) was granted a Royal Charter in 1927. In addition, the first public demonstration of television was given on January 26, 1926, although TV did not become widely available until after WWII. Justin Phillips, *C. S. Lewis at the BBC: Messages of Hope in the Darkness of War* (London: HarperCollins, 2002), 18.

158 Lewis, "*De Descriptione Temporum*," 8.

159 C. S. Lewis, "Equality," in *C. S. Lewis: Essay Collection & Other Short Pieces*, ed. Lesley Walmsley (1943 essay reprint; London: HarperCollins, 2000), 668.

160 Lewis, "Priestesses in the Church?" 401.

161 Lewis, "Membership," 337.

day, such as Millicent Fawcett,[162] Emmeline and Christabel Pankhurst,[163] Emily Davison,[164] and Nancy Astor,[165] he was still in agreement with them about *the fact* that they ought to be given the right to vote, own property and get an education. Indeed, given the extreme anti-feminist, old-boy culture of both Oxford, which only began granting degrees to women in 1920,[166] and Cambridge, whose Magdalene College, Lewis's college, only started admitting women in 1988,[167] Lewis could arguably be seen as a fairly

---

162 Although pinpointing an exact date is impossible, it is reasonable to see Olympia de Gouges as the first modern feminist. In 1791, she wrote *A Declaration of the Rights of Women and of Female Citizens*, which argues that women are citizens as much as men – that if women have the right to go to the scaffold, then they should also have the right to go to Parliament; ironically, she was sent to the guillotine two years later. In 1792, England witnessed her first modern feminist: Mary Wollstonecraft. In her *Vindication of the Rights of Woman*, she fought for the right to vote and for equal education opportunities. Wollstonecraft's book was followed about a hundred years later by John Stuart Mill's *Subjection of Women* (1861), which argued for "complete equality in all legal, political, social and domestic relations" between men and women. John Stuart Mill, *The Subjection of Women* (1861 reprint; Mineola, NY: Dover Publication, 1997), 102. This led to the first British petition for women's suffrage (1867), which was followed in 1870 with a bill passed in Parliament that gave women limited rights to retain their property after marriage. This act was amended in 1883, giving women the right to acquire and retain any property deemed separate from that of their husbands'. However, the modern feminist movement picked up the pace in 1897, when the National Central Society for Women's Suffrage and the Central Committee for Women's Suffrage merged into the National Union of Women's Suffrage Societies (NUWSS). Under the leadership of its president, Millicent Fawcett, the NUWSS coordinated a range of law-abiding regional activities.

163 On October 10, 1904, the Woman's Social and Political Union (WSPU) was founded by six women, the most famous of whom were Emmeline and Christabel Pankhurst. Frustrated by the NUWSS's lack of success in obtaining women's rights, the WSPU became increasingly more confrontational to the point where Emmeline was eventually imprisoned. Marwick, *A History of the Modern British Isles, 1914-1999*, 43-53.

164 On June 4, 1913, Emily Davidson, a WSPU suffragette, was trampled to death by the king's horse when she threw herself in front of the animal in protest. Although this activity did little for women's rights, on February 16, 1918, a limited number of women – only propertied women over the age of thirty – were given the historical opportunity to vote for the first time.

165 On December 1, 1919, Lady Nancy Astor became the first British MP to take her seat in the House of Parliament. In the same month, the Sex Disqualification Removal Act made it illegal for women to be excluded from most jobs, and allowed them to hold judicial office and enter the professions. Women could then become magistrates, solicitors and barristers. About ten years later, on May 7, 1928, all women over the age of twenty-one were given the right to vote on the same terms as men.

166 Academic halls for women were first established at Oxford in the nineteenth century, yet although women had been able to attend degree level courses, they could not receive degrees until 1920.

167 Magdalene College, Cambridge, which offered Lewis the Chair of Medieval and

generous-minded conservative, especially considering the fact that he tutored an impressive number of female students (relative to the female population at Oxford[168]). Yet as I say, Lewis was no feminist, and his reasons for not being one were at least as much the product of deliberate philosophizing as an unthinking cultural bias – despite what most of his critics say.[169]

Third, although Lewis could not be clearly identified as either a high or a low churchman, he did believe that the Church was a hierarchy and so laymen ought to practice the *spiritual exercise* of proper subordination to their spiritual elders. It should be the delight of laymen, Lewis argued, to kneel when they accept the Eucharist, kiss the cross, and pray,[170] and it is helpful, as Lewis himself found out through practice, to confess one's sins to a priest, for while the priest does not forgive by his own power, he, according to the grand tradition of Christianity, acts as God's representative on Earth and thus should be respected:

> I am going to make my first confession next week, wh[ich] will seem
> odd to you, but I wasn't brought up to that kind of thing. It's an odd

Renaissance Literature, was "the last college in Cambridge (as well as Oxford) to admit female students." Peter Sager, *Oxford & Cambridge: An Uncommon History* (London: Thames & Hudson, 2005), 296.

168 During the 1913-1914 school year, of the seventy women enrolled at Oxford, 36% of them chose to specialize in English; this percentage would stay more or less the same despite the tenfold increase of women over the next ten years. Currie, "The Arts and Social Studies, 1914-1939," 110. While most of the female students at Oxford were tutored by female dons in their own halls, it was not uncommon for male dons to tutor female students. Janet Howarth, "Women," in *The History of the University of Oxford: Volume VIII; The Twentieth Century*, ed. Brian Harrison, 345-76 (Oxford: Oxford University Press, 1994), 346. Since Lewis was an English tutor, he received a higher percentage of female students for tutorials than most of the other tutors at Oxford.

169 See Candice Fredrick and Sam McBride, *Women Among the Inklings: Gender, C. S. Lewis, J. R. R. Tolkien, and Charles Williams* (London: Greenwood Press, 2001), 38. Karin Fry, "No Longer a Friend of Narnia: Gender in Narnia," in *The Chronicles of Narnia and Philosophy*, ed. Gregory Bassham and Jerry L. Walls, 155-66 (Chicago: Open Court, 2005), 155. Kort, *C. S. Lewis: Then and Now*, 157. Cathy McSporran, "Daughters of Lilith: Witches and Wicked Women in the Chronicles of Narnia," in *Revisiting Narnia: Fantasy, Myth and Religion in C. S. Lewis' Chronicles*, ed. Shanna Caughey, 191-204 (Dallas: Benbella Books, 2005), 193. Doris Myers, "Lewis in Genderland," *Christian Scholar's Review* 36, no. 4 (Summer 2007): 460. For my response to these critics, see Adam Barkman, "C. S. Lewis: Sexist and Masculine Idolater?'" *Inklings-Jahrbuch für Literatur und Ästhetik* (Forthcoming 2009).

170 "It delights me that there should be moments in the services of my own Church when the priest stands and I kneel." Lewis, "Membership," 338. Cf. Lewis, *The Screwtape Letters*, 747. Although Lewis felt that all laymen benefit from the *spiritual exercise* of kneeling when they pray, he did not think that spiritually mature people – and people too old physically to do so – need to worry about the position of the body so long as the mind and heart are right. Lewis, *Prayer: Letters to Malcolm*, 234.

experience. The *decision* to do so was one of the hardest I have ever
made. . . . However, *quod ubique quo dab omnibus!* [an abbreviation of
Id teneamus, quod ubique, quod semper, quod ab omnibus creditum est,
'Let us hold on to that which has been believed everywhere, always, by
everyone,' a passage taken from St. Vincent of Lerin's *Commonitorium*
4.3].[171]

The Church, supported by a mostly true tradition, is the witness to Myth
and so, Lewis believed, it should demonstrate the mythical truth inherent in
hierarchy, which means, for instance, that women, as subordinate to men,
should not be permitted to act as priestesses (as Lewis wrote in his 1948 essay
"Priestesses in the Church?" which was directed against the 1944 ordination
of Li Tim Oi, who became the first Anglican priestess[172]), for while Christ
called all people to be priests in the sense that all are worthy to come before
Him, only men can mythically or symbolically represent the masculinity of
God's truest nature:

> One of the ends for which sex was created was to symbolize to us the
> hidden things of God. One of the functions of human marriage is to
> express the nature of the union between Christ and the Church. We
> have no authority to take the living and seminal figures which God
> has painted on the canvas of our nature and shift them about as if they
> were mere geometrical figures. . . . This is what common sense will call
> 'mystical.' Exactly. The Church claims to be the bearer of revelation. If
> that claim is false then we want not to make priestesses but to abolish
> priests. If it is true, then we would expect to find in the Church an
> element which unbelievers will call irrational and which believers will
> call suprarational.[173]

Subsequently, Lewis agreed with St. Paul, who said Christians should see
themselves as members of differing dignity in a common body ("By *members*
(μέλη) [St. Paul] meant what we should call *organs*, things essentially
different from, and complementary to, one another: things differing not
only in structure and function but also in dignity"[174]) and Lewis agreed
with Chalcidius,[175] a fifth-century Christian Platonist, from whom Lewis

171 Lewis, *The Collected Letters of C. S. Lewis: Volume II*, 452 [October 24, 1940].
172 While Li Tim Oi became the first Anglican priestess, the Church of Scotland (the
   Anglican Church in Scotland) did not *formally* allow female ordination until 1968
   and the Church of England (the Anglican Church in England) until 1992. G. I. T.
   Machin, *Churches and Social Issues in Twentieth-Century Britain* (Oxford: Clarendon
   Press, 2006), 20.
173 Lewis, "Priestesses in the Church?" 401
174 Lewis, "Membership," 334.
175 Walter Hooper thinks that Lewis borrowed the idea of the celestial dance from
   Chalcidius (and not, presumably, some older source). Hooper, *Companion & Guide*,

borrowed the idea that all of existence is, or ought to be, a grand celestial
dance consisting of harmonious motions of justice and love:

> 'It is loaded with justice as a tree bows down with fruit. All is
> righteousness and there is no equality. Not as stones lie side by side,
> but as when stones support and are supported in an arch, such is His
> order; rule and obedience, begetting and bearing, heat glancing down,
> life growing up. Blessed be He!' . . . 'In the plan of the Great Dance
> plans without number interlock, and each movement becomes in its
> season the breaking into flower of the whole design to which all else
> had been directed. Thus each is equally at the centre and none are there
> by being equals, but some by giving place and some by receiving it, the
> small things by their smallness and the great by their greatness, and all
> the patterns linked and looped together by the unions of a kneeling
> with a sceptered love.'[176]

This notion of "each . . . equally at the centre and none . . . there by being
equals" is an idea that Lewis likely got from Charles Williams, who wrote:
"Hierarchic, republican, the glory of Logres," which Lewis took to mean:
"As willed necessity is freedom, so willed hierarchy becomes equality."[177]
That is, the only true equality in ontological or spiritual terms is that which
comes from love, the equal amount of love, for instance, that a ruler has for
his subject and a subject has for his master; it is a proportionate equality

---

531. However, Will Vaus thinks Lewis got the idea from St. Gregory of Nazianzus.
Will Vaus, *Mere Theology: A Guide to the Thought of C. S. Lewis* (Downers Grove, IL.:
InterVarsity Press, 2004), 16. And Jaime Vidal, who does even bother trying to trace
the origin of this idea, thinks it is from St. Bonaventure. Jaime Vidal, "The Ubiquitous
Center in Bonaventure and Lewis with Application to The Great Dance on Perelandra,"
CSL: The Bulletin of the New York C. S. Lewis Society 6, no. 5 (March 1975): 1-4.
Hooper, no doubt, is correct, not only because there is neither evidence that Lewis
knew St. Gregory of Nazianzus (Lewis was poorly read in the Greek Fathers) nor that he
cared for Bonaventure (who certainly did not originate the idea of the Celestial Dance),
but also because Lewis used the Latin name for the celestial dance – "*caelestis chorea*"
(literally "a dance belonging to heaven") – indicating that he was more familiar with the
Latin Chalcidius than the Greek St. Gregory. And of course, even more tellingly, Lewis
actually linked Chalcidius and the celestial dance explicitly in many places; hence, we
read: "Thus, for Chalcidius, the geocentric universe is not in the least anthropocentric.
If we ask why, nevertheless, the Earth is central, he has a very unexpected answer. It is so
placed in order that the celestial dance may have a centre to revolve about." Lewis, *The
Discarded Image*, 55. And, "In actual fact what Spenser has done is to make an image
of the whole of life, a hymn to the universe that he and his contemporaries believed
themselves to inhabit. . . . For the universe, as they conceived it, is a great dance or
ceremony or society. It is Chalcidius' *caelestis chorea* and Alanus' cosmic city of which
Earth is a suburb." Lewis, *Spenser's Images of Life*, 96.
176 Lewis, *Perelandra*, 340-1, 343.
177 Lewis, *The Arthurian Torso*, 142.

grounded in Augustine's definition of virtue as "properly ordered loves," loving each according to its place.[178] For example, a husband and wife may be equal in their love for each other, yet it is precisely in this equal love that there is a radical hierarchy, for the husband loves his wife by ruling her well, and the wife loves her husband by obeying him well. To reject the equality of love which results in radical hierarchy is ultimately – and not just in our families and at Church – to reject one of the most fundamental principles of Old Western Culture: "Now if once the conception of Hierarchy is fully grasped, we see that order can be destroyed in two ways: (1) By ruling or obeying natural equals, that is by Tyranny or Servility. (2) By failing to obey a natural superior or to rule a natural inferior – that is, by Rebellion or Remissness."[179]

***

The seventh element in Lewis's understanding of an Old Western Man is that such a man, as a lover of Nature, will have both a healthy balance of trust in, and distrust of, technology and industry, for while technology *per se* (i.e. insofar as it is the product of reason) is not bad, its abuse has done a lot of harm, fueling, among other things, the false myth of developmentalism – in particular, the belief that everything is getting better simply because our technology has been improving.[180]

Now Lewis's belief that Old Western Men are those who are wary of technology and industry and the economics that drive these must be understood in its proper context. From his earliest years in Belfast watching the "unsinkable" Titanic being built[181] to experiencing firsthand the application of technology in WWI,[182] from reading about the Nazis' abuse of genetics[183]

---

178 Augustine *The City of God* 15.22. Cf. "We must aim at what St. Augustine (is it?) called 'ordinate loves.' Our deepest concern should be for first things, and our next deepest for second things, and so on down to zero." Lewis, *Prayer: Letters to Malcolm*, 237.

179 Lewis, *A Preface to Paradise Lost*, 76-7.

180 Lewis, *"De Descriptione Temporum,"* 10. Hadot distinguishes these two attitudes towards technology as "Promethean" (i.e. the belief that we should use technology to rule Nature) and "Orphic" (i.e. the belief that we should use technology to live in harmony with Nature). Hadot, *The Veil of Isis*, 97.

181 Bleakley, *C. S. Lewis – at Home in Ireland*, 95.

182 "Homer's war was nothing akin to Lewis's war – except in that humans died." K. J. Gilchrist, *A Morning After War: C. S. Lewis and WWI* (New York: Peter Lang, 2005), 71.

183 The "science" practiced in Lewis's *That Hideous Strength* is largely modeled on that which he heard was happening in Nazi Germany. However, the Oxford don also warned that eugenics and the abuse of genetics could easily become a reality in England and the rest of the world.

to the creation of the A-bomb,[184] Lewis felt that the progress of science, which began in the Enlightenment and moved through the Industrial Revolution and Second Industrial Revolution, was a movement that, left unchecked, would ultimately result in "the abolition of man."[185] Lewis feared that Old Western Man's link to Nature, which is pre-Watt,[186] was increasingly being

---

184 In December 1945, Lewis wrote the poem "On the Atomic Bomb: Metrical Experiment," which reads:

> So; you have found an engine
> Of injury that angels
> Might dread. The world plunges,
> Shies, snorts, and curvets like a horse in danger.
>
> Then comfort her with fondlings,
> With kindly word and handling,
> But do not believe blindly
> This way or that. Both fears and hopes are swindlers.
>
> What's here to dread? For mortals
> Both hurt and death were certain
> Already; our light-hearted
> Hopes from the first sentenced to final thwarting.
>
> This marks no huge advance in
> The dance of Death. His pincers
> Were grim before with chances
> Of cold, fire, suffocation, Ogpu, cancer.
>
> Nor hope that his last blunder
> Will end our woes by rending
> Tellus herself asunder –
> All gone in one bright flash like driest tinder.
>
> As if your puny gadget
> Could dodge the terrible logic
> Of history! No; the tragic
> Road will go on, new generations trudge it.
>
> Narrow and long it stretches,
> Wretched for one who marches
> Eyes front. He never catches
> A glimpse of the fields each side, the happy orchards.

C. S. Lewis, "On the Atomic Bomb: Metrical Experiment," in *Poems*, by C. S. Lewis, ed. Walter Hooper, 64-5 (San Diego: Harcourt Brace Jovanovich, 1964), 64-5 [1.1-7.4].

185 This is the title of one of Lewis's books.

186 Although it is impossible to say exactly when the Industrial Revolution began, Lewis saw James Watt's creation of a new type of steam engine in 1769 as the beginning of the end for Old Western Man's connection with Nature. Lewis, *"De Descriptione Temporum,"* 10. Of course, as I have already mentioned, Lewis believed that Old Western Men continued to exist after the eighteenth century, but in regard to Nature, fewer and fewer

severed by the siren-call of power and money that came with mechanization. Moreover, the Oxford don believed that the modern industrialized West tempts people – often unintentionally, though Anthroposophists think otherwise[187] – with its machines and miracle-cures into viewing the pastoral, non-mechanized days of old as backward and foolish:

> Between Jane Austen and us, but not between her and Shakespeare, Chaucer, Alfred, Virgil, Homer, or the Pharaohs, comes the birth of the machine. This lifts us at once into a region of change far above all that we have hitherto considered. . . . How has it come about that we use the high emotive word 'stagnation,' with all its malodorous and malarial overtones, for what other ages would have called 'permanence?' Why does the word 'primitive' at once suggest to us clumsiness, inefficiency, barbarity? . . . Why does 'latest' in advertisements mean 'best?'[188]

The most astounding example of this is how most moderns now perceive Adam in the Garden of Eden: from a god-like king who lived a thousand years, Adam has been reduced to a mere monkey; from the father of this world, who could see into the essence of animals and bring out their names, Adam, God's greatest earthly creation, has been diminished to an ignorant Neanderthal.[189]

To rectify this false glamorization of technology at the expense of the pastoral past (which can also be over-glamorized as we saw earlier), Lewis made the first king of Narnia, King Frank, a technologically-ignorant man, a friend of the animals (perhaps partly inspired by Lewis's reading of Henry

---

remained. Of those who did remain, Lewis identified most closely with the Romantic poets, such as Wordsworth and Blake, who were wary of the Industrial Revolution.

187 Although both Lewis and Barfield agreed that the rise of "technological materialism" was a bad thing, Barfield, following Steiner, thought it was the work of "Luciferic" or "Ahrimanic powers." Adey, *C. S. Lewis's 'Great War' with Owen Barfield*, 29.

188 Lewis, "*De Descriptione Temporum*," 10.

189 "Adam was, from the first, a man in knowledge as well as in stature. He alone of all men 'has been in Eden, in the garden of God: he has walked up and down in the midst of the stones of fire.' He was endowed, says Athanasius, with 'a vision of God so far-reaching that he could contemplate the eternity of the Divine Essence and the cosmic operations of His Word.' He was 'a heavenly being,' according to St. Ambrose, who breathed the aether, and was accustomed to converse with God 'face to face.' 'His mental powers,' says St. Augustine, 'surpassed those of the most brilliant philosopher as much as the speed of a bird surpasses that of a tortoise.'" Lewis, *A Preface to Paradise Lost*, 117. However, it should be noted that not all the Fathers believed Adam to be so august; Irenaeus, for instance, saw Our First Father as a child who needed to fall in order to grow.

More[190]) and a man who can "use a spade and a plough."[191] Yet it is precisely because King Frank ruled well – i.e. remembered his place in the hierarchy, obeying Aslan and governing his subjects, including Nature, well – that he is paid such great homage in *The Last Battle*;[192] indeed, the homage that he is given reflects – said Lewis, speaking of *Paradise Lost* – what it would have been like for Adam had he not fallen:

> Adam would have been alive in Paradise, and to that 'capital seat' all generations 'from all the ends of the Earth' would have come periodically to do their homage (XI, 342). To you or to me, once in a lifetime perhaps, would have fallen the almost terrifying honour of coming at last, after long journeys and ritual preparations and slow ceremonial approaches, into the very presence of the great Father, Priest, and Emperor of the planet Tellus; a thing to be remembered all our lives.[193]

Subsequently, just as King Frank was called to be a guardian of Nature, which, of course, entailed controlling the mad dash of technology, the natural kings and queens of Narnia that followed him, we are told by Lewis, "saved good trees from being unnecessarily cut down," among other noble deeds.[194] And just as all the kings of Narnia imitated the first king in his respect for Nature, so too Old Western Men are called to imitate pre-fallen Adam in his noble appointment as protector of God's Earth, to be governors who are not afraid of technology and the product of reason, yet will not allow mechanization and industry to run amuck.

Therefore, it should come as no surprise that Lewis himself – the romantic Oxonian – was both an animal lover (he had dogs, cats and even rabbits for most of his life) and a Nature lover; thus, he wrote letters to newspapers protesting the elimination of open-deck ships between England

---

190 "I did a good deal of work on Henry More once: a beautiful man of whom it was said 'He was often so drunk with happiness that he had much ado to keep himself from falling down & kissing the very stones on the path.' He is also one of the earliest people to mention kindness to animals as a duty." Lewis, *The Collected Letters of C. S. Lewis: Volume III*, 613 [May 24, 1955].

191 Lewis, *The Magician's Nephew*, 129.

192 Lewis, *The Last Battle*, 169.

193 Lewis, *A Preface to Paradise Lost*, 118.

194 Lewis, *The Lion, the Witch and the Wardrobe*, 166. Cf. Margarita Carretero-González, "Sons of Adam, Daughters of Eve, and Children of Aslan: An Environmentalist Perspective on *The Chronicles of Narnia*," in *Fantasist, Mythmaker, & Poet*, vol. 2, *C. S. Lewis: Life, Works, and Legacy*, ed. Bruce Edwards, 93-114 (Westport, CT: Praeger, 2007).

and Ireland,[195] for example, and delighted in taking walks, like the Romantic poets, in the English countryside; in fact, the Oxford don enjoyed the latter so much so, that Tolkien, though not only for this reason, based the character of Treebeard – the leader of the Ents, the tree-people in *The Lord of the Rings* – on Lewis.[196] And this suggests to me that there was at least some affinity between Treebeard's attitude toward the Orc-induced genocide of trees in *The Two Towers*, and Lewis's attitude toward the destruction of Nature by industrial England. Moreover, I believe that this is also connected to one further point: both Lewis and Tolkien, to return to the point I raised a moment ago, saw a strong, mythical link between the just rule of a king (people) and trees (Nature) flourishing. In *Return of the King*, for instance, the Tree of the King remained withered until Aragorn returned to the throne, and in *The Magician's Nephew* and "Young King Cole" the wise kings planted, or *became*, trees that warded off evil.[197] Finally, Lewis (though not Tolkien) felt neither an inclination to buy a car nor when blackouts were enforced during WWII did he feel inconvenienced without electricity or modern "necessities."[198]

Nevertheless, it is one thing to denounce the abuse of technology and it is another to give an account of how such an abuse came about. Although I will return to this more fully in chapter eight, it needs to be mentioned that Lewis, following Augustine and the Christian tradition in general,[199] believed

195 C. S. Lewis, "Cross-Channel Ships," *The Times* (November 18, 1938): 12.
196 Humphrey Carpenter, *J. R. R. Tolkien: A Biography* (London: Unwin Paperbacks, 1978), 198.
197 C. S. Lewis, *The Magician's Nephew* (1955 reprint; London: Fontana, 1985), 162. C. S. Lewis, "Young King Cole," in *Poems*, by C. S. Lewis, ed. Walter Hooper (1947 poem reprint; San Diego: Harcourt Brace Jovanovich, 1964), 19 [49-72].
198 Lewis, *The Collected Letters of C. S. Lewis: Volume II*, 413 [May 9, 1940].
199 Of course, I am aware that not all the Fathers believed pride to be the arch sin. Irenaeus, Cyprian, Pseudo-Cyprian, Orientius and even Basil, to mention a few, believed Satan fell through envy, not pride. Neil Adkin, "Pride or Envy?" *Augustiniana* 34 (1984): 350. Moreover, Augustine was not even the first to formulate the theory that pride was the arch sin. Athenagoras, Origen, Athanasius, Ambrose, Jerome and Chrysostom all spoke loosely of pride being the arch sin, and there is also evidence to suggest that Homer (e.g. Achilles), Hesiod (e.g. Narcissus), Solon, Plato (e.g. "injustice") and especially Plotinus (e.g. *tolma*) thought something similar. William Green, *Initium Omnis Peccati Superbia: Augustine on Pride as the First Sin* (Berkeley, CA: University of California Press, 1949), 415. History speaks of "Augustinian pride" only because "Augustine," whom we must remember started out as a Platonist, "alone seems to have been aware of the incongruity [between the Fathers] and felt the need to solve it." Adkin, "Pride or Envy?" 350. Cf. Frank Riga, "Augustinian Pride and the Work of C. S. Lewis," *Augustinian Studies* 16 (1984): 129-36. Cf. Frank Riga, "Self-Love in Augustine and C. S. Lewis," *Cithara: Essays in the Judaeo-Christian Tradition* 26, no.2 (May 1987): 20-30. Cf. Katherine Rogers, "Augustinian Evil in C. S. Lewis's *Perelandra*," in *The Transcendent Adventure: Studies of Religion in Science Fiction/Fantasy*, ed. Robert Reilly, 83-99 (Westport, CT: Greenwood Press, 1985).

that the Fall was the result of pride – man loving himself inordinately, loving himself above God: "This sin has been described by Saint Augustine as the result of Pride, of the movement whereby a creature (that is, an essentially dependent being whose principle of existence lies not in itself but in another) tries to set up on its own, to exist for itself."[200] The result of this love, Augustine said (and Lewis underlined in his edition of *The City of God*), is self-love, not love of God: "We see then that the two cities were created by two kinds of love: the earthly city was created by self-love reaching the point of contempt for God, the Heavenly City by the love of God carried as far as contempt of self."[201] Fallen man, in other words, loves things in improper ways: his self-love leads to the unjust use of things around him. Subsequently, Lewis, applying Augustinian theology, saw magic during the Renaissance as a prime example of self-love, of man trying to control Nature for his own selfish end, an end incompatible with God's hierarchy and order. Although magic by and large left the stage after the Renaissance, Lewis believed that the spirit behind magic – man's pride, his self-love – was the same spirit in much of modern science and technology: "Magic and 'science' are twins *et pour cause*, for the magician and the scientist both stand together, and in contrast to the Christian, Stoic, or the Humanist, in so far as both make Power their aim, believe Power to be attainable by a technique, and in the practice of that technique are ready to defy ordinary morality."[202] Not, of course, as Lewis constantly insisted,[203] that science itself is bad, but that the desire to control and dominate things in an improper way is wicked (hence Lewis was opposed to vivisection,[204] and the villains in *That Hideous Strength*, not to mention Uncle Andrew,[205] are largely a group of power-hungry, materialistic scientists willing to move vivisection to its 'logical' conclusion and experiment on

---

200 Lewis, *The Problem of Pain*, 508. Cf. Augustine *The City of God* 14.14. Cf. Lewis, *Mere Christianity*, 398.

201 C. S. Lewis, underlining in his edition of *De Civitate Dei*, by Sancti Aurelii Augustini, 2 vols. (Lipsiae: in aedibus B. G. Teubneri, MCMIX; The Rare Book Collection, The University of North Carolina at Chapel Hill), [14.28].

202 Lewis, *The Collected Letters of C. S. Lewis: Volume II*, 475 [March 28, 1941].

203 Defending *That Hideous Strength* against the claim that it is "anti-science," Lewis wrote: "*That Hideous Strength* [Professor Haldane] has almost completely misunderstood. The 'good' scientist is put in precisely to show that 'scientists' as such are not my target." C. S. Lewis, "A Reply to Professor Haldane," in *Of This and Other Worlds*, by C. S. Lewis, ed. Walter Hooper (1946 essay reprint; London: Fount, 2000), 85.

204 C. S. Lewis, "Vivisection," in *C. S. Lewis: Essay Collection & Other Short Pieces*, ed. Lesley Walmsley (1947 essay reprint; London: HarperCollins, 2000), 696. Cf. Lewis, *Out of the Silent Planet*, 21.

205 Uncle Andrew is in many ways the archetypal evil scientist / magician. He cruelly experiments on guinea-pigs and sees animals only as something to use and exploit. Lewis, *The Magician's Nephew*, 26, 101.

people):

> The physical sciences, good and innocent in themselves, had already, even in Ransom's own time, begun to be warped, had been subtly manoeuvred in a certain direction. Despair of objective truth had been increasingly insinuated into the scientists; indifference to it, and a concentration upon mere power had been the result. Babble about the *élan vital* and flirtation with panpsychism were bidding fair to restore the *Anima Mundi* of the magicians. Dreams of far future destiny of man were dragging up from its shallow and unquiet grave the old dream of Man as God.[206]

One of the reasons that this movement towards science has become so perversely prominent in the modern era is, according to Lewis (who witnessed it firsthand at Oxford[207]), the shift from classical education, which grounded society in Old Western Culture,[208] to scientific and economic education, which detaches man from the arts and theology, which are the subjects that focus on the soul of man under God instead of on man and his power over Nature. As Lewis said in *The Pilgrim's Regress*, one of whose "contentions is that the decay of our old classical learning is a contributory cause of atheism,"[209]

> I remember that they passed Ignorantia some miles beyond her sister Superbia and that led the pilgrims to question their Guide as to whether the Ignorance of the Tough-minded and the Clevers would some day

---

206 Lewis, *That Hideous Strength*, 560. In his review of *That Hideous Strength*, George Orwell spoke truly of Lewis's "horror of modern machine civilization." George Orwell, "The Scientist Takes Over," review of *That Hideous Strength*, by C. S. Lewis, *Manchester Evening News*, August 16, 1945.

207 When Lewis started studying at Oxford, Greek and Latin were mandatory for all students. However, "From 1900 onward the Headmasters' Conference fought an increasingly bitter battle over compulsory Greek against a well organized Greek Defence Committee which was only finally defeated in Congregation in March 1920." Currie, "The Arts and Social Studies, 1914-1939," 111. Moreover, coinciding with the defeat of mandatory Greek was the rise of a "new modern-side Greats," which focused on "'the study of the foundations of nineteenth-century and present-day civilization in its three branches of philosophy, science and political economic and social development.'" Ibid., 112. The advent of the new "Greats" slowly reduced the prestige of the old "Greats" (i.e. *Literae Humaniores*), which meant that Greek and Latin literature, history and philosophy became more and more specialized disciplines instead of providing a broad understanding of the essentials of Old Western Culture. Finally, in 1960, compulsory Latin for scientists was eliminated all together. Jose Harris, "The Arts and Social Sciences, 1939-1970," in *The History of the University of Oxford: Volume VIII; The Twentieth Century*, ed. Brian Harrison, 217-50 (Oxford: Oxford University Press, 1994), 227.

208 Lewis, "Modern Man and His Categories of Thought," 617.

209 Lewis, *The Collected Letters of C. S. Lewis: Volume II*, 93 [December 17, 1932].

be cured. He said there was less chance of that now than there had ever been: for till recently the Northern people had been made to learn the language of Pagus 'and that meant,' said the Guide, 'that at least they started no further from the light than the old Pagans themselves and had therefore the chance to come at last to Mother Kirk. But now they are cutting themselves off even from that roundabout route.' . . . Their slaves are escaping further north and becoming dwarfs, and therefore the masters are turning all their attention to machinery, by which they hope to be able to lead their old life without slaves. And this seems to them so important that they are suppressing every kind of knowledge except mechanical knowledge.[210]

***

The eighth and final component in Lewis's understanding of an Old Western Man is that such a man will neither be skeptical of the power of reason nor distrustful of objective values in ethics and the arts. Since these issues will make up the bulk of chapters seven, eight and ten, I will, as before, try to be brief.

To begin with, we must remember that Lewis's most cherished belief is that people should not submit to anything against their better judgment. In Lewis's own case, this did not mean that he thought everything in Christianity, for instance, can be *verified* with Cartesian certainty à la logical positivism; rather, it meant that he believed in Christianity because he thought it the most *probable* philosophy. Thus, Lewis maintained that this attitude – this trust in reason – is the one that best represents the wisdom of Old Western Culture, for it avoids two opposing dangers.

The first danger in regard to reason is that of "those plaguey philosophers whom we call Logical Positivists."[211] These belonged to one of the early schools of modern analytic philosophy, and their claim was grounded in a radical empiricism and focus on linguistic meaning, asserting that nothing should be believed or accepted without verification; thus, for instance, they claimed metaphysical and theological assertions should not be believed since

210 Lewis, *The Pilgrim's Regress*, 207.
211 Lewis, *The Collected Letters of C. S. Lewis: Volume III*, 540 [December 5, 1954]. The father of positivism is French philosopher Auguste Comte (1798-1857). Comte divided the progress of mankind into three historical stages: (1) the Theological, which relies on supernatural agencies to explain what man can't explain otherwise; (2) the Metaphysical, in which man attributes effects to abstract but poorly understood causes; and (3) the Positive, which says that man now understands the scientific laws which control the world.

they cannot be verified in the manner of scientific inquiry.[212] Although it is undeniable that Lewis felt somewhat intimidated by the jargon of "these modern linguistic birds,"[213] he could not see why the principle of verification should be accepted.[214] Yet, as a product of the Spirit of the Age, this principle loomed large, and it was not until after Lewis's death that this principle was finally exposed for the sham that it was. Nevertheless, there is indication, even as far back as *The Allegory of Love*, that, following Etienne Gilson,[215] Lewis believed the scientific, anti-metaphysical mindset of logical positivism (not to mention, behaviorism) could be traced back through various elements in the Enlightenment to Aquinas's rather innocent separation of faith and reason:

> In dealing with the Middle Ages we are often tricked by our imagination. We think of plate armour and Aristotelianism. But the end of the Middle Ages is already in sight when these attractive things appear. And just as the lobster shell of steel gave to the warrior, along with the security, something of the inertia, of the crustacean, so it is possible, without disrespect to the great philosophical panoply in which Dante and Aquinas walked complete, to hint that those who wore it necessarily lost some of the grace and freedom of their forebears. The recovery of Aristotle's text dates from the second half of the twelfth century: the dominance of his doctrine soon followed. Aristotle is, before all, the philosopher of divisions. His effect on his greatest disciple, as M. Gilson has traced it, was to dig new chasms between God and

212 Ayer, *Language, Truth and Logic*, 14.

213 Lewis, *The Collected Letters of C. S. Lewis: Volume III*, 447 [March 26, 1954]. Cf. "During my time at Oxford (1946-50), a new way of doing philosophy, sometimes called the 'revolution in philosophy,' was in full bloom. While at Oxford . . . I saturated myself in this 'new philosophy,' which its many enemies described as 'linguistic' or 'ordinary language.'" Flew, *There is no God*, 37.

214 Concerning Wither in *That Hideous Strength*, Lewis wrote: "It was incredible how little this knowledge [of his failed plans] moved him. It could not, because he had long ceased to believe in knowledge itself. What had been in his far-off youth a mere aesthetic repugnance to realities that were crude or vulgar, had deepened and darkened, year after year, into a fixed refusal of everything that was in any degree other than himself. He had passed from Hegel into Hume, thence through Pragmatism, and thence through Logical Positivism, and out at last into the complete void. The indicative mood now corresponded to no thought that his mind could not entertain. He had willed with his whole heart that there should be no reality and no truth, and now even the imminence of his own ruin could not wake him." Lewis, *That Hideous Strength*, 720-1.

215 "Of scholastic philosophy and theology you probably know much more than I do. If by any chance you don't, stick to Gilson as a guide and beware of the people (Maritain in your Church, and T. S. Eliot of mine) who are at present running what they call 'neo-scholasticism' as a fad." Lewis, *The Collected Letters of C. S. Lewis: Volume II*, 142 [June 7, 1934].

the world, between human knowledge and reality, between faith and reason. Heaven began, under this dispensation, to seem farther off. The danger of Pantheism grew less: the danger of mechanical Deism came a step nearer. It is almost as if the first, faint shadow of Descartes, or even of 'our present discontents' had fallen across the scene.[216]

Although there was arguably an ever-increasing emphasis on empiricism (over and against rationalism) from medieval Scholasticism on through the Enlightenment, Lewis felt that since the ethical and religious atmosphere of these ages were still in line with Old Western Culture, the perversion of reason in terms of completely turning the scientific against the metaphysical – instead of seeing them both working together – occurred only in the late nineteenth century;[217] hence, against the reductive nature of logical positivism (and behaviorism), Lewis asked: "Surely the gap between Professor Ryle and Thomas Browne is far wider than that between Gregory the Great and Virgil? Surely Seneca and Dr. Johnson are closer together than Burton and Freud?"[218]

The second danger in regard to reason is that of the existentialists. As a self-confessed rationalist, it should come as no surprise that Lewis had little sympathy for existentialism and its denial that reason can discover objective Truth: "What 'existentially' means – unless it means 'melodramatically' or 'ostentatiously' or 'making no end of a fuss about it' – I have never been able to find out."[219] Indeed, when Lewis was asked to help start-up a new periodical, he proposed it be within the parameters of Old Western Culture, and the first thing he stated to this effect was that the periodical "would definitely and always exclude . . . Total Scepticism: i.e. attacks on reason and natural morality."[220] Existentialism, therefore, was something that Lewis felt was deeply opposed to Old Western Culture as a *philosophy*, yet his attitude toward the movement was not completely negative: he appreciated some

---

216 Lewis, *The Allegory of Love*, 87-8.
217 Lewis, "*De Descriptione Temporum*," 7.
218 Ibid., 5.
219 Lewis, *The Collected Letters of C. S. Lewis: Volume III*, 1012 [January 16, 1959].
220 Lewis, *The Collected Letters of C. S. Lewis: Volume II*, 773 [April 1947].

insights of theistic existentialists like Martin Buber,[221] Gabriel Marcel[222] and
Helmut Kuhn[223] (though not Søren Kierkegaard[224]), and he thought that

221 In 1942, Lewis picked up a copy of Martin Buber's *I and Thou*, and about ten years
later, he wrote, "Buber made one point well, but with some exaggeration" – that point
being a typical existential theistic emphasis on the Pseudo-Dionysian Way of Negation
or the separateness of God and man: "As Buber might say God is most fully real to
us as *Thou*, less so as *He*, least so as *It*. We must worship the *Thou*, not the *He* in our
own minds, which is just as much an image (therefore a possible *idol*) as a figure of
wood or stone." Lewis, *The Collected Letters of C. S. Lewis: Volume III*, 979 [October
13, 1958], 1173 [July 19, 1960]. Indeed, it is a tribute to Lewis's broadmindedness as a
philosopher that he could see into a philosophy he was largely antithetical to and find
the truth within; hence, in *Prayer: Letters to Malcolm*, Lewis the rationalist exclaimed:
"How good Buber is!" Lewis, *Prayer: Letters to Malcolm*, 236. Nevertheless, one truth
is hardly enough to make it compatible with the Old Western view of reason, and so
Lewis thought it "rather rot" overall. Lewis, *The Collected Letters of C. S. Lewis: Volume
II*, 528 [August 1, 1942]. That is, he complained of three major weakness: "I thought
that [Buber] ignored (1.) The Incarnation. He is a Jew. Our Lord, besides being the
divine *Thou* is also a historical character, who must be considered also as *He*. Indeed
this is the essence of our faith 'Crucified *under Pontius Pilate*' – date, & signature of
civil servant & all, crude, historical event. . . . (2.) The *Ye* or *You* (Plural) experience.
One's two best friends, or one's parents, or one's wife and daughter, at times are v[ery]
distinctly neither *Thou* nor *They* but 'You two.' . . . What I had not yet thought about
was your objection, that he ignores the *Me*. You are probably right. He might even have
said that just as the *Thou* is deeper than the *Me*, so the *I* is deeper than the *Me*. For I
believe self consciousness to be full of deception and that the object I call *me* and think
about (both in my moments of pride and in my moments of humility) is v[ery] different
from the *I* who thinks about it." Lewis, *The Collected Letters of C. S. Lewis: Volume III*,
631-2 [July 11, 1955].

222 A couple years after reading the atheistic Sartre, Lewis heard the Christian existentialist
Gabriel Marcel give a talk on existentialism, about which Lewis initially commented,
"It is definitely *not* my philosophy." Lewis, *The Collected Letters of C. S. Lewis: Volume
II*, 954 [July 5, 1949]. However, some years later, Lewis added, "To see him is to love
him: but it appeared to me that his thesis if taken seriously, sh[oul]d reduce him and
us to perfect silence – as the philosophy of Heraclitus did his disciples. The same holds
of Buber. What they mean by calling Aquinas and Augustine Existentialists I can't
understand: nor do I much like such labels." Lewis, *The Collected Letters of C. S. Lewis:
Volume III*, 24 [April 9, 1950]. Cf. Ibid., 979-80 [October 13, 1958].

223 In 1949, Lewis was asked by Dorothy Sayers if he would be willing to write a preface to
Helmut Kuhn's *Encounter with Nothingness: An Essay on Existentialism*, to which Lewis
promptly replied: "No – I know (and care) little about the Existentialist nonsense. I
wouldn't dream of writing a preface. I think it is mainly philosophical *melodrama*."
Lewis, *The Collected Letters of C. S. Lewis: Volume II*, 995 [November 9, 1949]. However,
twelve days after refusing to write the preface, Lewis actually read Kuhn's book and
really enjoyed parts of it. Ibid., 999 [November 21, 1949]. Indeed, Lewis himself soon
after became friends with Kuhn, who, interestingly enough, actually translated Lewis's
Great Divorce into German. Lewis, *The Collected Letters of C. S. Lewis: Volume III*, 582
[March 18, 1955].

224 Even though Lewis was able to find some value in existentialism, in particular, the

existentialism and subjectivism in general often had some *literary* merit; hence, he called Jean-Paul Sartre "a great rhetorician,"[225] and insisted that "[Friedrich] Nietzsche was a better poet than a philosopher."[226]

theistic variety, he was still largely opposed to it; hence, while a Christian existentialist like Kierkegaard (whose philosophy was intended largely as a corrective to Hegelianism) would have agreed with Lewis when the Oxford don complained about logical positivism – "Our intellectuals have surrendered first to the slave-philosophy of Hegel, then to Marx, finally to the linguistic analysts" – there would have been little else in common between the two philosophers. C. S. Lewis, "Willing Slaves of the Welfare State," in *C. S. Lewis: Essay Collection & Other Short Pieces*, ed. Lesley Walmsley (1958 essay reprint; London: HarperCollins, 2000), 748. Naturally, insofar as Kierkegaard – the father of existentialism and all that is best in Buber, Marcel and Kuhn – was a Christian, Lewis did not wish to criticize him too much, saying, at first, "I can't read [him] myself, but some find him useful," and then later admitting that since Charles Williams liked the Dane, "there must be a lot in him." Lewis, *The Collected Letters of C. S. Lewis: Volume III*, 1449 [June 8, 1962]. Cf. Ibid., 1273 [June 5, 1961]. However, when push came to shove, Lewis the rationalist, Lewis the Old Western Man, stated without hesitation: "Kierkegaard still means almost nothing to me." Ibid. 979 [October 13, 1958]. In fact, Corbin Scott Carnell says Lewis thought that reading Kierkegaard is "like walking in sawdust." Corbin Scott Carnell, *Bright Shadow of Reality*, 67.

225 Lewis, *The Collected Letters of C. S. Lewis: Volume III*, 1238 [February 13, 1961]. In 1947, five years after Lewis's first encounter with existentialism, he read Sartre's *Existentialism is a Humanism*, "[which] seemed, if pressed," Lewis jokingly commented, "to be the Berkeleyian metaphysic in the mind of an atheist with a bad liver!" Ibid., 24 [April 9, 1950]. Sartre's philosophy of "existence precedes essence" (i.e. that "there is no [objective] human nature because there is no God to conceive of it") had become prominent in Lewis's day. Jean-Paul Sartre, *Existentialism is a Humanism*, trans. Carol Macomber, ed. John Kulka (1947 reprint; New Haven: Yale University Press, 2007), 22. Consequently, as a lover of Truth, Lewis recommended that Sartrian philosophy be discussed at the Socratic Club. Lewis, *The Collected Letters of C. S. Lewis: Volume III*, 33 [June 12, 1950]. In fact, not only did he recommend Sartrian philosophy be discussed at the Socratic Club, but he himself wrote a critique entitled "A First Glance at Sartre," in which he expressed his objections to Sartre, arguing, as the Socratic Club secretary has recorded it, that Sartre's claim of total freedom is an illusion: "Mr. Lewis said: firstly, that to speak of Man collectively or in the plural, implies an essence in any case: secondly, that I cannot be committing others to my choice, unless I know them to be beings of the same essence as myself: thirdly, that to define man's end as liberty is very like assuming a universal form of right conduct. These parts of Sartre seemed to Mr. Lewis to be undigested lumps of Kant; all the agony which Sartre, paradoxically, would have us accept leads us back only to the old principles of political liberty. Such an argument typifies the modern habit of exaggeration. What Sartre really hates is the idea of goodness as conformity, and he is a moral fanatic like Robespierre. Mr. Lewis then explained his view that conformity to a rule is not the essence, but only the accident of goodness. Thus there *can* be a measure of inventiveness, and freedom, in some moral actions. Sartre's illusion is his claim of total freedom, which leaves us in the dark at an endless trial, without a judge." Hooper, "Oxford's Bonny Fighter," 160-1.

226 Lewis, *The Collected Letters of C. S. Lewis: Volume III*, 1420 [March 27, 1963]. Although Lewis may have come to this conclusion through his own reading of Nietzsche's *Beyond*

And just as an Old Western Man is one who asserts the power of reason to discover objective Truth, he is also one who believes in the ability of the individual to discern objective value. Hence, in *The Abolition of Man*, which was recently voted the seventh most important work of non-fiction of the past century,[227] Lewis laid the ground work for Old Western axiology, particularly in regard to ethical and aesthetic value.

As for ethical value, Lewis endorsed the traditional doctrine of the existence of a universal moral law that communicates to people objective moral principles.[228] Consequently, the Oxford don disagreed with (1) the relativism of Social Darwinists, such as Herbert Spencer,[229] (2) ethicists inspired by Albert Einstein's physical theory,[230] (3) Freudians who reduce all morality to sexual instinct, and (4) divine command ethicists like Karl Barth, who think man so utterly depraved that even his natural knowledge of right and wrong are fallen and cannot act as a reliable guide.[231]

As for aesthetic value, Lewis felt the trends of the nineteenth and twentieth century were utterly contrary to the relatively stable artistic expression in Old Western Culture, at least insofar as the arts reflect, or at least should reflect, objective norms. Borrowing I. A. Richards' term,[232] Lewis said that Old Western artistic norms should elicit "stock responses," which consist in

a deliberately organized attitude which is substituted for 'the direct free play of experience.' In my opinion such deliberate organization is one of the first necessities of human life, and one of the main

Good and Evil (the only Nietzschean work that we know Lewis read), it is just as likely that Lewis got this idea from Douglas Ainslie's preface to Benedetto Croce's *Philosophy of the Practical: Economic and Ethic*, in which Lewis would have read: "Friedrich Nietzsche, whose spasmodic paragraphs, full of genius but often empty of philosophy, show him to have been far more of a poet than a philosopher." Douglas Ainslie, preface to *Philosophy of the Practical: Economic and Ethic*, by Benedetto Croce (London: MacMillian, 1913), x-xi.

227 "The 100 Best Books of the Century: Non-Fiction," *The National Review*, www.nationalreview.com/100best/100_books.html (accessed on October 5, 2003).
228 Lewis, *The Abolition of Man*, 417.
229 Herbert Spencer (1820-1903) tried to base his ethics on the theory of evolution.
230 Although Einstein said nothing about ethics, many philosophers, such as Bertrand Russell, thought Einstein's General Theory of Relativity had important philosophical implications.
231 Concerning the local followers of Barth, Lewis wrote: "They don't think human reason or human conscience of any value at all: they maintain, as stoutly as Calvin, that there's no reason why God's dealings should appear just (let alone, merciful) to us." Lewis, *The Collected Letters of C. S. Lewis: Volume II*, 351 [February 18, 1940].
232 I. A. Richards, *Principles of Literary Criticism* (1924 reprint; London: Routledge, 2001), 188.

functions of art is to assist it. All that we describe as constancy in love or friendship, as loyalty in political life, or, in general, as perseverance – all solid virtues and stable pleasure – depends on organizing chosen attitudes and maintaining them against the eternal flux (or 'direct free play') of mere immediate experience.[233]

Thus, for instance, in the visual arts, Lewis strongly denounced the cubists,[234] dadaists,[235] surrealists[236] and Pablo Picasso, all of whom thrived on the abnormal:

> I am also working on a book sent [to] me to review, *Le Mystere de la Poesie* by a professor at Dijon, of which my feeling is 'If this is typical of modern France, nothing that has happened in the last three months [i.e. the beginning of WWII] surprises me' – such a mess of Dadaists, Surrealists, nonsense, blasphemy and decadence, as I could hardly have conceived possible. But one ought to have known for, now that I come to think of it, all the beastliest traits of our intelligentsia have

---

233 Lewis, *A Preface to Paradise Lost*, 54-5.
234 Cubism developed in France between 1907 and the early 1920's. The name "cubism" comes from an insult by another artist, Henri Matisse. He called a painting by Georges Braque: "petits cubes" or little cubes. Since the Renaissance, many artists believed perception and space were best shown with linear perspective, a mathematical system used to imitate Nature. Artists using these ideas show a fix point of view. Cubists, on the other hand, show more than one view at a time. A cubist painting may show the front of a face and the side of a face at the same time (e.g. Picasso's *Girl with Dark Hair*). Picasso and Braque were two cubists who showed how space could be *cut-up, distorted and transformed* into different planes and views. H. H. Arnason et al., *History of Modern Art*, 4th ed. (Singapore: Prentice Hall, 1998), 181-216. Because of this distortion, Lewis felt Cubism did not bring out stock responses.
235 "Dada," which is the French word for "hobbyhorse," was chosen randomly as the name for this art movement. During a meeting of young artists and war resisters in 1916 in Zurich, they stuck a paper knife into a French-German dictionary and selected the word it pointed to. They felt "dada" was a good fit for their art movement, which emphasized protest activities, despair regarding WWI, and distaste for what they thought were the bourgeois values of the art of the time. Dada art was nihilistic, anti-aesthetic and a reaction to the rationalization, rules and conventions of mainstream art. Ibid., 254-5. Because dadaists considered their work to be anti-art or art that defied reason, Lewis believed their movement was in conflict with Old Western Culture.
236 Surrealism is an invented word – "sur" means beyond or farther than, so "surreal" means to go beyond real. It was named this because surrealist art derives much of its meaning from Freud's theory of the unconscious. Surrealism grew out of the dada movement and flourished in Europe between WWI and WWII. Surrealism tried to meld the conscious and unconscious, the world of dreams and fantasy along with reality so that the line between these ideas was completely blurred. Maurice Nadeau, *The History of Surrealism* (Cambridge, MA: Belknap Press, 1989), 240-1. This blurring of reality and subsequent distortion of the normal, not to mention surrealism's manifesto declaring a revolution in art, caused Lewis to strongly denounce the movement.

come to them from France.[237]

And in the literary arts, Lewis targeted literary critics, such as I. A. Richards, F. R. Leavis and E. M. Tillyard, and writers such as the early T. S. Eliot[238] and "the Steins and Pounds and *hoc genus omne*, the Parisian riff-raff of denationalized Irishmen and Americans who have perhaps given Western Europe her death wound."[239]

As a result, Lewis believed that Old Western Culture demands, not only in the arts, but also in ethics and rationality, the universal, the normal and the stable; as the Oxford don wrote in his anti-modernist poem "A Confession":

> I am so coarse, the things the poets see
> Are obstinately invisible to me.
> For twenty years I've stared my level best
> To see if evening – any evening – would suggest
> A patient etherized upon a table
> In vain. I simply wasn't able.
> . . .
> I'm like that odd man Wordsworth knew, to whom
> A primrose was a yellow primrose, one whose doom
> Keeps him forever in the list of dunces,
> Compelled to live on stock responses,
> Making the poor best that I can
> Of dull things . . . peacocks, honey, the Great Wall, Aldebaran,
> Silver weirs, new-cut grass, wave on the beach, hard gem,
> The shapes of horse and women, Athens, Troy, Jerusalem.[240]

***

Although many of the issues raised in this chapter remain undeveloped (for the sake of the book as a whole), I trust that readers have a fairly clear idea not only of the culture Lewis was writing in – e.g. modernist, Darwinian, anti-classical, post-Christian etc. – but also how Lewis understood his own place in this culture – e.g. as an Old Western Man. Moreover, it is my opinion that even though the Oxford don showed some evidence of an unthinking cultural bias (e.g. towards eastern religions etc.), he was still remarkably aware of his own culture and biases therein.

---

237 Lewis, *The Collected Letters of C. S. Lewis: Volume II*, 437 [August 17, 1940].

238 Although Lewis had no use for the early T. S. Eliot, he came to love the man later on in life when they worked together on revising the Psalter. Hooper, *C. S. Lewis: Companion and Guide*, 654.

239 Lewis, *The Collected Letters of C. S. Lewis: Volume II*, 164 [May 23, 1935].

240 C. S. Lewis, "A Confession," in *Poems*, by C. S. Lewis, ed. Walter Hooper (1954 poem reprint; San Diego: Harcourt Brace Jovanovich, 1964), 1 [1.1-6, 3.3-10].

IV: C. S. Lewis, Philosopher

Throughout the first half of this book, I wanted to do three inter-related things: discuss the Oxford don's *definition of philosophy*, explore his *philosophical journey* and subsequently argue for his *identity as a philosopher*. To this end, I began by claiming that Lewis understood philosophy as the ancients did: as a way of life. Thus, in chapter one, I laid out the general criteria of philosophy as a way of life, which is (1) a choice (2) made in a cultural context (3) to follow wholeheartedly a certain group of people who (4) have a certain take on life which (5) demands training which (6) is the result of rational discourse, and which (7) ultimately leads to a fully converted life. Once this understanding of philosophy was in place, I was then in a position, in chapter two, to argue that largely as a result of his early training in classics and philosophy – from reading Plato at "Chartres" to studying dialectic with Kirkpatrick, from majoring in "Greats" philosophy to teaching philosophy at University College, Oxford – Lewis chose to follow the guidance of reason and perform numerous spiritual exercises, such as reading, meditating on literary images, prayer, chapel attendance and so on, in a genuine attempt to live according to what he thought was true; as he said, "I [was] trying to find out truth."[241] However, like Plato and others before him, Lewis knew from firsthand experience that without desire, reason was impotent to move man from false images and philosophies to truer ones. Thus, the Oxford don devoted much of his writings – and I devoted chapter three – to exploring the nature of that important affect in the soul called heavenly desire. Yet as we discovered, heavenly desire is a blanket word for many different desires that have many different, though broadly related, objects. My argument in chapter four, therefore, was to show how one object of heavenly desire, Myth, which is the mysterious and supra-rational aspect of God's fuller nature, entered Lewis's poetic imagination via mythical literature, whose mythical images, in turn were evaluated by Lewis's reason (i.e. as being potentially true or false) and became vital facts in Lewis's decision to convert to Neoplatonic Christianity, which Lewis understood as a philosophy since it is due to reason accepting the supra-rational that he converted. Finally, in order to show how the Oxford don completely fit with the ancient understanding of philosophy as a way of life, I needed to put him into his cultural context so that his cultural identity could be established. This was crucial not only to help us understand the content of his Neoplatonic Christianity *qua* Old Western Culture, but also to shed some light both on the Oxford don's irrational cultural biases and on the degree to which his philosophical mind was able to process and critique the culture of his day.

241 Lewis, *Mere Christianity*, 331.

Consequently, whether a person agrees with Lewis's views or not (I do not agree with everything he said), I think that it is undeniable that he should be called a *philosopher* – even if he is "a very minor philosopher"[242] – for like the ancient philosophers before him, Lewis made a choice in a certain cultural context (twentieth-century Oxford) to follow wholeheartedly a certain philosophy (Neoplatonic Christianity) which demanded training (prayer, mythmaking, reading etc.) which was the result of submission to reason, all of which ultimately led to a fully converted life:

> I am sure [Lewis] was aware of his shortcomings, but to me he seemed closer to God than I had ever imagined a man could be. Most Christians seem to have two kinds of lives, their so-called 'real' life and their so-called 'religious' one. Not Lewis. The barrier so many of us find between the visible and the invisible was just not there for Lewis. No one ever had less of a split personality.[243]

Thus, while people may continue to call Lewis a lay theologian, they would do well to remember that if Lewis was a theologian, he was first a philosopher.[244]

And so with Lewis's philosophical definition, journey and identity all in place, it is time to delve deeper into the particulars of the Oxford don's philosophy, starting with his views on First Philosophy: metaphysics.

---

242 "I was never a scientist and have long ceased to be even the very minor philosopher I once was." Lewis, *The Collected Letters of C. S. Lewis: Volume III*, 99 [March 25, 1951].

243 Walter Hooper, "C. S. Lewis: Oxford's Literary Chameleon of Letters," in *Behind the Veil of Familiarity: C. S. Lewis (1898-1998)*, ed. Margarita Carretero González and Encarnación Hidalgo Tenorio, 23-46 (Bern: Peter Lang, 2001), 25.

244 Cf. "Lewis was a philosopher and literary critic, not a theologian." Michael Travers, "The Letters of C. S. Lewis: C. S. Lewis as Correspondent," in *Scholar, Teacher, & Public Intellectual*, vol. 4, *C. S. Lewis: Life, Works, and Legacy*, ed. Bruce Edwards, 19-48 (Westport, CT: Praeger, 2007), 38.

Part II

The Branches of
Philosophy

Chapter Six

Metaphysics

"Man," underlined Lewis in his edition of *Essays of Schopenhauer*, "is an *animal metaphysicum*."[1] This sentiment, far from being merely an anthropological claim, in many ways sums up Lewis's view of man and philosophy, for we recall that in 1918, when he first began to get excited about philosophy, he went so far as to equate metaphysics with philosophy as a whole, and we have seen that the history of Lewis's philosophical journey has been largely a history of his metaphysics, which for him, as for Aristotle, would have included much of what we now call natural theology.

Since metaphysics, and not epistemology (as is usually the case these days), holds the position of honour in Lewis's philosophy – existence preceding knowledge of existence – it is right that the second half of this book, wherein I propose to do an in-depth study of Lewis's view of the various branches of philosophy, begins with metaphysics (and thus, with *some* natural theology, an important part of which we already looked at in chapter three). Subsequently, herein I will examine three broad themes – spirit and matter, essence and existence, and eternity and time – all of which will demonstrate Lewis's evolving thoughts on prime reality. My hope is that despite Lewis being "a hard man to pin down metaphysically,"[2] I will be able to make some metaphysical connections, particularly in regard to the relationship between his idealism and later thoughts, which heretofore have been either ignored or understood poorly.[3]

---

1   C. S. Lewis, underlining in his edition of *Essays of Schopenhauer*, by Arthur Schopenhauer, trans. Mrs. Rudolf Dircks (London: Walter Scott Publishing, 1908; The Rare Book Collection, The University of North Carolina at Chapel Hill), 122.
2   Barfield, *Owen Barfield on C. S. Lewis*, 108.
3   See Adam Barkman, "C. S. Lewis and Philosophy as a Way of Life: An Essay on Being and Becoming," *Lamp-Post: The Bulletin of the Southern-California C. S. Lewis Society* 29, no. 3 and 30, no. 4 (Fall and Winter 2005): 3-15 and 3-15.

I: Spirit and Matter

To discuss Spirit and matter is to ask about what constitutes the building blocks of reality. For Berkeley, for instance, this becomes a question of *substance*. However, since Lewis's metaphysics are rather eclectic, the language of substance is often misleading. Thus, I will simply try to speak of Spirit and matter as what constitutes reality, and will use substance, in this section at least, only when it is explicitly used by the particular philosopher in question. Also, while the issue of Spirit and matter has a lot of overlap with that of essence and existence, I will try to keep these separate as much as possible for the time being.

Lewis's earliest metaphysical position was Lucretian materialism (a type of "popular realism"), which, we recall, claims that everything, including the gods, is matter. Little needs to be added to what I have already said in chapter two, save for two things. First, during this phase Lewis the materialist's poetry was very anti-spiritual; hence, in an unpublished poem he spoke of "cold Platonic Forms."[4] Second, it is essential to keep in mind that Lewis, from his earliest days until the day he died, insisted that both the argument from design / teleological argument (which attempts to prove with certainty the existence of God through the design of the universe)[5] and the cosmological argument (which tries to prove with certainty[6] that the universe needs a First Cause) fail.[7] My reason for reminding us of this point is twofold. Firstly, it demonstrates an unusual, if not in some sense an admirable, speed

---

4   C. S. Lewis, "And After This They Sent Me," in "The Unpublished Short Poetry of C. S. Lewis," by Don King, *VII: An Anglo-American Literary Review* 15 (1998): 81.

5   If, however, one were to follow Houston Craighead and equate Lewis's argument from reason with the argument from design or teleological argument proper, one could argue that Lewis changed his mind about the argument from design. Houston Craighead, "C. S. Lewis' Teleological Argument," *Encounter* 57, no. 2 (Spring 1996): 171-85. Nevertheless, most have rightly distinguished between the argument from reason and the teleological argument.

6   Although Lewis opposed the cosmological argument as *absolute* proof for the existence of God, he did think that it was very *probable* that God caused the world to begin: "If there ever was a life which sprang of its own accord out of purely inorganic universe, or a civilization which raised itself by its own shoulder-straps out of pure savagery, then this event was totally unlike the beginnings of every subsequent life and every subsequent civilization. . . . You have to go outside the sequence of engines, into the world of men, to find the real originator of the Rocket. Is it not equally reasonable to look outside Nature for the real Originator of the natural order?" C. S. Lewis, "Two Lectures," in *C. S. Lewis: Essay Collection & Other Short Pieces*, ed. Lesley Walmsley (1945 essay reprint; London: HarperCollins, 2000), 731.

7   "What I ought to have said was that the Cosmological argument is, for some people at some times, ineffective. It always has been for me." Lewis, *The Collected Letters of C. S. Lewis: Volume III*, 195 [May 28, 1952].

bump in Lewis's philosophy, for it shows that one of the greatest apologist of the twentieth century was utterly unimpressed by arguably one of the most powerful proofs for the existence of God (i.e. the argument from design) as testified by the recent theistic conversion of the great atheistic philosopher Antony Flew.[8] This oddity, in other words, is a good demonstration of Lewis's philosophical honesty, particularly in regard to natural theology. Secondly, Lewis's belief that the argument from design was weak helps us, importantly, to focus on other metaphysical considerations Lewis was dealing with as he shifted his views on what is really real.

From Lucretian dualism and the rejection of the argument from design, Lewis moved on to a kind of Manichean dualism which, of course, expounded the belief in two prime realities: Spirit and matter, the former being divine and the latter being evil. This dualism, however, was short lived as Lewis quickly returned to materialism – this time to a Stoical version – largely out of fear or at least distrust of the supernatural (and the popular). As a Stoical materialist Lewis did not deny the possibility of God's existence, but, much like Kant, he thought it unimportant, for he believed prime reality could be explained without reference to a divine being.

But this all changed when Lewis became an idealist because he came to see that only the divine could ground rationality (among other things); indeed, Lewis likely accepted at least a part of his 1924 summary of Locke's proof for the existence of God, for it demonstrated the need for a source of consciousness:

> We know God's existence by the following demonstration: I, at least, exist: but nothing comes from nothing: therefore there must be an eternal something. Again, a derivative Being must have all its powers from the same source whence it had being. But I have powers. Therefore the Being that originated me has great power. Again, I have consciousness: but it is impossible that consciousness c[oul]d emerge from the action of the unconscious. Therefore the original Being was conscious (chap. 10).[9]

---

8   Flew, "My Pilgrimage from Atheism to Theism," 198. As I mentioned in the introduction, Flew attended the Socratic Club meetings, whose president was C. S. Lewis and whose motto was the Socratic dictum "follow the argument wherever it leads;" indeed, it is interesting to note that while Flew and Lewis disagreed about the argument from design, both men converted to theism because they thought theism true; hence, Flew, for instance, spoke of his "pilgrimage of reason," and said, "C. S. Lewis's Socratic Club was open for business during the heyday of the new philosophy [i.e. logical positivism], and the Socratic principle I saw exemplified there – of following the evidence wherever it may lead – increasingly became a guiding principle in the development, refinement, and sometimes reversal of my own philosophical views." Flew, *There is a God*, 85, 42.

9   Lewis, "The Moral Good – Its Place Among the Values," 18.

This is extremely important to keep in mind because not only does it show that rationality was one of the reasons for Lewis's belief in the divine, but it also laid the groundwork for Lewis's argument from reason for the existence of God as it was presented many years later in *Miracles* and which Erik Wielenberg summarizes as follows:

> 1. If Naturalism [or Materialism] is true, then knowledge exists only if natural selection could produce a capacity for knowledge starting with creatures with no such capacity.
>
> 2. But natural selection could not produce a capacity for knowledge starting with creatures with no such capacity.
>
> 3. So: If Naturalism is true, then knowledge does not exist (from 1 and 2).
>
> 4. But knowledge does exist.
>
> 5. So: Naturalism is false (from 3 and 4).
>
> 6. If knowledge exists and Naturalism is false, then there is a supernatural, eternal, self-existent, rational Being that is the ultimate source of all knowledge.
>
> 7. Therefore, there is a supernatural, eternal, self-existent, rational Being that is the ultimate source of all knowledge (from 4, 5, and 6).[10]

The connection, then, between Lewis's idealism and his later argument against naturalism began when Lewis became an idealist (even though, it must be added, Lewis the absolute idealist was obliged to see Spirit as a mashing together of both truth and error[11]). Nevertheless, the link between rationality and divinity was not the only connection between Lewis's early idealism and his later metaphysical views.

One of the particularities of Lewis's metaphysics completely ignored by scholars is how Lewis the Christian – not Lewis the idealist – could claim on the one hand that God "likes matter"[12] (1941) and yet on the other hand tell his former pupil Christopher Derrick that "God is a Berkeleyian Idealist"[13]

---

10   Wielenberg, *God and the Reach of Reason: C. S. Lewis, David Hume and Bertrand Russell*, 101.

11   "Distinctions of . . . true and false . . . spring up only with the creation of souls and a world. Outside that world they are meaningless." Lewis, *Clivi Hamiltonis Summae Metaphysices Contra Anthroposophos Libri II*, 52-3.

12   Lewis, *Mere Christianity*, 360.

13   Derrick, *C. S. Lewis and the Church of Rome*, 213. Martin Moynihan, another of Lewis's pupils, also testifies to Lewis's enduring respect for Berkeley; Moynihan wrote of his tutor: "Lewis thought Berkeley's [philosophy] sufficient (nothing exists or can exist

(1956[14]). As far as I know, no one has even mentioned this dilemma, much less tried to reconcile these apparent contradictory claims by the mature Lewis. Moreover, since I myself have claimed that Lewis's Christian philosophy is an eclectic Neoplatonism, it is necessary that we understand what exactly Lewis meant by matter when he was an idealist and whether or not any such connotations carried over into his later Neoplatonic Christianity.

In his 1924 lecture notes on Berkeley, Lewis the subjective or Berkeleyan idealist summarized the Bishop's argument against matter *qua* material substratum thus:

> It is evident that ideas and those bundles of ideas we call objects exist only in the mind. Some hold, however, that our ideas are copies of Things outside the mind. But if these things are perceptible they too will be ideas: if not – how can colour be a copy of the invisible or hardness or the intangible. . . . Nothing but an idea can be like an idea. . . . Again, if there were external objects we obviously c[oul]d not know this by sense: still less by inference since we know from dreams that we can have the ideas without external objects. Nor is this the easiest method of accounting for our experience: since the action of matter upon consciousness is admittedly inscrutable. Lastly, if there were no external world we sh[oul]d still have the same reasons for believing in it. In order to conceive things independent of mind we should have to 'conceive them unconceived.'[15]

Berkeley's idealism, which Lewis largely endorsed, maintains that the objects we perceive – a general word for Berkeley meaning any way a person has ideas before himself – in the external world are not material things that have certain qualities, i.e. things with "absolute" or perception-independent existence, but are simply collections of qualities, which, as it turns out, are nothing more than sensible ideas which can only exist in minds or spirits – the only true substance. Berkeley's immaterialism, therefore, denies the existence of matter, but not of the external world *qua* collection of sensible

---

without God)." Martin Moynihan, "C. S. Lewis and T. D. Weldon," *VII: An Anglo-American Literary Review* 5 (1984), 103.

14 Lewis tutored Derrick in 1940, but the context of the conversation between Lewis and Derrick indicates that Lewis made this claim while he was living in Cambridge, meaning that this conversation took place sometime after 1954. Since the first letter we have between Lewis and Derrick is dated 1956, wherein Lewis talked about meeting up with his "old acquaintance" (i.e. someone he had not met in years), it is likely that Lewis the Christian accepted this link between God and Berkeley at least until 1956 and no doubt for the remainder of his life, given that he died in 1963. Lewis, *The Collected Letters of C. S. Lewis: Volume III*, 774 [August 2, 1956].

15 Lewis, "The Moral Good – Its Place Among the Values," 34.

ideas, for while we can in no way show that there is an undetectable material substratum lying behind the perceptible qualities of things (i.e. our own perceptions), it is obvious there are things that are not ourselves, namely, the sensible ideas we perceive. Subsequently, if the external world is simply a mass of sensible ideas, which, of course, are wholly passive, the external world must exist in an active mind or spirit, for ideas cannot exist if they are not perceived by mind or spirit. Hence, while finite spirits – people, angels, et al. – can perceive some ideas, it takes a much stronger Spirit to maintain the steady and uniform flow of sensible ideas that constitute the external world and our total experience. Lewis, the then philosophy professor, explained:

> Now if the Esse = Percipi [is] an idea, there is nothing in an idea but what we find in it. Since, then, we <u>find</u> no power or activity in our ideas, there <u>is</u> none. Therefore the cause of our ideas cannot be itself an idea: and we have proved that it cannot be an external, material world. Therefore it must be an active spirit: for we experiment in ourselves the power of spirit to excite ideas – tho[ugh] we have no <u>idea</u> of this active power: for ideas are passive and cannot represent it. But if only will produces ideas, and my will does <u>not</u> produce <u>all</u> my ideas, some other will must. The ideas produced by that other are stronger and more regular than those we produce ourselves and = 'Nature.' Thus there is a distinction between 'Real things' & 'Chimaeras.' We are not taking away the reality of things: we, of all men, believe our senses.[16]

Finally, while spirits have ideas, "the immediate object of sense or understanding," they do not have ideas of spirits, for spirits are active while ideas are passive; thus, spirits conceive of themselves and others in terms of "notions," which are those things "perceived by attending to the passions and operations of the mind."[17] That is, ideas are sensory, meaning that they are either the content of states of sensory awareness or the copies of such in memory and imagination, while notions are concepts of spirit – the self, via immediate intuition; other finite spirits, via inference; and Spirit, via "reflexion and reasoning;"[18] Lewis summarized it thus:

> It is no difficulty that we have no idea of spirits – wh[ich] as we showed we <u>cannot</u> have. Even if we had a new spirit-sense given us we c[oul]d only get new ideas from it, wh[ich] being like all ideas inactive c[oul]d not be like the active. The 'idea of spirit' is a contradiction in terms. Nor can we have an idea wh[ich] is <u>like</u> a spirit 'so far as it goes' tho[ugh] leaving out the thinking & power & perceiving: for these are just what

---

16   Ibid., 34-5.
17   Berkeley, *Of the Principles of Human Knowledge*, 89 [1.1.].
18   Berkeley, *Three Dialogues between Hylas and Philonous*, 221 [232].

make a spirit. The existence of other finite spirits I know by inference. 'I perceive several motions, changes and combinations of ideas that inform me there are certain particular agents like myself which accompany them and concur in their production' (145). But it is plain that most of the ideas I perceive must come from a single omnipotent spirit, who is therefore 'known as certainly and immediately as any other mind or spirit whatsoever.' It need not be objected that this involves the direct action of God in many monstrous phenomena: this is not repugnant to his goodness. Regularity being the greater good on the whole.[19]

Following his summary of Berkeley's metaphysics, Lewis went on to critique three aspects of the Bishop's project: (1) Berkeley's rejection of universals, which we already discussed in the previous chapter and which we know Lewis was troubled by; (2) Berkeley's explanation for how we can know relations, "for these, like matter, will be neither ideas nor thinkers;"[20] and (3) Berkeley's proof for the existence of other finite spirits. This latter point in particular is helpful for our understanding of Lewis's metaphysics, for the Oxford don was bothered by the fact that if one were to be a consistent subjective idealist, then one would have to admit that the ideas in each mind must be "numerically distinct from the 'same' idea in any other mind. And, when we have taken away the material world, we cannot explain how one mind can excite ideas in another."[21] Consequently, Lewis thought "that the ideas I call 'Jones talking must like all other ideas be excited by God in me: in which case Jones becomes (like matter) an otiose third term or 'occasion.'"[22] Ultimately, because of the quasi-solipsism that Lewis perceived in Berkeley's subjective idealism,[23] the young don was forced to interpret Berkeley in a more suitable fashion, saying, "What Berkeley really seems to mean is that there is a common world of sensibilia which is directly accessible to us all:

19   Lewis, "The Moral Good – Its Place Among the Values," 36.
20   Ibid., 38. Although Lewis's discussion of relations is often sparse and difficult to follow, it is worth noting that the Oxford don did spend quite a bit of time researching this topic, especially when he became an absolute idealist. For example, both Bradley's critique of external relations and G. E. Moore's counter-critique were important to Lewis's idealist metaphysics. See Bradley, *Appearance and Reality*, 25-32. G. E. Moore, *Philosophical Studies* (1922 reprint; London: Routledge, 2002), 276-309. Lewis, *All My Road Before Me*, 353-4 [February 18-20, 1925].
21   Lewis, "The Moral Good – Its Place Among the Values," 38.
22   Ibid.
23   Lewis linked solipsism and subjective idealism in at least two places: (1) "The way is thus left open for subjective idealism or solipsism." Lewis, "The Moral Good – Its Place Among the Values," 30. (2) "Relapse into extreme subjective idealism, *at least*: more probably into solipsism." Lewis, *The Collected Letters of C. S. Lewis: Volume III*, 1636 [January 1928 "The Great War Letters," Series I, Letter 8].

ideal only in the sense that there is no substratum below the <u>sensibilitas</u>. But we do not know how this c[oul]d be worked out. What we actually get in Berkeley is a series of private worlds only held together by the goodness of God."[24] It is clear from these comments that Lewis the subjective idealist was pitting his love for consistency against his intuitions, the result of which is that Lewis took much, but not all, of Berkeley's philosophy with him and moved on to absolute idealism, which Lewis, as is evident in his Great War documents, clearly thought had better answers to the problem of how the external world could at once be ideal and yet act as a common meeting ground for finite spirits.

As an absolute idealist, Lewis still maintained his Berkeleyan belief that there is only one prime substance, spirit or mind, and that everything else is simply ideas (or relations or notions); hence, he said we only perceive qualities or ideas and not some apparent material substratum behind them: "All my perceptions, then, exist only in my soul."[25]

Moreover, Lewis the absolute idealist still concurred with Berkeley both that the material world is only a collection of sensible ideas that must exist in spirit and that finite spirit cannot maintain the existence of the entire material world within itself. Consequently, Lewis asserted the need for Spirit to maintain the existence of the material world *qua* collection of ideas in Itself.

However, because Lewis rejected Berkeley's quasi-solipsism, which was the result of effectively denying real contact between finite spirits (Spirit or myself being the only cause of ideas in me), Lewis needed to postulate a new way of maintaining the belief in real contact between finite spirits. Consequently, he rejected Berkeley's theistic assumption about the absolute separation between Spirit and finite spirits – between God and his rational creatures – because the separation between Spirit and finite spirits put a barrier, the real person of God, between my contact with other finite spirits since on Berkeley's account I cause ideas in others via God, not via myself. In the place of the theistic Spirit, Lewis put the pantheistic Spirit, who is nothing more than a compresence or totality of all finite souls and ideas – all individual souls being in fact only Appearances of Spirit and all ideas existing in It: "Since all things are Spirit, it becomes a question what we mean by the spiritual, distinguished as one element in life from others. The common view that spiritual is the opposite of material is mainly an error. For matter exists, together with souls, inside Spirit, and souls and matter

24   Lewis, "The Moral Good – Its Place Among the Values," 38.
25   Lewis, *Clivi Hamiltonis Summae Metaphysices Contra Anthroposophos Libri II*, 1.

are simply two aspects of the single creative act of Spirit."[26] Therefore, if all souls are really, objectively Spirit, then in a sense I do not know other souls as a "third term," but know them directly as part of my True Self; however, this needs to be qualified. The material world, which helps to separate myself *qua* Appearance of Spirit from other Appearances of Spirit, is necessary for individuality, yet it is in fact only an idea which all Appearances share *qua* objective Spirit. All Appearances of Spirit can, *contra* Berkeley's subjectivism, directly perceive the same objective material world and we are justified in speaking of universals[27] – and not just particulars – because our objective self, Spirit, perceives the objective material world, which we, as Appearances, perceive when we think rationally, objectively or spiritually. As Lewis says in his chapter on "Being" in *Clivi Hamiltonis Summae Metaphysices Contra Anthroposophos Libri II*:

> That is to say: if we grant the existence of souls other than mine, these souls will be unconnected with me, and to explain the conduct of those people whom I meet in my own world new 'souls' have to be introduced which are included in mine. The hypothesis of the souls outside my own therefore become otiose. Again, the hypothesis really supposes that an identical content (viz: 'the world') should be indefinitely repeated. There would thus be many worlds in number, but one in quality. But since their quality would be one, their multiplicity could have no meaning, apart from their inclusion in some system – e.g. as part of a single space or time, or as a manifold united by some mind which stood outside them all. But by hypothesis no such union between them is possible. Their multiplicity therefore would be sheer multiplicity, which is meaningless. Therefore the hypothesis of other souls outside my own is not only otiose but self contradictory. Therefore not only the bodies but also the souls of others exist only in my soul.[28]

Borrowing Berkeley's (fairly standard) belief that spirits or souls are active subjects while ideas are passive objects, and employing Alexandrian terminology, Lewis insisted that Spirit can never be Contemplated since to do so would be to treat a subject – indeed, *the* Subject – as an object,

---

26 Ibid., 35.
27 Ever since he was a Stoical materialist, Lewis believed in abstract universals. At times, this put him at odds with the worldviews of philosophers who he sought to follow. For instance, Lewis did not accept Berkeley's nominalism, nor did he feel comfortable making all universals concrete as absolute idealists like Bradley and Hegel did. Rather, Lewis's worldview should be seen as an original creation – errors, inconsistencies and all.
28 Lewis, *Clivi Hamiltonis Summae Metaphysices Contra Anthroposophos Libri II*, 5.

separating the oneness of Spirit and soul into a duality, which is implied in Contemplation. Consequently, Spirit can only be Enjoyed and it is precisely at those moments of Enjoying Spirit that the soul feels the great sense of oneness and connectedness with the "hidden glory" behind all Appearances. Furthermore, as we discussed in chapter four, souls – other Appearances of Spirit – cannot be Contemplated *qua* Spirit, but can only be Contemplated *qua* body, for if we were to Enjoy souls *qua* Spirit we would be Spirit *qua* the one Spirit and not Spirit *qua* individual souls; thus, the material world and bodies, which are objective ideas in Spirit, act as a tool of differentiation that separate souls from one another. Therefore, we need to Contemplate others *qua* their bodies, for in Contemplation we treat them, or rather their bodies, as objects, which is to say we treat them as a duality – myself and them – and not a singularity, Spirit.[29] Hence, absolute idealism gave Lewis the

---

29 The marginalia in the back of Lewis's edition of Aristotle's *Ethica Nicomachea* gives us some interesting information on the Oxford don's idealist understanding of matter; the layout and Lewis's comments are as follows:

> The difficulty about bodies is that if a man believes bodies to be real, he must of course believe his own body to be real. But then he will believe the accounts which physiologists give of perception, and sooner or later will regard all the coloured and tangible shapes wh[ich] we call matter, as appearances arising in his own mind, from physiological causes. But among the appearances his own body must be caused / coloured: therefore, the whole world, including his body will be inside his mind. True, there might be another world of bodies wh[ich] caused this world of appearances: but that does not matter, for the whole argument was about the perceptible bodies. He will now have fallen into a contradiction for because he believes in his own body he has been forced to disbelieve in all bodies: but as this involved disbelief in his own body wh[ich] caused disbelief in all the rest, he has now no reason left for his disbelief: yet if he abandons it for belief he must go thro[ugh] the same circle again.

> While the contemplated or the enjoyed differ in kind, the material and the psychological (much of which is contemplated) are only different in tendency. What is private to a single self at a single moment, is the lowest level, the merely psychological. What is private is a single self, but, for that self, permanent, in psychological approaching materiality. What is common to a few selves is on the border line. What is not public, which is a permanent object for the greatest number of selves is most material.

Characteristics of matter 1. resistant to (⊠ informable) will 2. common 3. contemplated Matter

1.   As a necessity if there is to be a plurality of selves knowing one another. For to know another self does not mean to enjoy its thinking etc., wh[ich] w[oul]d mean to be it, and thus to remove all plurality, but to contemplate what it enjoys. But to talk of something wh[ich] can be both contemplated from without and enjoyed from within is to talk of a living body or an incarnate soul. For to know an alien soul (in any world) is to apprehend what it can only be: and the difference between the being and the apprehending gives you at once a distinction between the soul itself and something that w[oul]d

metaphysical tools needed to explain how we can have knowledge of other finite spirits or souls (and yet still speak of difference).

However, as we know from chapter two, Lewis ultimately rejected absolute idealism in favor of Neoplatonic theism largely because absolute idealism could not be lived. Consequently, as a Neoplatonic theist and later as a Christian, Lewis came to believe that there is a strong separation between God and his creation: "*When I say that one is not the other* I am not referring primarily to the difference of quality or degree . . . but *to distinction of substance*: rejecting the whole-and-part relation in favour of the creator-creature one, i.e. unsaying what I said in the *Summa* [i.e. *Clivi Hamiltonis Summae Metaphysices Contra Anthroposophos Libri II*]."[30] However, because the absolute idealists were heavily influenced by Plato and the Neoplatonists, many of their ideas are similar,[31] although, of course, there are also some important differences. Subsequently, I want to examine three sets of these similarities and differences pertaining to Spirit and matter.

The first similarity and difference between idealism and Neoplatonic Christianity is the issue of the soul's relation to God.

As an absolute idealist, Lewis believed that souls are autonomous splinters of Spirit embodied in matter (which is an illusion but necessary to separate souls from each other) and their task in life is to will as Spirit wills: "The approximation of souls to this qualitative equality with the consciousness of Spirit constitutes their spirituality and an account of the spiritual life is nothing but an account of the modes in which the approximation takes place."[32] Consequently, the more autonomous the soul is (the more it "creates

be analogous to our 'body' – however it might differ from it in the detail of its laws of working.

    2.   As the resistant stuff. We have a specimen of a world without matter in fantasy, or with a minimum of matter of wh[ich] the result is that there is no value in it.

C. S. Lewis, marginalia in his edition of *Ethica Nicomachea*, by Aristotelis, ed. I. Bywater (Oxonii: E Typographeo Charedoniano, n.d.; The Rare Book Collection, The University of North Carolina at Chapel Hill), back of the book.

30 Lewis, *The Collected Letters of C. S. Lewis: Volume II*, 871-2 [August 19, 1948].

31 Indeed, because idealism and Platonism are so similar, it is interesting to see how Lewis the absolute idealist translated Plato into idealist terms. For example, at the beginning of chapter eight in Lewis's edition of Plato's *Republic*, Lewis summarized Plato's argument thus: "The True Nature of Philosophic Education being illustrated by the symbol of the strange captives. Socrates explains how this conversion from shadow knowledge to knowledge of Reality can be effected. Mathematics, Astronomy and Music while empirically useful also draw the mind towards the Absolute. Last of all the Absolute is studied in itself in Dialectic; and our philosophic ruler is fully trained."

32 Lewis, *Clivi Hamiltonis Summae Metaphysices Contra Anthroposophos Libri II*, 40.

itself"[33]), the *less* real it becomes: "The Better or the Spiritual consists in living more as a manifestation of Spirit and less as a separate soul."[34]

Similarly, the Platonist knows that souls, though not part of the One, are "fallen" in the sense that they once enjoyed intimate vision of the Forms – i.e. true Being – and were happy insofar as they kept their "eyes" on the higher Reality. For the Platonist, then, the happiness of the individual soul also depends on seeking Reality, which is represented by the Forms; consequently, for the soul to look away from the Forms is for it to "fall" through the Great Chain of Being and into matter, which is an inferior substance, co-eternal with Being (hence, Platonic dualism). The Neoplatonic account of the Fall is only slightly different as it maintains that everything that exists emanated from the One, and the very act of emanation is seen as a type of "rebellion" or desire to be autonomous and free;[35] thus, the many or *Nous* rebels or springs from the One and, depending on who you talk to, this emanation implies either a spiritual monism, much like absolute idealism, or a dualism similar to Plato's.[36] However, for both the Platonist and the Neoplatonist, the incarnated soul is a "becoming" as it is not pure Being, like the Forms or the Neoplatonic Trinity, nor pure non-being, which, for Plato, is the nothingness *below* matter, but for the Neoplatonist is matter itself, which is *evil* insofar as it is the absence of Being or Form (a doctrine owing something to Plato and something to Aristotle, who said that matter cannot exist without form).[37]

---

33   Ibid., 20.

34   Lewis, *De Bono et Malo*, 2.

35   Plotinus *Enneads* 3.8.8.

36   While I tend to interpret Neoplatonic emanation as implying a kind of monism, Lewis believed emanation implies dualism, for when he rejected God emanating the universe instead of creating it, he did so because emanation sounded too passive, not because it implied the defusing of the same substance in a less potent degree: "Nor am I suggesting a theory of 'emanations.' The differentia of an 'emanation' – literally an overflowing, a trickling out – would be that it suggests something involuntary. But my words – 'uttering' and 'inventing' – are meant to suggest an act." Lewis, *Prayer: Letters to Malcolm*, 270.

37   A. C. Lloyd gives a nice summary of what Neoplatonists after Plotinus *generally* subscribed to: "If we analyse it we find that it makes a theory by combining the following Platonic, Peripatetic and Stoic doctrines. (1) Form fails to master matter completely (*Timaeus*). (2) Matter has no qualities (*Timaeus* and Stoics). (3) Evil is only apparent inasmuch as in the context of the whole it is no longer evil (*Laws* VII and X, Stoics). (4) The cause of evil is soul (*Laws* X). (5) It is never caused by God (*Republic* and *Timaeus*). (6) Privation is not a contrary like a co-ordinate species (Aristotle). (7) Final causes are forms and entelechies (Aristotle). (8) Failures are without goals because they are unintentional (Stoics)." A. C. Lloyd, "Athenian and Alexandrian Neoplatonism," in *The Cambridge History of Later Greek and Early Medieval Philosophy*, ed. A. H. Armstrong, 302-25 (Cambridge: Cambridge University Press, 2005), 318.

What links these ideas to Lewis the Neoplatonic *Christian* is the Augustinian belief that at one time all of Creation looked toward God in obedience, wherein all creatures willing obeyed God's commandments, and so were united with Him. Moreover, the Platonic and Neoplatonic falls and the idealist's "soul creating itself" are similar to the Christian Fall, wherein Satan and other "becomings" proudly looked to the inferior – themselves, things mixed with non-being – instead of to the superior, Being itself – God.

However, while matter is strongly related to the Platonic, Neoplatonic and idealist falls, the Christian Fall has nothing to do with matter, for matter – whatever it is – was created by God and declared "good" long before Adam and Eve, who themselves likely did not differentiate spirit and matter,[38] fell. Concerning Chalcidius, a fifth-century Neoplatonist, Lewis wrote: "He discusses at great length whether *silva* (matter) is inherently evil, without once mentioning *the Christian doctrine that God made all things and pronounced them very good.*"[39] Since God commands Christians to guard the Earth and "be fruitful and multiply," it is not wrong to love material things; indeed, it is our duty. Furthermore, because Christians believe in the resurrection of the body and the sacraments, they ought to have a respect for matter which Platonists (and others[40]) do not: "Isn't Xtianity separated from the other religions just by the fact that it does *not* allow one to exclude or reject *matter?*"[41] Indeed, according to Lewis, the material world can even attain a

38 Relying on Barfield's understanding of "ancient unities" between things in the past like breath, spirit and wind, Lewis often discussed his view that early man saw things in more general, unrefined terms. Early man, in other words, saw things holistically which is at once a good thing – for harmony is good – and a bad thing – for things are not just one but also many and particular. Hence, Lewis said of Merlin: "'Matter and spirit . . . were confused. After him came the modern man to whom Nature is something dead – a machine to be worked, and taken to bits if it won't work the way he pleases. . . . Merlin represents what we've got to get back to in some different way.'" Lewis, *That Hideous Strength*, 648.
39 Lewis, *The Discarded Image*, 50-1 (emphasis mine).
40 "I've known nice (and nasty) Hindoos. I should have thought the nice ones were precisely 'Pagans,' if one uses Pagan not in the popular modern sense which means pretty nearly 'irrelgious,' – but strictly. I.e., I think all the extreme refinement and that spirituality which takes the form of despising matter, is very like Pythagoras and Plato and Marcus Aurelius. Poor dears: they don't know about the Sacraments nor the resurrection of the body." Lewis, *The Collected Letters of C. S. Lewis: Volume III*, 776 [August 3, 1956].
41 Lewis, *The Collected Letters of C. S. Lewis: Volume II*, 640 [February 5, 1945]. Cf. "I don't say the resurrection of this body will happen at once. It may well be that this part of us sleeps in death and the intellectual soul is sent to Lenten lands where she fasts in naked spirituality – a ghostlike and imperfectly human condition. I don't imply that an angel is a ghost. But naked spirituality is in accordance with his nature: not, I think,

kind of salvation, although this idea – and this is crucial for understanding the idealist influence on the Christian Lewis – owes much to the *idealist language* of the material world being ideas that can *only* exist in spirits:

> Matter enters our experience only by becoming sensation (when we perceive it) or conception (when we understand it). That is, by becoming soul. That element in soul which it becomes will, in my view, be raised and glorified; the hills and valleys of Heaven will be to those you now experience not as a copy is to an original, nor as a substitute to the genuine article, but as the flower to the root, or the diamond to the coal. It will be eternally true that they originate with matter; let us therefore bless matter. But in entering our soul as alone it can enter – that is, by being perceived and known – matter has turned into soul (like the Undines who acquired a soul by marriage with a mortal).[42]

And this brings me back to the question I asked earlier about how we can reconcile Lewis's belief in matter with his claim that God is a "Berkeleyian Idealist." Obviously, the first step to answering this question is to answer another question, one raised by Lewis the Christian: "what do we mean by 'matter'?"[43] The problem, of course, is that Lewis the Christian could easily claim to believe in matter *qua* the material world and yet still be a Christian idealist who simply thought matter *qua* the material world is a collection of sensible ideas. If this were the case, then the question would be answered and Lewis the Christian would be Lewis the idealist Christian instead of Lewis the Neoplatonic Christian. Hence, we need to find out what Lewis thought matter *is* and why he used Berkeleyan language to talk about God.

In a telling passage in *Prayer: Letters to Malcolm*, Lewis discussed a poem he wrote about God when he had just become a theist – "And thus you neither need reply / Nor can; thus, while we seem / Two talkers, thou art One forever, and I / No dreamer, but Thy dream" – after which he commented: "*Dream* makes it too like Pantheism."[44] This is important because Lewis's biggest criticism of Berkeley's brand of Christianity is that it is dangerously near pantheism or absolute idealism, both of which are obviously incompatible with orthodox Christianity. Hence, Lewis the Christian criticized Berkeley thus: "The chasm between the two points of view is so abrupt that desperate remedies have been adopted. Berkeleyian Idealists have denied the physical

---

with ours." Lewis, *Prayer: Letters to Malcolm*, 303.

42   Lewis, *Prayer: Letters to Malcolm*, 303.
43   Lewis, *The Collected Letters of C. S. Lewis: Volume III*, 873 [August 7, 1957].
44   Lewis, *Prayer: Letters to Malcolm*, 267.

process; extreme Behavourists, the mental."[45] On top of this, while Lewis did not think that the argument for the existence of matter (presumably, *qua* non-idea) was perfect, he did think that it was at least respectable: "I do not think there is a *demonstrative* proof (like Euclid) of Christianity, nor of the existence of matter, nor of the good will & honesty of my best & oldest friends. I think all three are (except perhaps the second) far more probable than the alternatives."[46] The evidence, therefore, seems to suggest that Lewis at least rejected the idealist understanding of matter *qua* sensible ideas, yet even if this is the case, it remains to be seen what Lewis thought matter was.

I believe that Lewis accepted the Augustinian or Neoplatonic Christian understanding of God and matter, which, rejecting both Plato's doctrine of the co-eternity of Spirit and matter and the Neoplatonist's spiritual monism (which in many ways is like Berkeley's idealism), says that God potentially contains matter *qua* idea of matter in Himself, yet matter itself is not contained in God but is that which God creates:

> [Concerning the claim that] matter is a part of God, Milton certainly rejects in *De Doctrina* I, vii, the orthodox teaching that God made the material universe 'out of nothing', i.e. not out of any pre-existing raw material. He holds it to be 'an argument of supreme power and goodness that such diversified, multi-form, and inexhaustible virtue' ([such] as that of matter) 'should exist and be substantially inherent in God'. Spirit, according to Milton, 'being the more excellent substance virtually and essentially contains within itself the inferior one'. It is not easy to understand this doctrine, but we may note that it does not fall into the heresy against which the doctrine of 'creation out of nothing' was intended to guard. That doctrine was directed against dualism – against the idea that God was not the sole origin of things, but found Himself from the beginning faced with something other than Himself. This Milton does not believe: if he has erred he has erred by flying too far from it, and believing that God made the world 'out of Himself'. And this view must *in a certain sense* be accepted by all Theists: in the sense that the world was modeled on an *idea* existing in God's mind, that God *invented* matter, that (*salva reverentia*) He 'thought of' matter as Dickens 'thought of' Mr. Pickwick. From that point of view it could be said that God 'contained' matter as Shakespeare 'contained' Hamlet. In fact, if Milton had been content to say that God 'virtually contains' matter, as the poet the poem or the

feet swiftness, he would (I believe) have been orthodox.[47]

My argument, therefore, is that Lewis was a Neoplatonic Christian in regard to matter because he believed that God, souls and matter – whatever they all are precisely – are *separate, irreducible* (i.e. non-ideal) things: "Next, I think we prob[ably] differ about the meaning of *creation*. I take it to mean 'to cause to be, without pre-existing material (= to cause both the form & matter of) something pre-conceived in the Causer's thought wh[ich], after creation, is other than the Cause.'"[48]

Thus, while Lewis almost certainly rejected Berkeley's metaphysics of matter (and God) in favor of Augustine's (i.e. Neoplatonic Christianity's), there is still the question as to why Lewis the Christian used Berkeleyan language to speak of God. For my part, I am convinced that he did so for two reasons. First, Berkeleyan metaphysics had had a huge impact on Lewis and so it should not come as a surprise that despite rejecting the core beliefs of subjective idealism, Lewis the Christian would still phrase things in idealist *language*; that is, it is the language, not the metaphysics, which are a stumbling block to people when they read Lewis philosophically. Second, some of Lewis's Neoplatonic Christian *beliefs* really do agree with those of an idealist like Berkeley; hence, readers can easily be confused about some of Lewis's philosophically ambiguous claims, such as this: "I presume that only God's attention keeps me (or anything else) in existence at all."[49] What is important to remember is that Lewis's metaphysics were Neoplatonic Christian even if his language was not always so.

The second similarity and difference between Lewis's idealism and Neoplatonic Christianity is the connection between the material world and individual souls. Aristotle, and to a lesser extent, Plato, would have agreed with Lewis the absolute idealist that matter or body is essential for differentiating individual souls (form needs matter). As a Christian (and to a lesser extent as a Platonist), Lewis continued to accept the insights of absolute idealism and Aristotelianism in regard to the material world being necessary for differentiating individuals and giving us a neutral field wherein souls can meet. For instance, in 1940, he wrote:

> Matter, which keeps souls apart, also brings them together. It enables each of us to have an 'outside' as well as an 'inside', so that what are acts of will and thought for you are noises and glances for me; you are enabled not only to *be*, but to *appear*: and hence I have the pleasure of

47   Lewis, *A Preface to Paradise Lost*, 89-90.
48   Lewis, *The Collected Letters of C. S. Lewis: Volume II*, 870 [August 19, 1948].
49   Lewis, *Prayer: Letters to Malcolm*, 235. Cf. Lewis, *Miracles*, 1132.

making your acquaintance. . . . Society, then, implies a common field or 'world' in which its members meet. If there is an angelic society, as Christians have usually believed, then the angels also must have such a world or field; something which is to them as 'matter' (in the modern, not the scholastic, sense) is to us.[50]

And he reiterated the same idea in 1963, the year he died:

I have called my material surroundings a stage set. A stage set is not a dream nor a nonentity. But if you attack a stage set with a chisel you will not get chips of brick or stone; you'll only get a hole in a piece of canvas and, beyond that, windy darkness. Similarly, if you start investigating the nature of matter, you will not find anything like what imagination has always supposed matter to be. You will get mathematics. From that unimaginable physical reality my senses select a few stimuli. These they translate or symbolize into sensations, which have no likeness at all to the reality of matter. Of these sensations my associative power, very much directed by my practical needs and influenced by social training, makes up little bundles into what I call 'things' (labeled by nouns). Out of these I build myself a neat little box stage, suitably provided with properties such as hills, fields, houses, and the rest. In this I can act.[51]

The third similarity and difference between Lewis's idealism and Neoplatonic Christianity is ontological hierarchy. As an absolute idealist, Lewis acknowledged that there may be a celestial hierarchy, a string of intermediaries who hold us in their minds, yet he believed that ultimately all of these intermediaries would be swallowed up in the one Spirit just as the largest Russian nesting doll swallows up all the smaller ones. Moreover, as we saw before, Lewis also acknowledged the possibility of invisible gods or spirits, but he thought that ultimately we cannot know them and they, as they are not themselves the one Spirit, would merely be higher forms of men:

If the gods existed they could be nearer than I to Sprit only <u>in the first sense</u>: as every man better than I is nearer than I to Spirit, shares in more of the enjoyment of Spirit. For if the gods were nearer to Spirit in the second sense they would be intermediaries. But if so, they would not be in our world. . . . The gods, then, if they exist are creatures and differ from us only in degree.[52]

50 Lewis, *The Problem of Pain*, 484.
51 Lewis, *Prayer: Letters to Malcolm*, 275.
52 Lewis, *Clivi Hamiltonis Summae Metaphysices Contra Anthroposophos Libri II*, 29.

On top of thinking a celestial hierarchy of some sort possible, Lewis believed there was a terrestrial hierarchy; indeed, he even maintained that just as we know people have souls by Contemplating their bodies and arguing from analogy, so too do we have good reason to think animals have (animated, not rational) souls: "The argument consists in showing that the behavior of beasts is in many points identical with the behavior which in ourselves we recognize as flowing from our souls: therefore that beasts have souls is the most probable hypothesis."[53] Finally, at the lowest rung of the hierarchy is "dead matter," which, for Lewis the idealist, is simply the empty fantasies that poets make, for as we know, all idealists are united by the common rejection of matter *qua* material substratum: "Is there any appearance which is contemplated only and not enjoyed: That is, is there lifeless or dead matter? Clearly there is: if no where else, at least in the worlds created by human poets."[54]

When Lewis became a Neoplatonic Christian, his belief in both a celestial and terrestrial hierarchy increased.[55] As a Platonist, Lewis acknowledged that there is a hierarchy of souls – vegetative, animated and rational – and that men, as rational souls, are subordinate to more powerful rational souls, who in turn are ruled by the Good: it was axiomatic for the Greeks "that all perfect things are prior to all imperfect things;"[56] as a Christian, moreover, Lewis believed that God is the ultimate anti-egalitarian, for not only is there a hierarchy between unanimated matter, vegetation, animals, men and angels, but he also believed that there is a hierarchy among everything of a given class – that God can choose to exalt Jacob higher than Esau[57] – simply because the good and happiness of each creature exists in obeying its natural superior and ruling its natural inferior; a hierarchy, even among men, is the means by which God creates something beautiful and holy;

53   Ibid., 32.
54   Ibid.
55   "It is my contention that Lewis's Narnia exerts its attractive force because it is a literary instantiation of a certain kind of metaphysics: a metaphysics of participation, of superfluity of being, of sacrament, in which beauty plays a central role. Lewis refers to this metaphysics as Platonic, though it is really Neo-Platonism as transformed by the Christian thinkers of the Middle Ages, with all of their sacramental, Trinitarian, and Incarnational commitments. It is a metaphysics that envisions the world as a place where every creature bears within itself the marks of its Creator." Michael Muth, "Beastly Metaphysics: The Beasts of Narnia and Lewis's Reclamation of Medieval Sacramental Metaphysics," in *C. S. Lewis as Philosopher: Truth, Goodness, and Beauty*, ed. David Baggett, Gary Habermas and Jerry Walls, 228-44 (Downers Grove, IL: InterVarsity Press, 2008), 229.
56   Lewis, *The Discarded Image*, 85.
57   Malachi 1:2-3. Lewis, *The Four Loves*, 78.

indeed, following Augustine, Lewis thought that if people really loved God first and above all else, then they would will His will, which is to serve God according to the place He has assigned them.[58] And as we discussed in the previous chapter (and will return to again in chapter eight and nine), this is what justice is: loving each thing according to its place and worth as defined by God. Consequently, Lewis's Neoplatonic Christianity allowed him to explore a far richer concept of ontological hierarchy, for in absolute idealism everything is ultimately boiled down to the One, but in Lewis's Neoplatonic Christianity, everything explodes into its own uniqueness to the extent that it obeys God; in fact, if the Christian gains his life by losing it, the non-Christian, the disobedient one, loses his life – his individuality, being and "derivative immortality attained in [its] relation [to God]"[59] – by trying to take it in his own way: "Thus," wrote Lewis, "the whole Indian [and absolute idealist] aim seems to me to be *backward* towards a sort of unity wh[ich] God deliberately rejected and not onward to the true one. If mere unity (as to union) is the aim, all Creation seems otiose."[60]

Moreover, everything in the hierarchy God has created ought, strictly speaking, to be called "nature," for that which is natural is that which is within the preordained limits or ability of the thing God has created. Thus, a purely spiritual creature like an angel should not be called a supernatural creature in its own right, but is supernatural only in the sense that it has the ability to do what is beyond *our* nature as men. In the most perfect sense, only God is supernatural, for only God can go beyond all natures:

> In its strict theological sense this distinction presents little difficulty. When any agent is empowered by God to do that of which its own *kind* or *nature* would never have made it capable, it is said to act *supernaturally*, above its *nature*. The story in which Balaam's ass speaks is a story of the *supernatural* because speech is not a characteristic of asinine *nature*. . . . Whatever a man is enabled to receive or do by divine grace, and not by the exercise of his own *nature*, is *supernatural*. Hence 'joy, peace and delight' (of a certain sort) can be described by Hooker as 'supernatural passions' (I, xi, 3). . . . To call the angels

58 Augustine *The City of God* 12.5.
59 C. S. Lewis, marginalia in his edition of *De Incarnatione*, by Athanasius, ed. Frank Leslie Cross (London: T. and A. Constable, 1939; The Rare Book Collection, The University of North Carolina at Chapel Hill), 7 [4.6].
60 Lewis, *The Collected Letters of C. S. Lewis: Volume II*, 880 [September 27, 1948]. Cf. David Allred, "The Platonic Foundation of the Great Divorce," http://cslewis.drzeus.net/papers/platonic.html (accessed on April 15, 2004). Cf. Rebecca Totaro, "Regaining Perception: The Ransom Trilogy as a Re-embodiment of the Neoplatonic Model," *CSL: The Bulletin of the New York C. S. Lewis Society* 22, no. 10 (August 1991): 1-11.

themselves *supernatural* is, at first sight, no less odd than if we called the future *supernatural*. But certainly modern usage allows us to speak of '*supernatural* beings.' It is a usage philosophically scandalous.[61]

Thus, if God is the only real supernatural being, then it is no wonder that Lewis, as a Neoplatonic Christian, called his metaphysics "supernaturalism" as opposed to naturalism (which, like Lewis's earlier materialism, denies the existence of things that can work outside of the total system of Nature). In this way, Lewis understood supernaturalism and the metaphysics of hierarchy to act as an analogy for earthly politics – where supernaturalism is metaphysical monarchy and naturalism is metaphysical democracy:

> The difference between the two views might be expressed by saying that Naturalism gives us a democratic, Supernaturalism a monarchial, picture of reality. The Naturalist thinks that the privilege of 'being on its own' resides in the total mass of things, just as in a democracy sovereignty resides in the whole mass of people. The Supernaturalist thinks that this privilege belongs to some things or (more probably) One Thing and not to others – just as, in a real monarchy, the king has sovereignty and the people have not. And just as, in a democracy, all citizens are equal, so for the Naturalist one thing or event is as good as another, in the sense that they are all equally dependent on the total system of things. Indeed each of them is only the way in which the character of that total system exhibits itself at a particular point in space and time. The Supernaturalist, on the other hand, believes that the one original or self-existent thing is on a different level from, and more important than, all other things.[62]

Moreover, since God is the king of the ontological hierarchy, His creation, though not an evil thing, is very small indeed compared to His creative power. As Lewis said upon reading Julian of Norwich's *Revelations of Divine Love*: "One thing in her pleased me immensely. *Contemptus mundi* is dangerous and may lead to Manicheanism. Love of the creature is also dangerous. How the good of each is won, and the danger rejected, in her vision of 'all that is made' as a little thing like a hazelnut 'so small I thought it could hardly endure.' Not bad, you see: just very, very small."[63]

---

61   C. S. Lewis, *Studies in Words*, 2nd ed. (1960 reprint; Cambridge: Cambridge University Press, 1996), 64, 66. "The gods of Greece were not really supernatural in the strict sense which I am giving to the word. They were products of the total system of things and included within it. This introduces an important distinction." Lewis, *Miracles*, 1106.

62   Ibid., 1105.

63   Lewis, *The Collected Letters of C. S. Lewis: Volume II*, 392 [April 16, 1940].

Before moving on, necessity demands that I clarify a common misunderstanding in regard to Lewis and hierarchy. While Lewis adopted Chalcidius's *"caelestis chorea"* or "celestial dance" as a term used to describe the ontological hierarchy that God has made – a term that beautifully shows that everything has its place and that justice and beauty flow from one's obedience to it – it would be a mistake to think that Lewis uncritically accepted the hierarchies of Chalcidius and the other Neoplatonists, for while Lewis thought that God was at the top (or center, depending on how one looks at it) of the hierarchy and that His Beauty or at least Goodness does in some sense move the whole host of creation below (or outwardly away from) Him, it is unclear if Lewis actually accepted, for instance, the Aristotelian idea of planetary intelligences – i.e angels that rule the planets, such as Bernardus Silvestris's "Oyarsa"[64] – or the *longaevi* or other such middle-creatures between angels and men.[65] While Lewis did, of course, acknowledge the possibility of all of these,[66] and indeed thought aliens very probable, we must remember that his fiction is not always an accurate depiction of his metaphysical beliefs. Thus, when I say that Lewis's mature metaphysics is Neoplatonic Christian, I do not mean to say that such follows one strict ontological hierarchy, such as that of Chalcidius or Bernardus Silvestris; rather, Lewis's Neoplatonism in regard to hierarchy should be taken very broadly.

II: Essence and Existence

While Spirit and matter are concerned with the question of what constitutes the basic building blocks of reality, essence and existence are concerned with whether such realities have being and what kind of natures these realities assume. Since we have little information about Lewis's opinion on these issues when he was a materialist, we can start with Lewis's idealist views.

In his 1924 essay "The Whole," Lewis, who was almost certainly an idealist at the time, accepted the distinction between essence and existence, declaring that everything participating in "the Whole" shares one universal in common – existence; hence, he wrote, "When I say that I am speaking of the Whole I mean nothing but this: that my propositions have for subject a

---

64 Lewis, *Out of the Silent Planet*, 137. C. S. Lewis, "Genius and Genius," in *Studies in Medieval and Renaissance Literature*, by C. S. Lewis, ed. Walter Hooper (1936 essay reprint; Cambridge: Cambridge University Press, 1998), 170.

65 Lewis, *The Discarded Image*, 122-38. Lewis, *Poetry and Prose in the Sixteenth Century*, 11. Lewis, *The Magician's Nephew*, 170.

66 "'If you go back further . . . all the gods, elves, dwarfs, water-people, fate, longaevi. You and I know too much to think they are just illusions.' 'You think there are things like that?' 'I think there were. I think there was room for them then, but the universe has come more to a point.'" Lewis, *That Hideous Strength*, 647.

class including all particulars which participate in the universal of existence. I exclude nothing that is: I include nothing that is not."[67] In addition, Lewis felt that essence precedes existence since he believed that there are some essences that are merely potentially existent:

> Or again, the essence of a locomotive engine is to be a vehicle moved by tangent pressure thro[ugh] wheels mechanically made to revolve. This example is more pertinent; for the essence of a locomotive engine was the same before the building of the Rocket, and was itself already contemplated by Stevenson. And this already gives us the idea of essence as separable from and prior to existence.[68]

Nevertheless, in this essay, Lewis did not sufficiently deal with potential existence as a form of existence, namely, how all essences eternally exist in the mind of Spirit.

However, what is extremely important to note is that even though Lewis was at this time a subjective idealist – a follower of Berkeley – he, as I mentioned in the previous chapter, did not follow the Bishop in rejecting the distinctions between universality and particularity and essence and existence. That is, while Berkeley rejected these distinctions because he rejected Aristotle's theory of abstraction (wherein the universal is abstracted from the particular),[69] Lewis accepted Aristotle's theory (which we will discuss more in the following the chapter). Although this might seem trivial, Berkeley's entire philosophy was set up in order to bypass abstraction (particularly as presented by Locke) and account for knowledge as the direct result of minds perceiving ideas and not material objects in the external world. Thus, the fact that Lewis the subjective idealist accepted Aristotle's theory of abstraction, the correspondence theory of truth, and the distinction between essence and existence shows that Lewis's interest in idealism was more motivated by the need to account for the source of reason and objective values than anything else.

Furthermore, even though some of Lewis's epistemological positions changed when he became an absolute idealist, he remained convinced of two things.

67　Lewis, "The Whole," 106.
68　Ibid., 108.
69　"But how ready soever I may be, to acknowledge the scantiness of my comprehension, with regard to the endless variety of spirits and ideas that might possibly exist, yet for anyone to pretend to a notion of entity or existence, *abstracted* from *spirit* and *idea* . . . is, I suspect, a downright repugnancy and trifling with words." Berkeley, *A Treatise Concerning the Principles of Human Knowledge*, 121 [1.81].

First, he continued to agree with Aristotle, whose *Metaphysics* he probably first read in 1927,[70] when the Greek distinguished between essence and existence; hence, in his Great War letters, Lewis declared, "Whatness does *not* contain actuality: the bringing before the mind *what* X is, is preliminary to the question *whether* X exists."[71] Because Lewis continued to accept the distinction between essence and existence, he was able to formulate his rejection of both the ontological argument, which tries to prove the existence of God from an understanding of His essence, and the teaching that declares every essence has existence, for some things, such as the occultist's illusionary belief that he has real knowledge of spirits, have imaginary essences without having any actual existence.

Second, maintaining the distinction between essence and existence, Lewis accepted the Kantian belief in the Noumenal and Phenomenal selves,[72] which, in Lewis's absolute idealism, become the Real I or Spirit and the subjective I or particular Appearance; thus, while a particular Appearance may have contingent existence as an Appearance, Spirit has necessary existence. The particular, contingent Appearance or soul, moreover, does not have any *Real* essence outside of Spirit, for the autonomy of the Appearance is a false autonomy and one which leads, quite literally, nowhere if it does not will Spirit. The identity of the Appearance, therefore, is absolutely tied to Spirit, for they are in fact one substance. However, while Lewis the absolute

---

70   In his edition of Aristotle's *Metaphysics*, Lewis underlined the following: "<u>Since the essence plainly attaches to the *form*, soul and 'to be soul' are the same, but 'to be man' and 'man'</u> are different, unless indeed the soul is to be called man." C. S. Lewis, underlining in his edition of *Metaphysics*, by Aristotle, ed. and trans. John Warrington (London: J. M. Dent and Sons, 1956; The Rare Book Collection, The University of North Carolina at Chapel Hill), 1028b35-1029a1-5. Although we do not know exactly when Lewis first read Aristotle's *Metaphysics*, Lewis said he ordered a copy back in 1927. Lewis, *All My Road Before Me*, 440 [January 26, 1927].

71   Lewis, *The Collected Letters of C. S. Lewis: Volume III*, 1633-4 [January 1928, "The Great War Letters" Series I, Letter 8]. This quotation agrees with what Lewis wrote in his edition of Santayana's *Platonism and the Spiritual Life*: "Existence as a whole is not contingent. The contingent is 'what would have been different if something else had been different': i.e. it is applicable only to my part in relation to other parts inside a given whole." C. S. Lewis, marginalia in his edition of *Platonism and the Spiritual Life*, by George Santayana (London: Constable and Co., 1927; The Marion E. Wade Center, Wheaton College), 35. Cf. "[Lewis] was no mere conduit of sources but could put ideas in the historical philosopher's long perspective. On 26 February 1953, I asked him to explain the puzzling metaphysical dichotomies between form-substance and form-matter. He defined them at length extempore, soon going beyond my comprehension." Alastair Fowler, "C. S. Lewis: Supervisor," in *C. S. Lewis Remembered*, ed. Harry Lee Poe and Rebecca Whitten Poe, 98-114 (Grand Rapids, MI: Zondervan, 2006), 101.

72   Lewis, *Surprised by Joy*, 1358.

idealist thought that particular Appearances do not have a core soul in the Aristotelian or Platonic sense of the word (i.e. one separate from Spirit), Lewis rejected both Hume's understanding of the substance (and therefore the soul), which is "nothing but a collection of simple ideas,"[73] and Mill's definition of an essence, which Lewis summarized in his edition of *A System of Logic* as "the sum of attributes connotated by the name 'A.'"[74]

As part of believing that the essence or nature of Spirit is the totality of all Appearances, Lewis had to accept that good and evil and everything else ultimately are like particular colours that make a painting beautiful and good in its total presentation. In other words, part of what it means to be Spirit is that every good and evil Appearance must somehow constitute the essence of Spirit:

> The impossibility of absolute evil is also shown by Plato (Republic Bk I) where he shows that a wicked state (and for Plato the state is the symbol of the soul) perseveres in existence only by the goodness that is in it, and if it were absolutely evil would cease to be. So Jesus said that Satan's kingdom could not stand if it were divided against itself; showing that even if we assume a species of superhumanly evil beings, even they can maintain themselves only by internal concord and good faith: that is, not by their evil, but by such goodness as they have. . . . In the same way before we reach such an absolutely evil soul we should have disintegrated soul life altogether and therefore rendered all evil impossible. Therefore there is no absolute evil.[75]

While we will return to the question of Lewis's ethics in chapter eight, it is important that Lewis the idealist believed that Spirit does not *have* Its attributes, such as being, reason, evil or goodness, but *is* Its attributes. Indeed, it is because of this, Bradley described Spirit as "suprapersonal,"[76] for while we cannot say Spirit *qua* totality of Appearances shows anger, love or other feelings, "it is personal and more."[77]

When Lewis became a theist and Christian, many of his views about Spirit and God remained the same as they had been when he was an idealist. Besides, of course, rejecting the belief that we are a part of God and that

---

73 Lewis, "The Moral Good – Its Place Among the Values," 39. Cf. Lewis, *Poetry and Prose in the Sixteenth Century*, 12-3.

74 C. S. Lewis, marginalia in his edition of *A System of Logic, Ratiocinative and Inductive*, by John Stuart Mill, vol. 1, 3rd ed. (London: John W. Parker, DCCCLI; The Marion E. Wade Center, Wheaton College), 122.

75 Lewis, *De Bono et Malo*, 3.

76 Bradley, *Appearance and Reality*, 531.

77 Ibid.

He is both goodness and evil, reason and nonsense, Lewis still believed that God is "the ultimate Being,"[78] the "*ens entium*,"[79] the "*ens realissimum*,"[80] and "the One Self-Existent Thing"[81]: "About Being and Reason – it is clear that something must be self-existent (wh[ich] I take it is what you mean by 'Being'). I claim to show that Reason must be self-existent. There cannot be two independent self-existents. So I conclude that Reason is, or is a characteristic of, Being."[82] And while it is unclear whose terminology – Berkeley's, Boethius's or someone else's – Lewis used when he spoke of God as "the Divine Substance,"[83] it is clear that his idealist understanding of Spirit *being* Its attributes, such as Being, Reason and Goodness, and not simply having them, was completely compatible with the orthodox Christian understanding; as Lewis wrote in his edition of Augustine's *City of God*: "God is a Trinity because He has three persons, and a unity because He is what He has, as a living being is the life that he has. . . . I.e. Substance and quality or existence and essence coincide in God."[84] Consequently, Lewis the Neoplatonic Christian continued to agree with absolute idealism in regard to God as the Necessary Being: "if we fully understood *what* God is we should see that there is no question *whether* He is."[85] And this, of course, is strongly related to Lewis's argument from desire, a variation, as we saw in chapter two, of the ontological argument, to which Lewis the Christian partially softened up.

While none of Lewis's Christian thoughts on the nature of God are particularly new, many people have found them hugely appealing. One of the reasons for this is that Lewis has, through an impressive literary style, reformed the modern misunderstanding of Plato's theory of Forms and made them highly imaginable to lay readers. Thus, while many ridicule the idea of Platonic Forms, declaring them vaporous things that float around somewhere "beyond existence" in a reality that is somehow felt to be less real than our own,[86] Lewis insisted that "Plato was not so silly as moderns think,"[87] pointing out that "the true Platonic *eidos* is not only a 'thing' over and above all the particulars but a better thing than they. Beauty-in-itself

78   Lewis, *The Four Loves*, 80.
79   "The Being of beings." Lewis, "Is Theism Important?" 56-7.
80   "The Real Being." Lewis, "Religion without Dogma?" 164.
81   Lewis, *Miracles*, 1105.
82   Lewis, *The Collected Letters of C. S. Lewis: Volume II*, 808-9 [October 20, 1947].
83   Lewis, *The Problem of Pain*, 550.
84   Lewis, marginalia in his edition of *De Civitate Dei*, 11.10.
85   Lewis, *Miracles*, 1165.
86   Lewis, *The Abolition of Man*, 405.
87   Lewis, *Prayer: Letters to Malcolm*, 279.

is more beautiful than all beautiful objects: they are indeed mere shadows of it. . . . [The *eidos*] must be the plentitude and perfection whereof only dim traces are found in actual living things."[88] Naturally, Lewis followed Augustine, Boethius and others in understanding Plato's Forms to be Ideas in the mind of God; consequently, what Lewis was actually doing when he defended Plato's theory of Forms was rehabilitating or re-invigorating our understanding of God's nature:

> God is basic Fact or Actuality, the source of all other facthood. At all costs therefore he must not be thought of as a featureless generality. If He exists at all, He is the most concrete thing there is, the most individual, 'organised and minutely articulated.' He is unspeakable not by being indefinite but by being too definite for the unavoidable vagueness of language. The words *incorporeal* and *impersonal* are misleading because they suggest that He lacks some reality which we possess. It would be safer to call Him *trans-corporeal, trans-personal*. Body and personality as we know them are the real negatives – they are what is left of positive being when it is sufficiently diluted to appear in temporal or finite forms. Even our sexuality should be regarded as the transposition into a minor key of that creative joy which in Him is unceasing and irresistible. Grammatically, the things we say of Him are 'metaphorical': but in a deeper sense it is our physical and psychic energies that are mere 'metaphors' of the real Life which is God. . . . The ultimate spiritual reality is not vaguer, more inert, more transparent than the images, but more positive, more dynamic, more opaque. Confusion between Spirit and soul (or 'ghost') has here done much harm. Ghosts must be pictured, if we are to picture them at all, as shadowy and tenuous, for ghosts are half-men, one element abstracted from a creature that ought to have flesh. But Spirit, if pictured at all, must be pictured in the very opposite way. Neither God nor even the gods are 'shadowy' in traditional imagination: even the human dead, when glorified in Christ, cease to be 'ghosts' and become 'saints.' . . . If we must have a mental picture to symbolise Spirit, we should represent it as something *heavier* than matter. . . . Silences in the physical world occur in empty places: but the ultimate Peace is silent through the very density of life. Saying is swallowed up in being.[89]

In this description, God is so real that He, Who is Spirit and Light, paradoxically becomes "the *opaque* centre of all existences, the thing that simply and entirely *is*, the fountain of facthood."[90] This visual Platonic

---

88 Lewis, *Studies in Words*, 296-7.
89 Lewis, *Miracles*, 1167-8, 1169.
90 Ibid., 1165 (emphasis mine).

Christianity, almost mystical in tone, is further illuminated by Lewis in *The Great Divorce*, where the heretical Episcopalian Ghost says of God: "Exists? What does Existence mean? You *will* keep on implying some sort of static, ready-made reality which is, so to speak, 'there,' and to which our minds have simply to conform. These great mysteries cannot be approached in that way. If there were such a thing . . . quite frankly, I should not be interested in it. God, for me, is something purely spiritual."[91] Those like the Ghost, Lewis argued, need to "beware, as Professor [Alfred North] Whitehead says, of paying God ill-judged 'metaphysical compliments.'"[92] This is to say when one calls God "infinite," one ought not to think of Him as a formless wisp that is everywhere; rather, He should be thought of as a "particular Thing" which, while remaining "*the* Absolute Being," has at the same time "a definite character": "The Hebrew writings here observe an admirable balance. Once God says simply I AM, proclaiming the mystery of self-existence. But times without number He says 'I am the Lord' – I, the ultimate Fact, have *this* determinate character, and not *that*."[93] Indeed, one of the chief differences between the absolute idealist's and the Christian's understanding of God is that absolute idealist scorns the personal aspects of God, while the Christian strongly emphasizes such personal or mythical aspects and believes they ought to be expected since if creatures – lesser things – have unique essences, how much more so must God, Who is the Ultimate Being. Hence, while Bradley's Spirit can hardly be called "suprapersonal" due to actually being a mashing together of all Appearances, the Christian God is truly "Beyond Personality" in the sense of being more personal than we – just as Spirit is heavier than matter: "If you are looking for something super-personal, something more than a person, then it is not a question of choosing between the Christian idea and the other ideas. The Christian idea is the only one on the market."[94] Thus, on top of being omniscient, omnipotent, simple, eternal and all the rest (we will talk about these shortly), God, according to Lewis, is truly our Father, King and Friend.

Moving on from the nature of God in Lewis's mature thought, I turn to the question of essence and existence in creatures, and when I do so, I immediately find two things that need to be addressed.

The first is that while God is the Necessary Being, creatures are contingent beings; that is, while every existing thing has an essence – "to exist means to be a positive Something, to have (metaphorically) a certain shape or structure,

---

91   Lewis, *The Great Divorce*, 1047.
92   Lewis, *Miracles*, 1164.
93   Ibid., 1164-5.
94   Lewis, *Mere Christianity*, 423.

to be this and not that"[95] – the mode of existence for creatures is not the same as the mode of existence for God. For instance, creatures do not necessarily have to be created – they, or more precisely, their essences, could forever exist as Ideas in the mind of God. God's Ideas, in other words, need not be given a different type of existence in creation: God's Idea of Socrates did not have to *become* Socrates:

> To say that God 'is a particular Thing' does seem to obliterate the immeasurable difference not only between what He is and what all other things are but between the very mode of His existence and theirs. I must at once restore the balance by insisting that derivative things, from atoms to archangels, hardly attain to existence at all in comparison with their Creator. Their principle of existence is not in themselves. You can distinguish *what* they are from the fact *that* they are. The definition of them can be understood and a clear idea of them formed without even knowing *whether* they are. Existence is an 'opaque' addition to the idea of them.[96]

The second is since God is "the source of being . . . the source of power,"[97] the existence and essence of all creatures is, as I said earlier, "derived."[98] Thus all things – vegetables, animals, men, angels, etc. – are at once like and unlike their Maker; in other words, there is a univocity and equivocity between God and His creation:

> You remember the two maxims Owen [Barfield] lays down in *Saving the Appearances*? On the one hand, the man who does not regard God as other than himself cannot be said to have a religion at all. On the other hand, if I think God other than myself in the same way in which my fellow-men, and objects in general, are other than myself, I am beginning to make Him as idol. I am daring to treat His existence as somehow *parallel* to my own. But He is the ground of our being. He is always both within us and over against us. Our reality is so much from His reality as He, moment by moment, projects into us. . . . To be discontinuous from God as I am discontinuous from you would be annihilation.
>
> . . . We must, no doubt, distinguish the ontological continuity between Creator and creature which is, so to speak, 'given' by the relation between them, from the union of wills which, under Grace, is reached by a life of sanctity. The ontological continuity is, I take it,

---

95   Lewis, *Miracles*, 1166.
96   Ibid., 1165.
97   Lewis, *The Problem of Pain*, 512.
98   Lewis, "Membership," 340.

unchangeable, and exists between God and a reprobate (or a devil) no less than between God and a saint. . . . Meanwhile, I stick to Owen's view. All creatures, from the angel to the atom, are other than God; with an otherness to which there is no parallel: incommensurable. The very word 'to be' cannot be applied to Him and to them in exactly the same sense. But also, no creature is other than He in the same way in which it is other than all the rest. He is in it as they can never be in one another. In each of them as the ground and root and continual supply of its reality. And also in good rational creatures as light; in bad ones as fire, as at first the smouldering unease, and later the flaming anguish, of an unwelcome and vainly resisted presence. . . . Therefore of each creature we can say, 'This also is Thou: neither is this Thou.'[99]

One of the consequences of Lewis's belief in the univocal relation between God and creation is that he believed that the real or perfect essence of every created thing first exists as an Idea in God's mind; indeed, there seems to be a Platonic Form of each particular creature which acts, to put it in Aristotelian language, as the "<u>end</u>"[100] or "perfection"[101] by which all creatures are individually judged and measured. That is, when created things are given existence – when God's Ideas are actualized in creation – they are instilled with Platonic *eros*, which causes them to desire to be whole or to become like the Idea God has of them: "Everything," Lewis summarized in his edition of Boethius's *Consolation of Philosophy*, "desires to realize its own proper nature."[102] Thus, for a thing to desire to be its perfect self is for a thing to desire its own good ("But in seeking to be itself a thing is seeking unity (=good)"[103]), and this is only to be found in Goodness Himself, God: "Therefore the end of all things is the good, or the single good Being (which are the same)."[104] It follows, then, that all creatures become more themselves – attain more happiness and are more fully actualized – the more they look to, and act like, God; that is, the more they exercise "creaturely participation in Divine attributes."[105] And since every individual essence is part of the

99   Lewis, *Prayer: Letters to Malcolm*, 268, 271.
100 C. S. Lewis, underlining in his edition of *De Re Publica*, by Aristotle, ed. Immanuelis Bekkerr (Oxonii: E Typographeo Academico, 1837; The Rare Book Collection, The University of North Carolina at Chapel Hill), 1252b33.
101 Lewis, *The Pilgrim's Regress*, 170.
102 C. S. Lewis, marginalia in his edition of *King Alfred's Old English Version of Boethius' De Consolatione Philosophiae*, by Boethius, trans. King Alfred, ed. Walter John Sedgewick (Oxford: Clarendon Press, 1899; The Rare Book Collection, The University of North Carolina at Chapel Hill), 4.3.
103 Ibid.
104 Ibid.
105 Lewis, *The Problem of Pain*, 496.

Great Chain of Being, it follows that the perfection and happiness of one thing may not, save insofar as we are talking about God *qua* the End of All Things, be the same for another thing:

> Your definition of gaiety is v[ery] much to the point. Perhaps one can carry it further. A creature can never be a perfect *being*, but may be a perfect *creature* – e.g. a good angel or a good apple-tree. Gaiety at its highest may be an (intellectual) creature's delighted recognition that its imperfection as a being may constitute part of its perfection as an element in the whole hierarchical order of creation. I mean, while it is a pity there sh[oul]d be bad men or bad dogs, part of the excellence of a good man is that he is *not* an angel, and of a good dog that it is *not* a man. This is an extension of what St. Paul says about the body & the members. A good toe-nail is not an unsuccessful attempt at a hair; and if it were conscious it w[oul]d delight in being simply a good toe-nail.[106]

Ultimately, however, although Lewis was skeptical of any philosophy of history, he did believe that things were moving more and more to the point where they will be either totally God's, which entails genuine individuality for the creature, or totally nothing: this is the "Great Divorce" which Lewis wrote about in so many of his books, including *That Hideous Strength*:

> 'Have you ever noticed,' said Dimble, 'that the universe, and every little bit of the universe, is always hardening and narrowing and coming to a point? . . . I mean . . . [i]f you dip into any college, or school, or parish, or family – anything you like – at a given point in its history, you always find that there was a time before that point when there was more elbow room and contrasts weren't quite so sharp; and that there's going to be a time after that point when there is less room for indecision and choices are even more momentous. Good is always getting better and bad is always getting worse: the possibilities of even apparent neutrality are always diminishing. The whole thing is sorting itself out all the time, coming to a point, getting sharper and harder. Like in the poem about Heaven and Hell eating into merry Middle Earth from opposite ends. . . . Perhaps the whole time-process means just that and nothing else. But it's not only in questions of moral choice. Everything is getting more itself and more different from everything else all the time. Evolution means species getting less and less like one another. Minds get more and more spiritual, matter more and more material.'[107]

---

106 Lewis, *The Collected Letters of C. S. Lewis: Volume III*, 1252 [April 5, 1961].
107 Lewis, *That Hideous Strength*, 645-6.

All creatures, but especially rational souls, will either experience heavenly delight, authentic selfhood,[108] solidity,[109] sonship,[110] and godhood,[111] or utter misery, darkness, slavery, monotony, ghosthood,[112] and "sameness."[113] "There therefore comes a time," wrote Lewis, "when the creature is fully *built*, irrevocably attached either to God or to itself. This irrevocableness is what we call Heaven or Hell."[114] Yet to say all of this is only to speak generally of the existence and essence of creatures. What needs to be shown is how Lewis's essentialism works itself out more particularly, especially in regard to three things: Nature (including animals), nations and people.

As a romantic Platonist and lover of Nature, it should come as no surprise that Lewis believed Nature as a whole has "her essence"[115] – a core identity and not simply a collection of attributes:

> God need not create this Nature. He might have created others, He may have created others. But granted *this* Nature, then doubtless no smallest part of her is there except because it expresses the character He chose to give her. It would be a miserable error to suppose that the dimensions of space and time, the death and rebirth of vegetation, the unity in multiplicity of organisms, the union in opposition to sexes, and the colour of each particular apple in Herefordshire this autumn, were merely a collection of useful devices forcibly welded together. They are the very idiom, almost the facial expression, the smell or taste, of an individual thing. The *quality* of Nature is present in them all just as the Latinity of Latin is present in every inflection or the 'Correggiosity' of Correggio in every stroke of the brush.[116]

Of course, if Nature has a particular essence, then it is not a stretch to say that particular vegetation and animals are also thus unique. But note: merely having an essence does not tell us anything more than that God loves diversity and particularity; hence, while Lewis claimed each animal has a unique essence, he did not think they have rational souls: animals have animated souls or "sentience,"[117] and vegetation has vegetative souls or "bare life," but humans and angels have rational souls and thus are more like God

108 Lewis, *Mere Christianity*, 464.
109 Lewis, *The Great Divorce*, 1040.
110 Lewis, *Mere Christianity*, 421.
111 Lewis, "The Weight of Glory," 105.
112 Lewis, *Miracles*, 1168.
113 Lewis, *Mere Christianity*, 464.
114 Lewis, *The Collected Letters of C. S. Lewis: Volume II*, 585 [July 20, 1943].
115 Lewis, *Miracles*, 1149.
116 Ibid., 1148.
117 Lewis, *The Problem of Pain*, 540.

than animals and vegetation (although these are like God insofar as they resemble the Ideas He has of them).

Nevertheless, while Lewis strongly emphasized the difference between animals and men, he, as we know, was a great lover of ontological hierarchy, and so teased out some interesting ideas concerning the possibility of animals growing into their personalities. That is, just as matter can attain a kind of salvation by being taken into the soul via perception, so too might animals (and all of Nature) attain a kind of "derivative immortality"[118] insofar as they are included under the umbrella of man, who in turn is taken into God at the End of Days:

> Man was appointed by God to have dominion over the beasts, and everything a man does to an animal is either a lawful exercise, or a sacrilegious abuse, of an authority by Divine right. The tame animal is therefore, in the deepest sense, the only 'natural' animal – the only one we see occupying the place it was made to occupy, and it is on the tame animal that we must base all our doctrine of beasts. Now it will be seen that in so far as the tame animal has a real self or personality, it owes this almost entirely to its master. If a good sheepdog seems 'almost human' that is because a good shepherd has made it so. I have already noted the mysterious force of the word 'in.' I do not take all the senses of it in the New Testament to be identical, so that man is *in* Christ and Christ is *in* God and the Holy Spirit *in* the Church and also *in* the individual believer in exactly the same sense. . . . I am now going to suggest – though with great readiness to be set right by real theologians – that there may be a sense, corresponding, though not identical, with these, in which those beasts that attain a real self are *in* their masters. That is to say, you must not think of a beast by itself, and call that a personality and then inquire whether God will raise and bless *that*. You must take the whole context *in* which the beast acquires its selfhood – namely 'The-goodman-and-the-goodwife-ruling-their-children-and-their-beasts-in-the-good-homestead.'[119]

Shortly after writing this, Lewis said that when he wrote "tame," he did not mean "broken" or "enslaved;" hence, he said of Nature as a whole: "The 'vanity' to which she was subjected was her disease, not her essence. She will be cured in character: not tamed (Heaven forbid) nor sterilized. We shall still be able to recognize our old enemy, friend, playfellow and foster-mother, so

---

118 Ibid., 546.

119 Ibid., 545. In his edition of Aristotle's *Politics*, Lewis underlined the following: "The same holds good of animals in relation to men; for tame animals have a better nature than wild and <u>all tame animals</u> are better off when they are ruled by man; for then they are preserved." Lewis, underlining in his edition of *De Re Publica*, 1254b10-12.

perfected as to be not less, but more, herself."[120] I believe it is important for us to be aware of Lewis's originality here, for few men have so wonderfully described ontological hierarchy and salvation therein as Lewis has on this subject; indeed, who can forget Lewis's description of Mr. Bultitude the bear "trembl[ing] on the very borders of personality" when in the presence of Ransom?[121]

Nevertheless, while Nature and all her inhabitants have individuality, albeit in differing degrees, they are not merely particular things. That is, while Lewis thought the evolutionary process was one of the tools by which God shapes the individuality of Nature (separating Barfield's "ancient unities"[122]), we must remember that even when it was at odds with the rest of his philosophy (i.e. materialism, subjective idealism and absolute idealism), Lewis believed in universals. Thus, while admitting that there are individual lions, for instance, there is certainly a universal Lionness in which all particular lions participate.[123] And the same is true of Nature: it is because Nature has objective value and the power to provoke universal responses in us that Lewis agreed with Coleridge when the romantic poet said it is more correct to call a waterfall "sublime" than to call it "pretty": "The reason why Coleridge agreed with the tourist who called the cataract sublime and disagreed with the one who called it pretty was of course that he believed inanimate nature to be such that certain responses could be more 'just' or 'ordinate' or 'appropriate' to it than others."[124]

Of course, this combination of particularity and universality is not just true of Nature and her inhabitants, for all things are, in varying degrees, combinations of these two. And this, as we discussed in the last chapter, also includes cultures and nations, which Lewis believed have their own unique quality or *telos*.[125] That is, as with all created things, every nation exists as a perfect Idea in the mind of God and as such every nation has a perfect destiny if they will only strive after it. For instance, the true essence of Britain is what Lewis, following Chrétien de Troyes, calls "Logres;"[126] King Arthur, being a

---

120 Lewis, *Miracles*, 1149.

121 Lewis, *That Hideous Strength*, 672.

122 Ibid., 621.

123 Lewis, *The Problem of Pain*, 547.

124 Lewis, *The Abolition of Man*, 404.

125 C. S. Lewis, "What France Means to You," in *We Remember C. S. Lewis: Essays & Memoirs*, ed. David Graham, 1-5 (1944 article reprint; Nashville: Broadman & Homan Publishers, 2001), 3.

126 C. S. Lewis, underlining in his edition of *Arthurian Romances: Lancelot*, by Chrétien de Troyes, trans. W. WisterComfort (London: J. M. Dent, n.d.; The Rare Book Collection, The University of North Carolina at Chapel Hill), 287. It should be noted that while

good king who strove to establish Logres, almost succeeded in pulling "this whole society together,"[127] but ultimately failed and "Logres [sank] into mere Britain."[128] Likewise, the true essence of France was most evident during the First Crusade and when "goddess Reason" ruled,[129] and this ought to make sense if we accept Lewis's claim that the more a thing draws near to God – as love (the First Crusade) and reason cause a thing to do – the more the thing becomes itself. Passing over Lewis's comments about China and Germany in this regard,[130] the Oxford don's most romantic Platonic[131] comment about the essence of nations is in *The Last Battle*, where we are told that a thing becomes more real the closer it is to the center, which, of course, is a place of permanence and pure actuality (since the center of a circle does not require motion to be everywhere at the same time), for once a thing is in the direct center, as opposed to being on the outer ring, the thing is closest to God and hence its true self:

> 'The Eagle is right,' said the Lord Digory. 'Listen, Peter. When Aslan said you could never go back to Narnia, he meant the Narnia you were thinking of. But that was not the real Narnia. That had a beginning and an end. It was only a shadow or copy of the real Narnia which has always been here and always will be here: just as our own world, England and all, is only a shadow or copy of something in Aslan's real world.' . . . 'It's all in Plato, all in Plato: bless me, what *do* they teach them at these schools!'
>
> . . .
>
> 'I see,' [Lucy] said. 'This is still Narnia, more real and more beautiful

---

Charles Williams's fascination with Arthuriana and Logres likely had some influence on Lewis's understanding of Logres as seen in *That Hideous Strength*, the actual word was well-known to the Oxford don long before he met Williams. Indeed, Lewis's edition of *Arthurian Romances: Lancelot* is dated "1928," and he only began writing to Williams in 1936. Lewis, *The Collected Letters of C. S. Lewis: Volume II*, 183 [March 11, 1936].

127 Lewis, *That Hideous Strength*, 375.

128 Lewis, *The Arthurian Torso*, 157. Cf. Lewis, *That Hideous Strength*, 655, 738-9. Lewis, *The Voyage of the Dawn Treader*, 15.

129 Lewis, "What France Means to You," 3. Cf. C. S. Lewis, "Tragic Ends," a review of *The Death of Tragedy*, by George Steiner, *Encounter* 18, no. 2 (February 1962): 101.

130 Lewis, "What France Means to You," 4. Lewis, "Edmund Spenser, 1552-99," 145. Lewis, *Reflection on the Psalms*, 341.

131 Plato himself would have denied that nations have essences since he believed that a nation is an attribute of one or another perceptible image of the Real Polis. Consequently, Lewis is best understood as a *romantic* Platonist when he said that nations have essences, for he likely followed Romantics like Burke and Novalis when they spoke of the essence of a nation. See Dieter Sturma, "Politics and the New Mythology: the Turn to Late Romanticism," in *The Cambridge Companion to German Idealism*, ed. Karl Ameriks, 219-38 (Cambridge: Cambridge University Press, 2006), 231.

than the Narnia down below, just as *it* was more real and more beautiful than the Narnia outside the stable door! I see . . . world within world, Narnia within Narnia.'

'Yes,' said Mr Tumnus, 'like an onion: except that as you go in and in, each circle is larger than the last.'[132]

With the essence and existence of Nature and nations explained, this leaves the essence and existence of man. It ought to be clear by now that Lewis rejected the Humean, Millian and existential belief that man is merely a collection of attributes. However, while Lewis acknowledged that men have particular essences and souls, his ontology beyond that is often difficult to follow.

For instance, despite claiming in one place that God creates the "form and matter" which make up the particular man,[133] Lewis, in another place, questioned Aristotle's understanding of substance and indeed the Philosopher's categories in general:

> I know very well that in logic God is a 'substance'. Yet my thirst for quality is authorized even here: 'We give thanks to thee for thy great glory.' He *is* this glory. What He is (the quality) is no abstraction from Him. A personal God, to be sure; but so much more than personal. To speak more soberly, our whole distinction between 'things' and 'qualities', 'substances' and 'attitudes', has no application to Him. *Perhaps it has much less than we suppose even to the created universe.*[134]

Following up on this, Lewis even appeared to have challenged one of the most basic philosophical distinctions – the difference between substance and accident: "And I find 'substance' (in Aristotle's sense), when stripped of its own accidents and endowed with the accidents of some other substance, an object I cannot think."[135] Leaving aside Lewis's Neoplatonic disposition for the moment, this comment seems extremely difficult for the Oxford don to defend, for how, on this account, could he honestly say that Socrates without his left leg would cease to be Socrates? And did Lewis really find it so hard to imagine Kafka in the body of a cockroach? Even more disturbing is that this opinion cannot be explained away as the product of Lewis's early inconsistent idealism, for this distrust of certain Aristotelian distinctions seems to have been progressive. For example, in 1939 we read:

132 Lewis, *The Last Battle*, 160-1, 170.
133 Lewis, *The Collected Letters of C. S. Lewis: Volume II*, 870 [August 19, 1948].
134 Lewis, *Prayer: Letters to Malcolm*, 279 (emphasis mine).
135 Ibid., 289.

A man whom I know dreamed that he was at Falstaff's funeral; and as the mourners were saying that they had lost only the mortal husk of Sir John and that the real man awaited them in a better world, my friend awoke crying out, 'But we've lost his *fatness*'! I am not sure about the theology of this, but I approve the sentiment. Where personality is in question I will not give up a wrinkle or a stammer.[136]

And eight years later, in 1947, we read again: "God's creative freedom is to be conceived as the freedom of a poet: the freedom to create a consistent, positive thing with its own inimitable flavour. Shakespeare need not create Falstaff: but if he does, Falstaff *must* be fat."[137] And of course if this is not enough, all of the quotations above which challenge Aristotle's categories and distinctions are taken from *Prayer: Letters to Malcolm*, which was published the year Lewis died (1963).

I believe that the answer to these apparent inconsistencies is to be found in *how* Lewis is read. That is, despite the sheer number of quotations we have in which Lewis seems to have rejected the substance / accident distinction, I think these passages must be read either poetically (*The Personal Heresy*) or pastorally (*Prayer: Letters to Malcolm*), and not philosophically. Thus, in all likelihood, Lewis the philosopher accepted something like the distinction between substance and accident, but Lewis the poet or Lewis the lay pastor rejected it, desiring (perhaps half-informed by his earlier, confused idealism) to emphasize God's love of the particular right down to the last hair. If this, or something like it, is the case, then the particularity and universality of man is preserved and Lewis's Neoplatonic metaphysics are internally consistent. However, it would be philosophically irresponsible of me not to point out Lewis's lack of clarity in this matter.

Of course, this still leaves open the question as to the *quality* of the human essence. For example, does the fact that a man has an essence and, more importantly, a rational soul, prove his immortality as Plato thought? While this topic has more to do with ethics than metaphysics, and as such, will be largely deferred until chapter eight, one thing is worth mentioning here: if "a man's spiritual health is exactly proportional to his love for God," the reverse will also be true.[138] That is, if the soul in Heaven becomes its true self – if, to put it metaphysically, "What was sown as a becoming rises a being"[139] – then the evil soul will lose its essence and existence in exact proportion to his evil choices; it, in other words, will sink deeper into the "shadowlands" instead of

136 Lewis, *The Personal Heresy*, 54.
137 Lewis, *Miracles*, 1148.
138 Lewis, *The Four Loves*, 6.
139 Lewis, *Prayer: Letters to Malcolm*, 303.

transcending them.[140] Moreover, because, as I have said before, "all <u>natures</u> are good"[141] and existence is good,[142] and because existence and essence were usually linked in Lewis, a totally evil creature would be non-existent (hence, Satan is not totally evil, for he exists). Consequently, Lewis agreed with Neoplatonic Christians such as Augustine and especially Boethius, in whose *Consolation of Philosophy* Lewis noted: "For to be = to be oneself and to be bad is to relinquish that *as far as possible*."[143] For Boethius and Lewis, not to mention Plato,[144] a rational man can, poetically speaking,[145] devolve "into a beast," as Boethius put it,[146] or return to a "dumb beast," as Lewis said of his Narnian animals,[147] if they reject God, the source of all essences and existence. Nevertheless, metaphysically speaking, rational creatures do not seem to be able to go completely out of existence, even though they can diminish to mere "dust" and "ashes."[148] That is, despite the fact that Lewis likely borrowed from Friedrich von Hügel the idea that Sheol is a place "where the soul leads to a shrunken existence,"[149] Lewis's interpretation of the aforementioned "dust" and "ash" – his metaphysics of Hell in other words – is fairly original, for he argued that just as fallen man lost "his original

---

140 Lewis, *The Last Battle*, 163.

141 Lewis, marginalia in his edition of *De Civitate Dei*, 11.23. Cf. Lewis, *A Preface to Paradise Lost*, 66.

142 "There is a dignity and poignancy in the bare fact that a thing exists." Lewis, "Is Theology Poetry?" 12. Cf. Lewis, *Mere Christianity*, 348.

143 Lewis, marginalia in his edition of *King Alfred's Old English Version of Boethius's De Consolatione Philosophiae*, 109.

144 "And if, in that shape, he still refraineth not from wickedness he shall be changed every time, according to the nature of his wickedness, into some bestial form after the similitude of his own nature." Plato *Timaeus* 42c.

145 "Plato clearly said that the souls of wicked men may be re-incarnated as women, and if that doesn't cure them, finally as beasts. But we are not, says Chalcidius, to suppose that he meant literally. He only means that, by indulging your passions, you will, in this present life, become more and more like an animal." Lewis, *The Discarded Image*, 52-3.

146 "So he who having left goodness aside has ceased to be a man, since he cannot pass over into the divine state, turns into a beast." Boethius *The Consolation of Philosophy* 4.3.

147 "'Creatures, I give you yourselves,' said the strong, happy voice of Aslan. '. . . And I give you myself. The dumb beasts whom I have not chosen are yours also. Treat them gently and cherish them but do not go back to their ways lest you cease to be Talking Beasts. For out of them you were taken and into them you can return. Do not so.'" Lewis, *The Magician's Nephew*, 109.

148 Lewis, *The Great Divorce*, 1063. Lewis, *The Problem of Pain*, 537.

149 Friedrich von Hügel, *Essays and Addresses on the Philosophy of Religion* (1921 reprint; Eugene, OR: Wipf and Stock Publishers, 2001), 26. Of course, the general idea that Sheol or Hades is a place of diminished persons was well known to Lewis through Homer and other sources, but it is the explicitly metaphysical terminology that von Hügel uses that likely influenced Lewis. Cf. Lewis, *Reflections on the Psalms*, 329.

specific nature,"[150] so too will men in Hell not really be men at all, but will rather become "ex-men," "damned ghosts," or "man-shaped stains."[151] Thus, Christ's "I never knew you" is echoed by a certain woman in Heaven who *literally* no longer recognizes her utterly diminished husband,[152] and Hell, we are told by Lewis, is like a pantheistic maw where the stronger, in their prideful self-love, devour the weaker,[153] and cause all beauty and diversity to be mangled together and pushed ever closer to "non-entity."[154]

III: Eternity and Time

The final metaphysical category I want to discuss is Lewis's understanding of eternity and time, which inevitably entails a discussion on causality and at least a partial discussion of such theological issues as God's simplicity, impassibility, omniscience and omnipotence and their relation to man's freewill and destiny.

As with most of Lewis's writings on metaphysics and natural theology, we have very few of his thoughts on eternity and time from his materialist and dualist phases. However, it is important to keep in mind Lewis's strong affinity with the heroic gods of Norse mythology, who were mortal (i.e. in time) and yet still chose to act heroically. Although Lewis would later come to believe in eternal life, he always admired this element in Norse mythology and it influenced him in many important ways as we shall see in this chapter and again in chapter eight.

When Lewis moved beyond Stoical materialism and into subjective idealism, he appears to have agreed with Berkeley in rejecting time as an abstraction. Lewis summarized the Bishop thus: "We are rid of many atheistical arguments. Our rejection of abstract ideas also frees us from many puzzles. Thus we need not worry over Time, once we grasp that there is no Time 'abstracted from the succession of ideas in our minds.' The duration of a spirit 'may be estimated by the number of ideas or actions succeeding each other in that same spirit.'"[155] Berkeley's rejection of time made sense for Lewis because if everything is ideal (spiritual) and subjective (non-abstract), then a spirit simply experiences a concrete thought followed by another concrete thought and there is absolutely no meaning to the word "time" besides this

---

150 Lewis, *The Problem of Pain*, 512.
151 Ibid., 537. Lewis, *The Great Divorce*, 1037.
152 Ibid., 1088.
153 "[Satan's] dream is of the day when all shall be inside him and all that says 'I' can say it only through him." Lewis, *The Screwtape Letters*, 737.
154 Lewis, *The Problem of Pain*, 538.
155 Lewis, "The Moral Good – Its Place Among the Values," 35.

concrete, subjective mental experience. In other words, there is no uniform time which is infinitely divisible and which all experience,[156] and the only thing that is truly eternal is Spirit or God.[157]

However, as we discussed in previous chapters, Lewis's early philosophical beliefs were often in conflict with his poetic impulses. One such conflict or tension is found in the young subjective idealist's 1924 lecture notes on "The Good – Its Place Among the Values,"[158] in an apparent summary of the fifth meditation of Descartes' *Meditation on First Philosophy*. In this "summary," Lewis mentioned nothing about Descartes' actual fifth meditation, but rather wrote poetically about the philosophical differences between Zeus, who represents the transcendent, eternal god, and Odin, who represents the immanent, time-bound god. It is clear from this summary that Lewis the subjective idealist, who, metaphysically speaking, should have been sympathetic with Zeus, clearly favored Odin:

> Zeus, in the graver pictures of him, sits immovably on some cold mountain top far beyond the region of clouds and storms. He 'neither slumbers nor sleeps' and his nod shakes Olympus. Such a god, from the first, invites metaphysical treatment. We know that the people who talked thus of Zeus will sooner or later talk of the One, and the Form of the Good which is beyond existence. . . . [He] has [nothing] to do with Time. But Odin is a spirit rooted in Time. He waits for the twilight of the gods. He has no true immortality, only longevity: no one ever thought of him as young. This seriousness of mortality raises him above the frivolous Zeus, while the mortal irritation depresses him below the Zeus of Phidias. And being in Time, he is also in the struggle. He has descended into Hel, been tortured between two fires, hung on the tree Yggdrasil, starved, grown grey, and lost an eye. If we look for his parallel in the Greek stories we shall find it not in the 'easily living' gods but rather in the resourceful, stubborn, hand-bitten Ulysses. But even Ulysses reached home in the end, while Odin expects no final victory. He is the type of the man 'up against it.'[159]

The tension that Lewis experienced between his Berkeleyan metaphysics on the one hand and his poetic love for stoical, time-bound nature on the

156 Berkeley, *A Treatise Concerning the Principles of Human Knowledge*, 127 [1.98].
157 Ibid., 136 [1.117].
158 Although these Descartes lectures are found in the document labeled "The Moral Good – Its Place Among the Values" (MS-76) by Wheaton College, Wheaton has mislabeled these lectures. But as I mentioned in chapter four, for the sake of referencing, I shall continue to *cite* "The Good – Its Place Among the Values" as "The Moral Good – Its place Among the values."
159 Lewis, "The Moral Good – Its Place Among the Values," 62.

other was not fully resolved – though truthfully it was not much discussed – when Lewis became an absolute idealist.

At that time, Lewis remained in many ways sympathetic with Berkeley's denial of time, although the Oxford don softened this slightly by agreeing with Bradley, who said that time is a mere Appearance, the collection of which constitutes Reality; hence, time exists, but it is a flawed thing that strives after a timelessness it can never attain: "Time in fact is 'before' and 'after' in one," wrote Bradley, "and without this diversity it is not time. But these differences cannot be asserted of the unity; and, on the other hand and failing that, time is helplessly dissolved. . . . Thus, in asserting itself, time tries to commit suicide as itself, to transcend its own character and to be taken up in what is higher."[160] Indeed, insisting that "we . . . not confuse eternity with time,"[161] Lewis claimed that the Absolute or Spirit is the only eternal or timeless thing because only Spirit is the pure subject that can never be treated as an object, for to treat Spirit as an object (a real impossibility, as I mentioned earlier) is to Contemplate it: it is to treat it as a particular thing or time-bound Appearance. Thus, "since Spirit is never an object it is not subject to time, space, or relations."[162] To clarify this, we have to remember that Lewis believed that a particular soul can Contemplate other souls only as embodied fragments of the Absolute; that is, if, *per impossible*, we could contemplate the naked soul, the two souls would be absorbed into one and thus would be Spirit, the pure subject and *not* a subject Contemplating an object. Consequently, it would be better to say that while Spirit or the Absolute is the only pure, and hence eternal, subject, all souls *qua* their Real Selves are part of this pure subject and so all souls are also eternal insofar as they are aspects of the Absolute. Time, and indeed all of creation, then, is merely a manifestation of the eternal Spirit:

> The Creation and annihilation of souls by the Spirit must not be confounded with the birth and death of men in Time. The Spirit is not in Time and does not create in Time. This may be understood by . . . [an] analogy: for as the dramatic Time which the actions of Hamlet are supposed to occupy in the play tells us nothing of the actual times at which Shakespeare enjoyed his Hamlet consciousness, so the times of human birth and death tell us nothing of the Spirit's mode of creation. If for the sake of language we represent the Spirit as being in Time, we may say that whenever the Spirit enjoys my soul

---

160 Bradley, *Appearance and Reality*, 39, 207.
161 C. S. Lewis, *Replies to Objections in Detail* (Unpublished "Great War" document [1929?]; The Marion E. Wade Center, Wheaton College), 116.
162 Lewis, *Clivi Hamiltonis Summae Metaphysices Contra Anthroposophos Libri II*, 7.

it creates me (in the very moment of that enjoyment) and whenever it ceases to do so I am annihilated: so that if (again for the sake of language) we could suppose that Spirit had suspended for a million years that thinking which makes our world and then resumed it, no interval would appear to us at all.[163]

While Lewis's absolute idealism may seem harsh and deterministic, the Oxford don adamantly denied the charge, for he believed that when particular souls, aspects of Spirit, are "created" or "annihilated," they are not done so by a whimsical deity, but are done so by the souls themselves *qua* their Real Selves or Spirit.[164] Hence, souls are free both to create and annihilate themselves; however, it must be admitted that in another sense souls can never escape the determinism of their own nature as Spirit, the totality of all souls. As a result, the true freedom of individual souls lies in their ability to do their duty or will as Spirit / their True Selves wills, which in one sense destroys their individuality and yet in another sense awakens them to who they really are: "I do not contend that the poet (or anyone or anything) can be free except in the sense that to utter the truth of Spirit is freedom."[165] Although the ethical implications of this will be discussed in chapter eight, it must be added to this that the death of an individual soul in time is not equivalent to annihilation, for annihilation is a technical term for Lewis which means the relapse of soul into Spirit. Hence, the soul attains eternal life not by committing suicide, but by willing as Spirit wills or "annihilating" itself *qua* Spirit:

> In the same way when I as Spirit cease to separate and to contemplate the elements that make up the particular soul called 'myself,' I may be said either to annihilate that soul or to awake it from death into real life. Therefore in this sense, even the individual soul is eternal and blessed and truly living, on this condition, that it will consent to die: for it has been shown that the soul maintains or abandons its separation from Spirit, [which] is its life, at its own will. But this voluntary death of the soul must not be confounded with the death of the person in Time.[166]

In sum, the good of souls is not to be found in time, but in eternity, for to seek our good here, or to expect God to produce good in time (such as Christians believe), is ultimately to chase after an idol:

---

163 Ibid., 18-9.
164 Ibid., 21.
165 Lewis, *Replies to Objections in Detail*, 115.
166 Lewis, *Clivi Hamiltonis Summae Metaphysices Contra Anthroposophos Libri II*, 22.

By losing each such moment as we have it, we cannot attain absolute good [in time]. . . . For as von Hügel said, we have a horror of endless succession as such, whether filled with happiness or misery [and this] is witness that our home is only in eternity. There is therefore, in reality, no divine plan or design of 'producing' good in Time. The whole series of endless Time, however filled whenever the predominance of evil comes, early or late . . . is the image of Spirit, and therefore, of good.[167]

Of course, when Lewis became a Christian, many of his views about eternity and time changed. Perhaps the biggest change was in regard to his low (philosophical) opinion of time, for time, Lewis the Christian knew, is the good creation of God and is something in which He has chosen to act. The immanence of God and particularly the Incarnation, then, forced Lewis to abandon many of his idealist views of time and history. Yet, it must at once be admitted that Lewis did not always speak clearly about the causality between time and eternity, and this, I believe, is once again largely due to his idealist language conflicting with his Neoplatonic Christian metaphysics.

Lewis's Christian understanding of eternity and time is largely that of Augustine, Boethius and von Hügel (the latter was a modern Catholic theologian who Lewis read when he was an absolute idealist and subsequently enjoyed and recommended to many[168]). All of these men were Neoplatonic Christians in regard to eternity and time, and so on top of the specific Christian elements in their philosophies, there were many important Platonic elements as well. The most important of these is Plato's doctrine that time is "a movable image of Eternity."[169] In Platonic Christian, but not necessarily Hebrew,[170] terms, this means that God, who alone is eternal, created time;

---

167 Lewis, *De Bono et Malo*, 17-8.

168 Lewis, *The Collected Letters of C. S. Lewis: Volume II*, 529 [August 19, 1942], 775 [May 6, 1947], 915 [February 4, 1949]. Lewis, *The Collected Letters of C. S. Lewis: Volume III*, 228 [September 23, 1952], 526 [November 14, 1954], 616 [June 5, 1955].

169 Plato *Timaeus* 37d.

170 "In Psalm 90 (v. 4) it had been said that a thousand years were to God like a single yesterday; in 2 Peter 3:8 – not the first place in the world where one would have looked for so metaphysical a theology – we read not only that a thousand years are as one day but also that 'one day is as a thousand years.' The Psalmist only meant, I think, that God was everlasting, that His life was infinite in time. But the epistle takes us out of the time-series altogether. As nothing outlasts God, so nothing slips away from Him into a past. The later conception (later in Christian thought – Plato had reached it) of the timeless as an eternal present has been achieved. Ever afterwards, for some of us, the 'one day' in God's courts which is better than a thousand, must carry a double meaning." Lewis. *Reflections on the Psalms*, 384. It should be noted that the idea of God being everlasting and not eternal has become more popular these days and so if Lewis were writing today, no doubt he would address this issue in greater detail instead of just

consequently, just as man is called the image of God, so is man's time-bound life an image of God's eternal life (hence, Lucy always finds Aslan a little larger as *she* grows, for the larger she becomes the more she becomes like eternity[171]). While God dwells in an "Eternal Now" and thus experiences "ABC" at one moment, time-bound creatures experience "A" in the past, "B" in the present, and "C" in the future.[172] In more Aristotelian terms, God is like the center of a circle and as such sees, without moving, the entire circumference of the circle (i.e. time) at one moment.

Lewis strongly endorsed this doctrine ("I firmly believe God's life is non-temporal"[173]) because, even as an idealist, he had felt that time always entailed loss – the loss of moments to the past – and thus misery – the misery of losing and never attaining wholeness: "Time is a defect of reality since by its v[ery] nature any temporal being loses each moment of its life to get the next."[174] As a result, the True Happiness of creatures is to be found in that which never changes – "All that is not eternal is eternally out of date"[175] – and it is this after which the Platonic *eros* in the souls of people desires; indeed, because we were made in the image of God and called to be His children (i.e. complete persons), it should come as no surprise that people long for God *qua* Eternity, Wholeness and Happiness:

> The Eternal may meet us in what is, by our present measurements, a day, or (more likely) a minute or a second; but we have touched what is not in any way commensurable with lengths of time, whether long or short. Hence our hope finally to emerge, if not altogether from time (that might not suit our humanity) at any rate from the tyranny, the unlinear poverty, of time, to ride it not to be ridden by it, and so to cure that always aching wound ('the wound man was born for') which mere succession and mutability inflict on us, almost equally when we are happy and when we are unhappy. For we are so little reconciled to time that we are even astonished at it. 'How he's grown!' we exclaim, 'How time flies!' as though the universal form of our experience were again and again a novelty. It is as strange as if a fish were repeatedly surprised at the wetness of water. And that would be strange indeed;

---

assuming that all Christians believe God is eternal.

171 "'Welcome, child,' he said. 'Aslan,' said Lucy, 'you're bigger.' 'That is because you are older, little one,' answered he. 'Not because you are?' 'I am not. But every year you grow, you will find me bigger.'" Lewis, *Prince Caspian*, 124. For more on this, see chapter eight.

172 Augustine *The City of God* 11.21. Boethius *The Consolation of Philosophy* 5.6. von Hügel, *Essays and Addresses on the Philosophy of Religion*, 93. Lewis, *Miracles*, 1234.

173 Lewis, *The Collected Letters of C. S. Lewis: Volume II*, 915 [February 4, 1949].

174 Ibid.

175 Lewis, *The Four Loves*, 86.

unless of course the fish were destined to become, one day, a land animal.[176]

This doctrine, needless to say, is different than that of absolute idealism, which claims that men are really eternal *qua* their Real Selves, for Neoplatonic Christians like Augustine, Boethius and Lewis believe that any hope creatures have of eternal life comes from the grace of God, who is emphatically not a creature. But of course for the Neoplatonic Christian, this also raises many problems, the largest of which is that of causality: causality between God and creation and causality between creation and God.

To begin with, there is the problem of God's eternal nature limiting Him from true interaction with His creation. Thus, Aristotle wrote: "Just as human intellect . . . is subject to the limitations of time, so is the divine self-thought throughout eternity."[177] In response to this quotation, Lewis exclaimed, "Nonsense!"[178] – nonsense, of course, because according to Christians, God's eternal and transcendent nature, far from implying limitation, suggests true freedom and the possibility of immanence: "The doctrine that God was under no necessity to create," wrote Lewis, "is not a piece of dry scholastic speculation. It is essential."[179] Because God is simple, and hence impassible and unchangeable (for that which is simple is complete, neither gaining nor losing anything),[180] Lewis maintained that when God created the world (which we know He did from scripture), He did so out of neither obligation nor need. Indeed, the only limitation on God's freedom is God's own nature. That is, *pace* men like Duns Scotus and William of Ockham, who believe that God's freedom transcends His other attributes, Lewis agreed with men like Augustine and Boethius, who said that God never acts against His own nature. Let us consider two examples of this.

First, because God's nature is good, all of God's free acts must be good:

> Perhaps this is not the 'best of all possible' universes, but the only possible one. Possible worlds can mean only 'worlds that God could have made, but didn't.' The idea of that which God 'could have' done involves a too anthropomorphic conception of God's freedom. Whatever human freedom means, Divine freedom cannot mean indeterminacy between alternatives and choice of one of them. Perfect goodness can never debate about the end to be attained, and perfect wisdom cannot debate about the means most suited to achieve it. The

176 Lewis, *Reflections on the Psalms*, 384.
177 Aristotle *Metaphysics* 1075b1.
178 Lewis, marginalia in his edition of *Metaphysics*, 1075b1.
179 Lewis, *The Four Loves*, 80.
180 "God, we believe, is impassible." Lewis, *Prayer: Letters to Malcolm*, 255.

freedom of God consists in the fact that no cause other than Himself produces His acts and no external obstacle impedes them – that His own goodness is the root from which they all grow and His own omnipotence the air in which they all flower.[181]

Second, because God's nature is rational, all of God's free acts must be rational: "nonsense remains nonsense even when we talk it about God."[182] Moreover, what this means in terms of causality is that such things as miracles are logically possible, and they are so, according to Lewis, because God, as the supernatural Creator standing outside of Nature, can introduce new events into Nature, which are then taken up by the normal laws of Nature (if there are such things), causing a new outcome: "It is therefore inaccurate to define a miracle as something that breaks the laws of Nature. It doesn't. . . . The divine art of miracle is not an art of suspending the pattern to which events conform but of feeding new events into that pattern."[183]

Be that as it may, it is one thing to say that God is impassible, totally free and incapable of working against His own nature, and another to show how this works out in regard to creation, particularly in regard to apparently free, rational creatures like men. The problem, of course, is if God is impassible then in what sense can there be real communion between God and creation? The doctrine of God's impassibility is problematic not only for things like prayer but for all apparently free acts of creatures.

Despite process theologian Charles Hartshorne's insistence that Lewis's Christianity is utterly tied to "orthodox metaphysics,"[184] by which he means the metaphysics of Neoplatonic Christianity, Lewis did not always feel satisfied with the either / or answers of men like Augustine (for while Lewis was a Neoplatonic Christian, he was never afraid of challenging the past, as we saw in chapter five). Thus, instead of either holding tightly to the doctrine of God's impassibility to the point of saying that God only communes with us via His ideas of us, or lowering God to the human level and making Him dependent on our incarnated selves for new knowledge (hence limiting His omniscience), Lewis insisted that "strictly causal thinking is . . . inadequate when applied to the relation between God and man."[185] The Oxford don

---

181 Lewis, *The Problem of Pain*, 486. Cf. "'Dearest,' said Aslan, 'I will show you both what I can, and what I cannot, do.'" Lewis, *The Last Battle*, 140.

182 Lewis, *The Problem of Pain*, 482.

183 Lewis, *Miracles*, 1143.

184 Charles Hartshorne, "Philosophy and Orthodoxy: Reflections upon C. S. Lewis' *The Problem of Pain* and *The Case of Christianity*," *Ethics* 54, no. 4 (July 1944): 298.

185 Lewis, *Prayer: Letters to Malcolm*, 256.

pointed out that "[s]cripture just sails over the problem,"[186] and, interestingly enough, we even see him trying to find room in Aristotle – since Lewis was ever the philosopher – for a similar interpretation:

> Then again, is the contrast between Agape (God active coming to man passive) and Eros (man by desire ascending to God qua passive object of desire) really so sharp? [Nygren] might accuse me of a mere play upon words if I pointed out that in Aristotle's 'He moves as the beloved' . . . there is, after all, an active verb, χινεῖ ["moves"]. But is this merely a grammatical accident – is it not perhaps the real answer? Can the thing really be conceived in one way *or* the other? In real life it feels like both, and both, I suspect, are the same.[187]

Although Lewis's language of both / and is dangerously close to the language of absolute idealism (I am Spirit and Spirit is me), I believe that Lewis was simply trying to find the most satisfactory way of saving appearances and remaining faithful to scripture: "There is no question, of course, of individuals melting down into a kind of spiritual continuum such as Pantheistic systems believe in; that is excluded by the whole tenor of our faith. But there may be a tension between individuality and some other principle."[188] To explain his both / and method, Lewis gave us the following advice, which should remind us of his insistence that mythical or super-rational elements ought not to be utterly reduced to theological abstractions, for the likely result of such is distortion of Truth:

> In the end we must admit a two-way traffic at the junction. At first sight no passive verb in the world would seem to be so utterly passive as 'to be created.' Does it not mean 'to *have been* nonentity?' Yet, for us rational creatures, to be created also means 'to be made agents.' We have nothing that we have not received; but part of what we have received is the power of being something more than receptacles. . . . [Y]ou must admit that Scripture doesn't take the slightest pains to guard the doctrine of Divine Impassibility. We are constantly represented as exciting the Divine wrath or pity – even as 'grieving' God. I know this language is analogical. But when we say that, we must not smuggle in the idea that we can throw the analogy away and, as it were, get in behind it to a purely literal truth. All we can really substitute for the analogical expression is some theological abstraction. . . . By itself, the abstraction 'impassible' can get us nowhere. It might even suggest something far more misleading than the most *naïf* Old Testament

186 Ibid.
187 Lewis, *The Collected Letters of C. S. Lewis: Volume II*, 153 [January 8, 1935]. Cf. Lewis, *The Problem of Pain*, 495. Lewis, *The Discarded Image*, 113.
188 Lewis, *The Problem of Pain*, 515.

picture of a stormily emotional Jehovah. Either something inert, or something which was 'Pure Act' in such a sense that it could take no account of events within the universe it had created. . . . I suggest two rules for exegetics. (1) Never take the images literally. (2) When the *purport* of the images – what they say to our fear and hope and will and affections – seems to conflict with the theological abstractions, trust the purport of the images every time.[189]

According to Lewis, reason tells us that there are two truths – our agency and God's impassibility – which cannot satisfactorily be reconciled under our present rational limitations; therefore, we ought to maintain both truths and try to please God as best we can therewith.

And this solution of Lewis's is, in many ways, similar to his solution for how God's omniscience and our freewill relate. The problem is that if God is omniscience, omnipotence and goodness, then how is it possible for humans to be free, for would not these divine attributes, so the question goes, determine everything? Indeed, would this not make God the author of evil, for if He determines everything, whence evil? While the problem of evil will be addressed in chapter eight, the metaphysics of this general dilemma demands an answer now. And the answer that Lewis gives is precisely that of Augustine and Boethius, both of whom maintained that human freedom is compatible with God's foreknowledge, for "strictly speaking, He never *fore*sees anything; He simply sees [everything in His Eternal Now]."[190] Consequently, God knows all our real[191] future acts without necessarily being the cause of them; that is, it is true to say both that God knows everything and man has real freedom: "I think God can make things which not only . . . *seem* to have a partial independent life, but really have it."[192]

Needless to say, if God's freedom is limited by His own attributes, how much more so must man's freedom – true freedom though it is – be limited by God, and although we will discuss these limitations more in the next chapter, it is important to note that Lewis spoke of these limitations with

189 Lewis, *Prayer: Letters to Malcolm*, 256, 257.

190 Lewis, *The Discarded Image*, 89.

191 Although Lewis rarely discussed modality and the notion of possible worlds (e.g. possible actions or choices), he likely believed both that possible worlds are maximally possible states of affairs and that the actual world is that maximally possible state of affairs that actually obtains. Hence, in *Prince Caspian*, we read, "'You mean,' said Lucy rather faintly, 'that it would have turned out all right – somehow? But how? Please, Aslan! Am I not to know?' 'To know what *would* have happened, child?' said Aslan. 'No. Nobody is ever told that.' 'Oh dear,' said Lucy. 'But anyone can find out what *will* happen,' said Aslan." Lewis, *Prince Caspian*, 125.

192 C. S. Lewis, "The Seeing Eye," in *C.S. Lewis: Essay Collection & Other Short Pieces*, ed. Lesley Walmsley (1963 essay reprint; London: HarperCollins, 2000), 62.

reference to Bradley, an absolute idealist (albeit he could have cited Plato, Aristotle or Augustine as well), and not with reference to proponents of so-called negative freedom: "Later in his essay Burnaby seems to suggest that human wills are the one radically unpredictable factor in history. I'm not happy about this. Partly because I don't see how the gigantic negative which it involves could be proved; partly because I agree with Bradley that unpredictability is not the essence, or even a symptom, of freedom."[193] Consequently, man's freedom, according to Lewis, is a modest freedom since God has a destiny or plan for each creature, even though free creatures have the ability to refuse certain (but not all) things that God sets before them: "If I were asked what was common to both attitudes [magic and science] I would hazard the guess that it is something negative. Both have abandoned an earlier doctrine of Man. That doctrine had guaranteed him, on his own rung of the hierarchical ladder, his own limited freedom and efficacy."[194] Thus, Lewis's taxonomy of this issue would look as follows: Omniscience is God's knowledge of every free or determined act, Providence is what God makes come to pass, destiny is merely the plan or hope God has for each thing, Divine Freedom means freedom according to the Divine Nature, and human freedom means freedom within the limits God has set.

To conclude, throughout this chapter we have seen both how Lewis developed his metaphysical ideas over the course of his life, and also how he continued to use older concepts and language to process and explain his newer views; thus, James Patrick is absolutely right when he says that in Lewis's last writings, the Oxford don "returned to the old idealistic strains;"[195] however, as I have tried to point out, this return was more figurative than literal. Additionally, we have also seen that on the one hand, Lewis was not afraid to develop Neoplatonic ideas further than most have done, for instance, in regard to the essences of nations, yet on the other hand, he did not feel as compelled as many other Neoplatonists, such as Augustine, to hash out metaphysical answers to questions which remain shrouded in mystery, for instance, in regard to how God can really relate to people. Consequently, with Lewis's metaphysics laid out as much as possible, I now turn to his view of psychology, logic and epistemology in an attempt to expand on some of the things that we have just discussed.

---

193 Lewis, *Prayer: Letters to Malcolm*, 249.
194 Lewis, *Poetry and Prose in the Sixteenth Century*, 13-4.
195 James Patrick, "Reason in Chesterton and Lewis," *Chesterton Review* 17, no. 3 and 4 (August and November 1991): 355.

Chapter Seven

Psychology, Logic and Epistemology

Having discussed Lewis's understanding of the nature of ultimate reality, I now want to focus on one particular element of this reality: man. Specifically, I want to examine Lewis's psychology – both his belief concerning the inner workings of the soul (i.e. the intellect, will, imagination, unconscious, passions etc.) and his understanding of how this relates to both God and the physical world (i.e. the mind-body connection, the mind-world connection and the mind-God connection).

Naturally, all of this is intimately connected with both logic, which is the science of reasoning, and epistemology, the branch of philosophy that deals with how we know things. As a result, I will devote the remainder of this chapter to explaining Lewis's views on such things as logic, reason, authority, experience, faith and grace, and tying these together with things related to both epistemology and psychology which I have already mentioned in previous chapters, such as heavenly desire, sensitive imagination, deliberative or romantic imagination, phantasy, mysticism, existentialism, logical positivism and the argument from reason.

Furthermore, while there has been plenty of material published on Lewis's epistemology over the years,[1] most of what has been published has,

---

1   See, for instance: John Cox, "Epistemological Release in *The Silver Chair*," in *The Longing for a Form: Essays on the Fiction of C. S. Lewis*, ed. Peter Schakel, 159-70 (Grand Rapids, MI: Baker Book House, 1977). Richard Cunningham, *C. S. Lewis: Defender of the Faith* (Philadelphia: Westminster Press, 1967), 67-70. Stephen Thorson, "'Knowledge' in C. S. Lewis's Post-Conversion Thought: His Epistemological Method," *VII: An Anglo-American Literary Review* 9 (1988): 91-116. Robert Holyer, "C. S. Lewis – The Rationalist?" *Christian Scholar's Review* XVIII (Spring 1989): 148-67. Kevin Kinghorn, "Virtue Epistemology: Why Uncle Andrew Couldn't Hear the Animals Speak," in *The Chronicles of Narnia and Philosophy: The Lion, the Witch, and the Worldview*, ed. Gregory Bassham and Jerry Walls, 15-26 (Chicago: Open Court, 2005). Dallas Willard, "Truth in the Fire: C. S. Lewis and Pursuit of Truth Today," http://www.dwillard.org/articles/artview.asp?artID=68 (accessed October 13, 2003).

with the possible exception of the work by Victor Reppert, Erik Wielenberg and Stephen Thorson, been fairly superficial, failing to a large extent to address not only the connections between Lewis's early and later theories of knowledge, but also the specifically Anglican debt therein. On top of this, I have found no study that has properly addressed the Freudian and Aristotelian influences in Lewis's complex psychology. Consequently, I hope that all of this will be made clearer at the end of this chapter.

I: Psychology

When Lewis was a materialist, he thought man was a material thing that somehow attained (presumably material) rationality. This, of course, was the view of the Epicureans and Stoics, both of whom Lewis followed in his youth, and it is the view of modern-day naturalists as well. It is evident in his writing that Lewis did not believe his materialism was inconsistent with his belief in the mind's power to attain objective Truth or discover objective value in the world.

However, when he became an idealist, Lewis came to see the inconsistency of his materialism, namely, his claim both that man can be rational *and* that the material world is all that exists, that the material world is "the ultimate Fact . . . a vast process in space and time which is *going on of its own accord*."[2] The problem, which was brought up in chapter two, is the difficulty in maintaining the trustworthiness of our rational faculty without a Supreme Spirit or God, who is the source and standard of all rationality, for how, it was asked, can our reason be trusted if it is the result of a non-rational cause? Lewis's strict materialism could not account for this:

> Barfield convinced me that the positions we had hitherto held left no room for any satisfactory theory of knowledge. We had been, in the technical sense of the term, 'realists;' that is, we accepted as rock-bottom reality the universe revealed by the senses. But at the same time we continued to make for certain phenomena of consciousness all the claims that really went with a theistic or idealistic view. We maintained that abstract thought (if obedient to logical rules) gave indisputable truth, that our moral judgement was 'valid,' and our aesthetic experience not merely pleasing but 'valuable.' . . . Barfield convinced me it was inconsistent. If thought were a purely subjective event, these claims for it would have to be abandoned. If one kept (as rock-bottom reality) the universe of the senses, aided by instruments and co-ordinated so as to form 'science,' then one would have to go much further – as many have since gone – and adopt a Behaviouristic

---

2   Lewis, *Miracles*, 1104.

theory of logic, ethics, and aesthetics. But such a theory was, and is, unbelievable to me. . . . Unless I were to accept an unbelievable alternative, I must admit that mind was no late-come epiphenomenon; that the whole universe was, in the last resort, mental; that our logic was participation in a cosmic *Logos*.[3]

Indeed, Lewis became so convinced that man's rationality needed an objective, rational source, that he turned his previous view of man on its head and denied that man had in any sense a material substratum; according to Lewis the subjective idealist, man was simply a spirit or rational mind and his material body was merely an idea.

And this was similar to the view of Lewis the absolute idealist, save for two things. First, while Lewis the absolute idealist thought that man was a combination of soul and matter, he believed that both of these elements were simply different *modes* in which Spirit, the totality of all souls and matter (all Appearances), existed. Second, although Lewis became an idealist partly because he thought idealism could explain man's rational soul, the Oxford don ultimately had to deny that the True Self or Spirit was rational, for if all Appearances are part of Spirit, then error just as much as truth, is a part of man's True Self: "Distinctions of . . . true and false . . . spring up only with the creation of souls and a world. Outside that world they are meaningless."[4]

When Lewis became a Christian, many things, of course, changed in regard to his doctrine of man and God. For instance, Lewis came to see that man's share in divine Reason was not simply his share in *himself*: "Reasoning doesn't 'happen to' us: we *do* it. Every train of thought is accompanied by what Kant called 'the *I think*.' The traditional doctrine that I am a creature to whom God has given reason but who is distinct from God seems to me much more philosophical than the theory that what appears to be my thinking is only God's thinking through me."[5] In addition, even though metaphysical grounding for man's rationality was one of the reasons Lewis became an idealist in the first place (hence, setting the stage for his argument from reason for the existence of God), Lewis the absolute idealist's theoretical belief that rationality belongs to the world of Appearances was something that Lewis the Christian could not accept: "Doubtless, by definition," Lewis the Christian insisted, "God was Reason itself."[6]

---

3   Lewis, *Surprised by Joy*, 1364, 1365.
4   Lewis, *Clivi Hamiltonis Summae Metaphysices Contra Anthroposophos Libri II*, 52-3.
5   Lewis, *Miracles*, 1121.
6   Lewis, *Surprised by Joy*, 1376. Cf. "Since our Beloved became a man, how should Reason in any world take on another form?" Lewis, *Perelandra*, 199.

None of this, of course, made Lewis particularly original. In fact, when he went on to say that the image of God in man (man's "divine spark" as Plato put it[7]) is not so much the mind-body composite as it is the mind or rational soul, he was simply following Augustine, Boethius and countless others. However, although he did not always say so consistently,[8] Lewis believed that man as a *whole*, and not just the divine image in man, is an "amphibian"[9]: a rational soul plus a body, or a rational soul plus "brother ass" as he, following St. Francis of Assisi, affectionately called his corporeal nature.[10]

Nevertheless, as we saw in the previous chapter, Lewis was far from uniform in his language concerning the nature of man. In one place he followed the Platonists in speaking of man as a soul-body composite and in another he followed the Aristotelians in speaking of him as a hylomorphic compound of form (soul) and matter (body). Furthermore, because of the nature of the books he was writing (popular apologetics), Lewis did not always limit himself to philosophical language; indeed, in a number of places he used explicitly Pauline or biblical terms, declaring man a composite of spirit, soul and body.[11] For example, in his edition of James Moffat's *The New Testament: A New Translation*, Lewis wrote the following about Hebrews 6:8: "Comments says this does <u>not</u> mean 'dividing soul <u>from</u> spirit': but 'tearing asunder the inmost recesses of soul <u>and</u> spirit.'"[12] Naturally, for the sake of explaining Lewis's philosophy, this language must be untangled and examined.

As I noted in chapter four, Lewis largely modeled his Christian psychology on Aristotle's – though, of course, being the eclectic he was, made a few additions to his theory thanks to insights from the Romantics, Santayana, Freud, Boethius, Augustine and Bradley.

In most general terms, this means that Lewis accepted Pythagoras, Plato and Aristotle's doctrine of the three types of soul:

7   Plato *Timaeus* 41d.

8   For example, in one essay Lewis spoke far too generally, "We are spirits, free and rational beings." Lewis, "On Living in an Atomic Age," 365.

9   Lewis, *The Screwtape Letters*, 756.

10   Lewis, *The Four Loves*, 64-5.

11   "It was good that we should have to lay down our precious refinement at the very doorstep of the church; good that we should be cured at the outset of our inveterate confusion between *psyche* and *pneuma*, nature and supernature." Lewis, "Christianity and Culture," 72. Cf. Lewis, *The Collected Letters of C. S. Lewis: Volume II*, 632 [December 6, 1944]. Cf. Lewis, *Miracles*, 1230-1.

12   C. S. Lewis, marginalia in his edition of *The New Testament: A New Translation*, by James Moffat (London: Hodder & Stoughton, 1926; The Rare Book Collection, The University of North Carolina at Chapel Hill), Hebrews 6:8.

> The Rational Soul, which gives man his peculiar position, is not the only kind of soul. There are also Sensitive Soul and Vegetable Soul. The powers of Vegetable Soul are nutrition, growth and propagation. It alone is present in plants. Sensitive Soul, which we find in animals, has these powers but has sentience in addition. It thus includes and goes beyond Vegetable Soul, so that a beast can be said to have two levels of soul, Sensitive and Vegetable. . . . Rational Soul similarly includes Vegetable and Sensitive, and adds reason. . . . All three kinds of soul are immaterial[13]

Man's "three-storied soul,"[14] therefore, is made up of a rational part and two non-rational parts. Moreover, it cannot be emphasized enough, as Lewis summarized in his edition of Aristotle's *Ethics*, "that the 'parts of the soul' are only a metaphor," for man, in fact, only has one soul.[15]

The vegetative, and especially the sensitive, part of man's soul are, in Pauline terms, the soul or *psyche* proper.[16] In Aristotelian terms, both the vegetable and sensitive parts of the soul are non-rational, but, as we read in Lewis's underlining in his edition of *Ethics*, the sensitive part of the soul is closer to rationality than the vegetative part:

> Thus we see that the irrational part, as well as the soul as a whole, is double. One division of it, the vegetative, does not share in rational principle at all; the other, the seat of the appetites and of desire in general, does in a sense participate in principle, as being amenable and obedient to it (in the sense in fact in which we speak of 'paying heed' to one's father and friends, not in the sense of the term 'rational' in mathematics). And that principle can in a manner appeal to the irrational part, is indicated by our practice of admonishing delinquents, and by our employment of rebuke and exhortation generally.[17]

Although Lewis did not say a lot about the vegetative part of the soul, he did write quite a bit about the sensitive part of the soul. For our purposes here, I think it would be helpful to use Lewis's outline in *The Discarded Image* of Albert the Great's division of the sensitive soul into five senses and five wits as a guide to Lewis's own psychology of the sensitive soul,[18] for it makes sense that Lewis, a Christian and an Aristotelian in regard to psychology

---

13   Lewis, *The Discarded Image*, 153, 154.
14   Ibid., 153.
15   Lewis, marginalia in his edition of *Ethica Nicomachea*, 1138b.
16   Lewis, "Christianity and Culture," 72.
17   Lewis, marginalia in his edition of *Ethica Nicomachea*, 1103a.
18   Aristotle himself only thought there were three parts to the sensitive soul: sense-perception, desire and local motion. Aristotle *De Anima* 414b1.

(he made ample use of Aristotle's *De Sensu*[19]), would have been attracted to, and possibly influenced by, the psychology of one of the greatest Christian Aristotelians.[20] This said, it cannot be stressed enough that while Lewis acknowledged the five senses, his interpretation of the five wits – common sense, imagination, estimation, memory and phantasy – was not always consistent with Albert the Great nor even Aristotle. Consequently, I want to examine each of the five wits, and any other aspects of the sensitive soul not included in the model, to see how Lewis understood them. To this end, I begin with common sense.

Common sense in the philosophical sense of the word refers not to things that people generally know but rather to the specific faculty of the sensitive soul that collects, unifies and compares the material *sensations* (not ideas or images) of the five senses. Lewis explained it thus:

> Albertus gives it two functions: (a) 'It judges of the operations of a sense so that when we see, we know we are seeing;' (b) it puts together the data given by the five senses . . . so that we can say an orange is sweet or one orange is sweeter than another. . . . Common sense is that which turns mere sensations into coherent consciousness of myself as subject in a world of objects. It is very close to what some call Apperception. . . . The difficulty of becoming aware of it arises from the fact that we are never without it except in states which cannot, for that very reason, be fully remembered. Partial anesthesia, when we have sentience without full consciousness, is one of them.[21]

Although I can find no mention of this faculty of the soul in Lewis's corpus beyond what he said of it in *The Discarded Image*, it is likely that he believed there to be such a faculty since Lewis was an Aristotelian in most other aspects of his psychology and epistemology, which, as we shall see, would have entailed the existence of such a faculty.

The imagination – that is, the sensitive imagination – was heavily discussed in chapter four, yet it is worth recalling that Lewis largely followed

19 In his Arden edition of *Hamlet*, Lewis wrote, "Aristotle De Sensu 436A. The external senses are found in all creations wh[ich] have the power of locomotion." C. S. Lewis, marginalia in his edition of *Hamlet*, by William Shakespeare, in "C. S. Lewis's Annotations to His Shakespeare Volumes," by Lionel Adey, *CSL: The Bulletin of the New York C. S. Lewis Society* 8, no. 7 (May 1977): 7.

20 "In Albertus Magnus one finds the most comprehensive psychology of imagination and the best example of the evolution of the Aristotelian tradition." Murray Wright Bundy, *The Theory of Imagination in Classical and Medieval Thought* (Urbana, IL: The University of Illinois Press, 1927), 266.

21 Lewis, *The Discarded Image*, 164-5.

Aristotle in acknowledging the existence of this faculty. It is the part of the sensitive soul impressed, literally, with the material sensations from the common sense. Once in the imagination, these material sensations become immaterial "images," which are mental pictures of things experienced in the present.

"Estimation," Lewis wrote, "covers much of what is now covered by the word *instinct*,"[22] and as such, we find many cases of this non-rational awareness in Lewis writings:

> In English the word *instinct* is often loosely used for what ought rather to be called appetite: thus we speak of the sexual instinct. *Instinct* in this sense means an impulse which appears in consciousness as desire, and whose fulfillment is marked by pleasure. . . . Desire is directed to the concrete – this woman, this plate of soup, this glass of beer. . . . But instinct is also, and more properly, used to mean Behaviour as if from knowledge. Thus certain insects carry out complicated actions which have in fact the result that their eggs are hatched and their larvae nourished: and since . . . we refuse to attribute conscious design and foreknowledge to the agent we say that it has acted 'by instinct.'[23]

From the images retained in the sensitive imagination, estimation / instinct seeks out "intentions" (*intentiones*), which are, for the lack of a better word, things toward which the soul moves – things which are not present in the original images in the imagination, yet are not separable from them.[24] Through the "intentions" uncovered by estimation / instinct, the soul has the power to decide whether a given thing is desirable or undesirable, friend or foe: literally, the soul gains insight as to whether it should "tend" toward or away from a given thing. It is important to note that one of the major differences between the sensitive imagination and estimation / instinct is that of emotions or passions, for while the sensitive imagination is utterly factual and emotionless, estimation / instinct is the cause of many passions – of pain, pleasure, fear, etc. Consequently, in many places, Lewis echoed Plato and Aristotle in insisting that instincts, passions and "mere Nature"[25] not "be given a dictatorship in [the] soul,"[26] for these are merely part of the animal nature in man – i.e. the sensitive part of the soul – and so ought to be ruled by the rational, divine part.

---

22 Ibid., 162.
23 Lewis, "On Ethics," 307.
24 Bundy, *The Theory of Imagination in Classical and Medieval Thought*, 189.
25 Lewis, *The Abolition of Man*, 426.
26 Lewis, "On Ethics," 309.

Moreover, while instinct was covered under what Aristotle called "desire," an appetitive impulse in the sensitive part of the soul, it would be a mistake to think that all forms of appetite belong to the sensitive part of the soul. Aristotle said that "appetite will be found in all three parts" of the soul,[27] which means that while all animals have an appetite for their good, heavenly desire, for instance, is a desire or appetite for the Good that goes beyond mere Nature: it is a rational wish or will, and so belongs to the rational – specifically human as opposed to animal – part of the soul: "*Instinct*," wrote Lewis in reference to spiritual desire, "again dangerous. Neither you nor I believe this gift to be a merely biological phenomenon."[28]

Memory, like imagination, is another tricky word in Lewis's corpus, and it is even trickier because the Oxford don often spoke of it as if its meaning were obvious: "The inward Wits are memory, estimation, imagination, phantasy, and common wit. . . . Of these, memory calls for no comment."[29] The difficulty with memory is that it needs to be clearly differentiated not only from the sensitive imagination and estimation / instinct, but also from within, for memory is two-part: what I will call the sensitive memory and the rational memory.

The sensitive memory is the repository and conserver of the intentions, which, as we know, are uncovered by estimation / instinct. Thus, just as the sensitive imagination is the repository of images, which came from the sensations of common sense, so is the sensitive imagination the repository of intentions from estimation / instinct. There are three things that differentiate the sensitive imagination from the sensitive memory: (1) their objects, either images or intentions (*quasi* ideas); (2) their mode of being: the sensitive imagination is strictly passive, while the sensitive memory can also be active as "there is an act of reference beyond the 'intentions' and image to the thing itself;"[30] and (3) time: while the sensitive imagination is strictly concerned with the images of the present moment, the sensitive memory is also concerned with past images and intentions. Although we cannot be certain that Lewis accepted all of these distinctions, being an Aristotelian in most other aspects of psychology and epistemology and being one who surely believed animals have some sort of basic memory, Lewis almost certainly accepted this faculty as it was generally laid out by Aristotle or Albert the Great.

---

27   Aristotle *De Anima* 432b5.
28   Lewis, *The Collected Letters of C. S. Lewis: Volume III*, 628 [July 4, 1955].
29   Lewis, *The Discarded Image*, 162.
30   Bundy, *The Theory of Imagination in Classical and Medieval Thought*, 192.

Yet things are a bit more problematic when one discusses Lewis's view of the rational memory. The main reason is this: while Aristotle acknowledged that memory, like imagination, extends beyond the sensitive part of the soul and into the rational part, he denied the immortality of either type of memory, the intellect being the only aspect of the individual that is impassible and therefore immortal (and even this – the immortality of the intellect – is unclear as David Ross, the great Oxford Aristotelian, who likely taught Lewis himself, pointed out[31]). In other words, Aristotle's denial of the immortality of memory, which was in direct contrast to Plato, was ultimately a denial of personal immortality, which, needless to say, even for a Christian such as Lewis who thought little of such things, was totally unacceptable as it was in direct opposition to biblical teachings.

As for the function of the rational memory, Lewis likely believed two things.

First, following Plato (Platonic *eros*), the Romantics (*Sehnsucht*) and Augustine (God-softened heavenly desire), Lewis almost certainly thought that heavenly desire resides in the rational memory. It is true that he sometimes spoke as if he thought there was no innate knowledge, and hence, no knowledge dormant in heavenly desire and the rational memory; for instance, he declared himself, "an empirical theist,"[32] and insisted in an essay on ethics, "You will not suspect me of trying to reintroduce in its full Stoical or medieval rigour the doctrine of Natural Law. Still less am I claiming as the source of this substantial ethical agreement anything like Intuition or Innate Ideas."[33] Nevertheless, in the first instance, as we recall from chapter three, Lewis called himself "an empirical theist" because he argued his way to belief in God, yet as he himself pointed out, he already had an idea of God *before* he began his dialectic of desire since "the form of the desired is in the desire;"[34] and in the second instance, this quotation comes from an essay in which the Oxford don was merely arguing for the *fact* of objective values in ethics: he was not arguing about the epistemological *foundations* of such facts; thus, when this quotation is read in context of the larger essay, and indeed, in the context of Lewis's larger body of work, it is clear that he believed we have innate knowledge of many things. Consequently, we are justified in saying that he almost certainly believed heavenly desire to reside in the rational memory.

---

31   David Ross, *Aristotle* (1923 reprint; London: Routledge, 1996), 156.
32   C. S. Lewis, quoted in *C. S. Lewis: A Biography*, by Roger Lancelyn Green and Walter Hooper, 111.
33   Lewis, "On Ethics," 312.
34   Lewis, *Surprised by Joy*, 1371.

Second, the rational memory also seems to be the repository which stores the ideas that reason or the active intellect has abstracted from the imagination and then processed and analyzed. Interestingly, in regard to the function of memory, Lewis drew insights from two unlikely sources: Wordsworth and Santayana.

Wordsworth's influence on Lewis's understanding of the rational memory has to do with the Romantic poet's insistence that the best poetry comes from *reflection* upon one's past experiences:

> All good poetry is the spontaneous overflow of powerful feelings: but though this is true, Poems to which any value can be attached, were never produced on any variety of subjects but by a man, who being possessed of more than usual organic sensibility, had also thought long and deeply. For our continued influxes of feelings are modified and directed by our thoughts, which are indeed the representatives of all our past feelings; and, as by contemplating the relation of these general representatives to each other we discover what is really important to men.[35]

This sentiment becomes admirably clear in Lewis's *Out of the Silent Planet*, where we read:

> Ransom found this difficult. At last he said: 'Is the begetting of young not a pleasure among the *hrossa*?'
>
> 'A very great one, *Hmān*. This is what we call love.'
>
> 'If a thing is a pleasure, a *hmān* wants it again. He might want the pleasure more often than the number of young that could be fed.' It took Hyoi a long time to get the point.
>
> 'You mean,' he said slowly, 'that he might do it not only in one or two years of his life but again?'
>
> 'Yes.'
>
> 'But why? Would he want his dinner all day or want to sleep after he had slept? I do not understand.'
>
> 'But a dinner comes every day. This love, you say, comes only once while the *hross* lives?'
>
> 'But it takes his whole life. When he is young he has to look for his mate; and then he has to court her; then he begets young; then he rears them; *then he remembers all this, and boils it inside him and makes it into poems and wisdom.*'[36]

---

35   William Wordsworth, "Preface to *Lyrical Ballads*," in *William Wordsworth: The Major Works* (Oxford: Oxford University Press, 2000), 598.

36   Lewis, *Out of the Silent Planet*, 63 (emphasis mine).

While reflection upon memory is hardly interesting, it is significant to note that Wordsworth convinced Lewis that the experience of a given thing was not enough in itself, but needs to be remembered in order for it to reach its truest form. Memory, in other words, has, among other things, a perfecting power: "I have to thank you both," wrote Lewis in a 1959 letter, "for a present, as well as for a past pleasure: for I find already that my visit begins to mature very nicely in the cellars of my memory and bids fair to be a great wine for many years. That, you know, is the real test."[37]

And this is closely related to Santayana's influence on Lewis's theory of the rational memory. We recall from chapter four, Lewis the absolute idealist made use of Santayana's idea that myths need to be "disenchanted" – they need to be acknowledged as untrue – in order for them to achieve their real power, at which point they are "re-enchanted" and then employed to the betterment of man in terms of aesthetic experience. While Lewis came to reject this theory of myth, he did not reject the American philosopher's insight, for in Lewis's essay "Talking about Bicycles," the Oxford don expanded on Santayana's terminology and suggested that there are four "ages" that people go through: the Unenchanted, which is where something is seen in a dispassionate, matter-of-fact way; the Enchanted, where something becomes special and exciting to the self; the Disenchanted, where the self becomes disillusioned about that something; and, if the self makes it, the Re-enchanted, where the self regains, not foolishly, but wisely, the true essence of the thing and appreciates its wonderful uniqueness.[38] The importance of this in regard to memory is that Lewis did not *just* emphasize, as most do, the power of memory to distort the truth, or the power of memory to capture the truth as it is, or even, as Wordsworth did, the power of memory to perfect an experience, but he *also* made the extremely important point that memory has the power to illuminate a past experience in a way that is both *true* and *different* from the way the experience first occurred:

> Memory itself is the supreme example of the four ages. Wordsworth, you see, was Enchanted. He got delicious gleams of memory from his early youth and took them at their face value. He believed that if he could have got back to certain spots in his own past he could find there the moment of joy waiting for him. You are Disenchanted. You've begun to suspect that those moments, of which the memory is now so ravishing, weren't at the time quite as wonderful as they now seem. You're right. They weren't. Each great experience is

37   Lewis, *The Collected Letters of C. S. Lewis: Volume III*, 1050 [May 19, 1959].
38   C. S. Lewis, "Talking about Bicycles," in *C. S. Lewis: Essay Collection & Other Short Pieces*, ed. Lesley Walmsley (1946 essay reprint; London: HarperCollins, 2000), 690.

> *a whisper*
> *Which Memory will warehouse as a shout.*

But what then? Isn't the warehouse just as important because a particular kind of polarized light between past and present happens to be the mechanism that brings it into focus? Isn't it a fact about mountains – as good a fact as any other – that they look purple at a certain distance?[39]

Phantasy is the part of the sensitive soul which, we ought to partially recall, is chiefly responsible for comparing, uniting and dividing not only images in the sensitive imagination but also intentions in estimation / instinct. Just as common sense organizes the material sensations of the five senses, so does phantasy organize the immaterial images and intentions of the sensitive imagination and estimation / instinct.

However, while phantasy is clearly responsible for the creation of meaning on a very basic level, Lewis, following Aristotle, the Romantics, Tolkien and others, posited a second type of imagination, the deliberative or romantic imagination, which belongs exclusively to the rational soul and works with the active intellect or reason in creating deeper levels of meaning and art. Consequently, if one aspect of Lewis's psychology needs to be emphasized above any other, it ought to be the difference between the various meanings of imagination as used by the Oxford don, for scholars have been sorely ignorant of these important divisions, the result of which has been an enormous outpouring of superficial readings of the work of a fairly sophisticated mind. However, it is hard to completely blame scholars for failing to make these distinctions, for Lewis's own language is often sloppy and constantly requires untangling. As a test of this, let us consider the following quotation: "For the spiritual evils which we share with the devils (pride, spite) are far worse than what we share with the beasts: and sensuality really arises more from the imagination than from the appetites; which, if left merely to their own animal strength, and not elaborated by our imagination, would be fairly easily managed."[40] If we are not careful, we might be tempted to think that the imagination Lewis mentions here is that of the sensitive soul – either the sensitive imagination or phantasy – yet because the Oxford don associates it with the "spiritual" and contrasts it with the animal, it is clear that the kind of imagination he means here is the deliberative or romantic imagination, which belongs solely to the rational soul.

---

39   Ibid., 692.
40   Lewis, *The Collected Letters of C. S. Lewis: Volume III*, 1384 [November 26, 1962].

Hugging the line between the sensitive part of the soul and rational part of the soul is the unconscious. Lewis, of course, learned about this mysterious presence from Freud. However, the Oxford don had already been used to this dualistic way of thinking about the self on account of both Bradley's distinction between Appearances and Reality (which later became Lewis the absolute idealist's soul and Spirit respectively[41]) and Kant's distinction between the Noumenal and Phenomenal self: "The fruit of this experience [of feeling as though I was dying] was that when, some years later, I met Kant's distinction between the Noumenal and Phenomenal self, it was more to me than an abstraction. I had tasted it; I had proved that there was a fully conscious 'I' whose connections with the 'me' of introspection were loose and transitory."[42] Naturally, Kant's Noumenal and Phenomenal self, Bradley's Appearances and Reality and Freud's conscious and unconscious self are all vastly different, yet what is important is that Lewis recognized a division in the self which ultimately became a division between the conscious self (which was itself divided into the Contemplated and Enjoyed self respectively) and the unconscious self: "We need a threefold division [of the soul]," wrote Lewis

---

41 Bradley's idealism was much the same as T. H. Green's, whose epistemology Lewis summarized as follows: "Argument runs thus. Knowledge of nature = knowledge of unalterable relations or of facts recognized as such. But this can not result from experience, if experience means the mere <u>succession</u> of feelings. For a series of psychical events is not the knowledge that there is a series. The knowledge implies an eternal subject - i.e. in so far as my consciousness is a becoming (A, B, C) I cannot know that B follows A. To know this I must distinguish myself from A, B, C. Objects related by succession are [...] related not successive (h 306). When a whole is known, all its parts must be 'present together' (h 65). Only what does not 'become' can know a becoming. This involves a very sharp antithesis between <u>knowing</u> and consciousness. In so far as we change we cannot know it in so far as we know that we change, we are unchanging. Difficult to see what is meant by a series of psychical events wh[ich] we cannot know at all; yet that wh[ich] we know as changing must be such a series. The argument really cuts thro[ugh] the true mystery - that the self must somehow change and somehow be the same. Of course if state A ended and then B began as a new 'thing' then there would have to be a third permanent 'thing' to know that this had happened, but then its consciousness w[oul]d be divided from the consciousness of A in the same way that I am divided from <u>You</u> whereas the [...] whole [...] is that I recognize that the same I was A and then B and <u>am</u> the same. The Bergsonian method must be on the right track here. . . . I am not, something that <u>jumps</u> from A to B but the moving itself. I am not first at A, then at B; in wh[ich] case there w[oul]d have to be an eternal subject to know both. I am the AB becoming wh[ich] knows itself as becoming, and the shifting wh[ich] of that becoming into A + B is arbitrary. On any other view you set a tireless subject wh[ich] <u>knows</u> a becoming something but that something has to be an unknowing conscious event wh[ich] seems to = unconscious conscious." C. S. Lewis, marginalia in his edition of *Prolegomena to Ethics*, by T. H. Green, ed. A. C. Bradley, 5th ed (Oxford: Clarendon Press, 1924; The Marion E. Wade Center, Wheaton College), xxx.

42 Lewis, *Surprised by Joy*, 1358.

the Christian, "the Unconscious, the Enjoyed, and the Contemplated."[43]

Since the unconscious was not part of Aristotle's model of the soul, it is difficult to say how, precisely, it fits into Lewis's psychology; however, it seems that it must be intimately connected with memory,[44] and perhaps genetic predispositions in, or "planetary" effects on,[45] the soul. Freud himself defined the unconscious "as the foundation of all psychical life," and went on to say that "[t]he unconscious is the larger circle that includes the smaller circle of the conscious. Everything conscious has an unconscious preliminary stage, whereas the unconscious is able to remain at that stage and lay claim to the full value of a psychical function."[46] In other words, the unconscious is the vast ocean of our psychical life, some of which eventually becomes the preconscious or subconscious, which then has the ability to become the conscious. Lewis seems to have followed Freud in this regard, for he wrote:

> And what am I? The façade is what I call consciousness. I am at least conscious of the colour of those walls. I am not, in the same way, or to the same degree, conscious of what I call my thoughts: for if I try to examine what happens when I am thinking, it would, I well know, turn out to be the thinnest possible film on the surface of a vast deep. The psychologists have taught us that.[47]

43 Ibid., 1371.

44 As far as we know, the only work by Freud that Lewis read is *Introductory Lectures on Psychoanalysis*, in which Freud, in his eighteenth lecture, made a strong link between memory and the unconscious. Sigmund Freud, *Introductory Lectures on Psychoanalysis*, trans. James Strachey, ed. James Strachey and Angela Richards (1917 reprint; New York: Penguin, 1984), 324-5 [3.18].

45 Lewis was always fond of noting that the medieval church never condemned planetary effects on the soul, provided that these effects were understood as predispositions in the soul and not as effects that somehow negate freewill: "[The medieval church did not condemn] the general doctrine of planetary influences in natural objects, historical events, and human psychology." Lewis, *The Collected Letters of C. S. Lewis: Volume III*, 863 [July 1, 1957]. Because of both Lewis's defence of planetary influences and his delight in hierarchy and the natural heavens, it is reasonable to ask whether Lewis believed the planets to have some effect on human personality and the unconscious.

46 Sigmund Freud, *Interpreting Dreams*, trans. J. A. Underwood (1899 reprint; Toronto: Penguin, 2006), 628 [7f]. Cf. "Let us therefore compare the system of the unconscious to a large entrance hall, in which the mental impulses jostle one another like separate individuals. Adjoining this entrance hall there is a second, narrower, room – a kind of drawing-room – in which consciousness, too, resides." Freud, *Introductory Lectures on Psychoanalysis*, 336 [3.19].

47 Lewis, *Prayer: Letters to Malcolm*, 274. Cf. "Five senses; an incurably abstract intellect; a haphazardly selective memory; *a set of preconceptions and assumptions so numerous that I can never examine more than a minority of them – never become even conscious of them all.* How much of total reality can such an apparatus let through?" C. S. Lewis, *A Grief Observed* (1961 reprint; Toronto: Bantam Books, 1976), 85.

Consequently, in order to have a healthy psyche, complexes and neuroses, which Lewis said flatly are "not . . . sin but . . . disease,"[48] have to be cured, and painful experiences which have been repressed have to be discovered through introspection, recollection and interpretation; thus, Lewis wrote:

> I see no reason why a Christian sh[oul]d not be an analyst. Psychoanalysis after all merely defines what was always admitted, that the moral choices of the human soul operate inside a complex non-moral situation. Even Hamlet knew that 'the devil' was 'very potent' with men of the melancholy complexion – i.e. men with certain complexes, which really gives the whole thing in a nutshell.

> The Christian view would be that every psychological situation, just like every degree of wealth or poverty, talent or stupidity etc., had its own peculiar temptations and peculiar advantages, that the worst could always be turned to a good use and the best c[oul]d always be abused to one's spiritual ruin. In fact 'all fortune is good' as Boethius said.

> This doesn't mean that it w[oul]d be wrong to try to cure a complex any more than a stiff leg: but it does mean that if you can't, then, so far from the game being up, life with a complex, or with a stiff leg, is precisely the game you have been set.[49]

However, while Lewis always insisted that psychoanalysis can be healthy, that people have an unconscious, "that infantile sexual experience of the sort described by Freud does occur in all human beings,"[50] and that "there is some force in the wish-fulfillment doctrine,"[51] he rejected the Freudian idea that all desire is latent or unconscious sexual desire, and cautioned us against too much introspection, for while introspection can uncover repression, it can also distort the situation because as soon as the self Contemplates itself, its subject matter changes and eludes the Contemplating self. Speaking of his own conversion to Christianity in this regard, Lewis wrote: "Self-examination did of course continue. But it was at stated intervals, and for a practical purpose; a duty, a discipline, an uncomfortable thing, no longer a hobby or a habit. To believe and to pray were the beginning of extroversion. I had been, as they say, 'taken out of myself.'"[52] Thus, as we saw in much of our discussion about The Great War, Lewis, while admitting the unconscious, generally preferred

48   Lewis, *Mere Christianity*, 378. Cf. Lewis, *The Collected Letters of C. S. Lewis: Volume III*, 330 [May 18, 1953].
49   Lewis, *The Collected Letters of C. S. Lewis: Volume II*, 373-4 [March 26, 1940].
50   Lewis, "Psycho-Analysis and Literature," 291-2.
51   Lewis, *The Pilgrim's Regress*, 80.
52   Lewis, *Surprised by Joy*, 1378-9.

to set it aside, focusing his energy instead on the Contemplation of ideas and the Enjoyment of God, the self and others. Indeed, it is for this reason that while Lewis went to weekly confession and knew that he had to be aware of his own motives and actions, he quit writing in his journal and was afraid that confession might become an "orgy of egoism."[53] Consequently, psychoanalyzing the self for unconscious motivations is a good thing to an extent,[54] but it can also be both a hindrance insofar as things like wish-fulfillment may, in some circumstances, actually be useful,[55] and dangerous insofar as the psychical gaze stays too long on the self, which, as Lewis had learned from Augustine, can easily lead to pride, the arch-sin; hence, "[t]o admire Satan [in *Paradise Lost*] . . . is to give one's vote for . . . a world . . . of incessant autobiography."[56]

Above the sensitive part of the soul and the unconscious is, in Platonic and Aristotelian language, the rational part of the soul, or, in Pauline language, spirit or *pneuma*. It is the part of the soul which men share, in some measure, with angels, but not with animals (not, of course, that this is to say that the rational soul is *always* superior to the sensitive soul, for man *qua* animal may experience some pleasures that angels can never experience[57]). It is because

---

53   Lewis, *The Collected Letters of C. S. Lewis: Volume II*, 452 [October 24, 1940].

54   "My allusion to the psychotherapists was a fling at the increasing modern habit of seeing *all* personal difficulties in terms of disease and cure, and so reducing things that are really moral or intellectual or both to the pathological level. In your case there certainly does seem to be a pathological element. And of course it is 'proper' to make all efforts after relief." Lewis, *The Collected Letters of C. S. Lewis: Volume III*, 1023 [February 18, 1959].

55   "Do you think 'wishful thinking' is as dangerous as people make out now-a-days? All our people . . . go through the miseries of the last war by a series of wishful delusions. They always thought it was going to be over next month or next spring or next year. Did this do harm? I am inclined to think it helped them to get thorough bit by bit what they couldn't have faced at all if they had formed any true estimate of its extent. And I think I remember something like that as a boy – successfully completing a walk far too long for one and feeling 'If I'd known it was that length I could never have done it at all.' I suspect that modern psychology – at least, modern semi-popular psychology – plays about with the reserves of the soul very dangerously." Ibid., 44 [July 26, 1950].

56   Lewis, *A Preface to Paradise Lost*, 102.

57   "'The angels . . . have no senses; their experience is purely intellectual and spiritual. That is why we know something about God which they don't. There are particular aspects of His love and joy which can be communicated to a created being only by sensuous experience. Something of God which the Seraphim can never quite understand flows into us from the blue of the sky, the taste of honey, the delicious embrace of water whether cold or hot, and even from sleep itself.'" C. S. Lewis, "Scraps," in *C. S. Lewis: Essay Collection & Other Short Pieces*, ed. Lesley Walmsley (1945 essay reprint; London: HarperCollins, 2000), 346. A similar, though not identical, notion is found in Kant, who believed that only rational beings with sense perception could experience the beautiful.

man is a rational soul that he is able to not only desire knowledge for its own sake (another very Aristotelian idea in Lewis[58]), commit acts of virtue,[59] and make scientific advancements, but can also close his mind to knowledge, commit atrocious sins and squander all that he has. Now while Lewis was largely Aristotelian in his understanding of the sensitive soul, he was far more eclectic in regard to the rational soul, which, if we were to collect all that he said about this soul into a uniform theory, would be divided into five faculties: (1) reason, which is subdivided into intellect and discursive reason; (2) conscience, which is the faculty of moral intelligence; (3) freewill; (4) rational memory, in which I included heavenly desire; and (5) deliberative or romantic imagination. Since the latter two have already been discussed, I will focus my energy on reason, conscience and freewill.

Reason, as a faculty of the rational soul, is two-part in Lewis's psychology, though usually he spoke of it, as he did with memory, simply as one thing: "by *Reason* I meant 'the faculty whereby we recognize or attain necessary truths' or 'the faculty of grasping self-evident truths or logically deducing those which are not self-evident.'"[60] On top of this, the Oxford don often made strong links not only between reason and speech, for speech is intimately connected with knowledge, but also between reason and conscience. Consequently, it is extremely important that all of these concepts and relations be clarified.

---

58   The idea of knowledge for its own sake is something that Lewis likely got from Aristotle's *Metaphyiscs*; in fact, the Oxford don even alluded to it in *Till We Have Faces* when he described the contents of the Fox's library: "[S]ome of the conversations of Socrates . . . a book of Heraclitus; and a very long, hard book (without metre) which begins *All men by nature desire knowledge*." Lewis, *Till We Have Faces*, 977. Cf. "One of the things that distinguishes man from the other animals is that he wants to know things, wants to find out what reality is like, simply for the sake of knowing. When that desire is completely quenched in anyone, I think he has become something less than human." Lewis, "Man or Rabbit?" 352. Cf. "I mean the pursuit of knowledge and beauty, in a sense, for their own sake, but in a sense which does not exclude their being for God's sake. An appetite for these things exists in the human mind, and God makes no appetite in vain." Lewis, "Learning in Wartime," 583. We will discuss this idea more in the next chapter.
59   Concerning the possibility of aliens, Lewis wrote: "Supposing there were, have any of these animals what we call 'rational souls'? By this I include not merely the faculty to abstract and calculate, but the apprehension of values, the power to mean by 'good' something more than 'good for me' or even 'good for my species.' If instead of asking, 'Have they rational souls?' you prefer to ask, 'Are they spiritual animals'? I think we shall both mean pretty much the same." C. S. Lewis, "Religion and Rocketry," in *C. S. Lewis: Essay Collection & Other Short Pieces*, ed. Lesley Walmsley (1958 essay reprint; London: HarperCollins, 2000), 232.
60   Lewis, *The Collected Letters of C. S. Lewis: Volume III*, 129 [July 14, 1951].

Following Aristotle,[61] Boethius and others, Lewis sometimes made a division – though far from consistently – between *intellectus*, or the intellect, which grasps truths in a simple, intuitive way, and *ratio*, or discursive reason, which reasons from the truths of the intellect to discover new truths.[62]

The intellect is the highest part of reason, and, as we shall see, the highest part of the rational soul according to Lewis, for it is the intellect that grasps self-evident truths, without which all our thoughts would be in vain: "If nothing is self-evident, nothing can be proved."[63]

Discursive reason is less dignified than the intellect, for it does not immediately see objective truths or Reality, but must work from the self-evident truths seen by the intellect in order to attain new truths. As Lewis said to Barfield already back in 1927: "Agreed (by you and me, also by Kant, Coleridge, Bradley etc) that discursive reason always fails to apprehend reality, because it never grasps more than an abstract relational framework."[64] To put it another way, whereas the intellect has to do with certainty, universality and objectivity, discursive reason has to do with probability and particularity; by the intellect, God knows all things and angels know some things, and by a combination of intellect and discursive reason, men know some things.

The job of reason in both its facets, however, is to think. Yet, "thinking" is a difficult word, for it implies something like an inner *language*. Consequently, because *Logos* is not merely thought but also word, Lewis, and most Christians before him, often made a strong connection between reason and speech. Indeed, in George Herbert's *The Temple*, another book that Lewis listed in his top ten influences on his philosophy of life, we read of the Bishop's amazement that God would give men rational language: "O that Thou shouldst give dust a tongue"[65] – sentiments echoed by Lewis in *The Magician's Nephew*:

> The Lion opened his mouth, but no sound came from it; he was
> breathing out, a long, warm breath; it seemed to sway all the beasts
> as the wind sways a line of trees. Far overhead from beyond the veil

---

61　In chapter six of *Miracles*, Lewis quoted from Aristotle's *Metaphysics* in regard to the intellect and self-evident truths: "For as bats' eyes are to daylight so is our intellectual eye to those truths which are, in their own nature, the most obvious of all." Lewis, *Miracles*, 1129.

62　Lewis, *The Discarded Image*, 157.

63　Lewis, *The Abolition of Man*, 414.

64　Lewis, *The Collected Letters of C. S. Lewis: Volume III*, 1600 [1927, "The Great War Letters" Series I, Letter 1].

65　George Herbert, *The Temple*, in *The Works of George Herbert* (Hertfordshire: Wordsworth Editions, 1994), 71 ["Deniall" 4.1].

of blue sky which hid them the stars sang again: a pure, cold, difficult music. Then there came a swift flash like fire (but it burnt nobody) either from the sky or from the Lion itself, and every drop of blood tingled in the children's bodies, and the deepest, wildest voice they had ever heard was saying:

'Narnia, Narnia, Narnia, awake. Love. Think. Speak. Be walking trees. Be talking beasts. Be divine waters.'[66]

Closely connected with reason is conscience or the faculty of moral intelligence. Indeed, reason and conscience are so closely connected that Lewis, following the ancients and much of Old Western Culture, often grouped them together.[67] The reason for the intimacy between these two faculties is, as Lewis explained in *Studies in Words*, largely etymological:

Greek *oida* and Latin *scio* mean 'I know.' . . . *Suneidesis* [related to *oida*] and *conscientia* [related to *scio*] could be either the state (or act) of sharing knowledge or else simply knowledge, awareness, apprehension – even something like mind or thought. . . . When Tertullian speaks of convictions lodged in our 'innate *conscientia*' or Lactantius of what is 'clear to our *conscientia*' some sense like 'mind' or 'understanding' is required. . . . In its new sense *conscience* is the inner lawgiver: a man's judgement of good and evil. It speaks in the imperative, commanding and forbidding. But, as so often, the new sense does not replace the old. The old lives on and the new is added to it, so that conscience now has more than one meaning. . . . Theologians and scholars are aware of this and draw the necessary distinctions. Aquinas, who claims to be conforming to the 'common use of language,' says that *conscientia* is an application of our knowledge to our own acts, and that this application occurs in three ways. (1) We judge that we have done this or that. (2) We judge that something ought, or ought not to be done. (3) We judge that our past act was good or bad. The first is conscire in the classical sense. The second, which really includes the third (*syteresis* or *synderesis*) is something quite different; something which will be named, according to the system we employ, practical

---

66 Lewis, *The Magician's Nephew*, 108.
67 Notice how Lewis used the same argument from reason for the existence of God to defend not only logical reasoning but also moral reasoning: "Two views have been held about moral judgements. Some people think that when we make them we are not using our Reason, but are employing some different power. Other people think that we make them by our Reason. I myself hold this second view. . . . If we are to continue to make moral judgements . . . then we must believe that the conscience of man is not a product of Nature [i.e. material, matter]. It can be valid only if it is an offshoot of some absolute moral wisdom, a moral wisdom which exists absolutely 'on its own' and is not a product of non-moral, non-rational Nature." Lewis, *Miracles*, 1128.

reason, moral sense, reflection, the Categorical Imperative, or the super-ego. *Conscientia* in this second sense can be said to 'bind' and 'impel' (*instigare*), and can of course be obeyed or disobeyed" [ST. Ia, lxlx, art. 13]. . . . [Jeremy Taylor, following Aquinas, said] under the name *conscience* we must also include 'that which is called *synteresis*, or the general repository of moral principles.'[68]

This is to say that conscience belonged to reason because both were concerned with *reasoning*. Thus, Aristotle, Lewis's most important influence in this regard, spoke of three types of reasoning – scientific or theoretical, deliberative or practical, and productive – and made these three, each in their own way (as I touched on before), deal with matters of both Truth and morality;[69] as Lewis wrote:

> But when we turn to practical reason the ruinous effects are found operating in full force. By practical reason I mean our judgement of good and evil. . . . Until modern times no thinker of the first rank ever doubted that our judgements of value were rational judgements or that what they discovered was objective. It was taken for granted that in temptation passion was opposed, not to sentiment, but to reason. Thus Plato, thought, thus Aristotle, thus Hooker, Butler and Doctor Johnson.[70]

---

68   Lewis, *Studies in Words*, 181, 182, 194. Cf. Lewis, *The Allegory of Love*, 100.
69   Aristotle *Ethics* 1139b1-15, 1146b5-10.
70   Lewis, "The Poison of Subjectivism," 658. Cf. "We must therefore either extend the word Reason to include what our ancestors called Practical Reason and confess that judgments such as *society ought to be preserved* (though they can support themselves by no reason of the sort that Gaius and Titus demand) are not mere sentiments but are rationality itself; or else we must give up at once, and for ever, the attempt to find a core of 'rational' value behind all the sentiments we have debunked." Lewis, *The Abolition of Man*, 410-1. Cf. "The belief that to recognize a duty was to perceive a truth – not because you had a good heart but because you were an intellectual being – had roots in antiquity. Plato preserved the Socratic idea that morality was an affair of knowledge; bad men were bad because they did not know what was good. Aristotle, while attacking this view and giving important place to upbringing and habituation, still made 'right reason' (ὀρθός λόγος) essential to good conduct. The Stoics believed in a Natural Law which all rational men, in virtue of their rationality, saw to be binding on them. St. Paul has a curious function in this story. His statement in Romans (ii. 14 *sq.*) that there is a law 'written in the hearts' even of Gentiles who do not know 'the law,' is in full conformity with the Stoic conception, and would for centuries be so understood. Nor, during those centuries, would the word *hearts* have had merely emotional associations. The Hebrew word which St. Paul represents by καρδία would be more nearly translated 'Mind;' and in Latin, one who is *cordatus* is not a man of feeling but a man of sense." Lewis, *The Discarded Image*, 160. Cf. "A modern logician would say that the Law is a command and that to call a command 'true' makes no sense; 'The door is shut' may be true or false but 'Shut the door' can't. But I think we all see pretty well what the

Lewis's own language in regard to conscience and reason was heavily influenced by Aristotle, but it was also sufficiently blended with the language of St. Paul, Kant,[71] George MacDonald,[72] and others to the point where the faculty of reason was divided into intellect and deliberative reason, both of which, in different ways, pertained strictly to matters of Truth and falsity, and theoretical and practical reason,[73] again both in different ways, came to be identified with a separate faculty, conscience, which dealt strictly with matters of right and wrong: "He has provided a rich, beautiful world for people to live in," wrote Lewis of God, "He has given them intelligence to show them how it can be used, and conscience to show them how it ought to be used."[74] Consequently, theoretical reason is to the faculty of conscience what intellect is to the faculty of reason (they have to do with self-evident and universal truths: either of logic or the universal moral law), and practical reason or wisdom, which Lewis confusingly sometimes simply called "Conscience,"[75] is to the faculty of conscience what deliberative reason is to the faculty of reason (they have to do with argument from self-evident

---

Psalmists mean. They mean that in the Law you find the 'real' or 'correct' or stable, well-grounded, directions for living." Lewis, *Reflections on the Psalms*, 341.

71 Immanuel Kant, *The Metaphysics of Morals*, in *The Cambridge Edition of the Works of Immanuel Kant: Practical Philosophy*. trans. and ed. Mary Gregor (Cambridge: Cambridge University Press, 1999), 529 [6:399-40].

72 George MacDonald, whom Lewis referred to as his "master," preferred to speak of "conscience" rather than reason in regard to morality: "She was sorely troubled with what is, by huge discourtesy, called a bad conscience – being in reality a conscience doing its duty so well that it makes the whole house uncomfortable." George MacDonald, quoted in *George MacDonald: An Anthology*, by C. S. Lewis (1947 reprint; London: Simon & Schuster, 1996), 133.

73 Note the language Lewis used in regard to value and morality: "An open mind, in questions that are not ultimate, is useful. But an open mind about the ultimate foundations either of Theoretical or of Practical Reason is idiocy. If a man's mind is open on these things, let his mouth at least be shut. He can say nothing to the purpose. Outside the *Tao* there is no ground for criticizing the *Tao* or anything else." Lewis, *The Abolition of Man*, 416-7. However, sometimes Lewis, following Aristotle, spoke of theoretical reason in regard to non-moral matters: "As long as this dethronement refers only to the theoretical reason, it cannot be wholehearted. The scientist has to assume the validity of his own logic . . . even in order to prove that it is merely subjective." Lewis, "The Poison of Subjectivism," 657.

74 C. S. Lewis, "The Trouble with 'X' . . .," in *C. S. Lewis: Essay Collection & Other Short Pieces*, ed. Lesley Walmsley (1948 essay reprint; London: HarperCollins, 2000), 358. Cf. "And what did God do? First of all He left us conscience, the sense of right and wrong." Lewis, *Mere Christianity*, 352.

75 "We are now judging the useful by some other standard (whether we call it Conscience, or Practical Reason, or Law of Nature or Personal Preference)." C. S. Lewis, "The Humanitarian Theory of Punishment," in *C. S. Lewis: Essay Collection & Other Short Pieces*, ed. Lesley Walmsley (1949 essay reprint; London: HarperCollins, 2000), 706-7.

and universal truths). The disparity between conscience and reason is rarely emphasized in Lewis's writings, but in his essay "Why I Am Not a Pacifist," the Oxford don made it clear that the difference between these two faculties is most clearly marked in regard to temptation and man's fallen nature:

> The main difference between Reason and Conscience is an alarming one. It is thus: that while the unarguable intuitions on which all depend are liable to be corrupted by passion when we are considering truth and falsehood, they are much more liable, they are almost certain to be corrupted when we are considering good and evil. For then we are concerned with some action to be here and now done or left undone by ourselves. And we should not be considering that action at all unless we had some wish either to do or not do it, so that in this sphere we are bribed from the very beginning.[76]

On top of the difference both between reason and conscience and (within conscience) between theoretical and practical reason, Lewis also spoke of an element in conscience distinct from merely knowing right and wrong (theoretical reason) and merely applying the principles of right and wrong to real situations in the world (practical reason). This third element in the faculty of conscience is what Socrates identified with a daemon and Paul identified as the inner workings of the Holy Spirit; it is, in Lewis's words, "the thing that moves us to do right [and] has absolute authority."[77] And it is precisely this third "element" in the conscience that marks Lewis as one who not only understood the intricacies of secular ethics but also was able to combine these intricacies with Christian psychology; hence, Lewis insisted: "God whispers to us in our pleasures, *speaks in our conscience*, but shouts in our pain."[78]

The freewill or will is the final faculty of the rational soul I want to discuss. While Lewis, as we have seen, was largely Aristotelian in regard to psychology, he was forced, to some extent, to look elsewhere for a definition of the will for the simple reason that Aristotle had no clear conception of it;[79] indeed, Augustine is often credited as being the first to formulate the

76   C. S. Lewis, "Why I Am Not a Pacifist," in *C. S. Lewis: Essay Collection & Other Short Pieces*, ed. Lesley Walmsley (London: HarperCollins, 2000), 283.

77   Ibid., 284.

78   Lewis, *The Problem of Pain*, 518 (emphasis mine). In regard to the Holy Spirit working through conscience, consider the following sub-headings that Lewis put in his revised edition of *The Pilgrim's Regress*: *"John decides to live virtuously but at once meets an obstacle – Conscience tells him he can and must pass it by his own efforts – Traditional Christianity says he cannot"* and *"Fear is too suspicious, and the natural conscience too proud."* Lewis, *The Pilgrim's Regress*, 85, 91.

79   For most of the ancient Greeks, the soul was moved by desires (not a "will") and ruled

understanding of the will *qua* faculty.[80] Lewis's definition of the will as "the ultimate choosing part" of the rational soul,[81] consequently, is likely a combination of Bradley, Kant and Christians like Hooker, MacDonald and, of course, Augustine.

Yet even with this definition in hand, the will is still one of the most difficult faculties of the soul to explain, particularly in regard to its *place* in the soul. For instance, on the one hand, Lewis identified the will as the "heart"[82] or the part of the soul that "makes personality one;"[83] that is, he spoke of the will as "the real central man, the thing that chooses,"[84] called "the new Self, the new Will,"[85] and said unambiguously, "By central self or spirit I mean chiefly the Will."[86] On the other hand, as we know from Lewis's metaphysics, the Oxford don followed Augustine and others when he insisted that the will – God's will or man's will – must be subordinate to reason (and conscience); true freedom, therefore, is not negative freedom, in which the will is unrestricted, but rather true freedom is the liberty that comes from submitting the will to the dictates of reason, which, of course, comes from, and indeed is a part of, God. As a result of these two claims – the centrality of the will on the one hand and the superiority of reason on the other – readers are often confused as to how exactly Lewis envisioned these two faculties working together. Consequently, it is worthwhile trying to unravel this, and any other, relationship that may arise.

---

by reason. Lewis, of course, rejected any identification between the desires and will: "Choice may be no (morally) better than appetite or will power than desire. But if anyone says they're the *same*, then I w[oul]d have to say that a man dying of thirst, with no possibility of getting a drink, *chooses* a glass of water or *wills* to drink. Appetite and desire may exist to the Nth where there is no question of will or choice. . . . You keep on identifying the antithesis of Desire > < Will with the antithesis Evil > < Good. When I control my desire for sleep in order to fornicate, or my laziness in order to plan revenge, I am controlling innocent desire by evil will. The real distinction is between what *happens in & to me* (Desire) and what I *do* (Will)." Lewis, *The Collected Letters of C. S. Lewis: Volume III*, 1581 [1948].

80 Charles Kahn, "Discovering the Will: From *Aristotle* to *Augustine*," in *The Question of 'Eclecticism': Studies in Later Greek Philosophy*, ed. John Dillon and A. A. Long, 234-59 (Berkeley: University of California Press, 1988), 235. Bonnie Kent, "Augustine's Ethics," in *The Cambridge Companion to Augustine*, ed. Eleonore Stump and Norman Kretzmann, 205-33 (Cambridge: Cambridge University Press, 2001), 222.

81 Lewis, *The Collected Letters of C. S. Lewis: Volume II*, 632 [December 6, 1944].

82 Lewis, *The Screwtape Letters*, 753. Lewis, *The Collected Letters of C. S. Lewis: Volume II*, 194 [May 23, 1936].

83 Ibid., 764 [February 23, 1947].

84 Lewis, *Mere Christianity*, 379.

85 C. S. Lewis, "Three Kinds of Men," in *C. S. Lewis: Essay Collection & Other Short Pieces*, ed. Lesley Walmsley (1943 essay reprint; London: HarperCollins, 2000), 315.

86 Lewis, *The Collected Letters of C. S. Lewis: Volume II*, 632 [December 6, 1944].

One of the things that separated the early Christian philosophers, such as Augustine and Boethius, from the early pagan philosophers, such as Plato and Aristotle, is the doctrine of the Fall. Plato, and to a lesser extent, Aristotle, believed that no one would willingly do evil; thus, sin was the result of ignorance and education was the key to salvation. Augustine, being both a man heavily tempted by lust and a careful reader of scripture, came to see that that men like himself and St. Paul were often caught up in very non-Greek conflicts between knowing what is right on the one hand and yet still doing what is wrong on the other; hence, the Bishop of Hippo concluded – and this conclusion was accepted by Lewis – that the Fall and subsequent evil was not so much a matter of ignorance as it was of a well-made will (for God, by His very nature, can only make good things) which ultimately chose evil over good; as we read in Lewis's heavily annotated edition of Augustine's *City of God*:

> For nothing causes an evil will, since it is the evil will itself which causes the evil act; and that means that the evil choice is the efficient cause of an evil act, whereas there is no efficient cause of an evil choice; since if anything exists, it either has, or has not, a will. If it has, that will is either good or bad; and if it is good, will anyone be fool enough to say that a good will causes an evil will?[87]

That is, in the Garden of Eden, man had full knowledge of his duty to God via his reason and thus, since his will was not yet fallen, simply had to turn the gaze of his will to his reason in order to act rightly: nothing, in other words, forced his will to look away from reason. However, man turned his will away from the clarity of reason and so was punished in kind; that is, he, and subsequently, his descendents, were punished with a will that – at least according to Lewis (Augustine takes it further) – has an extremely hard time obeying reason and is easily moved by mere appetite:

> As regards the Fall, I submit that the general tenor of scripture does not encourage us to believe that our knowledge of the Law has been depraved in the same degree as our power to fulfill it. . . . In that very chapter (Romans 7) where [Paul] asserts most strongly our inability to keep the moral law he also asserts most confidently that we perceive the Law's goodness and rejoice in it according to the inward man.[88]

---

87   Lewis, underlining in his edition of *De Civitate Dei*, 13.6.

88   Lewis, "The Poison of Subjectivism," 663. Cf. "Since the Fall consisted in man's Disobedience to this superior, it was punished by man's loss of Authority over his inferiors; that is, chiefly, over his passions and his physical organism (De Civ. Dei, XIV, 15). Man has called for anarchy: God lets him have it. . . . [A]fter the Fall understanding ceased to rule and the will did not listen to understanding, both being

The relationship – and question of dignity – between the will and reason, therefore, ought to be fairly clear by now: the will is truly the innermost man and its weakness more tragic than the weakness of reason – sin being worse than ignorance – yet even so, man, without knowledge and wisdom, cannot attain true manhood; indeed, without the sovereign judgment of reason, the will is moved by every whim of the appetites and passions; hence, in *The Great Divorce*, a certain lady dwelling on the outskirts of Heaven begs her sinful, vaporous husband, saying, "'Listen to reason.'"[89] Consequently, the proper hierarchy in man – though we must always remember that all internal divisions are merely formalities[90] – ought to be reason firstly ruling the will, which, as the house of all the non-intellectual virtues (more on this in the next chapter), in turn controls the deliberative imagination, then the sensitive soul and finally the fairly innocent body:

> 'You are always dragging me down,' said I to my Body. 'Dragging *you* down' replied my Body. 'Well I like that! Who taught me to like tobacco and alcohol? You, of course, with your idiotic adolescent idea of being 'grown –up.' My palate loathed both at first: but you would have your way. Who put an end to all those angry and revengeful thoughts last night? Me, of course, by insisting on going to sleep. Who does his best to keep you from talking too much and eating too much by giving you dry throats and headaches and indigestion? Eh?' 'And what about sex?', said I. 'Yes, what about it?' retorted the Body. 'If you and your wretched imagination would leave me alone I'd give you no trouble. That's Soul all over; you give me orders and then blame me for carrying them out.'[91]

Sadly, Lewis did not attempt to answer fellow Oxonian philosopher Gilbert Ryle[92] concerning how the rational soul *can* control the body – i.e. the mind-

---

subjected to usurping appetite. . . . When Reason is disobeyed 'upstart Passions catch the government.'" Lewis, *A Preface to Paradise Lost*, 70.

89 Lewis, *The Great Divorce*, 1087.

90 "The Pagans, by their lights, may wisely have constructed a hierarchical scheme of Man, Reason ruling Passion politically and Soul ruling body despotically. . . . But in Christ . . . [i]f the whole man is offered to God, all disputes about the value of this or that faculty are, as it were, henceforth out of date." Lewis, *The Collected Letters of C. S. Lewis: Volume II*, 194 [May 23, 1936].

91 Lewis, "Scraps," 346-7.

92 We ought to recall that Lewis and Ryle were part of Oxford's exclusive, six-member "Philosopher's Tea," and although when these two men where part of this society, Ryle had yet to write *The Concept of Mind*, in which he rejected mind-body dualism or "the ghost in the machine," Lewis would have been well-aware of his colleague's famous attack on mind-body dualism. Gilbert Ryle, *The Concept of Mind* (London: Hutchinson, 1949), 15.

body problem[93] – yet what is important is that this harmony of man, where the will is in full conformity to reason (and conscience) and hence to God, really makes sense out of many of Lewis's more perplexing comments, such as "When I say 'intellect' I include will. Attention is an act of will. Intelligence in action is will *par excellence*;"[94] "The prayer preceding all prayers is, 'May it be the real I who speaks. May it be the real Thou that I speak to;'"[95] and "I would say that the most deeply compelled action is also the freest action. By that I mean, no part of you is outside the action. It is a paradox. I expressed it in *Surprised by Joy* by saying that I chose, yet it really did not seem possible to do the opposite."[96]

However, if psychological harmony means the subjective self willing God's objective will and if the freest act is the one most in conformity with reason and hence the will of God, then how is it that so many Lewis scholars over the years have come to regard the deliberative imagination – of all things – as the most exalted faculty in Lewis's mature thought? Peter Schakel, for example, who has influenced an entire generation of Lewis scholars and for whom I have high regard, declares that during the 1940s, Lewis thought that

93　Even though Lewis did not address the mind-body problem, he did discuss the history of some theories related to this problem: "This perennial problem presented itself to the medieval thinker in two forms . . . (1) How can the soul, conceived as an immaterial substance, act upon matter at all? . . . (2) 'It is not possible to pass from one extreme to another but by a mean.' This is the old maxim from *Timaeus* 31b-c. . . . This deep-seated principle would probably have moved the medievals to put something in between soul and body even if the psycho-physical question did not in all periods offer us the raw edge that I have indicated. And this principle made it certain in advance that their method of coping with the raw edge would be to supply a *tertium quid*. . . . This *tertium quid*, this phantom liaison-officer between body and soul, was called *Spirit* or (more often) the *spirits*. It must be understood that this sense does not at all overlap with the sense which enables us to speak of angels or devils or ghosts as 'spirits.' To pass from the one meaning to the other would be merely to make a pun. . . . [*Spirits*] were, putting it bluntly, to be like the aether of nineteenth-century physics, which, for all I could ever learn of it, was to be and not to be matter. This doctrine of the spirits seems to me the least reputable feature in the Medieval Model. If the *tertium quid* is matter at all (what have density and rarity to do with it?) both ends of the bridge rest on one side of the chasm; if not, both rest on the other." Lewis, *The Discarded Image*, 166-7. For more on this, see Lewis's unpublished notes on Alcaeon of Croton. C. S. Lewis, "The 'Seat of the Soul' in [the] Brain – Alcmaeon of Croton" (Unpublished notes; The Marion E. Wade Center, Wheaton College), 1. On my count there has been only one essay published on the mind-body problem in Lewis's writings; however, this essay has almost nothing to do with what Lewis actually wrote. It is more a development of Lewis's ideas. See J. D. Memory, "C. S. Lewis and the Mind-Body Identity Thesis," *CSL: The Bulletin of the New York C. S. Lewis Society* 5, no. 10 (August 1974): 17-8.
94　Lewis, *A Grief Observed*, 85.
95　Lewis, *Prayer: Letters to Malcolm*, 276.
96　Lewis, "Cross-Examination," 553.

reason was more important than the imagination, but then later, in the 1950s, "reversed" this order.[97] My problem with Schakel's analysis is threefold. First, Schakel's failure to distinguish – not just in the passage in question, but throughout his entire book – the different types of imaginations and reasons makes it clear that he is unfamiliar with the deeper sources behind Lewis's epistemology, which, needless to say, is strong evidence that he misunderstood Lewis.[98] Second, Schakel has a poor understanding of Lewis's Great War development, for if he really understood this debate, he would have known that the key element of disagreement between Barfield and Lewis was over, as Lewis argued, the inability of the imaginations to judge their own content. In other words, not just from *Till We Have Faces* onward, but from The Great War onward, Lewis agreed that the imaginations could have visions of things greater than that which can be grasped by the intellect, not to mention by discursive reason; however, Lewis always asserted that even myths, those concrete universal things that refuse to be allegorized or whittled down by reason, must be judged by reason as being either true or false, for if the images in the imagination cannot be so judged, then there is no way to say that one myth is truer than another, or one religion better than the next. Third, Lewis's insistence that myth cannot be fully interpreted by reason is *not* a new development which came in the 1950s as a result of the Oxford don's defeat at the hands of Anscombe, but rather was something that Lewis insisted on very early on. Thus, if Schakel simply means that Lewis thought myth could not be *fully* interpreted by reason, then I should agree with him, though I would still disagree with his 1950s time marker; however, if he – as others have interpreted him – means that the imaginations, presumably, the deliberative imagination, somehow became the most dignified faculty in Lewis's psychology in the 1950s, then I hope that I have shown that this is balderdash, for human reason, though a humble master (it is not omnipotent), resides in the citadel of the soul, meaning, among other things, that reason alone judges the imagination and its images via the will, for if it did not, then it would be impossible to distinguish true myth from false myth. That

---

97   Schakel, *Reason and Imagination in C. S. Lewis*, 127. Furthermore, in his essay "Seeing and Knowing: the Epistemology of C. S. Lewis's *Till We Have Faces*," Schakel falsely states, "By the early 1950s Lewis's ideas about knowledge, reason and the imagination had been modified or broadened considerably." Peter Schakel, "Seeing and Knowing: the Epistemology of C. S. Lewis's *Till We Have Faces*," *VII: An Anglo-American Literary Review* 4 (1983), 90.

98   In his later book *Imagination and the Arts in C. S. Lewis*, Schakel does a better job of making some of these distinctions; however, even these distinctions lack the sense of philosophy which Lewis assumed when he made them. Peter Schakel, *Imagination and the Arts in C. S. Lewis: Journeying to Narnia and Other Worlds* (Columbia, MO: University of Missouri Press, 2002), 4.

is, Lewis knew that Christianity, despite being a revealed, mythical religion, demanded the kingship of reason, for it is reason that says, "this myth appears true, yet I do not understand what it means;" or, to put it in Lewis's own words: "It is rational not to reason, or not to limit oneself to reason, in the wrong place; and the more rational a man is the better he knows this."[99]

II: Logic

In its most basic definition, logic is the science that deals with both valid inferences, either deductive, which moves an argument to a necessary conclusion, or inductive, which moves an argument to a probable conclusion, and all of their attending fallacies, either formal, which are mistakes pertaining to how a (deductive) syllogism is set up, or informal, which are mistakes of content, largely pertaining to the meaning of terms used. The ancients largely identified logic with dialectic, which is, as Lewis said, "concerned with proving."[100]

Now needless to say, logic was extremely important to Lewis. His mother, Florence, obtained First Class Honours in logic from Queen's University, Belfast,[101] and Lewis's personal letters indicate that even from a very early age, the future don was a budding logician: "If bounty on the part of his weary audience could stop the sermon of the philosopher," Lewis wrote to his father in 1914, "I should be compelled to close our controversy of the paradise and inferno: but even the four, crisp, dainty postal orders (for which many thanks) cannot deter me from exposing the logical weakness of your position."[102] On top of this, Lewis's great tutor, Kirkpatrick, was, we recall, as close to "being a purely logical entity" as a man could be, and Lewis's philosophical training at Oxford, his years of teaching philosophy (which included teaching logic), and his apologetic work, make logic an important topic for us to discuss, particularly since no Lewis scholar, to the best of my knowledge, has discussed the Oxford don's love of reason with special reference to the actual science of reasoning itself: logic. Indeed, because most scholars have ignored the difference between logic and Lewis's general understanding of reason and judgment – because they have not paid careful attention to the Oxford don when he himself remarked, "We should remember that, after all, 'logic' is the

99   Lewis, "Priestesses in the Church?" 398. Lewis also insisted that Shakespeare believed the same thing and so summarized the Bard's thoughts on the matter as follows: "Reason, in fact, rationally recognizes what is beyond reason." Lewis, *Poetry and Prose in the Sixteenth Century*, 509.
100 Lewis, *The Discarded Image*, 189.
101 Green and Hooper, *C. S. Lewis: A Biography*, xxi.
102 Lewis, *The Collected Letters of C. S. Lewis: Volume I*, 90 [November 8, 1914].

name not of a kind of judgment but of the science which attempts to give a formal account of the faculty of judgment"[103] – it is important that we briefly look at Lewis's history in regard to this science.

During his time with Kirkpatrick and at Oxford as a student, Lewis studied logic both explicitly and implicitly; indeed, he likely had to do a section on logic for Classical Honours Moderations,[104] and he certainly could not have escaped the subject when he did "Greats" a year later. However, his seriousness for the subject greatly increased when he actually began teaching it at University College, Oxford during the mid-nineteen-twenties. At that time, particularly so in 1925, Lewis spent a lot of time working through the logic textbooks of Bradley, Mill and others. His marginalia in these textbooks is extremely interesting, for they reveal a mind convinced that logic was not merely a game, but was, as nearly every great philosopher had believed, a science grounded in the very nature of Ultimate Reality. In other words, Lewis thought logic was utterly connected to metaphysics – sentiments, incidentally, which he found difficult to avoid touching on during the philosophy tutorials he gave: "[E]veryone who has tried to teach mere Logic knows how difficult it is, especially with an intelligent pupil, to avoid raising questions which force us into metaphysics."[105]

In order to give readers a sense of Lewis's engagement with his logic textbooks, I will give three examples of such. The first example is from Mill's *A System of Logic*, in which Mill, after much argument, stated: "[B]ut if we call the class itself the genus, we must not talk of predicating the genus"[106] – thoughts which Lewis summarized thus: "The difficulty seems to be that in order to know that a class is a real <u>genus</u> you have to know that its members differ from other things <u>by an infinite series of differences known and unknown</u>. How many common differences justify the faith that we can go on finding differences ad lib?"[107] The second example is from Bradley's *Principles*

103 Lewis, *The Collected Letters of C. S. Lewis: Volume III*, 1616 [July 3, 1927 "The Great War Letters" Series I, Letter 3].

104 "I am still reading the philosoph[y] book: there is something to be said for reading so little, you take it in better. Of course in work I am reading as fast [as] I can & am more than half way through the Iliad. I have to read all Homer, all Virgil, all Demosthenes & all Cicero, besides four Greek plays and a special subject instead of verse. *I think in my case it will be logic, but am not quite sure.*" Lewis, *The Collected Letters of C. S. Lewis: Volume I*, 434 [February 16, 1919] (emphasis mine).

105 Lewis, *The Discarded Image*, 188.

106 John Stuart Mill, *A System of Logic, Ratiocinative and Inductive*, vol. 1, 3rd ed. (London: John W. Parker, DCCCLI), 136.

107 Lewis, marginalia in his edition of *A System of Logic, Ratiocinative and Inductive*, vol. 1, 136.

of Logic, in which Bradley wrote: "For the present it may prove sufficient to remember that inferences being an ideal construction and involving therefore an ideal centre, are premise[s that] must be taken as true beyond the limits of a particular subject."[108] Following this quotation, Lewis commented:

> If we are to infer anything from (A=B) B must be something capable of having <u>other</u> attributes than its relation to A, something that we can move about and see from different sides, in the confidence that it will still be B i.e. we must treat it not as 'this' wh[ich] is rigidly particular but as a 'such' or <u>what</u> or content – a universal or, more generally, we infer not from the <u>existence</u> of B but from its content, from some character it has (e.g. equality to A): and contend are all universals. If I understand him, he seems right.[109]

And finally the third example is from H. W. D. Joseph's *Introduction to Logic*, in which Lewis read – "We do not assume that there are griffins, and enquire whether they possess the predicate of existence"[110] – but which the young Oxford don challenged:

> But <u>Griffins</u> must be the name of something actual (e.g. of a representation) before we can ask if Griffins exist. That we are pointing to something when we ask such a question is shown [. . .] the fact that [. . .] to a deaf man we might find ourselves saying 'we weren't asking if Griffins existed we were asking if Griffins existed.' Do we not really assume <u>Griffins</u> and then ask, do they inhabit that part of the world wh[ich] I have labelled external or that part wh[ich] I have labelled 'imaginary'?[111]

Yet, as informative as it is to catch a glimpse of Lewis puzzling over logical concepts in his textbooks, it is even more instructive for us to consider his unpublished Great War document *Note on the Law of Contradiction*, in which we see the young Oxford don making his most telling remarks about logic. The document itself is a follow-up to *Clivi Hamiltonis Summae Metaphysices Contra Anthroposophos Libri II*, and largely has to do with Lewis the absolute idealist, who in theory ought to have been sympathetic to Hegelian modes of reasoning, arguing against the Hegelian "logic" of thesis, antithesis and

108 Bradley, *The Principles of Logic*, vol. 2, 296.
109 C. S. Lewis, marginalia in his edition of *The Principles of Logic*, by F. H. Bradley, vol. 2 (London: Oxford University Press, 1922; The Marion E. Wade Center, Wheaton College), 296.
110 H. W. D. Joseph, *An Introduction to Logic* (Oxford: Clarendon Press, 1916), 166-7.
111 C. S. Lewis, marginalia in his edition of *An Introduction to Logic*, by H. W. D. Joseph (Oxford: Clarendon Press, 1916; The Marion E. Wade Center, Wheaton College), 166-7.

synthesis as (poorly) presented by Barfield, the Anthroposophist. The fact that
Lewis the absolute idealist would attack Hegelian logic is extremely telling,
for it shows that even though the Oxford don had employed such Hegelian
logic in his own metaphysics – Reality being the synthesis of all the theses
and antitheses of Appearances[112] – he could not bring himself to fully reject
traditional logic, for it was precisely traditional logic that brought him, for a
spell, to absolute idealism. Thus, *Note on the Law of Contradiction* makes it
clear that Lewis was, as I have insisted throughout, a genuine philosopher,
for only one who genuinely loved Truth would write this – "[The Law of
Contradiction] will be defended as the <u>Foundation</u> . . . of all argument"[113]
– or this:

> For this it is stated that we may use the Law when we 'choose.' If the
> word 'choose' implies anything arbitrary – e.g. that The Law may be
> used or neglected at will – this doctrine is tantamount to the denial
> of the Law as a whole. For to say that in any given case The Law may
> be used or neglected means that in any such case a contradiction may
> be true and also cannot be true. But this proposition itself is a denial
> of the law. . . . It should be noticed that the very argument which the
> critic [i.e. Barfield] uses in attempting to overthrow the Law is itself
> based on the Law. For he argues;
>
> 1. A vegetable is and is not etc.
>
> 2. Therefore, a vegetable is self contradictory.
>
> 3. But if this were true, and The Law of Contradiction were also true,
> these two truths w[oul]d be contradictory.
>
> 4. But truths cannot be contradictory.
>
> 5. Therefore, The Law of Contradiction is untrue.
>
> It will be at once apparent that step 4 is simply a statement of the Law
> of Contradiction. . . . If the critic's conclusion (5) is true, then his own
> argument, since it involves (4) is invalid. . . . Has any man in the cause
> of freedom so immovably bound himself hand and foot?[114]

Furthermore, since *Note on the Law of Contradiction* was penned as a
response to Barfield's comments on *Clivi Hamiltonis Summae Metaphysices
Contra Anthroposophos Libri II*, which was written in November 1928, *Note*

---

112 Again: "Distinctions of . . . true and false . . . spring up only with the creation of souls
   and a world. Outside the world they are meaningless." Lewis, *Clivi Hamiltonis Summae
   Metaphysices Contra Anthroposophos Libri II*, 53. .
113 C. S. Lewis, *Note on the Law of Contradiction* (Unpublished "Great War" document
   [1929?]; The Marion E. Wade Center, Wheaton College), 110.
114 Ibid., 111-3.

on the Law of Contradiction was probably written in the first half of 1929, which was just before Lewis became a theist. Consequently, it is likely that *Note on the Law of Contradiction*, which could easily be read alongside any of Lewis's theistic or Christian writings, helped clarify for the Oxford don – though sadly, not for Barfield – the logical problems involved in absolute idealism.

When Lewis became a Christian, his love of logic continued. In both his published and unpublished work, we can find many examples of him pointing out such fallacies as *"ad verecundiam,"*[115] *"ad ignorantiam,"*[116] *"ad hominem,"*[117] *"ad juidicium,"*[118] "equivocation,"[119] "red herring,"[120] "mares nest,"[121] *"non sequitur,"*[122] "undistributed middle,"[123] and "question-begging":

> If I object to what you said, I object not as a friend or as a guest, but as a logician. If you are going to argue with me on the points at issue between our churches, it is obvious that you must argue *to* the truth of your proposition, not *from* it. The opposite procedure only wastes your time and leaves me to reply, moved solely by embarrassment, *tu sei santo ma tu non sei filosofo*! ['You are a holy one, but you are no philosopher!'].[124]

In addition to these fallacies, Lewis even named five of his own: (1) "The Promethean Fallacy in Ethics," which, according to Lewis the idealist, falsely insists that even though people are a part of the Whole, they can still critique the Whole as if they were standing outside of the Whole; (2) "The Fallacy of Introspection," which, inspired by Alexander, falsely states that when

115 Lewis, "The Moral Good – Its Place Among the Values," 20.
116 Ibid.
117 Ibid.
118 Ibid.
119 Lewis, *Clivi Hamiltonis Summae Metaphysices Contra Anthroposophos Libri II*, 2, 6.
120 Lewis, *The Collected Letters of C. S. Lewis: Volume III*, 1616 [July 3, 1927 "The Great War Letters" Series I, Letter 3].
121 In his edition of William Empson's *Structure of Complex Words*, Lewis wrote a poem at the end of chapter three: "Each book by Empson read, becomes a land / Transformed by some malign enchanters word; / Each breaking land a double-entendre yields / And teeming Mares build nest in all his fields." C. S. Lewis, unpublished poem in his edition of *The Structure of Complex Words*, by William Empson (London: Chatto & Windus, 1951; The Rare Book Collection, The University of North Carolina at Chapel Hill), 100.
122 Lewis, *The Discarded Image*, 161.
123 Ibid.
124 Lewis, *The Collected Letters of C. S. Lewis: Volume II*, 150 [December 26, 1934]. Cf. Lewis, "The Moral Good – Its Place Among the Values," 21. Cf. Lewis, *Miracles*, 1102.

people examine their own trains of thoughts, real thoughts do not cease and words, mental pictures or physical sensations are not all that remain;[125] (3) "Bulverism," which is Lewis's name for *ad hominem* arguments, and which was, without a doubt, the fallacy he loved pointing out the most as we can gather not only from his essay "Bulverism,"[126] but also from his comments in his unpublished material, such as his edition of Reinhold Niebuhr's *Interpretation of Christian Ethics*, in which Lewis mentioned the fallacy on three different pages: page 133, 172 and 197;[127] (4) "The Gyges Fallacy" ("If there were an invisible man in the room it would look empty – The room does look empty. Therefore there is an invisible man in it");[128] and (5) "The Fallacy of Maximum Differentiation," about which he wrote the following:

> A thing is most itself, in the sense of being most recognizable, when it is most unlike everything else: but this does not mean that it is then in its best state. If you want to find out whether whisky is a spirit, you may take some neat whisky and apply a lighted match to it: but if you want a drink you may prefer to mix it with soda water. I do not think the best poetry is that which contains the fewest elements proper to prose. I think the greatest prose and poetry are least unlike each other, and that Dante has proved it.[129]

Moreover, on top of engaging in the negative action of pointing out fallacies, Lewis also engaged in the positive action of decrying the neglect of logic. Thus, in 1947, he told Dorothy Sayers that "[w]e badly need to

---

125 "As an empiricist Hume is entitled to use his principle [i.e. if there is no impression, there is no idea] . . . only if he can show an absolute certainty that the only possible materials of knowledge are impressions and the faint copies (ideas) derived from them. He feels certain of this because he falls into the same fallacy of 'introspection' as Berkeley. It is true that if at any moment you stop a train of thought to find what is 'in your mind' all you get is either <u>words</u>, <u>mental pictures</u> or <u>physical sensations</u>. But at the moment you begin 'introspecting' the real thought has ceased: it is not surprising, therefore, that you don't find it. But we <u>know</u> that the <u>pictures</u> etc. are not what we are thinking about." Lewis, "The Moral Good – Its Place Among the Values," 57.
126 C. S. Lewis, "Bulverism: Or the Foundation of Twentieth-Century Thought," in *C. S. Lewis: Essay Collection & Other Short Pieces*, ed. Lesley Walmsley (1941 essay reprint; London: HarperCollins, 2000), 589.
127 On page 133, we read: "But Bulverism isn't enough. An apprehension de finibus does not find relative good and evil (politics) easy to deal with;" on page 172, we read: "So irrelevantly [...] that here Bulverism is legitimate;" and on page 197, Lewis mentioned "Bulverism" again. Lewis, marginalia in his edition of *An Interpretation of Christian Ethics*, 133, 172, 197.
128 C. S. Lewis, review of both *Passion and Society*, by D. de Rougemont, and *The Bride of Christ*, by Claude Chavasse, *Theology* 40, no. 240 (June 1940): 460.
129 Lewis, *The Discarded Image*, 75.

revive formal logic,"[130] and in 1950 – importantly, just *after* Lewis's original argument against naturalism was defeated by Anscombe – he made the professor in *The Lion, the Witch and the Wardrobe* famously say,

> 'Logic!' said the Professor half to himself. 'Why don't they teach logic at these schools? There are only three possibilities. Either your sister is telling lies, or she is mad, or she is telling the truth. You know she doesn't tell lies and it is obvious that she is not mad. For the moment then and unless any further evidence turns up, we must assume that she is telling the truth.'[131]

However, as we can see even in this very quotation and despite what many defenders of Lewis would have us believe, the Oxford don's logic was not always perfect. Indeed, this quotation from *The Lion, the Witch and the Wardrobe*, to focus on it for a moment, is reminiscent of Chesterton's flawed "Trilemma" argument for the divinity of Christ, which Lewis himself appropriated and popularized in *Mere Christianity*. I say "flawed" because – *pace* David Horner[132] – to say that Jesus was either a liar, a lunatic or the Lord, just as to say Lucy is either a liar, a lunatic or a truth-teller, is to pose a false dilemma (Lewis's most common fallacy[133]); it is to deny any other interpretation than those presented – be it an alternative to the orthodox Christian interpretation of the biblical passages where Jesus's divinity is apparently declared or another reason for why Lucy might be wrong, such as her having had amnesia. Thus, I believe that if Christians want to find some value in the Trilemma argument, they need to change it into a probability argument and not a certainty argument. But again, I point out Lewis's logical inaccuracies both as one who has the highest respect for Lewis and his logical abilities and as one who does not want to overlook inconsistencies. Indeed, as I have said throughout, it is crucial that people know that Lewis both committed fallacies, though less than his critics heretofore have thought, and admitted his own limitations, such as he did after he lost his initial argument

---

130 Lewis, *The Collected Letters of C. S. Lewis: Volume II*, 778 [June 5, 1947].

131 Lewis, *The Lion, the Witch and the Wardrobe*, 47.

132 David Horner, *"Aut Deus Aut Malus Homo*: A Defense of C. S. Lewis's 'Shocking Alternative,'" in *C. S. Lewis as Philosopher: Truth, Goodness, and Beauty*, ed. David Baggett, Gary Habermas and Jerry Walls, 68-84 (Downers Grove, IL: InterVarsity Press, 2008).

133 "One of Lewis's most serious weaknesses as an apologist is his fondness for the false dilemma." Beversluis, *C. S. Lewis and the Search for Rational Religion*, 43. "[Lewis] is frequently accused of using questionable dichotomies, reducing an argument to two narrow possibilities while ignoring other valid positions." Steven Mueller, *Not a Tame God: Christ in the Writings of C. S. Lewis* (Saint Louis: Concordia Publishing House, 2002), 197.

with Anscombe, for if Lewis scholars are not prepared to admit a problem when we see one, then not only does it bespeak partisan bias but it also has the terrible effect of downplaying one of Lewis's greatest strengths, which is his ability, due to his love of Truth, to admit mistakes when he made them – as he did with Anscombe – and then push ahead to find a solution to the problem. As Lewis said less than two years before he died:

> I am on neither side in the present controversy [concerning the death penalty]. But I still think the abolitionists conduct their case very ill. They seem incapable of stating it without imputing vile motives to their opponents. If unbelievers often look at your correspondence column, I am afraid they may carry away a bad impression of our logic, manners and charity.[134]

III: Epistemology

Epistemology, the study of how we attain knowledge, was a subject of great interest to Lewis. However, as was often the case, the Oxford don seldom spoke systematically about his theories and so we are often forced to make conjectures to fill in things he left unsaid, especially in regard to his earlier years.

During his Lucretian materialist phase, Lewis, who we must remember was a lifelong rationalist and indeed a "critical rationalist,"[135] subscribed to epistemological realism, which maintains, as we recall from chapter two, that things in a given domain exist independently of knowledge or experience of them. Moreover, since Lewis had a high regard for reason and believed that it really provided him with objective Truth, he must have accepted what is known today as "the correspondence theory of truth," for this theory simply maintains, in the tradition of Plato's *Theaetetus* (a book Lewis later read but rarely mentioned[136]), that a belief (statement, proposition etc.) is true provided that there exists a fact that corresponds to it. For example, if the young Lewis perceived an apple and then thought about this perception and said, "I see an apple," this proposition would have been *true* because an apple really existed.

---

134 Lewis, *The Collected Letters of C. S. Lewis: Volume III*, 1302 [December 15, 1961].
135 While Lewis never differentiated between types of rationalisms, both Victor Reppert and David Rozema believe that Lewis was a "critical rationalist" – that is, a man who believes in the power of reason and the importance of evidence in belief-formation but also thinks that because human beings are finite (not to mention fallen), honest men can disagree about evidence and still be rational. Reppert, *C. S. Lewis's Dangerous Idea*, 44. David Rozema, "'Belief' in the Writings of C. S. Lewis," in *C. S. Lewis as Philosopher: Truth, Goodness, and Beauty*, ed. David Baggett, Gary Habermas and Jerry Walls, 144-58 (Downers Grove, IL: InterVarsity Press, 2008), 147.
136 Lewis, *All My Road Before Me*, 453 [February 17, 1927].

And since Lewis was an epistemological realist, he would have thought that the apple he perceived had material existence in the external world.

However, when Lewis became a pseudo-Manichean dualist he often spoke as one torn between realist and antirealist epistemologies (the latter of which states "that, with respect to a given domain, any full description of the objects of thought or experience in the domain has to make essential reference to the thinker or experiencer and the conditions under which the thinking or experience occurs"[137]); hence, Lewis wrote:

> If beauty were really in the tree, then two people who both had normal eyes would be bound to see the same beauty. But nothing is easier than to find two people one of whom would see beauty and other see no beauty in the same tree. Therefore the beauty cannot be in the tree but in some obscure and non-material point of view or relation between the mind of the perceiver and the sensations which the tree – very indirectly – causes in the mind.[138]

While Lewis followed Berkeley the antirealist in maintaining that secondary qualities, such as colour, are the product of Spirit or spirits interacting with man's spirit, Lewis was almost certainly a realist in regard to the object itself and its primary qualities, such as its hardness. And when he reconverted to materialism (i.e. Stoical materialism), it seems likely that he once again became a committed epistemological realist.

Yet with that said, when he became a subjective, and later, absolute, idealist, Lewis knew that he had to accept antirealist epistemology. Nevertheless, he was an uncomfortable antirealist since his Aristotelian or quasi-Aristotelian psychology works much better with realist epistemology and the correspondence theory of truth than with antirealist epistemology and Bradley's coherence theory of truth, which speaks of truth in terms of verifiability and involves the assumption that a belief is verified when it is part of an entire system of beliefs that is consistent and harmonious. Consequently, Lewis the confused absolute idealist wrote:

> To be sure the <u>Summa</u> [i.e. *Clivi Hamiltonis Summae Metaphysicos Contra Anthroposophos Libri II*] does not leave an absolute distinction between Subjective & Objective, such as found in [Epistemological] Realism [which entails the correspondence theory of truth]: but it by no means abolishes the distinction. The question 'Subjective or

---

137 A. C. Grayling, "Berkeley's Argument for Immaterialism," in *The Cambridge Companion to Berkeley*, ed. Kenneth Winkler, 166-89 (Cambridge: Cambridge University Press, 2005), 174.

138 Lewis, *The Collected Letters of C. S. Lewis: Volume I*, 377 [June 3, 1918].

Objective?' has an important meaning, provided you explain 'For whom?'[139]

Of course the tension in Lewis between his earlier correspondence theory of truth and his new leanings toward a coherence theory of truth is very much related to that tension in Lewis which I discussed earlier between traditional logic on the one hand and Hegelian logic on the other. That is, if Lewis accepted a coherence theory of truth, then he would have been forced to deny the absoluteness of Truth, to which he always seemed so attracted (and of which he later became a famous expounder). On the other hand, if Lewis continued to believe in the correspondence theory of truth (which we know he did when he first converted to idealism[140]), then it would have been difficult, but not impossible, for him to speak as strongly as he did in the defense of the law of non-contradiction (which he called "the law of contradiction"), for such a law, according to most absolute idealists, would not necessarily have been absolute in the *grand* scheme of things: thesis making way for antithesis and ultimately, synthesis.

Whatever the exact case may be in this matter, it is certain that there were difficulties in regard to the totality of Lewis's various philosophical beliefs when he was an idealist, for he never precisely said how his Aristotelian psychology, particularly in regard to the sensitive imagination and its entailment, the five senses, related to either his idealist metaphysics or his antirealist epistemology; his Great War letters admittedly discuss many of these things, but never in a very coherent way. Consequently, I would say that given Lewis's Aristotelian leanings in psychology and his stubborn refusal to give up traditional logic, Lewis the idealist never perfectly worked out his antirealist epistemology, particularly as it pertained to his theory of Truth; indeed, when he did get around to examining the coherency of his total worldview, he became a Christian.

And as a Christian, specifically, a Neoplatonic Christian, Lewis returned to a realist epistemology and the correspondence theory of truth, both of which fit well with his Neoplatonic metaphysics and Aristotelian psychology.[141] However, Lewis's philosophical language still remained imperfect since in

---

139 Lewis, *Replies to Objections in Detail*, 119.
140 In his 1924 essay "The Whole," Lewis – almost certainly a new convert to idealism – wrote, "You will complain that I have given an account <u>de facto</u> and not <u>de jure</u>. As a psychological fact it may be that this is how we come to believe in essence: but since I admit that propositions involving the word 'must' may be true, I am forced either to hold the coherence theory of truth (which I don't) or to explain what it is they correspond with in order to be true." Lewis, "The Whole," 114.
141 Willard, "Truth in the Fire: C. S. Lewis and Pursuit of Truth Today," 9.

The Discarded Image, for instance, he spoke of dialectic and epistemology synonymously:

> Dialectic is concerned with proving. In the Middle Ages there are three kinds of proof; from Reason, from Authority, and from Experience. We establish a geometrical truth by Reason; a historical truth, by Authority, by *auctours*. We learn by experience that oysters do or do not agree with us. . . . But unfortunately the word *experience* is not always used for the third type of proof. The variants are two. To learn by experience may be to *feel*; or, more misleading, knowledge by experience may be *preve* (that is, proof). Thus Chaucer opens his *Legend of Phillis* by saying that the maxim 'wikked frute cometh of a wikked tree' can be learned not only from authority but 'by preve;' that is, empirically. In the *Hous of Fame* there eagle says that the poet can 'fele' the theory of sound which he has just enunciated (826). In the *Knight's Tale* the line 'Ne who most felingly speketh of love' (A 2203) sounds very modern. But to 'speak feelingly' probably means to speak from first-hand experience.[142]

Despite Lewis's tendency to speak imprecisely in regard to philosophical terminology (which, as I have said before, may be forgiven to some extent because he did not always intend to write philosophically), we know that his Christian epistemology was identical to that which he ascribed in the aforementioned quotation to the general class of medieval, foundationalist[143] writers, who, incidentally, Lewis represented not with the epistemology of Augustine or Aquinas, but with that of the Anglican Aristotelian Richard Hooker, in whose *Of The Laws of Ecclesiastical Polity* Lewis underlined the following: "But of this we are sure, <u>that nature, Scripture, and experience</u> itself, have all taught the world to seek for the ending of contentions by submitting itself unto some judicial and definitive sentence, whereunto neither part that

---

142 Lewis, *The Discarded Image*, 189-90.
143 Given Lewis's foundationalism in epistemology – which he thought went back to antiquity and the Middle Ages – Lewis is much more in line with modern philosophers like Richard Swinburne and Basil Mitchell (Anglican philosophers) than Alvin Plantinga and Nicholas Wolterstorff (Calvinist philosophers); thus, while I think arguments against foundationalism are misguided, it is important to keep in mind that not all Christian philosophers would support Lewis's foundationalism: "A second case against Lewis as an apologist has been made because of recent developments in epistemology. In the last twenty years philosophers like Alvin Plantinga and Nicholas Wolterstorff have made compelling cases against any evidentalist defense of the rationality of religious belief." William Abraham, "C. S. Lewis and the Conversion of the West," in *Permanent Things: Toward the Recovery of a More Human Scale at the End of the Twentieth Century*, ed. Andrew Tadie and Michael Macdonald, 270-82 (Grand Rapids, MI: Eerdmans, 1995), 274.

contendeth may under any pretense or colour refuse to stand."[144] This is to say that just as medieval Aristotelian or Anglican epistemology was a matter of attaining knowledge via reason / nature, authority and experience, so too was Lewis's, for we are told in no uncertain terms: "Authority, reason and experience; on these three, mixed in varying proportions, all our knowledge depends."[145] Subsequently, in order to understand Lewis's epistemology better, I will examine these three elements and then end with a discussion on faith, which Lewis also thought was important for the attainment of knowledge.

To begin with, reason in regard to epistemology must be distinguished from reason in regard to psychology. The latter is the faculty of judgment, which is divided into two parts, as we saw, and the former is the judgment that takes place in this faculty. Furthermore, as a subcategory of this judgment, there is logic, which, during The Great War, Lewis said had only to do with giving a formal account of reason *qua* judgment, but which later on he often spoke of synonymously in terms of inference: "It therefore follows that all knowledge whatever depends on the validity of inference."[146]

Lewis believed we attain knowledge from reason in two ways, both of which correspond to the two parts of the faculty of reason. First, in our intellect, our reason just sees connections between things and knows they could not be otherwise; these self-evident or foundational truths are the highest form of objectivity a person can attain and Lewis, like many others, thought that a dogmatic assertion of them was fundamental to any knowledge claim[147] – hence, his rejection of existentialism. Second, in our deliberative reason, our reason moves from self-evident truths to infer or discover more truths. Naturally, because human reason is limited – and *not* because reason itself is fallen or flawed – people make mistakes when they use their deliberative reason:

144 C. S. Lewis, underlining in his edition of *Of the Laws of Ecclesiastical Polity*, by Richard Hooker, vol. 1 (London: J. M. Dent & Sons, 1925; The Rare Book Collection, The University of North Carolina at Chapel Hill), 117. Cf. "Hooker (*Laws of Ecclesiastical Polity*) is to me the great formulation of Anglicanism." Lewis, *The Collected Letters of C. S. Lewis: Volume II*, 647 [May 8, 1945].

145 Lewis, "Religion: Reality or Substitute?" 134. On the back of a handwritten manuscript of *Christian Behaviour*, Lewis summarized his epistemology thus: 'Knowledge = experience + logic." C. S. Lewis, "Christian Behaviour Outline," in *In Pursuit of C. S. Lewis: Adventures in Collecting His Works*, by Edwin Brown (Bloomington, IN: AuthorHouse, 2006), 79.

146 Lewis, "*De Futilitate*," 674.

147 In addition to logical and mathematical truths, Lewis believed that the intellect can also see some objective values as self-evident: "A dogmatic belief in objective value is necessary to the very idea of a rule which is not tyranny or an obedience which is not slavery." Lewis, *The Abolition of Man*, 426.

> We are only saying that total Reason – cosmic or super-cosmic Reason – *corrects* human imperfections of Reason. Now correction is not the same as mere contradiction. When your false reasoning is corrected you 'see the mistakes': the true reasoning thus takes up into itself whatever was already rational in your original thought. . . . To say that Reason is objective is to say that all our false reasonings could in principle be corrected by more Reason. . . . I have to add 'in principle' because, of course, the reasoning necessary to give us absolute truth about the whole universe might be (indeed, certainly would be) too complicated for any human mind to hold it together or even to keep on attending. But that, again, would be a defect in the human instrument, not in Reason.[148]

Consequently, where postmodern thinkers, for instance, think that man is incapable of attaining objective Truth because he is so mired in his own subjectivity, Lewis would rather say that while our reason is limited, our wills are fallen and our animal nature is in rebellion, rational argument can still provide us with real knowledge: "We never claimed to be impartial," wrote Lewis about the Socratic Club, "but argument is;"[149] or again, "Reason's duty (even for life's sake) [is not] to decide without evidence."[150]

Nevertheless, if "experience by itself proves nothing,"[151] then neither does reason, for reason always needs something to reason about: "It is Reason herself which teaches us not to rely on Reason only . . . [f]or Reason knows that she cannot work without material. . . . She will be the first to tell you to go and try experience."[152] Experience, in other words, provides the content for reason; or, as Lewis put it, "By *experience* I mean 'That part or result of any event which is presented to consciousness.'"[153]

In regard to experience, the first rule, according to Lewis, was "Look. Listen. Receive. Get yourself out of the way,"[154] and the second rule was rational evaluation. However, while Lewis thought the job of reason is to judge the huge variety of often contradictory experiences that enter the soul through the senses and subsequently appear as images, he remained mum on how we attain universal principles, not saying whether they are innate in the soul or whether they are abstracted from one's experiences by reason.

---

148 Lewis, "*De Futilitate*," 678.
149 Lewis, "The Founding of the Oxford Socratic Club," 592.
150 Lewis, *The Pilgrim's Regress*, 76.
151 C. S. Lewis, "Miracles," in *C. S. Lewis: Essay Collection & Other Short Pieces*, ed. Lesley Walmsley (1942 essay reprint; London: HarperCollins, 2000), 107.
152 Lewis, *Miracles*, 1167.
153 Lewis, *The Collected Letters of C. S. Lewis: Volume II*, 928 [March 28, 1949].
154 Lewis, *An Experiment in Criticism*, 19.

Whatever the case may be, Lewis felt that when "one's reason and . . . one's experience produce different results" – meaning, I take it, that when one's objective knowledge and one's subjective experience demonstrate different outcomes – then one must follow the stability of proven, rational truths.[155] Thus, while Lewis acknowledged the necessity of experience and even thought it an "honest thing,"[156] he was worried that people would blindly follow their own experiences and ignore the larger universal principles: "When it comes to virtue, experience, as Kant tells us, is the mother of illusion;"[157] or, as Lewis had the devil Screwtape say: "*Experience*, in the peculiar sense we [devils] teach [people] to give it, is, by the by, a most useful word. A great human philosopher nearly let our secret out when he said that where Virtue is concerned 'Experience is the mother of illusion;' but thanks to a change in Fashion . . . we have largely rendered his book innocuous."[158]

Although authority follows reason and experience in Lewis's medieval Aristotelian or Anglican epistemology, authority, by which the Oxford don largely meant the testimony of others, may reasonably be considered a subcategory of experience: "For of course authority, however we value it in this or that particular instance, is a kind of evidence."[159]

Indeed, from employing an Aristotelian *isogoge* in his writings[160] to commenting approvingly in his edition of Dante's *De Monarchia* ("I shall show both by Reason and Authority that the Romans ruled de jure"[161]), Lewis demonstrated that authority is an important part of our experience and constitutes an enormous amount of the evidence we have for our beliefs.

---

155 Lewis, "Religion: Reality or Substitute?" 135.

156 "What I like about experience is that it is such an honest thing. You may take any number of wrong turns; but keep your eyes open and you will not be allowed to go very far before the warning signs appear. You may have deceived yourself, but experience is not trying to deceive you. The universe rings true wherever you fairly test it." Lewis, *Surprised by Joy*, 1345-6.

157 Lewis, *Poetry and Prose in the Sixteenth Century*, 77.

158 Lewis, *The Screwtape Letters*, 813.

159 C. S. Lewis, "On Obstinacy in Belief," in *C. S. Lewis: Essay Collection & Other Short Pieces*, ed. Lesley Walmsley (1955 essay reprint; London: HarperCollins, 2000), 208.

160 "Aristotle often begins his argument with what he calls an Isagoge, a collection of instances which is not, if I understand the matter, intended (like Mill's induction) to prove a general principle, but merely to open our eyes to it. The following instances are meant to form such an isagoge." C. S. Lewis, "High and Low Brows," in *C. S. Lewis: Essay Collection & Other Short Pieces*, ed. Lesley Walmsley (1939 essay reprint; London: HarperCollins, 2000), 421. Cf. Lewis, *The Discarded Image*, 188.

161 C. S. Lewis, marginalia in his edition of *De Monarchia*, by Dantis Alligherii, ed. Carolum Witte (Vindobonae: Sumptibus Guilielmi Braumuller, 1874; The Rare Book Collection, The University of North Carolina at Chapel Hill), 39.

However, while authority is a kind of experience, particularly, the experience of others' opinions, Lewis often focused this further and associated authority – more in keeping with Christianity than Aristotle[162] – with revelatory testimony. Hence, the great prophets are in contact "with the unseen . . . with something objective,"[163] which they in turn pass on to others as authority. And as we discussed in chapter four, Lewis thought that this kind of authority would give us information above reason, yet, as always, he did not think that such authority should be accepted without reason judging the mystery or myth to be worth believing, all things considered: "One of the things my reason tells me is that I ought to check the results of my own thinking by the opinions of the wise. I go to authority because reason sends me to it."[164] Thus, on the one hand, Lewis appreciated the general Protestant devotion to scripture, but on the other hand, he also thought that Protestant thought was often "an exaggeration . . . of Pauline theology,"[165] and so he tended to agree with Hooker (again) in denouncing – no doubt somewhat unfairly – "Puritan hatred of knowledge,"[166] insisting not only that reason needs to evaluate revelation but also that revelation needs to be interpreted by other authority or the general Christian tradition if it is to remain orthodox: "even when we cite Scripture," Lewis commented in his edition of Otto's *The Idea of the Holy*, "the interpretation depends on human authority."[167]

Yet if Lewis's rationalism really held the day as I claim it did, it still remains to be seen how the Oxford don saw faith fitting into his epistemology. In his essay "Is Theism Important?" Lewis carefully distinguished between two types of faith: "[Faith] may mean (a) a settled intellectual assent. In that sense faith (or 'belief') in God hardly differs from faith in the uniformity of nature or in the consciousness of other people. . . . (b) a trust, or confidence,

---

162 Bundy, *The Theory of Imagination in Classical and Medieval Thought*, 441.

163 Lewis, *Prayer: Letters to Malcolm*, 265.

164 Lewis, "Christianity and Culture," 83. Cf. "On Reason and Revelation: If the claim 'there has been a revelation' is in fact false, then no doubt the acceptance of the supposed revelation will usually involve errors in reasoning. But there is no opposition in principle between Reason and Revelation: for of course those who accept Revelation believe that Reason leads them to regard it *as* a Revelation. In fact, the relation between Reason and Revelation is like that between Reason and sense-experience: i.e. both supply Reason with materials which she cannot spin out of herself." Lewis, "C. S. Lewis on Rationalism: (Unpublished Notes)," 89.

165 Lewis, *Poetry and Prose in the Sixteenth Century*, 33.

166 Lewis, marginalia in his edition of *Of the Laws of Ecclesiastical Polity*, 101.

167 Lewis, marginalia in his edition of *The Idea of the Holy*, 274. Cf. "When [the Puritans] and their Bibles were alone together, what strange fantastical opinion soever at any time entered into their heads, their use was to think the Spirit taught it them." Lewis, underlining in his edition of *Of the Laws of Ecclesiastical Polity*, 135.

in the God whose existence is thus assented to. This involves an attitude of the will. It is more like our confidence in a friend."[168]

Faith-A, in other words, is not some secret knowledge to which we must blindly cling, but is really the type of faith that is the result of reason proving certain things about God, such as His existence, His timelessness, etc. It is valuable as a kind of natural knowledge of God, and as such is often the first step toward Christianity: "But here, as in everything else," the devil Screwtape advised his nephew, "the way must be prepared for your moral assault by darkening [your patient's] intellect."[169] However, while this type of faith is very valuable, it is simply the child of reason, not having been implemented in action via the will; consequently, it is not a complete faith: "Correct thinking will not make good men of bad ones; but a purely theoretical error may remove ordinary checks to evil and deprive good intentions of their natural support."[170]

Faith-B, however, is a more complete faith as it flows from reason, into the will and finally into correct moral action, the performance of which eventually causes the development of virtue. Faith-B is a rational endurance in a true belief or a reasonable trust in a person who you already know with Faith-A; thus, Faith-B "moves us from the logic of speculative thought into what might perhaps be called the logic of personal relations;"[171] it is "the art of holding on to things your reason has once accepted, in spite of your changing moods;"[172] "it is the power of continuing to believe what we once honestly thought to be true until cogent reasons for honestly changing our minds are brought before us."[173] Men at once have to "train"[174] this faith by consciously willing Truth, and yet because they are weak and sinful, it must

---

168 Lewis, "Is Theism Important?" 54.
169 Lewis, *The Screwtape Letters*, 791.
170 Lewis, "The Poison of Subjectivism," 657.
171 Lewis, "On Obstinacy in Belief," 215. Cf. "The saying 'Blessed are those that have not seen and have believed' has nothing to do with our original assent to the Christian propositions. It was not addressed to a philosopher inquiring whether God exists. It was addressed to a man who already believed that, who already had a long acquaintance with a particular Person, and evidence that that Person could do very odd things, and who then refused to believe one odd thing more, often predicted by that Person and vouched for by all his closest friends. It is a rebuke not to skepticism in the philosophic sense but to the psychological quality of being 'suspicious.' It says in effect, 'You should have known me better.'" Ibid.
172 Lewis, *Mere Christianity*, 410.
173 Lewis, "Religion: Reality or Substitute?" 135.
174 Lewis, *Mere Christianity*, 410.

also be a "gift"[175] by the "motive power"[176] of God, grace:

> When we exhort people to Faith as a virtue, to the settled intention
> of continuing to believe certain things, we are not exhorting them to
> fight against reason. The intention of continuing to believe is required
> because, though Reason is divine, human reasoners are not. When
> once passion takes part in the game, the human reason, unassisted by
> Grace, has about as much chance of retaining its consistency in the
> mouth of a blast furnace. . . . Reason may win truths; without Faith
> she will retain them just so long as Satan pleases. . . . If we wish to be
> rational, not now and then, but constantly, we must pray for the gift of
> Faith, for the power to go on believing not in the teeth of reason but in
> the teeth of lust and terror and jealousy and boredom and indifference
> that which reason, authority, or experience, or all three, have once
> delivered to us for truth.[177]

Consequently, the more a person is empowered in his will not only to
hold onto what he knows is right but also to perform this in the world, the
more the person grows in understanding, and vice versa. This formula for the
attainment of knowledge, which states that moral character is essential to the
furtherance of knowledge, is Platonic and Aristotelian in origin and is known
today as virtue epistemology. Needless to say, Lewis's medieval Aristotelian
or Anglican epistemology is a type of virtue epistemology and indeed there
is almost no aspect of his epistemology that he stressed more, for we read
again and again: "Virtue – even attempted virtue – brings light; indulgence
brings fog;"[178] "The rebellion of the will is nearly always accompanied with
some fogging of the intelligence;"[179] "What you see and hear depends a good
deal on where you are standing: it also depends on what sort of person you
are;"[180] "I am astonished at the reward in *knowledge* given here and now to

---

175 "I doubt whether religious people have ever supposed that Faith-B follows automatically
     on the acquisition of Faith-A. It is described as a 'gift' (e.g. I Corinthians 12: I-II;
     Ephesians 2:8). As soon as we have Faith-A in the existence of God, we are instructed
     to ask from God Himself the gift of Faith-B." Lewis, "Is Theism Important?" 55.
176 Lewis, *The Collected Letters of C. S. Lewis: Volume II*, 189 [April 24, 1936].
177 Lewis, "Religion: Reality or Substitute?" 137-8. Cf. "Christians have often disputed as
     to whether what leads the Christian home is good actions, or Faith in Christ. I have
     no right really to speak on such a difficult question, but it does seem to me like asking
     which blade in a pair of scissors is more necessary. A serious moral effort is the only
     thing that will bring you to the point where you throw up the sponge. Faith in Christ is
     the only thing to save you from despair at that point: and out of that Faith in Him good
     actions must inevitably come." Lewis, *Mere Christianity*, 415.
178 Ibid., 386.
179 Lewis, *The Collected Letters of C. S. Lewis: Volume II*, 929 [March 28, 1949].
180 Lewis, *The Magician's Nephew*, 116.

even very feeble attempts at obedience;"[181] "There is an ignorance of evil that comes from being young: there is a darker ignorance that comes from doing it, as men by sleeping lose the knowledge of sleep;"[182] and "Sin may recur because the original temptation continues; but quite apart from that, sin of its very nature breeds sin by strengthening sinful habit and weakening the conscience."[183] Hence, the dwarfs in *The Last Battle* cannot truly see their way out of the barn because they refused to act rightly; Uncle Andrew cannot hear the animals – including Aslan – talking because his heart was hardened ("Now the trouble about trying to make yourself stupider than you really are is that you very often succeed"[184]); and Wither in *That Hideous Strength* "had willed with his whole heart that there should be no reality and no truth, and now even the imminence of his own ruin could not wake him."[185]

I could go on with many more examples, but already I have crossed over into the next chapter, which has to do with ethics, and to which, with confidence that Lewis's psychology, logic and epistemology have been laid out sufficiently, I now turn.

---

181 Lewis, *The Collected Letters of C. S. Lewis: Volume II*, 202 [July 28, 1936].
182 Lewis, *Perelandra*, 335.
183 Lewis, *The Problem of Pain*, 531.
184 Lewis, *The Magician's Nephew*, 117.
185 Lewis, *That Hideous Strength*, 721.

Chapter Eight

Ethics

In previous chapters, I have touched on various aspects of Lewis's moral philosophy. For instance, in chapter two, I mentioned the influence of Morris, Russell and other noble pagans on Lewis's budding moral awareness; in chapter three, there was some talk about the relationship between duty and happiness; in chapters five and six, the Oxford don's Christian understanding of the Fall, hierarchy, justice and Natural Law were discussed; and in chapters three and seven, the theological virtues of hope and faith and the role of the conscience were brought up. However, given the importance of ethics in Lewis's philosophy, a detailed discussion is long overdue.

Since ethics is the branch of Lewis's philosophy perhaps easiest to understand and most commonly associated with his popular apologetics and theology, there have been many studies on this topic; Gilbert Meilaender's *The Taste for the Other: The Social and Ethical Thought of C. S. Lewis* is probably the best of these.[1] Nevertheless, where Meilaender's book and the others come up short is in their insufficient understanding of Lewis's ethical growth and the ethicists with whom the Oxford don grappled. As I have recently pointed out,[2] inattention to, and ignorance of, Lewis's ethical development vis-à-vis

---

1 Gilbert Meilaender, *The Taste of the Other: The Social and Ethical Thought of C. S. Lewis* (Grand Rapids, MI: Eerdmans, 1980).

2 Adam Barkman, "'The Uncreative Spell': St. Augustine and C. S. Lewis on Pride," *CSL: The Bulletin of the New York C. S. Lewis Society* 39, no. 2 (March-April 2008): 1-16. Adam Barkman, "'Made for Infinite Happiness': Boethian Happiness in C. S. Lewis," *Lamp-Post: The Bulletin of the Southern-California C. S. Lewis Society* (Forthcoming). Adam Barkman, "Some Comments about the Future of Lewis Scholarship," *Lamp-Post: The Bulletin of the Southern-California C. S. Lewis Society* 29, no. 3 (Fall 2005): 21-4. Adam Barkman, "'The Shame of Glad Surrender Stood Confessed': C. S. Lewis and Confession," *CSL: The Bulletin of the New York C. S. Lewis Society* 36, no. 4 (July-August 2005): 1-15. Adam Barkman, "Some Ancient Philosophical Sources in C. S. Lewis' Practical Ethics," in *Surprised by Faith: Conversion and the Academy; A Collection of Papers Commemorating the 75th Anniversary of the Conversion of C. S. Lewis,* ed. Daryl McCarthy et al., 161-80 (Cambridge: Cambridge Scholar's Press, 2007).

his critical engagement with authors like Lucretius, Plato, Aristotle, Hume, Kant, Green, Bradley, Boethius and Augustine has led to a distorted view of the Oxford don's philosophy. Consequently, in this chapter, I will emphasize the development of Lewis's ethical theory, and I will do so in the context of two major, though admittedly interrelated, themes: happiness and duty, which mostly have to do with the theoretical, and virtue and vice, which mostly have to do with the practical.

I: Happiness and Duty

Lewis was baptized into Christianity – into Irish Anglicanism – when he was born, and subsequently was taught the rules of the Church and his ethical duties to God. This, Lewis later acknowledged, was a very good thing, for as he mentioned in *The Pilgrim's Regress*, "knowledge of broken law precedes all other religious experiences;"[3] in other words, if he had not been taught his duties to God when he was young, it would have been harder for him to recognize the need for his repentance later on.

However, according to the Oxford don, the flaw of his Christian education lay in the fact that the Church seemed to emphasize *only* duty and *never* happiness. On top of this, Lewis felt that given the great difficulty it took to obey the laws of the Church, the fearful punishments that were constantly emphasized for those who did not do so, and the general hypocrisy of most churchgoers ("'I shouldn't bother about it all too much if I were you,"[4] said the Steward to John), Lewis's attempt to be dutiful to God soon overwhelmed him and subsequently he found some relief in the Epicurean eudaimonian ethics – ethics which aim at happiness *qua* the avoidance of pain and fear – which characterized his Lucretian materialist phase. This is to say that Lewis's earliest years were largely characterized by anxiety, discouragement, hatred and revolt, and the persona he assumed in

Adam Barkman, "Aristotelian Ethics in C. S. Lewis' Philosophy," *CSL: The Bulletin of the New York C. S. Lewis Society* 38, no. 2 (March-April 2007): 1-9. Adam Barkman, "Augustinian Will and Aristotelian *Phronesis* in C. S. Lewis' Theory of Moral Action," *Inklings-Jahrbuch für Literatur und Ästhetik* 24 (2006): 117-42. Adam Barkman, review of *The Collected Letters of C. S. Lewis: Volume III; Narnia, Cambridge and Joy; 1950-1963*, by C. S. Lewis, ed. Walter Hooper, *Christian Scholar's Review* 37, no. 1 (Fall 2007): 117-9. Adam Barkman, review of *The Chronicles of Narnia and Philosophy: The Lion, the Witch and the Worldview*, ed. Gregory Bassham and Jerry L. Walls, *Christian Scholar's Review* 35, no. 4 (Summer 2006): 537-40. Adam Barkman, review of *The Collected Letters of C. S. Lewis: Volume Two; Books, Broadcasts and War; 1931-1949*, by C. S. Lewis, ed. Walter Hooper, *Philosophia Christi* 7, no. 1 (2005): 227-231.

3   Lewis, *The Pilgrim's Regress*, 19.
4   Ibid., 21.

these years was, as I mentioned in chapter four, that of Prometheus or Loki; that is, like Prometheus, who defied Zeus (who "keeps law within his own will"⁵) and was chained to a rock in punishment, or Loki, who defied Odin and was subsequently banished from Asgard, Lewis saw his rebellion against what he perceived to be the enslaving, arbitrary laws of Christianity as a just, romantic struggle; hence, of his poem *Loki Bound*, Lewis wrote: "My Loki was not merely malicious. He was against Odin because Odin had created a world though Loki had clearly warned him that this was a wanton cruelty. Why should creatures have the burden of existence forced on them without their consent?"⁶

While it is clear that Lewis, like his philosophical heroes Lucretius⁷ and (to a lesser extent) Schopenhauer,⁸ saw his ethics in terms of escape from pain and fear (what I call "negative happiness"), the future don largely failed to live in accordance with his own Epicurean eudaimonian ethics, for while his rejection of God and divine command ethics (which says that a person has the duty to obey God's arbitrary will) ought to have liberated him to pursue an unheroic,⁹ tranquil, unemotional ethical life resulting in pleasure *qua* the absence of pain and fear, in fact his adolescent philosophy and ethics were largely a kind of quasi-heroic pessimism, in which the only duty he recognized was just rebellion and the only happiness – not to mention pleasure – he found was in non-moral activities, such as reading. Moreover, while Lewis feared and hated emotion because of his father's emotional outbursts, the abuse he suffered for showing his feelings at school,¹⁰ and his attempted Epicureanism, between his initial fear of God and his subsequent hatred of all duties to Him, there was never – again, paradoxically, given his

---

5   In Aeschylus's *Prometheus Bound*, Lewis read Prometheus say: "Zeus, I know, is ruthless, and keeps law within his own will." Aeschylus *Prometheus Bound* 184-5. Cf. "The truth still holds while Zeus still holds the throne: the one who acts must suffer – that is law." Aeschylus *Agamemnon* 1591-3.

6   Lewis, *Surprised by Joy*, 1309.

7   Lucretius *On the Nature of Things* 860.

8   Arthur Schopenhauer, "On the Vanity of Existence," in *Essays and Aphorisms*, trans. R. J. Hollingdale, 51-4 (London: Penguin, 1970), 54.

9   Adam Barkman, "Was Epicurus a Buddhist? An Examination and Critique of the Theories of Negative Happiness in Buddha and Epicurus," *Ethica: An International Journal for Moral Philosophy* 7, no. 2 (December 2008): 287-94. Cf. "The Epicurean philosophy is . . . not a philosophy of heroes." Fredrick Copleston, *A History of Philosophy: Volume I; Greece and Rome* (New York: Doubleday, 1993), 411.

10   With reference to his rejection of his father's emotional outbursts, Lewis later said of the abuse he suffered at the hands of Robert Capron at Wynyard School: "You will remember that I had already learned to fear and hate emotion; here was fresh reason to do so." Lewis, *Surprised by Joy*, 1262.

philosophy – any phase in Lewis's entire life that was more emotional and tumultuous than that of his Lucreatian materialist days.

Nevertheless, despite explicitly saying that he knew about only divine command ethics, which makes all morality simply the arbitrary command of God, and pragmatic ethics, which makes all morality simply laws of convenience that support a given society,[11] Lewis the Lucreatian materialist read many authors who exposed him not only to the idea that there is a universal moral law not depending on God's arbitrary will, but also to the idea that Goodness is more than mere morality; indeed, many of the authors Lewis read at this time would become some of his favorite ethicists during his later years. For instance, (1) Plato showed the young Lewis that happiness, satisfaction or fulfillment consists in conforming one's life to the moral absolutes, which participate in the Good, which, in its supremacy, is beyond existence, and whose utter opposite, evil, is non-being or nothingness;[12] (2) Samuel Johnson, whose life is recorded in *Life of Johnson*, a book Lewis listed in his top ten influences on his philosophy of life, was another important moralist[13] whom Lewis read very early on and whom Lewis later cited as an important moral figure;[14] (3) book four of Virgil's *Aeneid* gave Lewis a taste for the beauty of moral duty (though it was still, admittedly, a command of the gods) in the form of Aeneas denying his hedonistic desire to stay with Dido in Carthage instead embracing his duty to found New Troy / Rome ("Meanwhile Aeneas the True longed to allay [Dido's] grief and dispel her sufferings with kind words. Yet he remained obedient to the divine command, and with many a sigh, for he was shaken to the depths by the strength of his love, returned to his ships."[15]); (3) *The Odyssey, Beowulf, Sir Gawain and*

---

11   "Hitherto I had always thought there were only two possible views of morals: either, if you believed in a religion, that they were a god-imposed law; or, if you did not, that they were merely rules for convenience – 'The rules of our prison-house' as Blake called them." Lewis, *The Collected Letters of C. S. Lewis: Volume I*, 343 [November 4, 1917].

12   Plato *Republic* 508e.

13   "Mr. Samuel Johnson . . . is one of the best moral writers which England has produced." James Boswell, *Life of Johnson* (London: Oxford University Press), 307 [July 14, 1763].

14   Lewis, "The Poison of Subjectivism," 658.

15   Virgil *The Aeneid* 4.390-5. Cf. "Such was Dido's entreaty; and her poor, unhappy sister carried the tearful messages between them. But all these appeals left Aeneas quite unmoved. He was deaf to every plea, for destiny barred the way and a divine influence checked his inclination to listen kindly. He stood firm like a strong oak-tree toughened by the years when northern winds from the Alps vie together to tear it from the soil, with their blasts striking on it now this side and now that; creaking, the trunk shakes, and leaves from on high strew the ground; yet still the tree grips among the rocks below, for its roots stretch as far down towards the abyss as its crest reaches up to airs of heaven. Like the tree, the hero was battered this side and that by their insistent pleas, and deeply his brave heart grieved. But his will remained unshaken. The tears rolled down, but

the Green Knight, The Works of Sir Thomas Malory, The Faerie Queene, The Countess of Pembroke's Arcadia, Paradise Lost, The Pilgrim's Progress, The Well at the End of the World and other works of mythology and fantasy all provided Lewis with instances of the beauty inherent in the heroic, which is part of the moral law; and (4) although George MacDonald had no moral influence on Lewis at this time, Lewis later credited MacDonald with exposing him to the idea that Goodness is more than moral duty:

> I should have been shocked in my teens if anyone had told me that what I learned to love in *Phantastes* was goodness. But now that I know, I see there was no deception. The deception is all the other way round – in that prosaic moralism which confines goodness to the region of Law and Duty, which never lets us feel in our face the sweet air blowing from 'the land of righteousness,' never reveals that elusive Form which if once seen must inevitably be desired with all but sensuous desire – the thing (in Sappho's phrase) 'more gold than gold.'[16]

But while he was exposed to these important ideas on Goodness, happiness and duty early on, Lewis took many years to fully embrace the truth in all of them.

Nonetheless, when Lewis went off to fight in WWI, he had three ethical experiences which shook his Epicurean eudaimonian – happiness-first – ethics, and propelled him in the *general direction* of deontological – duty-first – ethics, which stress not obedience to God's arbitrary will (divine command ethics), but obedience to *something like* the moral law within.

First, Lewis met fellow soldier Laurence Johnson, who was "moving toward Theism" and who Lewis believed was a man genuinely devoted to doing what is right not because God commanded him to do so, but because he thought it right.[17]

Second, just as Lewis the Lucretian materialist had been exposed to Goodness in MacDonald, so was Lewis the budding pseudo-Manichean dualist charmed by moral goodness when he read some essays by Chesterton:

> Strange as it may seem, I liked [Chesterton] for his goodness. I can attribute this taste to myself freely (even at that age) because it was a liking for goodness which had nothing to do with any attempt to be

---

without effect." Ibid., 440-9.
16   Lewis, preface to *George MacDonald: An Anthology*, xxxiv.
17   Lewis, *Surprised by Joy*, 1354.

good myself. I have never felt that the dislike of goodness which seems to be quite common in better men than me. 'Smug' and 'smugness' were terms of disapprobation which had never had a place in my critical vocabulary. I lacked the cynic's nose, the *odora canum vis* or bloodhound sensitivity for hypocrisy or Pharisaism. It was a matter of taste: I felt the 'charm' of goodness as a man feels the charm of a woman he has no intention of marrying.[18]

Third, Lewis began to see the beauty of morality *qua* morality when, as we discussed in chapter two, he read *William Morris: His Work and Influence*, in which Lewis discovered that morality is not merely an arbitrary divine command, nor simply a set of pragmatic rules set up by society, but rather is a kind of art, the proper performance of which leads to genuine loveliness and uprightness.[19] Although Lewis was probably unaware of it at the time, Morris was a eudaimonist very much like Lewis the Lucretian materialist.[20] Nevertheless, what Lewis took away from Morris was their mutual admiration for Norse mythology, particularly, Lewis the young soldier discovered, the notion of the heroic gods fighting bravely for what is right despite being aware that they will ultimately fail.[21] Although it is difficult to gauge the influence of this manly, non-pessimistic,[22] ethical motif on Morris's ethics, it

---

18   Ibid., 1354.

19   Lewis, *The Collected Letters of C. S. Lewis: Volume I*, 343 [November 4, 1917].

20   "We do not know what we ourselves are or what the world is, nor, if it comes to that, do we know what poetry, or art, or happiness is. One thing is quite certain to me, and that is that our beliefs, whatever they be, whether concerning God, or nature, or art, or happiness, are in the end only of account in so far as they affect the right doings of our lives; so far, in fact, as they make ourselves and our fellows happy." William Morris in M. L. Blumenthal, "William Morris, Heretic Among Socialists," a review of *William Morris and the Early Days of the Socialist Movement*, by J. Bruce Glasier, *The New York Times*, July 24, 1921. Cf. "Morris [is a] Pagan and Hedonist. . . . [He] is more willing to believe that if you are happy you will be good." Holbrook Jackson, *Dreamers of Dreams: The Rise and Fall of 19th Century Idealism* (New York: Farrar, Straus and Co., n.d.), 152.

21   "For one so enamoured of 'the Northernness' these doomed Eddaic gods – the very type of Stoical Romanticism – had a strong appeal." Lewis, "William Morris," 226.

22   In his essay "William Morris," which was written during his Christian phase, Lewis pointed out the beauty of the non-pessimistic ethics of Morris: "Morris has 'faced the facts.' This is the paradox of him. He seems to retire far from the real world and to build a world out of his wishes; but when he has furnished the results stands out as a picture of experience ineluctably true. No full-grown mind wants optimism or pessimism – philosophies of the nursery where they are not philosophies of the clinic; but to have presented in one vision the ravishing sweetness and the heart-breaking melancholy of our experience, to have shown how the one continually passes over into the other, and to have combined all this with a stirring practical creed, this is to have presented the *datum* which all our adventures, worldly and other-worldly alike, must take into

certainly impacted Lewis's beliefs about good and evil, duty and happiness. Consequently, Lewis's Lokian persona slowly began to give way to an identification with the Norse gods in general. Nevertheless, I should add that the destruction of Lewis's Lokian persona was also assisted by Lewis's greater appreciation for the heroics of the common man who fought in the war. In other words, Lewis felt he could no longer withdraw himself into the self-satisfaction of his own mind and the ethics attached with such a proud retreat; rather, he was exposed to many very ordinary men, who, like the Norse gods, fought honestly and heroically for a good higher than the self and the self's concern with freedom from pain.[23]

We can see, then, that Lewis's ethics during his pseudo-Manichean dualist phase began to develop from a fairly selfish, soft and superficial Epicurean eudaimonian ethics, which only focused on the avoidance of pain, into a more deontological ethic that at times seemed excessively ascetic:

> You [Arthur Greeves] accuse me of talking, 'as your own father might talk': and perhaps that is one thing you may find in me now – a vein of asceticism, almost of puritan practice without the puritan dogma. I believe in no God, least of all in one that would punish me for the 'lusts of the flesh': but I do believe that I have in me a spirit, a chip, shall we say, of universal spirit; and that, since all good & joyful things are spiritual & and non-material, I must be careful not to let matter (=nature=Satan, remember) get too great a hold on me, & dull the one spark I have.[24]

Now some might be tempted to see Lewis's new quasi-deontological ethics as coming from his philosophical interest in Berkeley, but this would be a mistake, for Berkeley's ethics, which rejected universals and hence also the existence of a universal moral law, were divine command ethics – ethics no different than those of the church Lewis grew up in. Thus, while we can name many potential sources for Lewis's new theory of ethics – certain elements in Plato and others like him, his wartime friends, certain elements

account." Ibid., 231.

23   During WWI, Lewis said: "I came to know and pity and reverence the ordinary man." Lewis, *Surprised by Joy*, 1356. Also consider the following lines that Lewis wrote during WWI: "Thank God that there are solid folk / Who water flowers and roll the lawn, / And sit and sew and talk and smoke, / And snore all through the summer dawn. / Who pass untroubled nights and days / Full-fed and sleepily content, / Rejoicing in each other's praise, / Respectable and innocent." C. S. Lewis, "In Praise of Solid People," in *Spirits in Bondage: A Cycle of Lyrics*, ed. Walter Hooper (San Diego: Harcourt Brace & Company, 1984), 42 [1-8].

24   Lewis, *The Collected Letters of C. S. Lewis: Volume I*, 379 [June 3, 1918].

in Schopenhauer,[25] Romantic poets with Gnostic leanings, etc. – what we must ultimately conclude is that Lewis's pseudo-Manichean dualist ethics were opposed to eudaimonian ethics, or at least eudaimonian ethics *qua* temporary pleasure, for such ethics, Lewis had come to think, were the symptom of an unmanly, cowardly will – one that could be bribed with feel-good, but ultimately false, answers:

> I *can* feel otherwise about the lusts of the flesh: is not desire merely a kind of sugar-plum that nature gives us to make us breed, as she does the beetles and toads so that both we and they may beget more creatures to struggle in the same net: Nature, or the common order of things, has really produced in man a sort of Frankenstein who is learning to shake her off. For man alone of all things can master his instincts.[26]

And this excessively ascetic quasi-deontological ethic quite naturally developed during Lewis's Stoical materialist phase; however, what is interesting to note is that when Lewis remembered the time between his pseudo-Manichean dualist phase and his Stoical materialist phase, he hardly acknowledged his own moral improvement which occurred during the war; thus he wrote: "When I came first to the University I was nearly without a moral conscience as a boy could be. Some faint distaste for cruelty and for meanness about money was my uttermost reach – of chastity, truthfulness, and self-sacrifice I thought as a baboon thinks of classical music."[27]

In spite of this, Lewis did admit that just as he was positively influenced by moral friends, like Johnson, during the war, so was he also positively influenced by moral friends, such as Barfield, after the war. And by being surrounded by men who looked to the objective moral law for guidance and genuinely tried to be good men, Lewis said that his own morality, and moral theory, began to improve:

> By the mercy of God I fell among a set of young men (none of them, by the way, Christians) who were sufficiently close to me in intellect and imagination to secure immediate intimacy, but who knew, and

25 Although Schopenhauer largely belonged to Lewis's Lucretian materialist phase, the German philosopher's influence on Lewis was multifaceted and it is easy to see an essay like Schopenhauer's "On Ethics" influencing certain elements in Lewis's dualist metaphysics and ethics: "No thinking person can remain in doubt that moral freedom is never to be sought in nature but only outside of nature. It is metaphysical; in the physical world it is impossible." Arthur Schopenhauer, "On Ethics," in *Essays and Aphorisms*, trans. R. J. Hollingdale, 133-47 (London: Penguin, 1970), 142-3.
26 Lewis, *The Collected Letters of C. S. Lewis: Volume I*, 375 [May 29, 1918].
27 Lewis, *The Problem of Pain*, 488.

tried to obey, the moral law. Thus their judgement of good and evil was very different from mine. . . . The new moral judgements never entered the mind as mere reversals (though they do reverse them) of previous judgements. . . . But the test is that the recognition of the new standards is accompanied with the sense of shame and guilt: one is conscious of having blundered into society that one is unfit for.[28]

In addition to moral friends, books played an important part in the development of Lewis's ethics. As we recall from chapter two, during his "New Look" or Stoical materialist phase, Lewis read a lot of philosophy, much of which was for his "Greats" program; in regard to ethics, the future Oxford don read such works as Mill's *Utilitarianism*, Hume's *Treatise of Human Nature* and *Of Morals*, Croce's *Philosophy of the Practical: Economic and Ethic*, Hobbes's *Leviathan*, Cicero's *On Good and Bad Ends*, Bradley's *Ethical Studies*, Plato's *Republic*, Aristotle's *Ethics*, and Kant's *Metaphysics of Morality*. Lewis the Stoical materialist rejected Mill's utilitarian ethics (which says that an action is morally right only if it produces as much utility or happiness as any other action[29]) because Lewis felt that such failed to account for universal moral value; Lewis likewise rejected Hume's sentiment-grounded precursor to utilitarian ethics,[30] for Lewis felt it contained many of the errors of his Lucretian materialist phase: "[I] read Hume's *Of Morals*. This contains nearly all my own fallacies in ethics – which look more fallacious in another person's language;"[31] Lewis thought Croce's eudaimonian, idealist ethics unrealistic,[32] saying in one place that the Italian Philosopher's belief that pain is always a sign an action is not yet fully good is "not . . . ethics for <u>human beings</u> at all;"[33] Lewis had little use for the egoistic, authoritarian ethics of Hobbes, who believed that the laws of nature were essentially dictates of egoistic prudence concerning self-preservation which, when shared

---

28 Ibid.

29 John Stuart Mill, *Utilitarianism*, ed. Geraint Williams (London: J. M. Dent, 1999), 7.

30 David Hume, *An Enquiry Concerning the Principles of Morals*, ed. J. B. Schneewind (Indianapolis: Hackett Publishing, 1983), 16 [1.1]. Cf. "Morality . . . is more properly felt than judged of." David Hume, *A Treatise of Human Nature*, ed. Ernest Mossner (New York: Penguin, 1985), 522 [3.1.2].

31 Lewis, *All My Road Before Me*, 51 [June 18, 1922].

32 "Finally, the theory that *subordinates* pleasure or happiness, utility or economy, to duty, to virtue, to moral activity, is to be rejected." Croce, *Philosophy of the Practical: Economic and Ethic*, 361.

33 Croce wrote, "The good action, as such, always brings with it satisfaction as pleasure, and the pain said to accompany it . . . shows that the action <u>is not altogether good</u>," about which Lewis commented, "In that case you are not writing ethics for <u>human beings</u> at all." C. S. Lewis, marginalia in his edition of *Philosophy of the Practical: Economic and Ethic*, by Benedetto Croce, trans. Douglas Ainslie (London: St. Martin's, 1913), 358.

by enough people (who do not know these laws as absolute), culminates in free surrender to the absolute will of a stable commonwealth;[34] and Lewis, oddly,[35] thought Cicero a dull windbag,[36] whose critique of the ethics of the Epicureans, Stoics and Academics, *On Good and Bad Ends*, "[was] not [a] very inspired work."[37] And while Bradley's ethical theory was important to Lewis during his idealist phases, and Plato's and Aristotle's were important during his theist and Christian phases, Kant's, and to a lesser degree, Plato's, ethics were important during Lewis's Stoical materialist phase. However, while I now want to examine the influence of Kant on Lewis's ethical theory, it is important for us to keep in mind that Lewis's philosophy was always eclectic, meaning, for instance, that he could at once approve of some parts of Croce's aesthetics and also disapprove of his ethics,[38] or value Freud's critique of divine command ethics and also disapprove of the way he justified sexual immorality.[39] Thus, as we examine Kant's ethics – particularly in regard to

---

34   Thomas Hobbes, *Leviathan*, ed. C. B. Macpherson (New York: Penguin, 1985), 189 [1.14]. Cf. Lewis, *Studies in Words*, 62.

35   I find it a bit unusual that at no point in his entire life did Lewis ever really appreciate Cicero, whose high view of ethics – his combination of Stoical, peripatetic and Platonic ethics (Cicero *On Good and Bad Ends* 4.26.43) – should have been attractive to the Oxford don during his Stoical materialist, and certainly during his theist and Christian, phases. The only possible Ciceronian influence I can find on Lewis is Lewis's Great War document entitled *De Bono et Malo*, the title of which the Oxford don likely got from either Cicero's *On Good and Bad Ends / De Finibus Bonorum et Malorum* or Aquinas's *De Bono et Malo*.

36   "I dined the other night at an Italian Professor's, who is a Fellow of Magdalen, and sat next to a Frenchwoman who has met Mussolini. She says he is a rhetorician, and escapes from questions he doesn't want to answer into a cloud of eloquence. I asked if she thought him a charlatan. She said no: he quite believes all his own gas, like a school boy, and is carried away by it himself. It interested me very much as being true to type – Cicero must have been just that sort of man." Lewis, *The Collected Letters of C. S. Lewis: Volume I*, 682 [March 30, 1927].

37   Lewis, *All My Road Before Me*, 66 [July 8, 1922].

38   "After Arnold came the vogue of Croce, in whose philosophy the aesthetic and logical activities were made autonomous forms of 'the spirit' co-ordinate with the ethical." Lewis, "Christianity and Culture," 71. Although this essay was written during Lewis's Christian phase, it could very well have been written during his Stoical materialist phase, for Lewis the Stoical materialist did not think that the aesthetic and the moral were on the same level. As we shall see, the moral was always higher for Lewis.

39   Concerning Sophocles's *Oedipus Rex*, Freud wrote: "For fundamentally it is an amoral work: it absolves men from moral responsibility, exhibits the gods as promoters of crime and shows the impotence of the moral impulses of men which struggle with crime. . . . [But] the difficulty is overcome by the pious sophistry that to bow to the will of the gods is the highest morality even when it promotes crime." Freud, *Introductory Lectures on Psychoanalysis*, 374 [3.21]. While Lewis agreed with Freud in rejecting Sophocles's divine command ethics and the notion that the will of the gods is the highest morality, Lewis was more hesitant when Freud wrote the following: "It is true

happiness, duty and the moral law – we should try to see in what sense Lewis the Stoical materialist should be called a Kantian in regard to ethics and in what sense he should not.

Kant, like Lewis, was brought up in the spirit of the pietist and puritan movement. Although Kant had reverence for God and called himself a Christian, his approach to religion was almost exclusively through the consciousness of moral obligation. The reason for this is complicated, but it is worth examining.

Moved by Hume's critique of causality, which maintained that we can never prove causality through empirical means (which Hume thought were the only means to knowledge), Kant proposed a "Copernican Revolution," which stated that objects conform to the human mind instead of the other way around.[40] Since the structure of the human mind is constant, objects always appear to it in certain ways. Because of this, people can make universal scientific judgments, which are good for both actual and possible experience.

However, while Kant agreed with philosophers like Plato, saying that there are certain universal principles, such as those of the moral law, which reason derives from within itself, he claimed that these principles can only be known on occasion of experience. A child, in other words, is not born with the ideas of morality; rather, when a child experiences a certain situation, reason derives the moral truths from within itself. These principles, in particular those of morality, are *a priori* concepts in the sense that they are not derived from experience but are applied to and in a sense govern experience: "That all our knowledge begins with experience there can be no doubt. . . . But though all our knowledge begins *with* experience, it does not follow that it all arises *out of* experience."[41]

---

we are not reformers but merely observers; nevertheless, we cannot help observing with a critical eye and we have found it impossible to side with conventional sexual morality or to form a very high opinion of the manner in which society attempts the practical regulation of the problems of sexual life. We can present society with a blunt calculation that what is described as its morality calls for a bigger sacrifice than it is worth and that its proceedings are not based on honesty and do not display wisdom." Ibid., 485 [3.27]. The reason why Lewis was fairly skeptical of sexuality in general and non-traditional sexuality in particular was because, at least during his pseudo-Manichean dualist phase, he started to associate sexuality, instincts and the body with evil, hence his earlier comment: "I *can* feel otherwise about the lusts of the flesh: is not desire merely a kind of sugar-plum that nature gives us to make us breed, as she does the beetles and toads so that both we and they may beget more creatures to struggle in the same net."

40   Kant, *Critique of Pure Reason*, 110 [BXVi].
41   Ibid., 136 [B1].

C.S. Lewis & Philosophy as a Way of Life

When Kant called moral judgments *a priori*, he meant that they were *synthetic a priori* judgments; and by this he meant two things. First, moral judgments are *synthetic* in that the predicate of a proposition is not already contained in the concept of the subject, for instance, to say that "all bodies are heavy" is synthetic (and not analytic) since the idea of heaviness is not contained in the concept of body as such.[42] Second, moral judgments are *a priori* since the truth of a claim such as "it is wrong to lie" is always true regardless of experience and time; it is a universal truth and not merely a generalization.

Now since all our knowledge, even *a priori* truths, are known on the occasion of experience, people cannot have theoretical knowledge of realities which are not given in sense-experience or which are incapable of being so given; consequently, supersensible reality is not open to people as an object of theoretical knowledge, and so God, the soul's immortality etc. are beyond proof or disproof.[43] Thus, Kant believed his criticism of metaphysics opened the way for practical or moral faith, which rests solely on the moral consciousness and practical reason and not on any specific metaphysics or theology.

Thus, whereas theoretical reason is directed towards knowledge, practical reason is directed towards choice in accordance with the moral law. And while this may sound almost Aristotelian, the major difference between Kant and Aristotle is that whereas the German Philosopher thought the moral law arose in reason on occasion of experience but not from experience, the Greek Philosopher said that reason abstracts the truths of the moral law *from* the particular experience and then re-applies the universals as judgment according to the particular circumstance.

Yet what is fundamental to Kant's ethics is his deontology. That is, Kant believed that any form of eudaimonian ethic (which makes the desire for happiness prior to duty to the moral law) a corrupt ethic. The German Philosopher believed the only unqualified good in the world was the good will, for only the good will acts purely out of duty for duty's sake, which Kant took to be the sign of a genuine moral act: "The greatest perfection of a human being is to do his duty *from duty*."[44] Of course, this means that an act is moral not simply if it acts in accordance with the moral law, but only if it acts for the sake of the moral law.

---

42 Ibid., 142 [B11].
43 Ibid., 117 [BXXX].
44 Kant, *The Metaphysics of Morals*, 523 [6:392].

One of the consequences of this was that Kant apparently believed that the less inclination or desire people have to perform certain moral obligations, the more ethical the acts are when they are actually performed. This, of course, put Kant squarely at odds with the eudaimonist tradition going back to Plato and especially Aristotle, who said that the better we become, the more we enjoy acting morally. Thus, while Plato and Aristotle would have agreed with Kant that the moral law or Right Reason is universal – indeed, while they likely would have approved of Kant's categorical imperative, which states that a person should "act upon a maxim [i.e. a subjective principle of volition] that can also hold as a universal law"[45] – Plato and Aristotle would have thought it impossible for Kant to act solely for duty's sake and hence with anything like a "pure" will.

As for Kant's influence on Lewis, there are arguments both for and against, though I believe the arguments for are stronger.

First, James Patrick has argued that although we no longer have a copy of Lewis's 1922 essay "Hegemony of Moral Value," we are justified in seeing this essay as a critique of Kantian, utilitarian and Platonic ethics since according to Patrick, this essay was largely the foundation for the lectures on moral philosophy that Lewis gave in 1924, the outline for which looks as follows: "1. Introductory – Theory of Values (Empirical Study), 2. Objectivity of Value, 3. Statement of Problem, 4. Same Continued, 5. Philebus & Republic, 6. Critique, 7. Utilitarian Ethics, 8. Critique, 9. Kantian Ethics, 10. Critique, 11. Fundamental errors of both these theories, 12. Practical Hegemony of the Moral Value, 13. Basis of Obligation, 14. Summary."[46] While we do know that Lewis's 1922 "Hegemony of Moral Value" differentiated between

---

45 Ibid., 379 [6:225].

46 C. S. Lewis, "Hegemony of Moral Value Outline" (Unpublished notes [1924]; Marion E. Wade Center, Wheaton College), 1. Hegemony means dominance or supremacy, hence, "Hegemony of Moral Values" could also be called "The Supremacy of Moral Values" or even "The Supremacy of the Universal Moral Law." Cf. James Patrick, "The Heart's Desire and the Landlord's Rules: C. S. Lewis as a Moral Philosopher," in *The Pilgrim's Guide: C. S. Lewis and the Art of Witness*, ed. David Mills, 70-85 (Grand Rapids, MI: William B. Eerdmans, 1998), 70.

morality and ethics,[47] discussed Kantian ethics, argued against hedonism,[48] and agreed with Plato[49] that "no pleasure could be considered bad, considered in itself."[50] Patrick is probably stretching it when he says that this essay was largely unchanged in subsequent years, for between 1922 and 1924, Lewis underwent a philosophical shift, converting from materialism to idealism. In addition, Patrick shows imprecision when he asserts that the Lewis of the 1922 "Hegemony of Moral Value" was "a convinced eudaemonist,"[51] for during Lewis's Stoical materialist phase, Lewis appears to have explicitly denied eudaimonism, saying of a conversation he had with his friend: "I agreed with him that most of us could find positive Satanic badness down there somewhere, the desire for evil not because it was pleasant but because it was evil."[52] Moreover, Patrick's denial that Lewis was once a Kantian in

47   "A word on the point of view. Meaning of Ethics. Various notions. The 'study of moral conduct' might mean an objective empirical study – a branch of anthropology. W[oul]d enquire what psychological facts of the moral order are actually to be found in different races etc. I endeavour to account for them as evolutionary products & the like. This not what we call ethics. In ethics we find questions as to what we mean by right. What is the standard: why ought we to do it. Difference between ethics illustrated by example. Science of sound as branch of physics (Theory of Music). But theory of music also different from a normative work from budding composers. In the same way ethics are different from moralizing." Lewis, "Hegemony of Moral Value Outline," 2.

48   "I tried to get on with my dissertation, having finished my attack on Hedonism and arrived at Kant." Lewis, *All My Road Before Me*, 96 [August 30, 1922].

49   In *Republic*, but especially in *Philebus*, Plato argued that most pleasures accompany pain and therefore are not good in and of themselves; however, Plato insisted that "the *pleasantness* of pleasures is not in dispute." Plato *Philebus* 13a-b.

50   "All morning I sat in the dining room and worked on my dissertation, trying to prove that no pleasure could be considered bad, considered in itself. I found it necessary to descend into pathology and rather doubt if I have done wisely." Lewis, *All My Road Before Me*, 98 [September 1, 1922]. Although this comment may *prima facie* appear to be against the Kantian notion that the only unqualified good is the good will, Kant, as Lewis noted in his 1925 annotations in his edition of *Critique of Practical Reason*, did not deny that there were other good things: "[Kant] argues that gifts and talents cannot be good without qualification (a) because, without good will, they may be mischievous: i.e. Dangerous or unfelicific. But so may the good will without knowledge. Therefore either it is not good without qualification, or things can be good without qualification even tho[ugh] they can, if circumstances demand, become 'pernicious.' (b) because, without good will, they do not satisfy an impartial spectator. But they dissatisfy us only qua undeserved. Now if nothing but the good will is good how can the good will deserve anything but more of itself? For surely 'what the good will deserves' = something really good. I.e. if you deny the idea of merit, the bad man's prosperity ought not to dissatisfy us. If you admit the idea of merit, then other things must be good beside the good will. But he doesn't mean that the good will is the only or whole good (see p. 12)." Lewis, marginalia in his edition of *Critique of Practical Reason*, n.8.

51   Patrick, *The Magdalen Metaphysicals*, 127.

52   Lewis, *All My Road Before Me*, 191 [February 5, 1923]. This comment, however, *may* have been more rhetorical than philosophical.

regard to ethics is based on *The Pilgrim's Regress*, in which, Patrick correctly observes, Vertue is eventually shown the need for desire, but also in which, as Patrick failed to notice, Vertue is depicted as *originally* having been a Stoic or Kantian who came to see the need for desiring happiness; thus, if Vertue in some measure represents Lewis's ethical journey, then it is likely that Lewis was at one time a Kantian or Stoic like Vertue.

Second, it is true that Lewis probably felt some discomfort with the Kantian implication that the good man does not enjoy performing his moral duty; for instance, in his annotations in his edition of Kant's *Critique of Practical Reason*, Lewis wrote:

> It is certain that we sh[oul]d all prefer a society where all the actions of the members flowed spontaneously from natural love to a society of misanthropes always treating each other well from a pure sense of duty. It is very hard to treat this as a purely hedonistic reference. On the other hand we <u>do</u> really attribute more moral value to a reformed drunkard for refraining from drink than to a <u>naturally</u> temperate man or to the coward who forces himself to stand than to the <u>naturally</u> brave man. In short it seems to be only in this special case (i.e. of the naturally benevolent and dutifully beneficent) that we feel any great difficulty in K[ant]'s distinction. Perhaps 'love,' in this sense, cannot really be a mere πάθος [*pathos*] like natural courage?[53]

Nevertheless, it must be added that this objection or concern about Kantian ethics was only expressed in 1925, when Lewis was already an idealist, and it only took root in 1931, when he became a Christian, and so it would be wrong to give it too much weight as an argument against a Kantian influence during Lewis's Stoical materialist phase.

Third, although Lewis likely learned about the distinction between loving something disinterestedly or for its own sake and loving something "interestedly" or as a means to an end from Aristotle, Lewis also found this principle in Kant, and since it was a distinction that Lewis made quite a bit of use of, we could also see this, if we were so inclined, as another potential Kantian influence.[54] Indeed, even the lesson Lewis learned from Jenkin

---

53 Lewis, marginalia in his edition of *Critique of Practical Reason*, lv.
54 Of *Dymer* being published, Lewis wrote: "But I cannot say simply that I desire not my fame but that of the poem. In the impossible case of an exactly similar poem written by someone else and winning success I should be very far from content. Though no one else need know that the approved poem is mine, I at least must know it. The feeling is not, therefore, a disinterested love for Dymer simply as a poem I happen to like." Lewis, *The Collected Letters of C. S. Lewis: Volume I*, 928 [March 6, 1926].

about trying to enjoy the quiddity of everything[55] – i.e. enjoying each thing as an end – was a lesson that Lewis had theoretically already learned from Aristotle and Kant.

Fourth, while Lewis's 1921 essay "Optimism" was clearly influenced by the non-pessimistic,[56] stoical spirit of the Norse gods – who implied that true freedom is willed necessity – it is also possible to see this essay as reflective of the Kantian choice to will duty for duty's sake, regardless of personal happiness.[57] Indeed, this seems to have become clearer in subsequent years, for while the Norse gods and Morris could merely provide Lewis with the impulse to reject the "carrot of immortality," they could not provide him with a universal ethic that secured his belief that his "moral judgement was 'valid.'"[58] Patrick appears to have thought that Lewis's Stoical materialist belief that our moral judgment is valid is from Plato and not Kant. While I agree with Patrick that Plato's ethical theory influenced "Hegemony of Moral Values" (Lewis spoke of "sit[ting] under the one tree in our tiny strip

---

55 Lewis, *Surprised by Joy*, 1359.

56 Lewis's non-pessimistic attitude was similar to that of Bertrand Russell, who wrote, "The slave is doomed to worship Time and Fate and Death, because they are greater than anything he finds in himself, and because all his thoughts are of things which they devour. But, great as they are, to think of them greatly, to feel their passionless splendour, is greater still. And such thought makes us free men; we no longer bow before the inevitable in Oriental subjection, but we absorb it and make it a part of ourselves. To abandon the struggle for private happiness, to expel all eagerness of temporary desire, to burn with passion for eternal things – this is emancipation, and this is the free man's worship. . . . United with his fellow men by the strongest of all ties, the tie of a common doom, the free man finds that a new vision is with him always, shedding over every daily task the light of love." Russell, "A Free Man's Worship," 114-5. Indeed, Lewis himself later said that when one realizes that there is no point in cursing the heavens, one ceases to be a pessimist: "When once one had dropped the absurd notion that reality is an arbitrary alternative to 'nothing,' one gives up being a pessimist (or even an optimist). There is no sense in blaming or praising the Whole, nor, indeed, in saying anything about it. Even if you persist in hurling Promethean or Haryesque defiances at it, then, since you are part of it, it is only the same Whole which through you 'quietly declaims the cursings of itself' – a futility which seems to me to vitiate Lord Russell's stirring essay on 'The Worship of a Free Man.' . . . One must . . . 'accept' the universe; totally, with no reservations, loyally." Lewis, *Surprised by Joy*, 1362. Yet despite Lewis's theoretical rejection of pessimism during his Stoical materialist phase, he was still haunted by the ghost of Schopenhauer from time to time: "Like me, [Barfield] has no belief in immortality etc., and always feels the materialistic pessimism at his elbow." Lewis, *All My Road Before Me*, 40 [May 24, 1922].

57 "The positive concept of freedom is that of the ability of pure reason to be of itself practical. But this is not possible except by the subjection of the maxim of every action to the condition of its qualifying as universal law." Kant, *The Metaphysics of Morals*, 375 [6:214].

58 Lewis, *Surprised by Joy*, 1364.

of garden and read a little of the good Plato"[59]), it is also clear that Kant and Plato would have agreed that there is a universal ethic; the difference between the two philosophers was a difference of metaphysical grounding or the lack thereof – not of ethical content or subsequent duty. Thus, based solely on the argument that "Hegemony of Moral Value" was a defense of the universal moral law, it is hard to argue that Lewis was not a Kantian. Indeed, given Lewis the Stoical materialist's likely rejection of eudaimonism and his disbelief in the Platonic metaphysics that ground morality (not to mention the comment of one of his examiners who said that Lewis thought "Plato is always wrong"[60]), Lewis was almost certainly more Kantian than Platonic; consequently, I believe we can see the following as an example of a Kantian expansion on the ethics of the Norse gods:

> I said I had lately been suffering from *timor mortis conturbat me* ['The fear of death is troubling me"]: Jenkin was in the same state – the suffocating feeling. He also said his great trouble was to know which is the real ideal. Was one to crush the physical desires altogether – to be pagan or puritan? He added however that he had a fear of knowing the real ideal for certain – it might be a startler. I was much interested in this. . . . [Jenkin] asked whether one ought to think about Death or put it out of one's mind: since we could never find out what it meant. I said one wanted to go on thinking about it till one reached a point of view from which it didn't matter whether you were immortal or not. One wanted to find a value wh[ich] was quite full in one moment and independent of time.[61]

Consequently, we can see that although Patrick has given us some reasons to question Lewis's debt to Kant and although Robert Houston Smith is partially correct when he says that Lewis "did not bother to master" the thought of Kant,[62] I believe the future Oxford don largely adopted Kantian ethics during his Stoical materialist phase; thus, if we overlook his non-pessimism, we may reasonably see Lewis during this time as a budding Kirkpatrick, who, we recall, was "like some ancient Stoic standing fast in the Roman decadence."[63]

59   Lewis, *The Collected Letters of C. S. Lewis*, 533 [March 18, 1921].
60   Lewis, *All My Road Before Me*, 53 [June 21, 1922].
61   Ibid., 141 [November 21, 1922]. Cf. "After breakfast . . . [I] did a Philosophy paper. I think I put in some good work on the importance of Time to ethics and on generalization: but my answer to the Kant question was uneven and I foolishly wrote a lot of poor pudding about Pragmatism." Ibid., 109 [September 27, 1922].
62   Robert Houston Smith, *Patches of Godlight: The Pattern of Thought of C. S. Lewis* (Athens, GA: University of Georgia Press, 1981), 22.
63   Lewis, *The Collected Letters of C. S. Lewis: Volume I*, 535 [March 28, 1921].

However, already back in 1922, the seeds of Lewis's next ethical phase – idealist ethics – were planted: "I believe a modern poem about [the] Ultimate must not be, like *Paradise Lost*, about good and evil but must exhibit what Hegel calls dialectic."[64] Although Lewis did not embrace idealism for at least another full year after writing this, it is clear that he was trying to make sense of idealism and its ethics, which dominated Oxford at the time. When Lewis finally converted from (Stoical) materialism to idealism, he said he did so because Barfield – who had himself recently converted to Anthroposophy, possibly due to eudaimonian promises of immortality[65] – had shown him that, among other things, absolute moral values could not be grounded in materialism since materialism says that all things are physical and temporary, which is to say that nothing – even the moral law – is eternal and absolute.

Almost as soon as Lewis became an idealist (the differences between the types of which is not very important for our discussion of ethics), Lewis began researching the philosophy of Cambridge Platonist Henry More, whose ethics, interestingly, did not influence Lewis at all. Shortly after this, Lewis wrote his essay "The Promethean Fallacy in Ethics," in which he attempted to critique Bertrand Russell's ethical position as laid out in "The Worship of a Free Man."[66] Russell's position, we recall, was more or less the same as Lewis's during his pseudo-Manichean dualist and Stoical materialist phases, which is to say that both Russell and Lewis had argued for the autonomous individual freely willing the dictates of Fate and thus overcoming Fate's tyranny. As an idealist, Lewis's problem with this position was that both his earlier self and Russell did not understand that if materialism is true, then *everything* is a part of the Whole, and thus it is nonsense to talk about people willing Fate as if people could somehow stand outside of the Whole and do otherwise; of Russell, Lewis wrote: "He does not face the real difficulty – that our ideals are after all a natural product, facts with a relation to all other facts, and cannot survive the condemnation of the fact as a Whole. The Promethean attitude would be tenable only if we were really members of some other whole outside the real whole: wh[ich] we are not."[67] Lewis's idealist understanding helped him to see that it is pointless to defy Fate and the whole; rather, he believed that any true ethic must take into account, and appreciate the fact, that Reality is one even if Appearances are many.

---

64   Lewis, *All My Road Before Me*, 112 [October 2, 1922].
65   Ibid., 254 [July 7, 1923].
66   Ibid., 282 [January 8, 1924].
67   Ibid., 281 [January 5, 1924].

Thus, Lewis's early idealist position was that while everything is ultimately one large spiritual Reality, the moral law, which dictates right and wrong (but, *pace* Arthur Balfour, is not necessarily connected to religion[68]), still exists and is valuable. That is, Lewis both agreed with the idealists that ethics need to be grounded in spiritual Reality and he continued to maintain with Kant – as is evident in Lewis's 1924 revision of "Hegemony of Moral Value" – that the moral law is important and must be obeyed:

> Pasley denounced me as an *a priori* philosopher who made human institutions subservient to my internal notions of right and wrong: but of course it took only a familiar bit of argument to show him that he did the same. I was forced to admit that the pleasure we took in action was, other things being equal, the less the temptation the greater the crime.[69]

And it is with these loosely connected ethical ideas in mind that Lewis approached the lectures he delivered when he was teaching philosophy at University College, Oxford. As we recall, the first set of lectures focused on "The Good – Its Place Among the Values" and the second set of lectures focused on "The Moral Good – Its Place Among the Values." In his lectures on "The Good" – which, as I mentioned in chapter four, are mislabeled "The Moral Good – Its Place Among the Values" by Wheaton College[70] – Lewis the idealist summarized and commented on *certain* ethical claims by Locke, Hume and Berkeley (sadly, the sections on Kant are missing). For the sake of

---

68 Although Arthur Balfour's *Theism and Humanism* later became one of the most important influences on Lewis's philosophical thought, during Lewis's early idealist phase, the Oxford don read Balfour's book while doing research for his essay "The Promethean Fallacy in Ethics" and subsequently "reject[ed] the kind of solution offered in [it]." Ibid., 283 [January 9, 1924]. The kind of solution – i.e. the ethical solution – Balfour offered was that "at no time has the mass of mankind treated morals and religion as mutually independent." Balfour, *Theism and Humanism*, 59. That is, while Lewis the idealist agreed with Balfour that moral values cannot be maintained if their origin is purely naturalistic, Lewis the idealist did not want to make a strong link between the moral law and religion.

69 Lewis, *All My Road Before Me*, 290 [February 24, 1924]. Shortly after this, Lewis spoke – in very Kantian terms – of his "antinomy of practical reason." Ibid., 304 [March 13, 1924].

70 As I mentioned in chapter four, Wheaton College has mislabelled "The Good – Its Place Among the Values" "The Moral Good – Its Place Among the Values." Again, there are two reasons why Wheaton's labelling system is mistaken. First, the lecture notes that Wheaton has called "The Moral Good" are dated "1924," but as Walter Hooper has indicated in *All My Road Before* (page 348), the lectures that Lewis delivered in 1924 were "The Good" not "The Moral Good." Second, the content of the lectures at Wheaton are not primarily concerned with ethics; hence, it is unlikely that they would be called "The Moral Good."

seeing Lewis the philosopher at work, I want to examine Lewis's summary and critique of these philosophers and their ideas on duty and happiness (insofar as Lewis touched on them).

As for his lectures on Locke, Lewis began with a quotation from *An Essay Concerning Human Understanding*: "But what Duty is, cannot be understood without a Law; nor a law be known or supposed without a law maker, or without reward and punishment."[71] Following this quotation, Lewis summarized Locke thus:

> Nor are there innate moral principles, tho[ugh] there are the innate tendencies to seek pleasure and avoid pain. We see that no moral law is universally recognized for true: indeed to become capable of truth or falsehood it w[oul]d have to [have] the proposition: 'It is ones duty to' and duty is meaningless without a lawgiver & rewards & punishments – wh[ich] are certainly not innate ideas. Lord Herbert's list of innate moral truths (v. his De Veritate) is a complete failure, involving a petitio. The most opposite principles come to seem innate to different men, thus the influence of early, and therefore unremembered, inculcation.[72]

While Lewis agreed with Locke that a duty cannot be understood apart from a law and while Lewis had come to recognize the need for some sort of metaphysical grounding for the moral law, Lewis neither believed in the law maker as Locke understood it – i.e. the God of Christianity – nor did Lewis agree that reward and punishment (save for the reward of finding one's true self) be important considerations in ethics.[73] Moreover, although Lewis felt there was some merit in Locke's critique of innate ideas, Lewis the Kantian (using arguments from Leibniz) still believed that the moral law could be known *a priori* on the occasion of experience:

> This part of Locke's work may be regarded as good polemic against the traditional doctrine [of innate ideas]. Where it fails is in recognition of the need which that doctrine was attempting, tho[ugh] clumsily enough, to satisfy. Leibniz, in his reply to Locke, comes much nearer to realizing the true issue – namely, the difference in kind between empirical and a priori truth. Our implicit knowledge of certain truths,

---

71   John Locke, *An Essay Concerning Human Understanding*, ed. Roger Woolhouse (New York: Penguin, 1997), 64 [1.2.12]. Lewis, "The Moral Good – Its Place Among the Values," 6.

72   Ibid., 8.

73   That is, Lewis did not agree with what he perceived to be Locke's quasi-hedonism, which the Oxford don summarized thus: "Good = Pleasure. Moral Good = action whose conformity to some draws upon a good from the lawmaker." Ibid., 11.

argues Leibniz, is not the same as a faculty simply of knowing them, but as a faculty of knowing them in a particular way. For Leibniz, the doctrine of innate ideas can be restated in a much less objectionable form than that which Locke had attacked. . . . Our mind is so constructed that it can generate certain truths from its own resources. It is true, as Locke says, that experience must furnish us with the ideas which make the matter of knowledge and that no knowledge is prior to experience. But this does not mean that knowledge is derived from experience: on the contrary while experience gives us objects to know it is our own resources that enable us to know them. In this point Leibniz is certainly in advance of Locke. Leibniz – in our modern language – regards knowledge as a co-operation of mind and things: Locke endeavours to deduce all knowledge from experience and leaves to the mind the passive role of simply seeing what is given. This attempt leads to two opposite kinds of errors. We find Locke, on the one hand, trying to read into 'mere' experience things that mere experience cannot give: and, on the other hand, treating as mere fictions of the mind that which is really an essential part of our knowledge of reality.[74]

As for other matters of Lockian ethics, Lewis likely agreed with the Englishman that (1) "Man is not free 'to will or not to will' for he must always 'will either A or Not-A,'"[75] (2) "It is the continuity of self consciousness that makes the Person or Self . . . the seat of moral responsibility,"[76] and (3) "Moral relations are between actions & some rule to wh[ich] actions are referred."[77]

As for his lectures on Hume, Lewis summarized the Scottish Philosopher's views on duty and happiness thus:

Since morality has an influence on the passions, and reason has no influence on the passions, the rules of morality cannot be the conclusions of Reason. Again, reason can prove only truth or falsehood: but our volitions and actions can neither be true nor false. The only sense in wh[ich] an act may be unreasonable is the sense of 'being founded on a mistake of fact' wh[ich] plainly does not make it immoral. Reasonableness & the reverse admit of no degrees: rightness & wrongness do. Nor can we save 'rational ethics' by saying that immorality is a mistake or right: for this supposes an existing right to be judged by reason, independent of the j[u]dgm[e]nts we make about it: and they, not it, w[oul]d be reasonable or unreasonable. Again, if

---

74 Ibid., 24-5.
75 Ibid., 10.
76 Ibid., 11.
77 Ibid.

morality were demonstrable by reason it must be either a matter of fact or a relation. But <u>what</u> relation? Even if we knew this, we sh[oul]d still have to prove how a relation can affect the will as obligation. Again the very same <u>relation</u> (e.g. incest) wh[ich] is wrong in man is right in beasts: if you say it is innocent in the beast <u>because</u> he 'knows no better' you are putting the morality in something outside the relation. The irrationality might hinder a beast from seeing right but c[oul]d not hinder right from existing – if it were really a relation. . . . The perceptions of moral good & evil are, then, impressions or <u>feelings</u> of pleasure and pain, 'of a particular kind,' wh[ich] we experience in character & action. To feel <u>such</u> pleasure & pain is to feel a character to be good or bad. Not <u>every</u> pleasure wh[ich] a character gives us is moral: 'only what we get when it' is considered in general without reference to our particular interest. Ethics, therefore, has only to ask <u>why</u> certain kinds of actions, considered in this way, give us uneasiness or pleasure.[78]

Although Lewis's critique of Hume's philosophy was very extensive, the Oxford don did not say anything in his lecture notes about Hume's rejection of "rational ethics." However, marginalia in the Oxford don's edition of Hume's *Treatise of Human Nature* reveal that Lewis the idealist thought that Hume, like Russell, had committed "The Promethean Fallacy in Ethics;" thus, for instance, Lewis underlined the following in Hume – "<u>All beings in the universe, considered in themselves, appear entirely loose and independent of each other</u>" – after which the Oxford don commented: "His fundamental error."[79] In other words, as an idealist who believed everything is connected and as an *a priori* philosopher in regard to ethics, Lewis could not accept the radical individualism and sentiment-grounded ethics of Hume. Nevertheless, Lewis did (oddly, as we shall see) praise Hume for his "great merit" in regard to pointing out the "distinction between the *is* and the *ought*."[80]

As for his lectures on Berkeley, Lewis said next to nothing about the Bishop's ethics – that is, apart from his critique of Berkeley's nominalism. However, because Lewis was metaphysically a subjective idealist when he prepared these lectures, it is well worth noting that Lewis showed almost no affinity to Berkeley in regard to ethics. There are two reasons for this. First, though a subjective idealist, Lewis was never happy with Berkeley's rejection of universals and hence the universal moral law. Second, Lewis was

78   Ibid., 50.

79   C. S. Lewis, marginalia in his edition of *A Treatise of Human Nature*, by David Hume, vol. 2 (London: J. M. Dent & Sons, 1911; The Marion E. Wade Center, Wheaton College), 174 [3.1.1].

80   Lewis, "The Moral Good – Its Place Among the Values," 59.

opposed to Berkeley's divine command theory, which maintained that things are moral because of God's arbitrary will. Given these two factors, it is only fair to conclude that Lewis's ethical theory throughout his idealist phases was probably more absolute idealist than subjective idealist.

That is, we know that Lewis had read the major ethical works of the major British absolute idealists (i.e. Green's *Prolegomena to Ethics*, Bradley's *Ethical Studies* and Bosanquet's *Suggestions in Ethics*) in or before 1924 – in other words, when Lewis first converted to idealism.[81] However, since Lewis rarely mentioned Bosanquet's ethics after first reading about them,[82] it is likely that Green's and Bradley's ethics were the dominate *idealist* influences on the ethics of Lewis's idealist phase. Thus, in order to help us understand to what extent Lewis the idealist borrowed from the ethical theories of Green and Bradley and to what extent he remained a Kantian and an original thinker, it is worth briefly examining the ethical theories of Green and Bradley.

Green owed a lot to the revival of Greek thought at Oxford in the latter half of the nineteenth century; in particular, the eudaimonian, self-perfection ethics of Plato and Aristotle helped move Green away from the hedonism and utilitarianism which dominated the day.[83] Yet despite the influence of Plato and Aristotle, Green's ethics were also shaped by German idealism, especially that of Hegel. Thus, Green agreed with Plato and Aristotle both that man desires happiness *qua* self-realization above all else and that this is achieved through correct moral action; however, as a typical absolute idealist, Green understood self-realization or happiness not only to be true freedom (i.e. the freedom that comes from concrete obedience to the moral law and the Eternal Consciousness) but also to be the state in which finite minds or spirits realize their true natures *as* the Eternal Consciousness.[84] Nevertheless, it must be insisted that as with Plato and Aristotle, Green believed that such

81 Although I can find no record of it, George Sayer claimed that Lewis read (presumably) the first edition of Bradley's *Ethical Studies* before 1922. Sayer, *Jack*, 162. We know from Lewis's diary that the Oxford don read Bosanquet's *Suggestions in Ethics* in May 1924 (i.e. before Lewis began lecturing on "The Good"). Lewis, *All My Road Before Me*, 323 [May 15, 1924]. And the marginalia in his edition of Green's *Prolegomena to Ethics* indicate that Lewis read this book in December 1924 (i.e. after Lewis finished his lectures on "The Good" but before he started his lectures on "The Moral Good").

82 The only other mention of Bosanquet (and presumably his ethics) is in *The Pilgrim's Regress*, where "Bernard" praises the wine of "Mother Kirk." Lewis, *The Pilgrim's Regress*, 145.

83 T. H. Green, *Prolegomena to Ethics*, ed. A. C. Bradley (1834 reprint; New York: Thomas Y. Crowell, 1969), 169 [3.1.163].

84 John Skorupski, "Green and the Idealist Conception of a Person's Good," in *T. H. Green: Ethics, Metaphysics, and Political Philosophy*, ed. Maria Dimova-Cookson and W. J. Mander, 47-75 (Oxford: Clarendon Press, 2006), 50.

self-realization and self-transcendence can only be effectively achieved in a society where "each has primarily to fulfill the duties of his station;"[85] indeed, Green went beyond Plato and Aristotle by insisting that right moral action consists in contributing to a good common to all individuals: "a good for which there can be *no competition*."[86]

Following Green, Plato and Aristotle, Bradley believed that the end of morality is happiness *qua* "self-realization;"[87] moreover, with Green, Bradley believed that such happiness, self-realization or true freedom can only be achieved when a person identifies his private will with the universal will, which is the will of society or abstract moral law made *concrete* in the laws of society. Hence, he thought that the moral law is given content by being made concrete in the laws of society, and also that morality becomes relative to the society and indeed relative to the person in society since each person has his duties which he must perform given his place or station in the larger organism.[88] Nevertheless, Bradley did not want to say – though it is not clear how he could say otherwise – that morality is mere social conformity, for he believed that individuals in society can critique the laws of society. While this may seem contradictory given that such a critique seems to presuppose an abstract moral law, Bradley said that such antinomies – indeed, all of good and evil – are the stuff of morality and the world of Appearances, which is ultimately transcended in Reality.[89] In addition to all this, Bradley thought that total determinism and total indeterminism were fatal to ethics, for man must both be free (*contra* determinism) and remain himself (*contra* indeterminism) in order to be held responsible for his actions.[90] Related to this, he also argued against both the Kantian ethics of duty for duty's sake, saying that such are too abstract and formal,[91] and utilitarian or hedonist ethics,

---

85   Green, *Prolegomena to Ethics*, 192 [3.2.183].
86   Ibid.
87   Bradley, *Ethical Studies*, 125.
88   Ibid., 180.
89   Bradley, *Appearance and Reality*, 197.
90   Bradley, *Ethical Studies*, 12.
91   "So we see 'duty for duty's sake' says only, 'do the right for the sake of the right;' it does not tell us what right is; or 'realize a good will, do what a good will would do, for the sake of being yourself a good will.' And that is something; but beyond that it is silent or beside the mark. . . . We saw that duty's universal laws are not universal, if that means they can never be overruled, and that its form and its absolute imperative are impractical. What after all remains is the acting for the sake of a good will, to realize oneself by realizing the will which is above us and higher than ours, and the assurance that this, and not the self to be pleased, is the end for which we have to live. But as to that which the good will is, it tells us nothing, and leaves us with an idle abstraction." Ibid., 159.

insisting that self-realization and not pleasure is the good or happiness.[92]

The influence of Green and Bradley – not to mention Kant and Plato – on Lewis's idealist ethics is best seen in two important Great War documents: the section on "Value" in *Clivi Hamiltonis Summae Metaphysices Contra Anthroposophos Libri II* and *De Bono et Malo*. I believe that by examining these two documents, we can get an excellent picture of Lewis's idealist beliefs concerning duty and happiness.

Now as we recall from earlier chapters, Lewis the absolute idealist believed that souls and matter are simply two aspects of Spirit. Since this is the case, Lewis faced many challenges as to how he could explain the good life or spiritual life. What he decided was that the spiritual life must be something that occurs in the life of the soul and not in Spirit as such.[93] To explain how the soul, which is at all times Spirit, can be more spiritual at one moment than at another, Lewis used a modified version of Plato's allegory of the cave:

> Let us suppose a man standing between a lantern and a white wall, and able to look only in the direction of the wall, but able either to approach it or to recede from it. . . . As he approaches it, the shadow which he casts upon the wall will grow larger and finally cover the whole wall so that it will have no outline. As he recedes from the wall, the shadow will become clearer and smaller and progressively more recognizable as a human form. Such a man might speak of that which he saw when he was furthest from the wall as 'human' and that which he saw when nearest to the wall as the opposite: but he would be in error if he forgot that all the appearances were equally 'human' in themselves.[94]

Lewis used this analogy and others to show how, without relapsing into Spirit, individual souls "can more or less re-awake the consciousness of their participation in Spirit."[95] However, while Lewis thought that this made it clear *that* the spiritual life was possible for souls, he felt that *how* such was possible, and *what* the spiritual life consisted in, required further explanation.

Thus, Lewis gave the following account of the spiritual life: the creation of souls necessarily required the creation of matter – a resisting field that

---

92   "Happiness . . . neither means a pleasure nor a number of pleasures. It means in general the finding of himself, or the satisfaction of himself as a whole, and in particular it means the realization of his concrete ideal life." Ibid., 96.
93   Lewis, *Clivi Hamiltonis Summae Metaphysices Contra Anthroposophos Libri II*, 36.
94   Ibid., 37.
95   Ibid., 38.

helps to differentiate one soul from another; yet matter, by its very nature, often resists the will of individual souls, and this resistance gives rise to pleasure and pain, and subsequently the passions, which, with the exception of heavenly desire (more on this later), tend to distract the soul from the spiritual life;[96] that is, although people are born into a world where they, through their passions, warp, and thus cannot see clearly, things as they really are, people can transcend this state in two steps. First, they have to learn to control their passions and learn to see things as they really are – that is, as they are in the mind of their True Selves or Spirit. Second, they have to attain a level of consciousness in which the soul as Spirit wills the things to be as they are.[97] This is to say that the spiritual life consists in the approximation of souls to a kind of "qualitative equality with the consciousness of Spirit;" or, if one prefers, the spiritual life is an account of the *modes* in which this approximation takes place.[98] No doubt influenced by Aristotle and Kant, Lewis said that these modes can de divided into the practical and the theoretical.

The practical mode of the spiritual life is primarily concerned with the moral good.[99] It has to do – said Lewis the Kantian – with right willing, which is – said Lewis the absolute idealist – willing *as* Spirit wills or treating an object with the impartiality or disinterestedness of Spirit (i.e. treating objects as ends or enjoying them for their own sake).[100] Consequently, an action is said to be immoral if it is determined by the passions and performed based on hedonistic principles of pain and pleasure; however, as we shall discuss more in a moment, it is not immoral if – against Kant, but with Green and Bradley – it is done out of a desire for self-realization or unity with Spirit.

---

96   Ibid., 39.

97   Ibid., 40. As Mr. Wisdom tells John, "I am the lawgiver: but I am also the subject. I, the Spirit, impose upon the soul which I become, the laws she must henceforth obey: and every conflict between the rules and our inclinations is but a conflict of the wishes of my mortal and apparent self against those of my real and eternal. 'I ought but I do not wish' – how meaningless the words are, how close to saying, 'I want and I do not want.' But once we have learned to say 'I, and yet not I, want,' the mystery is plain." Lewis, *The Pilgrim's Regress*, 148.

98   Lewis, *Clivi Hamiltonis Summae Metaphysices Contra Anthroposophos Libri II*, 40.

99   Lewis spoke of "the good of action, or will, which we call moral good." Lewis, *De Bono et Malo*, 7.

100   "No doubt a man may make both yielding and repentance too easy by reflecting that his action will in any case 'produce good.' But this comes from a false moral philosophy which placed the value of right action not in the form of right willing itself but in the consequences. The true doctrine can be studied in Kant and the Baghavat-Gita (on the fruits of action)." Ibid., 13.

The theoretical mode of the spiritual life has to do with understanding "that the law of right willing . . . is merely what I at my deepest level really will," which is to say, coming to see *what* the Spirit wills.[101] Given this, and noting that Lewis made no mention of obeying the Spirit's will as made concrete in the laws of society, Lewis thought he could reconcile Kant with Green and Bradley (minus their emphasis on society), saying: "a sound theory of ethics, such as was propounded by Kant, would of itself imply the metaphysics [of absolute idealism]."[102]

As for any value-comparison between the practical and theoretical modes of the spiritual life, Lewis insisted that "moral good is neither better nor worse than any other good."[103] Indeed, as we shall see, by establishing a series of hierarchies both in and between the theoretical and practical, Lewis attempted to show how the complete spiritual life needs both the theoretical and the practical.

Concerning the hierarchy in the theoretical mode or the hierarchy of "the first stage in the spiritual life," Lewis listed from lowest to highest: science, history, art and philosophy. Science is at the lowest level of the first stage of the spiritual life because Lewis thought that even though science is spiritual in that it must observe its objects *impartial* to any pleasure or pain, it, nevertheless, begins with motives from the passions (i.e. curiosity) and remains arbitrary and therefore limited in what it studies.[104] History follows science, and is more spiritual than it, "in so far as the objects contemplated [by history] are viewed with equal freedom from passions and are less abstract: in contemplating [the objects of history] we therefore see something less unlike what spirit sees."[105] Art is above both science and history because, as I touched on in chapter four and will address again in chapter ten, it shows greater concreteness than history,[106] greater coherence (within its subject) than science,[107] and just as much disinterestedness as both;[108] thus, art gives

---

101 Lewis, *Clivi Hamiltonis Summae Metaphysices Contra Anthroposophos Libri II*, 41.
102 Ibid.
103 Ibid., 42.
104 Ibid., 42-3.
105 Ibid., 44.
106 "Art may then be defined as that which presents objects to us with the greatest concreteness, being allowed in return to dispense with all consideration whether these objects are subjective or objective." Ibid., 45.
107 "[Art] is . . . more completely systematic than science: for we understand all the reciprocal relations within a play or a story more fully than science can ever understand the world." Ibid.
108 Art is disinterested "for the objects, not being asserted as real, do not tempt the passions." Ibid.

us an *image* of the spiritual life. Finally, philosophy is "far transcending" science, history and art since in philosophy a person knows *that* he is Spirit and *that* he wills the objects that seem to condition him;[109] however, while the philosopher recognizes that all the objects he apprehends are part of Spirit, he cannot achieve the complete spiritual life until he supplements his theoretical "that" with the practical "as."

Thus, the second stage of the spiritual life begins with the practical *act* of charity or morality. According to Lewis, charity is on a stage above – though as we shall see, it cannot do without – philosophy (as he defines it here), for charity is not concerned with abstractly knowing *that* other souls are ultimately one with a person's own self, but rather it is concerned with *experiencing* or tasting the concreteness of people as such.[110] In short, charity or morality disinterestedly wills the existence of others since it wills their existence *as* Spirit wills their existence. Nevertheless, charity or morality is not the complete spiritual life since it only focuses on willing the existence of "neighbouring souls" and not the entire world.[111]

Consequently, the complete spiritual life must bring together both the theoretical mode (the first stage) and the practical mode (the second stage), and this, Lewis implied, is accomplished in three steps.

First, the complete spiritual life requires a person to bring together the best of science, history, art, philosophy and charity: "If it is possible to attain a mode of experience which should be as unhampered in its range as Science, as concrete as History, as disinterested as Art, as free from the great primary abstraction as Philosophy, and as consciously co-operative with Spirit as Charity, we should have found the supreme form of the spiritual life."[112]

Second, the complete spiritual life requires a good memory, for through the use of memory, in which, we recall, heavenly desire resides, people can firmly hold in their minds, and deeply desire unity with, Spirit while at the same time remaining in "the Valley of Humiliation"[113] – i.e. remaining completely aware that they are still souls and that any hope of soul becoming Spirit *qua* Spirit is misplaced; as Mr. Wisdom told John,

> Abandon hope: do not abandon desire. . . . [W]hat you desire is no state of yourself at all, but something, for that very reason, Other and Outer. And knowing this you will find tolerable the truth that you cannot attain it. That the thing should *be* is so great a good that when

109 Ibid., 46.
110 Ibid., 47.
111 Ibid., 48.
112 Ibid., 48-9.
113 Lewis, *The Pilgrim's Regress*, 138.

you remember 'it is' you will forget to be sorry that you can never have it. . . . Wanting is better than having. The glory of any world wherein you can live is in the end appearance: but then, as one of my sons has said, that leaves the world more glorious yet.[114]

And third, the complete spiritual life or good life requires the use of the (deliberative) imagination. However, the truly spiritual man does not use his imagination to make art or even myth; rather, he uses his imagination to know and feel as Spirit knows and feels.[115] True, Lewis would later use some of this insight when he spoke of mythmaking as a spiritual exercise, but here he meant something more radical:

> To others it will appear that we have fallings from us and vanishings and that the outward world becomes a prospect in the mind: justly, for we are then pure Spirit so far as we go (for we are still limited, else would not be soul) and all is in our mind. Or it may seem to be simply a kind of love for the object, because we are its creator and will it into being. Others feel that what seemed dead things are charged with life, and people the hills and trees with vague personality: nor are they wrong, for we share the life of the Spirit which knows itself alive beneath all its vesture. But all alike know that such moments are our highest life. For their continuation would be the redemption of the world. . . . This highest form of the spiritual life I call imagination.[116]

Now from all of this we can say a few things about the ethics of Lewis's idealism. Firstly, Lewis, like Vertue in *The Pilgrim's Regress*, agreed with Kant and others that the moral law must disinterestedly be obeyed: "All thinking about health or riches, or about happiness, or about the possible survival of

---

114 Ibid., 141, 142.
115 In the house of Wisdom [i.e. absolute idealism], Contemplation re-awakens John's imagination when she shows John that by the moonlight (i.e. through his imagination), he can see the Island (i.e. Heaven), which now "seemed to him . . . more real [than ever before]." Ibid., 135.
116 Lewis, *Clivi Hamiltonis Summae Metaphysices Contra Anthroposophos Libri II*, 51. Borrowing a line from Berkeley, Lewis summarized this idea in *The Pilgrim's Regress* thus: "All this choir of heaven and furniture of earth are imaginations: not your imaginations nor mine, for here we have met in the same world, which could not be if the world was shut up within my mind or yours. Without doubt, then, all this show of sky and earth floats within some mighty imagination. . . . We must say that the world is not in this mind, or in that, but in Mind itself, in that impersonal principle of consciousness which flows eternally through us, in perishable forms. . . . I am the Imaginer: I am one of his imaginations. The Island is nothing else than the perfection and immortality which I possess as Spirit eternal, and vainly crave as mortal soul. . . . I have it and lo! the very having is the losing: because at every moment I, as Spirit, am indeed abandoning my rich estate to become that perishing and imperfect creature in whose repeated deaths and rebirths stands my eternity." Lewis, *The Pilgrim's Regress*, 146, 147.

the soul after death, or about god or the gods, or demons, is to be counted dangerous, as we count it dangerous to dwell on topics that inflame our passions in grosser, though it may be less fatal, ways;"[117] however, Lewis, like John in *The Pilgrim's Regress*, agreed with Green, Bradley and other absolute idealists in saying that since the moral law – in one mode or another – *is* the will of one's True Self, a person, *pace* Kant, needs to *desire* (with a heavenly desire) unity with Spirit or one's True Self, which, of course, leads to happiness *qua* self-realization (i.e. "the spiritual life").[118] Secondly, Lewis agreed with the Norse gods, Kant and the absolute idealists when they maintained that true freedom is willed necessity, or at least that true freedom is positive freedom (e.g. willing one's duty) and not negative freedom (i.e. willing without any coercion). Thirdly, while in his 1924 "Hegemony of Moral Value" Lewis may have followed Bradley in maintaining that Kant's ethics were too formal and abstract, and while Lewis theoretically ought to have rejected the absoluteness of the universal moral law, Lewis's marginalia in his edition of *Ethical Studies* – not to mention all of his Great War documents and his lectures (in particular the one in which he praised Hume for his distinction between the "ought and the is"[119]) – reveal that the Oxford don was very uncomfortable with making the concrete laws of society the highest form of

---

117 Lewis, *Clivi Hamiltonis Summae Metaphysices Contra Anthroposophos Libri II*, 68. Cf. "If we obey through hope and fear, in that very act we disobey: for the rule which we reverence most, whether we find in it our own hearts or on the Steward's card, is the rule which says that a man must act disinterestedly. To obey the Landlord thus, would be to disobey. But what if we obey freely, because we agree with him? Alas, this is even worse. To say that we agree, and obey because we agree, is only to say again that we find the same rule written in our hearts and obey *that*. If the Landlord enjoins *that*, he enjoins only what we already purposed to do, and his voice is idle. . . . In either case the mystery of the rules remains unsolved, and the Landlord is a meaningless addition to the problem." Lewis, *The Pilgrim's Regress*, 140.

118 "In the presence of these thoughts [such as, *why* do one's duty?] traditional morality falters – Without Desire [i.e. heavenly desire] it finds no motive: with Desire, no morality." Ibid., 123. Or again, as Mr. Wisdom said: "Remember what we have said of the Island. Because I am and am not Spirit, therefore I have and have not my desire. The same double nature of the word 'I', explains the rules. I am the lawgiver: but I am also the subject. I, the Spirit, impose upon the soul which I become, the laws she must henceforth obey: and every conflict between the rules and our inclinations is but a conflict of the wishes of my mortal apparent self against those of my real and eternal. 'I ought but I do not wish' – how meaningless the words are, how close to saying, 'I want and I do not want.' But once we have learned to say 'I, and yet not I, want,' the mystery is plain." Ibid., 148.

119 We recall that in 1924, Lewis the idealist said that Hume's "great merit" was his "distinction between the *is* and the ought." This critique is remarkable because it went against his budding absolute idealism: for example, in *Ethical Studies*, Bradley tried as hard as he could to get "rid of the opposition of 'ought' and 'is.'" Bradley, *Ethical Studies*, 203.

morality; for instance, when Bradley wrote – "We have found the end, we have found self-realization, duty, and happiness in one – yes, we have found ourselves, when we have found our station and its duties, our function as an organ in <u>the social organism</u>" – Lewis could only reply with two exclamation marks: "!!"[120] Furthermore, when Bradley inconsistently spoke like a Kantian who believes that the moral law can critique the laws of society, saying – "Again, the moral man need not find himself realized in the world. . . . <u>[I]t is necessary to remark that the community in which he is a member may be in a confused or rotten condition, so that in it right and might do not always go together</u>" – Lewis, in true Kantian fashion, wrote, "At Last!"[121]

And it is this final point – the absoluteness of the moral law and the moral good – which gave Lewis the absolute idealist the same kind of trouble[122] he had when he struggled with the conflict between traditional logic and Hegelian logic. That is, just as traditional logic and love of Truth had led Lewis to idealism, which then demanded that he abandon his concept of Truth, so did the need for a metaphysical grounding for the universal moral law help convince Lewis that he should become an idealist, but once the universal moral law was grounded in absolute idealist metaphysics, it ceased to be universal. Lewis's struggle with this contradiction is clearly seen when one examines his progression into absolute idealism. For instance, in 1926, Lewis the idealist – still with Kantian leanings in regard to the absoluteness of the moral law – pointed out: "Again, in your pantheistic conclusion, should you not show that you are aware of some of the moral difficulties? I mean, if the spirit grows in the grass etc, and in the cancer and the murderer, if it does everything, must it not be simply the neutral background of good and evil?"[123] However, in 1927, Lewis the absolute idealist – now with Bradleyan

---

120 C. S. Lewis, marginalia in his edition of *Ethical Studies*, by F. H. Bradley, 2nd ed. (London: Clarendon Press, 1927; The Marion E. Wade Center, Wheaton College), 163.

121 Ibid., 203.

122 Lewis the absolute idealist was far from alone in finding the absoluteness of the moral law and the moral good troublesome: "Evil . . . [is] something with which the more severe renditions of Absolute Idealism had severe philosophical difficulties." Andrew Vincent, "Metaphysics and Ethics in the Philosophy of T. H. Green," in *T. H. Green: Ethics, Metaphysics, and Political Philosophy*, ed. Maria Dimova-Cookson and W. J. Mander, 76-105 (Oxford: Clarendon Press, 2006), 98.

123 Lewis, *The Collected Letters of C. S. Lewis: Volume III*, 1500 [1926]. Cf. "This evening to the Univ[ersity] Philosophical Society after dinner to hear McMurray of Balliol read a paper. . . . The moral judgement for him is primarily the judgement 'This is evil,' wh[ich], since he is a Bradleyan, means 'the whole is such that this is evil' and he finds a difficulty about the universe being logically coherent and morally incoherent." Lewis, *All My Road Before Me*, 322 [May 8, 1924].

leanings in respect to the moral law – half-heartedly declared: "from the spiritual point of view every . . . cancer is good and beautiful."[124] Since Lewis was no fool, it is worth examining his *De Bono et Malo* to see how he could even momentarily forsake the universal moral law and the absoluteness of the moral good.

To begin with, we know Lewis understood the moral good to be part of the good or spiritual in general. On the one hand, this means that the moral man is a person who treats things as ends in themselves: concerned with valuing things for their own sake and willing and seeing as Spirit wills and sees, the moral man is primarily an extrovert; as a result, he ultimately loses himself to Spirit as a unity that is perfected. On the other hand, the immoral man is a person controlled by his passions: concerned only with how he can use others for his own pleasure, he is primarily an introvert; [125] as a result, he ultimately loses himself to Spirit as a thing that is disintegrated or broken down: "The evil soul loses herself by internal disintegration: the good soul loses herself by being supplemented and perfected."[126] Consequently, treating things, in particular, people, as ends and not means seems to be at the heart of Lewis's concept of the moral good, and it is *tempting* to see this Kantian principle as embodying an absolute goodness. In addition to this, Lewis's Platonic declarations that "Evil . . . is privative" and "Absolute Evil . . . [is] nothing"[127] seems to indicate that he believed in an absolute good, for according to Plato, who Lewis was apparently following, Good and evil are opposites, and if evil does not exist, then the Good must really exist. Indeed, following a quasi-Platonic, and not a Nietzschean,[128] position, Lewis even went on to declare that "Spirit is 'beyond' good and evil."[129]

However – against the notion that Lewis believed in an absolute good – what the Oxford don picked up on was precisely Plato's error. That is, when Plato declared that the Good is beyond Being, he spoke nonsense, for if the Good is beyond Being, then our understanding of the Good must have no relation to the Good beyond Being; likewise, when Lewis said that Spirit is beyond the good, he meant "that what we call good is only the copy or faint

124 Lewis, *Clivi Hamiltonis Summae Metaphysices Contra Anthroposophos Libri II*, 52.
125 "The morality which does not love sense . . . [is] suspect." Ibid., 54.
126 Lewis, *De Bono et Malo*, 4.
127 Ibid., 2.
128 We know that Lewis "began Nietzsche's *Beyond Good and Evil*" when he first became an idealist. Lewis, *All My Road Before Me*, 314 [April 11, 1924]. And we also know that he was not impressed by him: "More Nietzsche. So far there is nothing new about it – just what the ordinary egoist has always believed and acted on." Ibid., 314 [April 12, 1924].
129 Lewis, *De Bono et Malo*, 5.

echo of Spirit;"[130] however, in order for him to speak of the good as a copy of Spirit it means either that Spirit is the supreme good – which Lewis denied[131] – or that the good does not fully apply to Spirit. And indeed, it is this latter option Lewis opted for since he believed that both good and evil add to the supremacy of Spirit, which surpasses both of them:

> It is sometimes asked how Spirit, being all, can be good, since some things (and all includes these) are evil. Now it is clear, and most easily seen in art, that a good whole may contain parts which, taken severally (i.e. mis-taken as wholes) would be bad. Now a soul, so long as it maintains itself as a separate soul, is just a part so isolating itself and claiming to be a whole: and the badness of such a soul no more conflicts with the goodness of Spirit than the ugliness of a given colour (in isolation) conflicts with the beauty of the picture in which it occurs. . . . There is therefore no difficulty in the doctrine that what appears phenomenally in space and time as a plurality of goods and evils (even mostly evils) may nevertheless, as it really is in Spirit, be absolutely good.[132]

While this might sound like a good explanation of good and evil, it is, in fact, a false analogy, for while all colours are good, not all actions are.

Ultimately, all Lewis the absolute idealist could do was at once declare the moral law bankrupt (and not necessarily in favor of the concrete laws of society either[133]) and at the same time call for absolute disinterested devotion

---

130 Ibid.

131 "I meant that we do not in ourselves experience nor in others find essence of states absolutely good or bad: i.e. good, bad are in a position like that of big & little." C. S. Lewis, *Commentarium in Tractatum De Toto et Parte* (Unpublished "Great War" document [1929?]; The Marion E. Wade Center, Wheaton College), 1. In addition to the influence of the British Idealists, it is quite possible that Spinoza's *Ethics*, which Lewis both studied and taught, had some influence on Lewis's belief that nothing is good or evil for God. Baruch Spinoza, *The Ethics*, trans. Samuel Shirley, ed. Seymour Feldman (Cambridge: Hackett, 1992), 57 [1.appendix]. However, if there is a Spinozean element in Lewis, it is a shallow one, for Lewis's reason for saying Spirit is beyond good and evil (i.e. Spirit is the combination of all appearances) is different than Spinoza's (i.e. God is infinite and lacks nothing; therefore, He never acts for some good end since "good" is a term only used for things that lack).

132 Lewis, *De Bono et Malo*, 6. In *The Pilgrim's Regress*, John was tempted by some "brown girls," who represented lust. However, after John escaped their traps, he studied in the house of Mr. Wisdom, who represents absolute idealism, and soon began to reconsider the "evil" of the brown girls, saying, "'And yet – is not brown as necessary to the spectrum as any other colour?'" Lewis, *The Pilgrim's Regress*, 152.

133 Although the following passage might appear to be a statement about people choosing to obey the concrete laws of society in place of the abstract moral law, it is actually about those people who will *as* Spirit wills as opposed to those who merely will *what* Spirit

to it[134] – devotion which leads to a kind of happiness of soul in Spirit which those who do not obey the law do not enjoy.

Now as we recall, what helped Lewis convert from absolute idealism to theism was both the books he was reading and his discomfort with the impracticality of absolute idealist ethics; indeed, as I suggested in chapter two, these two elements very likely played off each other, for the books that Lewis was reading were broadly Neoplatonic Christian in nature – that is, they were books declaring both that the Good had absolutely *nothing* to do with evil, and that the Good demanded uncompromising moral action. However, before any particular authors can be discussed in regard to influencing Lewis's theistic understanding of happiness and duty, it must be pointed out that at the time of his theistic conversion, Lewis the absolute idealist momentary lost all of his eudaimonism and declared himself to be very much like the Old Testament Jews, who, Lewis rightly and wrongly maintained,[135] followed God without any promise of immortality or, presumably, happiness *qua* self-realization:

> It may be asked whether my terror was at all relieved by the thought that I was now approaching the source from which those arrows of Joy had been shot at me ever since childhood. Not in the least. No slightest hint was vouchsafed me that there ever had been or ever would be any connection between God and Joy. If anything, it was the reverse. I had hoped that the heart of reality might be of such a kind that we can best symbolize it as a place; instead, I found it to be a Person. For

wills: "For a man could not choose spiritually (i.e. morally, universally) to be a hand, since in this very act, as I have shown, he affirms himself as 'brains.'" Lewis, *De Bono et Malo*, 18.

134 "Any answer to the question Why must begin with the word BECAUSE: and if the action in question is chosen 'because of' some end beyond itself, then <u>that</u> end will be good in its own right: or if not that, then some other beyond it. But if we come to ground nowhere, but choose every act as a means to a means (<u>ad infinitum</u>) no action can begin at all. The same may be seen <u>a posteriori</u>. For if we ask a man why he is hurrying and he replies 'To catch a train': and we ask him again 'Why' and so on: in the end he is bound to answer <u>either</u> 'This is my duty' <u>or</u> 'This is my pleasure': that is <u>either</u> 'This is the manifestation of universal good demanded by my time & place – in willing this I will as Spirit' <u>or</u> 'This is my particular good – this is what I as soul regard as my end.' And if you asked him why he ought to do his duty, or why he liked pleasure, he would justly leave you unanswered as a fool." Ibid., 8.

135 While Lewis was no doubt right that the Jews chose to follow God without any promise of eternal life, the Oxford don probably did not do justice to the concept of "Deuteronomic Theology," which is a simple doctrine of retribution stating that God will bless those who keep the covenant and curse those who do not. Thus, it is impossible to say whether the Jews followed God first because He is Good, or first because He would reward them for following Him. Arnold, *Encountering the Old Testament*, 147.

all I knew, the total rejection of what I called Joy might be one of the demands, might be the very first demand he would make upon me. There was no strain of music from within, no smell of eternal orchards at the threshold, when I was dragged through the doorway. *No kind of desire was present at all.*

My conversion involved as yet no belief in a future life. I now number it among my greatest mercies that I was permitted for several months, perhaps for a year, to know God and to attempt obedience without even raising that question. My training was like that of the Jews to whom He revealed Himself centuries before there was a whisper of anything better (or worse) beyond the grave than shadowy and featureless *Sheol*. And I did not dream even of that. There are men, far better men than I, who have made immortality almost the central doctrine of their religion; but for my own part I have never seen how a preoccupation with that subject at the outset could fail to corrupt the whole thing. I had been brought up to believe that goodness was goodness only if it were disinterested, and that any hope of reward or fear of punishment contaminated the will. If I was wrong in this (the question is really much more complicated than I then perceived) my error was most tenderly allowed for. I was afraid that threats or promises would demoralize me; no threats or promises were made. The commands were inexorable, but they were backed by no 'sanctions.' God was to be obeyed simply because [H]e was God. Long since, through the gods of Asgard, and later through the notion of the Absolute, He had taught me how a thing can be revered not for what it can do to us but for what it is in itself. That is why, though it was a terror, it was no surprise to learn that God is to be obeyed because of what He is in Himself. If you ask why we should obey God, in the last resort the answer is, 'I am.' To know God is to know that our obedience is due to Him. In [H]is nature His sovereignty *de jure* is revealed.[136]

While the lack of heavenly desire at the time of Lewis's theistic conversion is surprising but not so surprising given the greater emphasis Lewis generally put on deontological considerations, what *is* surprising, or at least well worth noting, is the grace he experienced: "The old doctrine is quite true you know,"

---

136 Lewis, *Surprised by Joy*, 1377-8 (emphasis mine). Cf. "It is surely, therefore, very possible that when God began to reveal Himself to men, to show them that He and nothing else is their true goal and the satisfaction of their needs, and that He has a claim upon them simply by being what He is, quite apart from anything He can bestow or deny, it may have been absolutely necessary that this revelation should not begin with any hint of future Beatitude or Perdition. . . . Later, when, after centuries of spiritual training, men have learned to desire and adore God, to pant after Him 'as pants the hart', it is another matter. For then those who love God will desire not only to enjoy Him but 'to enjoy Him forever', and will fear to lose Him." Lewis, *Reflections on the Psalms*, 330.

wrote Lewis, less than a year after his conversion to theism, "– that one must attribute everything to the grace of God and nothing to oneself."[137] That is, more (but not less) than following Goodness and Truth for their own sake's, Lewis said that at the time of his theistic conversion he felt the absolute unity of freedom and necessity which was only made possible by grace and which ultimately helped the Oxford don do (but not yet desire) unreservedly as he ought.

Consequently, after becoming a theist who believed in a single good God,[138] Lewis realized that the gap in his absolute idealist ethics between his theory and practice was unacceptable ("I had pretty well known that my ideal of virtue would never be allowed to lead me into anything intolerably painful"[139]). Hence, Lewis came to see that he could no longer hold onto the satanic lie which stated that he was the creator of his own soul; as John in *The Pilgrim's Regress* said: "Above all it grew upon him that the return of the Landlord had blotted out the Island: for if there still were such a place he was no longer free to spend his soul in seeking it, but must follow whatever designs the Landlord had for him."[140]

One of "the designs" God had for Lewis after his theistic conversion was that he should further refine his understanding of the relationship between duty and happiness, and one of the ways in which this was made possible was through the books Lewis was reading both before, and during, his theist phase. The major authors who influenced Lewis in this regard were the pagans Plato and Aristotle, and the Christians William Law, Thomas Traherne, Jacob Boehme, Boethius, and Richard Hooker. While I will take up some of these authors in the next section, it is important to note that most of these authors were deeply committed to rational, eudaimonian ethics, which maintain that heavenly desire – i.e. the desire for happiness *qua* self-

---

137 Lewis, *The Collected Letters of C. S. Lewis: Volume I*, 877 [January 30, 1930].

138 "There could be no question of going back to primitive, untheologised and unmoralised, Paganism. The God whom I had at last acknowledged was one, and was righteous." Lewis, *Surprised by Joy*, 1380.

139 Ibid., 1376. Compare this to the discussion in *The Pilgrim's Regress* between the Man (i.e. Jesus) and John: "'You have heard from Wisdom how the rules were yours and not yours. Did you not mean to keep them? And if so, can it scare you to know that there is one who will make you able to keep them?' 'Well,' said John. 'I suppose you have found me out. Perhaps I did not fully mean to keep them – not all – or not all the time. And yet, in a way, I think I did. It is like a thorn in your finger, sir. You know when you set about taking it out yourself – you mean to get it out – you know it will hurt – and it does hurt – but somehow it is not very serious business – well, I suppose, because you feel that you always *could* stop if it was very bad. Not that you intend to stop. But it is a very different thing to hold your hand out to a surgeon to be hurt as much as *he* thinks fit. And at *his* speed.'" Lewis, *The Pilgrim's Regress*, 160-1.

140 Ibid., 163.

realization – is crucial, and yet because happiness can only be achieved by a creature acting according to its nature – in man's case, acting rational since he is a rational soul – man can only be happy when he obeys reason, which, among other things, tells man that he ought to obey the universal moral law, which is a reflection of God's own *nature* (and not His arbitrary will). Hence, Lewis the theist came to agree (1) with Plato that "God [is] never a cause of Evil;"[141] (2) with Aristotle that "Happiness [is] the only end never sought as a means"[142] and that "it lies in the Exercise of [man's] faculties according to their Excellences, with Reason;"[143] (3) with Law that "[we need] to act to the excellency of our rational nature"[144] and that "all degrees of love are degrees of happiness;"[145] (4) with Traherne that "'[God] must lead you out of this world to *learn your wants* . . . for till you find them you will never be happy;'"[146] (5) with Boeheme that "the foundation of hell is manifested, namely, in self-hood, and in the false will;"[147] (6) with Boethius that "[e]verything desires to realize its own proper nature"[148] and that "[a]ll creatures in obeying God realize their own will;"[149] and (7) with Hooker that "'[a]ll men desire to lead in this world a happy life'"[150] and that "[the] Human Law of Nature . . . or Reason . . . [or] the light of Reason" is a copy of the "1ˢᵗ Law Eternal," which is "God's [B]eing . . . [which] giv[es] Law to the working . . . and limit[s] His operations by the Good."[151]

In order to give the reader a clear picture of Lewis's theistic understanding of duty and happiness, six important changes from, or at least modifications of, his idealist understanding of these ought to be mentioned.

141 Lewis, marginalia in his edition of *RES PVBLICA*, 379c.

142 Lewis, marginalia in his edition of *Ethica Niocomachea*, 1097a15.

143 Ibid., 1097a20.

144 C. S. Lewis, underlining in his edition of *A Serious Call to a Devout Life*, by William Law (London: J. M. Dent & Sons, 1926; The Rare Book Collection, The University of North Carolina at Chapel Hill), 52.

145 Ibid., 126.

146 Lewis, *The Collected Letters of C. S. Lewis: Volume I*, 914 [July 8, 1930]. Cf. "By ceasing for a moment to consider my own wants I have begun to learn better what I really wanted." Lewis, "The Weight of Glory," 102-3.

147 C. S. Lewis, marginalia in his edition of *The Signature of all Things with other Writings*, by Jacob Boehme (London: J. M. Dent & Sons, 1926; The Rare Book Collection, The University of North Carolina at Chapel Hill), 267.

148 Lewis, marginalia in his edition of *King Alfred's Old English Version of Boethius' De Consolatione Philosophiae*, 92 [4.3].

149 Ibid., 98 [4.4].

150 In Lewis, *Studies in Words*, 274.

151 Lewis, marginalia in his edition of *Of the Laws of Ecclesiastical Polity*, on the inside of the cover of book one.

First, rejecting any absolute idealist argument that would reduce the moral law to the will of the nation or government, Lewis returned to his Kantian belief in the universality of the moral law. As the Oxford don would argue much later:

> [Clare] meant that [the man in question] had not only a legal but a moral right to act as he did. In other words, Clare is – or would be if she thought it out – a classical moralist after the style of Thomas Aquinas, Grotius, Hooker and Locke. She believes that behind the laws of the state there is a Natural Law.
>
> I agree with her. I hold this conception to be basic to all civilsation. Without it, the actual laws of the state become an absolute, as in Hegel. They cannot be criticized because there is no norm against which they should be judged.[152]

Second, Lewis coupled his belief in the universal moral law with Neoplatonic Christian metaphysics, which, deriving insight from Plato, Boethius and Hooker, maintained that the universal moral law is a true reflection of God's perfect nature, wherein there is no evil whatsoever. What this meant is that Lewis no longer thought that Spirit was beyond good and evil; rather, he had come to see that God is identical with the Good and evil is a perversion of this; as Lewis would say some years after his conversion:

> Confronted with a cancer or a slum the Pantheist can say, 'If you could only see it from the divine point of view, you would realize that this also is God.' The Christian replies, 'Don't talk damned nonsense.' For Christianity is a fighting religion. It thinks God made the world – the space and time, heat and cold, and all the colours and tastes, and all the animals and vegetables, are things that God 'made up out of His head' as a man makes up a story. But it also thinks that a great many things have gone wrong with the world that God made and that God insists, and insists very loudly, on our putting them right again.[153]

Third, Lewis the idealist had correctly believed that using, instead of enjoying, things is often a symptom of pride (the anti-moral state of mind). However, Lewis the idealist had also thought that his True Self was God, which not only had demonstrated outrageous pride, but also had given Lewis leave to break the moral laws should he so wish since he, as the totality of

---

152 C. S. Lewis, "We Have No 'Right to Happiness,'" in *C. S. Lewis: Essay Collection & Other Short Pieces*, ed. Lesley Walmsley (1963 essay reprint; London: HarperCollins, 2000), 389. Cf. "Freedom and what Hegelians call '*true* freedom' are almost mutually exclusive." Lewis, *Studies in Words*, 106.

153 Lewis, *Mere Christianity*, 344.

everything, made all the laws anyway; thus, as a theist, Lewis accepted what was true in his idealism (that pride is using things inappropriately or using things which should not be used) and rejected the false (that man is God). Indeed, as we will discuss in greater detail later, an important consequence of Lewis's conversion to theism was his awareness of his own sinful heart: "What worries me," Lewis wrote one year before becoming a Christian, "is *Pride* – my besetting sin."[154] Indeed, combining insight from Alexander about the danger of Contemplating one's own mind, from Freud about the vastness (and perversity) of the unconscious, from Kant about the risk of impure motives, and from numerous Christian writers, like Augustine, Boehme and Law, who warned about the dangers of pride and false self-love, Lewis the theist became extremely critical of his own motives; he even went so far as to stop writing in his journal, for he came to see such a preoccupation with the self as a potential danger to spiritual growth:

> One of the first results of my Theistic conversion was a marked decrease (and high time, as all readers of this book will agree) in the fussy attentiveness which I had so long paid to the progress of my own opinions and the states of my own mind. For many healthy extroverts self-examination first begins with conversion. For me it was almost the other way around. Self-examination did of course continue. But it was (I supposed, for I cannot quite remember) at stated intervals, and for a practical purpose; a duty, a discipline, an uncomfortable thing, no longer a hobby or a habit. To believe and to pray were the beginning of extroversion. I had been, as they say, 'taken out of myself.' If Theism had done nothing else for me, I should still be thankful that it cured me of the time-wasting and foolish practice of keeping a diary.[155]

Fourth, after his conversion to theism, Lewis came largely to agree with Plato, Aristotle, Augustine, Boethius, Hooker and others who believed both that morality begins with heavenly desire or the desire for happiness *qua* self-realization, and that this desire quickly leads to the recognition of moral duties,[156] which are grounded in God, who is the source all Goodness and

---

154 Lewis, *The Collected Letters of C. S. Lewis: Volume I*, 878 [January 30, 1930]. Cf. "*Pride*, on the other hand, is the mother of *all* sins, and the original sin of Lucifer – so you are rather better off than I am. You at your worst are an instrument unstrung: I am an instrument strung but preferring to play itself because it thinks it knows the tune better than the Musician." Ibid., 882 [February 10, 1930]. At the beginning of chapter fourteen of *Surprised by Joy* – the chapter dealing with Lewis's conversion to theism – the Oxford don quoted George MacDonald, who wrote: "The one principle of hell is – 'I am my own.'" Lewis, *Surprised by Joy*, 1367.

155 Ibid., 1378-9.

156 Cf. "However, one cannot be too careful: one must try to hold fast to ones duties (I wish

Being, meaning, of course, that to disobey God or the Good is to lose one's very existence and happiness. Thus, while rejecting the idea that desire for, and obedience to, God is actually desire for, and obedience to, himself, Lewis the theist continued to maintain his absolute idealist belief that a moral act is not, *pace* Kant, ruined by eudaimonian desire.

Fifth, although we only have records of Lewis's understanding of freedom from both his idealist and Christian phases, we can fairly confidently say that during his theistic phase, Lewis still maintained the insight of the Norse gods, Russell, Kant and Bradley that true freedom is willed necessity, or at least that true freedom is willing the dictates of the moral law, which, because it has its root in God, the ground of all Being, must be obeyed if a person is to exist and flourish; hence, as Lewis said when he was a Christian:

> Later in his essay Burnaby seems to suggest that human wills are the only radically unpredictable factor in history. I'm not happy about this. Partly because I don't see how the gigantic negative which it involves could be proved; partly because I agree with Bradley that unpredictability is not the essence, nor even a symptom, of freedom. (Did you see they've reprinted Ethical Studies? The baiting of Arnold, wholly just and in Arnold's own manner, is exquisite.)[157]

Sixth, recalling that Lewis the idealist refused to declare the moral good superior to the good in general, we ought not to be too surprised that Lewis the theist – a man who even more adamantly denied that the end of man is moral duty – went beyond this stalemate, declaring a substantial difference between "holiness" (i.e. the Good: the totality of God's nature) and "mere morality" (i.e. the moral good: a reflection of God's nature that must be obeyed no matter what).[158] The seeds of holiness, we remember, were planted in Lewis long ago when he first read George MacDonald and this MacDonaldian idea (which of course Lewis also found in many other writers,

---

I did) which are the prose of spiritual life and not learn to depend too much on these delightful moments." Lewis, *The Collected Letters of C. S. Lewis: Volume I*, 878 [January 30, 1930]. Cf. "I think the thing is to obey the ordinary rules of morality: subject to them, to be guided by those impulses which *feel* the most serious and innocent as opposed to those that *feel* trivial and shamefaced: but for ultimate justification & results to trust to God." Ibid., 932-3 [August 28, 1930]. Cf. "Grumble not at thy lot." C. S. Lewis, underlining in his edition of "The Communings with himself of Marcus Aurelius Antoninus," by Marcus Aurelius, trans. C. R. Haines (London: William Heinemann, 1930; The Rare Book Collection, The University of North Carolina at Chapel Hill), 103 [5.5].

157 Lewis, *Prayer: Letters to Malcolm*, 249.

158 Lewis, *The Collected Letters of C. S. Lewis: Volume I*, 901 [June 7, 1930].

such as Morris[159]) set the stage for some of the Oxford don's most important writings about the beauty of God's moral nature and the even greater beauty of God's complete nature, of which morality is only a part.

Two years after becoming a theist, Lewis converted to Christianity, and as a Christian (who of course admitted the secular foundation of his Christian ethics[160]), he wrote an enormous amount about duty and happiness. In particular, there are three issues – corresponding to three kinds of men[161] – worth discussing: (1) Lewis's defense of the universal moral law and man's

---

159 "The beauty of the actual world, the vague longings wh[ich] it excites, the inevitable failure to satisfy these longings, and over all the haunting sense of time & change making the world heart breakingly beautiful just because it slips away. . . . All this, I thought, [Morris] gave to perfection: but of what this longing really pointed to, of the reason why beauty made us homesick, of the reality *behind*, I thought he had no inkling. . . . Now in *Love is Enough* he raises himself right out of his own world. . . . For the first (and last?) time the light of *holiness* shines through Morris' romanticism, not destroying but perfecting it. Reading this . . . has shown me that in my fear of sensual cheat wh[ich] lurked at the back of my old romantic days (see Dymer VII) I have aimed at too much austerity and even dishonoured love altogether. I have become a dry prig. I do hope I am not being mocked – that this is not merely the masked vanguard of a new sensuality. But I verily believe not. In this light I shall come back to Morris and all that world. I have the key now and perhaps can stand the sweetness safely. For this too is a feature of life that becomes gradually clearer: namely that the road is always turning round and going back to places we seemed to have left – but they are different (yet in a way the same) when you come to them the second time." Ibid., 911 [July 1, 1930]. "You have I think misunderstood what I said about the return from austerity. I never meant for a moment that I was beginning to doubt whether absolute chastity was the true goal – of that I am certain. What I meant was that I began to think that I was mistaken in aiming at this goal by the means of a stern repression and even a contemptuous distrust of all that emotional & imaginative experience wh[ich] seems to border on the voluptuous: whether it was well to see in certain romances and certain music nothing but one more wile of the enemy: whether perhaps the right way was not to keep alive in ones soul tenderness & luxuriousness always reaching out to *that of which* (on my view) sex must be the copy." Ibid., 913 [July 8, 1930].
160 "The difference I am drawing between moral and non-moral good comes . . . from secular ethics." Lewis, *The Collected Letters of C. S. Lewis: Volume II*, 447 [October 12, 1940].
161 "There are three kinds of people in the world. The first class is of those who live simply for their own sake and pleasure, regarding Man and Nature as so much raw material to cut up into whatever shape may serve them. In the second class are those who acknowledge some other claim upon them – the will of God, the categorical imperative, or the good of society – and honestly try to pursue their own interests no further than this claim will allow. . . . But the third class is of those who can say like St. Paul that for them 'to live is Christ' (Philippians 1:21). These people have got rid of the tiresome business of adjusting the rival claims of Self and God by the simple expedient of rejecting the claims of Self altogether. The old egoistic will has been turned around, reconditioned, and made into a new thing. The will of Christ no longer limits theirs; it is theirs." Lewis, "Three Kinds of Men," 315.

duty to it, (2) his critique of eudaimonism *qua* selfish pleasure, and (3) his defense of eudaimonism *qua* the desire for self-realization, which ultimately becomes a selfless desire to see that the Good be praised even if the self is lost.

As for the universal moral law, Lewis the Neoplatonic Christian still maintained both that man's duty to the moral law is often painful and costly,[162] especially given man's fallen state,[163] and that obedience to the moral law would be rational and required even if God did not exist. Thus, even though Lewis is rightly famous for his moral argument for the existence of God as found in book one of *Mere Christianity* ("Right and Wrong as a Clue to the Meaning of the Universe"), we must remember that he accepted the existence of the rational-but-painful universal moral law long before he believed in God. Thus, he could say of his old philosophy tutor, E. F. Carritt: "Doing what we think right, on the other hand, is not the same as glorifying God. I fully agree with Mr. Carritt that *a priori* we might expect the production of whatever is 'good' to be one of our duties. If God had never spoken to man, we should be justified in basing the conduct of life wholly on such *a priori* grounds."[164] Consequently, while Lewis would have been pleased that Francis Collins, the head of the Human Genome Project, converted to Christianity largely because of Lewis's moral argument for the existence of God,[165] Lewis

---

162 Hence, from his earliest years onward, Lewis spoke highly of literature such as the *Aeneid* or the *Hippolytus*, which showed the beauty and value of painful obedience. For instance, he said: "I've just re-read the *Aeneid* again. The effect is one of the immense *costliness* of a vocation combined with a complete conviction that it is worth it. The whole story is littered with the cost – Creusa, Dido, Anchises, Palinurus, Pallas, Lausus, Camilla." Lewis, *The Collected Letters of C. S. Lewis: Volume I*, 750 [December 26, 1946].

163 "We agree with Kant so far as to say that there is one right act – that of self-surrender – which cannot be willed to the height by fallen creatures unless it is unpleasant." Lewis, *The Problem of Pain*, 522.

164 Lewis, "Christianity and Culture," 84.

165 "I went to visit a Methodist minister who lived down the street to ask him whether faith made any logical sense. He listened patiently to my confused (and probably blasphemous) ramblings, and then took a small book off his shelf and suggested I read it. . . . The book was *Mere Christianity* by C. S. Lewis. In the next few days, as I turned its pages, struggling to absorb the breadth and depth of the intellectual arguments laid down by this legendary Oxford scholar, I realized that all of my own constructs against the plausibility of faith were those of a schoolboy. Clearly I would need to start with a clean slate to consider this most important of all human questions. Lewis seemed to know all of my objections, sometimes even before I had quite formulated them. He invariably addressed them within a page or two. When I learned subsequently that Lewis had himself been an atheist, who had set out to disprove faith on the basis of logical argument, I recognized how he could be so insightful about my path. It had been his path as well. . . . The argument that most caught my attention, and most

probably would not have been shocked that atheist-turned-theist Antony Flew found this argument less than compelling:

> HABERMAS: 'So, take C. S. Lewis's argument for morality as presented in *Mere Christianity*. You didn't find that to be very impressive?'
>
> FLEW: 'No, I didn't.'
>
> HABERMAS: 'Although you disagreed with him, did you find him to be a very reasonable sort of fellow?'
>
> FLEW: 'Oh yes, very much so, an eminently reasonable man.'[166]

This said, however, Erik Wielenberg is correct when he understands Lewis the Christian (just like Lewis the theist) to have been saying that God does not *have* His properties, such as moral Goodness, but *is* His properties; however, Wielenberg goes *slightly* astray, for Lewis did not claim, as Wielenberg thinks he did, that God *is* the universal moral law ("A more likely interpretation is that Lewis is suggesting that God is identical to the moral law"[167]); rather, Lewis claimed that God *is* Goodness and the universal moral law is a *reflection* of this:

> If I had any hesitation in saying that God 'made' the Tao, it would only be because this might suggest that it was an arbitrary creation (*sic volo sic jubeo*), whereas I believe it to be the necessary expression, in terms of temporal existence, of what God of his own righteous nature necessarily is. One would indeed say of it *genitum, non factum*, for is not the Tao the Word Himself considered from a particular point of view? . . . In other words, I think (with Hooker) <u>not</u> that certain things are right because God commanded them, but that God commanded them because they are right.[168]

Thus, in *The Voyage of the Dawn Treader*, for example, Lewis depicted Aslan obeying His own rules: "'Aslan!' said Lucy almost a little reproachfully. 'Don't

rocked my ideas about science and spirit down to their foundation, was right there in the title of Book One: 'Right and Wrong as a Clue to the Meaning of the Universe.' While in many ways the 'Moral Law' that Lewis described was a universal feature of human existence, in other ways it was as if I was recognizing it for the first time." Francis Collins, *The Language of God: A Scientist Presents Evidence for Belief* (New York: Free Press, 2007), 21-2.

166 Flew and Habermas, "My Pilgrimage from Atheism to Theism: A Discussion between Antony Flew and Gary Habermas," 200-1.

167 Wielenberg, *God and the Reach of Reason: C. S. Lewis, David Hume, and Bertrand Russell*, 66.

168 Lewis, *The Collected Letters of C. S. Lewis: Volume III*, 1227 [January 11, 1961]. Cf. Lewis, "The Poison of Subjectivism," 663.

make fun of me. As if anything *I* could do would make *you* visible!' 'It did,' said Aslan. 'Do you think I wouldn't obey my own rules?'"[169] Indeed, in *The Last Battle*, one of the ways that the Anti-Christ figure, Puzzle the Donkey, who was controlled by the False Prophet figure, Shift the Ape, was recognized as a fraud was due to his violating the universal moral law – something that Aslan would never do despite the fact that "he is not a tame lion":

> Up till now the King and Jewel had said nothing: they were waiting until the Ape should bid them speak, for they thought it was no use interrupting. But now, as Tirian looked round on the miserable faces of the Narnians, and saw how they would all believe that Aslan and Tash were one and the same, he could bear it no longer.
>
> 'Ape,' he cried with a great voice, 'you lie. You lie damnably. You lie like a Calormene. You lie like an Ape.'
>
> He meant to go on and ask how the terrible god Tash who fed on the blood of his people could possibly be the same as the good Lion by whose blood all Narnia was saved. If he had been allowed to speak, the rule of the Ape might have ended that day; the Beasts might have seen the truth and thrown the Ape down. But before he could say another word two Calormene struck him in the mouth with all their force.[170]

Now a large part of what it means to say that the moral law is absolutely binding (and a true reflection of God's nature) is that its axioms are both self-evident and absolute premises in moral propositions; thus, Lewis, still a Kantian in this regard,[171] insisted, "The ultimate ethical injunctions have always been premises, never conclusions. Kant was perfectly right on that point at least: the imperative is categorical. Unless the ethical is assumed from the outset, no argument will bring you to it."[172] Consequently, while

---

169 Lewis, *The Voyage of the Dawn Treader*, 123.

170 Lewis, *The Last Battle*, 37. Cf. Ibid., 24, 29, 34, 41, 43. Cf. Adam Barkman, "'First to Aslan and Truth': Images of Christ in *The Last Battle*," *Pilgrimage* 13, no. 3 (May 2006): 12-5.

171 Hence, in *The Pilgrim's Regress*, Lewis described Immanuel (Kant) as one whose "appearance and constitution were those of a prize fighter;" thus, we are told, Kant "'might as well go to Mother Kirk [Christianity] straight away.'" Lewis, *The Pilgrim's Regress*, 145, 144. Of course, I only say that Lewis was a Kantian in regard to the moral law because he started out as one, not because he failed to add other voices to his already established belief. Hooker and Aquinas, for instance, were important additions in this respect; for instance: "I have now had my first week of term. Monday and Tuesday were quiet days, with evenings to myself which I spent in finding out what Thomas Aquinas had to say on the Law of Nature." Lewis, *The Collected Letters of C. S. Lewis: Volume II,* 402 [April 28, 1940].

172 Lewis, "On Ethics," 313. Cf. "If we ask: 'Why ought I to be unselfish?' . . . This is where I do stop. Men ought to be unselfish, ought to be fair." Lewis, *Mere Christianity*, 333.

admitting trivial differences and perversions, Lewis, much in line with the
newest trends in postcolonial theory,[173] denied that there were in fact a
plurality of moral laws and fundamental ethical injunctions:

> Did Christian Ethics really enter the world as a novelty, a new, peculiar
> set of commands, to which a man could be in the strict sense *converted*?
> I say converted to the practical ethics: he could of course be converted
> to the Christian faith, he could accept, not only as a novelty, the deity
> and resurrection of Jesus, the Atonement, the forgiveness of sins. . .
> . [But] the idea (at least in its grossest and most popular form) that
> Christianity brought a new ethical code into the world is a grave error.
> If it had done so, then we should have to conclude that all who first
> preached it wholly misunderstood their own message: for all of them,
> its Founder, His precursor, His apostles, came demanding repentance
> and offering forgiveness, a demand and an offer both meaningless
> except on the assumption of a moral law already known and already
> broken. . . . The savage has had as many generations of ancestors as the
> civilised man: he is the man who, in the same number of centuries,
> either has not learned or has forgotten, what the rest of the human
> race know. I do not see why we should attach much significance to
> the diversity and eccentricity (themselves often exaggerated) of savage
> codes. And if we turn to civilised man, I claim that we shall find far
> fewer differences of ethical injunction than is now popularly believed.
> . . . We are not really justified in speaking of different moralities as we
> speak of different languages or different religions.
>
> You will not suspect me of trying to reintroduce in its full Stoical or
> medieval rigour the doctrine of Natural Law. Still less am I claiming
> as the source of this substantial ethical agreement anything like
> Intuition or Innate Ideas. Nor, Theist though I am, do I here put
> forward any surreptitious argument for Theism. My aim is more timid.
> It is even negative. I deny that we have any choice to make between
> clearly differentiated ethical systems. I deny that we have any power
> to make a new ethical system. I assert that wherever and whenever
> ethical discussion begins we find already before us an ethical code
> whose validity has to be assumed before we can even criticize it.[174]

173 "Lewis's argument about cross-cultural similarities has increasing credibility in
contemporary postcolonial theory. . . . Theorists are beginning to recognize a violence
that is a counterpart to the construction of the Same, namely, the construction of the
Wholly Other. . . . The lines of similarity between cultures that Lewis draws in his
appendix to *The Abolition of Man* . . . suggest a salutary recognition that other peoples
are not only different from but also like us." Kort, *C. S. Lewis: Then and Now*, 90.
174 Lewis, "On Ethics," 305, 321-3. Cf. "What is common to Zarathustra, Jeremiah, Socrates,
Gautama, Christ and Marcus Aurelius, is something pretty substantial." Lewis, *The
Problem of Pain*, 501. Cf. "The number of actions about whose ethical quality a Stoic,

Subsequently, in works like *The Abolition of Man* (which was compared to Alasdair MacIntyre's *After Virtue* by philosopher Basil Mitchell,[175] and was an important book to philosopher George Grant[176]), Lewis maintained his firm conviction that the axioms of the universal moral law need to be employed in ethical judgments so that man, who was created to obey God, can both enact God's will on Earth[177] and be in harmony with himself. To these ends,

an Aristotelian, a Thomist, a Kantian, and a Utilitarian would agree is . . . very large. The very act of studying diverse ethical theories, as theories, exaggerates the practical differences between them." C. S. Lewis, "Meditation on the Third Commandment," in *C. S. Lewis: Essay Collection & Other Short Pieces*, ed. Lesley Walmsley (1941 essay reprint; London: HarperCollins, 2000), 304. Cf. In *An Interpretation of Christian Ethics*, Reinhold Neibur wrote: "The fact is that Christianity as a whole always had to borrow from some scheme of rationalism to complete its ethical structure" – after which, Lewis commented: "Truer to say that Christianity never professed to offer a new ethic! Therefore, of course, look over the human ethic wh[ich] is the only one there ever has been." Lewis, marginalia in his edition of *An Interpretation of Christian Ethics*, 216. Cf. "Rifles may flower and terrapins may flame / But truth and reason will be still the same. / . . . / Fashions in polysyllables may fright / Those Charlies on the Left of whom you write; / No wonder; since it was from them you learned / How white to black by jargon can be turned, / . . . / Yet your shrill covin-politics and theirs / Are two peas in a single pod – *who cares / Which kind of shirt the murdering Party wears? /* Repent! Repent! Some feet of sacred ground, / A target to both gangs, can yet be found, / Sacred because, though now it's no-man's-land, / There stood your father's house; there you should stand." C. S. Lewis, "To the Author of 'Flowering Rifle,'" in *Poems*, by C. S. Lewis, ed. Walter Hooper (1939 poem reprint; San Diego: Harcourt Brace Jovanovich, 1964), 65 [1-2, 7-10, 13-9] (emphasis mine).

175 "I think it is very interesting, the convergence between Alasdair MacIntyre's argument – both in *After Virtue* and in his most recent book *Whose Justice? Which Rationality?* – and the line that Lewis was taking in *The Abolition of Man*. . . . The point of convergence between MacIntyre and Lewis is that, like Lewis, MacIntyre argues that there is a central moral tradition which one can't dispense with – which can be developed, but which can't be altogether rejected." Basil Mitchell and Andrew Walker, "Reflections on C. S. Lewis, Apologetics, and the Moral Tradition," 16-7, 18. Cf. Basil Mitchell, "C. S. Lewis on the Abolition of Man," 177.

176 "Sheila Grant told me that the Appendix to *The Abolition of Man* had meant a great deal to her, George and many others when it was published (phone conversation Oct. 25 2001). It is this notion of natural law or the Tao that Grant was to use and make much of in his writings." Dart, "C. S. Lewis and George Grant: A Tale of Two Anglican Tories," 5.

177 "The Order of the Divine mind, embodied in the Divine Law, is beautiful. What should a man do but try to reproduce it, so far as possible, in his daily life? . . . [Psalm 18] is not priggery nor even scrupulosity; it is the language of a man ravished by a moral beauty. If we cannot at all share his experience, we shall be the losers. Yet I cannot help fancying that a Chinese Christian – one whose own traditional culture had been the 'schoolmaster to bring him to Christ' – would appreciate this Psalm more than most of us; for it is an old idea in that culture that should above all things be ordered and that its order should reproduce a Divine order." Lewis, *Reflections on the Pslams*, 341.

man, through his reason and conscience, needs to grasp the principles of the moral law, which are what God wills because He is Good, and then employ them in particular circumstances thus exercising proper control of his will, emotions, instincts and body (more on this in the next section):

> This conception in all its forms, Platonic, Aristotelian, Stoic, Christian, and Oriental alike, I shall henceforth refer to for brevity simply as 'the Tao.' . . . It is the doctrine of the objective value, the belief that certain attitudes are really true, and others really false, to the kind of thing the universe is and the kind of things we are. Those who know the Tao can hold that to call children delightful or old men venerable is not simply to record a psychological fact about our own parental or filial emotions at the moment, but to recognize a quality which *demands* a certain response from us whether we make it or not. I myself do not enjoy the society of small children: because I speak from within the Tao I recognize this as a defect in myself – just as a man may have to recognize that he is tone deaf or colour blind. And because our approvals and disapprovals are thus recognitions of objective value or responses to an objective order, therefore emotional states can be in harmony with reason (when we feel liking for what ought to be approved) or out of harmony with reason (when we perceive that liking is due but cannot feel it). No emotion is, in itself, a judgment; in that sense all emotions and sentiments are alogical. But they can be reasonable or unreasonable as they conform to Reason or fail to conform. The heart never takes the place of the head: but it can, and should, obey it. . . . If we did not bring to the examination of our instincts a knowledge of their comparative dignity we could never learn it from them. And that knowledge cannot itself be instinctive: the judge cannot be one of the parties judged; or, if he is, the decision is worthless and there is no ground for placing the preservation of the species above self-preservation or sexual appetite.[178]

---

178 Lewis, *The Abolition of Man*, 405-6, 412. Cf. "To surrender to all our desires obviously leads to impotence, disease, jealousies, lies, concealment, and everything that is the reverse of health, good humour, and frankness. For any happiness, even in this world, quite a lot of restraint is going to be necessary; so the claim made by every desire, when it is strong, to be healthy and reasonable, counts for nothing. Every sane and civilised man must have some set of principles by which he chooses to reject some of his desires and to permit others." Lewis, *Mere Christianity*, 384. Cf. "The times and places in which marriage depends on Eros are in a small minority. Most of our ancestors were married off in early youth to partners chosen by their parents on grounds that had nothing to do with Eros. They went to the act with no other 'fuel,' so to speak, than plain animal desire. And they did right; honest Christian husbands and wives, obeying their fathers and mothers, discharging to one another their 'marriage debt,' and bringing up families in the fear of the Lord. Conversely, this act, done under the influence of a soaring and iridescent Eros which reduces the role of the senses to a minor consideration, may yet be plain adultery, may involve breaking a wife's heart, deceiving a husband. . . . *It has*

Indeed, Lewis was convinced that if people did not accept the axioms of the moral law, they would have a very hard time humbly acknowledging their own sinfulness, which, if unconfessed, ultimately leads to damnation.[179] Thus, while moral imperatives (which do not need to be actualized in heaven: more on this later) precede, or become apparent on the occasion of, sin,[180] it is possible for sinful people to dull, or explain away, these moral imperatives. For this reason, Lewis felt that it was urgent that Christian philosophers and theologians defend the universal moral law and recall people to a healthy[181] sense of shame when they violate its ethical injunctions:

> Whatever these doctrines [of repression and inhibitions] mean, the
> impression they have actually left on most people is that the sense

---

not pleased God that the distinction between a sin and a duty should turn on fine feelings. This act, like any other, is justified (or not) by far more prosaic and definable criteria; by the keeping or breaking of promises, by justice or injustice, by charity or selfishness, by obedience or disobedience. My treatment rules out mere sexuality – sexuality without Eros – on grounds that have nothing to do with morals; because it is irrelevant to our purpose." Lewis, *The Four Loves*, 59-60 (emphasis mine).

179 Humility and shame are the keys to repentance and salvation. Thus, Lewis said when he just converted to Christianity: "Of course one sees, from all history and from ones own circle, that the people who already have a high intellectual and moral tradition of their own are, of all people, the least likely to embrace Christianity. Fancy converting a man like J. S. Mill!" Lewis, *The Collected Letters of C. S. Lewis: Volume II*, 70 [April 8, 1932].

180 Even Adam and Eve must have known the moral law *before* they ate the fruit of the Tree of the Knowledge of Good and Evil, for if they had not known it, then they would not have understood that it was their *duty* not to eat of that fruit; hence, Lewis said in a different context: "It would be the mockery of a tyrant to forgive a man for doing what he had never been forbidden until the very moment at which the forgiveness was announced." Lewis, "On Ethics," 305. Lewis, consequently, must have disagreed with B. G. Sanders – at least insofar as Sanders was talking about earthly man – when the Oxford don underlined the following: "The conscious knowledge of morality does not precede sin. . . . The real function of law, and of morality in general, is not so much to prevent men from sinning, which it in fact does not do, but to convince men of sin after the evil act has been committed." C. S. Lewis, underlining in his edition of *Christianity after Freud*, by B. G. Sanders (London: Geoffrey Bles, 1949; The Rare Book Collection, The University of North Carolina at Chapel Hill), 84, 85.

181 Obviously, Lewis did not think that it was healthy for those who have confessed and received forgiveness to continue dwelling on their former sin and shame: "Remember what St. John says 'If our *heart* condemn us, God is stronger than our heart.' The *feeling* of being, or not being, forgiven & loved, is not what matters. One must come down to brass tacks. If there is a particular sin on your conscience, repent & confess it. If there isn't tell the despondent devil not to be silly." Lewis, *The Collected Letters of C. S. Lewis: Volume III*, 962 [July 21, 1958]. Cf. "We must beware of the Past, mustn't we? I mean that any fixing of the mind on old evils beyond what is absolutely necessary for repenting our own sins and forgiving those of others is certainly useless and usually bad for us." Ibid., 1274 [June 5, 1961]. Cf. Lewis, *Prayer: Letters to Malcolm*, 286-7.

of Shame is a dangerous and mischievous thing. We have laboured to overcome that sense of shrinking, that desire to conceal, which either Nature herself or the tradition of almost all mankind has attached to cowardice, unchastity, falsehood, and envy. We are told to 'get things out into the open,' not for the sake of self-humiliation, but on the grounds that these 'things' are very natural and we need not be ashamed of them. But unless Christianity is wholly false, the perception of ourselves which we have in moments of shame must be the only true one; and even Pagan society has usually recognized 'shamelessness' as the nadir of the soul. . . . [Thus] a recovery of the old sense of sin is essential to Christianity. . . . Thomas Aquinas said of suffering, as Aristotle had said of shame, that it was a thing not good in itself; but a thing which might have a certain goodness in particular circumstances. That is to say, if evil is present, pain at recognition of the evil, being a kind of knowledge, is relatively good; for the alternative is that the soul should be ignorant of the evil, or ignorant that the evil is contrary to its nature, 'either of which,' says the philosopher, 'is *manifestly* bad.[182]

Despite all of this, Lewis, who at different times spoke of both himself and Jesus as "moralists,"[183] constantly felt the need to address those who challenged the existence of the universal moral law.

The first group of people Lewis addressed in regard to the existence of the universal moral law was fellow Christians who rejected such a law. From

182 Lewis, *The Problem of Pain*, 498, 535. Cf. "I think that what I mainly want to talk about is the Law of Nature, or objective right and wrong. It seems to me that the N.T., by preaching repentance and forgiveness, always *assumes* an audience who already believe in the Law of Nature and know they have disobeyed it. In modern England we cannot at present assume this, and therefore most apologetic begins a stage too far on. The first step is to create, or recover, the sense of guilt." Lewis, *The Collected Letters of C. S. Lewis: Volume II*, 470 [February 10, 1941].

183 "The overwhelming majority of [Jesus's] utterances are in fact addressed neither to thought nor to the imagination, but to the 'heart' – i.e. to the will and the affections. . . . I shudder to use so bleak a word as 'moralist,' but I think it less untrue than 'poet' or 'philosopher.'" Lewis, *The Collected Letters of C. S. Lewis: Volume II*, 191-2 [May 23, 1936]. "When you invite a middle-age moralist to address you, I suppose I must conclude, however unlikely the conclusion seems, that you have a taste for middle-age moralizing. I shall do my best to gratify it." C. S. Lewis, "The Inner Ring," in *C. S. Lewis: Essay Collection & Other Short Pieces*, ed. Lesley Walmsley (1944 essay reprint; London: HarperCollins, 2000), 721. Cf. "Even as a moralist [Langland] has no unique or novel 'message' to deliver. As a cure for all our ills he can offer us only the old story – do-well, do-better, and do-best. His advice is as ancient, as 'conventional,' if you will, as that of Socrates; not to mention names more august. It is doubtful whether any moralist of unquestioned greatness has ever attempted more (or less) than the defence of the universally acknowledged; for 'men more frequently require to be reminded than informed.'" Lewis, *The Allegory of Love*, 158-9.

literary history to annotations in his books, Lewis strongly disagreed with Christians like Calvin, Thomas Cartwright and Barth, for Lewis understood all of these, in varying degrees, to be proponents of divine command ethics, which, as we recall, states that something is right because God arbitrarily commands it. Divine command ethicists like radical Calvinists "belittl[e] . . . the Law of Nature"[184] because they believe that man is so fallen and depraved that man's concept of good and evil cannot possibly be accurate. Thus, while Lewis agreed with them that man is fallen, the Oxford don did not think that this implied that man's understanding is fallen and unable to grasp objective Truth and values: "The doctrine of Total Depravity – when the consequence is drawn that, since we are totally depraved, our idea of good is worth simply nothing – may thus turn Christianity into a form of devil-worship."[185] Consequently, Lewis agreed with historians like F. M. Powicke[186] and theologians like Hooker in saying that the radical Puritans and Calvinists must, because of their belief in man's fallen intellect, be considered anti-intellectual:

> To Hooker Cartwright was the opponent of reason, the light of Nature: it was in answer to that aspect of Cartwright's teaching that Hooker, to our endless joy, drew out all the tranquil beauty of the old philosophy. Certainly there is in Cartwright a core of what we may venture, very loosely, to call Barthianism: a flattening out of all things into common significance before the inscrutable Creator. . . . [Hooker] feels as his deepest enemy what I have called the 'Barthianism' of the puritans, the theology which set a God of inscrutable will 'over against' the 'accursed nature of Man' with all its arts, sciences, traditions, learning, and merely human virtues. . . . Hooker is always insisting that the real universe is much more complex than that. 'All things which are in the Church ought to be of God. But they may be

184 C. S. Lewis, marginalia in his edition of *The Medieval Contribution to Political Thought: Thomas Aquinas, Marsilius of Padua, Richard Hooker*, by A. P. D'Entreves (Oxford: Oxford University Press, 1939; The Marion E. Wade Center, Wheaton College), 99.

185 Lewis, *The Problem of Pain*, 487. In *An Interpretation of Christian Ethics*, Niebuhr claimed that "A genuine prophetic faith reaches a transcendence in which the conflict between man and nature is overcome, even when the conflict defies every effort of rational comprehension" – to which Lewis replied: "i.e. we know that what we call evil is 'good' in that divine sense of the word 'good' wh[ich] (p. 240) is totally unknown Boojumolatory!" Lewis, marginalia in his edition of *An Interpretation of Christian Ethics*, 241.

186 In his homemade index at the back of F. M. Powicke's book *The Reformation in England*, Lewis mentioned the "ANTI-INTELLECTUALISM of the extreme Puritans." C. S. Lewis, marginalia in his edition of *The Reformation in England*, by F. M. Powicke (Oxford: Oxford University Press, 1941; The Rare Book Collection, The University of North Carolina at Chapel Hill), index.

two ways accounted such.' . . . Certain powers are given to princes 'altogether by human right,' 'at men's discretion,' and yet princes may hold these same powers 'by divine right.' 'Unto kings by human right, honour by very divine right is due.' . . . For explicit divine injunction, embodied in scripture, is but 'a part of that rule' which were created to live by. . . . There is another part, no less God-given, which Hooker calls 'nature,' 'law rational, which men commonly used to call the Law of Nature,' 'the light of Reason.' The most permanent value of Hooker's work lies in his defence of that light.[187]

As we can see, Lewis thought it completely unacceptable to set up a "bibliocracy,"[188] which would make the Bible the only source of our knowledge of good and evil, not only because he believed the Bible itself spoke of a universal moral law,[189] but also because he held that if certain biblical stories conflict with our conscience, we should prefer to maintain that God is Good rather than the Bible is perfectly inerrant:

> On my view one must apply something of the same sort of explanation to, say, the atrocities (and the treacheries) of Joshua. I see the grave danger we run by doing so; but the dangers of believing in a God whom we cannot but regard as evil, and then, in a mere terrified flattery calling Him 'good' and worshipping Him, is still greater danger. The ultimate question is whether the doctrine of the goodness of God or that of the inerrancy of Scripture is to prevail when they conflict. I think the doctrine of the goodness of God is the more certain of the two. Indeed, only that doctrine renders this worship of Him obligatory or even permissible. . . . But . . . having said all this,

---

187 Lewis, *Poetry and Prose in the Sixteenth Century*, 449, 453-4. Cf. Steve Lovell, "C. S. Lewis and the Euthyphro Dilemma," http://www.theism.net/article/29 (accessed on March 18, 2005).

188 As we know from earlier, Lewis strongly disagreed with Cartwright, about whom Lewis wrote: "Thus all human tradition, all doctrines of Natural Law, and (equally) the new theory of sovereignty, are swept away to make room for what may be called a bibliocracy, the rule of the Book." Lewis, *Poetry and Prose in the Sixteenth Century*, 447.

189 Although Lewis likely came to this belief from his own reading of scripture, he also came across it in his edition of A. P. D'Entreves' *Natural Law*, wherein Lewis underlined the following: "Natural Law is that which is contained in the Scriptures. . . . [These words of Aquinas] mean that the law of nature is embodied in the Scriptures. But they also mean that the Scriptures do not contradict the law of nature. The evidence of reason and that of Revelation are correlative. The Christian religion is no longer a 'folly,' a flat contradiction of human nature and the abolition of the old Adam. Worldly and godly wisdom must be reconciled. Reason and faith are not incompatible." C. S. Lewis, underlining in his edition of *Natural Law: An Introduction to Legal Philosophy*, by A. P. D'Entreves (London: Hutchinson House, 1951; The Marion E. Wade Center, Wheaton College), 36.

we must apply it with fear and trembling. *Some* things which seem to us bad may be good. But we must not consult our consciences by trying to feel a thing good when it seems to us totally evil. We can only pray that *if* there is an invisible goodness hidden in such things, God, in His own good time will enable us to see it. If we need to.[190]

All of this is to say that Lewis thought Christians ought to worship God because of His "authority *de jure*,"[191] and not because of his authority *de facto*: "When a rationalist accuses certain Christians, say the seventeenth-century Calvinists, of devil worship, he does not mean that they worshipped a being whom they regarded as the devil; he means that they worshipped as God a being whose character the rationalist thinks diabolical."[192] Needless to say, Lewis thought such pseudo-devil worship "dangerous"[193] because it made Christians servile cowards[194] and not men who, in the words of the *Theologica Germanica*, "live in pure submission and obedience to the Eternal Good"[195]:

> If God's moral judgement differs from ours so that our 'black' may be His 'white', we can mean nothing by calling Him good; for to say 'God is good', while asserting that His goodness is wholly other than ours, is really only to say 'God is we know not what.' And an utterly unknown quality in God cannot give us moral grounds for loving or obeying Him. If he is not (in our sense) 'good' we shall obey, if at all, only through fear – and should be equally ready to obey an

---

190 C. S. Lewis, quoted in *C. S. Lewis and the Search for Rational Religion*, by John Beversluis, 156-7.

191 C. S. Lewis, review of *Paradise Lost in Our Time: Some Comments*, by Douglas Bush, *The Oxford Magazine* 65 (February 13, 1947): 216.

192 Lewis, "A Reply to Professor Haldane," 90. In his notes on Henry More, Lewis wrote, "Yet Judaism was given by God: Paganism, by Angels or evil spirits. The latter in some places have put out the natural light of reason in their votaries: whose extinction, as among the Quakers, is an invitation to the Devil." Lewis, "Henry More," 95.

193 "Only one further step was left to be taken, and Grotius took it in the *De Jure Belli ac Pacis* (1625). There he asserts that the Law of Nature, actually derived from God, would be equally binding even if we supposed that no God existed. It is another way of saying that good would still be good if stripped of all power. It is the extreme opposite of the Calvinist view which comes near to saying that omnipotence must be worshipped even if it is evil, that power is venerable when stripped of all good; and it is no doubt incomparably less dangerous to theism." Lewis, *Poetry and Prose in the Sixteenth Century*, 49.

194 Cf. "Servile fear is, to be sure, the lowest form of religion." Lewis, *Prayer: Letters to Malcolm*, 272.

195 *Theologica Germanica* (N.p.: Kessinger, n.d.), 18 [10]. Cf. "So it is good and just and right that the Good should be loved before God. And thus God loves not Himself as Himself, but as the Good." Ibid., 59 [32].

omnipotent Fiend.[196]

The second group of people Lewis addressed in regard to the existence of the universal moral law was the atheists who rejected such a law. Although Lewis rarely labeled them as such, these atheists usually belonged to two basic groups: behaviorists and materialist scientists, and atheist existentialists and pragmatists.

Behaviorists–called "Conditioners"[197] by Lewis–and materialist scientists are those who, among other things, reject the idea of a universal moral law in the name of "science," claiming that morality is nothing more than a byproduct of the evolutionary process. As a result, many of these scientists approach ethics as utilitarians who, seeing survival of the fittest as the one universal principle, argue that ends justify the means and subsequently often support things like euthanasia, abortion, and vivisection.[198] According to a lost paper by Lewis entitled "If We Have Christ's Ethics, Does the Rest of the Christian Faith Matter?" scientism popularizer H. G. Wells,[199] not to mention materialist scientists like J. B. S. Haldane and Conrad Waddington, were seen by Lewis as "faddists" who failed "to understand the actual condition of Man."[200] As he had done earlier in his life with Hume's sentiment-grounded morality,[201] Lewis attacked Wells, Haldane, Waddington and others for

---

196 Lewis, *The Problem of Pain*, 487.

197 Lewis, *The Abolition of Man*, 422.

198 "The victory of vivisection marks a great advance in the triumph of ruthless, non-moral utilitarianism over the old world of ethical law; a triumph in which we, as well as animals, are already victims, and of which Dachau and Hiroshima marks the more recent achievements. In justifying cruelty to animals we put ourselves also on the animal level. We choose the jungle and must abide by our choice." Lewis, "Vivisection," 696.

199 Although Wells was neither a scientist nor a philosopher, his influence on popular imagination in regard to man-made morality was immense: "Few would claim for Mr. H. G. Wells a place among the original thinkers of his time, but as a popular educator and gospeller his significance for our present studies is not negligible. For no English writer of our day has done more to captivate the mind of the masses with dreams of scientific progress and the complete resourcefulness and self-sufficiency of Man." Gwilym Griffith, *Interpreters of Man: A Review of Secular and Religious Thought from Hegel to Barth* (London: Lutterworth Press, 1944), 168.

200 These quotations are actually from the précis of this paper as found in the *Socratic Digest* and reprinted in Hooper, "Oxford's Bonny Fighter," 143.

201 Largely drawing on insight that he received when he read, and critiqued, Hume's ethics, Lewis the Christian wrote the following: "From propositions about fact alone no *practical* conclusion can ever be drawn. *This will preserve society* cannot lead to *do this* except by the mediation of *society ought to be preserved*. *This will cost you your life* cannot lead directly to *do not do this*: it can lead to it only through a felt desire or an acknowledged duty of self-preservation. . . . We must therefore either extend the

supposing morality to be either merely programmed behavior or subjective feelings.[202] If morality were either of these, Lewis believed, there would be no way to make meaningful value judgments, for even when one denies that there are universal "oughts," one cannot help but presuppose such "oughts." Thus, Lewis felt that the flaw of the behaviorists and materialist scientists is that they choose one universal moral law, such as the duty of general beneficence, and, without realizing that they are presupposing an axiom of the moral law, denounce all other moral duties as meaningless byproducts of evolution: "The Innovator, for example, rates high the claims of posterity. He cannot get any valid claim for posterity out of instinct or (in the modern sense) reason. He is really deriving our duty to posterity from the Tao; our duty to do good to all men is an axiom of Practical Reason, and our duty to do good to our descendants is a clear deduction from it."[203] Consequently, instead of being

---

word Reason to include what our ancestors called Practical Reason and confess that judgments such as *society ought to be preserved* (though they can support themselves by no reason of the sort that Gaius and Titius demand) are not mere sentiments but are rationality itself; or else we must give up at once, and for ever, the attempt to find a core of 'rational' value behind all the sentiments we have debunked. The Innovator will not take the first alternative, for practical principles known to all men by Reason are simply the *Tao* which he has set out to supersede. He is more likely to give up the quest for a 'rational' core and to hunt for some other ground even more 'basic' and 'realistic.'" Lewis, *The Abolition of Man*, 410-1.

202 In *That Hideous Strength*, the character Frost, who represented the ethical theories of Waddington, said: "Motives are not the causes of action but its by-products. . . . All motives . . . [are] subjective epiphenomena." Lewis, *That Hideous Strength*, 659. Cf. Lewis, "A Reply to Professor Haldane," 86.

203 Lewis, *The Abolition of Man*, 414. Cf. "Creative Evolution is 'the religion of the Twentieth Century.' This religion has its great commandment: 'Life must not cease. That comes before everything.'" Lewis, *Studies in Words*, 300. Cf. "As soon as Ransom had finished, Weston continued, 'Life is greater than any system of morality; her claims are absolute. It is not by tribal taboos and copy-book maxims that she has pursued her relentless march from the amoeba to man and from man to civilization.' 'He says,' began Ransom, 'that living creatures are stronger than the question whether an act is bent or good – no, that cannot be right – he says it is better to be alive and bent than to be dead – no – he says, he says – I cannot say what he says, Oyarsa, in your language. But he goes on to say that the only good thing is that there should be very many creatures alive. He says there were many other animals before the first men and the later ones were better than the earlier ones; but he says the animals were not born because of what is said to the young about bent and good action by their elders. And he says these animals did not feel any pity.'" Lewis, *Out of the Silent Planet*, 121-2. Cf. "The general law is Beneficence. Then comes the laws that give certain people a prior claim on your beneficence: people to whom your beneficence is pledged by a promise (Justice), or who have already benefited you (Gratitude), or who are specially weak and pitiable (Mercy) or fellow-citizens (Patriotism) or relatives (Family Affection). They are all perfectly sound, but the last two must not be allowed to over-ride the others. What

able to escape the universal moral law, behaviorists and materialist scientists – and indeed all skeptics of the moral law who choose only one axiom of the moral law – simply end up developing a system of ethics which is "singularly poor in content," for "[i]ts solitary command, compared with the richly articulated codes of Aristotle, Confucius, or Aquinas, suggests that it is a mere residuum; as the arts of certain savages suggest that they are the last vestige of a vanished civilization."[204] Indeed, when one reads a behaviorist tract like B. F. Skinner's *Beyond Freedom and Dignity*, which incidentally directed many of its attacks against Lewis's *Abolition of Man*,[205] one cannot help but feel that Lewis's critique of behaviorist and scientific materialist ethics was largely correct.

Existentialists of either the religious or atheistic type are those who simply deny that we can have knowledge of objective Truth and values; while existentialists can become proponents of things like divine command ethics or anarchy, many existentialists become pragmatists – those who maintain that since people cannot know objective Truth and values and since people do not want to believe in some arbitrary divine law or let chaos run amuck, it is best to think of morality and law in terms of what works. Often such existentialists and pragmatists reject the concept of a universal moral law because they observe that in practice, many axioms of the universal moral law conflict and hence cannot be truly universal since if there is a conflict, then one moral law must not be true.

Using Aristotelian language, Lewis agreed with the existentialists and others when he said that "moral decisions do not admit of mathematical certainty;"[206] indeed, the Oxford don even conceded that the moral law allows

I meant in the passage was that Racialism, setting up to be the supreme duty, is the rebellion of one particular moral law against moral law in general." Lewis, *The Collected Letters of C. S. Lewis: Volume II*, 699 [January 16, 1946]. Cf. Kant, *The Metaphysics of Morals*, 6:402.

204 Lewis, "On Ethics," 307.
205 "'What is now under attack,' said Maslow, 'is the 'being' of man.' C. S. Lewis put it quite bluntly: Man is being abolished. There is clearly some difficulty in identifying the man to whom these expressions refer. Lewis cannot have meant the human species, for not only is it not being abolished, it is filling the earth. . . . We are told that what is threatened is 'man *qua* man,' or 'man in his humanity,' or 'man as Thou not It,' or 'man as a person not a thing.' . . . What is being abolished is autonomous man – the inner man . . . the man defended by the literatures of freedom and dignity. His abolition has been long overdue. . . . Science does not de-humanize man, it de-homunculizes him. . . . To man *qua* man we readily say good riddance." B. F. Skinner, *Beyond Freedom & Dignity* (1971 reprint; Cambridge: Hackett, 2002), 200-1.
206 Lewis, "Why I Am Not a Pacifist," 293. Cf. "Now our treatment of [politics] will be adequate, if it achieves that amount of precision which belongs to its subject matter. The same exactness must not be expected in all departments of philosophy alike. . . . It is

for "deepening" and "changes of emphasis" from within;[207] nevertheless, he adamantly denied that the moral law is relative, contending that errors in moral judgment are, as we shall see more in the next section, due to one, or a combination, of the following: man getting the facts wrong,[208] man's fallen will,[209] and / or man's failure to develop the virtue of prudence:

---

equally unreasonable to accept merely probable conclusions from a mathematician and to demand strict demonstrations from an orator." Aristotle *Ethics* 1094b12-14, 25-26.

207 Lewis, "On Ethics," 306. Cf. "Those who understand the spirit of the *Tao* and who have been led by that spirit can modify it in directions which that spirit itself demands. Only they can know what those directions are. The outsider knows nothing about the matter. . . . So far from being able to harmonize discrepancies in its letter by penetration to its spirit, he merely snatches at some one precept, on which the accidents of time and place happen to have riveted his attention, and then rides it to death – for no reason that he can give. . . . This is why Aristotle said that only those who have been well brought up can usefully study ethics: to the corrupted man, the man who stands outside the *Tao*, the very starting point of this science is invisible. He may be hostile, but he cannot be critical: he does not know what is being discussed." Lewis, *The Abolition of Man*, 416-7.

208 "But one word before I end. I have met people who exaggerate the differences, because they have not distinguished between differences of morality and differences of belief about facts. For example, one man said to me, 'Three hundred years ago people in England were putting witches to death. Was that what you call the Rule of Human Nature or Right Conduct?' But surely the reason we do not execute witches is that we do not believe there are such things. If we did – if we really thought that there were people going about who had sold themselves to the devil and received supernatural powers from him in return and were using these powers to kill their neighbours or drive them mad or bring bad weather – surely we would all agree that if anyone deserved the death penalty, then these filthy quislings did? There is no difference of moral principle here: the difference is simply about matter of fact." Lewis, *Mere Christianity*, 330. We can see this kind of dispute about the facts in *On Liberty*, where John Stuart Mill wrote, "Another grand determining principle of the rules of conduct, both in act and forbearance, which have been enforced by law or opinion, has been the servility of mankind towards the supposed preferences or aversions of their temporal masters or of their gods. This servility, though essentially selfish, is not hypocrisy; it gives rise to perfect genuine sentiments of abhorrence; it made men burn magicians and heretics." – about which Lewis commented: "Nonsense. They burned them in self-defence." C. S. Lewis, marginalia in his edition of *On Liberty*, in *Utilitarianism, Liberty and Representative Government*, by John Stuart Mill (London: J. M. Dent & Sons, 1922; The Marion E. Wade Center, Wheaton College), 70.

209 Of an example of man's fallen will clouding his moral judgment, considering the following example: "In the same way [as with the Hebrews] we cannot be certain that the comparative absence of vindictiveness in the Pagans, though certainly a good thing in itself, is a good symptom. This was borne in upon me during a night journey taken early in the Second World War in a compartment full of young soldiers. Their conversation made it clear that they totally disbelieved all that they had read in the papers about the wholesale cruelties of the Nazi *régime*. They took it for granted, without argument, that this was all lies, all propaganda put out by our own government to 'pep up' our troops. And the shattering thing was, that, believing this, they expressed not the slightest anger.

In thus recalling men to traditional morality I am not of course maintaining that it will provide an answer to every particular moral problem with which we may be confronted. M. Sartre seems to me to be the victim of a curious misunderstanding when he rejects the conception of general moral rules on the ground that such rules may fail to apply clearly to all concrete problems of conduct. Who could ever have supposed that by accepting a moral code we should be delivered from all questions of casuistry? Obviously it is moral codes that create questions of casuistry, just as the rules of chess create chess problems. The man without a moral code, like the animal, is free from moral problems. The man who has not learned to count is free from mathematical problems. A man asleep is free from all problems. Within the framework of general human ethics problems will, of course, arise and will sometimes be solved wrongly. This possibility of error is simply the symptom that we are awake, not asleep, that we are men, not beasts or gods. If I were pressing on you a panacea, if I were recommending traditional ethics as a means to some end, I might be tempted to promise you the infallibility which I actually deny. But that, you see, is not my position.[210]

Thus, for example, in the case where a Nazi asks a man protecting a Jew if he is in fact protecting a Jew – that is, in the case where a person is apparently forced to decide between lying or betraying someone to murder – Lewis came to think[211] that the lie, if it is in fact a lie since there is no evil

---

That our rulers should falsely attribute the worst crimes to some of their fellow-men in order to induce other men to shed their blood seemed to them a matter of course. They weren't even particularly interested. They saw nothing wrong in it. Now it seemed to me that the most violent of the Psalmists – or, for that matter any child wailing out 'But it's not fair' – was in a more hopeful condition than these young men. If they had perceived, and felt as a man should feel, the diabolical wickedness which they believed our rulers to be committing, and then forgiven them, they would have been saints. But not to perceive it at all – not even to be tempted to resentment – to accept it as the most ordinary thing in the world – argues a terrifying insensibility. Clearly these young men had (on that subject anyway) no conception of good and evil whatsoever." Lewis, *Reflections on the Psalms*, 324.

210 Lewis, "On Ethics," 313-4. Cf. "But here also it is reasonable to combine a firm belief in the objective validity of goodness with a considerable skepticism about all our particular moral judgements. To say that they all require correction is indeed to say both that they are partially wrong and that they are not merely subjective facts about ourselves." Lewis, "*De Futilitate*," 679.

211 While the context is different, the early Christian Lewis *may* have agreed with Kant that it is always wrong to tell a lie; hence, concerning social lying (and not a more ambiguous form), Lewis's brother, Warnie, reported: "I had an argument with [C. S. Lewis] on the ethics of social lying, he maintained that a lie must not be told, even in indifferent matters, as a conversational counter in talking with a fool, I denying this strenuously." Warren Lewis, *Brothers and Friends: The Diaries of Major Warren Hamilton Lewis*, ed.

deception involved, is not worse than betrayal: "I've often puzzled over the question of the obligatory life – for I am sure wherever it is permissible it is obligatory. The case I am clear about is where an impertinent question forces you *either* to lie *or* to betray a friend's secret (for to say 'I won't tell you' is often tantamount to answering 'Yes')."[212]

In addition to defending universal rational ethics against the charge that it is too formal and impractical, Lewis also went on the offensive, pointing out that any kind of relativist position – be it existentialist, pragmatic, etc. – would be, if worse came to worst, unable to reject indisputably evil morality, such as that of the Nazis:

> What was the sense in saying that the enemy were in the wrong unless Right is a real thing which the Nazis at bottom knew as well as we did and ought to have practiced? If they had had no notion of what we mean by right, then, though we might still have had to fight them, we could no more have blamed them for that than for the colour of their hair. . . . If no set of moral ideas were truer or better than any other, there would be no sense in preferring civilised morality to savage morality, or Christian morality to Nazi morality. In fact, of course, we all do believe that some moralities are better than others. We do believe that some of the people who tried to change the moral ideas of their own age were what we would call Reformers or Pioneers – people who understood morality better than their neighbours did. Very well then. The moment you say that one set of moral ideas can be better than another, you are, in fact, measuring them both by a standard, saying that one of them conforms to that standard more nearly than the other. . . . If your moral ideas can be truer, and those of the Nazis less true, there must be something – some Real Morality – for them to be true about.[213]

In fact, as we shall see more of in the next chapter, the end result for most of those who reject the universal moral law (and rationality[214]) is a type of pragmatic social structure in which the powerful can, by changing the laws to suit their needs (à la Niccolò Machiavelli), control the majority.[215] Thus,

---

Clyde Kilby and Marjorie Lamp Mead (San Francisco: Harper & Row, 1982), 148 [July 10, 1934].

212 Lewis, *The Collected Letters of C. S. Lewis: Volume III*, 1000 [December 15, 1958].

213 Lewis, *Mere Christianity*, 324, 329.

214 Hence, like a good pragmatist, the Un-man in *Pereladra* "regarded intelligence simply and solely as a weapon, which it had no more wish to employ in its off-duty hours than a soldier has to do bayonet practice when he is on leave. Thought was for it a device necessary to certain ends, but thought in itself did not interest it." Lewis, *Perelandra*, 260.

215 Uncle Andrew is a perfect example of such a pragmatist: a man who, disbelieving in any kind of universal moral law, maintains both that belief in such is good for the average Joe, but he, knowing better, stands outside of it and is thus able to do as he pleases:

although Lewis, under the influence of Aristotle and Kant, spoke favorably of practical reason, the Oxford don largely used the word "practical" as a synonym for the pejorative word "pragmatic;" hence, he spoke of the "practical" Orual,[216] the "practical" Uncle Andrew,[217] the "practical" White Witch, Shasta's "practical" uncle,[218] the "practical" Nikabrik,[219] the "practical" Busby,[220] and the "practical" Susan.[221]

Now Lewis's defense of the universal moral law and our duty toward it was what motivated him to reject false eudaimonism or worldly hedonism. Nevertheless, we must not forget that already back when Lewis wrote "Hegemony of Moral Value," he tried to "prove that no pleasure could be considered bad, considered in itself."[222] As we should expect, then, as a Neoplatonic Christian, Lewis continued in this Platonic belief, only adding

---

"'That promise I did not keep.' 'Well, then, it was jolly rotten of you,' said Digory. 'Rotten?' said Uncle Andrew with a puzzled look. 'Oh, I see. You mean that little boys ought to keep their promises. Very true: most right and proper, I'm sure, and I'm very glad you have been taught to do it. But of course you must understand that rules of that sort, however excellent they may be for little boys – and servants – and women – and even people in general, can't possibly be expected to apply to profound students and great thinkers and sages. No, Digory. Men like me, who possess hidden wisdom, are freed from common rules just as we are cut off from common pleasures. Ours, my boy, is a high and lonely destiny.' As he said this he sighed and looked so grave and noble and mysterious that for a second Digory really thought he was saying something rather fine. But then he remembered the ugly look he had seen on his Uncle's face the moment before Polly had vanished: and all at once he saw through Uncle Andrew's grand words. 'All it means,' he said to himself, 'is that he thinks he can do anything he likes to get anything he wants.'" Lewis, *The Magician's Nephew*, 24.

216 "Orual lives the practical life and is, after many sins, saved." Lewis, *The Collected Letters of C. S. Lewis: Volume III*, 874 [August 7, 1957].

217 Explaining why Uncle Andrew does not hear the animals talking when everyone does, Lewis wrote: "He watched them very hard of course; but he wasn't really interested in seeing what they were doing, only in seeing whether they were going to make a rush at him. Like the [White] Witch, he was dreadfully practical." Lewis, *The Magician's Nephew*, 116.

218 Shasta's uncle "didn't know what lay to the North. Neither did he care. He had a very practical mind." Lewis, *The Horse and His Boy*, 12.

219 "'And anyway,' Nikabrik continued, 'what came of the Kings and their reign? They faded too. But it's very different with the Witch. They say she ruled for a hundred years: a hundred years of winter. There's power, if you like. There's something practical.' 'But, heaven and earth!' said the King, 'haven't we always been told that she was the worst enemy of all? Wasn't she a tyrant ten times worse than Miraz?'" Lewis, *Prince Caspian*, 145.

220 Lewis, *That Hideous Strength*, 381.

221 Lewis spoke of "the practical Susan," who later, in *The Last Battle*, failed to enter the New Narnia because she was too taken up with fashion and the immediate concerns of the world. Lewis, *Prince Caspian*, 107. Lewis, *The Last Battle*, 129.

222 Lewis, *All My Road Before Me*, 98 [September 1, 1922].

that Plato's "mixed pleasures"[223] – those pleasures which give momentary
and deceptive relief, such as scratching an itch – are like "the pleasures of the
mind which are intrinsically evil. The pleasure, say, of having a grievance."[224]
Yet this is only to say that while these mixed pleasures do not exist in Heaven,
they are still good in regard to their pleasantness – even if not in regard
to the circumstance in which this pleasantness occurs; hence, in the New
Narnia, Lucy says that "one can't feel afraid, even if one wants to."[225] And
so because all pleasures considered in themselves are good and act, similar to
Plato's position in the *Phaedrus*, as pointers toward the source of all pleasure,
God,[226] Lewis claimed both that God is "a hedonist at heart"[227] and that it
is an "absurd fancy" to imagine that "devils are engaged in the disinterested
pursuit of something called Evil."[228] Consequently, even though Lewis
sometimes spoke as if people could really desire something other than their
happiness,[229] he did not seriously believe this,[230] for even the Ghost in *The*

---

223 Plato *Philebus* 50d.
224 Lewis, *Prayer: Letters to Malcolm*, 284.
225 Lewis, *The Last Battle*, 164.
226 "I was learning the far more secret doctrine that *pleasures* are shafts of the glory as
it strikes our sensibility. As it impinges on our will or our understanding, we give it
different names – goodness or truth or the like. But its flash upon our sense and mood
is pleasure. . . . These pure and spontaneous pleasures are 'patches of Godlight' in the
woods of our experience. . . . [Hence] Joy is the serious business of Heaven." Lewis,
Prayer: Letters to Malcolm, 280, 281-2, 282-3.
227 Lewis, *The Screwtape Letters*, 794.
228 Ibid., 737. "Wickedness, when you examine it, turns out to be the pursuit of some
good in the wrong way. You can be good for the mere sake of goodness: you cannot be
bad for the mere sake of badness. You can do a kind action when you are not feeling
kind and when it gives you no pleasure, simply because kindness is right; but no one
ever did a cruel action simply because cruelty is wrong. . . . Goodness is, so to speak,
itself: badness is only spoiled goodness." Lewis, *Mere Christianity*, 348. In his edition
of Augustine's *Confessions*, Lewis also noted: "SIN always seeks some real good, 80, 82,
84, 86." Lewis, marginalia in his edition of *Confessions*, at the end of volume 1.
229 "This week I have been reading . . . Cicero's *De Legibus*. . . . [Y]ou might suppose [it] to
be rather a bromide, but it is perfectly delightful. It's in a dialogue form, and held out of
doors. Isn't this nice? – 'But I've another reason for liking this place which can't effect
you in the same way. My brother and I are 'on our native heath' here. We come of an old
family hereabouts: all round here you find our sacred places, our own people, and all the
relics of our forebears.' . . . All very ordinary and obvious, of course, but, like Boswell,
so full of sense and leisure and happiness. Does it occur to you that people have written
of that sort of thing in almost all ages but our own? I begin to suspect that the world is
divided not only into the happy and the unhappy, but into those who *like* happiness and
those who, odd as it may seem, really don't." Lewis, *The Collected Letters of C. S. Lewis:
Volume II*, 334-5. [January 28, 1940].
230 Lewis mentioned "the preference of the will for love rather than hatred, and happiness
rather than misery." Lewis, "Why I Am Not a Pacifist," 283.

Great Divorce who does not appear to desire happiness, in fact does so under the guise of duty *qua* happiness.[231] Thus, against Erik Wielenberg's claim that it is possible for people to desire evil for its own sake,[232] Lewis would have answered him by saying, for instance, that one man pursues a bottle of port because he thinks – mistakenly – that this will make him happy, while another man pursues Truth and acts in obedience to the moral law because he thinks – correctly – that this will make him happy.[233]

And speaking of which, Lewis was always careful to separate True Happiness not only from false happiness or temporary pleasure but also from mere moral duty. That is, while admitting that deontological ethics are more noble than eudaimonian ethics *qua* hedonism (including "theological hedonism" or service rendered to either a good or evil god who rewards his followers with immortality[234]), Lewis – still from his days as an absolute

---

231 "'If the thirst of Reason is really dead,' said the Spirit, and then stopped as though pondering. Then suddenly he said, 'Can you, at least, still desire happiness?' 'Happiness, my dear Dick,' said the Ghost placidly, 'happiness, as you will come to see when you are older, lies in the path of duty.'" Lewis, *The Great Divorce*, 1047.

232 Wielenberg quotes passages from both Augustine's *Confessions* and Lewis's diary written during his Stoical materialist phase as evidence that Lewis the Christian was wrong when he said that no one loves evil for its own sake. Wielenberg, *God and the Reach of Reason: C. S. Lewis, David Hume and Bertrand Russell*, 72-3. But as I have shown, Lewis the Christian rejected the idea of loving evil for evil's sake. Cf. Lewis, *An Experiment in Criticism*, 25.

233 "Which of the religions of the world gives to its followers the greatest happiness? While it lasts, the religion of worshipping oneself is the best. I have an elderly acquaintance of about eighty, who has lived a life of unbroken selfishness and self-admiration from the earliest years, and is, more or less, I regret to say, one of the happiest men I know. From the moral point of view it is very difficult! I am not approaching the question from that angle. As you perhaps know, I haven't always been a Christian. I didn't go to religion to make me happy. I always knew a bottle of port would do that. If you want a religion to make you feel really comfortable, I certainly don't recommend Christianity." Lewis, "Answers to Christianity," 325. For more examples of people taking comfort in false forms of happiness, consider the following: "After that, the Head's friend's saw that the Head was no use as a Head, so they got her made an Inspector to interfere with other Heads. And when they found she wasn't much good even at that, they got her into Parliament where she lived happily ever after." Lewis, *The Silver Chair*, 206. "(And when the others returned he [the cowardly man who did not finish the voyage to the End of the World] felt so out of things that he deserted on the voyage home at the Lone Islands, and went and lived in Calormen, where he told wonderful stories about his adventures at the End of the World, until at last he came to believe them himself. So you may say, in a sense, that he lived happily ever after." Lewis, *The Voyage of the Dawn Treader*, 165.

234 "That the profit should be located in another world makes, as Tyndale clearly sees, no difference. Theological hedonism is still hedonism. Whether the man is seeking heaven or a hundred pounds he can still 'but seeke himself' (*Prologue to Numbers*). . . . Christianity

idealist – believed that deontological ethics are inferior to eudaimonian ethics *qua* self-realization because the deontologist fails to realize that the end of man is not morality (the moral good), but something that, while always requiring morality and obedience to the moral law, is something far more that morality (the Good): "The Holiness of God is something more and other than moral perfection: His claim upon us is something more and other than moral perfection: His claim upon us is something more and other that the claim of moral duty."[235]

Thus, on the one hand, Lewis believed that although Kant's criterion for a moral act is unrealistic,[236] the German was right insofar as moral duty is often necessary regardless of how people feel. However, on the other hand, Lewis believed that although Aristotle's theory of leisure was unduly soft,[237]

---

is in constant danger of relapsing into theological hedonism. It had so relapsed in the eighteenth century when Boswell could say (without contradiction from Johnson) that the doctrine of future rewards and punishments was its very essence." Lewis, *Poetry and Prose in the Sixteenth Century*, 188, 189. As with Lewis, Charles Williams also rejected theological hedonism and the "carrot of immortality": "He vehemently denied that he had any natural desire for life after death." Lewis, "Preface," in *Essays Presented to Charles Williams*, xii. Cf. "Progress, for me, means increasing goodness and happiness of individual lives. For the species, as for each man, mere longevity seems to me a contemptible idea." Lewis, "Willing Slaves of the Welfare State," 746.

235 Lewis, *The Problem of Pain*, 502.

236 "If God were a Kantian, who would not have us till we came to Him from the purest and best motives, who could be saved?" Ibid., 521.

237 Although Lewis usually erred on the side of being too deontological, it appears that at one point shortly after his conversion to Christianity, he became excessively eudaimonistic, oversubscribing to Aristotle's theory of happiness and leisure: "The Purpose of education has been described by Milton as that of fitting a man 'to perform justly, skillfully, and magnanimously all the offices both private and public, of peace and war.' Provided that we don't overstress 'skillfully' Aristotle would substantially agree with this, but would add the conception that it should also be a preparation for leisure, which according to him is the end of all human activity. 'We wage war in order to have peace; we work in order to have leisure.' Neither of them would dispute that the purpose of education is to produce the good man and the good citizen, though it must be remembered that we are not here using the word 'good' in any narrowly ethical sense. The 'good man' here means the man of good taste and good feeling, the interesting man, and almost the happy man. With such an end in view education in most civilized communities has taken much the same path; it has taught civil behaviour by direct and indirect discipline, has awakened the logical faculty by mathematics or dialectic, and has endeavored to produce right sentiments – which are to the passions what right habits are to the body by steeping the pupil in the literature both sacred and profane on which the culture of the community is based. . . . Human life means to me the life of beings for whom the leisured activities of thought, art, literature, conversation are the end, and the preservation and propagation of life merely the means. That is why education seems to me so important: it actualizes that potentiality for leisure." C. S. Lewis, "Our English Syllabus," in *Rehabilitations: And Other Essays*, by C. S. Lewis (London: Oxford

Aristotle was closer to the mark than Kant since Aristotle knew that man can take delight in being obedient to the moral law; that is, because acting virtuously is the rational thing to do and since man's nature is rational and man's happiness is found in acting according to his nature,[238] man can attain happiness by obeying the moral law, which, moreover, is only *one* component of the happy life:

> Kant thought that no action had moral value unless it were done out of pure reverence for the moral law, that is, without inclination, and he has been accused of a 'morbid frame of mind' which measures the value of act by its unpleasantness. All popular opinion is, indeed, on Kant's side. . . . Yet against Kant stands the obvious truth, noted by Aristotle, that the more virtuous a man becomes the more he enjoys virtuous actions. What an atheist ought to do about this conflict between the ethics of duty and the ethics of virtue, I do not know: but as a Christian I suggest the following solution. . . . God's will is determined by His wisdom which always perceives, and His goodness which always embraces, the intrinsically good. But when we have said that God commands things only because they are good, we must add that one of the things intrinsically good is that rational creatures should freely surrender themselves to their Creator in obedience. The

University Press, 1939), 81, 83. Shortly after writing this paper, Lewis retracted some of what he had written: "I have been intending ever since I got [your letter] to let you know that I think your criticisms on my Aristotelian idea of leisure are largely right. I wouldn't write that essay now. In fact I have recently come to the conclusion that a besetting sin of mine all my life has been one which I never suspected – laziness – and that a good deal of the high sounding doctrine of leisure is only a defence of *that*. . . . If I still wanted to defend my old view I sh[oul]d ask you why *toil* appears in Genesis not as one of the things God originally created and pronounced 'very good,' but as a punishment for sin, like death. I suppose one w[oul]d point out in reply that Adam was a gardener before he was a sinner, and that we must distinguish two degrees and kinds of work – the one wholly good and necessary to the animal side of the *animal rationale*, the other a punitive deterioration of the former due to the Fall." Lewis, *The Collected Letters of C. S. Lewis: Volume II*, 422-3 [July 16, 1940]. Yet even though Lewis thought that the temptation of leisure is dangerous, he still maintained, as we shall see, that there are true elements in leisure – namely, enjoyment and the beauty of rest; hence, Lewis told an American woman: "Don't be too convinced that God really wants you to do all sorts of work you needn't do. Each must do his duty 'in that state of life to which God has called him.' Remember that a belief in the virtues of doing for doing's sake is characteristically feminine, characteristically American, and characteristically modern: so that *three* veils may divide you from the correct view! . . . Just you give Mary a little chance as well as Martha!" Lewis, *The Collected Letters of C. S. Lewis: Volume III*, 720 [March 19, 1956].

238 Lewis agreed with Tolkien in saying the following: "Since, in Tolkien's view, [subcreation] is one of man's proper functions, delight naturally arises whenever it is successfully performed." Lewis, "On Three Ways of Writing for Children," 509.

content of our obedience – the thing we are commanded to do – will always be something intrinsically good, something we ought to do even if (by an impossible supposition) God had not commanded it. But in addition to the content, the mere obeying is also intrinsically good, for in obeying a rational creature consciously enacts its creaturely role, reverses the act by which we fell, treads Adam's dance backwards, and returns. We therefore agree with Aristotle that what is intrinsically right may well be agreeable, and that the better man is the more he will like it; but we agree with Kant so far as to say that there is one right act – that of self-surrender – which cannot be willed to the height by fallen creatures unless it is unpleasant.[239]

To take another example, Lewis agreed that "unselfishness" (a negative good) is morally commendable, but it is not as perfect as "charity" (a positive good) since whereas unselfishness seems to exclude delight and happiness, charity is a much richer term, implying satisfaction in being good:

If you asked twenty good men what they thought the highest of the virtues, nineteen of them would reply, Unselfishness. But if you had asked almost any of the great Christians of old he would have replied, Love. You see what has happened? A negative term has been substituted for a positive, and this is of more than philosophical importance. The negative idea of Unselfishness carries with it the suggestion not primarily of securing good things for others, but of going without them ourselves, as if our abstinence and not their happiness was the important point. I do not think this is the Christian virtue of Love. The New Testament has lots to say about self-denial, but not about self-denial as an end in itself. We are not told to deny ourselves and to take up our crosses in order that we may follow Christ; and nearly every description of what we shall ultimately find if we do so contains an appeal to desire. If there lurks in most modern minds the notion that to desire our own good and earnestly to hope for the enjoyment of it is a bad thing, I submit that this notion has crept in from Kant

---

239 Lewis, *The Problem of Pain*, 522. Because Lewis agreed with Aristotle that virtue is lovely, the Oxford don also agreed with poets like Sidney and Spenser, who Lewis understood to have propagated this notion: Of the "golden" poet of the sixteenth century, Lewis wrote: "His aim is indeed ethical as well as aesthetic, *docere et delectare, docere delectando, jucunda doctrina*. But this is part of the loveliness, for virtue is lovely, not merely obligatory; a celestial mistress, not a categorical imperative." Lewis, *Poetry and Prose in the Sixteenth Century*, 322. Related to this, Lewis said of Spenser: "In sum, then, evil is solemn, good is gay. Evil means starvation, good glows with what Blake calls 'the lineaments of gratified desire.' Evil imprisons, good sets free. Evil is tired, good is full of vigour. The one says, Let go, lie down, sleep, die; the other, All Aboard! Kill the dragon, marry the girl, blow the pipes and beat the drum, let the dance begin." Lewis, *Spenser's Images of Life*, 95.

and the Stoics and is no part of the Christian faith. . . . We must not be troubled by unbelievers when they say that this promise of reward makes the Christian life a mercenary affair. There are different kinds of reward. There is the reward which has no natural connection with the things you do to earn it, and is quite foreign to the desires that ought to accompany those things. Money is not the natural reward of love, that is why we call a man mercenary if he marries a woman for the sake of her money. But marriage is the proper reward for a real lover, and he is not a mercenary for desiring it. . . . There is also [another] case, which is more complicated. An enjoyment of Greek poetry is certainly a proper, and not a mercenary, reward for learning Greek; but only those who have reached the stage of enjoying Greek poetry can tell from their own experience that this is so. The schoolboy beginning Greek grammar cannot look forward to his adult enjoyment of Sophocles as a lover looks forward to marriage. . . . He has to begin by working for marks, or to escape punishment, or to please his parents, or, at best, in the hope of a future good which he cannot at present imagine or desire [in the full sense of the word]. His position, therefore, bears a certain resemblance to that of the mercenary; the reward he is going to get will, in actual fact, be a natural or proper reward, but he will not know that till he has got it. Of course, he gets it gradually; enjoyment creeps in upon the mere drudgery, and nobody could point to a day or an hour when the one ceased and the other began. But it is just in so far as he approaches the reward that he becomes able to desire it for its own sake; indeed, the power of so desiring it is itself a preliminary reward. . . . The Christian, in relation to heaven, is in much the same position as this schoolboy. Those who have attained everlasting life in the vision of God doubtless know very well that it is no mere bribe, but the very consummation of their earthly discipleship; but we who have not yet attained it cannot know this in the same way, and cannot even begin to know it at all except by continuing to obey and finding the first reward of our obedience in our increasing power to desire the ultimate reward. Just in proportion as the desire grows, our fear lest it should be a mercenary desire will die away and finally be recognized as an absurdity. . . . Gospel replaces law, longing transforms obedience, as gradually as the tide lifts a grounded ship.[240]

---

240 Lewis, "The Weight of Glory," 96-7. Cf. "The grand problem is that of 'Unselfishness.' Note, once again, the admirable work of our Philological Arm in substituting the negative unselfishness for the Enemy's positive Charity. Thanks to this you can, from the very outset, teach a man to surrender benefits not that others may be happy in having them but that he may be unselfish in forgoing them. That is a great point gained. Another great help, where the parties concerned are male and female, is the divergence of view about Unselfishness which we have built up between the sexes. A woman means

Thus, still denying that "mere morality"[241] is the end of life ("The rescue

---

by Unselfishness chiefly taking trouble for others; a man means not giving trouble to others. As a result, a woman who is quite far gone in the Enemy's service will make a nuisance of herself on a large scale than any man except those whom Our Father has dominated completely; and, conversely, a man will live long in the Enemy's camp before he undertakes as much spontaneous work to please others as a quite ordinary woman may do every day. Thus while the woman thinks of doing good offices and the man of respecting other people's rights, each sex, without any obvious unreason, can and does regard the other as radically selfish." Lewis, *The Screwtape Letters*, 806. "If we were perfected, prayer would not be a duty, it would be delight. Some day, please God, it will be. The same is true of many other behaviours which now appear as duties. If I loved my neighbour as myself, most of the actions which are now my moral duty would flow out of me as spontaneously as song from a lark or fragrance from a flower. Why is this not so yet? Well, we know, don't we? Aristotle has taught us that delight is the 'bloom' on an unimpeded activity. But the very activities for which we were created are, while we live on earth, variously impeded: by evil in ourselves or in others. Not to practise them is to abandon our humanity. To practise them spontaneously and delightfully is not yet possible. This situation creates the category of duty, the whole specifically *moral* realm. . . . It exists to be transcended. Here is the paradox of Christianity. As practical imperatives for here and now the two great commandments have to be translated 'Behave *as if* you loved God and man.' For no man can love because he is told to. Yet obedience on this practical level is not really obedience at all. And if a man really loved God and man, once again this would hardly be obedience; for if he did, he would be unable to help it. Thus the command really says to us, 'Ye must be born again.' Till then, we have duty, morality, the Law. A schoolmaster, as St Paul says, to bring us to Christ. We must expect no more of it than of a schoolmaster; we must allow it no less. I must say my prayers today whether I feel devout or not; but that is only as I must learn my grammar if I am ever to read the poets. . . . But the school-days, please God, are numbered. There is no morality in Heaven. The angels never knew (from within) the meaning of the word *ought*, and the blessed dead have long since gladly forgotten it. This is why Dante's Heaven is so right, and Milton's, with its military discipline, so silly. . . . We can picture unimpeded, and therefore delighted, action only by the analogy of our present play and leisure. Thus we get the notion that what is as free as they would have to matter as little." Lewis, *Prayer: Letters to Malcolm*, 297-8. Cf. "That the spiritual life transcends both intelligence and morality, we are probably all agreed. But I suppose it transcends them as poetry transcends grammar, and does not merely exclude them as algebra excludes grammar." Lewis, "Christian Reunion," 397. Cf. "There is *nowhere* this side of heaven where one can safely lay the reins on the horse's neck. It will never be lawful simply to 'be ourselves' until 'ourselves' have become sons of God." Lewis, "The Sermon and the Lunch," 344.

241 "Mere *morality* is not the end of life. You were made for something quite different than that. J. S. Mill and Confucius (Socrates was much nearer the reality) simply didn't know what life is about. . . . Morality is indispensable: but the Divine life, which gives itself to us and which calls us to be gods, intends for us something in which morality will be swallowed up. We are to be re-made. All the rabbit in us is to disappear – the worried, conscientious, ethical rabbit as well as the cowardly and sensual rabbit. . . . We shall find underneath it all a thing we have never yet imagined: a real man, an ageless god, a son of God, strong, radiant, wise, beautiful, and drenched in joy." Lewis, "Man or Rabbit?" 355. "Christian ethics . . . makes duty a self-transcending concept and endeavours to

of drowning men is . . . a duty worth dying for, but not worth living for"[242]),
Lewis continued to maintain that man was "made for eternal happiness,"[243]
which, since man was "made for God,"[244] is "the fruition of God"[245] or
Beatitude.[246] *However*, Lewis thought that while heavenly desire and "need-
love" are a necessary part of life, this kind of love – this desire for Happiness
and God – is still only *eros*:

The first distinction I made was therefore between what I called Gift-

---

escape from the region of mere morality." Lewis, "On Ethics," 304. Cf. "Morality exists
to be transcended. We act from duty in the hope that someday we shall do the same acts
freely and delightfully." C. S. Lewis, "The Novels of Charles Williams," in *C. S. Lewis:
Essay Collection & Other Short Pieces*, ed. Lesley Walmsley (1949 essay reprint; London:
HarperCollins, 2000), 576. Cf. "I think all Christians would agree with me if I said
that though Christianity seems at the first to be all about morality, all about duties and
rules and guilt and virtue, yet it leads you on, out of all that, into something beyond."
Lewis, *Mere Christianity*, 416.
242 Lewis, "Learning in Wartime," 582.
243 "I take it, it has nothing in the world to do with trying to pretend that the enemy is
'not so bad after all' or that his sins 'don't matter,' or that he is really lovable. Not a bit.
It's the old business about 'loving the sinner and hating the sin' wh[ich] becomes alive
to me when I realize that this is what I do to myself all the time. In fact I provisionally
define Agape as 'steadily remembering inside the Gestapo-man there is a thing wh[ich]
says I and Me just as you do, which has just the same grounds (neither more nor less)
as your 'Me' for being distinguished from all its sins however numerous, which, like
you, was made by God for eternal happiness – remembering, and always acting for the
real interests of that thing as far as you can.'" Lewis, *The Collected Letters of C. S. Lewis:
Volume II*, 409 [May 4, 1940]. Cf. "God wants to give you a real and eternal happiness."
C. S. Lewis, "Answers to Questions about Christianity," in *C. S. Lewis: Essay Collection
& Other Short Pieces*, ed. Lesley Walmsley (1944 essay reprint; London: HarperCollins,
2000), 320. Cf. "What a state we have got into when we can't say 'I'll be happy when
God calls me' without being afraid one will be thought 'morbid.' After all, St. Paul
said just the same. If we really believe what we say we believe – if we really think that
home is elsewhere and that this life is a 'wandering to find home,' why should we not
look forward to the arrival." Lewis, *The Collected Letters of C. S. Lewis: Volume III*, 1056
[June 7, 1959].
244 Lewis, *The Four Loves*, 87.
245 In "Christianity and Culture," Lewis spoke of "the true end of man (fruition of God)."
Lewis, "Christianity and Culture," 84. And in his edition of Augustine's *City of God*,
Lewis summarized Augustine thus: "The Platonists first defined [Happiness] as the
fruition of god." Lewis, marginalia in his edition of *De Civitate Dei*, 7.9. Cf. Lewis, *The
Last Battle*, 156.
246 "Hence our notion of Heaven involves perpetual negations; no food, no drink, no sex,
no movement, no mirth, no events, no time, no art. . . . Against all of these, to be sure,
we set one positive: the vision and enjoyment of God. And since this is an infinite good
we hold (rightly) that it outweighs them all. That is, the reality of the Beatific Vision
would, or will, outweigh, would infinitely outweigh, the reality of the negations."
Lewis, "Transposition," 274-5.

love and Need-love. The typical example of Gift-love would be that love which moves a man to work and plan and save for the future well-being of his family which he will die without sharing or seeing; of the second, that which sends a lonely or frightened child to its mother's arms. . . . There is no doubt which was more like Love Himself. Divine Love is Gift-love. . . . And what, on the other hand, can be less like anything we believe of God's life than Need-love? He lacks nothing, but our Need-love, as Plato saw is 'the son of Poverty.' . . . [But] we must be cautious about calling Need-love 'mere selfishness.' *Mere* is always a dangerous word. . . . I do not say that man can never bring to God anything at all but sheer Need-love. Exalted souls may tell us of a reach beyond that. But they would also, I think, be the first to tell us that those heights would cease to be true Graces, would become Neo-Platonic or finally diabolical illusions, the moment a man dared to think that he could live on them and henceforth drop out the element of need. . . . It would be a bold and silly creature that came before its Creator with the boast 'I'm no beggar. I love you [constantly and perfectly] disinterestedly.'[247]

Consequently, Lewis believed that once a man truly realizes that his own happiness is found in making his will God's, then, and only then, can man's love (*eros*) – aided by grace[248] – become like God's "gift-love" (*agape*);[249] thus, in Heaven, man is happy, not just in knowing, in his small way, as God knows, but willing, as far as possible, as God wills: "Didn't people dispute once whether the final vision of God was more an act of intelligence or of love? That is probably another of the nonsense questions."[250] That is, once man truly loves things, including God,[251] as God loves them, which is to say, as "appreciative-pleasures" or for their own sake,[252] then, and only then, can

---

247 Lewis, *The Four Loves*, 5, 6.

248 "Morality is a mountain which we cannot climb by our own efforts." Lewis, "Man or Rabbit?" 356.

249 "Divine Gift-love – Love Himself working in a man – is wholly disinterested and desires what is simply best for the beloved." Lewis, *The Four Loves*, 81.

250 Lewis, *A Grief Observed*, 89.

251 "One needs the sweetness to start one on the spiritual life but, once started, one must learn to obey God for his own sake, not for the pleasure." Lewis, *The Collected Letters of C. S. Lewis: Volume II*, 13 [November 8, 1931]. "Believing first in reunion with the Beloved, and then, for the sake of the reunion, believing in Heaven, and finally, for the sake of Heaven, believing in God – this will not work." Lewis, *The Four Loves*, 87.

252 "Pleasures of Appreciation . . . make us feel that something has not merely gratified our senses in fact but claimed our appreciation by right. . . . In the Appreciative pleasures, even at their lowest, and more and more as they grow up into the full appreciation of all beauty, we get something that we can hardly help calling *love* and hardly help calling *disinterested*, towards the object itself." Lewis, *The Four Loves*, 12-3. Cf. "I mean the pursuit of knowledge and beauty, in a sense, for their own sake, but in a sense

man transcend both himself[253] and the duty / happiness distinction.[254]

Putting the concept of valuing something for its own sake in Christian terms, Lewis maintained not only that God's sovereignty gives each thing a unique nature and puts each thing in its proper place, but also that God's justice demands each thing be valued as an end in itself. Needless to say, the opposite of this is pride, which constantly focuses on the self[255] and endeavors to treat each thing as a means to satisfying the self.[256] Now obviously, Lewis

which does not exclude their being for God's sake." Lewis, "Learning in Wartime," 583. Cf. The devil Screwtape remarks: "Quite trivial things such as a fondness for country cricket or collecting stamps or drinking cocoa . . . I grant you, have nothing of virtue in them; but there is a sort of innocence and humility and self-forgetfulness about them which I distrust. The man who truly and disinterestedly enjoys any one thing in the world, for its own sake, and without caring two-pence what other people say about it, is by that very fact fore-armed against some of our subtlest modes of attack." Lewis, *The Screwtape Letters*, 768. Cf. Lewis, *The Four Loves*, 27. Cf. Lewis, "Man or Rabbit?" 352.

253 "But in reading great literature I become a thousand men and yet remain myself. . . . Here, as in worship, in love, in moral action, and in knowing, I transcend myself; and am never more myself than when I do." Lewis, *An Experiment in Criticism*, 141.

254 In *Perelandra*, Lewis, through the persona of Ransom, suggested that the angels in Heaven do not distinguish between duty and happiness, work and leisure: "'They [the Oyarsa] never have that experience [of waiting]. You and I are conscious of waiting, because we have a body that grows tired or restless, and therefore a sense of cumulative duration. Also we can distinguish duties and spare time and therefore have a conception of leisure. It is not like that with him.'" Lewis, *Perelandra*, 168. Cf. "The Scotch catechism says that man's chief end is 'to glorify God and enjoy Him forever'. But we shall then know that these are the same thing. Fully to enjoy is to glorify. In commanding us to glorify Him, God is inviting us to enjoy Him." Lewis, *Reflections on the Psalms*, 361. Cf. "Everyone will admit that choice is essentially conscious; to choose involves knowing that you choose. Now Paradisal man always chose to follow God's will. In following it he also gratified his own desire, both because all the actions demanded of him were, in fact, agreeable to his blameless inclination, and also because the service of God was itself his keenest pleasure. . . . The question 'Am I doing this for God's sake or only because I happen to like it?' did not then arise, since doing things for God's sake was what he chiefly 'happened to like.' His Godward will rode his happiness like a well-managed horse, whereas our will, when we are happy, is carried away in the happiness as in a ship racing down a swift stream." Lewis, *The Problem of Pain*, 521. Cf. "The man is a true man who chooses duty: he is a perfect man who at length never thinks of duty, who forgets the name of it." George MacDonald in Lewis, *George MacDonald: An Anthology*, 83.

255 Hence, Lewis the Neoplatonic Christian continued in his distrust of introspection and excessive focus on the self: "On the whole, you know, I feel that self-examination should be confined to examining one's *conduct*. One's *state* in general I don't think one knows much about." Lewis, *The Collected Letters of C. S. Lewis: Volume II*, 202 [July 28, 1936].

256 In *The Screwtape Letters*, Lewis had the devil Screwtape say, "We can produce this sense of ownership not only by pride but by confusion. We teach [people] not to notice

did not mean that it is sinful or immoral, for instance, to *use* a pig – i.e. bacon – as a *means* to satisfying hunger: he was Aristotelian enough to appreciate that not all using is necessarily bad.[257] Nevertheless, Lewis did believe that in the process of killing the pig, the man ought to refrain from cruelty and indeed (almost like the Native Americans of old), ought to give thanks for the pig and appreciate its own unique characteristics. The man who always enjoys things for their own sake (even if he also needs to use them appropriately), therefore, is – far from being a mindless member of the "herd"[258] – rather a true connoisseur of life. Indeed, owing debts to Norse mythology, absolute idealism, Augustine,[259] and others, Lewis believed that when a man enjoys each thing as it is meant to be enjoyed and loves each thing for its own sake, he becomes the truly just man, who, because his subjective identity becomes so wrapped up in God's, would rather, if it were possible, see this justice and goodness prevail over and against his own subjective happiness:

> And even now, even if – let's make an impossible supposition – His voice, unmistakably His, said to me, 'they have mislead you. I can do nothing of that sort for you. My long struggle with the blind forces is nearly over. I die, children. The story is ending' – would that be a moment for changing sides? Would not you and I take the Viking way: 'The Giants and Trolls win. Let us die on the right side, with

the different senses of the possessive pronoun – the finely graded differences that run from 'my boots' thorough 'my dog,' 'my servant,' 'my wife,' 'my father.' . . . Even in the nursery a child can be taught to mean by 'my teddy bear' *not* the old imagined recipient of affection to whom it stands in a special relation (for that is what the Enemy will teach them to mean if we are not careful) but 'the bear I can pull to pieces if I like.'" Lewis, *The Screwtape Letters*, 792. Although not immoral, the man who reads a book simply as a means of killing time or the like is less than ideal: "The distinction can hardly be better expressed than by saying that the many *use* art and the few *receive* it." Lewis, *An Experiment in Criticism*, 19.

257 In regard to knowledge (all forms of which are good, though they are not all equally good) Aristotle said that theoretical knowledge should be pursued for its own sake, practical knowledge should be pursued as a means to conduct, and productive knowledge should be pursued as a means to making something useful or beautiful. Aristotle *Ethics* 1094a1-5.

258 Niebuhr wrote the following: "So pervasive is the optimism and unilateral simplicity of modern morality that even a Anglo-Catholic theologian, under its influence, can arrive at the foolish conclusion that the Christian conception of love is practically identical with the 'herd complex'" – after which Lewis noted: "I heartily agree." Lewis, marginalia in his edition of *An Interpretation of Christian Ethics*, 105.

259 In his edition of Augustine's *City of God*, Lewis underlined the following: "We see then that the two cities were created by two kinds of love: the earthly city was created by self-love reaching the point of contempt for God, the Heavenly City by the love of God carried as far as contempt for self." Lewis, underlining in his edition of *De Civitate Dei*, 14.28.

Father Odin.'[260]

And, if this were not enough, Lewis believed that after man transcends both his moral duties and his own rational desires – precisely at the point when he dies to his selfish ways and views himself with perfect justice – only then is his true self revealed: "Creatures grow further apart as they increase in perfection. Good, as it ripens, becomes continually more different not only from evil but from other good."[261] Indeed, Lewis maintained (with Aquinas and against Scotus[262]) that only when a man becomes his true self can he experience genuine freedom,[263] wherein, as the Oxford don said

---

260 Lewis, *Prayer: Letters to Malcolm*, 301. Cf. "I don't often use *the kingdom, the power and the glory*. When I do, I have an idea of the *kingdom* as sovereignty *de jure*; God, as good, would have a claim on my obedience even if He had no power. The *power* is the sovereignty *de facto* – He is omnipotent. And the *glory* is – well, the glory; the 'beauty so old and new', the 'light from behind the sun.'" Ibid., 241-2. Cf. "I think it is well, even now, sometimes to say to ourselves, 'God is such that if (*per impossible*) [H]is power could vanish and His other attributes remain, so that the supreme right were forever robbed of the supreme might, we should still owe Him precisely the same kind and degree of allegiance as we now do.'" Lewis, *Surprised by Joy*, 1378.

261 Lewis, *The Great Divorce*, 1025.

262 In his essay "Heaven as the Home of the Free: The Primacy of the Will in Duns Scotus," John Médaille claims that Lewis's understanding of the Beatitude "is a more Thomistic view, but preserves the Scotist requirement for liberty." John C. Médaille, "Heaven as the Home of the Free: The Primacy of the Will in Duns Scotus," http://www.medaille.com/primacy.html (accessed February 2, 2005), 13. Although Lewis did not use these terms, Médaille is probably wrong, for like Aquinas and unlike Scotus, Lewis believed that in Heaven a Christian both would and could never fall away from God: "You may ask, do I then think that moral value will have no place in the state of perfection? Well it sounds a dreadful thing to say, but I'm almost inclined to answer No. It is never presented in Scripture in terms of service is it? – always in terms of suggesting fruition – a supper, a marriage, a drink. . . . May not that be one of the divine jokes – to see people like Marcus Aurelius and [Matthew] Arnold & [John Stuart] Mill at last submitting to the fact that they can give up being *good* and start receiving good instead. I don't mean, of course, 'can begin being bad,' but that when the *beata necessitas non peccandi* ['the blessed necessity of not sinning'] is attained, the will – the perilous bridge by wh[ich] we get home – will cease to be the important thing or to exist, as we now know it, at all. The sword will be beaten into a ploughshare. The supreme volition of self-surrender is thus a *good suicide* of will: we will thus once, in order to will no more." Lewis, *The Collected Letters of C. S. Lewis: Volume II*, 463-4 [January 18, 1941].

263 "[T]he blessed, forever submitting to obedience, become through all eternity more and more free." Lewis, *The Problem of Pain*, 538.

Augustinianly,[264] "'everything is allowed.'"[265]

II: Virtue and Vice

With the theoretical issues of morality – i.e., issues of duty and happiness – already addressed, all that remains to be discussed are the practical issues of morality, in particular, those relating to virtue and vice. Needless to say, because Lewis's understanding of virtue and vice changed throughout his life, it is impossible to define these two from the outset.

Now during his early Christian and subsequent Lucretian materialist phase, Lewis never directly addressed the topic of virtue and vice. However, a few things are worth mentioning.

Although Lewis was surrounded by many dutiful people, he never got a deep sense from any of them that virtue was something lovely and worth pursuing for its own sake: Lewis's cousin Quartus, for instance, was "gracious, childlike, deeply and religiously humble and abounding in charity," yet "the conception of duty [seemed to have] dominated his life;"[266] Lewis's teacher Smewgy taught Lewis manners ("To be in Smewgy's form was to be in a measure ennobled"[267]), but these manners were largely without a philosophical foundation. Perhaps the best example Lewis received of virtue being lovely and worth pursuing was from the books he was reading: Malory, Spenser and Milton, for example, certainly depicted the loveliness of virtue and virtuous action, and, indeed, we can see their influence in Lewis's childhood stories of Animal-Land, which demonstrated some stock responses in regard to the attractiveness of chivalry; however, while these stories certainly did some good, their impact was, again, minimal:

> I think that all things, in their way, reflect heavenly truth, the imagination not least. 'Reflect' is the important word. This lower life of the imagination is not a beginning of nor a step towards, the higher life of the spirit, merely an image. In me, at any rate, it contained no element either of belief or of ethics; however far pursued, it would

264 "This view of yours about desire is, I suppose, Augustinian. *Habe caritatem et fac quod vis* ["Have charity, and do as you will"]. This is certainly sound, but not perhaps very practical: for it implies *Donec caritatem habens, noli facere quod vis* ["until you have charity, do not do as you will"]. I wholly agree with what you say about escaping from the circle of morality into the love of God: in fact you have written an excellent commentary on St. Paul's view of the 'Law.'" Lewis, *The Collected Letters of C. S. Lewis: Volume II*, 194 [May 23, 1936].
265 Lewis, *The Last Battle*, 130.
266 Lewis, *Surprised by Joy*, 1269.
267 Ibid., 1308.

never have made me either wiser or better. . . . [Concerning heavenly
desire] no moral question was involved; I was at this time as nearly
non-moral on that subject as a human creature can be.[268]

Subsequently, Lewis, who was largely unaware of the beauty and
importance of virtue, did not succeed in harnessing his emotions in a healthy,
rational way (i.e. he showed poor "emotional intelligence"[269]), for when he
lost his faith in Christianity, he failed to say so honestly, and so was driven,
when it came time for his Confirmation, to lie to his father out of fear, which
then lead to a whole string of vices: "As Johnson points out, where courage
is not, no other virtue can survive except by accident. Cowardice drove me
into hypocrisy and hypocrisy into blasphemy."[270] Consequently, while Lewis
did not theorize about vice at this time, he himself became increasingly more
vicious: Lewis the coward and blasphemer soon became Lewis the fornicator,
who, indulging in masturbation and fantasizing about sadistic acts,[271] soon

268 Ibid., 1340, 1341-2.
269 Although the concept of emotional intelligence is a very new thing, it basically has to do
with the ability to understand emotions in ourselves and others. Generalizing slightly,
it is a new way of saying an old truth: the fully developed human being is one who
(rationally) understands, and thereby controls to some extent, his emotions. Daniel
Goleman, *Emotional Intelligence*, 10th ed. (New York: Bantam, 2006).
270 Lewis, *Surprised by Joy*, 1337. Although Lewis, following Augustine, always denied that
it is a good thing to pit one vice against another, Lewis admitted that his cowardice
protected him against becoming overly interested in magic and the occult. Ibid.,
1345. Nevertheless, Lewis certainly did not like being a coward; hence, in *The Quest of
Bleheris*, he wrote, "For believe me Galahad [Arthur Greeves], in all the sorrows of life
there is none greater than this, when a young man who has dreamed of might deeds
beholds at last the likeness of his own being and knows it for a coward." Lewis, *The
Quest of Bleheris*, 19.
271 Lewis, *The Pilgrim's Regress*, 28. Lewis's interest in sadism is a fairly well-documented
event. For instance, he signed-off many of his letters to Arthur Greeves "Philomastix,"
which means "whip-lover," and said the following about Rousseau: "I have . . . started a
very interesting work 'Les Confessions' de Rousseau – <qui avait, lui aussi un penchant
pour la verge qui consacre a ce sujet adorable quatre pages.> Altogether a 'really rather
lovely' book. <His taste is altogether for suffering rather than inflicting: which I can feel
too, but it is a feeling more proper to the other sex.>" Lewis, *The Collected Letters of C. S.
Lewis: Volume I*, 282 [February 20, 1917]. Despite the many failures of his book, David
Holbrook's *The Skeleton in the Wardrobe* does a good job of linking Lewis's early interest
in sadism with the whippings and abuse he suffered at school. David Holbrook, *The
Skeleton in the Wardrobe: C. S. Lewis's Fantasies; A Phenomenological Study* (Lewisburg:
Bucknell University Press, 1991), 91, 93. Although Lewis would later reject sadism as
such, he did abstract one true element from it, which, as we shall discuss in the next
chapter, is that gender inequality – with ruling men and submitting wives – is an erotic
necessity. Lewis, *The Four Loves*, 66. Alan Jacobs has wondered how Lewis would have
explained his early interest in sadism, but, as I have mentioned, I am sure that Lewis
simply would have acknowledged such an interest and, while denying the bad, would

realized that such acts left a "habit of sin behind."[272] Finally, Lewis became a proud Lokian prig, who thought himself superior to those around him and who wanted nothing more than to be left alone and call his soul his own.[273]

However, as we recall, when Lewis went to fight in WWI, his morality slowly began to improve. Lewis's friendship with virtuous men like Laurence Johnson was one of the most important reasons for this:

> The important thing was that [Johnson] was a man of conscience. I had hardly till now encountered principles in anyone so nearly of my own age and my own sort. The alarming thing is that he took them for granted. It crossed my mind for the first time since my apostasy that the severer virtues might have some relevance to one's own life. I say 'the severer virtues' because I already had some notion of kindness and faithfulness to friends and generosity about money – as who has not till he meets the temptation which gives all their opposite vices new and more civil names? But it had not seriously occurred to me that people like ourselves, people like Johnson and me who wanted to know whether beauty was objective or how Aeschylus handled the reconciliation of Zeus and Prometheus, should be attempting strict veracity, chastity or devotion to duty.[274]

Although Lewis's moral life was poor at this time, he did know, from his readings in Plato and possibly Aristotle, that moral education often begins with first *doing* the right thing, and then later acquiring the right motive for such (more on this shortly):

> I had taken it that they [chastity, duty etc.] were not our subjects. There was no discussion between us on the point and I do not think he ever suspected the truth about me. I was at no pains to display it. If this is hypocrisy, then I must conclude that hypocrisy can do a man good. To be ashamed of what you were about to say, to pretend that something which you had meant seriously was only a joke – this is an ignoble part. But it is better than not to be ashamed at all. And the distinction between pretending you are better than you are and beginning to be better in reality is finer than moral sleuthhounds conceive. I was, in intention, concealing only a part: I accepted his principles at once, made no attempt internally to defend my own 'unexamined life.' When a boor first enters the society of courteous

---

have accepted the good. Alan Jacobs, *The Narnian: The Life and Imagination of C. S. Lewis* (San Francisco: HarperSanFrancisco, 2005), 287.

272 Lewis, *The Pilgrim's Regress*, 30.
273 Lewis, *Surprised by Joy*, 1342.
274 Ibid., 1352.

people what can he do, for a while, except imitate the motions? How can he learn except by imitation?[275]

During his pseudo-Manichean dualist phase, Lewis put particular emphasis on chastity and courage; nevertheless, the process of becoming virtuous was a long one and it should not surprise us that throughout his next philosophical phase, Stoical materialism, Lewis remained a man of mixed moral character at best: for instance, on the one hand, he denounced cruelty to animals[276] and expressed his admiration of chivalry,[277] and on the one hand, he remembered his past drunkenness without shame[278] and was seen by some as timid.[279]

In regard to duty and happiness, Lewis the Stoical materialist was, of course, a Kantian, but in regard to virtue and vice it is harder to say what he was since he rarely discussed virtue and vice at the time. If Lewis was a Kantian in regard to virtue and vice during his Stoical materialist phase, then he would have seen virtue not, as Aristotle had said, as a means between two vices, but rather as "the moral strength of a human being's will in fulfilling his *duty*, a moral *constraint* through his own lawgiving reason, insofar as this constitutes itself an authority *executing* the law."[280]

Yet whatever the case may have been, when Lewis converted to subjective idealism and then absolute idealism, his ethics, while still partially Kantian,[281] became more Greenian or Bradleyan; however, because Lewis had spent an enormous amount of time studying the ethics of Plato and Aristotle, particularly, in the years just before he became a theist,[282] and because Green,

---

275 Ibid., 1345-5.

276 When Lewis's Aunt Lily told him about the cruel practices that some of the Oxford medical students were engaged in, Lewis declared, "After that I no longer defended Oxford again nor ever shall." Lewis, *All My Road Before Me*, 143 [November 25, 1922].

277 "[Jenkin and I] talked of *Troilus* and this led us to the question of chivalry. I thought the mere ideal, however unrealized, had been a great advance." Ibid., 121 [October 18, 1922].

278 Concerning his room at Oxford in 1917, Lewis wrote: "Here I first was brought home drunk." Ibid., 125 [October 25, 1922].

279 Examiners at Magdalen said that Lewis's "fault is timidity" – that he had "to much caution in letting [himself] go." Ibid., 127 [October 27, 1922].

280 Kant, *The Metaphysics of Morals*, 6:405.

281 For instance, in some of his Great War documents, Lewis spoke of morality, virtue and charity synonymously and then said, in a very Kantian, un-Aristotelian matter, that "virtue carr[ies] obligations." Lewis, *De Bono et Malo*, 9.

282 In regard to Aristotle, for instance, between 1926 and 1930, Lewis's diary entries and letters contain numerous references to Aristotle's ethical dualogy, *Ethics* and *Politics*, which, we know, were starting to play an increasingly more important role in Lewis's

and to a lesser degree, Bradley, combined Platonic and Aristotelian insight in regard to ethics with absolute idealist metaphysics,[283] Lewis's idealist understanding of virtue and vice showed signs of a Platonic-Aristotelian, and later, when Lewis started teaching English literature, Christian, influence.

Since these three influences – Platonic, Aristotelian and Christian – only became more pronounced from Lewis's idealist days onward, their impact on Lewis's idealist, theist and Christian phases need to be addressed. To this end, I will start by discussing Plato and then move on to Aristotle and finally Christianity.

As for Plato, he believed that God loves those who are most like Himself, which is to say that God loves those who are good and virtuous.[284] In addition, Plato insisted that although the pursuit of virtue is a means of attaining happiness *qua* self-realization, virtue, which is acquired through habituation,[285] is not something that can be discarded once happiness has been attained, for virtue is also integral to happiness. Concerning the nature of virtue, Plato sometimes spoke as if virtue were simply wisdom or knowledge; thus, coupled with the idea that no one would willingly do evil (for everyone desires to be happy), Plato came to the conclusion that ignorance is nearly equivalent to vice. However, while wisdom and virtue are often equated, Plato, of course, acknowledged the existence of other virtues, such as courage (which controls the passionate part of man), temperance (which unifies the passionate part of man and the appetitive part of man under the rule of reason) and justice (which sees that every part of the soul performs its proper function in true harmony). Nevertheless, the reason that wisdom and virtue are often equated is because all the other virtues seem to require wisdom; indeed, since *all* virtues seem to require each other, Plato usually spoke of the unity or oneness of virtue.[286]

---

ethical theory. See Lewis, *All My Road Before Me*, 383 [May 1, 1926], 384 [May 2, 1926], 385 [May 3, 1926], 397 [May 17, 1926], 434 [January 22, 1927]. Lewis, *The Collected Letters of C. S. Lewis: Volume I*, 857 [January 2, 1930], 909 [June 22, 1930].

283 Chapter five of Green's *Prolegomena to Ethics* is dedicated solely to Platonic and Aristotelian conceptions of virtue.

284 Plato *Republic* 613a7-b1.

285 "I call 'education' the initial acquisition of virtue by the child, when the feelings of pleasure and affection, pain and hatred, that well up in his soul are channelled in the right courses before he can understand the reason why. Then when he does understand, his reason and his emotions agree in telling him that he has been properly trained by inculcation of appropriate habits." Plato *The Laws* 653.

286 Not all Plato scholars agree that Plato spoke thus. Gareth Matthews, for instance, claims that at least in Plato's early dialogues, the character of Socrates "doesn't know at all what virtue is." Gareth Matthews, *Socratic Perplexity and the Nature of Philosophy* (Oxford: Oxford University Press, 2006), 45.

Although it is impossible to say precisely what any one particular person learned from another, there are four general areas where Plato's theory of virtue and vice likely influenced Lewis's own: (1) the definition of virtue, (2) the unity and particular functions of the four cardinal virtues, (3) the relation between virtue and education, and (4) virtue's share in happiness.

The first Platonic influence on Lewis's theory of virtue and vice is in regard to the definition of virtue. Lewis agreed with Plato (and later, Aristotle) that virtue (*aretē*) is "a perfection;"[287] and, as we shall discuss shortly, Lewis later adapted this definition of virtue to Augustine's, which maintains that virtue is "properly ordered loves."

The second Platonic influence on Lewis's theory of virtue and vice is in regard to the unity and particular functions of the four Cardinal virtues. As an idealist, theist and Christian, Lewis agreed with Plato both that there are four Cardinal virtues – "PRUDENCE [i.e. practical reason], TEMPERANCE, JUSTICE AND FORTITUDE"[288] – and that these are a unity: "Plato rightly taught that virtue is one."[289] However, it should be added that when Lewis became a Christian, he also acknowledged the existence of both the three theological virtues – faith, hope and charity – and a few other virtues, such as chastity[290] and courtesy.[291] While I will discuss the theological virtues, especially charity, later, I now want to briefly describe the function of each of the Cardinal virtues and some of their opposing vices.

Practical reason or prudence, Lewis said, "lies in 'the masterly administration of the unforeseen;'"[292] it is "practical common sense, taking the trouble to think out what you are doing and what is likely to come of it."[293] Broadly speaking, Lewis agreed with Plato that reason is opposed to ignorance; however, while Plato thought ignorance was the sole cause of vice, Lewis made ignorance one of the two "daughters of the Enemy" (the other daughter, pride, will be addressed later).[294] Indeed, as I discussed in the

---

287 Lewis, *The Problem of Pain*, 504.
288 Lewis, *Mere Christianity*, 369.
289 Lewis, *The Problem of Pain*, 502.
290 Lewis, *Mere Christianity*, 381.
291 Ibid., 374.
292 Lewis, *Prayer: Letters to Malcolm*, 248.
293 Lewis, *Mere Christianity*, 369.
294 Lewis, *The Pilgrim's Regress*, 164-5. Cf. "Hatred we can manage. The tension of human nerves during noise, danger, and fatigue, makes them prone to any violent emotion and it is only a question of guiding this susceptibility into the right channels. If conscience resists, muddle him. Let him say that he feels hatred not on his own behalf but on that of the women and children, and that a Christian is told to forgive his own, not other people's enemies. In other words let him consider himself sufficiently identified with

previous chapter, Lewis, a virtue epistemologist before there was a name for such, agreed with Plato (and Aristotle) that because of the interconnectedness of the virtues, ignorance often leads to vice and virtue often leads to knowledge:

> The right direction leads not only to peace but to knowledge. When a man is getting better he understands more and more clearly the evil that is still left in him. When a man is getting worse he understands his own badness less and less. A moderately bad man knows he is not very good: a thoroughly bad man thinks he is all right. This is common sense, really. You understand sleep when you are awake, not while you are sleeping. . . . Good people know about both good and evil: bad people do not know about either.[295]

As a result, Lewis felt very strongly that people need to develop the virtue of practical reason or prudence:

> Nowadays most people hardly think of Prudence as one of the 'virtues.' In fact, because Christ said we could only get into His world by being like children, many Christians have the idea that, provided you are 'good,' it does not matter being a fool. But that is a misunderstanding. . . . St Paul points out, Christ never meant that we were to remain children in *intelligence*: on the contrary. He told us to be not only 'as harmless as doves,' but also 'as wise as serpents.' He wants a child's heart, and a grown-up's head. . . . He wants every bit of intelligence we have to be alert at its job, and in first-class fighting trim.[296]

Courage or fortitude is the virtue that prevents the *thuymos* or passionate part of the man from descending into vice like cowardice (the one vice which no one is proud of[297]) or brutal hatred (a vice Lewis the idealist, theist and

---

the women and children to feel hatred on their behalf, but *not* sufficiently identified to regard their enemies as his own and therefore proper objects of forgiveness." Lewis, *The Screwtape Letters*, 815.

295 Lewis, *Mere Christianity*, 380. This quotation probably owes something to George MacDonald, who said, "A beast does not know that he is a beast, and the nearer a man gets to being a beast the less he knows it." Lewis, *George MacDonald: An Anthology*, 141.

296 Lewis, *Mere Christianity*, 369-70.

297 In *The Screwtape Letters*, the devil Screwtape advises his nephew thus, "But hatred is best combined with Fear. Cowardice, alone of all the vices, is purely painful – horrible to anticipate, horrible to feel, horrible to remember; Hatred has its pleasures. It is therefore often the *compensation* by which a frightened man reimburses himself for the miseries of Fear. The more he fears, the more he will hate. And Hatred is also a great anodyne for shame. To make a deep wound in his charity, you should therefore first attack his courage. . . . We have made men proud of most vices, but not of cowardice. Whenever we have almost succeeded in doing so, the Enemy permits a war or an

Christian struggled with for a while[298]). The importance of courage to Lewis is easily seen in comments like – "courage is not simply *one* of the virtues, but the form of every virtue at the testing point"[299] – and writings like the first chapter of *The Abolition of Man*, "Men without Chests" (which, incidentally, was the title used by Francis Fukuyama when he, acknowledging his debt to Lewis, wrote about *thuymos* in *The End of History and the Last Man*[300]). According to Lewis, courage "faces danger as well as . . . 'sticks it' under pain."[301] In fact, because courage can only be tested in the midst of trial and pain, Lewis believed that God intentionally allows us – in this fallen world,

---

earthquake or some other calamity, and at once courage becomes so obviously lovely and important even in human eyes that all our work is undone, and there is still at least one vice of which they feel genuine shame. . . . In the last war, thousands of humans, by discovering their own cowardice, discovered the whole moral world for the first time. In peace we can make many of them ignore good and evil entirely; in danger, the issue is forced upon them in a guise to which even we cannot blind them. There is here a cruel dilemma before us. If we promoted justice and charity among men, we should be playing directly into the Enemy's hands; but if we guide them to the opposite behaviour, this sooner or later produces (for He permits it to produce) a war or a revolution, and the undisguisable issue of cowardice or courage awakes thousands of men from moral stupor. . . . [R]emember, the *act* of cowardice is all that matters; the emotion of fear is, in itself, no sin and, though we enjoy it, does us no good." Lewis, *The Screwtape Letters*, 815, 816. Cf. "Absolute obedience to your instinct for self-preservation is what we call cowardice." Lewis, "We Have No 'Right to Happiness,'" 390.

298 "So I will say it after all: that I seem to have been supported in respect to chastity and anger more continuously, and with less struggle, for the last ten days or so than I often remember to have been." Lewis, *The Collected Letters of C. S. Lewis: Volume I*, 877 [January 30, 1930]. Cf. "This same spiritual law works terribly in the opposite direction. The Germans, perhaps, at first ill-treated the Jews because they hated them: afterwards they hated them much more because they had ill-treated them. The more cruel you are, the more you will hate; and the more you hate, the more cruel you will become – and so on in a vicious circle for ever." Lewis, *Mere Christianity*, 404.

299 Lewis, *The Screwtape Letters*, 816.

300 In *The Abolition of Man*, Lewis spoke of men who lack the proper passions and stock responses, such as the desire for justice and notion that courage is lovely, as "men without chests." Lewis, *The Abolition of Man*, 408. Fukuyama appropriated this phrase in *The End of History and the Last Man*, saying that without *thuymos* ("the spirited part of man") and the desire for "recognition," which Fukuyama, following Hegel, thinks is basic to all people, liberal democracies cannot stand: "The attempt of liberal politics in the Hobbes-Locke tradition to banish the desire for recognition from politics or to leave it constrained and impotent left many thinkers feeling quite uneasy. Modern society would henceforth be composed of what C. S. Lewis called 'men without chests': that is, people who were composed entirely of desire and reason, but lacking that proud self-assertiveness that was somehow at the core of man's humanity in earlier ages." Francis Fukuyama, *The End of History and the Last Man* (Toronto: Free Press, 1992), 188.

301 Lewis, *Mere Christianity*, 371.

in this "'vale of soul-making'"[302] – to experience pain[303] in order to help us develop this virtue; hence, in *The Lion, the Witch and the Wardrobe*, Aslan stopped everyone from helping Peter fight Maugrim the wolf because He wanted Peter to grow brave ("'Back! Let the Prince win his spurs'"[304]), and in *Perelandra*, Ransom was shown that courage is a kind of good hatred: "It is perhaps difficult to understand why [the thought of attacking the Un-Man] filled Ransom not with horror but with a kind of joy. The joy came from finding at last what hatred was made for. . . . He rejoiced in the perfect congruity between his emotion and its object."[305] In addition, Lewis believed that without courage, practical reason could not rule the appetites: "Without the aid of trained emotions the intellect is powerless against the animal organism."[306] Consequently, while the virtues cannot really be separated,[307]

302 Lewis, *The Problem of Pain*, 527. Lewis could have gotten this phrase from any number of people: Athanasius, Bosanquet, John Keats et al.

303 Concerning Lewis's argument that God uses pain to help people grow, while John Beversluis thinks that this argument fails because many atheists do not suffer enough, Erik Wielenberg suggests that if anything, the argument might fail because too few atheists suffer enough! Beversluis, *C. S. Lewis and the Search for Rational Religion*, 117. Wielenberg, *God and the Reach of Reason: C. S. Lewis, David Hume and Bertrand Russell*, 43, 47, 52. Nevertheless, Wielenberg admits both that human ignorance does not allow us to judge God's love for people based on the pain we empirically see these people undergoing and that there are some types of evil, such as "non-victim-improving natural child suffering," that Lewis's argument does not satisfactorily account for. While I agree with Wielenberg that human ignorance accounts for our inability to judge God's love for people, I think that Wielenberg is wrong when he maintains that Lewis's argument cannot account for "non-victim-improving natural child suffering" – e.g. that of a child who suffers a disease at childbirth which does not necessarily help him morally improve. First of all, the existence of such pain is questionable. Second of all, we must remember that God judges a child only according to what it has been given, and so if the child has been given next to nothing, then the child is responsible for next to nothing; hence, even if a child suffers pain that does not improve him in this life, the shear fact that he underwent such pain will be taken into account in Heaven and justice will be done. Cf. Reppert, "The Ecumenical Apologist,"23. Cf. James Petrik, "In Defense of C. S. Lewis's Analysis of God's Goodness," *International Journal for Philosophy of Religion* 36 (1994): 51-2.

304 Lewis, *The Lion, the Witch and the Wardrobe*, 119.

305 Lewis, *Perelandra*, 285.

306 Lewis, *The Abolition of Man*, 407.

307 In a less philosophical moment – that is, when he was doing the BBC show "The Anvil" – Lewis spoke of courage as a layman might and not in the more Platonic or philosophical sense which he actually embraced and which denies that a person can be brave without also being wise; thus, for instance, Lewis said very un-philosophically of animals (who are not rational): "It's perfectly obvious that you can have courage without being a Christian. Lots of Nazis are courageous, lots of animals are courageous." C. S. Lewis, "The Anvil," in *Mere Christianity: Anniversary Edition*, by C. S. Lewis, ed. Walter Hooper (1943 essay reprint; New York: Macmillan, 1981), 208.

courage – coupled with the appropriate gentleness – is the virtue of choice for the warrior and warrior-king; thus, Plato said the guardians ought to be "fierce among his enemies and mild at home,"[308] and Lewis agreed, insisting that the man of chivalry, the knight, "is not a compromise or happy mean between ferocity and meekness; he is fierce to the *n*th and meek to the *n*th. . . . [He] is a work not of nature but of art; of that art which has human beings, instead of canvas or marble, for its medium."[309]

Temperance or self-control, which has to do with unifying the passionate or emotional part of man and the appetitive part of man under the rule of reason, was defined by Lewis as "going the right length and no further."[310] That is, while courage has to do with the specific control of the emotions or passions, which, we recall from chapter seven, arise from the instincts / estimation, temperance has to do with proper control of the unity of the passions and appetites; thus, the vices which temperance particularly struggles against are those of the animal – e.g. sloth, lust, etc. – and not of the devil – pride, envy, etc. As for Lewis himself, we know that in addition to hatred and the diabolical vices of pride and envy,[311] he struggled with the following vices throughout his idealist, theist and Christian phases: (1) until about five or six years after his conversion to Christianity, Lewis admitted that laziness was one of his chief vices;[312] (2) at the age of fifty-eight, Lewis admitted that talking too much was one of his lifelong vices;[313] and (3)

308 C. S. Lewis, marginalia in his edition of *TIMAEVS*, by Plato, in *PLATONIS OPERA TOMVS IV* (Oxonii: E Typograheo Clarendoniano, 1899; The Rare Book Collection, The University of North Carolina at Chapel Hill), 17c.

309 C. S. Lewis, "The Necessity of Chivalry," in *C. S. Lewis: Essay Collection & Other Short Pieces*, ed. Lesley Walmsley (1940 essay reprint; London: HarperCollins, 2000), 717, 719. Cf. "Seneca says 'for *natura* does not give virtue; it is an art to become good.' It might mean simply 'We are not born with all the virtues, they don't come of their own accord. We have to work at them.'" Lewis, *Studies in Words*, 47.

310 Lewis, *Mere Christianity*, 370.

311 In a letter to his friend Arthur Greeves, Lewis listed each of their particular vices: "LUXURIA [unchastity] C. S. L . . . IRA [anger] C. S. Lewis . . . SUPERBIA [pride] C. S. L . . . INVIDIA [envy] C. S. L." Lewis, *The Collected Letters of C. S. Lewis: Volume I*, 882 [February 10, 1930].

312 "I have recently come to the conclusion that a besetting sin of mine all my life has been one which I never suspected – laziness." Lewis, *The Collected Letters of C. S. Lewis: Volume II*, 422-3 [July 16, 1940].

313 "Except when speaking to one's Confessor, Doctor, or Lawyer (where the opposite holds) I suppose the rule is 'When in doubt, don't tell.' At least I have nearly always regretted doing the opposite and never once regretted holding my tongue. (Talking too much is one of my vices, by the way)." Lewis, *The Collected Letters of C. S. Lewis: Volume III*, 738 [April 15, 1956]. In another instance, Laurence Harwood, one of Lewis's godsons, said of Lewis: "He loved to swim and, when we lived in Sussex after the war, would often insist on an early-morning dip in the local lake before breakfast. He would be

from his Lucreatian materialist days until his Christian conversion, Lewis struggled with lust and unchastity,[314] which, of all the vices save for pride, the Oxford don theorized about the most; for instance, as an idealist, Lewis saw lust and masturbation as the soul's abuse of matter,[315] and as a Christian, Lewis, drawing insight from Augustine and Charles Williams,[316] said that lust engenders false images in the imagination, which, when subsequently desired, produce a bizarre incestuous love of self that ultimately develops into something nearly indistinguishable from pride, which is the false love of self: "For me the real evil of masturbation w[oul]d be that it takes an appetite which, in lawful use, leads the individual out of himself to complete (and correct) his own personality in that of another (and finally in children and even grandchildren) and turns it back: sends the man back into the prison of himself, there to keep a harem of imaginary brides."[317]

conversing incessantly with my father, sometimes even as he left the diving board for a belly-flop into the water. I was convinced that he could talk under water, because when his head eventually emerged, the words he uttered seemed to be several stages along the line of his thought." Laurence Harwood, *C. S. Lewis, My Godfather: Letters, Photos and Recollections* (Downers Grove, IL: IVP Books, 2008), 89.

314 Lewis, *The Collected Letters of C. S. Lewis: Volume I*, 882 [February 10, 1930]. As with cowardice, Lewis believed that lust was something that most people are ashamed of; hence, in *The Great Divorce*, the bookshop in Hell covers its shameful merchandise with very respectable stuff: "However far I went I found only dingy lodging houses, small tobacconists, hoardings from which posters hung in rags, windowless warehouses, good stations without trains, and bookshops of the sort that sell *The Works of Aristotle*." Lewis, *The Great Divorce*, 1029. From a letter by Kingsley Amis, we know that this bookstore is one which sells pornography: "As for books and writers, I picked up old C. S. L; who bought me a drink; said he was an Ulsterman, explained to me why pornographic bookshops always have *The Works of Aristotle* in the window." Kingsley Amis, *The Letters of Kingsley Amis*, ed. Zachary Leader (London: HarperCollins, 2000) [April 29, 1951].

315 "The morality which does not love sense . . . [is] suspect. This was expressed theologically in Aquinas by the doctrine that even sexual pleasure was greater before the Fall. What is condemned as sensuality means (a) The soul not wholly incarnating its will in matter, but dwelling upon the subjective images of desire and using matter merely as fuel for them (delicatus homo etiam cum [...] frui videatur re vera masturbator est) ['Even an effeminate man seems to enjoy . . . in fact, he is a masturbator'] (b) The soul pursuing material pleasures in defiance of morality, which has by right the commanding voice in the spiritual life. The soul which loves matter, in our sense, would in practice be both chaste and temperate." Lewis, *Clivi Hamiltonis Summae Metaphysices Contra Anthroposophos Libri II*, 54.

316 Concerning Arthur and Morgause in Charles Williams's Arthurian poems, Lewis wrote: "For that is the horror of Incest: it offends against the law of exchange, the strain gives itself not to another strain but only back to itself. It is a physiological image of that far more abominable incest which – calling it Gomorrah – Williams studies in *Descent into Hell*: the final rejection of all exchange whereby the heart turns to the *succubus* it has itself engendered." Lewis, *The Arthurian Torso*, 130.

317 Lewis, *The Collected Letters of C. S. Lewis: Volume III*, 758 [June 3, 1956].

Justice was defined by Lewis as "fairness" since "it includes honesty, give and take, truthfulness, keeping promises, and all that side of life."[318] Although it is not immediately obvious, justice as fairness is precisely Plato's definition of justice, for he thought that a thing – be it a faculty in the soul or a person in society – is just and fair when it performs its proper function in true harmony. Thus, although Lewis felt that Plato's *Republic* was overrated,[319] the Oxford don agreed with the *Republic* that "the Reason, the Desires and the Combative Elements . . . must perform their proper functions: The Reason ruling the Desires by aid of the Combative;"[320] indeed, "We were told it all long ago by Plato. As the king governs by his executive, so Reason in man must rule the mere appetites by means of the 'spirited element'. The head rules the belly through the chest."[321]

The third Platonic influence on Lewis's theory of virtue and vice is in regard to the relation between virtue and education. In his edition of Plato's *Laws*, Lewis summarized Plato, saying that "right education" – which is primarily moral education – is a matter of "habituation."[322] Following Plato (and later, Aristotle), Lewis insisted that when children are very young, their rational and moral faculties have not yet developed; however, this is not a

---

318 Lewis, *Mere Christianity*, 371.

319 Of Cambridge, Lewis said, "You can even meet unmistakable classical scholars who don't assume the *Republic* and the *Ethics* as common ground; who behave for all the world as if these (the left and right lung of Oxford humanization) were just two classical texts like any others. It is shocking and refreshing (I never myself thought the *Republic* quite deserved its Oxonian status)." Lewis, "Interim Report," 639.

320 Lewis, marginalia in his edition of *RES PVBLICA*, at the end of book four.

321 Lewis, *The Abolition of Man*, 407. Compare this quotation to Lewis's summary of book four in his edition of Plato's *Republic*: "After further discussion of the state, Socrates returns to the main subject of Justice. By elimination the city proved just in virtue of each caste, fulfilling its own function. In the individual, therefore, justice must be similar. That is, the Reason, the Desires and the combative elements, corresponding to the Ruling, Military and Civilian castes, must perform their proper functions: The Reason ruling the Desires by the aid of the Combative." Also compare this to Lewis's underling in his edition of Aristotle's *Metaphysics*: "For the soul rules the body with a <u>despotical rule</u>, whereas the intellect rules the appetites with a <u>constitutional and royal</u> rule. And it is clear that the rule of the soul over the body, and of the mind and the rational element over the passionate, is natural and expedient; whereas <u>the equality</u> of the two or the <u>rule of the inferior</u> is always hurtful. The same holds good of animals in relation to men; for tame animals have a better nature than wild and <u>all tame animals</u> are better off when they are ruled by man; for then they are preserved. Again, <u>the male is by nature superior</u>, and the female inferior; and the one rules and the other is ruled." Lewis, underlining in his edition of *Metaphysics*, 1254b1.

322 C. S. Lewis, marginalia in his edition of *Leges*, by Plato, in *PLATONIS OPERA TOMVS V*, ed. Ioannes Burnet (Oxonii: E Typograheo Clarendoniano, 1899; The Rare Book Collection, The University of North Carolina at Chapel Hill), 652b, 654b.

reason to neglect moral education, for virtue is a matter of habituation or "good pretending;"[323] it is a process by which children, even before they mentally mature, are exposed to axiologically-sound influences – influences which, using the phrase Lewis borrowed from Richards, elicit stock responses ("Every virtue is a *habitus* – i.e. a *good* stock response"[324]). Thus, Lewis wrote,

> Now [obedience and ruling] require . . . a certain training or habituation if [they are] to be done well: and indeed the habit of command, or of obedience, may often be more necessary than the most enlightened view as to the ultimate moral grounds for doing either; and certainly, where there is no training, the enlightened views will either be ineffective, or effective at the cost of great nervous tension. You can't begin training a child to command until it has reason and age enough to command someone or something without absurdity. You can at once begin training it to obey: that is, teaching it the act of obedience *as such* – without prejudice to the views it will later hold as to who should obey whom, or when, or how much. Just as you try to train it in *courage* [etc.].[325]

While critics might see this Platonic moral education system as brainwashing, Lewis adamantly denied it, claiming that in this moral educational system and others like it, "[Teachers] did not cut men to some pattern they had chosen. They handed on what they had received: they initiated the young neophyte into the mystery of humanity which over-arched him and them

---

323 "There are two kinds of pretending. There is a bad kind, where the pretence is there instead of the real thing; as when a man pretends he is going to help you instead of really helping you. But there is also a good kind, where the pretence leads up to the real thing. When you are not feeling particularly friendly but know you ought to be, the best thing you can do, very often, is to put on a friendly manner and behave as if you were a nicer person than you actually are. And in a few minutes, as we have all noticed, you will be really feeling friendlier than you were. Very often the only way to get a quality in reality is to start behaving as if you had it already. That is why children's games are so important. They are always pretending to be grown-ups – playing soldiers, playing shop. But all the time, they are hardening their muscles and sharpening their wits so that the pretence of being grown-up helps them to grow up in earnest." Lewis, *Mere Christianity*, 441-2. Cf. "The rule for all of us is perfectly simple. Do not waste time bothering whether you 'love' your neighbour; act as if you did. As soon as we do this we find one of the great secrets. When you are behaving as if you loved someone, you will presently come to love him." Ibid., 404.

324 Lewis, "Christianity and Culture," 82.

325 Lewis, *The Collected Letters of C. S. Lewis: Volume II*, 372 [March 26, 1940]. Cf. "Obedience is one of the virtues [the student] has come to [the teacher] to learn." Lewis, "Our English Syllabus," 85.

alike. It was but old birds teaching young birds to fly."[326]

The fourth and final Platonic influence on Lewis's theory of virtue and vice is in regard to virtue's share in happiness. Lewis agreed with Plato (and, as with nearly all of the previous points, also with Aristotle) that although virtue is a means to happiness, it is also an essential part of happiness; hence, virtue should be valued for its own sake and evil men are always punished simply by being what they are. However, while pagans Plato and Aristotle said different things about what the happy life would ultimately be like, Lewis, borrowing insight from the Christian Boethius,[327] insisted that virtue constitutes not only part of our temporary happiness, but also part of our eternal Happiness – our Happiness in Heaven:

> We might think that the 'virtues' were necessary only for this present life – that in the other world we could stop being just because there is nothing to quarrel about and stop being brave because there is no danger. Now it is quite true that there will probably be no occasion for just or courageous acts in the next world, but there will be every occasion for being the sort of people that we can become only as the result of doing such acts here. The point is not that God will refuse you admission to His eternal world if you have not got certain qualities of character: the point is that if people have not got at least the beginnings of those qualities inside them, then no possible external conditions could make a 'Heaven' for them – that is, could make them happy with the deep, strong, unshakable kind of happiness God intends for us.[328]

Thus, while vicious people may, in this life, attain what they think will make them happy, they can find no lasting satisfaction in it, for True Happiness always requires virtue; as Aslan said of the White Witch:

> 'This is what happens to those who pluck and eat fruits at the wrong time and in the wrong way. The fruit is good, but they loathe it ever after. . . . [The Witch will always be young because she ate from the tree since] things always work according to their nature. She has won

---

326 Lewis, *The Abolition of Man*, 422. Cf. "But I think Digory would not have taken an apple for himself in any case. Things like Do No Steal were, I think, hammered into boys' heads a good deal harder in those days than they are now." Lewis, *The Magician's Nephew*, 147.

327 Summarizing part of the argument in book four of Boethius's *Consolation of Philosophy*, Lewis wrote: "The good are always rewarded and the wicked always punished, by the mere fact of being what they are. Evil power and evil performance are the punishment of evil will, and it will be infinite since the soul is immortal (as philosophy, no less than Theology asserts)." Lewis, *The Discarded Image*, 86.

328 Lewis, *Mere Christianity*, 371.

her heart's desire; she has unwearying strength and endless days like a goddess. But length of days with an evil heart is only length of misery and already she begins to know it. All get what they want: they do not always like it.'[329]

Consequently, God wants to perfect people morally – He, as Lewis already knew when he was an idealist, wants to polish people like mirrors[330] – for only then can He Who Is Perfect reveal Himself to imperfect people;[331] indeed, as Orual asked: "How can [the gods] meet us face to face till we have faces?"[332]

Now as for Aristotle, his theory of virtue and vice is much more developed than Plato's, although Aristotle's impact on Lewis's conception of these is

329 Lewis, *The Magician's Nephew*, 162.

330 In one of his Great War documents, Lewis wrote: "We should be as clear glasses for Spirit to see through." Lewis, *Clivi Hamiltonis Summae Metaphysices Contra Anthroposophos Libri II*, 49. As a theist and then later as a Christian, Lewis continued to use this metaphor: "You can put this another way by saying that while in other sciences the instruments you use are things external to yourself (things like microscopes and telescopes), the instrument through which you see God is your whole self. And if a man's self is not kept clean and bright, his glimpse of God will be blurred – like the Moon seen through a dirty telescope. That is why horrible nations have horrible religions: they have been looking at God through a dirty lens. . . . The command *Be ye perfect* is not idealistic gas. Nor is it a command to do the impossible. He is going to make us into creatures that can obey that command. He said (in the Bible) that we were 'gods' and He is going to make good His words. If we let Him – for we can prevent Him, if we choose – He will make the feeblest and filthiest of us into a god or goddess, a dazzling, radiant, immortal creature, pulsating all through with such energy and joy and wisdom and love as we cannot now imagine, a bright stainless mirror which reflects back to God perfectly (though, of course, on a smaller scale) his own boundless power and delight and goodness. The process will be long and in parts very painful, but that is what we are in for. Nothing less. He meant what He said." Lewis, *Mere Christianity*, 426, 452-3.

331 "God can show Himself as He really is only to real men." Ibid., 426.

332 Lewis, *Till We Have Faces*, 1013. "This was a letter from C. S. Lewis to Dorothea Conybeare, who had asked him to explain the title of his book *Till We Have Faces*. He pointed out that it was a quotation from a remark in the book itself (p. 305), 'How can they (i.e. the gods) meet us face to face till we have faces?' 'The idea,' he continued, 'was that a human being must become real before it can expect to receive any message from the superhuman; that is, it must be speaking with its own voice (not one of its borrowed voices), expressing its actual desires (not what it imagines that it desires), being for good or ill, not any mask, veil or *persona*.'" Rose Macaulay, *Letters to a Sister from Rose Macaulay*, ed. Constance Babington Smith (London: Collins, 1964), 261. As I mentioned in chapter five, Orual, whose name is also Maia, which is probably related to the Hindu word for "Appearances," is thus contrasted with the gods, who represent Reality. No doubt, this is an example of Lewis appropriating absolute idealist terms to elucidate general Christian truth.

about the same as Plato's.

According to Aristotle, happiness consists in virtuous action, where virtue is understood to be both moral and intellectual excellence, and which does not necessarily exclude pleasure or some external goods. Subsequently, following Plato, Aristotle believed that virtuous character, which all people have the capacity for, is developed through practice or training. That is, although children, for instance, do not necessarily start with knowledge of good and evil, children can form good habits, such as truth-telling, simply by obeying the instructions of their moral teachers and parents. Over time, children can come to understand that what they were taught and what they did, such as truth-telling, is right because what they were taught and what they did was right in itself.

Virtue, therefore, is a disposition, but so, it must be added, is vice. The difference between these two dispositions is of degree: virtue, which we must remember is a perfection of goodness, is found in the mean between two extremes, which are themselves vices. For instance, courage, though an extreme good, is the mean between rashness, which is the excess of confidence, and cowardice, which is the privation of confidence. In order to decide what the mean is in each particular case, which, it should be noted, is relative to each person since each person's capacity is different, the person needs to draw on practical reason, which allows him to determine the correct action in the particular circumstance through mediation with "Right Reason": "Excellence, then, is a state concerned with choice, lying in a mean relative to us, this being determined by reason and in the way in which the man of practical wisdom would determine it."[333] Since practical reason, which Aristotle called *phronēsis* and Lewis usually called prudence, is necessary for the determination of all the other virtues, Aristotle, similar, but not identical, to Plato, thought there was a kind of unity to the virtues.[334] Nevertheless, I should add that Aristotle's perfectly virtuous man – the magnanimous man – is unlike both Plato's and Christianity's ideal man, for Plato did not emphasize external goods as much as Aristotle (who even went so far as to dedicate two chapters in *Ethics* to the excellence of friendship[335]) and Christianity has always had trouble with the magnanimous man's focus on self-respect or "good" pride over and against humility.

---

333 Aristotle *Ethics* 1106b36-110712.

334 Ibid., 1144b19-20.

335 While Plato – as we can gather from dialogues like *Lysis* – did think that friendship or *philia* was a good thing, he did not emphasize it as much as Aristotle. Indeed, as I said, Aristotle emphasized all external goods more than Plato.

Nevertheless, Aristotle did properly assert that moral activity presupposes freedom since people can only be held accountable for acts that they choose to perform. Pertaining to this moral freedom, Aristotle often spoke of the difference between (1) the temperate or virtuous man, who acts both *with* and *from* reason; (2) the continent man, who merely acts with reason, but not necessarily from the right reason or motive; (3) the incontinent man, who acts *in* ignorance, such as the man who acts foolishly under the influence of drink; (4) the man who acts *from* ignorance, such as the man who is unaware that too much drink is bad;[336] and (5) the vicious man, who does evil out of evil habit (there are two other types of man, the superhuman and the bestial, but they do not figure prominently into Aristotle's ethics). Yet despite all these distinctions (and good intentions), Aristotle still had a hard time escaping Plato's conclusion that no one willingly does evil.

As for Aristotle's influence on Lewis's theory of virtue and vice, we already know that as far back as his Stoical materialist phase, Lewis made use of the Aristotelian and / or Kantian distinction between loving something for its own sake and loving something as a means to an end; moreover, during that same time period, Lewis also agreed with both Aristotle and Kant (and disagreed with Hume[337]) that motive is fundamental to whether or not an action is virtuous: "[We must remember] that virtue is that form of the image of good which appears in action [and] that this virtue lies in motive and intention only."[338] Leaving aside all of these and other instances of Aristotelian influence, and setting aside the fact that Lewis actually translated Aristotle's poem about virtue into English ("Virtue, thou whom men with toil / Seek as their most precious spoil, / Gladly here in Greece for thy / Beauty, Virgin, men will die"[339]), we can add four more areas where

---

336 Lewis called the man who acts *in* ignorance one who acts "thro' ignorance," and he called the man who acts *from* ignorance one who acts "when . . . ignorant." Lewis, marginalia in his edition of *Ethica Nicomachea*, 1110a1-15.

337 In his 1924 lecture notes, Lewis critiqued Hume's theory of virtue and vice thus: "Hume offends against empiricism. He gives an account of virtues wh[ich] leaves out the distinction between moral virtues and mere 'gifts.' He then explains that distinction away. But that distinction is part of ordinary moral experience and therefore one of the phenomena that ethics must 'save.'" Lewis, "The Moral Good – Its Place Among the Values," 59. Although not directly related to this, Lewis added elsewhere: "It is evident on this view that virtue will be esteemed: but not that it deserves esteem." Lewis, marginalia in his edition of *A Treatise of Human Nature*, 286.

338 Lewis, *De Bono et Malo*, 14.

339 C. S. Lewis, "After Aristotle," in *Poems*, by C. S. Lewis, ed. Walter Hooper (1956 poem reprint; San Diego: Harcourt Brace Jovanovich, 1964), 80-1 [1-5]. Concerning this poem, Lewis wrote: "On the poem of Aristotle . . . [i]t would have been conventional to imagine the image of Virtue either as a mistress or as a task, but these two joined together – how much more flavour they have! Then, moreover, taking an image from

Lewis's theory of virtue and vice is specifically Aristotelian: (1) virtue being in the mean and this mean being relative to the person's capacity; (2) the differences between temperance, continence, incontinence, and vice; (3) the pleasantness, and not just the deeper happiness, that comes from virtue; and (4) the relation between friendship and virtue. Finally, though it marks precisely the opposite of agreement, Lewis constantly made reference to Aristotle's magnanimous man – a subject that I will address when I talk about Lewis's Christian influences.

The first specifically Aristotelian influence on Lewis's theory of virtue and vice is in regard to virtue being in the mean and this mean being relative to the person's capacity.

To begin with, Lewis agreed with Aristotle that virtue, as a perfection, is an extreme good; hence, in *The Pilgrim's Regress*, Virtue says to Mr Sensible,

> 'It is very odd that you should say that,' interrupted Virtue, 'for I also was brought up on Aristotle. But I think my text must have differed from yours. In mine, the doctrine of the Mean does not bear the sense you have given it at all. He specially says that there is no excess of goodness. You cannot go too far in the right direction. The line that we should follow may start from a middle point in the base of a triangle: but the further off the apex is, the better.'[340]

Moreover, Lewis agreed with Aristotle that virtue is found in the mean between two extremes; hence, he insisted both that "God will help us to moderate the excesses,"[341] and that

> [The Devil] always sends errors into the world in pairs – pairs of opposites. And he always encourages us to spend a lot of time thinking which is the worse. You see why, of course? He relies on your extra dislike of the one error to draw you gradually into the opposite one. But do not let us be fooled. We have to keep our eyes on the goal and go straight through between both errors. We have no other concern than that with either of them.[342]

---

duty to one's parents, he brings her in again, as Venus and at the same time as Juno imposing labour, to the heart and home and childhood years. Nor is this all; then, as if digging deeper, as if inserting the form of Virtue also into our physical nature, he has preferred her before sleep itself. In these verses, much more divinely than Menander, he has moulded an entire image of life." Lewis, *The Collected Letters of C. S. Lewis: Volume III*, 696-7 [January 26, 1956].
340 Lewis, *The Pilgrim's Regress*, 96.
341 Lewis, *Prayer: Letters to Malcolm*, 237.
342 Lewis, *Mere Christianity*, 440. Cf. The devil Screwtape says,"The use of Fashions in thought is to distract the attention of men from their real dangers. We [devils] direct

Finally, Lewis agreed that because each person's capacity differs – not only *qua* human being, but also *qua* male and female, etc. – the virtue and vice of each person will differ from person to person; thus, in his edition of Aristotle's *Politics* for instance, Lewis approvingly underlined Aristotle's comment that "the courage of a man is shown in commanding, of a woman in obeying," and summarized this principle thus: "each member of the relation must have his *proper* virtue;"[343] indeed, this idea was so fundamental to Lewis's thought that he repeated it again and again, saying: "You cannot judge any artifact except by using it as it was intended. It is no good judging a butter-knife by seeing whether it will saw logs;"[344] "You can't judge Christianity simply by comparing the *product* in those two people; you would need to know what kind of raw material Christ was working on in both cases;"[345] and

> When a man who has been perverted from his youth and taught that cruelty is the right thing, does some tiny little kindness, or refrains from some cruelty he might have committed, and thereby, perhaps, risks being sneered at by his companions, he may, in God's eyes, be doing more than you and I would do if we gave up life itself for a friend.[346]

The second specifically Aristotelian influence on Lewis's theory of virtue and vice is in regard to the differences between temperance, continence, incontinence (*akrasia*), and vice. Although Lewis, unlike Aristotle, had a clear conception of the will, he still made ample use of the distinctions Aristotle made on the spectrum of self-control. Thus, in his 1929-1930 Great War document *Commentatrium in Tractatum De Toto et Parte*, Lewis discussed incontinence or *akrasia*:

the fashionable outcry of each generation against those vices of which it is least in danger and fix its approval of the virtue nearest to that vice which we are trying to make endemic. The game is to have them all running about with fire extinguishers whenever there is a flood, and all crowding to that side of the boat which is already nearly gunwale under. Thus we make it fashionable to expose the dangers of enthusiasm at the very moment when they are all really becoming worldly and lukewarm; a century later, when we are really making them all Byronic and drunk with emotion, the fashionable outcry is directed against the dangers of mere 'understanding.' Cruel ages are put on their guard against Sentimentality, feckless and idle ones against Respectability." Lewis, *The Screwtape Letters*, 804. Cf. *"Every form has its proper corruption."* Lewis, *The Pilgrim's Regress*, 172. Cf. "With both the 'North' and the 'South' a man has, I take it, only one concern – to avoid them and hold the Main Road. . . . We were made to be neither cerebral men nor visceral men, but Men." Ibid., 11.

343 Lewis, underlining and marginalia in his edition of *De Re Publica*, 1260a17.
344 Lewis, "Christianity and Culture," 90.
345 Lewis, "Answers to Questions about Christianity," 326.
346 Lewis, *Mere Christianity*, 379.

Do sleep & ἀκρατία ["*akratia*," the older form of "*akrasia*,"] suspend the self in the same sense? . . . Is there no sense in wh[ich] love, friendship & knowledge suspend it? It appears to me that sleep, or, say the early stages of artificial anesthesia (since we know more about these) suspend or disintegrate the self in the sense of moving us towards your meaningless man i.e. we begin to fall apart into atoms of sensation & lose unity of apperception. There is this pain & that pain but no 'I' feeling this pain along with that pain. Now ἀκρατία seems to suspend the self in a different sense. The simple subject of many experiences seems to remain in tact on the cognitive side – temptation [...] to leave me well aware where I am, what I am doing – but it is the single will that is disintegrated. Chloroform breaks cognitive unity: ἀκρατία breaks volitional unity. The one moves towards the <u>zero</u> of self: the other towards dual personality. I.e. in keeping awake you resolve that Barfield shall be one rather than none: but in resisting temptation, you resolve that he shall be one rather than many.[347]

Of course the meaningfulness of this passage is only clear when we remember that Lewis the absolute idealist thought that goal of the soul is the pursuit of the spiritual life, which is to see as Spirit sees (the theoretical) and will as Spirit wills (the practical, which is concerned with "virtue or morality"[348]). Consequently, as we noted in the aforementioned passage, Lewis appropriated Aristotle's[349] theory of *akrasia* or incontinence to explain how the soul can be tempted away from willing as Spirit wills and hence putting a negative rift between soul and its True Self, Spirit. Moreover, when Lewis became a Christian, he still continued to affirm the difference between the vicious man

347 Lewis, *Commentatrium in Tractatum De Toto et Parte*, 1.

348 Lewis, *Clivi Hamiltonis Summae Metaphysices Contra Anthroposophos Libri II*, 40.

349 Although Plato also mentions *akrasia*, Aristotle's account of it is much more famous and Lewis's usage of this word reveals its Aristotelian origin. Of course, Lewis also read about incontinence in the medieval literature he was studying at the time; however, such medieval literature never used the Greek word *akrasia*, which Lewis himself used. Thus, for example, in his edition of *The Book of the Courtier*, Lewis underlined the following: "First we practice vertue or vice, after that, we are vertuous or vitious. . . . You have saide that Continence is an unperfect vertue, because it hath in it part of affection: and me seemeth <u>the vertue</u> (where there is in our mind a variance between reason and greedie desire) <u>which fighteth and giveth the victory to reason, ought to be reckoned more perfect</u>, than that which overcommeth, having neither greedie desire nor any affection to withstand it. . . . And likewise the other vertues are aided by affections, which in case they were clean taken away, <u>they woulde leave reason very feeble and faint, so that it shoulde litle prevaile, like a shipmaster that is without winde in a great calme.</u>" C. S. Lewis, underlining in his edition of *The Book of the Courtier*, ed. W. H. D. Ross (London: J. M. Dent & Sons, n.d.; The Rare Book Collection, The University of North Carolina at Chapel Hill), 268, 270-1, 272. We know from the final page of this book that Lewis read it a second time in March 1929.

and all other types of man, saying, "A man who is not a vulgar man may do a vulgar thing: you will find this explained in Aristotle's *Ethics*."[350] Indeed, in *Mere Christianity*, the third book of which owes a considerable debt to "the true subtlety and sagacity of Aristotle's *Ethics*,"[351] Lewis spoke of the difference between the temperate man and the continent man:

> There is a difference between doing some particular just or temperate action and being a just or temperate man. Someone who is not a good tennis player may now and then make a good shot. What you mean by a good player is a man whose eye and muscles and nerves have been so trained by making innumerable good shots that they can now be relied on. They have a certain tone or quality which is there even when he is not playing. . . . In the same way a man who preserves in doing just actions gets in the end a certain quality of character. Now it is that quality rather than the particular actions which we mean when we talk of a 'virtue.' This distinction is important [because] . . . [w]e might think that, provided you did the right thing, it did not matter how or why you did it – whether you did it willingly or unwillingly, sulkily or cheerfully, through fear or public opinion or for its own sake. But the truth is that right actions done for the wrong reason do not help to build the internal quality or character called a 'virtue,' and it is this quality or character that really matters. (If the bad tennis player hits very hard, not because he sees that a very hard stroke is required, but because he has lost his temper, his stroke might possibly, by luck, help him to win that particular game; but it will not be helping him to become a reliable player).[352]

The third specifically Aristotelian influence on Lewis's theory of virtue and vice is in regard to the pleasantness of virtue. Of course, Lewis had already learned from Plato that virtue is pleasant; however, while Plato maintained that virtues are mixed pleasures (since they are still accompanied by pain),[353] Aristotle thought that pleasure is the unimpeded activity of our

350 C. S. Lewis, "Period Criticism," in *C. S. Lewis: Essay Collection & Other Short Pieces*, ed. Lesley Walmsley (1946 essay reprint; London: HarperCollins, 2000), 488.

351 Lewis, *Poetry and Prose in the Sixteenth* Century, 52. Concerning the potential title for the third book in *Mere Christianity* (which was subsequently entitled "Christian Behaviour"), Lewis wrote: "The title, for you and me, w[oul]d be *Xtian Ethics*. What this is in the vernacular is doubtful. *Xtian Morals? – Xtian Morality? – Xtian Moral Standards – Xtian Behaviour?* . . . I think if Aristotle were writing now he'd call the Ethics 'Behaviour.' Or, w[oul]d they like *The Xtian Technique of Living*?" Lewis, *The Collected Letters of C. S. Lewis: Volume II*, 528 [August 15, 1942].

352 Lewis, Mere Christianity, 371. Cf. Lewis, *Studies in Words*, 331.

353 "The pleasures you could count as members of our household are the ones you called true and pure. In addition to these you should include in the mixture the pleasures which a healthy, self-controlled man has, and in general all those pleasures which accompany

natural (perfect) state and because virtue helps to restore us to our natural (perfect) state, true virtue must be wholly pleasurable – even though virtue is said to be good in itself.[354] Lewis agreed with Aristotle that true virtue is purely pleasant, for Lewis believed that virtues are a necessary part of our happiness in Heaven – a place where there is no pain or suffering. In fact, this idea is found in Dante's *Divine Comedy*, about which Lewis wrote:

> Dante sees Beatrice's beauty increase: he knows from this phenomenon that they have risen to yet another of the spheres – just as (for he is thinking of Aristotle) a man knows that he has increased in virtue when he finds increased pleasure in virtuous acts. But Dante is not content simply to say that he knows they have risen higher: he says that they have risen to a *larger* sphere. . . . [T]hese material and spatial spheres are really, in Dante's view, and not only poetically, correspondent to progressive degrees of grace and virtue and how exactly the ascent accomplished while looking at Beatrice and recognized only by what is seen in her corresponds to the moral advance accomplished while intent on something outside a man's self; and then think of the increased size of the sphere and how well that symbolizes the new spaciousness of life when a good *habitus* has been acquired.[355]

In a less obvious manner, we get the same idea in *Prince Caspian*, where Aslan, the Christ-figure, talks to the progressively more virtuous Lucy, saying, "'Welcome, child.' . . . 'Aslan,' said Lucy, 'you're bigger.' 'That is because you are older, little one,' answered he. 'Not because you are?' 'I am not. But every year you grow, you will find me bigger.'"[356] However, while acknowledging the absolute pleasantness of virtue itself, Lewis, in his Kantian-Christian manner (which I have already discussed in the previous section of this chapter), still thought that Aristotle did not make enough of internal conflict; consequently, I believe we can see the following passage from *The Allegory of Love* as a Kantian-Christian critique of, though certainly not a total rejection of, Aristotle:

---

 every kind of virtue, as if they were attendants on some deity." Plato *Philebus* 63e.

354 Aristotle *Ethics* 1153a13-17, 1172a20-25.

355 Lewis, "Dante's Similes," 74-5. Lewis may have also gotten this idea from Marco Polo: "When these Magi were presented to Christ, the youngest of the three adored him first; and it appeared to him that Christ was of his stature and age. The middle one came next, and then the eldest; and to each he seemed to be of his own stature and age. Having compared their observations, they agreed to go to worship him all together, and then he appeared to all of them at his true age." Marco Polo *The Travels of Marco Polo* 1.13.

356 Lewis, *Prince Caspian*, 124. Cf. Peter Schakel, *Is Your Lord Large Enough? How C. S. Lewis Expands Our View of God* (Downers Grove, IL: IVP, 2008), 14.

A ready way of indicating the nature [of moral experience in mid-to late antiquity] . . . will be to remind the modern student of a certain surprise which he probably felt when he first read the *Ethics* of Aristotle. For us moderns the essence of the moral life seems to lie in the antithesis between duty and inclination. Special moral theories may attempt to resolve it, and some of 'our late fantasticks' may try to look round it or over it; but it remains, nevertheless, the experience from which we all start. All of our serious imaginative work, when it touches morals, paints a conflict: all practical moralists sing to battle or give hints about the appropriate strategy. Take away the concept of 'temptation' and nearly all that we say or think about good and evil would vanish into thin air. But when we first opened our Aristotle, we found to our astonishment that this inner conflict was for him so little of the essence of the moral life, that he tended to thrust it into a corner and treat it almost as a special case – that of the [*akrates* or incontinent man]. The really good man, in Aristotle's view, is not tempted. Where we incline to think that 'good thews inforced with pains' are more praiseworthy than mere goodness of disposition, Aristotle coolly remarks that the man who is temperate at a cost is profligate: the really temperate man abstains because he likes abstaining. The ease and pleasure with which good acts are done, the absence of moral 'effort' is for him the symptom of virtue.

Now when we turn to the moralists who lived under the Roman Empire, all this is changed. I do not know whether they were better or worse than the contemporaries of Aristotle; but they were certainly more conscious of a difficulty in being good. 'Fight the good fight' – how oddly the words would sound in the *Ethics*! Under the Empire, they are on every moralist's lips. The examples which could be drawn from the writings of St. Paul alone would be enough to prove a far-reaching change. But the phenomenon is by no means a result of Christianity, however much Christianity may have done to deepen and perpetuate it.[357]

The fourth and final specifically Aristotelian influence on Lewis's theory of virtue and vice is in regard to friendship and virtue. Provided that we remember that Aristotle's word for virtue is wider than moral virtue – i.e. that a virtue is simply a perfection or excellence – we can say that Lewis agreed with Aristotle that friendship is a virtue since he believed that the man who has true friends is happier than he who has none: "Friendship is unnecessary, like philosophy, like art, like the universe itself (for God did not need to create). It has no survival value; rather it is one of those things which

---

357 Lewis, *The Allegory of Love*, 58-9.

gives value to survival."[358] Indeed, concerning his own situation, Lewis said, "My happiest hours are spent with three or four old friends in old clothes tramping together and putting up in small pubs – or else sitting up till the small hours in someone's college rooms talking nonsense, poetry, theology, metaphysics over beer, tea, and pipes. There's no sound I like better than adult male laughter."[359] However, if we understand virtue simply to mean moral virtue, then we must admit that Lewis thought friendship can be both an aid and a hindrance to virtue: "Friendship (as the ancients saw) can be a school of virtue; but also (as they did not see) a school of vice. It is ambivalent. It makes good men better and bad men worse."[360]

Now as for Lewis's comments about Aristotle's magnanimous man, these are best addressed in the context of the final influence on Lewis's theory of virtue and vice: Christianity, in particular, that of Augustine, which of course necessarily gives rise to the question of the problem of evil, or "the Problem of Pain," as Lewis called; that is, if God is omnipotent and perfectly moral, how is it possible for evil to exist? Since much of this has been touched on before and since men like Erik Wielenberg, Jerry Root,[361] Armand Nicholi Jr.,[362] Louis Markos,[363] and Thomas Talbott[364] have dealt with Lewis's answer to the problem of evil in greater detail than I can here, I will try to be brief and only focus on the issues not yet discussed.

To begin with, Lewis agreed with the biblical writers, Augustine and even Plato[365] that man was made for God. Although different authors give different reasons as to why man was created by God, Lewis believed that man was made to glorify God in a manner which was genuinely meaningful; that is to say, man was made to worship God freely or in a manner that allows man to choose between at least two options: "By grace He gives the higher creatures power to will His will ('and wield their little tridents'): the lower

358 Lewis, *The Four Loves*, 47.

359 C. S. Lewis, on the dust-jacket of *Perelandra* (N.p.: MacMillan, 1944).

360 Lewis, *The Four Loves*, 52. Cf. Lewis, "The Inner Ring," 728.

361 Jerry Root, "C. S. Lewis and the Problem of Evil," in *Lightbearer in the Shadowlands: The Evangelistic Vision of C. S. Lewis*, ed. Angus Menuge, 353-66 (Wheaton, IL: Crossway Books, 1997).

362 Armand Nicholi Jr., *The Question of God: C. S. Lewis and Sigmund Freud Debate God, Love, Sex, and the Meaning of Life* (New York: The Free Press, 2002), 187-215.

363 Louis Markos, *Lewis Agonistes: How C. S. Lewis Can Train Us to Wrestle with the Modern and Postmodern World* (Nashville: Broadman & Holman, 2003), 90-111.

364 Thomas Talbott, "C. S. Lewis and the Problem of Evil," *Christian Scholar's Review* 17 (1987): 36-51.

365 Because man was made for God, Plato believed that suicide was wrong, for man does not have the right to do what he pleases with the property of others.

ones simply execute it automatically."[366] Such freedom, of course, entails the existence of a neutral field in which it can be exercised, and if there is more than one free person in a given field, then these free willed persons will have the ability to influence each other either positively or negatively; hence, moral – and some "natural"[367] – evil is due to creaturely freedom. In regard to God and man, Lewis believed that man's free choice to love God is one thing God's omnipotence could never logically do, which is to say, paradoxically (or mythically), given that God is simple and lacks nothing, that man's free love must *somehow* add something to God – must *somehow* "be a real ingredient in the divine happiness."[368]

In addition to this, Lewis agreed with men like Plato, Aristotle, Augustine, Green and Bradley that all of reality is ordered in a hierarchy, the justice of which consists in each free thing acting according to its proper nature and in its proper place:

> The work of a Beethoven, and the work of a charwoman, become spiritual on precisely the same condition, that of being offered to God, of being done humbly 'as to the Lord.' This does not, of course, mean that it is for anyone a mere toss-up whether he should sweep rooms or compose symphonies. A mole must dig to the glory of God and a cock must crow. We are members of one body, but differentiated members, each with his own vocation. A man's upbringing, his talents, his circumstances, are usually a tolerable index of his vocation.[369]

Consequently, Lewis, Plato, Aristotle, Augustine, Green et al. all agreed that injustice consists in wicked "competition"[370] or in one thing trying to be what it is not; that is, injustice occurs when a given free thing treats another thing other than it ought to be treated: "'Can you be righteous,' asks Traherne, 'unless you be just in rendering to things their due esteem?'"[371]

For Augustine and Lewis, injustice amounts to disobedience since man's proper activities are revealed to his mind. Moreover, Lewis – not only as

---

366 Lewis, *Prayer: Letters to Malcolm*, 271. Cf. Lewis, *Mere Christianity*, 350.

367 Lewis agreed with the Bible (and Augustine) that some "natural" evils, such as diseases, are caused by the immoral wills of fallen angels. Lewis, *The Problem of Pain*, 516. However, as I discussed when I addressed Lewis's understanding of courage, Lewis thought that God himself allows *fallen* creatures to experience pain in order to help them grow.

368 Lewis, "The Weight of Glory," 102.

369 Lewis, "Learning in Wartime," 583.

370 Thus, the devil Screwtape says that in Hell "'to be' *means* 'to be in competition.'" Lewis, *The Screwtape Letters*, 782. Cf. "Pride is *essentially* competitive." Lewis, *Mere Christianity*, 398.

371 Thomas Traherne, quoted in *The Abolition of Man*, by C. S. Lewis, 404.

a Christian but also as a theist and an idealist – agreed with Augustine that injustice and disobedience spring from the will loving itself more (but also not less[372]) than it ought to; in other words, *pace* the chivalric knights' honour[373] and Aristotle's "sub-Christian" magnanimous man,[374] injustice

---

372 "Now, the self can be regarded in two ways. On the one hand, it is God's creature, an occasion of love and rejoicing; now, indeed, hateful in condition, but to be pitied and healed. On the other hand, it is that one self of all others which is called *I* and *me*, and which on that ground puts forward an irrational claim to preference. . . . The Christian must wage endless war against the clamour of the *ego* as *ego*: but he loves and approves selves as such, though not their sins. The very self-love which he has to reject is to him a specimen of how he ought to feel to all selves; and he may hope that when he has truly learned (which will hardly be in this life) to love his neighbour as himself, he may then be able to love himself as his neighbour: that is, with charity instead of partiality. The other kind of self-hatred, on the contrary, hates selves as such. It begins by accepting the special value of the particular self called *me*, then, wounded in its pride to find that such a darling object should be so disappointing, it seeks revenge, first upon the self, then on all. Deeply egoistic, but now with an inverted egoism, it uses the revealing argument, 'I don't spare myself' – with the implication 'then *a fortiori* I need not spare others' – and becomes like the centurion in Tacitus, *immitior quia toleraverat*." Lewis, "Two Ways with the Self," 298. In *That Hideous Strength*, when Jane was moving in the direction of righteousness, she was able to properly "rejoice . . . in the consciousness of her own beauty." Lewis, *That Hideous Strength*, 505.

373 Concerning the knightly mouse Reepicheep, Lewis wrote: "'Sir,' said the Mouse, 'I can eat and sleep and die for my King without one. But a tail is the honour and glory of a Mouse.' 'I have sometimes wondered, friend,' said Aslan, 'whether you do not think too much about your honour.'" Lewis, *Prince Caspian*, 177. Cf. Lewis, *The Allegory of Love*, 103.

374 "Self-renunciation is thought to be, and indeed is, very near the core of Christian ethics. When Aristotle writes in praise of a certain kind of self-love, we may feel, despite the careful distinctions which he draws between the legitimate and the illegitimate *Philautia*, that here we strike something essentially sub-Christian [*N.E.* bk 9, ch. 8]. . . . There are two kinds of self-hatred which look rather alike in their earlier stages, but of which one is wrong from the beginning and the other right to the end." Ibid., 297. Cf. "Those loved authors, so civilised, tolerant, humane, and enlightened, every now and then reveal that they are divided from us by a gulf. Hence the eternal, roguish tittering about pederasty in Plato or the hard pride that makes Aristotle's *Ethics* in places almost comic." Lewis, *Reflections on the Psalms*, 220. Cf. "*Arete* involves not simply 'being good' but being 'good *at*' a great many things (including morals), and Aristotle's conception of the happy life comes very close to our conception of the fully civilised life, in which the raw material (such as health, peace, and competence) provided by fortune is used by a master. Happiness is almost a *style*." Lewis, *Studies in Words*, 275-6. Cf. "The best elements in Aristotle's ethical thought contributed to this picture comparatively little. The doctrine of the Mean was dully and dutifully allegorized by Spenser in *Faerie Queene*, II. II. But what proved far more attractive was Aristotle's Magnanimous Man: the man who both had, and was entitled to have, a high opinion of his own worth. Hence, I believe, comes that astonishing absence of humility which separates Sidney's and Spenser's heroes so widely from those of Malory. 'This secret assurance of his own worthinesse,' says Sidney, 'always liues in the worthiest minds' (*Arcadia*, 1593, V). 'Oft

and disobedience spring from pride or the inordinate love of self: for Lewis the idealist, this meant loving the self *qua* soul instead of the self *qua* Spirit,[375] and for Lewis the Christian, this meant not loving the self as God

---

times nothing profits more,' says Milton, 'Then self-esteem grounded on just and right' (*P. L.* VIII. 571) – a beautifully exact account of Aristotle's Magnanimity. The contrast between the medieval and this 'philosophical' ideal comes out almost comically if we lay two passages side by side. In Gawain and the Green Knight the hero, traveling alone,

> had no fere but this fole bi frithes and downes
> And no gome but God bi gate with to karp (695).

Spenser's Guyon in the same situation

> every more himselfe with comfort feedes
> Of his own virtues and praise-worthie deeds (II. VII. 2)

I fear there is no hint of a smile on Spenser's face as he described this windy diet. . . . But, for many sixteenth-century men, as for the Stoics, Aristotle's Magnanimity was not magnanimous enough, 'for he saith,' complains Vives, 'that magnanimitie goeth about to seke honours. . . . But Plato, Cicero, Seneca and other place it rather in despising them' (*De Causis*, VI). . . . [The magnanimous man is] this unmoved, unconquerable, 'mortal god' (as Henry More calls him), if modified in one direction gives us Milton's Christ: if in another, his Satan." Lewis, *Poetry and Prose in the Sixteenth Century*, 54-5. Also consider the following comments Lewis made about Spenser's *Faerie Queene*: "*I labour to pourtraict in Arthure . . . the image of a brave knight, perfected in the twelve private morall virtues, as Aristotle hath devised* – yet already in the First Part of your poem you have introduced Holiness and Chastity, which Aristotle would never have dreamed of including among his virtues. *In the person of Prince Arthure I sette forth magnificence in particular, which virtue . . . . according to Aristotle . . . is the perfection of all the rest, and conteineth in it them all.* But that is not what you set forth at all. Certainly there is no trait of *megaloprepeia* (Magnificence) in his character, no slightest indication that he is a large spender. But there is probably a confusion of terms here, due to some bad Latin translation you were using. What you mean is Magnanimity, not Magnificence; megalopsychia, not megalo-prepeia. The crown of all the virtues is for Aristotle a right Pride or Magnanimity, which deserves and claims the highest honour. Now it is true that Alma shows the spring of Arthur's action to be Prays-desire (II, ix, 36-9). But even so, he has only as much resemblance to the Aristotelian megalopsychos as any good knight was bound to have." Lewis, *Spenser's Images of Life*, 137-8. Cf. "If [Spenser's Arthur] is Aristotelian 'Magnanimity,' in search of earthly glory, his deliverance of St. George is arrant nonsense. 'Magnanimity,' in this sense, cannot come to the rescue of Holiness; for whatever pagan character of the μεγαλόψυχος is not sin, belongs already to the Saint." Lewis, *The Allegory of Love*, 337. Despite all these examples, Lewis did not think magnanimity as such is a bad thing: he just thought that Aristotle's focus on it was dangerous; indeed, in *Out of the Silent Planet*, Lewis mentioned an example of good magnanimity, saying: "[Ransom's] headache was gone: he felt vigilant, courageous and magnanimous as he had seldom felt on Earth." Lewis, *Out of the Silent Planet*, 23.

375 "All souls will <u>what</u> Spirit wills: but good souls will <u>as</u> Spirit wills. Hence we pray not 'Thy will be done' wh[ich] w[oul]d be a [. . .] but 'Thy will be done <u>in earth as it is in Heaven</u>." Lewis, *De Bono et Malo*, 7.

commanded it to be loved, in particular, loving God below the self, hence, a confusion of "first and second things."[376] Consequently, Lewis's answer to the problem of evil – a problem that plagued him as late as his conversion to theism[377] – is that evil entered the world because man and angel were given freedom which they abused.

Now according to Augustine, because man chose to sin against God, he was cursed and could not return to God's court unless he were made pure again. This is where Christ came in. Because only God (He-Who-Is-Pure) can remove impurity, only God can take away man's sins. However, because God is perfectly just, He could not disregard Justice for the sake of impure man. Thus, God took on flesh to die for the sins of man in order to satisfy perfect Justice, and this act of God taking on flesh and dying constitutes the greatest virtue of all, Charity. Consequently, for Augustine, it is nonsense to talk about virtue without reference to love. Indeed, Augustine said that just as all the vices spring from pride, so do all the virtues spring from humility, obedience and "ordinate love."[378]

Lewis accepted Augustine's – and Christ's[379] – reduction of all the virtues

---

376 "[E]very preference of a small good to a great, or partial good to a total good, involves the loss of the small or partial good for which the sacrifice was made." C. S. Lewis, "First and Second Things," in *C. S. Lewis: Essay Collection & Other Short Pieces*, ed. Lesley Walmsley (1942 essay reprint; London: HarperCollins, 2000), 655.

377 For instance, despite Lewis's appreciation of Traherne, Lewis, being a philosopher who struggled deeply with the problem of evil, found some of Traherne's answers a bit thin: "I have been reading a little every evening in Traherne's *Centuries of Meditations*. . . . I think he suffers by making out everything much too easy and really shirking the problem of evil in all its forms: at least, as far as I have got, for it is unfair to say this of a book not yet finished. But apart from this he has extraordinary merits." Lewis, *The Collected Letters of C. S. Lewis: Volume I*, 914 [July 8, 1930]

378 Augustine *The City of God* 15.23. Cf. Ibid., 14.12.

379 Lewis actually credited Christ, not Augustine, with this idea: "Our Lord seems to reduce all virtue to active beneficence." Lewis, *The Problem of Pain*, 530.

(all the positive dispositions in the will[380]) to humble,[381] obedient[382] love; however, Lewis realized that Augustine was just putting a Christian face on what Plato had said long before, namely, that Plato's justice and Augustine's ordinate love mean loving each thing as it ought to be loved, which, for Augustine and Lewis, meant loving God above all else: "We must aim at what St Augustine . . . called 'ordinate loves'. Our deepest concern should be for first things, and our next deepest for second things, and so on down to zero – to total absence of concern for things that are not really good, nor means to good, at all."[383] Nonetheless, while Augustine felt that man could not love God at all without grace – meaning that the non-Christian's virtues

---

380 "Think of your man as a series of concentric circles, his will being the innermost, his intellect coming next, and finally his fantasy. You can hardly hope, at once, to exclude from all the circles everything that smells of the Enemy: but you must keep on shoving all the virtues outward till they are finally located in the circle of fantasy, and all the desirable qualities inward into the Will. It is only in so far as they reach the Will and are there embodied in habits that the virtues are really fatal to us. . . . All sorts of virtues painted in the fantasy or approved by the intellect or even, in some measure, loved and admired, will not keep a man from Our Father's house." Lewis, *The Screwtape Letters*, 753.

381 "[The Great Sin] is Pride or Self-conceit: and the virtue opposite to it, in Christian morals, is called Humility. . . . Do not imagine that if you meet a really humble man he will be what most people call 'humble' nowadays: he will not be a sort of greasy, smarmy person, who is always telling you that, of course, he is nobody. Probably all you will think about him is that he seemed a cheerful, intelligent chap who took a real interest in what *you* said to *him*. . . . He will not be thinking of humility: he will not be thinking about himself at all." Lewis, *Mere Christianity*, 398, 402. Cf. The devil Screwtape says, "No more lavish promises of perpetual virtue, I gather; not even the expectation of an endowment of 'grace' for life, but only a hope for the daily and hourly pittance to meet the daily and hourly temptation! This is very bad." Lewis, *The Screwtape Letters*, 770. It should be noted that Lewis himself became extremely humble later on in his life; hence, we read: "One of the things that make it easier to believe in Providence is the fact that in all trains, hotels, restaurants and other public places I have only once seen a stranger reading a book of mine, tho[ugh] my friends encounter this phenomenon fairly often. Things are really very well arranged." Lewis, *The Collected Letters of C. S. Lewis: Volume III*, 338 [June 16, 1953].

382 Lewis often spoke about "the habit of obedience." Lewis, *The Screwtape Letters*, 809. "I don't think Milton w[oul]d have seen the contrast – if you mean to suggest one – between virtue as obedience and virtue as reason. I'm not sure that I do myself, either!" Lewis, *The Collected Letters of C. S. Lewis: Volume II*, 548 [January 20, 1943].

383 Lewis, *Prayer: Letters to Malcolm*, 237. Cf. "St Augustine defines virtue as *ordo amoris*, the ordinate condition of the affection in which every object is accorded that kind of degree of love which is appropriate to it. Aristotle says that the aim of education is to make the pupil like and dislike what he ought. When the age for reflective thought comes, the pupil who has been thus trained in 'ordinate affections' or 'just sentiments' will easily find the first principles in Ethics; but to the corrupt man they will never be visible at all and he can make no progress in that science. Plato before him had said the same." Lewis, *The Abolition of Man*, 404-5.

were not true virtues – Lewis did not go quite this far since the he tended
to see degrees where Augustine (and Tertullian[384]) saw absolutes.[385] Thus, on
the one hand, Lewis agreed with Augustine that man can neither be saved[386]
nor consistently will the Good[387] except by God's grace (hence, Lewis agreed
with Hooker's Augustinian sentiment that "[o]ur very virtues may be snares
unto us"[388]); however, on the other hand, Lewis repeatedly pointed out the

---

384 Hence, in *The Pilgrim's Regress*, Neo-Angular tells Vertue, a follower of pagan ethics,
that he is "undoubtedly damned" and then goes on to quote Tertullian: "*Virtues
paganorum splendida vitia*" ["The virtues of the pagans are splendid vices"]. Lewis, *The
Pilgrim's Regress*, 109. Kathryn Lindskoog, *Finding the Landlord: A Guidebook to C. S.
Lewis's Pilgrim's Regress* (Chicago: Cornerstone, 1995), 60.

385 Although Lewis blocked off the following in his edition of Augustine's *City of God*, he
did not fully agree with the Saint: "The fact is that the soul may appear to rule the body
and the reason to govern the vicious elements in the most praiseworthy fashion; and yet
if the soul and reason do not serve God as God himself commanded that he should be
served, then they do not in any way exercise the right kind of rule over the body and
the vicious propensities. . . . Thus the virtues which the mind imagines it possesses, by
means of which it rules the body and the vicious elements, are themselves vices rather
than virtues, if the mind does not bring them into relation with God in order to achieve
anything whatsoever and to maintain that achievement. For although the virtues are
reckoned by some people to be genuine and honourable when they are related only to
themselves and are sought for no other end, even then they are puffed up and proud,
and so are to be accounted vices rather than virtues." Augustine *City of God* 19.25.

386 "John decides to live virtuously but at once meets an obstacle – Conscience tells him
he can and must pass it by his own efforts – Traditional Christianity says he cannot."
Lewis, *The Pilgrim's Regress*, 85. Cf. "But I cannot, by direct moral effort, give myself
new motives. . . . Everything which really needs to be done in our souls can be done
only by God." Lewis, *Mere Christianity*, 444. In *The Voyage of the Dawn Treader*, Eustace
cannot "un-dragon" himself: he needs Aslan to remove the scales. Lewis, *The Voyage of
the Dawn Treader*, 87.

387 "My reason for thinking that a mere statement of even the highest ethical principles is
not enough is precisely that to know these things is not necessarily to do them, and if
Christianity brought no healing to the impotent will, Christ's teaching would not help
us." Lewis, *The Collected Letters of C. S. Lewis: Volume II*, 605 [March 9, 1944]. Cf. "We
may, indeed, be sure that perfect chastity – like perfect charity – will not be attained by
any merely human efforts. You must ask for God's help. Even when you have done so, it
may seem to you for a long time that no help, or less help than you need, is being given.
Never mind. After each failure, ask forgiveness, pick yourself up, and try again. Very
often what God first helps us towards is not the virtue itself but just this power of always
trying again. For however important chastity (or courage, or truthfulness, or any other
virtue) may be, this process trains us in habits of the soul which are more important
still. It cures our illusions about ourselves and teaches us to depend on God. . . . The
only fatal thing is to sit down content with anything less than perfection." Lewis, *Mere
Christianity*, 385.

388 Lewis, underlining in his edition of *Of the Laws of Ecclesiastical Polity*, 23 [1.7]. Cf. The
devil Screwtape writes, "Our research department has not yet discovered . . . how to
produce *any* virtue. This is a serious handicap. To be greatly and effectively wicked a

good latent in the lesser of two evils ("'It's better for [the dufflepuds] to admire [the Chief Duffer] than to admire nobody'"[389]) and even – having more confidence in man's freedom than Augustine[390] – rejected the idea of "eternal security":

> The world does not consist of 100 per[cent] Christians and 100 per[cent] Non-Christians. There are people (a great many of them) who are slowly ceasing to be Christians but who still call themselves by that name: some of them are clergymen. There are other people who are slowly becoming Christians though they do not yet call themselves so. There are people who do not accept the full Christian doctrine about Christ but who are so strongly attracted by Him that they are His in a much deeper sense than they themselves understand. There are people in other religions who are being led by God's secret influence to concentrate on those parts of their religion which are in agreement with Christianity, and who thus belong to Christ without knowing it. For example, a Buddhist of good will may be led to concentrate more and more on the Buddhist teaching about mercy and to leave in the background (though he might still say he believed) the Buddhist teaching on certain other points. Many of the good Pagans long before Christ's birth may have been in this position. And always, of course, there are a great many people who are just confused in mind and have a lot of inconsistent beliefs all jumbled up together. Consequently, it is not much use trying to make judgements about Christians and non-Christians in the mass.[391]

man needs some virtue. What would Attila have been without his courage, or Shylock without self-denial as regards the flesh?" Lewis, *The Screwtape Letters*, 815. With William Law and others, Lewis believed that what appears on the surface to be virtue might actually be vice; hence, he wrote: "Two rules from W[illia]m Law must be always before our minds.

1.   'There can be no surer proof of a confirmed pride than a belief that one is sufficiently humble.'
2.   'I earnestly beseech all who conceive they have suffered an affront to believe that it is very much less than they suppose.'"

Lewis, *The Collected Letters of C. S. Lewis: Volume I*, 1243 [February 24, 1961]. Cf. The devil Screwtape says, "Your patient has become humble; have you drawn his attention to the fact? All virtues are less formidable to us once the man is aware that he has them, but this is specially true of humility." Lewis, *The Screwtape Letters*, 770.

389 Lewis, *The Voyage of the Dawn Treader*, 126. Cf. "The sins of the flesh are bad, but they are the least bad of all sins. All the worst pleasures are purely spiritual. . . . There are two things inside me, competing with the human self which I must try to become. They are the Animal self, and the Diabolical self. The Diabolical self is the worse of the two. That is why a cold, self-righteous prig who goes regularly to church may be far nearer to hell than a prostitute." Lewis, *Mere Christianity*, 386.

390 Lewis, *Prayer: Letters to Malcolm*, 256. Cf. Lewis, *The Great Divorce*, 1077.

391 Lewis, *Mere Christianity*, 455. Of course in fairness to Augustine, he did think that in

While Lewis thought the grace of God is offered to all people, he maintained that people need to accept grace in order to be purified and made whole: thus, there is no need for the heroic optimism of self that characterized Greek ethics;[392] rather, all that is required is a genuine, straightforward, rational confession: "Remember what St. John says 'If our *heart* condemn us, God is stronger than our heart.' The *feeling* of being, or not being, forgiven and loved, is not what matters. One must come down to brass tacks. If there is a particular sin on your conscience, repent and confess it. If there isn't, tell the despondent devil not to be silly."[393]

Nevertheless, once sins are confessed and grace is given, Lewis believed that man has a responsibility both to show gratitude to God for what He has done and to get on with the joint-business of developing virtue. Thus, there is a need for (1) acts of piety, such as prayer,[394] worship,[395] and giving alms to

---

this life it was difficult to determine who is saved and who is not; hence, he said that it is futile to say that the City of God can be visually represented on Earth.

392 Thus, in *The Pilgrim's Regress*, John, preparing to "dive" into the grace of Christ, rejects the advice of Mr. Humanist, who said: "'Mere atavism. You are diving to escape your real duties. All this emotionalism, after the first plunge, is so much *easier* than virtue in the classical sense.'" Lewis, *The Pilgrim's Regress*, 188. Cf. "But we know that some of *our own acts* have sprung from evil *will* . . . although we know better, and that what we need is not – or not *only* – re-education but repentance, God's forgiveness, and His Grace to help us to do better next time." Lewis, *The Collected Letters of C. S. Lewis: Volume III*, 330 [May 18, 1953].

393 Ibid., 962 [July 21, 1958].

394 Lewis often used the language of virtue – that is, of habit and disposition – when he spoke of prayer: "I don't think we ought to try to keep up our normal prayers when we are ill and over-tired. I would not say this to a beginner who still has the habit to form. But you are past that stage." Ibid., 567 [February 20, 1955].

395 Cf. "Every service is a structure of acts and words through which we receive a sacrament, or repent, or supplicate, or adore. And it enables us to do these things best – if you like, it 'works' best – when, through long familiarity, we don't have to think about it. . . . Thus my whole liturgiological position really boils down to an entreaty for permanence and uniformity. I can make do with almost any kind of service whatever, if only it will stay put. But if each form is snatched away just when I am beginning to feel at home in it, then I can never make any progress in the art of worship. You give me no chance to acquire the trained habit – *habito dell'arte*." Lewis, *Prayer: Letters to Malcolm*, 226. Cf. "That is why the Christian statement that only He who does the will of the Father will ever know the true doctrine is philosophically accurate. Imagination may help a little: but in the moral life, and (still more) in the devotional life we touch something concrete which will at once begin to correct the growing emptiness of our idea of God." Lewis, *Miracles*, 1167.

the poor;[396] (2) acts of penance,[397] such as fasting;[398] (3) spiritual exercises, which we have already discussed in chapter two;[399] and even (4) Purgatory,

---

396 Lewis was famous for his generosity to all those in need. Thus, Owen Barfield, who was in charge of Lewis's finances, said: "[Lewis] gave two-thirds of his income away altogether and would have bound himself to give the whole of it away if I had let him." Barfield, *Owen Barfield on C. S. Lewis*, 14. Cf. "Though endlessly generous (Jack had for years been giving two-thirds of his royalties to charity) both Lewis brothers lived in fear of penury which Jack told me had been instilled into them by their father who frequently warned them that they were likely to end up in a 'work house.'" Walter Hooper, introduction to *The Letters of C. S. Lewis to Arthur Greeves (1914-1963)*, by C. S. Lewis, ed. Walter Hooper (New York: Collier Books, 1979), 32. Cf. "I do most thoroughly agree with your father's principle about alms. It will not bother me in the hour of death to reflect that I have been 'had for a sucker' by any number of impostors; but it would be a torment to know that one had refused even *one* person in need. After all, the parable of the sheep and goats makes our duty perfectly plain, doesn't it. Another thing that annoys me is when people say 'Why did you give that man money? He'll probably go and drink it.' My reply is 'But if I'd kept [it] *I* should probably have drunk it.'" Lewis, *The Collected Letters of C. S. Lewis: Volume III*, 1376 [October 26, 1962]. Cf. "Charity – giving to the poor – is an essential part of Christian morality. . . . I am afraid the only safe rule is to give more than we can spare. In other words, if your expenditure on comforts, luxuries, amusements, etc., is up to the standard common among those with the same income as our own, we are probably giving away too little. . . . For many of us the great obstacle to charity lies not in our luxourious living or desire for more money, but in our fear – fear of insecurity. This must often be recognized as a temptation." Lewis, *Mere Christianity*, 375.

397 "Your problem, however, was not about sinful desires in that sense; rather about desires, intrinsically innocent and sinning, if at all, only by being stronger than the triviality of their object warrants. I have no doubt at all that if they are the subject of our thoughts they must be the subject of our prayers – whether in penitence or in petition or in a little of both: penitence for the excess, yet petition for the thing we desire." Lewis, *Prayer: Letters to Malcolm*, 237. Cf. "And always remember that poverty & every other ill, lovingly accepted, has all the spiritual value of voluntary poverty or penance." Lewis, *The Collected Letters of C. S. Lewis: Volume III*, 776 [August 3, 1956]. Cf. Ibid., 358 [August 10, 1953], 1355 [July 3, 1962].

398 "Everyone knows that fasting is a different experience from missing your dinner by accident or through poverty. Fasting asserts the will against the appetite – the reward being self-mastery and the danger pride: involuntary hunger subjects appetite and will together to the Divine will, furnishing on occasion for submission and exposing us to the danger or rebellion. . . . Ascetic practices, which in themselves strengthen the will, are only useful in so far as they enable the will to put its own house (the passions) in order, as a preparation for offering the whole man to God. They are necessary as a means; as an end, they would be abominable, for in substituting will for appetite and there stopping, they would merely exchange the animal self for the diabolical self." Lewis, *The Problem of Pain*, 529. Cf. "I practice the fast [before Communion] myself and habit has made it easy as regards food." Lewis, *The Collected Letters of C. S. Lewis: Volume III*, 629 [July 7, 1955].

399 "We – or at least I – shall not be able to adore God on the highest occasions if we have learned no habit of doing so on the lowest." Lewis, *Prayer: Letters to Malcolm*, 281-2. Cf.

which Lewis envisioned not as a place where a person earns his salvation, but rather as a place where a person can do something to show God that he understands that developed virtue – seeing as God sees and willing as God wills – is essential for man's Happiness in Heaven:

> The right view [of Purgatory] . . . [is] in Newman's *Dream*. There, if I remember rightly, the saved soul, at the very foot of the throne, begs to be taken away and cleansed. It cannot bear for a moment longer 'With its darkness to affront the light.' . . . Our souls *demand* Purgatory, don't they? Would it not break the heart if God said to us, 'It is true, my son, that your breath smells and your rags drip with mud and slime, but we are charitable here and no one will upbraid you with these things, nor draw away from you. Enter into the joy'? Should we not reply, 'With submission, sir, and if there is no objection, I'd *rather* be cleaned first.' 'It may hurt, you know.' – 'Even so, sir.'[400]

To conclude, even though this chapter has been lengthy, this was necessary since there was no topic Lewis wrote more about than ethics. Indeed, this chapter could have been much longer if I followed Gilbert Meilaender in combining Lewis's ethical and social thoughts. But instead, I chose to follow Aristotle, who saw ethics as preliminary to, but also part of, socio-political philosophy. And it is this branch of philosophy to which I now turn.

"When you are training soldiers in manoeuvres, you practice with blank ammunition because you would like them to have practiced before meeting the real enemy. So we must practice in abstaining from pleasures which are not in themselves wicked. If you don't abstain from pleasure, you won't be good when the time comes along. It is purely a matter of practice." Lewis, "Answers to Questions on Christianity," 321-2.

400 Lewis, *Prayer: Letters to Malcolm*, 293. Cf. "I had a tooth out the other day, and came away wondering whether we dare hope that the moment of death may be very like that delicious moment when one realizes that the tooth is really out and a voice says 'Rinse your mouth out with this.' 'This' of course will be Purgatory." Lewis, *The Collected Letters of C. S. Lewis: Volume III*, 1064 [July 7, 1959]. "I have often had the fancy that one stage in Purgatory might be a great big kitchen in which things are always going wrong – milk boiling over, crockery getting smashed, toast burning, animals stealing. The women have to learn to sit still and mind their own business: the men have to learn to jump up and do something about it. When both sexes have mastered this exercise, they go on to the next." Ibid., 1361 [July 31, 1962]. Cf. "There are some enlightened and progressive old gentlemen of this sort whom no courtesy can propitiate and no modesty disarm. But then I dare say I am a much more annoying person than I know. (Shall we, perhaps, in Purgatory, see our own faces and hear our own voices as they really were?)." Lewis, *Reflections on the Psalms*, 312. The best study of Lewis and purgatory is by David Clark. See David Clark, *C. S. Lewis: A Guide to His Theology* (Oxford: Blackwell, 2007), 131-49.

Chapter Nine

Socio-Political Philosophy

Socio-political philosophy is more or less an extension, or application, of ethics. Lewis's own interest in this type of philosophy is mixed, though not as much as some might think. For instance, most who are familiar with Lewis are aware that he wrote a smattering of essays on topics such as the inequality of the sexes, the Welfare State and democratic education; however, most of these same people dismiss Lewis's writings on gender without a second thought, follow Lewis's brother, Warnie, in speaking of the Oxford don's "contempt for politics and politicians,"[1] and, with the exception of men like Joel Heck,[2] think Lewis's writings on education irrelevant. While I certainly admit that Lewis's contribution to socio-political philosophy is not particularly original, I do think, as I have argued in recent years,[3] that he was

---

1   Warren Lewis, "Memoirs of C. S. Lewis," in *Letters of C. S. Lewis*, ed. Warren Lewis and Walter Hooper, 21-46 (San Diego: Harvest, 1993), 26. Ron Dart, Suzanne Bray, John West Jr., Richard John Neuhaus and Danny Adkison are the exceptions since they recognize some value in Lewis's political writings. See Suzanne Bray, "C. S. Lewis and Politics," *VII: An Anglo-American Literary Review* 20 (2003): 13-32. John West Jr., "Finding the Permanent in the Political: C. S. Lewis as a Political Thinker," in *Permanent Things: Towards the Recovery of a More Human Scale at the End of the Twentieth Century*, ed. Andrew Tadie and Michael Macdonald, 137-50 (Grand Rapids, MI: Eerdmans, 1995). John West Jr., "Politics from the Shadowlands: C. S. Lewis on Earthly Government," *Policy Review* (Spring 1994). Richard John Neuhaus, "C. S. Lewis in the Public Square," *First Things* (December 1998). Danny Adkison, "The Politics of C. S. Lewis Reconsidered," *CSL: The Bulletin of the New York C. S. Lewis Society* 15, no. 8 (June 1984): 4-6. Cf. Gregory Wolfe, "Lewis on the Nature of Politics: A Reply to Danny Adkison," *CSL: The Bulletin of the New York C. S. Lewis Society* 16, no. 1 (November 1984): 6-7. Cf. "One Year Ago in the Bulletin," *CSL: The Bulletin of the New York C. S. Lewis Society* 2, no. 10 (August 1971): 5. Cf. "Report of the 138th Meeting: April 10, 1981," *CSL: The Bulletin of the New York C. S. Lewis Society* 12, no. 6 (April 1981): 5-6.

2   Joel Heck, *Irrigating Deserts: C. S. Lewis on Education* (Saint Louis: Concordia Academic Press, 2005).

3   For example, see Adam Barkman, "C. S. Lewis and the Enduring Relevance of Monarchy," *CSL: The Bulletin of the New York C. S. Lewis Society* 37, no. 4 (July-August

a valuable voice for the enduring relevance of Old Western Culture, and as such ought to be given more consideration by socio-political philosophers.

Since most of Lewis's cultural background was discussed in chapter five, herein I will mainly focus on Lewis's actual ideas. As for the structure of this chapter, I have divided it into three main parts: the family, the state, and education – the Church, since it is more theological than philosophical, has been omitted.

I: The Family

Excluding a few Lewis scholars, such as Walter Hooper,[4] Peter Kreeft,[5] Kathryn Lindskoog,[6] Will Vaus,[7] and David Downing,[8] the majority of people who read Lewis – both friends[9] and foes alike – reject the Oxford don's theory of the family, or more specifically, his stance on gender and gender roles. For instance, Hugh Trevor-Roper, a colleague of Lewis's, thought him "a purple-faced bachelor and misogynist . . . periodically trembling at the mere apprehension of a feminine footfall;"[10] Candice Fredrick and Sam

---

2006): 1-15. Adam Barkman, "'All is Righteousness and there is no Equality': C. S. Lewis on Gender and Justice," *Christian Scholar's Review* 36, no. 4 (Summer 2007): 415-36. Adam Barkman, review of *The Collected Letters of C. S. Lewis: Volume III; Narnia, Cambridge and Joy; 1950-1963*, by C. S. Lewis, ed. Walter Hooper, *Philosophia Christi*, 10 no. 1 (2008): 262-5.

4 Walter Hooper, "C. S. Lewis and C. S. Lewises," in *G. K. Chesterton and C. S. Lewis: The Riddle of Joy*, ed. Michael Macdonald and Andrew Tadie, 33-52 (Grand Rapids, MI: Eerdmans, 1989), 38.

5 Peter Kreeft, "Gender and the Will of God: The Issue of Priestesses is Ultimately an Issue of God," http://lrc.edu/rel/blosser/Kreeft_gender.htm (accessed on May 19, 2005).

6 "C. S. Lewis has often been accused of misogyny, but the truth is that his attitude toward women was generally enlightened." Kathryn Lindskoog, "Women," in *The C. S. Lewis Readers' Encyclopedia*, ed. Jeffrey Schultz and John West Jr., 429-30 (Grand Rapids, MI: Zondervan, 1998), 429.

7 "Given Lewis's views on hierarchy and on the masculine and feminine aspects of life, it has been claimed that Lewis was a misogynist. However, one need only look at the facts of Lewis's life to know that he was not a hater of women." Vaus, *Mere Theology: A Guide to the Thought of C. S. Lewis*, 142.

8 "In the chronicles, it is usually the villains who make sexist remarks." David Downing, *Into the Wardrobe: C. S. Lewis and the Narnia Chronicles* (San Francisco: Jossey-Bass, 2005), 158.

9 "[S]ome who genuinely enjoy and value the writings of Lewis (including the Narnian stories) still question certain of his gender attitudes." Leland Ryken and Marjorie Lamp Mead, *A Reader's Guide Through the Wardrobe: Exploring C. S. Lewis's Classic Story* (Downers Grove, IL: InterVarsity, 2005), 147.

10 Hugh Trevor-Roper, *Letters from Oxford: Hugh Trevor-Roper to Bernard Berenson*, ed. Richard Davenport-Hines (London: Phoenix, 2007), 286.

McBride are adamant that Lewis was a "sexist;"[11] Stella Gibbons believes that Lewis's fiction is "narrow and unkind [toward women];"[12] Margaret Patterson Hannay sees some of Lewis's unpublished short stories as "marred by . . . misogynist themes;"[13] Michael White claims that "[w]omen are often attacked in [Lewis's *Chronicles of Narnia*];"[14] Karin Fry concurs, saying that "the *Chronicles* are indeed 'unfriendly' to the feminine;"[15] Courtney McKim Yates believes that "[t]he decay of strength in potentially formidable characters illustrates the misogynistic view of women that religion unavoidably presented in C. S. Lewis' works and life;"[16] Wesley Kort thinks that "Lewis shares the racist, sexist, and homophobic aspect of mid-twentieth-century white, male culture;"[17] and Andrew Adamson, the director of the latest movie version of *The Lion, the Witch and the Wardrobe*, said he changed one of the lines that Father Christmas says to Lucy and Susan ("Battles are ugly when women fight"[18] to "I hope you don't have to use [the weapons] because battles are ugly affairs"[19]) since Adamson considered the original line "a sexist aspect" of the novel.[20] In order to evaluate Lewis's apparent sexism and misogyny – and derivatively, his supposed perverse view of the family – a combination of cultural, chronological and philosophical considerations are necessary.

To begin with, we can say with some certainty that as a boy, Lewis was closer to his mother than his father. It is true that Lewis's boyhood stories of Animal-Land – stories with an abnormal emphasis on politics[21] – reveal a desire on Lewis's part to emulate his father, who talked unceasingly about Irish politics;[22] however, in temperament, Lewis was more like his rationalistic

11 Fredrick, *Women among the Inklings*, 159.
12 Stella Gibbons, "Imaginative Writing," in *Light on C. S. Lewis*, ed. Jocelyn Gibb, 86-101 (London: Geoffrey Bles, 1965), 93.
13 Margaret Patterson Hannay, *C. S. Lewis* (New York: Frederick Ungar, 1981), 252.
14 White, *C. S. Lewis: The Boy Who Chronicled Narnia*, 224.
15 Fry, "No Longer a Friend of Narnia: Gender in Narnia," 166.
16 Courtney McKim Yates, "The Girls of Narnia: Conflicts Between Religion and Gender in C. S. Lewis's Chronicles," http://www2.mcdaniel.edu/English/students/lit04/cyates.htm (accessed May 13, 2005).
17 Kort, *C. S. Lewis: Then and Now*, 157.
18 Lewis, *The Lion, the Witch and the Wardrobe*, 100.
19 Jamie Portman, "Adamson's Work on Shrek Made Narnia His Next Cheque," *The National Post* Friday, December 9, 2005 (PM6).
20 Ibid.
21 For instance, few ten year-olds would write the following: "Hacom used his power well. He called [the] counsel of chiefs corresponding to our modern parliament. Without its consent nobody could be punished, or rewarded, nor could any new law be enacted." C. S. Lewis, *Boxen: The Imaginary World of the Young C. S. Lewis*, ed. Walter Hooper (San Diego: Harcourt Brace Jovanovich, 1985), 43.
22 Concerning his father, Lewis wrote: "He was fond of oratory and had himself spoken

mother than his sentimental father. Indeed, when Lewis's mother died, Lewis, who was only ten years-old at the time, was devastated,[23] not only because he lost one of his parents, but also because he lost a much needed female-influence in his life. Although some critics have made a much bigger deal of this event than is called for, few would think that this did not factor into Lewis's early psychological makeup.

In subsequent years, Lewis's view of the family, and women in particular, developed due to six important factors.

First, although Lewis, like most heterosexual men, struggled with sexual temptations toward the fairer sex, both Lewis and his brother, Warnie, never had any desire to marry. Indeed, in 1922, Lewis spoke of "the horrors of marriage,"[24] and a few years later, he declared himself a confirmed bachelor.

Second, when Lewis was a student, he had few opportunities to socialize with the opposite sex; however, he was not as cut off from the company of women as some people have claimed,[25] for in 1922, Lewis moved into "Hillsboro" with his friend's mother (Mrs. Moore) and sister (Maureen), whom Lewis had promised to take care of when his friend (Patty Moore) died. The nature of Lewis's relationship with Mrs. Moore (who never divorced, but lived separately from her husband until her death) has been endlessly debated – with some even declaring that there was an initial sexual relationship between the two of them,[26] hence an implied "Oedipal situation;"[27] however, it seems clear to me that from day one, Lewis viewed Mrs. Moore as nothing more than a surrogate "mother"[28] and she viewed

---

on political platforms in England as a young man; if he had had independent means he would certainly have aimed at a political career." Lewis, *Surprised by Joy*, 1246.

23   Ibid., 1255.

24   Lewis, *All My Road Before Me*, 44 [June 3, 1922]. In 1923, Lewis recorded that he and Barfield "felt the same way about women and the home life and the unimportance of all the things that are advertised in common literature." Ibid., 278 [October 1923?].

25   Mary Stewart Van Leeuwen, for instance, mistakenly thinks that until the time of his marriage, Lewis largely lived in "a world without women." Mary Stewart Van Leeuwen, "A Sword Between the Sexes: C. S. Lewis's Long Journey to Gender Equality," *Christian Scholar's Review* 36, no. 4 (Summer 2007): 406.

26   Wilson, *C. S. Lewis: A Biography*, 106.

27   Joe Christopher, "Gender Hierarchies and Lowerarchies: A Response to Mary Stewart Van Leeuwen and Adam Barkman," *Christian Scholar's Review* 36, no. 4 (Summer 2007): 466.

28   "Some of those who have written about C. S. Lewis regarded his living with Mrs. Moore and Maureen as odd, even sinister. This was not the view of those of us who visited the Kilns [Lewis's home] in the thirties. There she was, a rather stately woman, sitting at the tea table. 'Mother, may I introduce Mr. Sayer, a pupil of mine?' is what he would say." Sayer, *Jack*, 154.

him as nothing more than an "adopted son,"[29] for indeed Lewis (at least) usually referred to her as mother and the evidence against this having been anything but an innocent relationship – even when Lewis was an atheist – is quite weak. Nevertheless, the important thing is that with Mrs. Moore and Maureen, Lewis constructed a new family, which, though it certainly put more distance between Lewis and his father, was on the whole positive not only because it exposed Lewis to much needed feminine influence, but also because it gave him a sense of home and family, which he had not had since his mother died: "'If not for [Mrs. Moore], I should know little or nothing about ordinary domestic life as lived by most people.'"[30] Indeed, it became even more a home after Warnie retired from the military and came to live with Lewis, the Moores and their servants at the "Kilns."

Third, as I mentioned in chapter five, although both Oxford and Cambridge only began admitting women to their colleges around the beginning of the twentieth century, Lewis tutored a higher percentage of women than most dons at Oxford. And though he, like the majority of Oxford dons,[31] neither appreciated having a lot of women about the university[32] nor was particularly thrilled about tutoring them (mostly because

29 Wilson, *C. S. Lewis: A Biography*, 65. Cf. Thomas Peter, *Simply C. S. Lewis: A Beginner's Guide to the Life of C. S. Lewis* (Wheaton, IL: Crossway Books, 1997), 65.
30 Sayer, *Jack*, 155.
31 Though more the opinion of the male students than the male dons, the following is an example of how women were generally viewed at Oxford at the beginning of the twentieth century: "Women dons shielded their pupils from the men, who in the 1920s tended anyway to regard them as bluestockings, socially somewhat inferior and unsuitable as partners." Harrison, "College Life, 1918-1939," 97. Cf. "Many male dons dislike women dons, and it is certainly rare to find a woman don who is welcomed in either professional or tutorial circles." John Betjeman, *John Betjeman's Oxford* (Oxford: Oxford University Press, 1990), 56.
32 Although Lewis wrote the following before he became a Christian, it is largely representative of his later views: "The Term has now been over some weeks, for which I am not sorry. It produced one public event of good omen – the carrying in Congregation of a Statute limiting the number of [women] at Oxford. The appalling danger of our degenerating into a woman's university (nay worse still, into *the* women's university, in contradistinction to Cambridge, *the* men's university) has thus been staved off. . . . But the question of the age of the anti-feminists is an interesting one: and the voting . . . revealed very consolatory facts. First came the very old guard . . . the full fed patriarchs of Corpus, the last survivors of the days when 'women's rights' were still new fangled crankery. They were against the women. Then came the very-nearly-as-old who date from the palmy days of J. S. Mill, when feminism was the new, exciting, enlightened thing. . . . They voted for the women. Then came the young and the postwar (I need not say I trust that I did my duty) who voted solid *against*. The arrangement is quite natural when you think it out. The first belong to the age of innocence when women had not yet been noticed: the second, to the age when they had been noticed but not yet found out:

he thought them academically less serious than men[33]), Lewis liked women *qua* women ("Who said I dislike women?"[34]) and his reputation with his female students (not to mention the girls he privately tutored at his home[35]) was generally very good. For instance, Rosamund Cowan said "[Lewis] treated us like queens;"[36] Joan O' Hare claimed that he showed her and her friend "impeccable courtesy;"[37] Patricia Berry insisted that "his manners to

---

the third to us. Ignorance, romance, realism." Lewis, *The Collected Letters of C. S. Lewis: Volume I*, 703 [July 9, 1927]. However, over the years, Lewis was seen as "courteous" and "unfailing kind" toward the few female dons he knew. Kathleen Lea, "Memories of Lewis as a Colleague," *Chesterton Review* 17, no. 3 and 4 (August and November 1991): 399.

33 For instance, when Lewis was a student – admittedly one going from the most difficult program at Oxford, "Greats," on to one of the easiest, English – he wrote the following: "I thus had plenty of time to feel the atmosphere of the English School which is very different from that of Greats. Women, Indians, and Americans predominate and – I can't say how – one feels a certain amateurishness in the talk and look of the people." Lewis, *All My Road Before Me*, 120 [October 16, 1922]. And in 1926, when Lewis was teaching both English and philosophy, he expressed surprise that out of all the women he was tutoring "hardly any of them had read the *Dialogues* [of Plato]." Ibid., 380 [April 28, 1926].

34 Lewis, *The Collected Letters of C. S. Lewis: Volume II*, 849 [April 8, 1948]. Moreover, in a letter to E. R. Eddison, Lewis denied being "a misogynist." Ibid., 546 [January 19, 1943]. When Chad Walsh told Lewis a story that he had heard about him, Lewis replied: "'The pleasant story about my locking myself in my room when a woman invaded the college precincts is – I regret to say – pure bosh. For one thing, women are wandering through 'the college precincts' the whole blessed day. For another, having taken female pupils of all ages, shapes, sizes, and complexions for about twenty years, I am a bit tougher than the story makes out. If I ever fled from a female visitor it was not because she was a woman but because she was a *bore*, or because she was the fifteenth visitor on a busy day.'" C. S. Lewis, quoted in *The Literary Legacy of C. S. Lewis*, by Chad Walsh (New York: Harcourt Brace Jovanovich, 1979), 17.

35 Concerning some of the schoolgirls who were living at Lewis's household during WWII, we read: "When, later, I told [Lewis] I wanted to go up to Oxford (University), he encouraged me, coached me in Latin, and even taught me a little Greek. . . . And how generous he was! When my mother, a widow, came to visit shortly before I sat for my entrance exam, Lewis made her an offer of financial assistance towards paying my university dues. His only stipulation was that it should be kept secret. My mother accepted; and thus it is largely due to his generosity that I was able to graduate, and later, take my master's degree. It is my understanding that he similarly helped 'Microbe' when she went on to train as a nurse." Patricia Heidelberger, "Part A: With Girls at Home," in *In Search of C. S. Lewis*, ed. Stephen Schofield, 53-4 (South Plainfield, NJ: Bridge, 1983), 54.

36 Rosamund Cowan, "Part A: With Women at College," in *In Search of C. S. Lewis*, ed. Stephen Schofield, 61-6 (South Plainfield, NJ: Bridge, 1983), 62.

37 Joan O'Hare, "Intellectual Development," in *We Remember C. S. Lewis: Essays & Memoirs*, ed. David Graham, 41-5 (Nashville: Broadman & Holman, 2001), 42.

the 'ladies of St. Hugh's' was most gracious;"[38] Rachel Trickett declared that "pupils who survived the combat of his tutorials learned to love and rely on his humanity and loyalty;"[39] Joan Pile claims, "Mr. Lewis was a good friend, and is one of my happy memories;"[40] Pat Wallsgrove maintains, "Mr. Lewis . . . always treated us with courtesy . . . and encouraged us to talk;"[41] Murial Jones remembered Lewis as "an extremely good teacher;"[42] Patricia Hunt held that "he was always perfectly polite, but rather distant in manner;"[43] and Mary Neylan (née Shelley), the granddaughter of the author of *Frankenstein*, converted to Christianity thanks to her former tutor.[44] In addition, Lewis's lectures were usually packed with female students: "Arts undergraduates were often farmed out to men tutors and were free, like the men, to choose whether to attend lectures or to go to lectures outside their subject given by such stars as C. S. Lewis."[45]

Fourth, besides Mrs. Moore, Maureen and his female students, Lewis maintained a very active epistolary correspondence with literally hundreds of women, mostly admirers of his Christian apologetics who were seeking his advice. For those who think Lewis uncharitable toward women or a misogynist, it would be a good idea to read some of these letters, for Lewis's sympathy with the plight of women is evident on every page; for example, we read:

> I think I can understand that feeling about a housewife's work being like that of Sisyphus (who was that stone rolling gentleman). But it is surely, in reality, the most important work in the world. What do ships, railways, mines, cars, government etc exist for except that people may be fed, warmed, and safe in their own homes? As Dr Johnson said, 'To be happy at home is the end of all human endeavour.' (1st to be happy, to prepare for being happy in our own real Home hereafter: 2nd, in the

38 Patricia Berry, "Part B: With Women at College," in *In Search of C. S. Lewis*, ed. Stephen Schofield, 67-70 (South Plainfield, NJ: Bridge, 1983), 70.

39 Rachel Trickett, "Uncrowned King of Oxford," in *We Remember C. S. Lewis: Essays & Memoirs*, ed. David Graham, 61-4 (Nashville: Broadman & Holman, 2001), 62.

40 Joan Pile, "Part C: With Women at College," in *In Search of C. S. Lewis*, ed. Stephen Schofield, 71-3 (South Plainfield, NJ: Bridge, 1983), 72.

41 Pat Wallsgrove, "Courtesy and Learning," in *We Remember C. S. Lewis: Essays & Memoirs*, ed. David Graham, 46-7 (Nashville: Broadman & Holman, 2001), 47.

42 Murial Jones, "Part C: With Women at College," in *In Search of C. S. Lewis*, ed. Stephen Schofield, 74-5 (South Plainfield, NJ: Bridge, 1983), 75.

43 Patricia Hunt, "Awe and Delight," in *We Remember C. S. Lewis: Essays & Memoirs*, ed. David Graham, 56-8 (Nashville: Broadman & Holman, 2001), 57.

44 Walter Hooper, "Mary Neylan," in *The Collected Letters of C. S. Lewis: Volume II; Books, Broadcasts, and the War 1931-1949*, ed. Walter Hooper, 1054-5 (San Francisco: HarperSanFrancisco, 2004), 1054-5.

45 Janet Howarth, "Women," 366.

meantime, to be happy in our houses.) We wage war in order to have peace, we work in order to have leisure, we produce food in order to eat it. So your job is the one for which all others exist.[46]

Fifth, as a confirmed bachelor and Oxford don (a job which generally entailed the absence of wife and child[47]), Lewis had little interest in having, raising or being around children, which, at least in regard to being around children, Lewis later recognized as "a defect" in himself.[48] However, during WWII, when some children from London were evacuated and came to stay at Lewis's house for a time,[49] the Oxford don found these children "delightful"[50] and without a doubt *The Lion, the Witch and the Wardrobe* owed much to this experience.[51] Moreover, over the years, Lewis became the godfather to four children (Maureen Blake, Laurence Harwood, Lucy Barfield and Sarah Neylan), to whom he showed great affection and generosity.[52]

And sixth, in 1956, Lewis married his friend Joy Gresham (née Davidman) so that she and her two sons could stay in England and, as far as Lewis knew,[53]

---

46   Lewis, *The Collected Letters of C. S. Lewis: Volume III*, 580 [March 16, 1955]. Lewis also gave an enormous amount of financial aid to women; for instance, he once wrote to his producer at the BBC and asked, "My Dear Fenn – I want, as before, to ask the BBC to pay my fees for these five talks directly to the following people in the following proportions, 1. To Miss Webb . . . 2. To the Clergy Widows Fund . . . 3. To Miss Burton." Lewis, *The Collected Letters of C. S. Lewis: Volume II*, 508 [February 9, 1942].

47   Lewis recorded an interesting story about Oxford philosopher F. H. Bradley's attitude toward children: "Carritt described someone's – Smith perhaps – going for a walk with Bradley the philosopher. Bradley kept rushing off to scold little boys who were throwing papers about or were 'just going to write their names on walls.' After these painful episodes he would ask 'Do you like children?' in a voice which led you, if you were wise, to reply, 'Not very much.' Then in a tender and encouraging voice, 'Do you like *dogs*?'" Lewis, *All My Road Before Me*, 50 [June 14, 1922].

48   Lewis, *The Abolition of Man*, 405.

49   Lewis, *The Collected Letters of C.S. Lewis: Volume II*, 270 [September 2, 1939].

50   In 1940, Lewis said that he "has a house full of really delightful refugee children (I am a bachelor and never appreciated children till the war brought them to me)." Ibid., 451 [October 24, 1940].

51   Lewis, *The Lion, the Witch and the Wardrobe*, 9.

52   Not only in life but also in death did Lewis show his godchildren generosity. Hence, his godchildren are the first of those to whom Lewis left a legacy in his will. C. S. Lewis, "The Last Will of C. S. Lewis," http://www.discovery.org/cslewis/articles/writingsspblcdmn/will.php (accessed on February 8, 2005), 1.

53   Although Joy was mistreated by her ex-husband, Bill, her reason for moving to England was probably more so she could be close to Lewis, with whom she had fallen in love, than to start a new life. Lyle Dorsett, *And God Came In: The Extraordinary Story of Joy Davidman; Her Life and Marriage to C. S. Lewis* (New York: Ballantine, 1983), 94. Cf. Brian Sibley, *C. S. Lewis Through the Shadowlands: The Story of His Life with Joy*

start a new life. Although Lewis did not consider this initial marriage to Joy a real marriage (i.e. a Christian marriage),[54] one year later, when she was dying of cancer and when he discovered that her former marriage had also not been a legitimate / Christian marriage since her ex-husband had been married before, Lewis and Joy decided that they wanted to have a Christian marriage, which, naturally enough, was consummated.[55] While everyone agrees that Lewis's understanding of the family was influenced by the addition of a wife and two step-children, some, such as Mary Stewart Van Leeuwen, have made a much bigger deal of this than others; in fact, Van Leeuwen has gone so far as to say that Lewis's marriage to Joy radically altered his entire philosophy of the family and gender roles – from gender hierarchy to gender equality:

> Lewis's three late books – *Till We Have Faces, The Discarded Image,* and *A Grief Observed* – are for various reasons among his least read. Hence we are left with the common portrait of Lewis as the unchanging defender of gender stereotypes and gender hierarchy. Many of his readers, including myself, wish that this shift on this issue – whatever its sources – had occurred earlier, and found its way into his much better-selling apologetic works and his novels for children and adults. But better late than never.[56]

As I have argued elsewhere[57] and will argue again for the sake of the readers, Van Leeuwen's belief that Lewis's marriage and post-marriage books reveal a rejection of gender hierarchy is completely false. However, before I can show why it is false, I first need to establish the nature of Lewis's belief in gender hierarchy and the family – at least until his marriage to Joy in 1956.

In previous chapters, we discovered that from his absolute idealist phase onward, Lewis believed that that the universe is a rigorous hierarchy, the justice of which consists in "proportionate equality" or each thing acting according to its proper nature and in its proper place.[58] Although it is likely that Lewis's idealist and theistic belief in ontological hierarchy entailed belief in both gender and age hierarchies, these latter types of hierarchy really only became pronounced during Lewis's Christian phase, when, importantly, he supported them not only with pagan philosophical theories, which reflect

---

Davidman (Grand Rapids, MI: Spire, 1999), 116.

54 Lewis, *The Collected Letters of C. S. Lewis: Volume III,* 669 [October 30, 1955].

55 "I prayed that when I buried my wife my whole sexual nature sh[oul]d be buried with her, and it seems to have happened." Ibid., 1303 [December 20, 1961].

56 Van Leeuwen, "A Sword Between the Sexes," 414.

57 Adam Barkman, "'We Must Go Back to Our Bibles': A Response to Mary Stewart Van Leeuwen," *Christian Scholar's Review* 36, no. 4 (Summer 2007): 445-54.

58 Aristotle *Politics* 1317b1.

universal values, but also with biblical revelation, such as I Corinthians, 6:16,[59] I Corinthians 11:3,[60] Malachi 1:2-3,[61] and Ephesians 5:25,[62] all of which speak not simply of an arbitrary cultural norm but rather a significant, mythical unveiling.

As for age hierarchy, Lewis agreed with both the Bible and the universal moral law that there should be a clear – but as with all relationships, a courteous[63] – hierarchy between parents and children. Thus, Lewis thought it "perverse" when children, such as Eustace Scrubb,[64] call their parents by their "Christian names,"[65] and believed it absolutely fundamental that when children grow up, they have a responsibility to take care of their aging parents: "Of course you *ought* to be dependent on your daughter and son-in-law. Support of parents is a most ancient and universally acknowledged duty. And if you come to find yourself dependent on anyone else you mustn't mind."[66] Lewis himself deeply regretted how he treated his own father,[67] yet it is clear from Lewis's life that he made up for this by his respectful treatment of Mrs. Moore as she got older.[68] However, in addition to parents and children, Lewis also hinted that a marriage between an older man and a younger woman is best,[69] and in regard to siblings, Lewis clearly endorsed a hierarchy between the elder and the younger; consequently, in *The Lion, the Witch and the Wardrobe*, he made Peter the unequivocal king of Narnia because he not only

---

59   Lewis, *The Collected Letters of C. S. Lewis: Volume II*, 394 [April 18, 1940].

60   C. S. Lewis, "Christianity and Literature," in *C. S. Lewis: Essay Collection & Other Short Pieces*, ed. Lesley Walmsley (1939 essay reprint; London: HarperCollins, 2000), 414. Cf. Lewis, *The Collected Letters of C. S. Lewis: Volume II*, 395 [April 18, 1940].

61   Lewis, *The Four Loves*, 78.

62   Ibid., 67.

63   "'Christian, seek not yet repose.' This does not mean, of course, that there is no difference between home life and general society. It does mean that home life has its own rule of courtesy – a code more intimate, more subtle, more sensitive, and therefore, in some ways more difficult, than that of the outer world." C. S. Lewis, "The Sermon and the Lunch," in *C. S. Lewis: Essay Collection & Other Short Pieces*, ed. Lesley Walmsley (1945 essay reprint; London: HarperCollins, 2000), 344.

64   "[Eustace] didn't call his Father and Mother 'Father' and 'Mother,' but Harold and Alberta." Lewis, *The Voyage of the Dawn Treader*, 7.

65   Lewis, "Membership," 335.

66   Lewis, *The Collected Letters of C. S. Lewis: Volume III*, 359 [August 10, 1953]. Cf. "There is authority of husbands over wives and parents over children." Lewis, "Membership," 336.

67   "I treated my own father abominably and no sin in my whole life now seems to be so serious." Lewis, *The Collected Letters of C. S. Lewis: Volume III*, 445 [March 24, 1954].

68   "In her declining years Mrs. Moore became . . . senile and grumbling. . . . [I]n April 1950 she went into a nursing home in Oxford where Lewis visited her every day." Hooper, *C. S. Lewis: Companion & Guide*, 714.

69   Lewis, *The Collected Letters of C. S. Lewis: Volume III*, 1402-3 [January 2, 1963].

is masculine and good, but also is the eldest sibling. Nevertheless, applying age hierarchy – like all matters of casuistry – is not always straightforward, and so we look in vain for easy solutions to conflicts between age hierarchy and other types of hierarchy. For instance, in *Perelandra*, the Queen (a woman) is said to be superior to Ransom (a man) because of her superior age, title, and probably also purity: "[The Queen] knew now at last that she was not addressing an equal. She was a queen sending a message to a queen [Eve] through a commoner [Ransom], and her manner to him was henceforth more gracious."[70]

As for gender hierarchy, while Mary Stewart Van Leeuwen, for example, is right that Lewis used many non-Christian sources, such as Aristotle, Freud and pagan mythology, to explain gender hierarchy, she is mistaken both to see Lewis's belief in gender hierarchy as *merely* the product of his earlier philosophical phases[71] and to think that Lewis's use of scripture is flawed (because he understood the Bible to teach gender hierarchy), for it is not Lewis, but rather feminists, who pick and choose scripture and, like the proud children of modernity that most of them are,[72] drain revelation of all its mythical power; thus, I agree with Lewis when he insisted that the Bible teaches salvation equality,[73] not gender equality:

---

70   Lewis, *Perelandra*, 203.

71   Van Leeuwen, "A Sword Between the Sexes," 399.

72   Needless to say, I agree with Lewis when he implied that the majority of feminists today are motivated by pride – an unjust desire to rearrange the cosmic order as one likes. Thus, concerning Jane in *That Hideous Strength*, Lewis wrote: "She had been conceiving this world as 'spiritual' in the negative sense – as some neutral, or democratic, vacuum where differences disappeared, where sex and sense were not transcended but simply taken away. Now the suspicion dawned upon her that there might be differences and contrasts all the way up, richer, sharper, and even fiercer, at every rung of the ascent. How if this invasion of her own being in marriage from which she had recoiled, often in the very teeth of instinct, were not, as she had supposed, merely a relic of animal life or patriarchal barbarism, but rather the lowest, the first, and the easiest form of some shocking contact with reality which would have to be repeated . . . on the highest level of all? 'Yes,' said the Director. 'There is no escape. If it were a virginal rejection of the male, He would allow it. Such souls can bypass the male and go on to meet something far more masculine, higher up, to which they must make a yet deeper surrender. But your trouble has been what old poets called *Daungier*. We call it Pride. You are offended by the masculine itself: the loud, irruptive, possessive thing – the golden lion, the bearded bull – which breaks hedges and scatters the carefully made bed. The male you could have escaped, for it exists only on the biological level. But the masculine none of us can escape. What is above and beyond all things is so masculine that we are all feminine in relation to it.'" Lewis, *That Hideous Strength*, 680.

73   For more on this, compare Galatians 3:24-8, Romans 10:9-12 and Colossians 3:9-11: (1) "Therefore the law was our disciplinarian until Christ came, so that we might be justified by faith. But now that faith has come we are no longer subject to a disciplinarian,

It is idle to say that men are of equal value. If value is taken in a worldly sense – if we mean that all men are equally useful or beautiful or good or entertaining – then it is nonsense. If it means that all are of equal value as immortal souls then I think it conceals a dangerous error. The infinite value of each human soul is not a Christian doctrine. God did not die for man because of some value he perceived in him. The value of each human soul considered simply in itself, not of relation to God, is zero. As St Paul writes, to have died for valuable men would have been not divine but merely heroic; but God died for sinners. He loved us not because we were lovable, but because he is Love. It may be that he loves all equally – he certainly loved all to the death – and I am not certain what the expression means. If there is equality it is in his love, not in us.[74]

Consequently, standing opposed to people who think that gender is merely a social construct,[75] Lewis strongly contended that "gender is a reality . . . more fundamental . . . than sex."[76] Hence, he thought that since sex,

---

for in Christ Jesus you are all children of God through faith. As many of you as were baptized into Christ have clothed yourselves with Christ. There is no longer Jew or Greek, there is no longer slave or free, there is no longer male and female; for all of you are one in Christ Jesus;" (2) "Because if you confess with your lips that Jesus is Lord and believe in your heart that God raised him from the dead, you will be saved. For one believes with the heart and so is justified, and one confesses with the mouth and so is saved. The Scripture says, 'No one who believes in him will be put to shame.' For there is no distinction between Jew and Greek; the same Lord is Lord of all and is generous to all who call on him;" (3) "Do not lie to one another, seeing that you have stripped off the old self with its practices and have clothed yourselves with the new self, which is being renewed in knowledge according to the image of its creator. In that renewal there is no longer Greek and Jew, circumcised and uncircumcised, barbarian, Scythian, slave and free; but Christ is all in all!"

74 Lewis, "Membership," 338. Cf. "It is not easy to get inside the skin of men long dead, and I find indications in Miss Mohl's work of a frame of mind specially unpropitious to the operation. When we read that *even in his own day*, Athens was more democratic than Aristotle's philosophy of government, and he was *already* considerably *behind the times*' (p. 11, italics mine), we become uneasy. And our fears are confirmed on p. 339, where the author speaks of 'a medieval conception that is now wholly lost: namely that every individual soul is of equal value in the eyes of the Deity and that all inequalities and injustices and sufferings in this world are blotted out in the next.'" C. S. Lewis, review of *The Three Estates in Medieval and Renaissance Literature*, by Ruth Mohl, *Medium Aevum* 3, no. 1 (February 1934): 68.

75 Thus, for instance, Lewis would have been against Yale theologian Miroslav Volf, who insists that gender "stems exclusively from the creaturely realm." Miroslav Volf, *Exclusion & Embrace: A Theological Exploration of Identity, Otherness, and Reconciliation* (Nashville: Abingdon, 1996), 170.

76 Lewis, *Perelandra*, 327-8. Cf. "Masculine and feminine, as Lewis sees them, are more than biological categories. They are metaphysical realities." Walsh, *The Literary Legacy of C. S. Lewis*, 17.

which is biological, is an inferior copy of gender, which is spiritual, God, Who is Spirit, must be gendered. Naturally enough, the Oxford don followed the general tradition of man, and, of course, the Bible, in declaring that God's essence, therefore, must not be merely masculine, but "the Wholly Masculine."[77] Lewis, of course, did not mean to imply that God does not have any feminine attributes (such as Wisdom) or that He cannot be spoken of with feminine metaphor (Lewis "love[d] Dame Julian [of Norwich],"[78] who made constant reference to God "our mother"[79]); rather, Lewis thought that at a *mythical* level, it is more accurate to describe the First Person in the Trinity as Father rather than Mother, the Second Person in the Trinity as Son rather than Daughter, and the Third Person in the Trinity as "It (or Him)" rather than She.[80] Although we know from chapter four that the very nature of the mythical rejects any reduction into abstract terms, it is useful to see what kind of connotations both the masculine and the feminine have in order to get a sense of how Lewis understood the relationship between these two.

To this end, Diana Pavlac Glyer is certainly right in saying that Lewis believed that masculinity cannot be reduced to authority and femininity to subordination;[81] however, it is equally true that Lewis believed that whatever masculinity and femininity are, masculinity entails authority and femininity entails subordination. Thus, implying that a masculine spirit is embodied in a male body and a feminine spirit is embodied in a female body (an argument, incidentally, against so-called transgendered people), Lewis held that man *qua* man has authority over women: "St. Paul tells us (I Corinthians 11:3)

---

77   C. S. Lewis, "Epigrams and Epitaphs," in *Poems*, by C. S. Lewis, ed. Walter Hooper (1956 poem reprint; San Diego: Harcourt Brace and Jovanovich, 1964), 136 [15.7]. Cf. "The Firste Fayre must nedes be of us concyued as masculine." Lewis, *The Collected Letters of C. S. Lewis: Volume II*, 541 [December 19, 1942]. Cf. "[Nature] has the master touch – the rough, male taste of reality. . . . For we are only creatures: our role must always be that of patient to agent, female to male, mirror to light, echo to voice." Lewis, *The Problem of Pain*, 480, 495.

78   Lewis, *The Collected Letters of C. S. Lewis: Volume III*, 558 [February 2, 1955].

79   Julian of Norwich *Revelations of Divine Love* [Long Text] 58.

80   Lewis, *Mere Christianity*, 433. It should be noted that the Hebrew word for "spirit" (note the small "s") is *rûah*, which despite being feminine, is not very significant because the Spirit is not very developed in the Old Testament. Furthermore, the Greek word for spirit or Spirit is *pneuma*, which is grammatically neuter, and the term used by John of the Spirit, *Paraclete* (John 14:26; 15:26; 16:13-4), is grammatically masculine. It appears clear to me that Lewis is perfectly correct in following the typical understanding of the Spirit as neuter or masculine.

81   Diana Pavlac Glyer, "'We are *All* Fallen Creatures and *All* Very Hard to Live With': Some Thoughts on Lewis and Gender," *Christian Scholar's Review* 36, no. 4 (Summer 2007): 478.

that man is the 'head' of woman. We may soften this if we like by saying that he means only man *qua* man and woman *qua* woman and that an equality of the sexes as citizens or intellectual beings is not therefore absolutely repugnant to his thought."[82] Naturally, Lewis thought that man's authority over woman must, like everything else, be exercised in its proper place – hence, for example, a given man on the street does not have proper authority over my wife. Nevertheless, Lewis and St. Paul's point is that injustice occurs when men and women act against their (gendered) natures – when men, in particular, husbands, either abuse their authority over, or refuse to lead, women,[83] and when women, in particular, wives, either fail to submit to, or are overly servile towards, men.[84]

Nonetheless, as indicated in his discussion of I Corinthians 11:3 (and expanded on in a private letter[85]), Lewis believed that while man *qua* man has authority over woman *qua* woman, he did allow for at least three qualifications: (1) men and women *qua* rational beings, (2) men and women *qua* certain kinds of job holders, and (3) men and women *qua* citizens.

As for (1), Lewis believed that because men and women are both rational beings,[86] it is an "impoverishment" if friendship does not arise between the

---

82   Lewis, "Christianity and Literature," 414. Cf. "The Headship doctrine is that of Christianity. I take it to be chiefly about man *as* man and woman *as* woman, and therefore about husbands and wives, since it is only in marriage that they meet *as* epitomes of their sex." Lewis, *The Collected Letters of C. S. Lewis: Volume II*, 395 [April 18, 1940].

83   For this reason, Lewis deplored "the old, misogynistic manner" of St. Jerome. C. S. Lewis, "Hero and Leander," in *Selected Literary Essays*, by C. S. Lewis, ed. Walter Hooper (1952 essay reprint; Cambridge: Cambridge University Press, 1969), 64. And Lewis disapproved of Digory's chauvinism: "'That's all *you* know,' said Digory. 'It's because you're a girl. Girls never want to know anything but gossip and rot about people getting engaged.' 'You looked exactly like your Uncle when you said that,' said Polly." Lewis, *The Magician's Nephew*, 50. Moreover, because men are supposed to rule benevolently over women, Lewis made the chivalric Prince Rilian say, "'I am glad, gentleman, that the foul Witch took to her serpent form at the last. It would not have suited well either with my heart or with my honour to have slain a woman.'" Lewis, *The Silver Chair*, 158.

84   In the general sense of the feminine Creation submitting to the masculine God, Arthur Mastrolia is right when he says that "Lewis loved the obedience of the Blessed Virgin Mary." Arthur Mastrolia, *C. S. Lewis and the Blessed Virgin Mary: Uncovering a 'Marian Attitude'* (Lima, OH: Fairway, 2000), 155.

85   In a letter to Mary Neylan, Lewis added other qualifications, such as career vocations. Lewis, *The Collected Letters of C. S. Lewis: Volume II*, 395 [April 18, 1940].

86   For instance, concerning Jill "June" Freud, who worked at Lewis's house during WWII, Lewis wrote, "Beauty and brains and virtue never dwell / Together in one place, the critics say. / Yet we have known a case / You must not ask her name / But seek it 'twixt July and May." Jill Freud, "Part B: With Girls at Home," in *In Search of C. S. Lewis*, ed.

sexes.[87] One need only look at Lewis's own friendships with women such as Ruth Pitter, Sister Penelope, Dorothy Sayers, and Joy Gresham to see how much he enjoyed the company and conversation of intelligent – even if some of them were "Amazon[ian],"[88] or "ogreish"[89] – women; in fact, it is clear that when Lewis said he "can't bear a 'man's man' or a 'woman's woman,'"[90] he believed that the ideal man is one whose essence is masculine but tempered by

Stephen Schofield, 55-60 (South Plainfield, NJ: Bridge, 1983), 57.

87 Lewis, *The Four Loves*, 68.

88 Lewis himself admitted that his wife, Joy, was "something of the Amazon." Lewis, *A Grief Observed*, 56. Also consider the following story that Joy's son Douglas recounts: "Walking in the wood one day, Mother cradling the gun under one arm, she and Jack [C. S. Lewis] suddenly came face to face with a youth armed with a long-bow and quiver of target arrows. 'What do you think you're doing here?' called out Jack. 'This is private property. Please leave at once.' 'Yer gonna make me' replied this man . . . and, nocking an arrow, he half drew his bow, raising it in threat. Jack immediately stepped in front of Mother to shield her, until he became uncomfortably aware that he was probably in more danger from behind than he was from the bowman. For as he heard the incredibly ominous double click of the breech bolt, he also heard Mother say in tones of chilled steel, 'God damn it, Jack, get out of my line of fire!'" Douglas Gresham, *Lenten Lands: My Childhood with Joy Davidman and C. S. Lewis* (San Francisco: HarperSanFrancisco, 1989), 86.

89 Concerning the British author Dorothy Sayers, Lewis wrote: "For all she did and was, for delight and instruction, for her militant loyalty as a friend, for courage and honesty, for the richly feminine qualities which showed through a port and manner superficially masculine and even gleefully ogreish – let us thank the Author who invented her." C. S. Lewis, "A Panegyric for Dorothy L. Sayers," in *C. S. Lewis: Essay Collection & Other Short Pieces*, ed. Lesley Walmsley (1958 essay reprint; London: HarperCollins, 2000), 570. It should be noted that despite his general high regard for Sayers, Lewis could not have meant it as a compliment when he called Sayers "ogreish" since in *That Hideous Strength*, Lewis described Fairy Hardcastle – a butch lesbian police officer – as an "ogress." Lewis, *That Hideous Strength*, 509. From what I can gather, Sayers appears to have been both like and unlike the typical British woman of the interwar period: "Yet if British culture was being feminized [during the interwar] period [1920-1930], British women themselves were being culturally refined in a fashion that could only be described as more 'masculine.' . . . British women in the interwar years were more commonly idealized as 'pals.' The pal was no retiring Victorian Miss. She had characteristics of the flapper, the big sister, and the public schoolboy: bright, spirited, a 'sport,' faithful and true, good in a tight spot." Siân Nicholas, "Being British: Creeds and Culture," in *The British Isles: 1901-1951*, ed. Keith Robbins, 103-36 (Oxford: Oxford University Press, 2006), 121.

90 Lewis, *The Collected Letters of C. S. Lewis: Volume III*, 158 [January 10, 1952]. Cf. "What you say about the *she* in you & the *he* in her certainly does *not* seem to me the plains of Gomorrah and *is* in some sense (*what* I don't well know) probably true." Ibid., 617 [June 5, 1955]. Cf. Concerning Pauline Baynes's illustrations in *The Chronicles of Narnia*, Lewis wrote: "Of course [her illustrations are] effeminate too. Don't like either the ultra feminine or the ultra masculine myself. I prefer *people*." Ibid., 639 [August 5, 1955].

feminine attributes,[91] and the ideal woman is one whose essence is feminine but tempered by masculine attributes.[92] Nevertheless, while Lewis thought that both men and women are rational, he – and here he has some support from modern research[93] – did not think that men and women in general have the same cognitive strengths. For instance, in typical Aristotelian language (which, despite Aristotle's false views of women,[94] does not deny the truth of Lewis's statement), the Oxford don spoke of "metaphysical energy" as "the proper glory of the masculine mind," and "the intense practicality and concreteness of the female [which is], no doubt, her glory and her proper contribution to the common wisdom of the race."[95]

As for (2), nowhere in his writings did Lewis insist that a woman's place is only in the home.[96] Hence, in this regard he championed greater vocational

---

91   Thus, for instance, Lewis always insisted that he, and his sex, did not cry enough. Ibid., 432 [February 22, 1954]. Moreover, Lewis reviled the link between manliness and empire, which, as Wendy Webster tells us, was still pervasive during his lifetime. Wendy Webster, *Englishness and Empire: 1939-1965* (Oxford: Oxford University Press, 2007), 182-217.

92   Hence, in regard to females, Lewis liked well-balanced girls like Aravis, "who always had been more interested in bows and arrows and horses and dogs and swimming." Lewis, *The Horse and His Boy*, 87. And he disliked overly dolled-up girls, such as the later Susan or Lasaraleen, or overly masculine women, such as Fairy Hardcastle or Spenser's Radigund. Lewis, *The Last Battle*, 129. Lewis, *The Horse and His Boy*, 87, 90. Lewis, *That Hideous Strength*, 509, 714. Lewis, *Spenser's Images of Life*, 105, 107.

93   "Molecular biology and brain imaging show that much of the mental differences between the sexes is nature, the imprint of hormonal activity on the prenatal brain, and not nurture, the pressures and morays of society." Gerald Schroeder, *The Hidden Face of God: Science Reveals the Ultimate Truth* (New York: Simon & Schuster, 2001. Cf. Lawrence Kohlberg, *Philosophy of Moral Development* (New York: Harper & Row, 1981).

94   Aristotle thought women are incomplete men, whereas Lewis thought that women are different from, but still subordinate to, men.

95   Lewis, "Modern Man and His Categories of Thought," 617-8. Oddly, Kathryn Lindskoog, who elsewhere denied that Lewis was sexist, claimed in her book *Sleuthing C. S. Lewis* that the essay "Modern Man and His Categories of Thought" was not written by Lewis because of, among other things, "the patently ridiculous gender generalizations in it." Kathryn Lindskoog, *Sleuthing C. S. Lewis: More Light in the Shadowlands* (Macon, GA: Mercer University Press, 2001), 113. My suspicion is that Linkskoog, in her desire to reveal Walter Hooper to be a fraud, over-stretched her case by finding fault with this perfectly Lewisian essay.

96   In *That Hideous Strength*, Jane appears to be the product of a literal reading of St. Paul's statement that women are saved by childbirth. Lewis, *That Hideous Strength*, 356. I Timothy 2:15. However, in a letter to his friends, Lewis made it clear that this was not his point: "[Jane] wasn't meant to illustrate the problem of the married woman and her own career in general: rather the problem of everyone who follows an *imagined* vocation at the expense of a real one." Lewis, *The Collected Letters of C. S. Lewis: Volume II*, 669-70 [September 11, 1945].

equality for women than many of his Christian contemporaries. However, flowing from his general principle that man *qua* man has authority over woman *qua* woman, Lewis strongly opposed priestly orders for women in the Church, almost certainly disagreed with direct combat roles for women in the military,[97] likely disapproved of women in the highest positions of authority in schools,[98] and, to a lesser extent, disliked queens who rule without a king over them: "Everyone knew that that it was contrary to natural and divine law that women should rule men. . . . Calvin knew as well as Knox that the rule of women 'was a deviation from the original and proper order of nature' and 'to be ranked, no less than slavery, among the punishments of the fall of man.'"[99]

As for (3), Lewis agreed with the woman's suffrage movement of his day when it maintained that men and women should be treated as equal voting, property-owning, and divorce-seeking *citizens*.[100] However, Lewis did not concede any of these points because he thought that men and women were *ontological* or *spiritual* equals; rather, he felt that in a fallen political system, the danger of men ruling tyrannically over women is greater than the danger of importing political values into the spiritual life. Hence, ontologically- or spiritually-speaking, Lewis believed in proportionate equality (i.e. equality for equals, though not all people are equals), whereas politically-speaking, he believed in numerical equality (i.e. equality for everyone regardless of ontological or spiritual differences).

Nonetheless, Lewis's radical separation of the secular (the state) and

---

97 Thus, while in *The Lion, the Witch and the Wardrobe* Lewis seemed completely against women fighting in battles, in *The Horse and His Boy*, Lucy, for instance, is allowed to shoot arrows from the side. Lewis, *The Horse and His Boy*, 152.

98 Lewis, *The Silver Chair*, 11. Cf. Walter Hooper, *Past Watchful Dragons: The Narnian Chronicles of C. S. Lewis* (New York: Collier Books, 1979), 48.

99 Lewis, *Poetry and Prose in the Sixteenth Century*, 198. While Lewis definitely agreed that a proper monarchy has a king ruling it, he still appreciated the mythical radiance that came when Queen Elizabeth was crowed: "You've got the Coronation right too: especially a sacrificial, even a tragic rite. And a symbol: for we (Man) have had laid on us the heavy crown of being lords of this planet, and the same contract between the frail, tiny person – the huge ritual goes for us all." Lewis, *The Collected Letters of C. S. Lewis: Volume III*, 348 [July 17, 1953]. Cf. Ibid., 343 [July 10, 1953].

100 "I should view with the strongest disapproval any proposal to abolish womanhood suffrage, or the Married Women's Property Act." Lewis, "Membership," 337. Cf. Lewis, *Mere Christianity*, 391-2.

the sacred (the Church[101]) is plagued with difficulties.[102] For instance, if the only real marriage is a Christian marriage, then did Lewis think a Hindu marriage or a Jewish marriage illegitimate? Moreover, if Lewis thought state marriages were spiritually meaningless, why did he – as it appears he did[103]

---

101 While I have mentioned some of Lewis's views about women in the Church in previous chapters, a few more things could be mentioned here since I will not formally discuss them in the body of this book. First, we recall from chapters four and five that Lewis rejected any notion of women acting as priestesses in the Church – this is to say that Lewis rejected any notion of women as *representing* men, for Christ is to the Church as man is to woman. Second, Evangelical writers are correct to point out that "there are also compelling biblical arguments [such as I Timothy 2:12] against placing women in headship, which Lewis didn't mention." David Mills, "Rationality and Revelation: C. S. Lewis and Lambeth," *Mandate* (July / August 1998), http://theroadtoemmaus.org/RDLb/12The/SxTh/WmO/WmODMlls.htm (accessed on May 6, 2005). Doubtless, Lewis's argument against priestesses in the Church is weakened because he did not appeal to scripture as much as he could have; however, in Lewis's defence, his approach to this issue – a more sacramental or Anglican approach – is a useful corrective for Protestants who rely too much on textual arguments. Third, unlike most traditionalists or complimentarians, Lewis neither thought that women were incapable of teaching men spiritual truths ("There were female preachers [in the New Testament]" Lewis, "Priestess in the Church," 399), nor did he think that women were incapable of baptizing men ("There is no doubt that laymen, and women, can baptize." Lewis, *The Collected Letters of C. S. Lewis: Volume III*, 134 [September 12, 1951]). Fourth, while some have pointed out that Lewis ignored the verse about "the priesthood of all believers," Lewis likely thought this verse referred to that fact that because of Christ, all believers can come before God without any other sacrifice – not that women can represent men in the Church. Fifth, Lewis believed that feminism in the Church was a potential (and as we know now, an actual) cause of schism and disharmony in the body of Christ; that is, he maintained that feminists who argue for women's rights in the Church are not merely wrong but are knowingly or unknowingly promoting sinful division; thus, in a letter to Dorothy Sayers, Lewis wrote: "I never wake up to anything till it's well under way, so news has only just reached me of a movement (starting, I believe, from Chinese Anglicans) to demand that women sh[oul]d be allowed Priests' Orders. I am guessing that, like me, you disapprove something which w[oul]d cut us off so sharply from all the rest of Christendom, and which w[oul]d be the very triumph of what they call 'practical' and 'enlightened' principles over the far deeper need that the Priest at the Altar must represent the Bridegroom to whom we are all, in a sense, feminine." Lewis, *The Collected Letters of C. S. Lewis: Volume II*, 860 [July 13, 1948]. For all these reasons, I find it absurd when Alan Jacobs claims that "if Lewis were writing today, he would surely leave [the subject of the ordination of women] alone." Jacobs, *The Narnian*, 254-5. For more on Lewis and the Church, see chapter four of Lyle Dorsett, *Seeking the Secret Place: The Spiritual Formation of C. S. Lewis* (Grand Rapids, MI: BrazosPress, 2004).

102 J. R. R. Tolkien, of all people, pointed out some of these difficulties in a three page letter to Lewis critiquing Lewis's theory of divorce as put forth in *Mere Christianity*. J. R. R. Tolkien, *The Letters of J. R. R. Tolkien*, ed. Humphrey Carpenter and Christopher Tolkien (London: HarperCollins, 1995), 60-2.

103 "What sh[oul]d the positive life of the homo[sexual] be? I wish I had a letter wh[ich] a

– oppose gay marriages of any sort? While I will not try to help Lewis out of these problems, it would be unfair to him to ignore the positive aspects of his theory of Christian marriage.

But what are these positive aspects? Besides his firm insistence on set gender roles in marriage (which has helped countless people, including a certain "Mrs. B," who claims that "the first influence that led me back to a right understanding of God's role for women was _Mere Christianity_"[104]) Lewis poured refreshing praise on the institution of marriage, saying of his own marriage that he "was never so happy before."[105] Additionally, I think that (1) he was right in seeing successful marriages as between "good people" and not "great lovers,"[106] (2) he put the right emphasis on a married couple's duty to have children (i.e. rejecting abortion[107] and contraceptives,[108] a Christian couple should see children as a great blessing[109]), (3) he rightly left the door

---

pious male homo[sexual], now dead, once wrote to me – but of course it was the sort of letter one takes care to destroy. He believed that his necessity _could_ be turned to spiritual gain: that there were certain kinds of sympathy and understanding, a certain social role which mere _men_ and mere _women_ c[oul]d not give. But it is all horribly vague – too long ago. Perhaps any homo[sexual] who humbly accepts his cross and puts himself under Divine guidance will, however, be shown the way. I am sure that any attempt to evade it (e.g., by mock- or quasi-marriage with a member of one's own sex _even_ if this does not lead to any carnal act) is the wrong way." Lewis, _The Collected Letters of C. S. Lewis: Volume III_, 472 [May 14, 1954].

104 Mrs. B, "Rebellion and Feminism: My Story," http://www.ladiesagainstfeminism.org/artman/publish/article_1363.shtml (accessed on May 25, 2005).

105 Lewis, _The Collected Letters of C. S. Lewis: Volume III_, 861 [June 25, 1957]. Cf. "My wife died in July, so my married life was very short; it surpassed in happiness all the rest of my life." Ibid., 1226 [January 10, 1961].

106 "When two people achieve lasting happiness, this is not solely because they are great lovers but because they are also – I must put it crudely – good people; controlled, loyal, fair-minded, mutually adaptable people." Lewis, "We Have No 'Right to Happiness,'" 391.

107 "It is merciful and Christian to remove the natural consequences of fornication by giving the girl a bed in a maternity ward and providing for the child's keep and education, but wrong to remove them by abortion or infanticide." Lewis, _The Collected Letters of C. S. Lewis: Volume III_, 91 [February 7, 1951]. Lewis's view of abortion is typical not only of the Christians of his day but also of the general public, for abortion was not made legal in England until the 1960s. Rodney Lowe, "Riches, Poverty, and Progress," in _The British Isles: 1901-1951_, ed. Keith Robbins, 197-228 (Oxford: Oxford University Press, 2006), 219.

108 Lewis was not absolutely opposed to contraceptives. Lewis, _The Collected Letters of C. S. Lewis: Volume II_, 18 [November 22, 1931]. However, he generally disapproved of them. Lewis, _The Collected Letters of C. S. Lewis: Volume III_, 600 [April 28, 1955]. Cf. Lewis, _That Hideous Strength_, 640. Cf. Lewis, _Studies in Words_, 298-9.

109 Lewis, _The Collected Letters of C. S. Lewis: Volume III_, 605-6 [May 8, 1955]. Cf. Lewis, _The Collected Letters of C. S. Lewis: Volume II_, 392 [April 18, 1940], 729 [July 29, 1946].

open to the possibility of marriage in Heaven ("If the lowest & most corrupt form of sexual union has some mystical 'oneness' involved in it . . . *a fortiori* the blessed & lawful form must have it *par excellence*"[110]), (4) he maintained the right balance between the theory and practice of marriage (i.e. although he grounded his understanding of marriage in grand metaphysical principles, he also appealed to many practical considerations[111]), (5) he gave the right amount of liberality toward Christian couples who want to get divorce (i.e. only because of adultery[112]), and (6) he placed the right restrictions on divorced Christians who want to get remarried (i.e. only for the innocent party or perhaps for no one at all[113]).

Now, heretofore, I have merely been trying to explain Lewis's theory of the family, and especially gender roles, up until the time of his own marriage in 1956. Yet as I mentioned earlier, it still remains for me to show that Mary Stewart Van Leeuwen is mistaken when she says that Lewis changed his mind about gender hierarchy, and hence, the family, after his marriage. I propose to deal with Van Leeuwen's thesis by systematically working through Lewis's post-1956 writings to look for continued evidence of his belief in gender hierarchy and by extension the traditional Christian family.

Cf. Lewis, *That Hideous Strength*, 750.

110 Lewis, *The Collected Letters of C. S. Lewis: Volume III*, 616 [June 5, 1955].

111 An example of practical considerations in marriage is the husband's role in protecting the family from, and representing the family to, the world. Lewis, *The Collected Letters of C. S. Lewis: Volume II*, 395 [April 18, 1940]. Lewis, *Mere Christianity*, 392-3.

112 Lewis, *The Collected Letters of C. S. Lewis: Volume III*, 189 [May 13, 1952].

113 "In B[isho]p Gore's 'Sermon on the mount' . . . I find the view that Christ forbade 'divorce in such a sense as allowed re-marriage.' The question is whether He made an exception by allowing divorce in such a sense as allowed re-marriage when the divorce was for adultery. In the Eastern Church re-marriage of the innocent party is allowed: not in the Roman. The Anglican B[isho]ps at Lambeth in 1888 denied re-marriage to the guilty party, and added that 'there has always been a difference of opinion in the Ch[urch] as to whether Our Lord meant to forbid re-marriage of the innocent party in a divorce.' . . . It w[oul]d seem then that the only question is whether you can divorce your husband in such a sense as w[oul]d make you free to re-marry. I imagine that nothing is further from your thoughts. I believe that you are free as a Christian woman to divorce him especially since the refusal to do so does harm to the innocent children of his mistress: but that you must (or should) regard yourself as no more free to marry another man than if you had not divorced him." Ibid. Cf. "My own very tentative idea w[oul]d be that you must always regard yourself as his wife, and therefore incapable of a second marriage while he lives: but that I'm not at all clear that this forbids you to 'divorce' him i.e. to give him *legal* freedom to make another marriage, tho[ugh] this w[oul]d not (in our eyes) be marriage in the full Christian sense. It might, however, prevent connections wh[ich] w[oul]d on *any* view be more sinful." Ibid., 562 [February 13, 1955].

Till We Have Faces, which is not only dedicated to Lewis's wife, Joy, but is also the book of Lewis's that best captures the female mind,[114] was published in 1956, the year Lewis got married. Unquestionably, this book owed a debt to Joy not only for her editorial comments and critique but also for her insight into the female psyche. It is unlikely Lewis could have written the book without her.

So what evidence does Van Leeuwen present to justify her claim that this was one of the books that shows Lewis was moving towards a more egalitarian view of gender? Sadly, all she presents us with is the claim that "[i]t is Lewis's only novel told through the voice of a female: a strong woman ruler on the fringes of the classical Greek world, struggling against pride and toward belief in a way that parallels Lewis' own journey to faith recorded in *Surprised by Joy*."[115] If I understand Van Leeuwen correctly, she seems to be saying that (1) a novel narrated in a woman's voice is evidence of egalitarianism, and (2) "the strong woman ruler," Orual, is someone Lewis sympathized with in an egalitarian fashion.

As for the first claim, that a story told through the voice of a woman is evidence of egalitarian leanings, little can be said. It might be evidence, but it might not be. A quick glance at the history of English literature reveals not only that many supporters of gender hierarchy wrote novels from a woman's perspective or at least with women as the central figures, but also that it is difficult to say what a person's theological or philosophical leanings are from what they write in a novel.

But even if one were to admit that it is possible to get something of a picture of an author's personal beliefs from the evidence found in his or her fiction (we will discuss this more in the next chapter), does this help Van Leeuwen's claim that Orual, the central figure in *Till We Have Faces*, is someone who Lewis sympathized with in an egalitarian fashion? Is there anything in Orual's character that Lewis himself admired and is there any philosophical truths being championed by her which Lewis himself accepted?

In fairness to the evidence, there is one passage in which a certain element of Orual's character may have been admired or at least well-understood by Lewis as it recalls Joy Davidman. Queen Orual says of Bardia, her chief soldier, "'He used me, and talked to me, more and more like a man. And this

---

114 "All female readers so far have approved the feminine psychology of [*Till We Have Faces*]: i.e. no masculine note intrudes." Ibid., 716 [March 4, 1956].
115 Van Leeuwen, "A Sword Between the Sexes," 411.

both grieved and pleased me.'"[116] This passage seems to foreshadow a passage in *A Grief Observed* where Lewis discussed the "masculine-like" friendship he was able to have with his wife:

> That's what I meant when I once praised her for her 'masculine virtues.' But she soon put a stop to that by asking how I'd like to be praised for my feminine ones. It was a good *riposte*, dear. Yet there was something of the Amazon, something of Penthesilea and Camilla. And you, as well as I, were glad it should be there. You were glad I should recognize it.[117]

Both of these passages agree with what Lewis wrote in *The Four Loves*, published in 1960, where he said that a marriage without real friendship is less than ideal (for an ideal marriage would have all the loves: affection, friendship, *eros* and *agape*). But are these passages a reflection of *egalitarianism*? There is no reason to think so. In fact, if a person looks closer at the evidence in *Till We Have Faces*, it becomes clear it is Psyche, and not Orual, whom Lewis would have us admire.

That is, whereas Orual has "the mind of an ugly woman"[118] and "lives the practical life"[119] (which, we recall, was a word almost always used negatively by Lewis), Psyche "is in some ways like Christ *not because she is a symbol of Him* but because every good man or woman is like Christ."[120] And here we need to notice two things. The first is that as a woman, Psyche cannot represent Christ as a symbol; only men can do that – sentiments that Lewis expressed back in his 1948 essay "Priestesses in the Church?": "To us a priest is primarily a representative, a double representative, who represents us to God and God to us. Sometimes the priest turns his back to us and faces East – he speaks to God for us: sometimes he faces us and speaks to us for God. We have no objection to a woman doing the first: the whole difficulty is about the second."[121] This does more than suggest that Lewis's belief in gender hierarchy was still in place in 1957. Yet if this is not enough, consider the second thing: since Psyche is Christ-like in the way every good person is, then what she does and says in the text in many ways ought to reflect Lewis's own beliefs. If this is granted, consider four quotations from Psyche: (1) she calls Cupid, her husband, "The *master* of my house;"[122] (2) she tells Orual

116 Lewis, *Till We Have Faces*, 950.
117 Lewis, *A Grief Observed*, 56.
118 Lewis, *The Collected Letters of C. S. Lewis: Volume III*, 874 [August 7, 1957].
119 Lewis, preface to *Till We Have Faces*, 846.
120 Lewis, *The Collected Letters of C. S. Lewis: Volume III*, 830 [February 10, 1957].
121 Lewis, "Priestesses in the Church?" 400.
122 Lewis, *Till We Have Faces*, 916 (emphasis mine).

the first time, "'Dear Maia, I am a wife now. It's no longer you that I must *obey*;'"[123] (3) she tells Orual a second time, "'*I'm not my own*. You forget, Sister, that I'm a wife;'"[124] and (4) again she tells Orual, "'Orual, I have a husband *to guide me now*.'"[125] All of these passages, far from proving some supposed egalitarianism in *Till We Have Faces*, simply reinforce Lewis's belief in gender hierarchy, and hence his traditional view of the family.

So, if in 1957 Lewis still held the same basic gender beliefs as he did before, what about the remaining two years of his marriage? In 1959, Lewis published "Screwtape Proposes a Toast," in which he wrote, "The claim to equality, outside the strictly political field, is made only by those who feel themselves to be in some way inferior."[126] This belief that political equality is the only valid form of equality is precisely in keeping with what Lewis had written in his 1943 essay "Equality":

> I do not think that equality is one of those things (like wisdom or happiness) which are good simply in themselves and for their own sakes. I think it is in the same class as medicine, which is good because we are ill, or clothes because we are no longer innocent. . . . Legal and economic equality are absolutely necessary remedies for the Fall, and protection against cruelty. But medicine is not good. There is no spiritual sustenance in flat equality. . . . Under the necessary covering of legal equality, the whole hierarchical dance and harmony of our deep and joyously accepted spiritual inequality should be alive.[127]

The evidence makes it clear, then, that continuing through 1959, Lewis accepted gender hierarchy. But what about the time during and after the death of his wife?

Van Leeuwen has claimed that *A Grief Observed* is further evidence (although we have not seen any evidence so far) of Lewis's supposed move towards egalitarianism. It is my opinion, however, that there is nothing in *A Grief Observed* which contradicts gender hierarchy. In fact, if Van Leeuwen had not been so selective in her choice of evidence, she would have found the clearest biblical arguments Lewis gives for gender hierarchy is in the book that he published just four months before he wrote *A Grief Observed*: *The Four Loves*.

123 Ibid., 918 (emphasis mine).
124 Ibid., 919 (emphasis mine).
125 Ibid., 935 (emphasis mine).
126 C. S. Lewis, "Screwtape Proposes a Toast," in *C. S. Lewis: Essay Collection & Other Short Pieces*, ed. Lesley Walmsley (1959 essay reprint; London: HarperCollins, 2000), 758.
127 Lewis, "Equality," 666, 667.

In *The Four Loves*, Lewis began by quoting I Corinthians 7:5 in defense of Paul's warning *against* marriage – indicating that the Oxford don's wedding to Joy had not softened his convictions about the purpose of marriage.[128] Nevertheless, Van Leeuwen does not seem to notice any of this, for the only thing she focuses on is Lewis's appropriation of pagan, mythical rituals to explain gender hierarchy in marriage:

> We have seen Lewis's complex theory of gender relations drew in large measure on classical mythology and philosophy and, to a lesser degree, on Jungian notions of archetypes functioning within a cumulative, collective human unconscious. Since most of this goes well beyond both the biblical record and the basic creeds of the Church, how did Lewis justify speaking with such authority as if it were *all* part of 'mere' – that is, basic – Christian belief?[129]

What Van Leeuwen has omitted, and this is vitally important for understanding *why* Lewis maintained a belief in gender hierarchy throughout his life, is what Lewis said *after* giving a preliminary mythical explanation of the relation between the genders. He wrote,

> But I dare not mention this Pagan sacrament without turning aside to guard against any danger of confusing it with *an incomparably higher mystery*. As nature crowns man in that brief action [the fertility rite], so *the Christian law has crowned him in the permanent relationship of marriage, bestowing – or should I say, inflicting? – a certain 'headship' on him*. This is a very different coronation. And as we could easily take the natural mystery too seriously, *so we might take the Christian mystery not seriously enough*. Christian writers (notably Milton) have sometimes spoken of the husband's headship with a complacency to make the blood run cold. *We must go back to our Bibles*. The husband is the head of the wife just in so far as he is to her what Christ is to the Church. He is to love her as Christ loved the Church – read on – and gave his life for her (Ephesians 5:25).[130]

In answer to Van Leeuwen, then, who asks how Lewis could justify including issues of gender hierarchy as if it were part of basic Christianity, we know

---

128 Lewis, *The Four Loves*, 62.

129 Van Leeuwen, "A Sword Between the Sexes," 409. It is interesting to note that Lewis explicitly denied that *Till We Have Faces*, for example, was more Jungian than Christian: "Your letter was cheering for *Till We Have Faces* has attracted less attention than any book I ever wrote. The names are just 'made up.' I expect some Jungianisms do come in but the main conscious prose work is Christian, not Jungian." Lewis, *The Collected Letters of C. S. Lewis: Volume III*, 1419 [March 26, 1963].

130 Lewis, *The Four Loves*, 67 (emphasis mine).

that Lewis justified gender hierarchy – "an incomparably higher mystery" than the pagan mystery – with *biblical authority*. It is "the Christian law" that taught Lewis, throughout the first fifty years of his life and at the time of his wife's death, about gender hierarchy.

Since this is the case, it is highly unlikely that Lewis would have abandoned his belief in gender hierarchy for any reason. So what about some of the supposed egalitarian passages in *A Grief Observed*? What does one say to passages like this – "Could a woman be a complete wife unless, for a moment, in one particular mood, a man felt almost inclined to call her Brother?"[131] Or this –

> For we did learn and achieve something. There is, hidden or flaunted, a sword between the sexes till an entire marriage reconciles them. It is arrogance in us to call frankness, fairness, and chivalry 'masculine' when we see them in a woman; it is arrogance in them, to describe a man's sensitiveness or tact or tenderness as 'feminine.' . . . Marriage heals this. Jointly the two become fully human. 'In the image of God created He *them*.' Thus, by a paradox, this carnival of sexuality leads us out beyond our sexes.[132]

Are these passages evidence of a new egalitarianism in Lewis? Do they suggest that Lewis abandoned his biblical reasons (not to mention natural ones) for his belief in gender hierarchy? The answer, I believe, is clearly, "no."

One could only mistake the first passage I quoted for a clear statement of egalitarianism if one were to overlook Lewis's precise wording ". . . for a moment, in one particular mood . . ."[133] The brotherly aspect of a wife is the friendship aspect of a wife, and Lewis most definitely believed that it was an "impoverishment" if a man could not have friendship with his wife. I myself can happily identify with what Lewis says about this aspect in regard to my own wife, yet it does not change the fact that she is still essentially feminine and I am in a position of benevolent authority over her: Paul tells us Christ is to the Church as man is to woman, and John tells us that Jesus calls us friends *if* we obey Him.[134] This is to say that friendship is not incompatible with hierarchy.

---

131 Lewis, *A Grief Observed*, 56.
132 Ibid., 57-58. Cf. Lewis, *Spenser's Images of Life*, 38.
133 This language is reflective of Lewis's generous mind. In another place, when discussing Spenser's feminine depictions of Christ, he wrote: "I do not say that this image, if rightly understood, is theologically shocking." C. S. Lewis, "Neoplatonism in Spenser's Poetry," in *Studies in Medieval and Renaissance Literature*, by C. S. Lewis, ed. Walter Hooper (1961 essay reprint; Cambridge: Cambridge University Press, 1998), 155.
134 John 15:14.

As for the second passage, there is again nothing here that contradicts Lewis's hierarchical beliefs. God creating man and woman in His image, for instance, is biblical – Genesis 1:26. Thus, it is my opinion that Lewis wrote this passage as a celebration of his deceased wife: he was both tearfully celebrating their marriage and delighting, very biblically, in the wholeness that marriage brings to people. He was experiencing what Adam felt when God made Eve for him, or what God, in some sense, feels when He is united with His wife, Israel, or Christ with His bride, the Church. Furthermore, when Lewis said that certain *attributes* should not be called "masculine" or "feminine" as they can be found in both sexes, he was not denying that each of the sexes are essentially masculine or feminine. Rather, he was saying what he had been saying all along: that a true man is not a savage "man's man," but is something of a benevolent, authoritative, sensitive and strong ruler, while a true woman is something of a gentle, feisty, modest, submissive partner. Both of the sexes share many of the same attributes, yet remain essentially different; both become one in marriage, yet remain individuals.

The final work Van Leeuwen lists as evidence of a move towards egalitarianism is *The Discarded Image*, which was written during Lewis's lifetime but published posthumously (1964). She claims that the absence of gender hierarchy in this book about medieval literature is evidence of egalitarianism. But after all we have seen so far, is this at all likely?

It is true that Lewis did not discuss gender hierarchy in this book, but he may not have done so for many reasons. To begin with, the book is not a theological, much less a fictitious, work, and so he may have deemed it inappropriate to discuss such things in a book designed for academia. But perhaps more to the point, why should we think that gender was such an important issue for an introduction to medieval literature? Lewis's goal in the book was far broader than gender, and he may not have thought the topic deserved any discussion. After all, Lewis had discussed animal hierarchy in other works but did not mention it in *The Discarded Image* either.[135] Furthermore, a careful look at Lewis's other academic books on literature reveal that – save for *A Preface to Paradise Lost* – Lewis largely ignored gender issues. His reasons for doing so are his own; we can only speculate.

Nevertheless, if one wished to push the issue, one *does* find some very telling references to gender hierarchy in his academic book published *even later* than *The Discarded Image*: *Spenser's Images of Life*. In this book, published in 1967, Lewis used the word "feminist" (presumably meaning something like "one who claims that the sexes are equal") in a purely *negative* way. He contrasted

---

135 Lewis, *Studies in Words*, 32.

the "feminine" Britomart – who, as we know from *The Faerie Queene,* is no pushover – with the "real feminist," Radigund. The language Lewis used is extremely telling and serves to illuminate some of the passages he wrote in previous works like *A Grief Observed,* where he said it is arrogance for men to say things like chivalry is "masculine" when it is also found in women. True femininity, which is submissive without being servile, is contrasted with one of its perversions – feminism – which seeks either authority over men (an obvious example of perverting God-ordained hierarchy) or "mere" equality with men (a more subtle, but far more dangerous, form of perverting hierarchy). One may object and say that Lewis is discussing *Spenser's* view of gender and not *Lewis's.* While it is true that Lewis did not write the characters of Britomart and Radigund, his interpretation of them is evidence of his own personal conviction; his language betrays his views:

> There is nothing of the virago or feminist about Britomart. True, she had temporarily taken the role of the knight errant. But she became one only in order to find her lover; her outlook has always been entirely feminine. . . . Radigund, on the contrary, is a real feminist. The motive of her aggression is explained to be revenge. She is revenging herself on all mankind because one man Bellodant rejected her love (v, iv, 30). And her vengeance takes the form of directly reversing the roles of the sexes. . . . [When Artegall foolishly yields to Radigund in battle] Radigund has him dressed as a woman and set to spin. . . . Here woman has usurped man's place in the hierarchy and man has abdicated it. Whereas Radigund consciously designs an empire over men (and in the long run fails in her undesign), Britomart's power, though real, is entirely unconscious.[136]

Lewis did not have to call Radigund a feminist; indeed, a feminist scholar would probably do one of two things: she would either refuse to label Radigund a feminist because Radigund is so repulsive in her lust for dominance, or she would sympathize with Radigund and call her a feminist. Lewis was not sympathetic with Radigund at all. His sympathy lay with Britomart, whose knightly character, he constantly tried to show, is perfectly compatible with a feminine essence.

As a result of all this, I believe it is perfectly clear that Lewis the Christian did not change his basic views about gender hierarchy, and subsequently, the family.

---

136 Lewis, *Spenser's Images of Life,* 105, 107.

II: The State

As we previously discussed, when Lewis was very young – under the age of eleven – he appears to have been somewhat interested in politics. That is, in addition to his 1908 essay on "Home Rule," which debated the pros and cons of Irish Home Rule,[137] Lewis wrote numerous stories about Animal-Land, which, though understandably superficial, artfully combined fantasy and politics. Naturally, these stories owed a considerable amount to Lewis's politically-mind father.

Nevertheless, after Lewis's mother died, Lewis became less attached to his father and (perhaps as a corollary) less interested in politics: "if a man talks to me for an hour about golf, war & politics, I know that his mind is built on different lines from mine."[138] Indeed, while we can only guess what Lewis's only realist novel, simply entitled "The Ulster Novel (1918)," would have been like if he had finished it, we do know that throughout the latter part of his Lucretian materialist phase, Lewis maintained that *if* he were ever to become interested in politics, he would "probably become a nationalist [i.e. a supporter of Irish Home Rule]."[139]

Yet despite his disinterest in politics, Lewis the Lucretian materialist and Lewis the pseudo-Manichean dualist did comment on the political theory he was reading at the time – namely that which is found in Plato's *Republic*. Bernard Bosanquet once said that "there is no sound political philosophy which is not an embodiment of Plato's conception;"[140] if this is the case, then it is no wonder Lewis hated politics, for not only as a teenager but also as a man did Lewis – with only a few qualifications (to be mentioned throughout) – loathe Plato's political theory. In fact, the first canto of Lewis's epic poem *Dymer* is a passionate attack on Plato's political, and by extension, educational, system.[141] Lewis's problem with Plato's ideal state is not that Plato had a low opinion of the average man's competence (Lewis agreed with

---

137 "When one says 'Home rule' he says in a word a most great parlamentary mater. It has its pros, and cons, and there is much to be said on both sides. It has its proctecters and assilants but I am going to pretect it when I grow up." C. S. Lewis, "Home Rule," in *The Lewis Papers: Memoirs of the Lewis Family, 1850-1930*, vol. 6, ed. Warren Lewis (The Marion E. Wade Center, Wheaton College), 112-3.

138 Lewis, *The Collected Letters of C. S. Lewis: Volume I*, 95 [November 17, 1914].

139 Ibid., 330 [July 24, 1917].

140 Bernard Bosanquet, *The Philosophical Theory of the State* (1899 reprint; London: MacMillian, n.d.), 7.

141 Lewis, preface to the 1950 edition of *Dymer*, 3-4.

that,[142] even in regard to the Irish[143]); rather Lewis's problem with Plato is that the Greek philosopher did not leave enough room for individual freedoms, such as freedom of vocation, freedom of marriage, freedom to own property, freedom to read what one likes, etc. Quite possibly born out of his disgust with colonialism and his support for Irish independence, Lewis the romantic philosopher could not tolerate the kinds of restrictions Plato put on the citizens of his republic; indeed, throughout his first three philosophical phases (and beyond), Lewis's distrust of political totalitarianism is palpable; hence, on the one hand, he denounced monarchy, saying: "I said I didn't care twopence about monarchy – the only real issue was civilisation against barbarism."[144] And on the other hand, (probably to the surprise[145] and chagrin of his leftist philosophy tutor, Carritt) Lewis equally condemned Leninism:

> Must civilized man sit at the feet of savages? It was excusable for the eighteenth century to indulge in dreams about the 'noble savage;' it is not excusable for us who have modern anthropology at our command. We know too well the characteristics of primitive society – the human sacrifices, the obscene and childish superstitions, the untroubled sensuality, the contented wallowing of the human animal in its native sty. Never again can we believe that by looking backward we shall find the forward road. . . . But it leaves untouched my deepest objection to the whole theory. There still remains one point in which

---

142 "What do you think of this latest outrage perpetuated by the slander, ignorance, and prejudice of the British nation on those who alone can support it? I mean of course the shameful way in which Prince Louis of Battenberg has been forced to resign. He is, I hear, the only man in the Admiralty who knows his job: he has lived all his life in England: his patriotism, loyalty, and efficiency are admitted by all who have a right to judge. And yet, because a number of ignorant and illiterate clods (who have no better employment than that of abusing their betters) so choose, he must resign. This is what comes of letting a nation be governed by 'the people.' 'Vox populi, vox Diaboli,' we must say, reversing the old but foolish proverb." Lewis, *The Collected Letters of C. S. Lewis: Volume I*, 88 [November 3, 1914].

143 Lewis spoke plainly of "narrow Ulster bigotry." Ibid., 566 [June 1921]

144 Lewis, *All My Road Before Me*, 191 [February 4, 1923].

145 Concerning his Lucretian materialist days, Lewis wrote: "Looking back on my life now, I am astonished that I . . . did not become a Leftist, Atheist, satiric Intellectual of the type we all know so well. All the conditions seem to be present. I had hated my pubic school. I hated whatever I knew or imagined of the British Empire. And though I took very little notice of Morris' socialism . . . continual reading of Shaw had brought it about that such embryonic political opinions as I had were vaguely socialistic. . . . It is true that I hated the Collective as much as any man can hate anything; but I certainly did not then realize its relations to socialism. I suppose that my Romanticism was destined to divide me from the orthodox Intellectuals as soon as I met them; and also that a mind so little sanguine as mine about the future and about common action could only with great difficulty be made revolutionary." Lewis, *Surprised by Joy*, 1343-4.

the society which Lenin anticipates will bear a fatal resemblance to primitive society. It will be one in which the collective will of the group or herd completely dominates over the individual. . . . I am not suggesting that these herd instincts always work badly: it is indeed a matter of pure chance how they work. They may enjoin what is really good and forbid what is really bad, and they may equally well do the opposite. But whatever they do, they do blindly. . . . The transition from animal to man is the transition from blind collective herd action, to intelligent action by the individual. . . . Here then lies the whole failure, for me, of Lenin's theory. To reach the non-political society in which the herd shall be all in all is, in effect, to dehumanize man: to return him to the condition of the gregarious animals, to elevate the pack above the individual and dethrone reason in favour of instinct. The state, even at its worst, is the preferable alternative of the two: if, at least, it is better to be an unhappy man than a happy sheep. The state always implies the dominance of the conscious reason of the individual over the mere instincts of the collective mass. It may be a dominance of one class over others guided by selfish cunning and cruelly exercised: but so long as the individual, not the collective instinct, is at the helm there will be some freedom and some hope for the future. In the herd-life there is no room for advance and no freedom, for the first signs of individual development will be ruthlessly repressed. . . . Even in absolute monarchy, as Dr. Johnson observed, if the king is too oppressive the people will rise up and cut his head off. When the positions are reversed, when the many are masters, this check is removed. The Proletarian despotism has nothing to fear: it is the only perfect tyranny.[146]

While it may be tempting to see some of these comments as merely the product of a youthful romanticism, this would be a mistake, for even as a Christian, Lewis – while finding some symbolic value in monarchy (more on this later) – passionately argued against political totalitarianism.

Nonetheless, although Lewis's political theory became slightly more sophisticated during his Stoical materialist and idealist phases thanks to his teaching political philosophy at Oxford (which covered such texts as Aristotle's *Politics* and Rousseau's *Social Contract*),[147] Lewis's political theory

---

146 Lewis, "On Bolshevism," 73, 74-5, 76, 78. For more on when this essay was written, see chapter five. Cf. "Cut them all down to a level; all slaves, all ciphers, all nobodies. All equals. Thus Tyrants could practice, in a sense, 'democracy.' But now 'democracy' can do the same work without any other tyranny than her own. No one need now go through the field with a cane. The little stalks will now of themselves bite the tops off the big ones. The big ones are beginning to bite off their own in their desire to Be Like Stalks." Lewis, "Screwtape Proposes a Toast," 760.

147 "While teaching English literature at Magdalen, Lewis helped in the history school by teaching political theory. He took the history students. His lectures covered Rousseau

still did not fit nicely into a box. For instance, while a person might be tempted to see Lewis the Stoical materialist as sympathetic with liberty-loving John Stuart Mill, we know from Lewis's annotations that he thought Mill "Wrong" about nearly everything.[148] Moreover, from the previous chapter, we know that even as an idealist, Lewis rejected the political theories of the British Idealists since he thought these theories were totalitarian (however, he did say he liked Bosanquet's *Theory of the State* "on the whole"[149]). The key, therefore, to understanding Lewis's political theory throughout his Stoical materialist and idealist phases is to keep in mind three things: (1) his romantic, anti-colonial feelings from his youth, (2) his commitment to Kantian, libertarian ethics, and (3) his endorsement of Aristotelian (and to a lesser extent, Platonic) checks and balances against political corruption (thus, for instance, Lewis often quoted Aristotle's phrase "<u>men do not become tyrants in order that they may not suffer cold</u>"[150] and repeatedly paraphrased Plato when he spoke of "necessity, the tyrant's plea"[151]).

---

and Aristotle, et al. He loved doing this." A. J. P. Taylor, "The Fun of the Thing," in *In Search of C. S. Lewis*, ed. Stephen Schofield, 117-22 (South Plainfield, NJ: Bridge, 1983), 118. Cf. "Waterfield . . . read an essay on Mill." Lewis, *All My Road Before Me*, 381 [April 29, 1926].

148 C. S. Lewis, marginalia in his edition of *Principle of Political Economy with Some of Their Applications to Social Philosophy*, Vols. I & II, by John Stuart Mill (London: John L. Parker, 1857; The Marion E. Wade Center, Wheaton College), 78, 79.

149 Lewis, *All My Road Before Me*, 41 [May 25, 1922].

150 Lewis, underlining in his edition of *De Republica*, 1267a14. Cf. "But where Mammon vacates the throne, how if Moloch takes his place? As Aristotle said 'Men do not become tyrants in order to keep warm.' All men, of course, desire pleasure and safety. But all men also desire power and all men desire the mere sense of being 'in the know' or in the 'inner ring,' of not being 'outsiders': a passion insufficiently studied and the chief theme of my story. When the state of society is such that money is the passport to all these prizes, then of course money will be the prime temptation." Lewis, "A Reply to Professor Haldane," 86. Cf. "What an answer, by the by, Wyvern was to those who derive all the ills of society from economics! For money had nothing to do with its class system. . . . Aristotle remarked, men do not become dictators in order to keep warm. If a ruling class has some other source of strength, why need it bother about money? Most of what it wants will be pressed upon it by emulous flatterers; the rest can be taken by force." Lewis, *Surprised by Joy*, 1307.

151 Lewis, marginalia in his edition of *RES PVBLICA*, 565c. Cf. "The rebellion of Satan and the tyranny of a Nimrod or a Charles are wrong for the same reason. Tyranny, the rule over equals as if they were inferiors, is rebellion. And equally, as Shakespeare's Ulysses saw, rebellion is tyranny. All Milton's hatred of tyranny is expressed in the poem: but the tyrant held up to our execrations is not God. It is Satan. He is the *Sultan* – a name hateful in Milton's day to all Europeans both as freemen and as Christians. . . . He is the Machiavellian prince who excuses his 'political realism' by 'necessity, the tyrant's plea.'" Lewis, *A Preface to Paradise Lost*, 78. Cf. "If I am not deceived, we are all at this moment helping to decide whether humanity shall retain all that has hitherto made humanity

When Lewis became a theist and Christian, he – though still unclear about many matters of political policy[152] – continued to endorse the three key convictions of his earlier phases; however, to these, as we know from chapter five, he added two more: (4) man is fallen and hence cannot be trusted with absolute power, and (5) symbolic monarchy is of great value. Since these two points are the spring from which most of Lewis's mature political ideas flowed, they are worth examining in detail.

As for man being fallen and hence unworthy of absolute power, Lewis likely came to accept this idea – nicely captured in Lord Acton's phrase: "all power corrupts, and absolute power corrupts absolutely"[153] – through a combination of agreeing with the Christian teaching about man's fallen will, reading enough history to know that absolute power almost always leads to tyranny, witnessing the abuses of colonialism in Ireland first hand, and living through two world wars and the beginning of the Cold War. All of these factors made Lewis unusually (and perhaps, overly) sensitive to even a hint of totalitarianism. Needless to say, then, Lewis rejected the theocracy of past Christian ages;[154] the communism of Plato, Karl Marx,[155] Vladimir Lenin,

---

worth preserving, or whether we must slide down into the sub-humanity imagined by Mr Aldous Huxley and George Orwell and partially realized in Hitler's Germany. For the extermination of the Jews really would have been 'useful' if the racial theories had been correct; there is no foretelling what may come to seem, or even to be, 'useful,' and 'necessity' was always 'the tyrant's plea.'" C. S. Lewis, "On Punishment: A Reply," in *C. S. Lewis: Essay Collection & Other Short Pieces*, ed. Leslie Walmsley (1954 essay reprint; London: HarperCollins, 2000), 709.

152 "Politics have really become unintelligible to the amateur now. In the old days when it was about votes for women or home rule for Ireland one could have an opinion: now I feel one's opinion, and therefore one's vote, is quite worthless." Lewis, *The Collected Letters of C. S. Lewis: Volume II*, 10 [October 24, 1931]. As we can see, John West Jr. is more or less correct when he says that Lewis's concern "was not policy but principle." West, "Finding the Permanent in the Political," 139.

153 Lord Acton, quoted in "Membership," by C. S. Lewis, 337.

154 "Theocracy has been rightly abolished not because it is bad that learned priest should govern ignorant laymen, but because priests are wicked men like the rest of us." Lewis, "Membership," 337. Tied to Lewis's criticism of theocracy is his distrust of church parades. C. S. Lewis, "Blimpophobia," in *C. S. Lewis: Essay Collection & Other Short Pieces*, ed. Lesley Walmsley (1944 essay reprint; London: HarperCollins, 2000), 602. Cf. Lewis, *Surprised by Joy*, 1305. In addition, it is worth noting that while Lewis usually appreciated Richard Hooker's theological writings, he did not like Hooker's writings about the intimate relation between Church and state.

155 "There are several kinds of [dwarfs], I gather, though I only distinguished two – a black kind with black shirts and a red kind who call themselves Marxomanni. They are all very fierce and apparently quarrel a good deal but they all acknowledge some kind of vassalage to this man Savage." Lewis, *The Pilgrim's Regress*, 116. Lewis once said that the Marxists were his "most hostile critics." Lewis, *The Collected Letters of C. S. Lewis:*

and Joseph Stalin;[156] and the fascism and imperialism of the Romans,[157] colonial Christendom,[158] the Nazis,[159] Benito Mussolini,[160] Francisco Franco,[161] António de Oliveira Salazar,[162] "Charn,"[163] "Calormen,"[164] and

---

Volume II, 707 [April 18, 1946].

156 "When you pray for Hitler & Stalin, how do you actually teach yourself to make the prayer real?" Ibid., 391 [April 16, 1940]. Cf. "I pray every night for the people I am most tempted to hate or despise (the present list is Stalin, Hitler, Mussolini, Mackenzie, Austen & Opie) and in the effort to make this real I have had to do a good deal of thinking." Ibid., 408 [May 4, 1940].

157 "I'm all for the Gauls myself and I hate all conquerors. But I never knew a woman who was not all for Caesar – just as they were in his life-time." Lewis, *The Collected Letters of C. S. Lewis: Volume III*, 1073 [August 11, 1959]. Incidentally, Lewis put Julius Caesar in Hell in *The Great Divorce*. Lewis, *The Great Divorce*, 1034.

158 "If our nation is really so much better than others it may be held to have either the duties or the rights of a superior being towards them. In the nineteenth century the English became very conscious of such duties: the 'white man's burden.' What we called *natives* were our wards and we their self-appointed guardians. This was not all hypocrisy. We did do them some good. But our habit of talking as if England's motive for acquiring an empire . . . had been mainly altruistic, nauseated the world. . . . If ever the book which I am not going to write is written it must be the full confession by Christendom of Christendom's specific contribution to the sum of human cruelty and treachery. Large areas of 'the World' will not hear us till we have publicly disowned much of our past. Why should they? We have shouted the name of Christ and enacted the service of Moloch." Lewis, *The Four Loves*, 21, 23. Given this statement by Lewis, I find it incredible how a supposed "defender" of Lewis like Gregg Easterbrook could claim that "[t]he sociological structure of Narnia is aristocratic and favors British imperialism." Gregg Easterbrook, "In Defense of C. S. Lewis," *The Atlantic Monthly* (October 2001), 3. With defenders like these, who needs enemies!

159 "I might agree that the Allies are partly to blame, but nothing can fully excuse the iniquity of Hitler's persecution of the Jews, or the absurdity of his theoretical position." Lewis, *The Collected Letters of C. S. Lewis: Volume II*, 128 [November 5, 1933].

160 "He spoke of lots of sub-species [of the cruel dwarfs] besides the Marxomanni – Mussolimini, Swastici, Gangomanni. . . . I can't remember them all." Lewis, *The Pilgrim's Regress*, 118.

161 Lewis, *The Collected Letters of C. S. Lewis: Volume II*, 368 [March 21, 1940]. Concerning his acquaintance Roy Campbell, who fought alongside Franco in the Spanish Civil War, Lewis wrote: "I loathed and loath Roy Campbell's particular blend of Catholicism and Fascism, and told him so." Lewis, *The Collected Letters of C. S. Lewis: Volume III*, 1401 [January 1963].

162 "All you tell me about China [concerning the communist takeover] is horrible, and I was shocked to read an article the other day about Portugal. I had got the idea that Salazar was (as if such a thing were possible!) a *good* dictator. But apparently Portugal is just like all the other totalitarian countries, indeed worse in one way, for the atrocities are done in the name of Christianity." Ibid., 1347 [May 31, 1962].

163 "Strong cruel empire[s] like Charn," we are told by Aslan, "[are] not the kindly land I mean [Narnia] to be." Lewis, *The Magician's Nephew*, 163.

164 "'These little barbarian countries that call themselves *free* (which is as much as to say, idle, disordered, and unprofitable),'" says the hateful dictator of Calormen, Tisroc, "'are hateful to the gods and to all persons of discernment.'" Lewis, *The Horse and His Boy*,

even (potentially) the entire human race.[165]

Against "the power philosophies of totalitarian states,"[166] Lewis supported democracy, which he, drawing on Aristotle's distinction between natural health and medicine,[167] believed would minimize – i.e. act as a temporary remedy for – the damage that man can inflict on his fellow man:

> I am a democrat because I believe in the Fall of Man. I think most people are democrats for the opposite reason. A great deal of democratic enthusiasm descends from the ideas of people like Rousseau, who believed in democracy because they thought mankind so wise and good that everyone deserved a share in the government. The danger of defending democracy on those grounds is that they're not true. And whenever their weakness is exposed, the people who prefer tyranny make capital out of the exposure. I find that they're not true without looking further than myself. I don't deserve a share in governing a hen-roost, much less a nation. Nor do most people – all the people who believe advertisements, and think in catchwords and special rumours. The real reason for democracy is just the reverse. Mankind is so fallen that no man can be trusted with unchecked power over his fellows.[168]

In his more optimistic moments, Lewis even cautiously praised more extreme forms of democracy, such as "Christian Socialism"[169] and "Distributivism"[170] (both of which argue for more economic equality without

---

97.

165 "We know what our race does to strangers. Man destroys or enslaves every species he can. Civilised man murders, enslaves, cheats, and corrupts savage man. Even inanimate nature he turns into dust bowls and slagheaps. There are individuals who don't. But they are not the sort that are likely to be our pioneers in space. Our ambassador to new worlds will be the needy and greedy adventurer or the ruthless technical expert. They will do as their kind has always done. What that will be if they meet things weaker than themselves, the black man and the red man can tell." Lewis, "Religion and Rocketry," 234-5.

166 Lewis, "The Poison of Subjectivism," 657.

167 Lewis, "Equality," 667.

168 Ibid., 666. Cf. Lewis, *The Collected Letters of C. S. Lewis: Volume II*, 455 [December 11, 1940].

169 Lewis, "Screwtape Proposes a Toast," 757.

170 G. K. Chesterton, one of Lewis's heroes, was an advocate of Distributivism. Hence, even if Lewis himself was not a distributivist, we can gather from the following statement by Curry in *That Hideous Strength* that Lewis was probably sympathetic with those who were: "'One sees now that Denniston would never have done. Most emphatically not. A brilliant man at that time, of course, but he seems to have gone quite off the rails since then with all his Distributivism and what not. They tell me he's likely to end up in a monastery.'" Lewis, *That Hideous Strength*, 362.

the totalitarian structures), and he even dared to hope that one day empires, and even large countries, would be broken up into smaller, self-governing regions which could thereby maintain their own unique essences[171]:

> I want what we certainly shan't get – a super-national state built out of units far smaller than existing nations: units like Wessex and Picardy, not like 'Britain' (a horrid word) and France. Units so small, and real, would then safely develop the greatest local diversity of language, culture, and custom. England did not achieve unity by a League of Barons. The Barons were (for all practical purposes) eliminated; the towns, the shires, and even parishes, survived. That is our model.[172]

Although Lewis did not think this model at all possible, he did believe that were it so, it would put politics in its proper, limited place, for "[a] sick society," Lewis once said with Stoic-Christian-Marxist[173] undertones, "must think much about politics."[174] Indeed,

> It is easy to think the State has a lot of different objects – military, political, economic, and what not. But in a way things are much simpler than that. The State exists simply to promote and to protect the ordinary happiness of human beings in this life. A husband and his wife chatting over a fire, a couple of friends having a game of darts in a pub, a man reading a book in his own room or digging in his own garden – that is what the state is for. And unless they are helping to increase and prolong and protect such moments, all the laws, parliaments, armies, courts, police, economics, etc., are simply a waste of time.[175]

---

171 As we discussed in chapters five and six, Lewis believed that each nation has its own unique essence, which is constantly, presumably by the deeds of its people, trying to actualize itself; hence, Lewis wrote: "About Logres – I do think there is a 'better England' always getting lost in, but always showing through, the actual one." Lewis, *The Collected Letters of C. S. Lewis: Volume III*, 466 [May 3, 1954].

172 C. S. Lewis, "C. S. Lewis," *Encounter* (December 1962).

173 "[M]edieval thought had inherited from both the Bible and the Stoics a sharp contrast between a lost, prehistoric state of innocence and the world as we actually know it, and that things like slavery and private property were normally attributed to the latter." Lewis, *Poetry and Prose in the Sixteenth Century*, 158. "The fundamental assumption of the Marxist theory is, as we saw, that the State is a disease." Lewis, "On Bolshevism," 72.

174 Lewis, "Membership," 334.

175 Lewis, *Mere Christianity*, 448. "To live his life in his own way, to call his house his castle, to enjoy the fruits of his own labour, to educate his children as his conscience directs, to save for their prosperity after his death – these are wishes deeply ingrained in white and civilised man. Their realization is almost as necessary to our virtues as to our happiness." Lewis, "Willing Slaves of the Welfare State," 750. "For the good life as (I suppose) you and I conceive it – independence, calling one's house one's castle, saying

Now despite reluctantly agreeing with democracy (and possibly more radical forms of it, such as Christian Socialism or Distributivism), Lewis did not support any particular political party (*pace* George Orwell, who was convinced that Lewis was a Tory out to subvert the Left[176]). It is true that Lewis generally said nice things about the Tory Prime Minister Winston Churchill and was grateful when the Prime Minister recommended him for the rank of Commander of the Order of the British Empire (which he turned down because, as usual,[177] he did not want to appear too political[178]); however,

---

'Mind your own business' to impertinent people, resisting bribes and threats *as a matter of course*, culture, honour, courtesy, un-assertiveness, the ease and elbow-room of the mind – all this is no natural endowment of the animal Man, but the fine flower of a privileged class. And because it is so fine a flower it breeds, within the privileged class itself, a desire to equalize, a guilty conscience about their privileges. (At least I don't think the revolt from below has often succeeded, or even got going, without this help from above). . . . But then, the moment you try to spread this good life you find yourself removing the very conditions of it both from the few and from the many, in other words for all. . . . The many, merely by being the many, annihilate the goals as soon as they reach them: as in this case of education that I started with. . . . Don't imagine that I am constructing a concealed argument in favour of a return to the old order. I know *that* is not the solution. But what is? Or are we assuming that there is a solution? Perhaps in a fallen world the social problem can in fact never be solved and we must take more seriously – what all Christians admit in theory – that our home is elsewhere." Lewis, *The Collected Letters of C. S. Lewis: Volume III*, 17-18 [March 12, 1950].

176 Concerning Lewis's *Beyond Personality*, Orwell wrote: "One reason for the extravagant boosting that these people always get in the press is that their political affiliations are invariably reactionary. Some of them were frank admirers of Fascism as along as it was safe to be so. That is why I draw attention to Mr C. S. Lewis and his chummy little wireless talks, of which no doubt there will be more. They are not really so unpolitical as they are meant to look. Indeed they are an out-flanking movement in the big counter-attack against the Left which Lord Elton, A. P. Herbert, G. M. Young, Alfred Noyes and various others have been conducting for two years past." George Orwell, "As I Please," *Tribune*, October 27, 1944. While Ron Dart and Humphrey Carpenter are not the conspiracy theorists that Orwell was, they do think that Lewis was a Tory. Carpenter, *The Inklings*, 206. Dart, "C. S. Lewis and George Grant: A Tale of Two Anglican Tories," 5.

177 John Lawlor, a former student of Lewis's, reports that when he asked Lewis to give money to support the Spanish government in its civil war, Lewis refused since he "could not contribute to anything that had an overtly political implication." John Lawlor, *C. S. Lewis: Memories and Reflections* (Dallas: Spence, 1998), 9.

178 "I feel greatly obligated to the Prime Minister [Winston Churchill], and so far as my personal feelings are concerned this honour would be highly agreeable. There are always however knaves who say, and fools who believe, that my religious writings are all covert anti-Leftist propaganda, and my appearance in the Honours List would of course strengthen their hands. It is better that I should not appear there. I am sure that the Prime Minister will understand my reason, and that my gratitude is and will be none the less cordial." Lewis, *The Collected Letters of C. S. Lewis: Volume III*, 147 [December 4, 1951].

Lewis always insisted that he was best described as a "political sceptic,"[179] and believed that Christians should not form their own party (to avoid distorting the truth of their religion) but rather should band together to offer their collective support to the party willing to represent their basic convictions:

> An interdenominational Christian Voters' Society might draw up a list of assurances about ends and means which every member was expected to exact from any political party as the price of his support. Such a society might claim to represent Christendom far more truly than any 'Christian Front;' and for that reason I should be prepared, in principle, for membership and obedience to be obligatory on Christians. 'So all it comes down to is pestering MPs with letters?' Yes: just that. I think such pestering combines the dove and the serpent. I think it means a world where parties have to take care not to alienate Christians, instead of a world where Christians have to be 'loyal' to infidel parties. Finally, I think a minority can influence politics only by 'pestering' or by becoming a 'party' in the new continental sense (that is, a secret society of murderers and blackmailers) which is impossible to Christians.[180]

Hence, "the practical problem of Christian politics is not that of drawing up schemes for a Christian society,"[181] wrote Lewis, who in another place mentioned what a "fully Christian society" would look like, "but that of living as innocently as we can with unbelieving fellow-subjects under unbelieving rulers who will never be perfectly wise and good and who will sometimes be very wicked and very foolish."[182]

However, in spite of his generally skeptical political convictions, Lewis believed in the improvement of the state.[183] In fact, as we know from chapter

---

179 "I doubt if I am a Tory. I am much more nearly a political sceptic." Ibid., 1371 [September 18, 1962]. American Republicans would do well to read Ron Dart's insightful critique concerning their slightly dishonest appropriation of Lewis to their party's ideology. Ron Dart, "C. S. Lewis: The Culture Wars," *Clarion: Journal of Spirituality and Justice*, http://www.clarion-journal.ca/article.php?story (accessed on December 3, 2004).

180 Lewis, "Meditation on the Third Commandment," 301-2.

181 A "fully Christian society" would shun "passengers or parasites," manufacturing of "silly luxuries and then of sillier advertisements to persuade us to buy them," "putting on airs," disrespect, and usury or the lending money at interest. Lewis, *Mere Christianity*, 374, 375.

182 Lewis, "The Humanitarian Theory of Punishment," 703. At a Socratic Club meeting, Lewis once said that "no nation emphatically *is* or is *not* a Christian nation." C. S. Lewis, quoted in "Oxford's Bonny Fighter," by Walter Hooper, 158.

183 As the devil Screwtape says, "Certainly we do not want to allow their Christianity to flow over into their political life, for the establishment of anything like a really just society would be a major disaster." Lewis, "Screwtape Proposes a Toast," 798.

eight, one of the things that set him apart from the skeptics of his time was precisely his confidence that all men can know the universal moral law, by which they can grow. Thus, while Lewis certainly thought that moral progress is more difficult for those with a lot of power than those with little power, he, being a proponent of "classical political theory [which supports] natural law, the value of the individual, [and] the rights of man,"[184] did think that good positive laws can be established by men constantly looking toward, and learning to apply, the universal moral laws; hence, King Peter and his siblings, we are told, "made good laws and kept the peace."[185] In particular, Lewis felt that good rulers of secular states will demonstrate the four cardinal virtues: prudence, courage, temperance, and justice, all of which are worth briefly addressing in the context of politics.

Prudence, as we recall from the previous chapter, is practical – though not *pragmatic*[186] – reason. This virtue is fundamental to any moral ruler since "government involves questions about the good for man, and justice, and what things are worth having at what price."[187] Following Aristotle, Lewis agreed that "political science is the supreme form of Prudence,"[188] for society is the supreme context in which matters of practical (but not theological or theoretical) ethics take place:

> This raises the question of Theology and Politics. The nearest I can get to a settlement of the frontier problem between them is this: that Theology teaches us what ends are desirable and what means are lawful, while Politics teaches what means are effective. Thus Theology tells us that every man ought to have a decent wage. Politics tells us by what means this is likely to be attained. Theology tells us which of

---

184 Lewis, "Willing Slaves of the Welfare State," 748.

185 Lewis, *The Lion, the Witch and the Wardrobe*, 166.

186 In *That Hideous Strength*, the evil pragmatic planners of N.I.C.E. have the following conversation: "'It's a long time since we had anyone in Politics.' 'Um – yes. There's still a considerable prejudice against Politics as an academic subject. I say, Feverstone, oughtn't we to give this new subject a leg up?' 'What new subject?' 'Pragmatometry.' 'Well now, it's funny you should say that, because the man I was beginning to think of is a politician who has also been going in a good deal for Pragmatometry. One could call it a fellowship in social Pragmatometry, or something like that.'" Lewis, *That Hideous Strength*, 440.

187 Lewis, "Willing Slaves of the Welfare State," 749.

188 Lewis, marginalia in his edition of *Ethica Niocomachea*, 1141a7. This understanding can also be found in a note that Lewis made in his edition of Dante's *De Monarchia*, where he summarized Dante thus: "[The Monarch] is to supply the major premises of the practical syllogism to the subordinate Princes, being to them as Wisdom [theoretical reason] is to Prudence [practical reason]." Lewis, marginalia in his edition of *De Monarchia*, 22.

these means are consistent with justice and charity. On the political question guidance comes not from Revelation but from natural prudence, knowledge of complicated facts and ripe experience.[189]

Unlike theological principles and theoretical reason, both of which have to do with universals, prudence draws on these universals in order to apply them to particular situations. The prudent ruler, therefore, is one who judges well in particular situations:

> The good king in Psalm 72:2 will 'judge' the people rightly; that is, he will 'defend the poor.' When God 'arises to judgement' he will 'help all the meek upon earth' (76:9), all the timid, helpless people whose wrongs have never been righted yet. When God accuses earthly judges of 'wrong judgement,' He follows it up by telling them to see that the poor 'have right' (82:2, 3).[190]

Consequently, the prudent ruler plans what society should be like and has the courage to defend it; however, according to Lewis, such a ruler, realizing that he too is fallible, will not lay down laws that are too restrictive or would lead to – as Lewis thought the laws of the England of his day lead to[191] – a police state:

> If 'planning' is taken in the literal sense of thinking before one acts and acting on what one has thought out to the best of one's ability, then of course planning is simply the traditional virtue of Prudence and not only compatible with, but demanded by, Christian ethics. But if the word is used (as I think you use it) to mean some particular politico-social programme, such as [the Welfare State] of the [Labour Party], then one c[oul]d only say after examining that programme in detail. . . . Where benevolent planning, armed with political or economic power, can become wicked is when it tramples on people's rights for the sake of their good.[192]

---

189 Lewis, "Christian Apologetics," 151.

190 Lewis, *Reflection on the Psalms*, 314-5.

191 On the final page of his edition of Tacitus's *Annals of Imperial Rome*, Lewis wrote the following: "August 16th 1921 . . . Re-read June 1953. It is a much less startling book now than in 1921: we have grown used to the police-state." C. S. Lewis, marginalia in his edition of *Annalivum*, by Cornelii Taciti, ed. C. D. Fisher (Oxonii: E Typographeo Clarendoniano, n.d.; The Rare Book Collection, The University of North Carolina at Chapel Hill), final page. Naturally, Lewis believed that the police state is largely heralded in by the secret police, who are "the common factor in all revolutions." Lewis, "A Reply to Professor Haldane," 89. Cf. Lewis, *The Lion, the Witch and the Wardrobe*, 57. Cf. Lewis, *That Hideous Strength*, 416-7.

192 Lewis, *The Collected Letters of C. S. Lewis: Volume III*, 92 [February 7, 1951].

Thus, the prudent ruler will focus on securing citizens' rights, and not, as so many have done in recent years, play on citizens' fears in order to take away their rights: "'Give up your freedom and I will make you safe' is, age after age, the terrible offer."[193]

Courage is the virtue that controls the passionate part of the soul. As we just touched on, this virtue is vital for rulers since a good, but cowardly, politician will never be able to act upon his convictions. Consequently, a courageous ruler will be like Socrates, who was not afraid to tell the truth even when it cost him his life, like Augustine's Christian emperor, who boldly confesses his mistakes,[194] and like King Frank (or Lancelot[195]), who maintains the proper balance of fierceness and gentleness:

> All the sharpness and cunning and quarrelsomeness which [King Frank] had picked up as a London cabby seemed to have been washed away, and the courage and kindness which he had always were easier to see. Perhaps it was the air of the young world that had done it, or talking with Aslan, or both. . . . 'Upon my word,' whispered Fledge to Polly. 'My old master's been changed nearly as much as I have! Why, he's a real master now.'[196]

Temperance is the excellence that unifies the passionate and appetitive parts of man under his reason. Lewis felt that this virtue was extremely important for rulers, who are constantly faced with the temptation of, among other things, greed – greed for money and greed for power. In particular, Lewis believed that because the link between science, technology, economics and politics is so strong in modern times, the state is increasingly becoming dependent on scientists and economists, neither of whom are experts in moral philosophy and the art of wise statecraft. Thus, Lewis the Christian Aristotelian[197] was uncomfortable that the government abolished its Usury

---

193 Ibid., 1104 [December 8, 1959].
194 Augustine *The City of God* 5.24.
195 Lewis, "The Necessity of Chivalry," 717.
196 Lewis, *The Magician's Nephew*, 154-5. Cf. "'Shasta – I mean Cor,' said Aravis. 'No, shut up. There's something I've got to say at once. I'm sorry I've been such a pig. But I did change before I knew you were a Prince, honestly I did: when you went back, and faced the Lion.'" Lewis, *The Horse and His Boy*, 172. Cf. "'Let *me* be killed,' cried the King. 'I ask nothing for myself. But come and save all Narnia.'" Lewis, *The Last Battle*, 45.
197 "There is one bit of advice given to us by the ancient heathen Greeks, and by the Jews of the Old Testament, and by the great Christian teachers of the Middle Ages, which the modern economic system has completely disobeyed. All these people told us not to lend money at interest; and lending money at interest – what we call investment – is the basis of our whole system. Now it may not absolutely follow that we are wrong. Some people say that when Moses and Aristotle and the Christians agreed in forbidding interest (or

Laws (which subsequently made the lending of money at interest legal), he thought modern business and economics favoured shoddy products over quality ones (since they keep the industry going),[198] and he feared both technocracies, which would put scientists in charge of state-planning,[199] and

'usury' as they called it), they could not foresee the joint stock company, and were only thinking of the private money-lender, and that, therefore, we need not bother about what they said. This is a question I cannot decide on. I am not an economist. But I should not have been honest if I had not told you that three great civilizations had agreed (or so it seems at first sight) in condemning the very thing on which we have based our whole life." Lewis, *Mere Christianity*, 375. Commenting on Thomas Wilson's *Discourse on Usury*, Lewis wrote: "Wilson's own views are expressed, often with great lucidity and energy, through the mouths of the Preacher and the Civilian. Some understanding of these views is the best preparation for seeing the *Merchant of Venice*. 'What is more against nature than that money should beget or bring forth money, which was ordained to be a pledge betwixt man and man . . . and not to increase itselfe as a woman doth that bringeth foorthe a childe, cleane contrarye to the firste institution of money': and again 'Nature cannot afoord yt that *once one of dead things* should become twice one.' I have ventured to italicize five words here because they reveal the whole point of the scene where Shylock attempts to justify his trade by Jacob's genetic stratagem with the flocks. The difference between cattle, which breed by nature, and *dead things* is the crux of the whole matter and Shylock blandly displays his incurable blindness. Throughout the *Discourse* there is real learning, real thought, and some passion." Lewis, *Poetry and Prose in the Sixteenth Century*, 291-2. Cf. [*The Merchant of Venice*] is not so much about men as about metals. The horror of usury lay in the fact that it treated metal in a way contrary to nature. If you have cattle they will breed. To make money – the mere medium of exchange – breed as if it were alive is a sort of black magic. The speech about Laban and Jacob is put into Shylock's mouth to show that he cannot grasp this distinction; and the Christians point out that friendship does not take 'A breed for barren metal.' C. S. Lewis, "Hamlet: The Prince or the Poem?" in *Selected Literary Essays*, by C. S. Lewis, ed. Walter Hooper (1942 essay reprint; Cambridge: Cambridge University Press, 1969), 96.

198 "Unless an article is so made that it will go to pieces in a year or two and thus have to be replaced, you will not get a sufficient turnover. A hundred years ago, when a man got married, he had built for him (if he were rich enough) a carriage in which he expected to drive for the rest of his life. He now buys a car which he expects to sell again in two years. Work nowadays must *not* be good." C. S. Lewis, "Good Work and Good Works," in *C. S. Lewis: Essay Collection & Other Short Pieces* (1959 essay reprint; London: HarperCollins, 2000), 378-9.

199 Lewis, "The Willing Slaves of the Welfare State," 749. Cf. "If you must reduce the romance to a proposition, the proposition would be almost the converse of that which the Professor supposes: not 'scientific planning will certainly lead to Hell,' but 'Under modern conditions any effective invitation to Hell will certainly appear in the guise of scientific planning' – as Hitler's regime in fact did. Every tyrant must begin by claiming to have what his victims respect and to give what they want. The majority in most modern countries respect science and want to be planned. And, therefore, almost by definition, if any man or group wishes to enslave us it will of course describe itself as 'scientific planned democracy.' It may be true that any real salvation must equally, though by hypothesis truthfully, describe itself as 'scientific planned democracy.' All the more reason to look very carefully at anything which bears that label." Lewis, "A

the Welfare State, introduced by the Labour party of Lewis's day, which, while admittedly helping some in need,[200] raised taxes, resulting in people becoming more and more dependent on state-run programs, such as public schools, instead of on programs that the individual selects for himself.[201] Furthermore, as we discussed in chapter five, Lewis feared that most politicians neglect their responsibility as guardians of Nature, and instead see the planet merely as a source of revenue and power. Thus, when Uncle Andrew (who admittedly is not a politician) arrived in Narnia, all he can think of is "the commercial possibilities" of the place, and not the wonder of a newly-formed world.[202] Of course, since statecraft must take into account *all* virtues, it would be an exaggeration to say that Lewis would have been a supporter of Al Gore had the former Vice President been around in Lewis's time; however, in my experience, people are often amazed how "green" Lewis, who was merely following God's commandments in Genesis, actually was.

Justice has to do with fairness, honesty and proper harmony. As we know, Lewis agreed with Aristotle that justice in a secular democracy ought to be of numerical, not proportionate, equality; consequently, while ontologically-speaking two people may be proportionally unequal – for instance husbands and wives in a Christian marriage – politically-speaking, all people are, in virtue of being human, numerically equal. In either case, however, justice still means giving to each his or her due.

In regard to particular aspects of political (numerical) justice, Lewis had quite a bit to say. For instance, concerning marriage, divorce and women's rights, Lewis, as we already know, separated secular and Christian marriages and believed that women should have the same rights as men, including the freedom to seek divorce; concerning gay rights, we know that he supported them politically,[203] though he did not morally approve of homosexual

---

Reply to Professor Haldane," 87.

200 Lewis, *The Collected Letters of C. S. Lewis: Volume III*, 1429 [June 10, 1963].

201 Lewis, "The Willing Slaves of the Welfare State," 750. Cf. "What *was* exceptional about Britain's welfare system was its centralization." Lowe, "Riches, Poverty, and Progress," 223.

202 Lewis, *The Magician's Nephew*, 103.

203 "I quite agree with you about Homosexuals: to make the thing criminal cures nothing and only creates a blackmailers' paradise. Anyway, what business is it of the State?" Lewis, *The Collected Letters of C. S. Lewis: Volume III*, 1154 [May 27, 1960]. For some reason, the following letter was left out of *The Collected Letters of C. S. Lewis: Volume III* and so I have included it here as it is found in *Letters of C. S. Lewis*: "I quite agree with the Archbishop that no *sin*, simply as such, should be made a *crime*. Who the deuce are our rulers to enforce their opinions about sin on us? – a lot of professional politicians, often venal time-servers, whose opinion on a moral problem in one's life we sh[oul]d attach very little value to. Of course many acts which are sins against God are

activity[204] nor gay marriage of any sort; in regard to state-censorship, Lewis was opposed to any unnecessary meddling by the government, and so while mourning the corruptness of the modern world, he said that "the lesser of two evils . . . is to abandon all moral censorship;"[205] as for abortion, Lewis only mentioned it once and, though he thought it immoral, said nothing about its legality; and concerning euthanasia, he opposed suicide purely based on authority,[206] and, though he appears to have thought that even a brain-dead

---

also injuries to our fellow-citizens, and must on that account, but only on that account, be made crimes. But of all the sins in the world I sh[oul]d have thought homosexuality was the one that least concerns the State. We hear too much of the State. Government is at its best a necessary evil. Let's keep it in its place." C. S. Lewis, *Letters of C. S. Lewis*, ed. Warren Lewis and Walter Hooper, revised ed. (San Diego: Harcourt Brace & Company, 1993), 473 [February 1, 1958].

204 "First . . . I take it for certain that the *physical* satisfaction of homosexual desires is sin. This leaves the homo[sexual] no worse off than any normal person who is, for whatever reason, prevented from marrying. Second, our speculations on the cause of the abnormality are not what matters and we must be content with ignorance. The disciples were not told *why* (in terms of efficient cause) the man was born blind (Jn. IX 1-3): only the final cause, that the works of God sh[oul]d be made manifest in him. . . . This suggests that in homosexuality, as in every other tribulation, those works can be made manifest: i.e. that every disability conceals a vocation, if only we can find it, wh[ich] will 'turn the necessity to glorious gain.' Of course, the first step must be to accept any privations wh[ich], if so disabled, we can't lawfully get. The homo[sexual] has to accept sexual abstinence just as the poor man has to forego otherwise lawful pleasures because he w[oul]d be unjust to his wife and children if he took them." Lewis, *The Collected Letters of C. S. Lewis: Volume III*, 471 [May 14, 1954]. Cf. Lewis, *Mere Christianity*, 378.

205 C. S. Lewis, "Sex in Literature," in *C. S. Lewis: Essay Collection & Other Short Pieces*, ed. Lesley Walmsley (1962 essay reprint; London: HarperCollins, 2000), 481.

206 "You must go on [to accomplish what God wants you to do in this life]. That is one of the many reasons why suicide is out of the question. (Another is the absence of any ground for believing that death *by that route* w[oul]d reunite you with her. Why should it? You might be digging an eternally unbridgeable chasm. Disobedience is not the way to get nearer to the obedient)." Lewis, *The Collected Letters of C. S. Lewis: Volume III*, 606 [May 8, 1955]. Cf. "You have made it sound at one point as if Episcopalians didn't think suicide a sin! but no doubt that is unintentional." Ibid., 688 [December 19, 1955].

person must live out his life,[207] he was not strongly committed to this.[208] As for other political issues related to justice, Lewis went into considerable detail pertaining to honesty in politics, war, retributive punishment and slavery, all of which I now want to examine.

Since justice implies honesty, Lewis, following Aristotle,[209] Hobbes and others, thought that adultery is a matter concerning the state since it has to do with breaking one's legal oath to another: "My own view – just to get it out of the way – is that [masturbation, perversion, fornication and adultery] are evils, but that the law should be concerned with none of them except adultery. Adultery is an affair for law because it offends the Hobbesian principle 'that men perform their covenants.'"[210] While this view may be surprising to some, especially given Lewis's liberality in politics, it makes perfect sense when one sees adultery as lying under oath.

Moreover, since Lewis believed honesty to be an essential part of justice, it is no wonder that he had little use for the election process, which he thought

207 "We know nothing about the life of imbeciles, less than we do about animals. I take it that where the brain does not function the spirit is hardly in this world at all. 'Not at Home' is the real message written across the imbecile's face. It is I think most unlikely that there is anything we c[oul]d recognize as suffering. The *real* child, the soul, is 'miles away.' It is connected with this invalid body and decaying brain only in order that it may go through the process of death which is the turnstile to the resurrection life. What the state of this almost absentee soul is at present no one can know. But you may find out one day that it was particularly blessed. It doesn't look like that of course. But think what wrong conclusions you w[oul]d draw from seeing an anaesthetized person, a drunk person, or even a sleeping person, if we knew nothing about chloroform, alcohol, or sleep." Lewis, *The Collected Letters of C. S. Lewis: Volume II*, 660 [June 7, 1945].

208 "I remember once I said to a doctor that I didn't see why the incurably sick shouldn't be given release from pain; and I remember what he said: 'You've had no clinical experience, Lewis. Like most of the people who talk like that, you're in robust health. You'll find that it's hardly ever the incurably sick who want to be released, whatever the pain is like. It's their families, who hate to see them suffer, and can't stand the emotional strain (or, of course, the worry and expense), that start saying, 'Doctor, he mustn't be allowed to suffer – far better to put him out of his misery.'" C. S. Lewis, quoted in "A Chance Meeting," by Charles Wrong, in *C. S. Lewis at the Breakfast Table and Other Reminiscences*, ed. James Como, 107-14 (San Diego: Harcourt Brace & Company, 1992), 111.

209 Although Lewis appears to have accepted the illegality of adultery from Hobbes, he also read about it in Aristotle, who said, "As to adultery, let it be disgraceful, in general, for any man or woman to be found in any way unfaithful when they are married, and called husband and wife. If during the time of bearing children anything of the sort occur, let the guilty person be punished with a loss of privileges in proportion to the offence." Aristotle *Politics* 1335b38-9, a1-2. In his edition of *Politics*, Lewis summarized Aristotle thus: "Punishment of adultery on either side." Lewis, marginalia in his edition of *De Re Publica*, 1335b38-9, a1-2.

210 Lewis, "Sex in Literature," 480.

to be largely an affair of "govertisement" or "government by advertisement"
– that is, charming politicians selling the people lies in order to get elected;[211]
as Lewis wrote in his poem "Lines During a General Election": "Their threats
are terrible enough, but we could bear / All that; it is their promises that bring
despair."[212] Consequently, Lewis was drawn to the minority of politicians,
such as Churchill, who dared to call a spade a spade,[213] and in *Prince Caspian*,
Caspian, like Plato's guardians and King Solomon, is shown to be a man
of true justice and honesty when he declares his own limitations to rule:
"'Welcome, Prince,' said Aslan. 'Do you feel yourself sufficient to take up
the Kingship of Narnia?' 'I – I don't think I do, Sir,' said Caspian. 'I'm only
a kid.' 'Good,' said Aslan. 'If you had felt yourself sufficient, it would have
been a proof that you were not.'"[214] However, while straight-talk can be a
sign of justice, Lewis was perceptive enough to know that such talk does not
always entail true content; hence, he said of Adolf Hitler: "We listened to
Hitler's speech together. I don't know if I'm weaker than other people: but it
is a positive revelation to me how *while the speech lasts* it is impossible not to
waver just a little. . . . Statements which I *know* to be untrue all but convince
me, at any rate for the moment, if only the man says them unflinchingly."[215]
Indeed, because Lewis took such subtle propaganda "to be the most wicked of
all actions – sowing the seeds of future cruelties by telling lies about cruelties
that were never committed,"[216] he largely rejected the media, recommending,
like a Noam Chomsky before his time, that people "abstain from reading
– and *a fortiori* from buying – a paper which you have once caught telling
lies."[217]

---

211 Lewis, *"De Descriptione Temporum,"* 8.
212 C. S. Lewis, "Lines During a General Election," in *Poems*, by C. S. Lewis, ed. Walter
     Hooper (San Diego: Harcourt Brace Jovanovich, 1964), 62 [1-2].
213 "There seem to be good prospects of putting Labour out, in spite of the fact that they
     are promising the earth, whereas Churchill, with his usual good sense, is promising
     nothing but hard times." Lewis, *The Collected Letters of C. S. Lewis: Volume III*, 142-3
     [October 18, 1951].
214 Lewis, *Prince Caspian*, 175.
215 Lewis, *The Collected Letters of C. S. Lewis: Volume II*, 425 [July 20, 1940]. Cf. "What a
     wonderful power there is in the direct appeal which disregards the temporary climate
     of opinion – I wonder is it the case that the man who has the audacity to get up in any
     corrupt society and squarely preach justice or valour or the like *always* wins? After all,
     the Nazis largely got into power by simply talking the old straight stuff about heroism
     in a country full of cynics and buggers." Ibid., 346 [February 11, 1940].
216 C. S. Lewis, "Private Bates," in *C. S. Lewis: Essay Collection & Other Short Pieces*, ed.
     Lesley Walmsley (1944 essay reprint; London: HarperCollins, 2000), 606.
217 C. S. Lewis, "After Priggery – What?" in *C. S. Lewis: Essay Collection & Other Short
     Pieces*, ed. Lesley Walmsley (1945 essay reprint; London: HarperCollins, 2000), 350.
     "[Lewis] thought the radio posed great danger as a tool of propaganda; we can only

Another issue related to justice is war. As one could probably gather from comments made throughout this book, Lewis was a lifelong advocate of chivalry and Augustine's just war theory. Thus, although he was not particularly excited about fighting in WWI, he did so, and, if we take him at his word and not overanalyze him as K. J. Gilchrist has done,[218] it appears as though he found the war uninteresting yet worth fighting;[219] for these reasons, Lewis (along with his future friend Tolkien[220]) did not leave the war jaded like so many of "the Lost Generation," but rather had a renewed conviction that just wars must be fought:

> The future of civilisation depends on the answer to the question, 'Can a democracy be persuaded to remain armed in peacetime?' If the answer to that question is No, then democracy will be destroyed in the end. But 'to remain armed' here means 'to remain effectively armed,' a strong navy, a strong air force, and a reasonable army are essentials. If they cannot be had without conscription, then conscription must be endured. For the sake of our national existence we are ready to endure the loss of liberty. But we are not ready to endure it for anything less.[221]

Indeed, in 1938, when Lewis actually articulated his theory of just war, he, though a patriot,[222] set patriotism aside as a minor point and argued thus:

guess at his response to present-day reports that most people receive most of their news from television." "'The Politics of C. S. Lewis': Report of the 140th Meeting," *CSL: The Bulletin of the New York C. S. Lewis Society* 12, no. 8 (June 1981): 3-5.

218 "The letters, diary, and poetry Lewis wrote through the years after he was wounded all show distinct signs of a continuing trauma." Gilchrist, *A Morning After War*, 153.

219 Lewis, *Surprised by Joy*, 1356-7. Although Lewis was no coward, Katrelya Angus slightly exaggerates when she says, "[Lewis] did far more than teach chivalry to his students within the cloistered walls; he brought chivalry out into the world through his books and radio broadcasts, thus setting an example for anyone who seeks to apply the knightly virtues to modern life. Hence, we can consider Lewis a pioneer of the concept of Chivalry Today. . . . Lewis himself was a *fierce fighter on the battlefield*, both as a soldier in France and as a philosopher in England, yet he was a kind gentleman and an inspiration to all. C. S. Lewis is one of the greatest historical figures to ever set foot on the stage of chivalry, and his work should be admired by all of today's knights in shining armor." Katrelya Angus, "C. S. Lewis: A Pioneer of Chivalry Today," *Chivalry Today*, http://www.chivalrytoday.com/Essays/Angus/Lewis-Chivalry.html (accessed on April 23, 2004): 1 (emphasis mine).

220 For more on Tokien and WWI, see John Garth, *Tolkien and the Great War: The Threshold of Middle-Earth* (London: HarperCollins, 2003).

221 Lewis, "Blimpophobia," 603.

222 As we know from chapter five, Lewis was a patriot; however, as we also know, he valued the higher claims of morality, such as loving one's neighbour, over and against the lower claims of morality, such as loving one's country. Thus, concerning extreme or inordinate patriotism, the devil Screwtape wrote: "I had not forgotten my promise to

About war – I have always believed that it is lawful for a Christian to bear arms in war when commanded by constituted authority unless he has very good reason (which a private person rarely has) for believing the war to be unjust. I base this 1. On the fact that Our Lord does not appear to have regarded the Roman soldiers as *ex officio* sinners. 2. On the fact that the Baptist told soldiers not to leave the army, but to be *good* soldiers. 3. On the opinion of St Augustine (somewhere in *De Civitate*). 4. On the general agreement of all Christian communities except a few sects – who generally combine pacifism with other odd opinions. I take the dicta in the Sermon on the Mount to be prohibitions of revenge, not as a counsel of perfection but as absolutely binding on all Christians. I do not think punishment inflicted by lawful authorities for the right motives is revenge: still less, violent action in the defence of innocent people. I cannot believe the knight errant idea to be sinful. Even in the very act of fighting I think charity (to the enemy) is not *more* endangered than in many necessary acts wh[ich] we all admit to be lawful.[223]

One year after writing this (at the outbreak of WWII, during which Lewis signed up as a Local Defence Volunteer[224]), he wrote a letter entitled "The Conditions for a Just War," in which he largely reiterated these same points ("if war is ever lawful, then peace is sometimes sinful"),[225] and one year after this, probably still remembering the scandal of the Oxford Union's 1933 resolve not to "fight for King and Country,"[226] he wrote an essay about the value of chivalry[227] and read a paper to a pacifist society at Oxford entitled "Why I Am Not a Pacifist," in which he forcefully, but courteously, argued against the pacifist position, saying: "[O]f course war is a very great evil. But that is not the question. The question is whether war is the greatest evil in

consider whether we should make the patient an extreme patriot or an extreme pacifist. All extremes, except extreme devotion to the Enemy, are to be encouraged." Lewis, *The Screwtape Letters*, 754. It is interesting to note that in his edition of *The City of God*, Lewis was intrigued that Augustine had so little patriotism: "This passage [4.5] is interesting historically for A[ugustine]'s completely individual outlook and inability to understand the racial or national feeling." Lewis, marginalia in his edition of *De Civitate Dei*, 4.5.

223 Lewis, *The Collected Letters of C. S. Lewis: Volume II*, 233-4 [October 5, 1938].
224 Ibid., 425 [July 20, 1940].
225 C. S. Lewis, "The Conditions for a Just War," in *C. S. Lewis: Essay Collection & Other Short Pieces*, ed. Lesley Walmsley (1939 essay reprint; London: HarperCollins, 2000), 768.
226 Paul Addison, "Oxford and the Second World," in *The History of the University of Oxford: Volume VIII; The Twentieth Century*, ed. Brian Harrison, 167-88 (Oxford: Oxford University Press, 1994), 167.
227 This essay, originally called "Notes on the Way," was later renamed "The Necessity of Chivalry."

the world, so that any state of affairs which might result from submission is certainly preferable. And I do not see any really cogent arguments for that view."[228]

Naturally, Lewis has had his share of critics; for instance, William White believes that "Lewis' reflections upon warfare are certain to strike many readers as inadequate, if not callous and uncompassionate,"[229] and Tony Campolo thinks that Lewis's arguments against pacifism are weak since he "didn't read anything prior to 300 AD;" indeed, Campolo insists, "If [Lewis] had [read any Christian material prior to 300 AD], he would have discovered that Tertullian and Origen were pacifists and the early church was pacifist."[230] While William White probably neglected to read *The Chronicles of Narnia*, in which Aslan tells King Frank to "be just and *merciful* and brave,"[231] Tony Campolo is certainly wrong when he thinks Lewis's argument against pacifism weak, for not only was Lewis familiar with both Tertullian, whom he quoted approvingly,[232] and Origen, whom he called a "heretical father,"[233] but he also dealt very well with both the philosophical problems of pacifism (e.g. justice needs strength[234]) and the biblical problems of pacifism (e.g. "Does anyone suppose that Our Lord's hearer understood Him to mean that if a homicidal maniac, attempting to murder a third party, tried to knock me out of the way, I must stand aside and let him get his victim?"[235]). Thus, Lewis disapproved of any unjust act in war, such as, *perhaps*, the use of atomic bombs ("A really modern weapon, a machine which a skill-less man can work by pressing a button, to the destruction of thousands, himself in safety, is disgusting"[236]); however, Lewis still thought that the just ruler and

228 Lewis, "Why I Am Not a Pacifist," 287. Cf. In his edition of Augustine's *City of God*, Lewis summarized the Saint thus: "Of course many died: but the mode and time of death is not what makes it an evil." Lewis, marginalia in his edition of *De Civitate Dei*, 1.12.

229 William Luther White, *The Image of Man in C. S. Lewis* (Nashville: Abingdon, 1969), 176.

230 Tony Campolo, quoted in "C. S. Lewis at 100," by Walter Unger, *M. B. Herald* 37, no. 20.

231 Lewis, *The Magician's Nephew*, 159 (emphasis mine).

232 "*Animus*," wrote Lewis, quoting from Tertullian's *De Anima*, "*est vir animae.*" Lewis, *The Collected Letters of C. S. Lewis: Volume II*, 716 [June 17, 1946]. Cf. "When Tertullian speaks of convictions lodged in our 'innate *conscientia*' or Lactantius of what is 'clear to our *conscientia*' some sense like 'mind' or 'understanding' is required." Lewis, *Studies in Words*, 182.

233 Lewis, *The Collected Letters of C. S. Lewis: Volume II*, 381 [April 11, 1940].

234 Lewis, "Why I Am Not a Pacifist," 287-8.

235 Ibid., 291.

236 Lewis, *The Collected Letters of C. S. Lewis: Volume III*, 803 [October 31, 1956]. While this letter seems to indicate that Lewis was opposed to the atomic bomb, he said in another, earlier letter: "The whole question of the atomic bomb is a very difficult one;

nation must be willing to go to war when the cause is just, such as Muslim aggression prior to the First Crusade[237] or Soviet hostility in the East.[238]

In addition to being a proponent of just wars, Lewis was also a supporter of retributive punishment. It is true, of course, that as a boy, Lewis hated the corporal punishment he received at school; however, this was largely because the punishment he received at school, especially at Wynard School under the authority of "the ogre hearted" Robert Capron,[239] was unjust; as Walter Hooper has pointed out:

> Corporal punishment was the method most favoured for the inculcation of learning in small boys up until recent times and some may still defend its effectiveness – as long as learning is the result. . . . While the pace of Victorian and Edwardian life was gentle, punishments could be very severe. Caning and floggings were considered as quite normal and even essential in school life. . . . [However, when a boy named Hickmotts was so badly beaten at Wynard] the elder Hickmotts . . . took legal proceedings against Capron in the High Court [and the school was eventually shut down].[240]

Thus, despite Lewis's unpleasant experience with corporal punishment growing up, he was soon convinced – especially during his Stoical materialist phase – that just, retributive punishment is necessary in order for society to run efficiently. As one can probably gather, Lewis grounded this conviction in the universal moral law, by which all people can understand what justice is – even if they disagree about particular cases or facts.

Consequently, Lewis opposed both exemplary punishment, which would make the punishment of a man *purely* exemplary, and the "humanitarian theory of punishment," which, using radical behaviorist methods, would try

---

the Sunday after the news of the dropping of the first one came through, our minister asked us all to join in prayer for forgiveness for the great crime of using it. But, *if* what we have since heard is true, i.e. that the first item on the Japanese anti-invasion programme was the killing of every European in Japan, the answer did not, to me, seem so simple as all that." Lewis, *The Collected Letters of C. S. Lewis: Volume III*, 77-8 [December 28, 1950].

237 Lewis, "What France Means to You," 1-2.

238 "At any rate both your country [the U. S. A.] and mine [Britain] have twice in our lifetimes tried the recipe of appeasing an aggressor and it didn't work on either occasion: so that it seems [sensible] to try the other way this time [with the Russians]." Lewis, *The Collected Letters of C. S. Lewis: Volume III*, 178-9 [April 3, 1952].

239 C. S. Lewis, "Heart-Breaking School," in "The Unpublished Short Poetry of C. S. Lewis," by Don King, *VII: An Anglo-American Literary Review* 15 (1998): 79-80.

240 Walter Hooper, "C. S. Lewis in Hertforshire's 'Belsen,'" *Hertfordshire Countryside* 37 (September 1982): 10, 18.

to "cure" the criminal instead of punishing him. Lewis's problem with both of these alternatives is that they deny the criminal,[241] the victim,[242] and the state, justice.

In the case of *purely* exemplary punishment, the state is only concerned with society's *perception* of the guilt of the criminal, and not with whether or not the punishment is just; that is, the state is not be concerned with the guilt or innocence of the criminal, but only with whether the punishment of the criminal will lead to the kind of behavior it wants its citizens to exhibit – a theory which Lewis thought "shockingly immoral."[243] Naturally, Lewis was not opposed to a just punishment which also, accidentally, acted as an example of what happens to criminals: he was only worried about a state that abandons justice and punishes people for its own end.

In the case of "humanitarian punishment," Lewis (with strong support from contemporary judicial theorists[244]) believed that without grounding in

---

241 "I urge a return to the traditional or Retributive theory [of punishment] not solely, not even primarily, in the interests of society, but in the interests of the criminal." Lewis, "The Humanitarian Theory of Punishment," 698.

242 In 1957, some young people broke into Lewis's house and stole some of his belongings. These young people were later arrested and Lewis was called in as a witness. What shocked Lewis was that the judge did not administer justice, but rather brushed off the actions of the young people as "stupid pranks" and made the young people, that is, their parents, pay a small fine. As a result of this, Lewis wrote an essay entitled "Delinquents in the Snow," in which he expressed his frustration that "criminal law increasingly protects the criminal and ceases to protect the victim." He went on to say that when the state fails to administer justice, especially to victims, anarchy and rebellion ensue. While it seems likely that Lewis wrote this essay more out of frustration than anything else, he did – in my opinion, wisely – suggest that minor protests and revolts help keep the state in line and the government just. C. S. Lewis, "Delinquents in the Snow," in *C. S. Lewis: Essay Collection & Other Short Pieces*, ed. Lesley Walmsley (1957 essay reprint; London: HarperCollins, 2000), 742-5. Lewis, *Reflections on the Psalms*, 325.

243 Lewis, *The Collected Letters of C. S. Lewis: Volume III*, 1299 [December 1, 1961].

244 "In 1949 Lewis declared: 'I think it essential to oppose the humanitarian theory of punishment, root and branch, wherever we encounter it.' Now, a quarter of a century later, Lewis has received weighty support from an unexpected quarter. A Working Party of the American Friends Service Committee has published two volumes: one, written by inmates undergoing the ultimate 'correction' in what are ominously designated Adjustments Centers, is entitled, *Maximum Security: Letters from California's Prisons*; the other, *Struggle for Justice: A Report on Crime and Punishment in America.* . . . The authors of the *Report* dissect the theory and practice of prison reform. Their blunt conclusion is that 'the reformist prescription is bankrupt.' . . . What remedy do the authors of this *Report* suggest as an alternative? They suggest that we should revert to the traditional practice of letting the punishment fit the crime." Stuart Barton Babbage, "C. S. Lewis and the Humanitarian Theory of Punishment," *Christian Scholar's Review* 2, no. 3 (1972): 233-4, 235.

the universal moral law, any attempt to mercifully cure a criminal would be based on the arbitrary remedy of the "straighteners," and would thus be "hideously immoral."[245] That is, if the penal system denies the universal moral law, then how, except by subjective opinion and convention, can it determine what is "good" and "merciful" for the criminal?

> I am ready to make both the protection of society and the 'cure' of the criminal as important as you please in punishment, but only on a certain condition; namely, that the initial act of thus interfering with a man's liberty be justified on grounds of desert. Like payment in purchase, or marriage as regards the sexual act, it is this, and (I believe) this alone, which legitimizes our proceeding and makes it an instance of punishment at all, instead of an instance of tyranny.[246]

Thus, on the one hand, Lewis certainly believed that rulers should be merciful: hence, Aslan the Judge declared, "Justice shall be mixed with mercy;"[247] however, on the other hand, Lewis was convinced that the word "mercy" was meaningless when it was separated from justice and the universal moral law, for "mercy, detached from justice, grows unmerciful;"[248] this is to say that mercy is not the disregarding of justice, but rather is the acknowledgement of, and then the release from the *guilt* of, the trespass once it has been asked for; obviously, however, this does not necessarily mean that the trespass goes *unpunished*.

Given all this, it is little surprise that for the first sixty years of his life – and probably for his entire life – Lewis was a supporter of capital punishment. If we follow Lewis's discussion of capital punishment chronologically, we know that from the 1930s through to the 1950s, he believed that even though "good men may legitimately differ,"[249] "capital punishment is compatible with Christianity,"[250] for, among other things, "[i]t is quite clear that St. Paul . . . approved of capital punishment."[251] However, in the 1960s, when capital punishment was abolished in England, Lewis revisited the debate, and, if he did not change his mind, he at least softened his views and demonstrated, as he had not done earlier, that he understood what the real issue was:

245 Lewis borrowed the word "straighteners" from Samuel Butler's book *Erewhon*, in which criminals are cured by "straighteners." Lewis, *The Collected Letters of C. S. Lewis: Volume III*, 1346 [May 25, 1962].
246 Lewis, "The Humanitarian Theory of Punishment," 707.
247 Lewis, *The Horse and His Boy*, 184.
248 Lewis, "The Humanitarian Theory of Punishment," 704.
249 Lewis, "Why I Am Not a Pacifist," 287.
250 Lewis, "The Conditions for a Just War," 767.
251 Lewis, *The Collected Letters of C. S. Lewis: Volume III*, 247 [November 8, 1952].

I do not know whether capital punishment should or should not be abolished, for neither the natural light, nor scripture, nor ecclesiastical authority seems to tell me. . . . The real question is whether a murderer is more likely to repent and make a good end three weeks hence in the execution shed or, say, thirty years later in the prison infirmary. No mortal can know. But those who have most right to an opinion are those who know most by experience about the effect of prolonged prison life. I wish some prison chaplains, governors and wardens would contribute to the discussion.[252]

The final issue in regard to justice is slavery. Given Lewis's youthful disgust with colonialism and totalitarian systems, it goes without saying that from his earliest days onward, Lewis thought that political slavery unjust. It is true, of course, that he sometimes sounded as if he were sympathetic with slavery; thus, he once wrote: "Aristotle said that some people were only fit to be slaves. I do not contradict him. But I reject slavery because I see no men fit to be masters."[253] Nevertheless, the sense of this passage is crucial: Lewis agreed with Aristotle that *if* some men (i.e. "natural slaves") lack deliberative reason, then the man with deliberative reason (i.e. "the natural master") will be just in ruling over them.[254] However, Lewis thought that no man lacks deliberative reason, and so speaking of "[the Greeks'] sin in owning slaves,"[255] Lewis insisted that political slavery is, in itself,[256] unnatural, unjust and un-

---

252 Ibid., 1299 [December 1, 1961].
253 Lewis, "Equality," 666.
254 In his edition of Aristotle's *Politics*, Lewis underlined the following: "For the soul rules the body with a <u>despotical rule</u>, whereas the intellect rules the appetites with a <u>constitutional and royal</u> rule. And it is clear that the rule of the soul over the body, and of the mind and the rational element over the passionate, is natural and expedient; whereas <u>the equality</u> of the two or the <u>rule of the inferior</u> is always hurtful. The same holds good of animals in relation to men; for tame animals have a better nature than wild and <u>all tame animals </u>are better off when they are ruled by man; for then they are preserved. Again, <u>the male is by nature superior</u>, and the female inferior; and the one rules and the other is ruled." Next to the "whereas" in this quotation, Lewis commented, "This gives the whole thing away. If the slave lacks reason himself but can apprehend it, then he is to the master not as body to soul but as ορεςις to νους, and the master's good sh[oul]d be kingly or political cf. 1254B – Eth. 1102 B." Lewis, underlining and marginalia in his edition of *De Republica*, 1254b1. Cf. "I am reading the *Politics* of Aristotle which contains one of the few reasoned defences of slavery in ancient literature – most of the ancients taking it for granted and therefore feeling no need to defend it. Very subtle, but I think I see his weak point." Lewis, *The Collected Letters of C. S. Lewis: Volume II*, 909-10 [June 22, 1930]. Cf. "It was of course recognized, as by Aristotle so by others, that servile status and servile character did not always coincide. Hence a fragment of Menander runs 'live in slavery with the spirit of a freeman (*eleutherós*) and you will be no slave.'" Lewis, *Studies in Words*, 112.
255 Lewis, *The Collected Letters of C. S. Lewis: Volume II*, 422 [July 16, 1940].
256 While a great Christian like St. Paul did not demand political freedom for slaves –

Christian;[257] as we read in *The Voyage of the Dawn Treader*:

> 'Secondly,' said Caspian, 'I want to know why you have permitted this abominable and unnatural traffic in slaves to grow up here, contrary to the ancient custom and usage of our dominions.'
>
> 'Necessary, unavoidable,' said his Sufficiency. 'An essential part of the economic development of the Islands, I assure you. Our present burst of prosperity depends on it.'
>
> 'What need have you of slaves?'
>
> 'For export, your Majesty. Sell 'em to Calormen mostly; and we have other markets. We are a great centre of the trade.'
>
> 'In other words,' said Caspian, 'you don't need them. Tell me what purpose they serve except to put money into the pockets of such as Pug?'
>
> 'Your Majesty's tender years,' said Gumpas, with what was meant to be a fatherly smile, 'hardly make it possible that you should understand the economic problem involved. I have statistics, I have graphs, I have –'
>
> 'Tender as my years may be,' said Caspian, 'I believe I understand the slave trade from within quite as well as your Sufficiency. And I do not see that it brings into the islands meat or bread or beer or wine or timber or cabbages or books or instruments of music or horses or armour or anything else worth having. *But whether it does or not, it must be stopped.*'
>
> 'But that would be putting the clock back,' gasped the governor. 'Have you no idea of progress, development?'
>
> 'I have seen them both in an egg,' said Caspian. 'We call it 'Going Bad' in Narnia. This trade must stop.'[258]

---

probably because he always believed that some form of slavery would be with us in this fallen world – he likely did not think that political slavery was ideal.

257 "If you read history you will find that the Christians who did the most for the present world were just those who thought the most of the next. The Apostles themselves, who set on foot the conversion of the Roman Empire, the great men who built up the Middle Ages, the English Evangelicals who abolished the Slave Trade, all left their mark on Earth, precisely because their minds were occupied with Heaven." Lewis, *Mere Christianity*, 406. Cf. "I think the best results are obtained by people who work quietly away at their objectives, such as the abolition of slave trade, or prison reform, or factory acts, or tuberculosis, not by those who think they can achieve universal justice, or health, or peace. I think the art of life consists in tackling each immediate evil as well as we can." Lewis, "Why I Am Not a Pacifist," 288.

258 Lewis, *The Voyage of the Dawn Treader*, 47-9 (emphasis mine). Cf. "'No, no, no,' howled the Beasts. 'It can't be true. Aslan would never sell us into slavery to the King of Calomen.' 'None of that! Hold your noise!' said the Ape with a snarl. 'Who said

Of course, as we know from before, none of this is to deny that, ontologically-speaking, man is the natural slave of God, who is our natural or proper master. Nor is it to deny that God, our natural master, could place a man (or another creature[259]) to rule over other men as a natural master *even if* such a master were not necessarily more rational, for such a rule would be the product of our natural master's – God's – lawful decree. Hence, Lewis agreed with Robert Filmer that Adam was the "lawful," natural, kindly, proper or God-appointed ruler of the planet, and with this understanding in mind, Lewis made the first man on Perelandra "the King,"[260] and in Narnia, we know that Caspian is called the "lawful king" because he is the descendent of the first king,[261] King Frank, whereas "King" Miraz is rebuked for the "unnatural murder of [his] kindly lord,"[262] Prince Rilian reprimands the Green Witch for plotting to murder the "natural lords" of some foreign lands,[263] and the White Witch is overthrown, whereupon "all names [are] restored to their proper owners."[264] The natural, lawful, kindly, proper or God-appointed ruler, therefore, "is one who inherits his lordship,"[265] which, of course, is to say that his lordship must ultimately be inherited from God – such as the lordship of husbands over wives. Consequently, since the natural master or ruler in Lewis's sense, though not in Aristotle's, is one who has inherited his authority from God, he has no right to abdicate his authority. For this reason, King Lune tells Prince Cor, "'Tis no question what thou wantest, Cor, nor I either. 'Tis in course of law. . . . The King's under the law,

anything about slavery? You won't be slaves. You'll be paid – very good wages too. That is to say, your pay will be paid into Aslan's treasury and he will use it all for everybody's good. . . . We'll be able, with the money you earn, to make Narnia a country worth living in. There'll be oranges and bananas pouring in – and roads and big cities and schools and offices and whips and muzzles and saddles and cages and kennels and prisons – Oh, everything.' 'But we don't want all those things,' said an old bear. 'We want to be free. And we want to hear Aslan speak himself.'" Lewis, *The Last Battle*, 34, 35. Cf. Lewis, *The Horse and His Boy*, 28, 117, 128-9. Cf. Lewis, *The Magician's Nephew*, 59, 77.

259 Cf. After Ransom's history lesson to the wise Sorns in *Out of the Silent Planet*, we read: "They were astonished at what he had to tell them of human history – of war, slavery and prostitution. 'It is because they have no Oyarsa,' said one of the pupils. 'It is because every one of them wants to be a little Oyarsa himself,' said Augray. 'They cannot help it,' said the old *sorn*. 'There must be rule, yet how can creatures rule themselves? Beasts must be ruled by *hnau* and *hnau* by *eldila* and *eldila* by Maledil. These creatures have no *eldila*.'" Lewis, *Out of the Silent Planet*, 91.

260 Lewis, *Perelandra*, 201.

261 Lewis, *Prince Caspian*, 151.

262 Ibid., 152.

263 Lewis, *The Silver Chair*, 149.

264 Lewis, *The Lion, the Witch and the Wardrobe*, 127.

265 Lewis, *Studies in Words*, 27.

for it's the law that makes him king. Hast no more power to start away from thy crown than any sentry from his post;'"[266] and Reepicheep the mouse refuses to let King Caspian abandon his kingship, saying,

> 'If it please your Majesty, we mean *shall* not,' said Reepicheep with a low bow. 'You are the King of Narnia. You break faith with all your subjects . . . if you do not return. You shall not please yourself with adventures as if you were a private person. And if your Majesty will not hear reason it will be the truest loyalty of every man on board to follow me in disarming and binding you till you come to your senses.'[267]

Of course, as I have said, Lewis would have supported Filmer's theory of the absolute sovereignty of the eldest line of Adam's posterity if such could have been known and if man were not fallen. However, since Lewis agreed with Locke's *Second Treatise of Government* that the eldest line of Adam's posterity cannot be known[268] and since man is fallen, the Oxford don rejected the doctrine of "Divine Right of Kings,"[269] embraced democracy, and strongly warned against any kind of modern, unnatural slavery, such as that which is entailed in Rousseau's General Will[270] and in the "slave-philosophy of Hegel . . . [and] Marx."[271]

Now this discussion concerning natural and unnatural authority unsurprisingly leads to Lewis's fifth and final key political conviction: the symbolic value of monarchy. As we know by now, Lewis followed Christian and pagan sources in repeatedly declaring God the absolute monarch of creation: "The birth of Christ is the arrival of the great warrior and the great

---

266 Lewis, *The Horse and His Boy*, 186-7.

267 Lewis, *The Voyage of the Dawn Treader*, 181-2.

268 Lewis, *The Collected Letters of C. S. Lewis: Volume II*, 314 [December 31, 1939]. John Locke, *Second Treatise of Government: An Essay Concerning the True Original, Extent and End of Civil Government*, ed. Richard Cox (Wheeling, IL: Harlan Davidson, 1982), 1 [1.4].

269 C. S. Lewis, "Lilies That Fester," in *C. S. Lewis: Essay Collection & Other Short Pieces*, ed. Lesley Walmsley (1955 essay reprint; London: HarperCollins, 2000), 372. Cf. Lewis, "Willing Slaves of the Welfare State," 749.

270 "[But] Hidden in the heart of this striving for Liberty there was also a deep hatred of personal freedom. That invaluable man Rousseau first revealed it. In his perfect democracy, you remember, only the state religion is permitted, slavery is restored, and the individual is told that he has really willed (though he didn't know it) whatever the Government tells him to do. From that starting point, *via* Hegel (another indispensable propagandist on our side) we easily contrived both the Nazi and the Communist state." Lewis, "Screwtape Proposes a Toast," 757. In another essay, Lewis condemned "the Russian slave camps." Lewis, "The Willing Slaves of the Welfare State," 747.

271 Ibid., 748.

king;"[272] "[The miracles and power that God has over Nature] proclaim that He who has come is not merely a king, but *the* King, her King and ours;"[273] "St Paul was impeached and banished and the world went on to the next step – the attack on the King Himself;"[274] "'Aslan?' said Mr Beaver 'Why, don't you know? He's the King.'"[275] Lewis understood God's kingship over all creation to be both literal and mythical, but *not*, as we recall from chapter four, metaphorical; hence, he concurred with John Seeley in saying that "[Christ's] Kingship is not figurative."[276] Moreover, ontologically-speaking, all of creation is a hierarchy, wherein proportionate equality is justice. Thus, all things have their natural rulers or kings by the decree of the High King Himself, God. Even our world was designed as a monarchy, with Adam at its head, but since Adam fell and the knowledge of his true heir was lost, all men, politically-speaking, must be treated as numerical equals in order to avoid unnatural tyranny.

Nevertheless, by making the hero of his *Cosmic Trilogy* a "King's man,"[277] Lewis agreed with Hugh Latimore that even the fallen monarchies of the world have some value: "Busy brains, wanton wits . . . say the name of a king is an odious name."[278]

Indeed, Lewis went much further than this, claiming, "Monarchy [is] the one element in our State which matters most."[279] What Lewis meant by this is that since even a fallen monarchy, and derivatively, a fallen aristocracy, bearers the image of mythical Reality, this fallen or broken image can still nourish people who are exposed to it:

> 'I think there are these four ages about nearly everything. Let's give them names. They are the Unenchanted Age, the Enchanted Age, the Disenchanted Age, and the Re-enchanted.'

272 Lewis, *Reflections on the Psalms*, 380.
273 Lewis, *Miracles*, 1200. This same idea is summarized by Lewis in his edition of St Athanasius's *On the Incarnation*, where we read: "He who gives Himself a virgin birth is the genius of all births: He who makes water wine is a King of all Waters." C. S. Lewis, marginalia in his edition of *De Incarnatione*, 29.
274 C. S. Lewis, "Modern Translations of the Bible," in *C. S. Lewis: Essay Collection & Other Short Pieces*, ed. Lesley Walmsley (1947 essay reprint; London: HarperCollins, 2000), 475.
275 Lewis, *The Lion, the Witch and the Wardrobe*, 74.
276 C. S. Lewis, marginalia in his edition of *Ecce Homo*, by John Robert Seeley (London: J. M. Dent & Sons, 1932; The Rare Book Collection, The University of North Carolina at Chapel Hill), 21.
277 Lewis, *That Hideous Strength*, 655.
278 C. S. Lewis, underlining in his edition of *Sermons*, by Hugh Latimore (London: J. M. Dent & Sons, 1926; The Rare Book Collection, The University of North Carolina at Chapel Hill), 150.
279 Lewis, "Myth Became Fact," 138.

. . . .

'That man on the other side of the bar thinks we've been talking politics.'

'I'm not sure that we haven't,' said I.

'You're quite right. You mean that Aristocracy is one other example? It was the merest Enchantment to suppose that any human being, trusted with uncontrolled powers over their fellows, would not use it for exploitation; or even to suppose that their own standards of honour, valour, and elegance (for which alone they existed) would not soon degenerate into flash-vulgarity. Hence, rightly and inevitably, the Disenchantment, the age of Revolutions. But the question on which all hangs is whether we can go to Re-enchantment.'

'What would that Re-enchantment be?'

'The realization that the thing of which Aristocracy was a mirage is a vital necessity, if you like, that Aristocracy was right: it was only the Aristocrats who were wrong. Or, putting it the other way, that a society which becomes democratic in *ethos* as well as in constitution is doomed.'[280]

Richard Neuhaus calls this "the C. S. Lewis trickle-down theory of politics"[281] since Lewis spoke of fallen monarchy as "the channel though which all the *vital* elements of citizenship – loyalty, the consecration of secular life, the hierarchical principle, splendour, ceremony, continuity – still trickle down to irrigate the dust-bowl of modern economic Statecraft."[282] Therefore, the best

---

280 Lewis, "Talking about Bicycles," 692. In *That Hideous Strength*, when Jane meets Ransom, she says of him: "This face was of no age at all. She had (or so she had believed) disliked bearded faces except for old men with white hair. But that was because she had long since forgotten the imagined Arthur of her childhood – and the imagined Solomon too. Solomon – for the first time in many years the bright solar blend of king and lover and lover and magician which hangs about that name stole back upon her mind. For the first time in all those years she tasted the word *King* itself with all linked associations of battle, marriage, priesthood, mercy, and power." Lewis, *That Hideous Strength*, 495. Cf. "Like the column of a palm-tree, like a dolomite tower, / Like the unbearable noon-day in the glare of its power, / So solemn and so radiant was Solomon to behold, / Men feared his immense forehead and his beard of gold." C. S. Lewis, "Solomon," in *Poems*, by C. S. Lewis, ed. Walter Hooper (1946 poem reprint; San Diego: Harcourt Brace and Jovanovich, 1964), 46 [3.1-4].

281 Neuhaus, "C. S. Lewis in the Public Square," 1.

282 Lewis, "Myth Became Fact," 139. Cf. "There was a good element in [Aristotle's theory of leisure] – the recognition, badly needed by modern commercialism, that the economic activities are not the *end* of man." Lewis, *The Collected Letters of C. S. Lewis: Volume II*, 422 [July 16, 1940]. Cf. "[We must guard against those who say that] politics [is] only economics." Lewis, "Transposition," 278.

of the fallen political structures is not a republican democracy, whose "thick-voiced Tannoy . . . blare[s] over Arthur's grave,"[283] but rather a constitutional monarchy or a democracy with a ceremonial monarchy.[284]

To sum up, on the one hand, Lewis the Christian loved and valued ontological hierarchy with its proportionate equality and rich mythical meaning; however, on the other hand, he was skeptical of the abuses that came with such on a political level, given the fallen nature of man. Thus, Lewis's entire political agenda was to navigate between these two factors and his solution was something like a democratic or even a quasi-socialist system which would maintain its ceremonial monarchy to spiritually nourish the people, and whose rulers would seek to draw out the unique essence of the nation but would do so with prudence, courage, temperance and justice mixed with mercy.

III: Education

As members of the middle-upper class, Lewis's parents both had the money to pay for, and understood the value of, good education for their children. Thus, starting at an early age, Lewis was educated at home by both his mother, who taught him French and Latin, and a governess who taught him everything else.[285] However, despite this promising start, Lewis experienced a string of bad luck at school. After his mother died, Lewis was sent to Wynyard School (England), where he suffered some abuse (hence Lewis nicknamed it "Belsen" after the German concentration camp) and so was withdrawn and placed in Campbell College (Ireland). But, because of health concerns, Lewis was pulled from Campbell after only one semester and moved to Cherbourg House (England), which was a preparatory school for Malvern College, which Lewis attended after Cherbourg. Nonetheless, realizing that his son was not cut-out for multi-pupil education – with all its pedophilia and power-games[286] – Albert, Lewis's father, took Lewis out of Malvern and sent him to Great Bookham to be tutored privately by W. T. Kirkpatrick. Consequently, in a matter of six years (1908-1914), Lewis had attended six different educational facilities, all of which, except for his time with

---

283 Lewis, "Lines During a General Election," 62 [10]. Cf. "Consequently, when the Pevensie children had returned to Narnia last time for their second visit, it was (for the Narnians) as if King Arthur came back to Britain, as some people say he will. And I say the sooner the better." Lewis, *The Voyage of the Dawn Treader*, 19.

284 Lewis, "Equality," 668. Lewis, *The Collected Letters of C. S. Lewis: Volume III*, 348 [July 17, 1953], 343 [July 10, 1953].

285 Lewis, *Surprised by Joy*, 1249.

286 Ibid., 1292-1311.

Kirkpatrick, Lewis "loathed,"[287] and indeed confessed that he "never hated anything so much, not even the front line trenches in World War I."[288]

Besides the unjust corporal punishment and the uncomfortable formal clothing,[289] Lewis hated his time at school because of the bullying. As we know, Lewis's Lucretian materialist phase was characterized by anguish, agnosticism and snobbery and much of this was due to the difficult time he had at school with the "Bloods" or student-oligarchy. In fact, not only did Lewis later link the tyrannical rule of the Bloods with the progressive element of a college that strove after world-domination,[290] but even as a mere fifteen year-old, he wrote an impressive essay ("Are Athletes Better Than Scholars?") in which he, as a Lokian intellectual, attacked the athleticism of the Bloods:

> If then we are to contrast the athlete with the scholar, regarding them as separate individuals, there can surely be but little doubt among reasonable persons as to which is the more beneficial to his fellow men. The days are long past when the mighty man of arms, the Goliath, the Aeneas, was the prop and pillar of his fatherland. Physical development matters little now a days on the battlefield and nothing at all in politics. The successful football player or cricket player achieves no material benefit for the country he supports. The Scholar on the other hand not only furnishes and improves his own mind, but also by the instruction he may impart, and the discoveries to which his learning may lead, benefits and glorifies his fellow beings. . . . Doubtless there are many persons – and more particularly amongst my own class – schoolboys – who would regard what I have been writing as rankert treason against an athletic code to which they demand conformity from all: there are those, believe me, who in England will become next summer engaged in a dangerous and even unequal war, [who] would still follow the doings of our cricket team in Australia with more interest than those of our army in the hostile land. . . . They should not blind themselves to the fact that athletic success is transitory, and will bear them no help when they are turned adrift in the world: learning, however, is everlasting and will always stand them in good stead. . . . Let it not however be inferred from what I said, that I condemn the pursuit of

287 C. S. Lewis, the dust-jacket of *Perelandra* (N.p.: MacMillan, 1944). Cf. Lewis, *Surprised by Joy*, 1316.

288 Lewis, *The Collected Letters of C. S. Lewis: Volume III*, 1325 [March 23, 1962].

289 Lewis, *Surprised by Joy*, 1256. Cf. Lewis, *Prince Caspian*, 170.

290 When Mark Studdock accidentally walked into a private gathering at N.I.C.E, we are told: "Shortly after his brief intrusion into it [the library] on that miserable morning he had discovered that his room, though nominally public, was in practice reserved for what one had learned, at school, to call 'bloods' and, at Bracton, 'the Progressive Element.'" Lewis, *That Hideous Strength*, 478.

athletics: far be it from me to oppose this healthy means of recreation.
. . . But while allowing that the pursuit of athletics is a wholesale
– nay, a necessary pastime – one cannot lose sight of the mistakes and
wrong ideas arising from an exaggerated estimation of their value.[291]

A few years after writing this, Lewis started to work on his epic poem *Dymer*,
into which he poured his "hatred of . . . public schools;"[292] however, this time,
his anger was not so much directed at the Bloods, but rather at the restrictive
nature of schools in general: "And twenty separate Boards of Education /
Closed round [Dymer]. He was passed through every test, / Was vaccinated,
numbered, washed and dressed, / Proctored, inspected, whipt, examined
weekly, / And for some nineteen years he bore it meekly."[293] Although it is
not helpful to overanalyze, we should remember that in Lewis's Lucretian
materialist mind there was a strong, irrational interplay between restrictive
schooling, bullying, colonialism, familial frustration and distance from
God.

While all this sounds quite bleak, Lewis's early education was not all
bad and he was able to become something that he could not have envisioned
years earlier.[294] Indeed, as we know from chapter two, Lewis's time with
Kirkpatrick was his model of what the ideal life would look like: studying,
eating, walking and talking. Thus, with the exception of some knowledge of
the classics he gained at Malvern College, Lewis the future scholar was largely
formed under the guidance of Kirkpatrick, who "thought the reverence owed
to boys was Truth."[295] Consequently, Kirkpatrick treated Lewis like a young
J. S. Mill (whose autobiography Lewis understandably loved[296]) or, as Lewis

---

291 Lewis, "Are Athletes Better Than Scholars?" 318-9.

292 Lewis, preface to the 1950 edition of *Dymer*, 3.

293 Lewis, *Dymer*, 8 [1.6.3-7]. Even when Lewis reconciled himself to education years later,
he still remembered his own hatred of school and, tongue-in-check, made Prince Cor
fearfully say, "Education and all sorts of horrible things are going to happen to me."
Lewis, *The Horse and His Boy*, 173.

294 Hence, based on his own experience, Lewis later wrote of education in general: "While
we are planning the education of the future we can be rid of the illusion that we shall
ever replace destiny. Make the plans as good as you can, of course. But be sure that
the final effect on every single boy will be something you never envisaged and will
spring from little free movements in your machine which neither your blueprint nor
your working model gave any hint of." C. S. Lewis, "My First School," in *C. S. Lewis:
Essay Collection & Other Short Pieces*, ed. Lesley Walmsley (1943 essay reprint; London:
HarperCollins, 2000), 596.

295 C. S. Lewis, "Old Kirk, Like Father Time Himself," in "The Unpublished Short Poetry
of C. S. Lewis," by Don King, *VII: An Anglo-American Literary Review* 15 (1998): 82.

296 Lewis read Mill's *Autobiography* at least three times ("Re-read . . . after many years .
. . Oct. 1959" "Again May 1962"), and so he would have been very familiar with the
first three chapters, in which Mill discussed his early education with his father. C. S.

later came to see it, as a "Lockian private pupil,"²⁹⁷ for both the young J. S. Mill and the Lockian pupil were tutored privately and, as was the case with Lewis, self-discovery along with some helpful "scaffolding" or Socratic midwifery was the teaching method of choice; thus, in *Surprised by Joy*, we read:

> We opened our books at *Iliad*, Book I. Without a word of introduction [Kirkpatrick] read aloud the first twenty lines or so in the 'new' pronunciation. . . . He then translated, with a few, a very few explanations, about a hundred lines. I had never seen a classical author taken in such large gulps before. When he had finished he handed me over Crusius' *Lexicon* and, having told me to go through again as much as I could of what he had done, left the room. It seems an odd method of teaching, but it worked.²⁹⁸

After Lewis left Kirkpatrick's, he went to University College, Oxford, where he took three Firsts – in Classical Honours Moderation, *Literae Humaniores* ("Greats") and English Language and Literature – in less than four years: a remarkable feat given that only five percent of all students attained First Class degrees.²⁹⁹ Although Lewis had some trouble entering Oxford due to the mathematical part of the entrance exam or "Responsions,"³⁰⁰ he more than proved himself once fully admitted; indeed, he took especially well to Oxford's tutorial system, wherein each student is assigned a tutor to whom the student reads a essay once a week and then receives personalized feedback: "Instead of listening to a professor lecture for an hour at a time three times a week, and later trying to remember as much as possible about what he or she had said when it came time for a test or examination, the emphasis at Oxford

---

Lewis, marginalia in his edition of *Autobiography*, by John Stuart Mill (Oxford: Oxford University Press, 1958; The Marion E. Wade Center, Wheaton College), 266.

297 "[The Master of New College] asked me about my previous education and when I told him of Kirk he exclaimed 'Oh, then you are the Lockian private pupil! Now that's very interesting.' He advised me to read Locke's *On Education* (I had already done so at Grendon in 1921) and Rousseau's *Emile* in the light of my own experience." Lewis, *All My Road Before Me*, 274 [October 18, 1923].

298 Lewis, *Surprised by Joy*, 1325.

299 Heck, *Irrigating Deserts*, 77.

300 Lewis, *Surprised by Joy*, 1351. Interestingly, although Lewis was poor at elementary mathematics, he "effectively [used] concepts from higher mathematics" to explain theological problems. David Neuhouser, "Higher Dimensions: C. S. Lewis and Mathematics," *VII: An Anglo-American Literary Review* 13 (1996): 58. Cf. Russell Howell, "Lewis's *Miracles* and Mathematical Elegance," in *C. S. Lewis as Philosopher: Truth, Goodness, and Beauty*, ed. David Baggett, Gary Habermas and Jerry Walls, 211-27 (Downers Grove, IL: InterVarsity Press, 2008).

was on the student and the development of his or her ideas."[301] Thus, besides attending the occasional voluntary lecture, Lewis's time at Oxford was in many ways an extension of his time with Kirkpatrick, which, of course, was excellent since the most recent research has shown that the tutorial system – with its focus on scaffolding, thought clarity, interpersonal relations, and adaptability to student needs, abilities, background, gender, learning style, temperament, etc. – is the most ideal form of education.[302]

Once Lewis finished studying at University College, he worked for one year as a sabbatical-fill in the philosophy department at New College and then was offered a fellowship, which he held for twenty-nine years, as tutor of English language and literature at Magdalen College (where, as we know, he also taught philosophy and history for a number of years). In regard to Lewis the educator there are three things worth discussing: (1) his relationship with his students, (2) his relationship with his colleagues, and (3) his theory of education.

Lewis's relationship with his students was something that appears to have improved over the years. For instance, when he was just starting out, he had to fight discouragement because his lectures were poorly attended,[303] he hurt some students because he was overly argumentative during tutorials,[304] and he soon realized that he could not assume that all students had the same knowledge: "And of course when one is trying to TEACH one can take nothing for granted. Hitherto I have always talked or read to people to whom I could say 'You remember Bradley's stunt about judgement' or 'The sort of business you get at the beginning of Kant.' But of course that won't do now."[305] Moreover, after a few years of teaching, Lewis discovered that an educator is in many ways responsible for the edification or corruption of his students: "[I] [h]ad a conversation with Slade, who gave up Greats a year ago. He tells me I was successful (when I was his tutor) of demolishing all his original beliefs in morals but not in replacing them. I don't know

---

301 W. Brown Patterson, "C. S. Lewis: Personal Reflections," in *C. S. Lewis: Remembered*, ed. Harry Lee Poe and Rebecca Whitten Poe, 89-97 (Grand Rapids, MI: Zondervan, 2006), 90.

302 Paul Eggen and Don Kauchak, *Educational Psychology: Windows on Classrooms*, 7th ed. (Upper Saddle River, NJ: Pearson, 2007), 45, 49, 63, 65, 83, 85, 98, 101.

303 Lewis, *The Collected Letters of C. S. Lewis: Volume I*, 635 [October 15, 1924].

304 George Sayer notes that "[w]hen [Lewis] first began tutoring, [he] was severe, harsh, and argumentative. . . . [But his] attitude toward his pupils became far gentler and more sympathetic within a few years, when he learned how to conceal his diffidence and sensitivity under a hearty and frequently humorous manner." Sayer, *Jack*, 199, 200.

305 Lewis, *The Collected Letters of C. S. Lewis: Volume I*, 634 [August 28, 1924].

how seriously he meant this."[306] In addition, even though Lewis would later become famous for mastering the art of explaining a difficult concept using simple words and ideas,[307] this art took time to develop as is evident in his awkwardly written 1933 novel, *The Pilgrim's Regress*.

Yet, as I said, improve, Lewis did. In 1940, he wrote *The Problem of Pain* and in 1941, he broadcasted the first book of *Mere Christianity* and authored *The Screwtape Letters* (which was later used as a textbook for the General Certificate of Education: Advanced Level[308]); following this, in 1942, he became the president of the Socratic Club, and from there on, he penned countless popular theological works, maintained continuous correspondence with hundreds of people seeking his learned advice, was given five honorary doctorates (from St. Andrew's, Laval, Manchester, Dijon and Lyon), and wrote an number of articles about teaching methods – notably, "Christian Apologetics," "Before We Can Communicate," "The Death of Words" and "Modern Translations of the Bible." In all of this, Lewis revealed himself to have been a master instructor and rhetor, able to understand his audience[309]

---

306 Lewis, *All My Road Before Me*, 451-2 [February 14, 1927]. However, in later years, Lewis probably underestimated his impact on his students: "And what he has done to me, doubtless I have done to others; I, who am exceptionally blessed in having been allowed a way of life in which, having little power, I have had little opportunity of oppressing and embittering others. Let all of us who have never been school prefects, NCOs, schoolmasters, matrons of hospitals, prison wardens, or even magistrates, give hearty thanks for it." Lewis, *Reflections on the Psalms*, 322.

307 Concerning his works of non-fiction, Lewis said, "But they have succeeded because I'm a professional teacher and explanation happens to be one of the things I've learned to do." Lewis, *The Collected Letters of C. S. Lewis: Volume III*, 503 [August 14, 1954].

308 Jocelyn Gibb, one of Lewis's editors, told Lewis that the Associated Examining Board for the General Certificate of Education (Advanced Level) had adopted the *Screwtape Letters* as one of the books in the 1955-56 syllabus. Lewis, *The Collected Letters of C. S. Lewis: Volume III*, 523 [November 12, 1954]. Cf. "W[oul]d you believe it: an American schoolgirl has been expelled from her school for having in her possession a copy of my *Screwtape*! I asked my informant whether it was a Communist school, or a Fundamentalist school, or an R. C. school, and got the shattering answer 'No, it was a *select* school.' That puts a chap in his place, doesn't it!" Ibid., 543 [December 17, 1954].

309 "I have been asked to write about the difficulties which a man must face in trying to present the Christian Faith to modern unbelievers. That is too wide a subject for my capacity or even for the scope of an article. The difficulties vary as the audience varies. The audience may be of this or that nation, may be children or adults, learned or ignorant. My own experience is of English audience only, and almost exclusively of adults. It has, in fact, been mostly of men (and women) serving in the RAF. This has meant that while very few of them have been learned in the academic sense of the word, a large number of them have had a smattering of elementary practical science, have been mechanics, electricians or wireless operators; for the rank and file of the RAF belong to what may almost be called 'the Intelligentsia of the Proletariat.' I have also talked to students at the Universities. These strict limitations in my experience must be kept

and teach them challenging concepts (without a hint of snobbery[310]) in their own language: "My task was therefore simply that of a *translator* – one turning Christian doctrine, or what he believed to be such, into the vernacular, into language that unscholarly people would attend to and could understand."[311]

And something similar appears to have been true for Lewis as a tutor and lecturer. Although Lewis was like the majority of Oxford dons, who saw their research as their real work,[312] he largely committed himself to doing the best job he could as a tutor and lecturer; thus, while (*pace* David Downing[313]) *some* students found Lewis an average or even irritating tutor,[314]

---

in mind by the readers. How rash it would be to generalise from such an experience I myself discovered on the single occasion when I spoke to soldiers. It became at once clear to me that the level of intelligence in our army is very much lower than in the RAF and that quite a different approach was required." C. S. Lewis, "God in the Dock," in *C. S. Lewis: Essay Collection & Other Short Pieces*, ed. Lesley Walmsley (1948 essay reprint; London: HarperCollins, 2000), 33.

310 "Twice lately in the *Church Times* I have seen protests of an inexplicable warmth against the practice of transliterating Greek words. This is said to be (a) useless to those who do not know Greek, and (b) irritating to those who do. But: (a) When I meet a Hebrew word transliterated I can remember it and use it, just as I would remember and use an English word that was new to me: but my visual memory is not good enough to retain, for future recognition, the Hebrew characters. I presume that many Greekless readers have the same experience about Greek words. (b) Why should it 'irritate' anyone? There is no sacrosanctity about the Greek types used in modern England. Those used in the Seventeenth century were very different. Plato could not have read either." C. S. Lewis, "And Less Greek," *Church Times* (July 20, 1962).

311 C. S. Lewis, "Rejoinder to Dr Pittenger," in *God in the Dock: Essays on Theology and Ethics*, by C. S. Lewis, ed. Walter Hooper (1958 essay reprint; Grand Rapids, MI: Eerdmans, 1970), 183.

312 "The typical Oxford don, however, was becoming someone who engaged in both teaching and research; increasingly he tended to regard the former, however necessary and rewarding, as essentially an interruption of the latter – of his 'own work,' as he would call it." Keith Thomas, "College Life, 1945-1970," in *The History of the University of Oxford: Volume VIII; The Twentieth Century*, ed. Brian Harrison, 189-216 (Oxford: Oxford University Press, 1994), 195. Cf. "You have doubtless been told – but it can hardly be repeated too often – that our colleges at Oxford were founded not in order to teach the young but in order to support masters of arts. In their original institution they are homes not for teaching but for the pursuit of knowledge. . . . We are not going to try to improve you; we have fulfilled our whole function if we help you to *see* some given tract of reality." Lewis, "Our English Syllabus," 84-5, 87.

313 Although an excellent Lewis scholar, Downing exaggerates when he says, "As a speaker and teacher, Lewis was unsurpassed." David Downing, *Planets in Peril: A Critical Study of C. S. Lewis's Ransom Trilogy* (Amherst, MA: The University of Massachusetts Press, 1992), 4.

314 Lewis's brother, Warnie, noted that C. Maurice Bowra "was irritated and bored by C. S. Lewis." C. Maurice Bowra, quoted in *Brothers and Friends*, by Warren Lewis, 283 [December 7, 1968]. "I am not sure that he was an outstandingly good tutor, although

a dull lecturer,[315] an unclear supervisor,[316] and a don who did not care about students as persons but only as tools to sharpen his own thought,[317] most of Lewis's former students (who ranged in number from three to thirty-eight a year[318]) agree that he was an excellent teacher. For instance, his female students (whom I discussed earlier) found Lewis courteous and challenging; Erik Routley says that "[i]f ever there were a man who exploded the slander that 'academic' means remote, dull, and inhuman, that man was Lewis;"[319] Luke Rigby claims that Lewis had "a true kindness that soon put a green and overawed freshman at his ease;"[320] Derek Brewer insists that Lewis "was an unusually good example of the ideal [tutor] . . . [even though] [h]e did not particularly enjoy it;"[321] John Lawlor recounts that he "passed from dislike and hostility to stubborn affection, and then to gratitude for the weekly bout [with Lewis] in which no quarter was asked or given;"[322] Kenneth Tynan found "the great thing about [Lewis] as a teacher of literature was that he could take you into the medieval mind and the minds of a classical writer;"[323] W. R. Fryer recounts, "I found [Lewis] – not surprisingly – the only good *tutor* . . . among the men who taught me at Oxford. . . . He was superhuman

it was wonderful to go to him, and incredibly inspiriting." Peter Bayley, "From Master to Colleague," in *C. S. Lewis at the Breakfast Table and Other Reminiscences*, ed. James Como, 77-86 (San Diego: Harcourt Brace & Company, 1992), 79.

315 "I never felt any warmth in my encounters with Lewis. No real human contact. . . . I wouldn't say Lewis was a good lecturer. He read word for word from his brief. For me at least he never really illuminated anything." Alan Rook, "The Butcher," in *In Search of C. S. Lewis*, ed. Stephen Schofield, 11-5 (South Plainfield, NJ: Bridge, 1983), 12, 13.

316 "A great teacher and a great writer need not be an efficient supervisor. Lewis was too permissive and left me to get on with things. . . . Yet he gave generously of his time, unlike most supervisors in those days." Fowler, "C. S. Lewis: Supervisor," 100.

317 "Lewis was interested in his pupils, not as persons, but, by deliberate policy, as well as inclination, only so long as they baited him and allowed him to win an argument." Norman Bradshaw, "Impressions of a Pupil," in *In Search of C. S. Lewis*, ed. Stephen Schofield, 17-27 (South Plainfield, NJ: Bridge, 1983), 25. "Lewis lacked the warmth to fire his students with enthusiasm. He lacked even the active interest in developing their capacities. . . . Either he was not a very good judge of character or his lack of interest in his students prevented him from assessing them accurately." George Bailey, "In the University," in *C. S. Lewis: Speaker & Teacher*, ed. Carolyn Keefe, 105-22 (Grand Rapids, MI: Zondervan, 1974), 115.

318 Heck, *Irrigating Deserts*, 113.

319 Erik Routley, "A Prophet," in *C. S. Lewis at the Breakfast Table and Other Reminiscences*, ed. James Como, 33-7 (San Diego: Harcourt Brace & Company, 1992), 36-7.

320 Luke Rigby, "A Solid Man," in *C. S. Lewis at the Breakfast Table and Other Reminiscences*, ed. James Como, 38-40 (San Diego: Harcourt Brace & Company, 1992), 39.

321 Brewer, "The Tutor: A Portrait," 41-2.

322 Lawlor, *C. S. Lewis: Memories and Reflections*, 9.

323 Kenneth Tynan, "Exhilaration," in *In Search of C. S. Lewis*, ed. Stephen Schofield, 3-9 (South Plainfield, NJ: Bridge, 1983), 7.

in the range of his knowledge and in the height of his intellectual vision;"[324] E. L. Edmonds mentions that "[l]ectures by Lewis . . . were a joy;"[325] Peter Philip remarks, "In four years I do not remember him missing a weekly tutorial with me more than two or three times;"[326] James Dundas-Grant says, "The great thing is [Lewis] made us *think*;"[327] Dom Bede Griffiths maintains that his tutorials with Lewis were "the beginning of a lasting friendship;"[328] Martin Moynihan declares Lewis "generous and forbearing" as a tutor;[329] Martin Lings says he owes Lewis "both for his encouragement . . . and also for his implacable criticism;"[330] W. J. B. Owen insists that "as a tutor [Lewis] was superb;"[331] J. I. Packer, who heard Lewis lecture once, says Lewis "was supposed to be the best lecturer in Oxford, and on that showing it could have been true;"[332] Roger Poole rhetorically asks, "What exactly was the magic element in Lewis's lecturing technique? It was the ability to ask questions no one had thought of;"[333] Penelope Fitzgerald recollects how Lewis generously told the students in the lecture hall that he would adapt himself "to the slowest note-taker;"[334] George Watson notes that there was always "an enormous audience" at Lewis's lectures;[335] Dabney Hart was impressed by Lewis's humility when he retraced a error he made during

324 Fryer, "Disappointment at Cambridge?" 29.

325 E. L. Edmonds, "C. S. Lewis, the Teacher," in *In Search of C. S. Lewis*, ed. Stephen Schofield, 37-52 (South Plainfield, NJ: Bridge, 1983), 43.

326 Peter Philip, "South African View," in *In Search of C. S. Lewis*, ed. Stephen Schofield, 93-6 (South Plainfield, NJ: Bridge, 1983), 94.

327 James Dundas-Grant, "From an 'Outsider,'" in *C. S. Lewis at the Breakfast Table and Other Reminiscences*, ed. James Como, 229-33 (San Diego: Harcourt Brace & Company, 1992), 230. Concerning one student who read a bad paper to him, Lewis said, "I applied the Socratic method, I think with some good results." Lewis, *All My Road Before Me*, 351 [February 14, 1925].

328 Dom Bede Griffiths, "Forty Years' Perspective," in *We Remember C. S. Lewis: Essays & Memories*, ed. David Graham, 32-5 (Nashville: Broadman & Holman, 2001), 34.

329 Martin Moynihan, "I Sleep but My Heart Watcheth," in *We Remember C. S. Lewis: Essays & Memories*, ed. David Graham, 36-40 (Nashville: Broadman & Holman, 2001), 38.

330 Martin Lings, "A Debt Repaid," in *We Remember C. S. Lewis: Essays & Memories*, ed. David Graham, 53-5 (Nashville: Broadman & Holman, 2001), 54.

331 W. J. B. Owen, "Splendid Tutor," in *We Remember C. S. Lewis: Essays & Memories*, ed. David Graham, 59-60 (Nashville: Broadman & Holman, 2001), 59.

332 J. I. Packer, "What Lewis Was and Wasn't," in *We Remember C. S. Lewis: Essays & Memories*, ed. David Graham, 6-8 (Nashville: Broadman & Holman, 2001), 7.

333 Roger Poole, "Lewis Lecturing," in *We Remember C. S. Lewis: Essays & Memories*, ed. David Graham, 70-7 (Nashville: Broadman & Holman, 2001), 72.

334 Penelope Fitzgerald, "Letter," in *We Remember C. S. Lewis: Essays & Memories*, ed. David Graham, 152-3 (Nashville: Broadman & Holman, 2001), 153.

335 Watson, "The Art of Disagreement," 77.

his lecture;[336] W. Brown Patterson claims, "[Lewis] would agree or disagree with me as he thought best. But in all his criticisms he sought to lead me to strengthen an argument, to express an idea more clearly, or to anticipate a difficulty;"[337] Paul Piehler remembers that "[g]rades or exam results seemed to be the last thing in [Lewis's] mind;"[338] Christopher Mead Armitage learned from Lewis's lectures that "the life of the mind, especially the search for the origins of ideas, mattered;"[339] Charles Wrong thought Lewis "an immensely formidable personality, and one who would not tolerate any falling off in scholarly standards;"[340] well-known Canadian novelist Robertson Davies mentions that he "attended lectures by Lewis and admired him greatly;"[341] M. A. Manzalaoui says that Lewis was "an outstanding lecturer and tutor in English literature, in philosophy and political theory;"[342] despite not having been a student of Lewis's, Walter Hooper tells us that Lewis, like all great teachers, had just as many "examples and illustrations" of the subject-matter he was lecturing on as he did of actual subject-matter;[343] and, though separated by an ocean, even the British POWs that Lewis taught during

---

336 Concerning a lecture Lewis was giving on *Samson Agonistes*, Dabney Hart wrote, "On the last morning Lewis began with a gracious retraction of a comment the afternoon before about Aristotle: that he had ignored the Dionysian elements in tragedy. Conversation in the evening with a better Aristotelian than himself led him to agree that possibly Aristotle had merely thought it unnecessary to mention what everyone took for granted. Lewis's careful attention to this correction struck me as significant for Lewis as much as for Aristotle and *Samson Agonistes*." Hart, *Through the Open Door*, 4.

337 Patterson, "C. S. Lewis: Personal Reflections," 91.

338 Paul Piehler, "Encounters with Lewis: An Interim Report," in *C. S. Lewis: Remembered*, ed. Harry Lee Poe and Rebecca Whitten Poe, 115-58 (Grand Rapids, MI: Zondervan, 2006), 120.

339 Christopher Mead Armitage, "Smartened Up By Lewis," in *C. S. Lewis: Remembered*, ed. Harry Lee Poe and Rebecca Whitten Poe, 159-60 (Grand Rapids, MI: Zondervan, 2006), 159.

340 Wrong, "A Chance Meeting," 107.

341 Robertson Davies, "Letter: January 22, 1979," in *We Remember C. S. Lewis: Essays & Memories*, ed. David Graham, 149 (Nashville: Broadman & Holman, 2001), 149.

342 M. A. Manzalaoui, "Narnia: The Domain of Lewis's Beliefs," in *We Remember C. S. Lewis: Essays & Memories*, ed. David Graham, 9-25 (Nashville: Broadman & Holman, 2001), 10.

343 "For the Prolegomena lectures Lewis had two notebooks at the dais. One notebook had, on the left-hand side, a very detailed outline of the subject-matter; on the right-hand side were numerous examples and illustrations from the authors he was talking about. The other notebook, which he called 'Thickening,' and which grew as time went on, contained further examples and illustrations which he had picked up in his reading and might bring into his lectures." Walter Hooper, "The Lectures of C. S. Lewis at the Universities of Oxford and Cambridge," *Christian Scholar's Review* 27, no. 4 (Summer 1998): 441.

WWII almost certainly gained a lot from the Oxford don's instruction.[344]

Nevertheless, if Lewis was, for the most part, an excellent teacher both in and out of the classroom, he had few friends among his colleagues at Oxford and was generally seen as incompetent in regard to university politics and matters of academic administration. That is, besides the Inklings – the group of Christian intellectuals who met once a week to discuss the books they were writing – and a few others, Lewis was largely ostracized by his Oxonian colleagues. The reason for this is twofold.

First, in fairness to Lewis's colleagues who did not like him, Lewis *was* (even by his own admission[345]) incompetent at academic administration and university politics: he was not very skilled at writing recommendation letters

---

344 "It would perhaps be going too far to say that the British prisoners of war can now read the Oxford Honours School of English in their camps. But they can do something like it. . . . On the cultural side I anticipate, along with much bad work, answers of real interest, for I believe that the necessary restriction on bulky works of criticism, literary history, and apparatus, by forcing the students to concentrate on the texts and to digest them more thoroughly and, above all, to find in one great author their chief commentary on another, may have certain positive advantages over the normal procedure." C. S. Lewis, "Open Letter," *The Christian News-Letter* 119 (February 4, 1942): 4. "Most recently of all, at Oxford, we have (first of all Faculties in Universities) conducted an Examination for Englishmen now behind barbed wire in Germany. We felt, as we read and re-read the answers, which told of so many hours usefully and delightfully passed in prison, that the labour had been immensely worthwhile." C. S. Lewis, "Is English Doomed?" in *C. S. Lewis: Essay Collection & Other Short Pieces*, ed. Lesley Walmsley (1944 essay reprint; London: HarperCollins, 2000), 436-7.

345 When Basil Willey, professor of English at the University of Cambridge, suggested that Lewis become the Chairman of the Faculty Board of English, Lewis replied: "No. It would never do. People so often deny their own capacity for business either through mock-modesty or through laziness that when the denial happens to be true, it is difficult to make it convincing. But I have been tried at this kind of job; and none of those who experienced me in office ever wanted to repeat the experiment. I am both meddlesome and forgetful. Quite objectively, I'd be a disaster." Lewis, *The Collected Letters of C. S. Lewis: Volume III*, 802 [October 26, 1956].

for students;[346] he rarely spoke at college meetings;[347] the one time he did get political was when he (successfully, though perhaps not wisely) helped Adam Fox – a divinity specialist and not a poetry expert[348] – become the Chair of Poetry;[349] and when Lewis was appointed vice-president of Magdalen, he was so forgetful and uncommitted to his responsibilities that he "was the only vice president of Magdalen within living memory not to be invited to undertake a second year of office, his first having been so disastrous."[350]

Second, and perhaps most important, though Lewis largely followed Oxford's social graces and avoided talking about religion with his students and colleagues,[351] he not merely broke but shattered the unwritten Oxonian

---

346 "[Lewis] once told me that a confidential reference (say, for a pupil) would always be strengthened if it contained some small item not entirely to the candidate's credit. He thought thereby the honesty of the reference would be more obvious. In fact, in my own experience of many committees before my retirement was that a referee's least hesitation was normally enough, in the large number of applications, to provide a reason for throwing out at least that application. On the other hand, in an open reference he once gave for me, he commented that I had good health. That would read today, and doubtless did then, as a friendly referee seeking desperately for something favorable to say." Derek Brewer, "C. S. Lewis: Sixty Years On," in *C. S. Lewis: Remembered*, ed. Harry Lee Poe and Rebecca Whitten Poe, 55-71 (Grand Rapids, MI: Zondervan, 2006), 67. While Lewis's recommendation letter for Derek Brewer sounds like a poor letter, many of the recommendation letters Lewis wrote were actually quite good. See C. S. Lewis, "Eric Bentley: An Appreciation," in *The Play and Its Critic: Essays for Eric Bentley*, ed. Michael Bertin (New York: University of America Press, n.d.), 4-7. C. S. Lewis, "Recommendation Letter for E. L. Edmonds," *The Canadian C. S. Lewis Journal* no. 59 (Summer 1987): 1. C. S. Lewis, "Recommendation Letter for N. Bradshaw," *The Canadian C. S. Lewis Journal* no. 7 (July 1979): 16. C. S. Lewis, "Recommendation Letter for Helen Tyrrell Wheeler," *The Canadian C. S. Lewis Journal* no. 67 (Summer 1989): 2.

347 "I don't remember Lewis ever speaking at a College meeting. He took hardly any interest in academic politics, nor in national politics, although Magdalen was noted for the active part it played in the former and 1937-1939 were years which saw passionate debate over the chances of war or peace than any other period in my lifetime." David Hunt, "Observations of a Magdalen Don," in *In Search of C. S. Lewis*, ed. Stephen Schofield, 123-5 (South Plainfield, NJ: Bridge, 1983), 124.

348 Despite being a divinity specialist, Fox had published some poems. Thus, believing in Fox's abilities, Lewis wrote, "So little were the merits of *Fox* perceived by his own age that his elevation to the Chair of Poetry in the University of Oxford is said to have excited wonder." C. S. Lewis, "From Johnson's *Life of Fox*," *The Oxford Magazine* 56 (June 9, 1938): 738. Nevertheless, in actuality, Fox appears to have been a weak candidate for the Chair of Poetry.

349 Fox, "At the Breakfast Table," 94-5.

350 Hugh Sinclair, "Forgetful Rudeness," in *We Remember C. S. Lewis: Essays & Memories*, ed. David Graham, 115-8 (Nashville: Broadman & Holman, 2001), 116.

351 "Rules, sometimes quite firmly enforced, prescribed conversational content and style. Religion, politics and women were the most likely topics for exclusion." Harrison,

rule that no non-divinity professor be actively engaged in religious – and at that, popular religious – activities. Consequently, Lewis quickly found himself excluded from the "inner ring" and the "progressive element" of the College, which treated him as an enemy and which he described with much disgust in "The Inner Ring," "Highbrows and Lowbrows" and *That Hideous Strength*. As James Houston, a former student at Oxford, said,

> I can deeply understand why Lewis wrote *That Hideous Strength*, because he is describing his own Magdalen Common Room, and the struggles and the sneers that he got there from his smart colleagues; nothing could be more outrageous to them than that a man should not only talk religion, but should publish it, and be known and have a reputation way beyond theirs because of religion and not scholarship. Thus, his scholarship tended to be overlooked by many in the 1950s, because he was too popular as a religious writer.[352]

The ultimate result of both Lewis's incompetence at school politics and the offence he caused his highbrow, anti-religious colleagues at Oxford was that he failed to attain a chair in the English department in spite of having published many important academic books and having given Oxford twenty-nine years of his life. Thus, when the University of Cambridge offered Lewis the Chair in Medieval and Renaissance Literature, he took it and, despite having to be separated from his friends and family in Oxford for the duration of the workweek, he enjoyed being at Cambridge very much. However, his enjoyment at Cambridge was not so much based on the lack of politics (there was: but he characteristically ignored it[353]) nor was it based on the lack of

---

"College Life, 1918-1939," 87.

352 James Houston, "Reminiscences of the Oxford Lewis," in *We Remember C. S. Lewis: Essays & Memories*, ed. David Graham, 129-43 (Nashville: Broadman & Holman, 2001), 137. Cf. "[I] think the Educational world is rather anti-me." Lewis, *The Collected Letters of C. S. Lewis: Volume III*, 144 [October 29, 1951].

353 "[Lewis] was essentially a college rather than a university man. He rarely seemed to be interested in the affairs of the university as a whole, or even (and this was a fault) in those of his own faculty. He never attempted to master regulations. He hardly ever read *The Reporter*, the university's official journal, and it was some time before he even discovered its existence. But as time went on, he became more and more interested in college affairs, in some, of course more than others. He was ignorant of anything to do with finance, and during debates on figures his eyes closed and he was even known to snore. But it might surprise some people to know that, when genuinely interested, administration did not entirely pass him by. I suspect that few could guess that one passage in *The Reporter* on a particular intricate subject dealing with the relationship between the university and the colleges was penned largely by the hand of C. S. Lewis." Richard Ladborough, "In Cambridge," in *C. S. Lewis at the Breakfast Table and Other Reminiscences*, ed. James Como, 98-104 (San Diego: Harcourt Brace & Company, 1992), 101-2.

hostility (he provoked many students and his own department was divided against him[354]); rather, Lewis enjoyed Cambridge because its environment was less atheistic than Oxford[355] and he was able to spend more time writing and reading: "I like Cambridge better all the time: also my new job – or rather my new leisure for I've never been so under-worked since I first went to school."[356]

Now despite Lewis's hatred of his public schooling, which was teacher-centered, and his fondness for his time with Kirkpatrick, which was student-centered, Lewis's theory of education for schoolchildren was rather teacher-centered and traditional; his view of post-secondary education, however, was more student-centered and Oxonian. Thus, for the most part, his educational theory could be called Aristotelian, for like Aristotle, Lewis emphasized three key things: (1) the purpose of early education is to "humanize" students or help them to achieve their full potential as human beings,[357] and part of what this means is to allow students to have "freeborn minds," which is only attainable with free or liberal education;[358] (2) since true freedom means positive freedom – freedom within the bounds of universal values – young

---

354 For instance, Lewis offended many English literature undergraduates with his comments in the school newspaper and his own department was – though not antagonistically, at least sharply – divided into those who supported Lewis and those who supported Lewis's arch-rival, F. R. Leavis: "The Faculty [of English] is a democracy. The most diverse conceptions of English meet and contend here. Almost every undergraduate conception is already represented on it. Because it is a democracy, no one conception is likely to secure a complete victory. Compromise is inevitable. . . . If (which heaven forbid) we were a dictatorship you could have a consistent scheme expressing a single conception. But this would be something narrower than a school of English. It would once have been a school of Q-ism; it might now be one of Leavisism or Willeyism, or even Lewisism." C. S. Lewis, "Correspondence," *Delta: The Cambridge Literary Magazine* no. 23 (February 1961): 6.

355 Lewis, *The Collected Letters of C. S. Lewis: Volume III*, 520 [November 1, 1954].

356 Ibid., 900 [November 27, 1957].

357 "Perhaps this will become clearer if we take a concrete instance. When a Roman father told his son that it was a sweet and seemly thing to die for his country, he believed what he said. He was communicating to the son an emotion which he himself shared and which he believed to be in accord with the value which his judgment discerned in noble death. He was giving the boy the best he had, giving of his spirit to humanize him as he had given of his body to beget him." Lewis, *The Abolition of Man*, 406. Cf. Lewis, "Our English Syllabus," 84. Cf. "I think I may say that of all the men we meet with, nine parts of ten are what they are, good or evil, useful or not, by their education." C. S. Lewis, underlining in his edition of *Some Thoughts Concerning Education*, by John Locke (Cambridge: Cambridge University Press, 1895; The Marion E. Wade Center, Wheaton College), 1 [1.1].

358 "I believe a man is happier, and happy in a richer way, if he has 'the freeborn mind.'" Lewis, "Willing Slaves of the Welfare State," 749.

students must be exposed to natural, proper, basic and general things, onto which they can then add subsequent knowledge; however, since young students do not have the knowledge to easily discern what is natural, proper, basic and general, teachers need to expose students to these things; (3) but because students develop – i.e. become more fully human and rational – over time, the amount of control the teacher exercises should decrease with students' ability to think for themselves; hence, early education should be teacher-centered and later education should be student-centered.

As for (1), Lewis agreed with Aristotle that whereas *vocational training* aims at preparing people –"slaves" – for *work*, *education* prepares people – "freemen" – for *life*:

> Neither [Aristotle nor Milton] would dispute that the purpose of education is to produce the good man and the good citizen, though it must be remembered that we are not here using the word 'good' in any narrowly ethical sense. The 'good man' here means the man of good taste and good feeling, the interesting and interested man, and almost the happy man. With such an end in view education in most civilized communities has taken much the same path; it has taught civil behaviour by direct and indirect discipline, has awakened the logical faculty by mathematics and dialectic, and has endeavoured to produce right sentiments – which are to the passions what right habits are to the body – by steeping the pupil in literature both sacred and profane on which the culture of the community is based. Vocational training, on the other hand . . . aims not at a good man but a good banker, a good electrician, a good scavenger, or a good surgeon.[359]

While Lewis was overly paranoid by the educational bills passed by the government after WWII which called for an increase in vocational training in order to rebuild the economy,[360] his warning to civilization still seems to be valid: "Our ideal must be to find time for both education and training: our danger is that equality may mean training for all and education for none.

---

359 Lewis, "Our English Syllabus," 81-2. Cf. "The only end of education is to restore our rational nature to its proper state." Lewis, underlining in his edition of *A Serious Call to a Devout Life*, 231 [18]. Cf. Lewis, *Studies in Words*, 127-30. Cf. Aristotle *Politics* 1342a1.

360 "As for the [the neglect of human capital formation], wartime developments had hinted at a fundamental reform of education and one that would pay greater attention than hitherto to vocational training. However, the Education Act, for all its benefits, did little to oust the status attached to intellectual, abstract activity in grammar and public schools." W. R. Garside, "Declining Advantage: the British Economy," in *The British Isles: 1901-1951*, ed. Keith Robbins, 163-96 (Oxford: Oxford University Press, 2006), 191.

. . . It is against this danger that schoolmasters have to fight, for if education is beaten by training, civilization dies."[361] Thus, closely following Aristotle, Lewis claimed that whereas training is necessary to support life, education is what makes life worth living, and while Lewis would later admit that he followed Aristotle too closely in seeing educated, leisured activity as the purpose or end of life,[362] he nevertheless believed that in an ideal world – in Heaven and in glimpses here on Earth – human life would mean "the life of beings for whom the leisured activities of thought, art, literature [and] conversation are the end."[363]

Consequently, although Lewis neither gave vocational training enough credit nor appreciated the fact that trained men can also be educated, he was certainly right not only in pointing out the error of our own time – i.e. the veneration of professionals, who would have been glorified slaves in the past – but also in emphasizing the importance of the humanities and religious

---

361 Lewis, "Our English Syllabus," 82.
362 "Your criticisms on my Aristotelian idea of leisure are largely right. I wouldn't write that essay ["Our English Syllabus"] now." Lewis, *The Collected Letters of C. S. Lewis: Volume II*, 422 [July 16, 1940].
363 Lewis, "Our English Syllabus," 83.

education[364] (often against the sciences[365]) for human self-actualization.

364 "The author of an article entitled 'Old School Ties for All,' in your last issue, speaks with confidence of the religious training given at English public schools. I hope he is right; but if he is, his position is so important that it deserves to be defended in some detail against the rather different conclusions . . . in Mr. B. J. Sandhurst's 'How Heathen is Britain.' May we hope that his will be done in a second article?" C. S. Lewis, "Public Schools," *The Church Times* 130, no. 4 (October 3, 1947): 417. Moreover, in *The Silver Chair* Lewis seemed critical of schools like Experiment House where "Bibles [are] not encouraged" and where students do not learn about "Adam and Eve." Lewis, *The Silver Chair*, 14, 42. However, because Lewis was doubtful of religious education remaining in schools, he usually said that people need to focus on converting teachers, rather than having schools teach religious education: "The restraints imposed on you by 'secular education' are, no doubt, very galling [e.g. not being allowed to receive religious education by the teachers]. But I wonder whether secular education will do us all the harm the secularists hope. Secular *teachers* will. But Christian teachers in secular schools may, I sometimes think, do more good precisely because they are *not* allowed to give religious instruction in class. At least I think that, as a child, I sh[oul]d have been very allured and impressed by the discovery – which must be made when questions are asked – that the teacher believed firmly in a whole mass of things he wasn't allowed to teach!" Lewis, *The Collected Letters of C. S. Lewis: Volume III*, 331-2 [May 20, 1953]. Cf. "About the lack of religious education: of course you must be grieved, but remember how much religious education has exactly the opposite effect to that which was intended, how many hard atheists come from pious homes." Ibid., 507 [September 19, 1954]. Cf. "I do not, therefore, think that our hope of re-baptising England lies in trying to 'get at' the schools. Education is not *in that sense* a key position. To convert one's adult neighbour (just free from school) is the practical thing. . . . If you make the adults of today Christian, the children of tomorrow will receive a Christian education." C. S. Lewis, "On the Transmission of Christianity," in *C. S. Lewis: Essay Collection & Other Short Pieces*, ed. Lesley Walmsley (1946 essay reprint; London: HarperCollins, 2000), 615.

365 As the scientist Weston says, "I do not call classics and history and such trash education." Lewis, *Out of the Silent Planet*, 22. "The conception of a 'liberal' curiosity and of the 'liberal' studies which exist to satisfy it is one we owe to Aristotle. 'We call a man *free* whose life is lived for his own sake, not for that of others. In the same way philosophy is of all studies the only free one: because it alone exists for its own sake.' Of course *philosophy* does not here mean, as now, the rump or residuum left by the specialization of the various sciences. And perhaps Aristotle would not, in any case, have allowed the word to cover history. That hardly matters. In his conception of a study pursued not for some end beyond itself but for its own sake he has provided most of the activities we carry on at the universities with their charter. Of course this conception (Aristotle meant it only for freemen) has always been baffling and repellent to certain minds. There will always be people who think that any more astronomy than a ship's officer needs for navigation is a waste of time. There will always be those who, on discovering that history cannot really be turned to much practical account, will pronounce history to be Bunk. Aristotle would have called this servile or banausic; we, more civilly, may Christian it Fordism." Lewis, "Is History Bunk?" 645. Cf. Lewis, *The Collected Letters of C. S. Lewis: Volume II*, 93 [December 17, 1932]. Cf. "In our own age we have seen the sciences beating back the humanities as humanism once beat back metaphysics." Lewis, *Poetry and Prose in the Sixteenth Century*, 31.

Hence, even though Lewis distrusted humanist / neoscholastic / perennialist emphasis on teaching "the Best Books" (which he always thought would be arbitrary[366] and could lead to a "Charientocracy" or "the rule of the *cultured*" in an arbitrary, highbrow sense of the word[367]), he certainly favored perennialist educational theory, which underscores positive freedom, well-grounded instruction and merit-based democratic education,[368] over and against other rival educational theories, such as behaviorism, which supports manipulation, or progressivism, which stresses negative freedom and experimental, non-merit-based democratic education.[369]

366 "'The best' could only have meant what a committee of four or five dons, brought up in a particular tradition, happened to think the best. We should have been dictating the course of future knowledge and taste on the authority of our existing taste and ignorance." Lewis, "Our Idea of an 'English School,'" 76. Cf. Lewis, "Our English Syllabus," 87-8. Cf. Lewis, *The Collected Letters of C. S. Lewis: Volume I*, 581 [August 7, 1921]. Cf. Lewis, *The Collected Letters of C. S. Lewis: Volume III*, 1082-3 [August 25, 1959]. Cf. Lewis, "*De Audiendis Poetis*," 3.

367 "What I think we are really in danger of is something that would be only one degree less intolerable [than theocracy], and intolerable in almost the same way. I would call it Charientocracy; not the rule of the saints but the rule of the χαρίεντες, the *venustiores*, the Hotel de Rambouillet, the Wits, the Polite, the 'Souls,' the 'Apostles,' the Sensitive, the *Cultured*, the Integrated, or whatever the latest password may be." Lewis, "Lilies That Fester," 372.

368 While Lewis almost certainly supported the (very democratic) Education Act of 1944, which gave free public schooling to all children up to the age of fifteen, he strongly insisted that the ethos of schools must not become democratic in regard to merit, for if all students are rewarded simply for being themselves and not for what they produce on a competitive scale, then society cannot be maintained. Marwick, *A History of the Modern British Isles: 1914-199*, 157. Lewis, "Democratic Education," 597. Despite endorsing the competitiveness that goes with true democratic education, Lewis was well aware that such could easily breed pride and sin: "This of course is what Democratic education means – give them all an equal start and let the winners show their form. Hence Equality of Opportunity in practice means ruthless Competition during those very years which, I can't help feeling, nature meant to be free and frolicsome. Can it be good, from the age of 10 to the age of 23, to be always preparing for an exam, and always knowing that your whole worldly future depends on it: and not only knowing it, but perpetually reminded of it by your parents and masters? Is this the way to breed a nation of people in psychological, moral, and spiritual health? . . . The old inegalitarian societies had at least this in their favour, that at least *some* of their members (the eldest sons of gentlemen living on inherited land, *and* the agricultural labourers with no chance to rise and therefore no thought of rising) were often really outside the competitive struggle. I have an uneasy feeling that much of the manliness and toughness of the community depended on them. I'm not idealizing such societies. The gentry were often bad, the peasantry often (perhaps nearly always) ill treated. I mean only that we haven't solved the problem. Or, generalizing this, I find the social problem insoluble. It is 'How to extend to all the good life which unequal societies have (sometimes) produced for the few.'" Lewis, *The Collected Letters of C. S. Lewis: Volume III*, 17-8 [March 12, 1950].

369 As the devil Screwtape says, "In a word, we may reasonably hope for the virtual abolition of education when *I'm as good as you* has fully had its way." Lewis, "Screwtape Proposes

As for (2), Lewis believed that in order to prevent humanity from slipping into the arbitrary tyranny of behaviorism and pragmatism (both of which deny that we can know objective values), children, such as Caspian[370] and Digory,[371] must be taught universal values and be given basic, general knowledge onto which they can continually build and from which they can find their niche. Thus, on the one hand, early childhood education should be teacher-centered, for only the teacher can show the child what is natural, proper and basic ("it [is] but old birds teaching young birds to fly"[372]); on the other hand, early education should also be a matter of exposing children to many different alternatives in order to give them the broad fundamentals and help them decide what interests them ("It is natural and necessary that we should begin by giving a boy the keys to some four or five chambers of knowledge which we think the best"[373]). Hence, we could say that while the teacher restricts the child by steering him away from the edges of irrationality, immorality, falsehood, etc., the teacher does not want to stunt the child's growth by restricting his movements in the safe fields of reason, morality, true facts etc. Consequently, the teacher is neither authoritarian nor permissive, but rather is *authoritative*: he tells young students what is good, and explains to older students why it is good; he is consistent, has high expectations for the students, understands his subject matter well, makes and enforces just rules – with physical force if necessary,[374] and models true behavior.[375]

---

a Toast," 761. Cf. Lewis, *The Abolition of Man*, 406. In *The Silver Chair*, "Experiment House" is a progressive school. Lewis, *The Silver Chair*, 13.

370 Cf. "The education in kingship that Caspian receives is completely opposite from the training of the Controllers implied by King and Ketley's *The Control of Language*. It is based on medieval political philosophy, the law that Bracton had ceased to study. It begins in earnest when Caspian's tutor, Dr. Cornelius, takes the young prince up on the roof to view the conjunction of the two planets, Victory and Peace. This expresses the medieval idea that the king must study divine law and then convey it to his people as positive law. The orderly movement of the 'great lords of the upper sky' symbolizes the law of God, and the king must imitate the order of Heaven in wise laws to govern the movements and relationships of his subjects. Thus Dr. Cornelius charges Caspian to do what he can to bring back 'the long-lost days of freedom' (48)." Doris Myers, *C. S. Lewis in Context* (Kent, OH: Kent State University Press, 1994), 136.

371 Lewis, *The Magician's Nephew*, 147.

372 Lewis, *The Abolition of Man*, 422.

373 Lewis, "Our Idea of an 'English School,'" 75.

374 "Eustace (of course) was at a school where they didn't have corporal punishment, so the sensation [of being spanked] was quite new to him." Lewis, *The Voyage of the Dawn Treader*, 31. Cf. "Obedience is one of the virtues [the pupil] has come to the [schoolmaster] to learn; his motive for reading one book and neglecting another must constantly be that he was told so." Lewis, "Our English Syllabus," 85.

375 "'Shasta didn't [run away]' snorted Bree. 'At least he ran in the right direction: ran *back*. And that is what shames me most of all. I, who called myself a war-horse and boasted

As for (3), despite not having had a theory of development as sophisticated as a Jean Piaget, a Lev Vygotsky or an Erik Erikson, Lewis appreciated that children develop over time and his educational theory took this into account. For instance, he agreed with Plato and Aristotle that at an early age children simply need to be told what is right and wrong and should be encouraged to play in a manner which is in agreement with objective values so that when they come of age, they will have the proper "stock responses" and proto-virtues in place. In addition, Lewis thought that schoolchildren need to focus more on academic basics, such as "grammar, dates, and prosody"[376] (but not spelling[377]), and not worry too much about expressing their views on the little knowledge they have gained.[378] However, Lewis maintained that

---

of a hundred fights, to be beaten by a little human boy – a child, a mere foal, who had never held a sword nor had any good nurture or example in his life!'" Lewis, *The Horse and His Boy*, 128.

376 C. S. Lewis, "The Parthenon and the Optative," in *C. S. Lewis: Essay Collection & Other Short Pieces*, ed. Lesley Walmsley (1944 essay reprint; London: HarperCollins, 2000), 444. Cf. "Before some audiences I should feel it my duty to insist rather strongly on the value of grammar." Lewis, "The Idea of an 'English School,'" 63. Cf. "Two of the most cogent essays [in Dorothy Sayers' *The Poetry of Search and the Poetry of Statement*] are 'The Work Tools of Learning' and the 'The Teaching of Latin,' but it would be too much to hope that they will influence educational practices." C. S. Lewis, "Rhyme and Reason," review of *The Poetry of Search and the Poetry of Statement*, by Dorothy Sayers, *Daily Telegraph* (December 1, 1963). Although Lewis spoke strongly of teaching schoolchildren the basics, he did not make it clear what subjects he thought should be studied in schools. Hence, we do not know if he would he have favored teaching, for instance, the seven liberal arts (Grammar, Dialectic, Rhetoric, Arithmetic, Music, Geometry, and Astronomy).

377 In agreement with the latest research, Lewis thought approximate spelling, as opposed to precise spelling, a better use of students' and teachers' time: "Nearly everything I have ever read about spelling reform assumes from the outset that it is necessary for us all to spell alike. Why? We got on for centuries without an agreed common orthography. Most men of my age remember censoring the letters of soldiers and know that even the wildest idiosyncrasies of spelling hardly ever made them unintelligible. . . . A few hard words will still have to be learned by everyone. But for the rest, who would be a penny the worse if *though* and *tho*, *existence* and *existance* . . . were all equally tolerated? As things are, surely Liberty is the simple and inexpensive 'Reform' we need? This would save children and teachers thousands of hours' work. It would also force those to whom applications for jobs are made to exercise their critical faculties on the logic and vocabulary of the candidate instead of tossing his letter aside with the words 'can't even spell.'" C. S. Lewis, "Spelling Reform," *The Times Educational Supplement* (Jan 1, 1960): 13. Cf. Eggen and Kauchak, *Educational Psychology*, 204

378 Lewis, "The Parthenon and the Optative," 444. Cf. Lewis, *An Experiment in Criticism*, 93. In "The Parthenon and the Optative" and "Is English Doomed?" Lewis criticized the Norwood Report, which was a government document recommending changes to schooling. While Lewis felt that the document endorsed students' critically engaging with literary texts instead of learning the basics of grammar and so on, he had not

once students go to university – once "education" (the process of receiving teaching) becomes "learning" (the pursuit of knowledge for its own sake)[379] – then students should focus on one particular area of study[380] and be treated as equals by their tutors, which is to say that students should then be able to express their opinions about the facts they have studied since they are both knowledgeable and developed. Yet even with this said, we do well to keep in mind that Lewis detested research degrees since he believed that university students still need to focus more on attaining knowledge and less on trying to be creative:

> The ['Research'] system was, I believe, first devised to attract the Americans and to emulate the scientists. . . . In science, I gather, a young student fresh from his First in the Tripos can really share in the work of one of his seniors in a way that is useful to himself and even to the subject. But this is not true of the man who has just got his First in English or Modern Languages. Such a man, far from being able or anxious . . . to add to the sum of human knowledge, wants to acquire a good deal more of the knowledge [he] already [has]. . . . To head him off from [this knowledge], to pinfold him in some small inquiry whose chief claim often is that no one has ever made it before, is cruel and frustrating.[381]

---

read the Report very carefully; as Joel Heck tells us: "In this, Lewis revealed the fact that he did not read carefully part III, chapter 4 of the report. Earlier, the authors had written: '[T]oo many boys and girls after leaving the Secondary School show themselves deficient in ability to master the thought of a passage or chapter and to express their ideas in writing or orally with precision and clarity.' Hence the authors recommended that more time be spent on the basics." Heck, *Irrigating Deserts*, 158-9.

379 "Now learning, considered in itself, has, on my view, no connexion at all with education. It is an activity for men – that is for beings who have already been humanized by this kneading and moulding process. . . . Learning is not education; but it can be used educationally by those who do not propose to pursue learning all their lives." Lewis, "Our English Syllabus," 84, 86. While "learning" in Lewis's sense here sounds selfish and unchristian, Lewis did add in another essay that the scholar can glorify God by countering false philosophies and promoting clear understanding. Lewis, "Learning in War-Time," 584.

380 "I think that the high lights chosen by his elders and the wide area of ordinary country explored on his own, are both necessary elements in a man's education. But I feel very strongly that the place for the selected high lights is the school, and the place for the other is the University." Lewis, "Our Idea of an 'English School,'" 75. Cf. "As Hegel saw, a perfect study of anything requires a knowledge of everything." Lewis, "Our English Syllabus," 87-8.

381 Lewis, "Interim Report," 642. "For Research as practiced at this and other universities to-day I make no defence. I detest it." Lewis, "Correspondence," 7. Cf. Lewis, "Our Idea of an 'English School,'" 77. Cf. Lewis, "Our English Syllabus," 84.

Now if Lewis's educational theory strikes us as a bit rigid and archaic, we are struck correctly, for while Lewis, like Plato and Aristotle before him, did correctly perceive the importance of giving children both correct stock responses and an introduction to the basics, he, like his masters, failed to appreciate how vital it is for young children to exercise all their faculties.[382] Moreover, while Lewis, a university professor, certainly spoke truer of university education than he did of early childhood education, it is still possible to see his contempt for research degrees as springing from a rather pessimistic view of cognitive development. But then, we must remember that Lewis was one of the best-read men of his generation and it was precisely because of his vast reservoir of knowledge that he was able to be as creative as he was. And it is with this in mind that I now turn to the final chapter of this book, which has to do with Lewis's aesthetics.

---

382 Eggen and Kauchak, *Educational Psychology*, 234-57.

Chapter Ten

Aesthetics

Aesthetics is the branch of philosophy that studies the nature of Beauty and art. While some people might be tempted to think that Lewis wrote more on aesthetic issues than on anything else, they would be mistaken, for whereas aesthetics has to do with broad, theoretical questions concerning Beauty and art, Lewis's writings on literary history, literary criticism and, to a lesser degree, literary theory are too specific. In addition, although people might point to Lewis's vast outpourings on Myth as evidence of his intense interest in aesthetics, these people would only be partly correct, for as I repeatedly stressed throughout chapter four, even though Myth touches Beauty and can indeed be made into art (myth), Myth is not identical to Beauty. Thus, while I will make many references to Myth herein, I will mainly focus on discussing the nature of Beauty and Lewis's broad theory of art. Let me also add that although I will go beyond the usual boundaries of aesthetics and discuss some aspects of literary theory and criticism, my reason for doing so is purely philosophical since Lewis's larger philosophical principles illuminate many of his literary principles and as such are important for scholars interested in Lewis's literary theory and criticism to be aware of.

I: Beauty

From previous chapters, we know both that the "first beauty" Lewis ever experienced was his brother's toy garden, and that he knew his experience of Beauty in the garden was something more than a subconscious erotic impulse.[1] Moreover, while Lewis's earliest aesthetic experiences were intensely mythical and sublime (hence, his love of Norse mythology and the "sublimity" of Lucretius[2]), Lewis the Lucretian materialist largely understood

---

1   Lewis, "Psycho-Analysis and Literary Criticism," 295.
2   "Theism is 'sublime': but if anyone thinks 'sublimity' theistic, let him read Lucretius." C. S. Lewis, review of *Longius and English Criticism*, by T. R. Henn, *The Oxford Magazine* 53 (December 6, 1934): 264.

these experiences to be those of Beauty.

And for the most part, this understanding continued into Lewis's pseudo-Manichean dualist phase, wherein thanks to Plato, Berkeley and others, he came to see Beauty as objective and as a synonym for Spirit; however, while Plato would have said that (material) Nature is beautiful insofar as it reflects (spiritual) Beauty, Lewis was deeply engrossed with Berkeleyan replies to Lockean epistemology, and so concluded that since we cannot know how sensations from the physical world can enter our minds, we have no right attributing any Beauty whatsoever to Nature:

> The thing in your last letter with which I most want to disagree is the remark about Beauty and nature; apparently I did not make myself very clear. You say that nature is beautiful, and that is the view we all start with. But let us see what we mean. If you take a tree, for instance, you call it beautiful because of its shape, colour and motions, and perhaps a little because of association. Now these colours etc are sensations in my eye, produced by vibrations on the aether between me and the tree: the real tree is something quite different – a combination of colourless, shapeless, invisible atoms. It follows then that neither the tree, nor any other material object can be beautiful in itself: I can never see them as they are, and if I could it would give me no delight. The beauty therefore is not in matter at all, but is something purely spiritual, arising mysteriously out of the relation between me & the tree: or perhaps as I suggest in my Song, out of some indwelling spirit behind the matter of the tree – the Dryad in fact ["Atoms dead could never thus / Wake the human heart of us, / Unless the beauty that we see / Part of endless beauty be, / Thronged with spirits that have trod / Where the bright foot-prints of God / Lie fresh upon the heavenly sod."[3]]. . . . You see the conviction is gaining ground on me . . . that Beauty is the call of the spirit in that something to the spirit in us.[4]

This is to say that largely because of his antirealism in regard to secondary qualities, Lewis denied the beauty of Nature; and because he was relatively humble, he denied that he himself was the cause of Beauty.[5] Thus, he attributed the idea of Beauty neither to Nature nor to himself but to Spirit or some relation between sprits.

Consequently, supported by such an elevated view of Beauty, Lewis's WWI art, i.e. his WWI poetry, was not overly-focused on ugliness, instability and despair, unlike most of the art produced around WWI – art such as T. S.

---

3   Lewis, *The Collected Letters of C. S. Lewis: Volume I*, 373 [May 23, 1918].
4   Ibid., 374 [May 29, 1918].
5   Ibid., 377 [June 3, 1918].

Eliot's "Waste land," Igor Stravinsky's *The Rite of Spring* or Marcel Duchamp's "Nude Descending a Staircase (No. 2)." Moreover, Lewis's wartime art was further bolstered against ugliness and despair by his habit of reading older, more tried-and-true works of literature:

> Both [Johnson] and all the other literary people whom I have met since I left home for Oxford, have made me feel how deep is my ignorance of modern, that is to say, *contemporary*, literature, especially poetry. I have often sat in amazed silence amid glib talk of Rupert Brooke, Masefield, Chesterton, Bottomley etc. But after all I suppose our steady nibbling at older works is a safe-guard against 'crazes' – deadly things that arise so easily about a new writer.[6]

Now when Lewis returned to Oxford after the war and converted to Stoical materialism, his theory of Beauty underwent two important changes. First, no longer committed to believing that Beauty is purely a spiritual quality, Lewis the materialist– partly due to Bergson's stress on the vitality and energy of life in general – was able to rescue his romantic, pre-war love of Nature; hence, he said later, "Nature never taught me that there exists a God of glory and of infinite majesty. I had to learn that in other ways. But nature gave the word *glory* a meaning for me."[7] Second, Lewis's appreciation of Nature's beauty was further honed by the lesson he learned from Jenkin (and Aristotle) that one must always try to relish the quiddity or essence of each thing and, insofar as it is just, treat each particular as an end in itself. As a result of these important changes, Lewis's aesthetic theory stressed six things: (1) Beauty is *not* simply expression, for *what* is expressed is important; (2) beautiful things do not appear to us as simple impressions, but are, in fact, a union of impressions; (3) Plato is right that beautiful things are often reminders of other beautiful things, and Wordsworth is right that the beauty remembered might perfect the beauty of a particular thing; (4) there is also a purely sensuous element in Beauty, for certain musical notes, for instance, satisfy certain nerves; (5) Beauty is not merely contemplative or theoretical, but is mostly an emotional stirring and an invitation to who-knows-what; and (6) Beauty must be objective, but it is unclear *how* it can be so; thus we read:

> I wonder what has to be done about your question of Beauty? The popular theory among contemporaries is that Beauty is simply expression: as soon as a shape or a sound becomes a means by which I find the expression or 'objectification' of myself, it is beautiful. That

---

6   Ibid., 342 [November 4, 1917].
7   Lewis, *The Four Loves*, 17.

is why (they say) that even things 'uncomely & broken' find their aesthetic value in the right place. Not satisfied with this view myself: for it makes it indifferent *what* is expressed. E. g. a face that expressed cruelty, stupidity or greed would be beautiful if only it expressed them thoroughly. They w[oul]d probably say that greed etc are themselves 'inexpressive' of the *idea* of the individual – the thing he is tending to be, his potential completeness. To me it seems that a great many different emotions are united in the perception of beauty: it may turn out to be not a simple thing but a result of unions. For one thing nearly all beautiful sights are to me chiefly important as *reminders* of other beautiful sights: without memory it would be a poor affair. The process presumably has a beginning but once going it grows like a snowball. Could it be the joy remembered ('Which now is sad because it has been sweet') is a necessary element in Beauty? There is too, I think, a purely sensuous element: that such and such notes or tints (*in themselves* – not in their combinations) just happen to satisfy our nerves of hearing & sight – as certain foods satisfy those of tastes. This w[oul]d be rather a condition of beauty, perhaps, than an element in it. One thing is plain, that the statements continually made about Beauty's being pure contemplation, stirring no impulse, being the antithesis of the practical or energizing side of us, are wrong. On the contrary beauty seems to me to be always an invitation of some sort & usually an invitation to we don't know what. A wood seen as 'picturesque' by a fool (who'd like a frame round it) may be purely contemplated: seen as 'beautiful' it seems rather to say 'come into me.' But this is getting away from your point – much more important – whether its objective & has a real right & wrong apart from our opinions. One always feels that it has. But I don't understand: it must be objective & yet how can it?[8]

Piecing this all together we may say that while Lewis had no metaphysical grounds for asserting the objectivity of Beauty (this may have been a relic from his pseudo-Manichean dualist phase), he believed that the work of art itself – be it natural or man-made – contains a unique essence or quality that is in itself either beautiful or ugly but always meaningful and whose beauty, which has the power to move man, can be recognized and given greater appreciation by man's reflection upon it. Consequently, this theory convinced Lewis the Stoical materialist that Beauty is actually able to elevate the individual to a more perfect mode of existence, for "aesthetic experience [is] not merely pleasing but 'valuable.'"[9]

Now immediately prior to his conversion to idealism, Lewis's interest

---

8   Lewis, *The Collected Letters of C. S. Lewis: Volume I*, 567-8 [July 1921].
9   Lewis, *Surprised by Joy*, 1364.

in aesthetics peaked. This was largely due to Barfield, who was Lewis's interlocutor during The Great War, and Lewis's philosophy tutor and renowned philosopher of art, E. F. Carritt, who pushed Lewis to read many aesthetic theories, such as those by Benedetto Croce[10] and George Santayana.[11] All of these men and their philosophies of Beauty fortified Lewis's belief that aesthetic experience is valuable,[12] which, of course, resulted in Lewis's idealist belief that art is an image of the spiritual life (more on this later).

However, Lewis did not agree with all that the aforementioned philosophers – or others – had to say. For instance, part of the reason why Lewis became an idealist in the first place was because he disagreed with Carritt, who claimed that materialism can make sense of Beauty.[13] In addition, Lewis deviated from many at Oxford who insisted that Beauty and moral Goodness are nearly synonymous ("I couldn't make [Herbert] Paton [a professor of philosophy at Oxford] admit any difference between art and virtue"[14]). And while Lewis agreed with Barfield in saying that the poetic should not be *reduced* to the prosaic, Lewis disagreed with Barfield, who claimed that the imagination produces *truth* rather than (even profound) *meaning*; hence, Lewis wrote,

> Have you so exhausted in your survey the horizons of the spiritual world that you are sure that there can be no other value than that one of Truth with which you seem at present most concerned, and that you can therefore affirm that if Beauty will not be taken in as a door keeper to Truth, or as Truth's domino, her occupation must be gone?

10 "Carritt made some interesting remarks on Croce's theory of universals. The true concepts (Truth, Beauty, etc.) are immanent, transcendent: the mathematical are *only* transcendent – that is, they have no particulars: the pseudo-concepts are only immanent, that is they are mere arbitrary groupings of particulars. He also drew my attention to the difference between Kant's early and later views of Noumena, which I must look up." Lewis, *All My Road Before Me*, 36 [May 17, 1922]. "[I] took Croce's *Essence of Aesthetic* out of Union. . . . I finished Croce: a difficult and provocative book. The different activities of the spirits apparently grow out of one another in a cycle. Emotion leads to image, and when we have made the image we want to understand: from understanding we turn to action which leads to new emotion and the cycle repeats. He assumes the unreality of matter, regarding it as we regard the news Queen Anne is dead." Ibid., 39 [May 23, 1922].
11 "I read Santayana's *Reason in Art* for an hour: very pugnacious and bracing and mostly true." Ibid., 182 [January 19, 1923].
12 Cf. "Beauty is no negligible or superfluous appendage to any man's life, but an aspect in which he must value his whole world. It is no luxury, but often an exacting and severe ideal. It is the salt without which life would be savourless." Carritt, *The Theory of Beauty*, 17.
13 Ibid., 21.
14 Lewis, *All My Road Before Me*, 356 [February 26, 1925].

> . . . From what you have said at various times I gather that your real reason is a fear lest, if the value we find in beauty cannot be claimed as a kind of Truth, it will turn out to be nothing but pleasure under a pompous name.[15]

Nevertheless, while Lewis believed that his idealism, in particular, his absolute idealism, could preserve his belief in the objectivity of Beauty and the distinctions between moral Goodness, Beauty and Truth, the logical incoherence of absolute idealism ultimately forced Lewis to recognize that in the long run, absolute idealism could preserve the objectivity of neither Truth, Goodness nor Beauty.

As a result, Lewis converted to theism and then to Christianity. Subsequently, he followed the Neoplatonic Christian tradition in maintaining that God is identical to Beauty and that "Beauty descends from God into nature;"[16] thus, in *The Magician's Nephew*, Lewis envisioned Aslan singing a heartbreakingly beautiful song to create the world of Narnia: "There were no words. There was hardly even a tune. But it was, beyond comparison, the most beautiful noise [Digory] had ever heard. It was so beautiful he could hardly bear it."[17] Moreover, following Plato in the *Phaedrus*, Lewis believed that while some things in Nature are more beautiful than others[18] (even though all things are fallen[19]), the beauty of each thing is only fully

---

15   Lewis, *The Collected Letters of C. S. Lewis: Volume III*, 1612, 1613 [1927 "The Great War Letters" Series I, Letter 2].

16   Lewis, *The Collected Letters of C. S. Lewis: Volume I*, 933 [August 28, 1930]. Cf. "Through [the body] God showed me that whole side of His beauty wh[ich] is embodied in colour, sound, smell and size." Lewis, *The Collected Letters of C. S. Lewis: Volume III*, 1384 [November 26, 1962]. Cf. Lewis, "The Trouble with 'X' . . ." 358.

17   Lewis, *The Magician's Nephew*, 93. While the idea of God or the gods creating the world through music is as old as Pythagoras, it is interesting to note that Lewis's friend Tolkien also used this idea in his work: "There was Eru, the One, who in Arda is called Ilúvatar; and he made first the Ainur, the Holy Ones, that were the offspring of his thought, and they were with him before aught else was made. And he spoke to them, propounding to them themes of music; and they sang before him, and he was glad." J. R. R. Tolkien, *The Silmarillion*, ed. Christopher Tolkien (London: Unwin Paperbacks, 1989), 15.

18   "Beauty is not democratic; she reveals herself more to the few than the many, more to the persistent and disciplined seekers than to the careless." Lewis, "Democratic Education," 598. Cf. "The idea that some preferences in art are really better than others cannot be got rid of." C. S. Lewis, "Different Tastes in Literature," in *C. S. Lewis: Essay Collection & Other Short Pieces*, ed. Lesley Walmsley (1946 essay reprint; London: HarperCollins, 2000), 466.

19   "It is enough to say there that Nature, like us but in her different way, is much alienated from her Creator, though in her, as in us, gleams of the old beauty remain." Lewis, "On Living in an Atomic Age," 365.

realizable when it is appreciated as a reflection of "eternal Beauty;"[20] hence, in *The Problem of Pain*, Lewis insisted that "each of the redeemed shall forever know and praise some one aspect of the Divine beauty better than any other creature can,"[21] and in *Perelandra*, Lewis wrote, "[T]he very beauty of [the King] lay in the certainty that [he] was a copy, like and not the same, an echo, a rhyme, an exquisite reverberation of the uncreated music prolonged in a created medium."[22] Consequently, this leads to two important points about what I call "aesthetic justice."

First, since God both gave quiddity, definition and meaning to all natural things and designed man such that he can recognize the nature and beauty of such things, man shows aesthetic justice when he relishes the particularity of all things – firstly as God has created them (Nature) and secondly as man justly rearranges what God has made (art). Needless to say, this aesthetic justice entails a doctrine of objective aesthetic value,[23] and as we recall from previous chapters, it also leads to the Platonic-Aristotelian pedagogical theory of Beauty, which states that training people to be aesthetically just – helping people to acquire proper habits or "stock responses" to things (e.g. "pain is black"[24]) – is fundamental not only because it leads to true aesthetic judgment, but also because true aesthetic judgment often leads to true moral judgment:

---

20 "[A]n author should never conceive himself as bringing into existence beauty or wisdom which did not exist before, but simply and solely as trying to embody in terms of his own art some reflection of eternal Beauty and Wisdom." Lewis, "Christianity and Literature," 416.

21 Lewis, *The Problem of Pain*, 551.

22 Lewis, *Perelandra*, 332.

23 Lewis, *The Personal Heresy*, 104.

24 "What is good or happy has always been high like the heavens and bright like the sun. Evil and misery were deep and dark from the first. Pain is black in Homer, and goodness is a middle point for Alfred no less than for Aristotle. To ask how these married pairs of sensibles and insensibles first came together would be great folly; the real question is how they ever came apart, and to answer that question is beyond the province of a mere historian." Lewis, *The Allegory of Love*, 44. Cf. "I am misrepresented. From that sentence a reader would gather that in my *Preface to Paradise Lost* I included the maxims 'Honesty is the best policy' and 'War is horrible' among the maxims with which I wished men to be habitually indoctrinated. This is not so. I wrote not 'Honesty is the best policy' but 'Virtue is lovely': not 'War is horrible' but 'Death is bitter.' I have no wish to defend my maxims at this point against those which have been substituted for them: my point is that they are different and indeed involve a difference of outlook which is fundamental." C. S. Lewis, "A Difference of Outlook," *The Guardian* (June 27, 1947): 283. Cf. Lewis, *That Hideous Strength*, 701.

That elementary rectitude of human response, at which we are so ready to fling the unkind epithets of 'stock,' 'crude,' 'bourgeois,' and 'conventional,' so far from being 'given' is a delicate balance of trained habits, laboriously acquired and easily lost, on the maintenance of which depends both our virtues and our pleasures and even, perhaps, the survival of our species.[25]

Second, if people try to establish any created thing – be it God-made or man-made – as the highest Beauty, they act aesthetically (and morally) unjustly, for while true Beauty, i.e. God, calls us *through* beautiful things, He warns us not to rest *in* beautiful things: "The books or music in which we thought the beauty was located will betray us if we trust to them; it was not *in* them, it only came *through* them."[26] Indeed, going beyond this and most aesthetic theories, Lewis insisted that true Beauty is not something that we merely want to ponder; rather, it is something that we long to be surrounded and filled by: "We do not merely want to *see* beauty, though, God knows even that is bounty enough. We want something else which can hardly be put into words – to be united with the beauty we see, to pass into it, to receive it into ourselves, to bathe in it, to become part of it."[27]

Because of Lewis's Neoplatonic Christian theory of Beauty – i.e. God is Beauty, Creation participates in Beauty, and man has a heavenly desire for, among other things, God *qua* Beauty – many scholars, such as Philip Tallon,[28] Peter Kreeft,[29] and Philip Harrold[30] have recognized that Beauty plays an important role in Lewis's philosophy, particularly in the various theodicies he constructs. It is true, of course, that few of these philosophers have stressed Lewis's important distinction between Myth and Beauty: while

25   Lewis, *A Preface to Paradise Lost*, 56-7.
26   Lewis, "The Weight of Glory," 98.
27   Ibid., 104.
28   Philip Tallon, "Evil and the Cosmic Dance: C. S. Lewis and Beauty's Place in Theodicy," in *C. S. Lewis as Philosopher: Truth, Goodness, and Beauty*, ed. David Baggett, Gary Habermas and Jerry Walls, 195-210 (Downers Grove, IL: InterVarsity Press, 2008), 199.
29   Peter Kreeft, "Lewis's Philosophy of Truth, Goodness, and Beauty," in *C. S. Lewis as Philosopher: Truth, Goodness, and Beauty*, ed. David Baggett, Gary Habermas and Jerry Walls, 23-38 (Downers Grove, IL: InterVarsity Press, 2008), 23.
30   Despite being completely wrong when he says that "Lewis was certainly aware of the social construction of knowledge [and] the inaccessibility of pure objectivity," Philip Harrold is right that Lewis's aesthetics played an important role in his philosophy and theology, particularly in regard to smuggling important truths "past the watchful dragons." Philip Harrold, "Stealing Past the Watchful Dragons: C. S. Lewis's Incarnational Aesthetics and Today's Emerging Imagination," in *Apologist, Philosopher, & Theologian*, vol. 3, *C. S. Lewis: Life, Works, and Legacy*, ed. Bruce Edwards, 183-208 (Westport, CT: Praeger, 2007), 193.

myth is an art, its value does not lie in its aesthetic nature (Beauty) but in its ability to communicate concrete universality (Myth);[31] however, most of these philosophers have rightly recognized Lewis's very orthodox insistence that all distinctions in God – be it between Truth, Goodness, Myth, or Beauty – are merely formal distinctions, which do not actually obtain in God's indivisible nature.

II: Art

Although Lewis never defined Beauty and only thrice defined art, we may say, for the sake of distinguishing this section from the previous one, that while Beauty is the attractive quality of a given thing, art is the body of knowledge that helps people use certain instruments to achieve certain practical (as opposed to theoretical) goals. Consequently, since I have already examined Lewis's theory of aesthetic quality (Beauty), I now want to examine his theory of aesthetic method (art).

Throughout his Lucretian materialist and pseudo-Manichean dualist phases, Lewis said little about the philosophy of art, for although he learned grammar, rhetoric and artistic appreciation at Wyvern College and greatly enjoyed reading and writing literature at all times, the only aspect of aesthetics he was interested in was the metaphysical and epistemological status of Beauty, which we have already discussed.

However, when he was hovering between Stoical materialism and idealism, he joined many literary and philosophical societies, such as the Philosopher's Tea and the Martlets,[32] and wrote quite a bit about the nature of art. From what I can gather, he appears to have held the following beliefs: (1) a work of art is not merely an "expression," but is an expression about, and therefore always dependent on, *something*; hence, he agreed with Plato that the "something" is ontologically greater than the art it inspired;[33] (2) a work of art is not primarily to be criticized and Contemplated (in Alexander's

---

31   While in earlier chapters I made some connection between Myth and the Sublime, those connections, such as between the *numinous*, Myth and the Sublime, were not formally made by Lewis. Additionally, it would be misleading to say that Lewis made any formal distinction between the Sublime and Beauty.

32   For more on the Martlets see Walter Hooper, "To the Martlets," in *C. S. Lewis: Speaker & Teacher*, ed. Carolyn Keefe, 47-84 (Grand Rapids, MI: Zondervan, 1974).

33   Lewis, *All My Road Before Me*, 197 [February 14, 1923]. Cf. "Thanks for the theory of poetry. The most valuable part of it, and the part which sh[oul]d be insisted on is that 'a poet who is only a poet is not the greatest poet.' The assumption that a great poem must have nothing in it but poetry has 'worked like madness in the brain' of too many of us." Lewis, *The Collected Letters of C. S. Lewis: Volume I*, 508 [September 25, 1920].

sense) but rather is to "be experienced and enjoyed;"[34] (3) biographical information is rarely necessary for art appreciation;[35] (4) *pace* Croce,[36] a work of art is fundamentally "a social thing": it exists to be communicated or at least potentially communicated;[37] (5) a work of art is that which has had a certain form (in the Platonic sense of the word) imposed upon it;[38] and (6) depending on the art form and the artist, art aims at such things as "vision," "exaltation," "inspiration," "criticism of life," "wisdom," "nobility," and so on.[39]

It is remarkable to note that from his Stoical materialist days onward, Lewis never changed his mind about any of these six points. Nevertheless, when he became an idealist, he did have to account for these six points in unique ways since he needed to fit his theory of art to his larger philosophical framework. Consequently, he defined art in various ways, such as "techne,"[40] "the craft of expression,"[41] "the transference from one soul to another of any

---

34 Lewis, *All My Road Before Me*, 198 [February 14, 1923].

35 The June 18, 1924 Martlets minutes record the following: "The minutes of the last meeting were read and carried; the President then called upon Mr. Lewis to read his paper on James Stephens. Mr. Lewis began by congratulating himself on *his entire ignorance of biographical detail* and proceeded forthwith to a critical appreciation of his author's works." Quoted in Walter Hooper, preface to *Selected Literary Essays*, by C. S. Lewis, ed. Walter Hooper, vii-xx (Cambridge: Cambridge University Press, 1969), xiii.

36 Croce, *The Essence of Aesthetic*, 33.

37 Lewis, *All My Road Before Me*, 198 [February 14, 1923].

38 Ibid., 199 [February 14, 1923].

39 In a letter to his friend Leo Baker, Lewis wrote, "It is in your 'Words used for the purpose they alone can serve' that you really get to the heart of [what poetry is]. All this talk that every critic gives us about vision etc is darkening counsil: for vision, exaltation, criticism of life etc are not poetry, but the subject of poetry: and not the peculiar subject of poetry but the subject of all art. What we want to find is – that which is proper to poetry alone: what is the method by which poetry *and no other art* performs the duties shared with all art? Doubtless you would answer that in the same way as I w[oul]d & come to a definition something like this 'Poetry is the art of utilizing the informal or irrational values of words to express that which can only be symbolized by their formal or conventional meanings.' These values include chiefly sound & association: also of course their 'group' sound or rhythms which are above and beyond their individual sounds: here is the meaning & justification of metre. Hence the value of the test 'Could this be said as well in prose?': if the answer is in the affirmative the poem is condemned. As to all those other things – inspiration, purpose, nobility, wisdom etc, there are two answers. (1.) These are not peculiar to the art of poetry but common to all art: it is unfair, therefore, to include them in the definition of poetry. (2) If a man was not an artist (i.e. had not these other possessions) he c[oul]d not have things inexpressible by ordinary speech to tell us, c[oul]d not therefore be a poet." Lewis, *The Collected Letters of C. S. Lewis: Volume I*, 508-9 [September 25, 1920].

40 Lewis, *Clivi Hamiltonis Summae Metaphysices Contra Anthroposophos Libri II*, 59.

41 Ibid.

experience in its concreteness, as opposed to the inference of its conceptual element only,"[42] and "that which presents objects to us with the greatest concreteness, being allowed in return to dispense with all consideration whether these objects are subjective or objective."[43] In order to understand these definitions, we need to consider four things.

First, Lewis argued that art is more concrete than history since history only focuses on the concreteness of Appearances, whereas art can see things as they are in Reality or as Spirit sees them. Art, in other words, can represent concrete universality.

Second, Lewis believed that within the limits of a particular work of art, such as the play *Hamlet*, art is more systematic than science "for we understand all the reciprocal relations within a play or a story more fully than science can ever understand the world."[44] While this seems like an outrageous claim, what Lewis meant was that whereas the systemization of science is rigid, set and legalistic, the systemization of art is fluid, spiritual and dependent on human interpreters in order to bring out all nuances. The difference, in other words, is between the letter of the law (science) and the spirit of the law (art).

Third, Lewis maintained that the principle job of art is to train people to be disinterested. He believed this was largely possible since the objects of art are not as real as other objects, and so do not tempt the passions as much. Consequently, art should teach people to appreciate things as they really are, and not as people, through desire and fear, would make, and thereby distort, them. While this latter point in particular seems odd and mistaken, especially given the value Lewis placed on being sensitive to the guidance of heavenly desire, we need to remember that for Lewis the idealist, far more often than not passions and emotions cause the individual to focus on his finite self, the soul, and his own feelings about things, instead of on his infinite self, Spirit, and how things really are from Spirit's all-encompassing point-of-view. As a result, the Oxford don thought that while it is acceptable for people to feel desire in the presence of Beauty and beautiful things, such desire is not the goal of art.

Fourth, because art is so concrete, systematic and disinterested, it gives people "a foretaste or shadow of the full consciousness of Spirit."[45] However, while Lewis disagreed with, for instance, Croce's creative antirealism, which

42 Ibid., 59-60
43 Ibid., 45.
44 Ibid.
45 Ibid.

states that aesthetic experience does not allow for any cognitive distinction between natural aesthetic experience (e.g. a storm) and artificial aesthetic experience (e.g. a fictitious storm),[46] Lewis did concede that "art cannot of itself assure us that the objects presented are more than the idlest subjective fancies."[47] For this reason, he thought that despite having value, art is still only an *image* of the spiritual life – a *representation* of the life of the soul when it wills and sees as Spirit wills and sees – rather than the life itself. And this, incidentally, accounts for the extension of Lewis's Stoical materialist belief that art is always expression about something, which, for him, implied the superiority (but not necessarily the aesthetic superiority[48]) of the something, e.g. a real tree, over and against the art, e.g. a painting of a tree. Additionally, the artist's dependence on real things or the things of Spirit – which may also be of mysterious things that the artist does not understand, such as Myth – entails that the artist's creativity lies in rearranging the things that Spirit created rather than, *pace* aesthetes who make the artist's "genius" supreme, bringing into existence something which previously did not exist; thus, "the poet . . . can be free [only] in the sense that to utter the truth of Spirit is freedom."[49]

Now as I said before, when Lewis became a theist and a Christian, most of his earlier beliefs about art remained with him. However, despite some fluctuation in regard to the stress he put on art and moralizing, the major change pertaining to art that occurred during Lewis's Christian phase was in de-emphasizing the importance of art:

---

46   "About Croce. Croce thinks that nothing assertive *or cognitive* can enter an aesthetic experience at all: that at the moment of enjoying a storm you cease to be aware that it is a real or imagined storm: the distinction disappears. I think that the knowledge of the object's reality or unreality survives and makes an aesthetic difference: that the fall of Rome differs aesthetically from the fall of Troy just because it is judged to be real. Not that the real is aesthetically better than the imaginary, but just aesthetically different. As a natural corollary, Croce thinks like you [Barfield] that there is strictly speaking no aesthetic experience of nature: for in being aesthetically experienced it ceases to be asserted as 'Nature': in fact you make your work of art out of it much as a painter does. This has always seemed to me untrue: the reality of the objects being to me the very differentia of my aesthetic experience of the [perceptible God]. Again, Croce regulates all so-called experience of nature to a very low level – as inchoate art: and in this I disagree with him. I have never considered my quarrel with the Croceans in connection with *poetry*." Lewis, *The Collected Letters of C. S. Lewis: Volume III*, 1625-6 [1927? "The Great War Letters" Series I, Letter 6].

47   Lewis, *Clivi Hamiltonis Summae Metaphysices Contra Anthroposophos Libri II*, 45.

48   Lewis, *The Collected Letters of C. S. Lewis: Volume III*, 1625-6 [1927? "The Great War Letters" Series I, Letter 6].

49   Lewis, *Replies to Objections in Detail*, 116.

At an early age I came to believe that the life of culture (that is, of intellectual and aesthetic activity) was very good for its own sake, or even that it was good for man. After my conversion, which occurred in my later twenties, I continued to hold this belief without consciously asking how it could be reconciled with my new belief that the end of human life was salvation in Christ and the glorifying of God.[50]

This is to say that even though Lewis the idealist had opposed those who glorified the "genius" of certain artists and who made aesthetic taste almost a spiritual value, he felt that his previous views of art, including his idealist view, made art more important than it really was. Consequently, he both agreed with his friend Charles Williams, whom he took to be saying "that poetry is after all only poetry. . . . It is not a substitute for philosophy or theology, much less for sanctification,"[51] and he criticized art-for-art's-sake aesthetes like Matthew Arnold,[52] Walter Pater,[53] Benedetto Croce,[54] I. A.

50 Lewis, "Christianity and Culture," 71.
51 Lewis, *The Arthurian Torso*, 121. Additionally, Lewis also agreed with Williams that theology is more than just poetry. Lewis, "Is Theology Poetry?" 10.
52 Lewis, "Christianity and Culture," 71. Concerning George Watson's book *The Literary Critics*, Lewis told Watson: "And your severities about Arnold and Leavis are just, besides being much better bred than A's own superciliousness or L's yahoo howls." Lewis, *The Collected Letters of C. S. Lewis: Volume III*, 1341 [May 12, 1962]. Cf. Lewis, *The Personal Heresy*, 65.
53 Critiquing Walter Pater's *Marius the Epicurean*, Lewis said that Pater tried to include the whole spiritual life in the life of pleasure on account of its beauty, but ultimately could not because "that is the refutation of aestheticism: for perfect beauty you need to include things which will at once show that mere beauty is not the sole end of life. If you don't include them, you *have* given up aestheticism: if you do, you *must* give it up Q.E.D." Lewis, *The Collected Letters of C. S. Lewis: Volume II*, 35 [January 10, 1932].
54 Lewis, "Christianity and Culture," 71.

Richards,[55] F. R. Leavis,[56] E. R. Carritt,[57] E. M. W. Tillyard,[58] the early T. S. Eliot,[59] and Harold Bloom,[60] all whom Lewis thought failed to truly[61] appreciate art and artistic genius precisely because they overvalued them:

> To my mind [art and literature] are only healthy when they are either (a) Definitely the handmaids of religious, or at least moral, truth – or (b) Admittedly aiming at nothing but innocent recreation or entertainment. Dante's alright, and *Pickwick* is alright. But the

---

55   Ibid., 72. Cf. "I'm sure you were right in tracing the *extreme* Richardian view to subjectivism. Since the real wholeness is not, for them, in the objective universe, it has to be located inside the poet's head. Hence the quite disproportionate emphasis laid by them, as by the Romantics before them, on the poet – to the exclusion of the object dealt with, the work of art as a *thing*, and the reader." Lewis, *The Collected Letters of C. S. Lewis: Volume II*, 468 [February 4, 1941]. Cf. Lewis, *An Experiment in Criticism*, 124-35. Cf. Lewis, "High and Low Brows," 432.

56   Lewis, "Christianity and Culture," 72. Cf. "You ought to have been spending . . . on Tolkien's 3 vol. *Lord of the Rings* the time you spent on [*Poetry and Prose in the Sixteenth Century*]. *The Lord* is the book we have all been waiting for. And it shows too, which cheers, that there are thousands left in Israel who have not bowed the knee to Leavis." Lewis, *The Collected Letters of C. S. Lewis: Volume III*, 774-5 [August 2, 1956]. Cf. "I suppose the head of F. R. Leavis in a charger would be rather too costly?" C. S. Lewis, quoted in *C. S. Lewis: Memories and Reflections*, by John Lawlor (Dallas: Spence Publishing, 1998), 47. Cf. "I'm for Christ against Epicurus, but no words can express my championship of Epicurus against *Scrutiny* [the journal Leavis edited], Existentialists, and 'all that.'" Lewis, *The Collected Letters of C. S. Lewis: Volume II*, 1003 [November 28, 1949]. Cf. "The very title *Scrutiny* characterizes the Leavisian approach to reading. Had Lewis founded a journal, he might have called it *Exploration*." Lionel Adey, *C. S. Lewis: Writer, Dreamer & Mentor* (Grand Rapids, MI: Eerdmans, 1998), 93. Cf. "For Leavis . . . the old tradition, based largely on the Classics and Christianity, was no longer valid: true moral guidance must now be sought in the qualities of great writers such as Shakespeare, Jane Austen or George Eliot, who had expressed a refined intelligence that transcended the limitations imposed by traditional codes, so offering human beings a way of living in the world which would be surer than that afforded by swimming along in the old European stream." John Beer, "Basil Willey: 1897-1978," *Proceedings of the British Academy*, vol. 66 (London: Oxford University Press, 1982), 484.

57   Lewis, "Christianity and Culture," 84.

58   Cf. Charles Beach, "C. S. Lewis vs. E. M. W. Tillyard: The Personal Heresy," *CSL: The Bulletin of the New York C. S. Lewis Society* 38, no. 1 (January-February 2007): 1-17.

59   Lewis, "Christianity and Culture," 72.

60   Although Lewis only knew Bloom when Bloom was a student at Cambridge, Lewis probably already sensed Bloom's tendency to elevate the Romantics, and in particular, William Blake, as a prophetic figure. Because of this – this strange forging of art and religion – along with some technical jargon, Lewis said of Bloom's book *The Visionary Company*: "This is one of the most difficult books I have ever read: harder than *Romans* and ten times harder than Aristotle." C. S. Lewis, "Poetry & Exegesis," review of *The Visionary Company, a Reading of English Romantic Poetry*, by Harold Bloom, *Encounter* 22, no. 6 (June 1963), 74.

61   Lewis, *An Experiment in Criticism*, 10.

great *serious irreligious* art – art for art's sake – is all balderdash; and, incidentally, never exists when art is really flourishing. In fact one can say of Art as an author I recently read says of Love (sensual love, I mean) 'It ceases to be a devil when it ceases to be a god.' Isn't that well put? So many things – nay, every real *thing* – is good if only it will be humble and ordinate. . . . One thing we want to do is to kill the word 'spiritual' in the sense in which it is used by writers like Arnold and Croce.[62]

As we know from previous chapters, Lewis believed that a thing is most itself when it acts according to its nature and place in God's hierarchy of values – which, in the case of art and artistic genius, is quite low: "I think we can still believe culture to be innocent after we have read the New Testament; I cannot see that we are encouraged to think it important."[63]

Now because Lewis the Christian lowered art on the scale of important activities in life, many of those around him misunderstood him. For instance, Peter Bayley, a former student of Lewis, said he was always disappointed that

62 Lewis, *The Collected Letters of C. S. Lewis: Volume II*, 390-1 [April 16, 1940]. In *The Great Divorce*, a painter is told: "'If you are interested in the country only for the sake of painting it, you'll never learn to see the country. . . . Every poet and musician and artist, but for Grace, is drawn away from love of the thing he tells, to love of the telling till, down in Deep Hell, they cannot be interested in God at all but only in what they say about Him.'" Lewis, *The Great Divorce*, 1066-7. Cf. "But wherever the truth may lie . . . I feel certain . . . that if we . . . overvalue art, then art itself will be the greatest sufferer; when second things are put first, they are corrupted." C. S. Lewis, "Sir Walter Scott," in *Selected Literary Essays*, by C. S. Lewis, ed. Walter Hooper (1956 essay reprint; Cambridge: Cambridge University Press, 1969), 215. Cf. "But the Christian knows from the outset that the salvation of a single soul is more important than the production or preservation of all the epics and tragedies in the world. . . . And *a posteriori* it is not hard to argue that all the greatest poems have been made by men who valued something else much more than poetry." Lewis, "Christianity and Literature," 419. In *The Renaissance and English Humanism*, Douglas Bush wrote, "The notion of art as self-expression and of criticism as aesthetic disinterestedness is quite modern, and it reached the logical end of its relatively short life in the gospel and practice of art for art's sake." To which, Lewis replied, "I shake hands with you on that." Lewis, *The Collected Letters of C. S. Lewis: Volume II*, 476 [March 28, 1941]. Cf. Lewis, *The Four Loves*, 63.
63 Lewis, "Christianity and Culture," 74. Concerning the medieval approach to the arts, Lewis wrote: "A chef, a surgeon, or a scholar, may be proud, even to arrogance, of his skill; but his skill is confessedly the means to an end beyond itself, and the status of the skill depends wholly on the dignity or necessity of that end. I think it was then like that with all the arts. Literature exists to teach what is useful, to honour what deserves honour, to appreciate what is delightful. The useful, honourable, and delightful things are superior to it: it exists for their sake; its own use, honour, or delightfulness is derivative from theirs. In that sense the art is humble even when the artists are proud; proud of their proficiency in the art, but not making for the art itself the high Renaissance or Romantic claims." Lewis, *The Discarded Image*, 214.

Lewis "never showed a trace of any aesthetic sense except about literature,"[64] and Hugh Trevor-Roper, one of C. S. Lewis's colleagues at Magdalene College, asked his friend Bernard Berenson, "Do you know C. S. Lewis? In case you don't let me offer a brief character sketch. Envisage (if you can) . . . the mind and thought of a Desert Father . . . preoccupied with meditations of inelegant theological obscenity: a powerful mind warped by a positive detestation of such profane frivolities as art, literature and (of course) poetry."[65] While Bayley ought to read both Lewis's *Experiment in Criticism*, which discusses more than just literature, and Peter Schakel's *Imagination and the Arts in C. S. Lewis*, which does a wonderful job of exploring Lewis's interest in arts such as dance, music, architecture, etc., Trever-Roper should simply peruse any of Lewis's poetry, fiction, literary history, literary criticism, etc. to discover that Lewis greatly appreciated the arts and *especially* poetry.[66] Thus, just like the wife who does not find her husband funny because his insight overshadows his humor, so were Lewis's specifically literary achievements often overshadowed by his popular apologetics and related works. And for this reason, the task before us is to see precisely what value Lewis the Christian put on the arts.

From previous chapters, we also know that Lewis agreed with Tolkien and others in saying that God has given man a deliberative imagination by which he can act as a "sub-creator" to God's Creator. *Pace* Dorothy Sayers,[67] Lewis did not think that this meant that man's ability to create is only

---

64 Bayley, "From Master to Colleague," 78.

65 Trevor-Roper, *Letters from Oxford*, 285.

66 Lewis always insisted that his favourite art is poetry. Lewis, *"De Descriptione Temporum,"* 8.

67 Although Sayers' understanding of man's sub-creative faculties can be interpreted generously, it is difficult not to feel that she overstressed them when she wrote, for instance, "If the common man is to enjoy the divinity of his humanity, he can come to it only in virtue and right of his making." Dorothy Sayers, *The Mind of the Maker*, 9th ed. (1941 reprint; London: Methuen & Co., 1947), 174. For this reason, Lewis took Sayers to task: "[T]he one serious dissatisfaction I feel with Miss Sayers book [*The Mind of the Maker*] . . . is a dissatisfaction on the practical, or pastoral, side rather than on the theoretical. I think that in an age when idolatry of human genius is one of out most insidious dangers Miss Sayers would have been prudent to stress more continuously than she does the fact that the analogy [between God's creating and man's 'creating'] *is* merely an analogy. I am afraid that some vainglorious writers may be encouraged to forget that they are called 'creative' only by a metaphor – that an unbridgeable gulf yawns between the human activity of recombining elements from a pre-existing world and the Divine activity of first inventing, and then endowing with substantial existence, the elements themselves." C. S. Lewis, review of *The Mind of the Maker*, by Dorothy Sayers, *Theology* 43, no. 256 (October 1941): 248. Cf. Diana Pavlac Glyer and Laura Simmons, "Dorothy L. Sayers and C. S. Lewis: Two Approaches to Creativity and Calling," *VII: An Anglo-American Literary Review* 21 (2004): 31-46.

quantitatively different than God's; rather, Lewis believed that there was a qualitative difference: i.e. whereas God creates out of nothing, man creates by simply rearranging things that God has already made:

> 'Creation' as applied to human authorship . . . seems to me an entirely misleading term. We make ἐς ὑποχειμενων ['with regard to what lies at hand'] i.e. we re-arrange elements He has provided. There is not a *vestige* of real creativity *de novo* in us. Try to imagine a new primary colour, a third sex, a fourth dimension, or even a monster wh[ich] does not consist of bits of existing animals stuck together! Nothing happens. And that surely is why our works (as you said) never mean to others quite what we intended: because we are re-combining elements made by Him and already containing *His* meanings. Because of those divine meanings in our materials it is impossible we sh[ould] ever know the whole meaning of our own works, and the meaning we never intended may be the best and truest one.[68]

Consequently, Lewis insisted that art is simple mimesis or imitation,[69] which exists not for the sake of the artist but for the sake of communication,[70] and which is appropriately used in five ways: (1) as a means of earning an income, (2) as a way of communicating knowledge to others, (3) as a cultural weapon, (4) as *praeparatio evangelica*, and (5) as a way of giving people pleasure.[71]

---

68 Lewis, *The Collected Letters of C. S. Lewis: Volume II*, 555 [February 20, 1943]. Cf. "When you listened to [Aslan's] song you heard the things he was making up: when you looked round you, you saw them." Lewis, *The Magician's Nephew*, 99. Cf. Lewis, *The Collected Letters of C. S. Lewis: Volume II*, 870-1 [August 19, 1948]. Cf. Lewis, *The Personal Heresy*, 21.

69 Lewis, "Christianity and Literature," 416. Cf. "Even in literature and art, no man who bothers about originality will ever be original: whereas if you simply try to tell the truth (without caring two pence how often it has been told before) you will, nine times out of ten, become original without ever having noticed it." Lewis, *Mere Christianity*, 465.

70 "When an artist is in the strict sense working, he of course takes into account the existing taste, interests, and capacity of his audience. These, no less than the language, the marble, or the paint, are part of his raw material; to be used, tamed, sublimated, not ignored nor defied. Haughty indifference to them is not genius nor integrity; it is laziness and incompetence. You have not learned your job." Lewis, "Good Work and Good Works," 383. "It still seems to me that the burden of proof rests on those who describe as 'private' compositions which their authors take pains to have multiplied by print and which are advertised and exposed for sale in shops. It is an odd method of securing privacy." Lewis, "Period Criticism," 487.

71 Although Lewis's essay "Christianity and Culture" only lists four reasons for art and culture – (1), (3), (4) and (5) – in other essays Lewis mentioned (2) as one of the chief reasons for producing and appreciating art; hence, Lewis said, "We must go to books for that which books can give us – to be interested, delighted, or amused, to be made merry or to be made wise." Lewis, *The Personal Heresy*, 68-9. And George Sayer reports that Lewis believed that a test of a good book is if it makes "you better, wiser and

As for (1), Lewis thought that one reason to practice the arts is simply to earn a living; this is to say that he felt God did not require Christian converts to find a new vocation so much as He required them to have a new attitude within the old vocation:

> Provided, then, that there was a demand for culture, and that culture was not actually deleterious, I concluded I was justified in making my living by supplying that demand – and that all others in my position (dons, schoolmasters, professional authors, critics, reviewers) were similarly justified; especially if, like me, they had few or no talents for any other career – if their 'vocation' to a cultural profession consisted in the brute fact of not being fit for anything else.[72]

Indeed, Lewis often expressed his gratitude that he made his money as an English professor and a not a professional theologian since he thought that being too close to theological matters would have dulled his interest in the divine:

> I think there is a great deal to be said for having one's deepest spiritual interest distinct from one's ordinary duty as a student or professional man. . . . St Paul's *job* was tent-making. When the two coincide I sh[oul]d have thought that there was a danger lest the natural interest in one's job and the pleasures of gratified ambition might be mistaken for spiritual progress and spiritual consolation: and I think clergymen sometimes fall into this trap. . . . Contrariwise, there is the danger that what is boring or repellent in the job may alienate one from the spiritual life. And finally [Francis Bacon] said 'None are so unholy as those whose hands are cauterized with holy things': sacred things may become profane by becoming matters of the job. You *now* want truth for her own sake: how will it be when the same truth is also needed for an effective footnote in your thesis? . . . I've always been glad myself that Theology is not the thing I earn my living by.[73]

This said, Lewis did not choose English because he thought it just as important as theology (*pace* what many evangelical academics believe nowadays[74]);

---

happier." C. S. Lewis, quoted in "George Sayer on C. S. Lewis' Definition of a Great Book," by Mark Koonz, *CSL: The Bulletin of the New York C. S. Lewis Society* 37, no. 5 (September-October 2006): 5.

72   Lewis, "Christianity and Culture," 78.

73   Lewis, *The Collected Letters of C. S. Lewis: Volume III*, 82-3 [January 5, 1951].

74   Dennis Hiebert, for instance, thinks that sociology (though not an art but a social science) is equally as important as theology: "To view sociology and theology, along with other disciplines, as engaging in real dialogue as equal anchor points of truth, or allies subject to the one Sovereign, clearly is to set a truly new agenda for evangelical scholarship." Dennis Hiebert, "Can We Talk? Achieving Dialogue between Sociology

rather, he felt that in his case his personal effectiveness for God would have suffered had he become a professional theologian (for more on this danger, read his excellent poem "The Apologist's Evening Prayer").

As for (2), Lewis distinguished between art that is *primarily* intended to be Contemplated or "to alter our opinions," such as *Genesis*, Plato's *Republic*, and Spinoza's *Ethics*, and art that is *primarily* intended to be Enjoyed or to allow us to "enter fully into the opinions" of others, such as *Paradise Lost*, *The Golden Ass*, and *The Prelude*.[75] Nevertheless, in both cases, art endeavors to give a person new experiences and knowledge regardless of whether or not the person agrees with the opinions of those he has just been exposed to; thus, concerning the question Why read? – which could also be rephrased, Why bother with art? – Lewis said, "The nearest I have yet got to an answer is that we seek an enlargement of our being. We want to be more than ourselves. . . . We are not content to be Leibnitzian monads. We demand windows."[76] Yet be that as it may, such knowledge and experiences can only be acquired *if* the art is good and *if* the person approaching the art really tries to receive the knowledge and experience being communicated. While I will discuss the aesthetic goodness of art later on, I think it is worth spending a bit of time discussing how people should approach a work of art.

To begin with, Lewis thought that it is okay for people to find personal meaning in a work of art – meaning, that is, which the artist did not intend to put in it. Hence, he noted that the word "Babylon" – a hated word in the Old Testament – is an example of a word that has acquired genuine beauty simply through the process of time,[77] and he acknowledged that an author is not always aware of all the meanings of his own work (such as Plato's portrayal of the just man who is hung from a tree). *Nevertheless*, Lewis's entire approach to life was so influenced by both Jenkin, Aristotle and Kant's insistence on treating things as ends in themselves and Alexander's distinction between Enjoyment and Contemplation that Lewis felt in order to do justice to a work of art (be it God-made or man-made), people should "get [themselves] out of

---

and Theology," *Christian Scholar's Review* 37, no. 2 (Winter 2008): 213-4.

75   "When we read the 'literature of knowledge' we hope, as a result, to think more correctly and clearly. In reading imaginative work, I suggest, we should be much less concerned with altering our own opinions – though this of course is sometimes their effect – than with entering fully into the opinions, and therefore also the attitudes, feelings and total experience, of other men. Who in his ordinary senses would try to decide between the claims of materialism and theism by reading Lucretius and Dante? But who in his literary senses would not delightfully learn from them a great deal about what it is like to be a materialist or a theist?" Lewis, *An Experiment in Criticism*, 85.

76   Ibid., 137, 138.

77   Hence, "There can be poetry without a poet." Lewis, *The Personal Heresy*, 16.

the way"[78] and try to appreciate the quiddity of each work of art,[79] which is to say to try and appreciate the work of art as *the artist intended*; thus, *contra* structuralism, deconstruction, and all those who champion "The Intentional Fallacy,"[80] Lewis said, "[The good reader] will read 'in the same spirit that the author writ.'"[81] And this, in turn, entails two things.

---

78   "The only imperative that nature utters is, 'Look. Listen. Attend.'" Lewis, *The Four Loves*, 16. "The first demand any work of any art makes upon us is surrender. Look. Listen. Receive. Get yourself out of the way. . . . In love we escape from our self into one another. In the moral sphere, every act of justice or charity involves putting ourselves in the other person's place and thus transcending our own competitive particularity. In coming to understand anything we are rejecting the facts as they are for us in favour of the facts as they are. . . . The secondary impulse is to go out of the self, to correct its provincialism and heal its loneliness. In love, in virtue, in the pursuit of knowledge, and in the reception of the arts, we are doing this. . . . In reading great literature I become a thousand men and yet remain myself. . . . Here, as in worship, in love, in moral action, and in knowing, I transcend myself; and am never more myself than when I do." Lewis, *An Experiment in Criticism*, 19, 138, 141. Precisely because Enjoyment or surrender to a work of art precedes Contemplation, Lewis never tired of reminding people that the search for motifs etc. must come *after* Enjoyment and *not during* Enjoyment: "'Motifs,' as Professor Tolkien has reminded us, are mere products of analysis. They do not, as 'motifs,' occur in concrete imaginative experience." C. S. Lewis, review of *The Other World, According to Descriptions in Medieval Literature*, by Howard Rollin Patch, *Medium Aevum* 20 (1951): 93. Cf. "I'm not quite sure what you meant about 'silly adventure stories without any point.' If they *are* silly, then having a point won't save them. But if they are good in themselves, and if by a 'point' you mean some truth about the real world wh[ich] one can take *out of* the story, I'm not sure that I agree. At least, I think that *looking for* a 'point' in that sense may prevent one sometimes from getting the real effect of the story in itself – like listening too hard for the words in singing which isn't meant to be listened to that way (like an anthem in a chorus)." Lewis, *The Collected Letters of C. S. Lewis: Volume III*, 388 [December 18, 1953].

79   "For me a novel, or any work of art, is primarily a *Thing*, an Object, enjoyed for its colour, proportions, atmosphere, its flavour – the Odyssey-ishness of the *Odyssey* or the Learishness of *K Lear*: but never, never (here is the real difference) as a personal acquaintance with the author." Ibid., 102 [March 27, 1951]. Cf. "[T]he *Romance of the Rose* could not, without loss, be re-written as the *Romance of the Onion*, and if a man did not see why, we could only send him back to the real world to study roses, onions, and love, all of them still untouched by poetry, still raw." Lewis, *The Personal Heresy*, 97. One of Lewis's greatest abilities was to perceive and describe the quiddity of particular things; for instance, he described Francis de Sales's Christianity as "Honeyed and floral," Spenser's as "grave and homely," and Pascal's as "grim but manly." Lewis, "On the Reading of Old Books," 440-1.

80   For example, Lewis would have disagreed with Michel Foucault, who wrote, "Criticism and philosophy took note of the disappearance – or death – of the author some time ago." Michel Foucault, "What Is an Author?" in *The Critical Tradition: Classic Texts and Contemporary Trends*, ed. David Richter, 889-99 (Boston: Bedford/St Martin's, 1998), 891.

81   Lewis, *An Experiment in Criticism*, 11.

First, people must be aware of the particular method or genre the artist is using so that the art is appreciated as it ought to be: "For you cannot judge any artifact except by using it as it was intended."[82] For example, Disney's *Beauty and the Beast* must be appreciated as a musical and Bon Jovi's "Always" must be appreciated as a rock song: "If we can't learn to like a work of art for what it is, we had best give it up. There is no point in trying to twist it or force it into a form it was never meant to have."[83] This point is particularly hard, for even though it is permissible to prefer one genre over another (this is what makes us unique), personal preference can easily be twisted into subjective hatred of the Other, resulting in a person unjustly blaming one work of art, such as a 2D fighter like *Street Fighter*, for not being another work of art, such as a 3D fighter like *Soul Caliber*.

Second, in order to treat a work of art justly, people need editors, commentators and literary historians – people who can elucidate things like the cultural context in which the art was made or the particular meaning of a word during a certain time period:

> That anything which takes us outside the poem and leaves us there is regrettable, I fully agree. But we may have to go outside it in order that we may presently come inside it again, better equipped. . . . A man who read the literature of the past with no allowance at all for the fact that manners, thought, and sentiments have changed since it was written, would make the maddest work of it. . . . When our aim is knowledge we must go as far as all available means – including the most intense, yet at the same time most sternly disciplined, exercise of our imaginations – can possibly take us. . . . We must clean the lens and remove the stain so that the real past can be seen better.[84]

---

82 Lewis, "Christianity and Culture," 90. Cf. "You will smile at the idea of a man actually reading *Comus* as a charm (*moly*) against lechery. So indeed w[oul]d I. But isn't that smile just the survival in us of the art-for-arts-sake poison? And is there any way of finding out the real quality of the old books until we make the experiment of reading them as they were meant to be read? It's at least worth trying." Lewis, *The Collected Letters of C. S. Lewis: Volume II*, 478 [March 28, 1941]. Cf. "Those who read poetry to improve their minds will never improve their minds by reading poetry. . . . The desirable habit of mind, if it is to come at all, must come as a by-product, unsought." Lewis, "Lilies that Fester," 369. Cf. "[The Bible] is, if you like to put it that way, not merely a sacred book but a book so remorselessly and continuously sacred that it does not invite, it excludes or repels, the merely aesthetic approach. You can read it as literature only by a *tour de force*. You are cutting the wood against the grain, using the tool for a purpose it was not intended to serve." C. S. Lewis, "The Literary Impact of the Authorised Version," in *Selected Literary Essays*, by C. S. Lewis, ed. Walter Hooper (1950 essay reprint; Cambridge: Cambridge University Press, 1969), 144.

83 Lewis, *Spenser's Images of Life*, 113.

84 Lewis, "*De Audiendis Poetis*," 1, 2.

As a literary historian and diachronic semanticist,[85] Lewis was very concerned with cleansed lens and spotless spectacles; however, he believed that many approaches to works of art, such as the psychological, biographical, anthropological, and historicist approaches, usually do more harm than good;[86] hence, "No inquirer needs to use Occam's razor more vigorously than the literary critic."[87] Lewis's reasons for thinking in this way goes back to (1) his idealist belief that joy is not, *pace* what many psychologists would say, repressed sexual desire, (2) his idealist belief that William Morris's romances are not to be read as biographical reflections of the author's socialist philosophy (a belief which ultimately culminated in Lewis's book *The Personal Heresy*), (3) his Christian-phase belief that anthropologists misrepresent stories of the Holy Grail when they falsely assume that everyone who wrote about the Holy Grail in the past was thinking of a pagan cauldron (which is the same as nowadays saying that everyone who pens a story about Superman is thinking about Moses and Nietzsche),[88] and (4) his Christian-phase belief

---

85   A diachronic semanticist is one who studies the history of particular words. For more on Lewis as a semanticist, read Lewis's fascinating but under read book *Studies in Words* and check out Michael Covington, "C. S. Lewis as a Semanticist," *CSL: The Bulletin of the New York C. S. Lewis Society* 13, no. 1 (November 1981): 1-6.

86   For other approaches to literary criticism that Lewis rejected, see Jerry Daniel, "The Taste of the Pineapple: A Basis for Literary Criticism," in *The Taste of the Pineapple: Essays on C. S. Lewis as Reader, Critic, and Imaginative Writer*, ed. Bruce Edwards, 9-27 (Bowling Green, OH: Bowling Green State University Popular Press, 1988).

87   C. S. Lewis, review of "Shakespeare and the Rose of Love," by John Vyvyan, *The Listener* (July 7, 1960).

88   Lewis, *"De Audiendis Poetis,"* 11. Cf. "Within a given story any object, person, or place is neither more nor less nor other than what the story effectively shows it to be. The ingredients of one story cannot 'be' anything in another story, for they are not in it at all. These supposedly identical ingredients are the abstract products of analysis. Within the concrete literary experiences we never meet them." C. S. Lewis, "The Genesis of a Medieval Book," in *Studies in Medieval and Renaissance Literature*, by C. S. Lewis, ed. Walter Hooper (1966 reprint; Cambridge: Cambridge University Press, 1998), 40. Cf. "It is not to be disputed that literary texts can sometimes be of great use to the anthropologist. It does not immediately follow from this that anthropological study can make in return any valuable contribution to literary criticism." C. S. Lewis, "The Anthropological Approach," in *Selected Literary Essays*, by C. S. Lewis, ed. Walter Hooper (1962 essay reprint; Cambridge: Cambridge University Press, 1969), 301. Cf. "In all [these approaches to Arthurian literature] I may seem to you – and you may be right – to be naively clinging to a modern idea of story telling. To some extent I am. The Scylla of our approach to old texts is of course this naïf modernity; we go into the past as the most regrettable type of English tourist goes abroad, carrying his Englishry with him and meaning by a 'good hotel' in Picardy that which is most like a hotel in Brighton. But there is Charybdis too – a tendency to forget that these foreigners, or these medievals, are after all human, to explain everything by dead disciplines (e.g. Rhetoric) even if this involves attributing to them strictly unimaginable states of mind.

that since man cannot discover an inner meaning in the historical process (by his natural powers), there is no use in critics, such as Hegel and Augustine, going to a work of art in order to uncover such meaning.[89] Thus, while Lewis thought some types of information enhance artistic appreciation, he believed other types do not.[90] As a result, he disapproved of Contemplating artists, preferring instead to Enjoy, and then after that, Contemplate their works of art: "Let it be granted that I do approach the poet; at least I do it by sharing his consciousness, not by studying it. I look with his eyes, not at him."[91] This said, while Lewis did not deny that some works of art have better internal qualities than others, he (reluctantly, for he disliked criticism in general[92]) thought that Contemplating and critiquing works of art should primarily be done by judging works of art by *how people approach them* – which is something we will discuss in greater depth shortly.

As for (3), Lewis agreed with Gregory the Great that one of the jobs of the arts is to act as a counter-cultural weapon, which, in turn, entails two things. First, the Christian artist has to be aware of culture and the arts; knowledge, in other words, is vital: "If we are to convert our heathen neighbours, we must understand their culture."[93] Second, the Christian artist must produce *quality* art; this, it is important to note, does not simply mean producing art that has a moral, for as Lewis pointed out, "Morality has spoiled literature often enough;"[94] rather, art that is to be used as a weapon must be *both* aesthetically good (i.e. it must have good *poiema*) and morally

---

I think you and I are both in more danger from Charybdis than from Scylla. Hence, am rather on my guard." Lewis, *The Collected Letters of C. S. Lewis: Volume III*, 1080 [August 22, 1959].

89   Lewis, "Historicism," 621.

90   In regard to literature, Lewis said he gained the most from editors, textual critics, commentators and lexicographers; the second most from literary historians; the third most from emotive critics (who pass on their enthusiasm for an author); and finally almost nothing from evaluative critics, concerning whom, Lewis asked, "Can I, honestly and strictly speaking, say with any confidence that my appreciation of any scene, chapter, stanza or line has been improved by my reading of Aristotle, Dryden, Johnson, Lessing, Coleridge, Arnold himself . . . Pater, or Bradley? I am not sure I can." Lewis, *An Experiment in Criticism*, 122. Although it is not relevant to this section, it is interesting to note that one of Lewis's greatest literary roles was that of an emotive critic; hence, Adam Fox said truly, "[Lewis] had the art . . . of interesting one in authors one had never read." Fox, "At the Breakfast Table," 94.

91   Lewis, *The Personal Heresy*, 11. Cf. "In my opinion all criticism should be of books, not of authors." Lewis, "The Genesis of a Medieval Book," 38.

92   Bruce Edwards, "Literary Criticism," in *Reading the Classics with C. S. Lewis*, ed. Thomas Martin, 330-48 (Grand Rapids, MI: Baker Academic, 2000), 346.

93   Lewis, "Christianity and Culture," 76.

94   Lewis, "The Novels of Charles Williams," 576.

good (i.e. it must have good *logos* and elicit proper stock responses);[95] hence, Lewis wrote:

> All I want to use is the distinction between the author as author and the author as man, citizen, or Christian. What this comes to for me is that there are usually two reasons for writing an imaginative work, which may be called the Author's reason and the Man's. If only one of these is present, then, so far as I am concerned, the book will not be written. If the first is lacking, it can't; if the second is lacking, it shouldn't. . . . While the Author is in this state [of desiring to write], the Man will of course have to criticize the proposed book from quite a different point of view. He will ask how the gratification of this impulse will fit with all the other things he wants, and ought to do or be. . . . The Author's impulse is a desire . . . and of course, like every other desire, needs to be criticized by the whole Man.[96]

95 While some have argued that aesthetic goodness is a form of moral goodness, Lewis rejected this, saying, "[Matters of morality], such as virtue and vice or love and hatred, besides being good or bad themselves make the possessor good or bad. [Matters of aesthetics] do not. . . . I am not pretending to know how this baffling phenomenon – the two kinds or levels of good and evil – is to be fitted into a consistent philosophy of values. But it is one thing to be unable to explain a phenomenon, another to ignore it." Lewis, "Christianity and Culture," 91. In regard to this passage, Brother Every questioned Lewis further, prompting this response from Lewis: "When we detect a mistake we also produce evidence of some moral defect. But a mistake in arithmetic is not the *same* as a sin (e.g. the sin may be only just above zero, where the mistake, as a mistake, is v[ery] serious). In the same way: if a poet were morally perfect, he w[oul]d make the best possible use of his talent. [Therefore] a defective use implies a moral imperfection. But the poetical fault is not the *same* as the moral." Lewis, *The Collected Letters of C. S. Lewis: Volume II*, 467 [January 28, 1941]. Shortly after this, Lewis wrote again to Brother Every and distinguished between three types of badness: "(1) 'Less goodness than we hoped or expected' e.g. bad dinner does not mean it was poisoned: second-rate art is the result; (2) 'Mere inefficiency, clumsiness, privation' e.g. bad sentences in essays, poor grammar or lack of invention: like a lisp or a limp; (3) 'positive badness – vulgarity, falsity, etc' this is the only one that has to do with moral evil but only in society not in the writer, for the writer might be a victim of it himself." Ibid., 468 [February 4, 1941]. Cf. Lewis, *An Experiment in Criticism*, 136.

96 C. S. Lewis, "Sometimes Fairy Stories May Say Best What's To Be Said," in *C. S. Lewis: Essay Collection & Other Short Pieces*, ed. Lesley Walmsley (1956 essay reprint; London: HarperCollins, 2000), 526, 527. Cf. "[T]he fact is that there is no *essential* qualification for criticism more definite than general wisdom and health of mind. To make such wisdom effective, many conditions may be necessary, such as a really good knowledge of the language and a wide experience of poetry." Lewis, *A Preface to Paradise Lost*, 116. Cf. "Literature written by Christians for Christians would have to avoid mendacity, cruelty, blasphemy, pornography, and the like, and it would aim at edification in so far as edification was proper to the kind of work in hand. But whatever it chose to do would have to be done by the means common to all literature." Lewis, "Christianity and Literature," 411-2. Cf. "Only a clever human can make a real Joke about virtue, or indeed about anything else; any of them can be trained to talk *as if* virtue were funny."

Thus, while Lewis would almost certainly have been disappointed with the vast majority of dull-bladed, poorly-written books that can be found in the average Christian bookstore, he likely would have approved of a well-forged movie like *The Passion of the Christ*. Moreover, while many of Lewis's own artistic creations did not start out as weapons intended for cultural warfare,[97] he did use many of his books – some in very humorous ways[98] – to combat false ideas in society: for instance, his *Cosmic Trilogy* was partially intended to counter the idea that aliens are evil and colonizing men are good.[99]

Nevertheless, while Lewis's *Cosmic Trilogy* may be morally good, it does not follow that it is also aesthetically so; and while I have no space to debate the pros and cons of particular works of art, I think Lewis's *Perelandra*, or at least parts of it, can be seen as an example of art as a weapon. Consider, for instance, the following passage where Ransom is debating whether or not to attack the Un-man:

> [Ransom's] fear, his shame, his love, all his arguments, were not altered in the least. The thing was neither more nor less dreadful than it had been before. The only difference was that he knew – almost as a historical proposition – that it was going to be done. He might beg, weep, or rebel – might curse or adore – sigh like a martyr or blaspheme like a devil. It made not the slightest difference. The thing was going to be done. . . . You might say, if you liked, that the power of choice had been simply set aside and an inflexible destiny substituted for it. On the other hand, you might say that he had been delivered from the rhetoric of his passions and had emerged into unassailable freedom. Ransom could not, for the life of him, see any difference between these two statements. Predestination and freedom were apparently identical. He could no longer see any meaning in the many arguments he had heard on this subject.[100]

This passage can be seen as a good example of art as weapon because its superstructure is grounded in rational and moral truths (man is free and God

Lewis, *The Screwtape Letters*, 764.

97 C. S. Lewis, "It All Began with a Picture," in *C. S. Lewis: Essay Collection & Other Short Pieces*, ed. Lesley Walmsley (1960 essay reprint; London: HarperCollins, 2000), 529. C. S. Lewis, "Unreal Estates," in *C. S. Lewis: Essay Collection & Other Short Pieces*, ed. Lesley Walmsley (1962 essay reprint; London: HarperCollins, 2000), 531. Lewis, "Cross-Examination," 555.

98 For an excellent look at Lewis's theory and use of humour, see Terry Lindvall, *Surprised by Laughter: The Comic World of C. S. Lewis* (London: Thomas Nelson, 1996).

99 For more on this see David Downing, "Rehabilitating H. G. Wells: C. S. Lewis's *Out of the Silent Planet*," in *Fantasist, Mythmaker, & Poet*, vol. 2, *C. S. Lewis: Life, Works and Legacy*, ed. Bruce Edwards, 13-34 (Westport, CT: Praeger, 2007).

100 Lewis, *Perelandra*, 279.

has a plan for everything) and it uses excellent poetic technique to portray that which cannot be appreciated on a purely abstract level. Lewis's art, in other words, supports and fleshes out true philosophy and theology, and the result of this is aesthetically and morally good art.

Moreover, perhaps the best example of Lewis's art as a weapon is his numerous essays and books on Christianity. While many people might not regard Lewis's Christian essays and books as art, such people would not be abiding by Lewis's Aristotelian definition of art, which states that an art is "a trained habit of using certain instruments to certain ends."[101] This is to say that since Lewis agreed with Aristotle[102] that *rhetoric* is an art – the art or method that uses the instrument of words to call the passions to the aid of reason in order to promote true action[103] – the rhetoric[104] that we see used in the service of Truth in Lewis's Christian essays and books, particularly where Lewis translates difficult philosophical concepts into everyday language,[105]

---

101 Lewis, *The Personal Heresy*, 103.

102 Lewis read Aristotle's *Rhetoric* and *Poetics*, and while the Oxford don made use of a few ideas in these books, Aristotle's largest influence on Lewis's theory of art was in regard to the means / ends distinction, which, incidentally, Aristotle did not apply to his own aesthetic theory. Aristotle's limited influence on Lewis's literary theory and rhetoric is illuminated a little by the following account by Nathaniel Micklem who writes: "I remember sending [Lewis] a copy of *The Labyrinth* with the observation that being, I supposed, a natural Aristotelian he would not approve such Platonic verse as mine. He replied that he did not find himself Aristotelian." Nathaniel Micklem, *The Box and the Puppets (1888-1953)* (London: Geoffrey Bles, 1957), 123. Cf. C. S. Lewis, "Ajax and Others," review of *On Aristotle and Greek Tragedy*, by John Jones, *The Sunday Telegraphy* 98, no. 6 (December 16, 1962).

103 "Very roughly, we might almost say that in Rhetoric imagination is present for the sake of passion (and, therefore, in the long run, for the sake of action), while in poetry passion is present for the sake of imagination, and therefore, in the long run, for the sake of wisdom or spiritual health – the rightness and richness of a man's total response to the world." Lewis, *A Preface to Paradise Lost*, 54.

104 On a number of occasions, Lewis referred to himself as a "rhetorician" or a "rhetor." Lewis, *The Collected Letters of C. S. Lewis: Volume I*, 713 [July 29, 1927]. Lewis, *The Collected Letters of C. S. Lewis: Volume II*, 444 [September 25, 1940]. Ibid., 766 [March 9, 1947]. For more on Lewis as a rhetorician, see Como, *Branches to Heaven: The Geniuses of C. S. Lewis*, 139-194. Cf. Greg Anderson, "A Most Potent Rhetoric: C. S. Lewis, 'Congenital Rhetorician,'" in *Scholar, Teacher, & Public Intellectual*, vol. 4, *C. S. Lewis: Life, Works, and Legacy*, ed. Bruce Edwards, 195-228 (Westport, CT: Praeger, 2007).

105 In regard to Truth, Lewis maintained, "The first thing we demand of a translator is that he should translate: questions of elegance come later." C. S. Lewis, "Basic Fears," *The Times Literary Supplement* (December 2, 1944): 583. Hence, concerning translating difficult theological ideas into common language, Lewis said, "If the real theologians had tackled this laborious work of translation about a hundred years ago, when they began to lose touch with the people (for whom Christ died), there would have been no place for me." Lewis, "Rejoinder to Dr Pittenger," 183. And this foundational belief – that

is a shining example of art as weapon. Thus, because nearly all who read Lewis's Christian writings see the beauty of Truth clearly, we may say in this case: "The result proves the excellence of the means. The clarity of the object proves that the lens we saw it through is good."[106]

As for (4), in addition to believing that quality Christian art can be a powerful cultural weapon, Lewis also thought that quality "sub-Christian" art or art within the broad spectrum of universal values, such as Virgil's *Aeneid* (pagan) or Tolkien's *Lord of the Rings* (non-explicit Christian), can move people in the direction of, and prepare people for, Christianity;[107] hence, "Galahad is the *son* of Lancelot."[108] In fact, as we discussed in chapter four, Lewis believed that non-Christian myths in general are the highest form of sub-Christian art, and as we discussed in chapter nine, most sub-Christian art – which so happens to be the majority of older art and a minority of

---

communicating the concept comes first and elegance comes second – influenced Lewis's translations of both difficult but true philosophy and difficult but false philosophy. An example of Lewis's translation of difficult but true philosophy is in "The Weight of Glory," where he reinvigorates the biblical teaching of Heaven by saying that "the leaves of the New Testament are rustling with the rumour that one day [we will get in]." Lewis, "The Weight of Glory," 104. And an example of Lewis's translation of difficult but false philosophy is in *Out of the Silent Planet*, where he critiques the Life-Force philosophy and colonialism of Weston, saying: "'It is in her right,' said Weston, 'the right, or, if you will, the might of Life herself, that I am prepared without flinching to plant the flag of man on the soil of Malacandra: to march on, step by step, superseding, where necessary, the lower forms of life that we find, claiming planet after planet, system after system, till our posterity – whatever strange form and yet unguessed mentality they may have assumed – dwell in the universe wherever the universe is habitable.' 'He says,' translated Ransom [to the angelic ruler, Oyarsa], 'that because of this it would *not* be a bent action – or else, he says, it *would* be a possible action – for him to kill you all and bring us here. He says he would feel no pity. He is saying again that perhaps they would be able to keep moving from one world to another and wherever they came they would kill everyone. I think he is now talking about worlds that go round other suns. He wants the creatures born from us to be in as many places as they can be. He says he does not know what kind of creatures they will be.'" Lewis, *Out of the Silent Planet*, 122-3. One of the things that made Lewis such an excellent translator is that he read so broadly and deeply that he really understood the concepts he was translating; thus: "No translation can give an author's style with perfect fidelity. No reading of very short extracts from the original can do it justice; for style depends not only on the occurrence of this or that feature but on its frequency. If we are to talk of Rainoldus's style at all, what, then, can we do but begin by reading a good many pages of him?" C. S. Lewis, "De Descriptione Temporum," *Essays in Criticism* 6, no. 1 (January 1956), 247.
106 Lewis, *An Experiment in Criticism*, 31.
107 For more on this see Joel Heck, "*Praeparatio Evangelica*," in *C. S. Lewis: Lightbearer in the Shadowlands; The Evangelistic Vision of C. S. Lewis*, ed. Angus Menuge, 235-58 (Wheaton, IL: Crossway Books, 1997).
108 Lewis, "Christianity and Culture," 80.

contemporary art[109] – is important in "humanizing" people.

However, while the route of sub-Christian art to Christianity was the one that Lewis himself took, the Oxford don was also well aware that such a route is by no means a sure path to the door of the Church (at which point, to be sure, one must actually convert). We can see in our own culture that despite the popularity of fantasy novels, superhero movies and role-playing video games, none of these have led to an abundance of Christian converts; indeed, in a culture like Japan's, where *manga* and *anime*, which are absolutely overflowing with universal values,[110] are read and watched by everyone, the percentage of Christians is among the lowest in the world.

As for (5), although in this fallen world, duty must always be on-guard against pleasure, Lewis, we recall, maintained that God is a Hedonist and therefore all true pleasures come from Him. Consequently, the Oxford don believed that people can and should go to the arts for pleasure, delight and

---

109 Not only for the sake of perpetuating stock responses but also for the sake of historical continuity did Lewis and the Inklings strongly oppose any attempts by other faculty members in the English department to abandon teaching Old English and allow modern literature to be taught: "The English faculty that was so notoriously conservative as to syllabus (compulsory Anglo-Saxon, nothing twentieth-century until 1970, a situation . . . that twentieth-century-hating Tolkien and his allies fought to preserve) was packed with unmutedly professing Christians, Roman Catholics in some number, including Tolkien, but especially Anglicans: laymen and laywomen such as C. S. Lewis and Charles Williams. . . . In the light of such attitudes it's small wonder that Oxford and Oxford English should have generated only a tiny handful of modernist or postmodernist writers." Valentine Cunningham, "Literary Culture," in *The History of the University of Oxford: Volume VIII; The Twentieth Century*, ed. Brian Harrison, 413-50 (Oxford: Clarendon Press, 1994), 437, 438. Cf. "The actual history of Eng[lish] Lit[erature] as a 'Subject' has been a great disappointment to me. My hope was that it would be primarily a historical study that w[oul]d lift people out of (so to speak) their chronological provincialism by plunging them into the thought and feeling of ages other than their own: for the arts are the best Time Machine we have. But all that side of it has been destroyed at Cambridge and is now being destroyed at Oxford too. This is done by a compact, well-organized group of whom Leavis is the head." Lewis, *The Collected Letters of C. S. Lewis: Volume III*, 1371 [September 18, 1962].

110 While a scholar like Anne Petty ought to be congratulated for seeing the connection between Tolkien and Japanese *anime* and *manga*, Petty is no *anime* and *manga* scholar, and so fails to see the universal values that permeate Japanese culture on account of these art forms; hence, she mistakenly writes, "Unlike the superhero, no one [in *anime*] is purely good or evil." Anne Petty, *Tolkien in the Land of Heroes: Discovering the Human Spirit* (Cold Spring Harbor, NY: Cold Spring Press, 2003), 257. Despite being cartoons, most *anime* embodies timeless themes and presents these themes in excellent artistic forms and hence would certainly have been valued by someone like Lewis. Cf. Adam Barkman, "Beyond Good? Beyond Evil? Beyond Your Wildest Imagination?" in *Transformers and Philosophy*, ed. John Shook and Liz Stillwaggon, 165-175 (Chicago: Open Court, 2009).

inspiration,[111] and indeed, because there are so many different kinds of arts (e.g. literature, dance, etc.) and modes of expression within each art (e.g. science fiction, comedy, etc.), the pleasures that people can get from the arts are extremely rich, diverse and vast;[112] they truly are a testimony to God's creative diversity and Beauty. Nonetheless, Lewis believed that a person must be aware of two things.

First, just because a person derives pleasure from a work of art, it does not follow that all works of art that produce pleasure are well-constructed and of a high aesthetic quality. Thus, while not denying that works of art really contain beauty,[113] Lewis said that because of the difficulty in establishing a *criterion* to *scrutinize* works of art, it is better to judge the aesthetic goodness of a work of art on the basis of how people approach the art.[114] To this end, he began by separating people into two categories – the user ("the many," "the unliterary") and the receiver ("the few," "the literary")[115] – and maintained that the user does not care about art in the same way as the receiver.[116] For instance, while the user might treat the *Venus de Milo* as pornography and only read books when utterly bored (preferring excitement over anything else[117]), the receiver might return again and again to the Louvre to marvel at

---

111 Lewis, "Christianity and Culture," 79. Cf. "[The Christian] has no objection to comedies that merely amuse and tales that merely refresh; for he thinks like Thomas Aquinas *ipsa ratio hoc habet ut quandoque rationis usus intercipiatur*. We can play, as we can eat, to the glory of God." Lewis, "Christianity and Literature," 419. Cf. "The growth of English Schools at Universities, the School Certificate, and the Educational Ladder – all excellent things – may yet produce unexpected results. I foresee the growth of a new race of readers and critics to whom, from the very outset, good literature will be an accomplishment rather than a delight." Lewis, "High and Low Brows," 431. Cf. "We read the humanists [Erasmus, Buchanan, et al.], in fact, only to learn about humanism; we read the 'barbarous' authors in order to be instructed or delighted about any theme they choose to handle." Lewis, *Poetry and Prose in the Sixteenth Century*, 20.

112 Lewis, *An Experiment in Criticism*, 133.

113 Lewis, "Different Tastes in Literature," 470.

114 Lewis, *An Experiment in Criticism*, 1.

115 "A work of (whatever) art can be either 'received' or 'used.' When we 'receive' it we exert our senses and imagination and various other powers according to a pattern invented by the artist. When we 'use' it we treat it as assistance for our own activities. . . . 'Using' is inferior to 'reception' because art, if used rather than received, merely facilitates, brightens, relieves or palliates our life, and does not add to it." Ibid., 88.

116 Lewis, "Different Tastes in Literature," 466.

117 "There must be a pleasure in such stories distinct from mere excitement." C. S. Lewis, "On Stories," in *C. S. Lewis: Essay Collection & Other Short Pieces*, ed. Lesley Walmsley (1947 essay reprint; London: HarperCollins, 2000), 493. It is interesting to note that while Lewis selected *The Three Musketeers* as an example of art that is generally *used* on account of its one-dimensional focus on action and excitement, Lewis's brother, Warnie, reread the book many times and declared it one of his favorites: "Last night I

the beauty of that Greek sculpture and delight, like Schopenhauer did,[118] in rereading his favorite books. Naturally, it goes without saying that whereas the receiver treats a work of art as it was intended to be treated, the user treats the work of art as he likes. Moreover, the receiver tries to value all aspects of a given work of art, such as the cinematography, script, acting, sound editing, etc. in a movie, and not just one aspect, such as the great action sequences. Consequently, the pleasure that a user gets from a work of art is no indication that the work of art is aesthetically good (e.g. the user can make better use of *Playboy* than he can of the *Venus de Milo*), while the pleasure that a receiver gets from a work of art is a reasonable indicator that there is something of value in the work of art – even if, Lewis constantly insisted, the work of art is a children's book[119] or a work that is not considered academic or highbrowed;[120] hence, he concluded by saying, "If all went ideally well we should end by defining good [art] as that which permits, invites, or even compels [receiving]; and bad, as that which does the same for [using]."[121]

Second, just because a person derives pleasure from a given work of art, it does not follow that the art is morally good or edifying. Hence, before ever being exposed to a work of art, a person must begin by deciding whether the work of art in question is worth experiencing or not, particularly in regard to potential moral damage it could cause. Then, once a person has decided that it is morally prudent to Enjoy or experience the work of art in question, he must give himself over to the work of art in order to get at the quiddity of, and with it, the unique pleasure that is derived from, the work of art:

> In good reading there ought to be no 'problem of belief.' I read Lucretius and Dante at a time when (by and large) I agreed with Lucretius. I have read them since I came (by and large) to agree with Dante. I cannot find that this has much altered my experience, or at all altered

---

finished [Dumas's] *Three Musketeers* once more, and find that it retains all its old magic. I don't know how many times I've read it." Warren Lewis, *Brothers and Friends*, 289 [February 25, 1969].

118 Although Lewis always seems to have valued rereading books, he underlined in his copy of the *Essays of Schopenhauer* "<u>Any kind of important books should immediately be read twice</u>." Lewis, underlining in his edition of the *Essays of Schopenhauer*, 48.

119 C. S. Lewis, "On Juvenile Tastes," in *C. S. Lewis: Essay Collection & Other Short Pieces*, ed. Lesley Walmsley (1958 essay reprint; London: HarperCollins, 2000), 476.

120 Lewis, "High and Low Brows," 421. Cf. "In art, we find on the one hand, purists and doctrinaires, who would rather (like Scaliger) lose a hundred beauties than admit a single fault, and who cannot believe anything to be good if the unlearned spontaneously enjoy it: on the other hand, we find the uncritical and slovenly artists who will spoil the whole work rather than deny themselves the indulgence of sentiment or humour or sensationalism." Lewis, preface to the third edition of *The Pilgrim's Regress*, 10.

121 Lewis, *An Experiment in Criticism*, 104,

my evaluation, of either. A true lover of literature should be in one way like an honest examiner, who is prepared to give the highest marks to the telling, felicitous and well-documented exposition of views he dissents from or even abominates.[122]

However, once the Enjoyment is complete (whenever that may be), the person should then Contemplate or rationally evaluate what he has experienced in order to ascertain what he has learned from the work of art (the knowledge the work contains), whether the work of art was executed well or not (its aesthetic nature), and, of course, whether the sentiments expressed in the work of art are those which one should support or condemn (its moral nature): "The only two questions to ask about a [work of art], in the long run, are, firstly, whether it is interesting, enjoyable, attractive, and secondly, whether this enjoyment wears well and helps or hinders you towards all the other things you would like to enjoy, or do, or be."[123] Thus, for instance, after reading T. S. Eliot's poem "The Waste Land" in presumably a receiving / Enjoying spirit, Lewis concluded that it was morally dangerous:

> The plea that [Eliot's] poems of disintegration are all satiric, are intended as awful warnings, is the common plea of all these literary traitors to humanity. So Juvenal, Wycherley, Byron excuse their pornography: so Eliot himself excuses Joyce. His intention only God knows. I must be content to judge his work by its fruits, and I contend that no man is fortified against chaos by reading the *Waste Land*, but that most men are by it infected with chaos.[124]

---

122 Ibid., 86.

123 Lewis, *A Preface to Paradise Lost*, 119-20. Although Lewis never developed it, he indicated in a few places that art with immoral *logos* or content will often result in an aesthetically-poor work of art: "For my own part, I do not believe that the poetic value of any poem is identical with the philosophic; but I think they can differ only to a limited extent, so that very poem whose prosaic or intellectual basis is silly, shallow, perverse, or illiberal, or even radically erroneous, is in some degree crippled by that fact." Lewis, "Shelley, Dryden, and Mr Eliot," 203. While Lewis is speaking poetically and not literally here, we can see that since *ultimately* Beauty and moral Goodness meet in God, *ultimately* they are both absent in God's opposite: nothingness, which is the *telos* of sin: "It is idle to point out to the perverted man the horror of his perversion: while the fierce fit is on, that horror is the very spice of his craving. It is ugliness itself that becomes, in the end, the goal of lechery; beauty has long since grown too weak a stimulant." Lewis, *That Hideous Strength*, 629. Hence, the Devil hates music and art. Lewis, *The Screwtape Letters*, 763.

124 Lewis, *The Collected Letters of C. S. Lewis: Volume II*, 163 [May 23, 1935]. Cf. "A bad book is to be deemed a real evil in so far as it can be shown to prompt to sensuality, or pride, or murder, or to conflict with the doctrine of Divine Providence, or the like. The other dyslogistic terms dear to critics (vulgar, derivative, cheap, precious, academic, affected, bourgeois, Victorian, Georgian, 'literary', etc.) had better be kept strictly on the taste side of the account." Lewis, "Christianity and Culture," 88.

Consequently, while many have come under the false impression that in regard to his most mature theory of art Lewis thought *all* works of art should be experienced by *all* people and should be done so without any critique at *all*,[125] we can see that by looking at the big picture, Lewis always believed that moral considerations – though rarely a straight forward matter[126] – were extremely important. Thus, although it is true that the Oxford don warned against people confusing literary style with morality[127] and called for an end to censorship in the arts,[128] we also know, for instance, that he thought vulgar language usually contaminates art,[129] and that young children should mainly read books of knowledge and those which elicit proper stock responses.[130]

125 Although George Musacchio is an excellent Lewis scholar, his confusion over Lewis's balance between art and morality in *An Experiment in Criticism* – Lewis's final book on literary theory – is a case in point. George Musacchio, *C. S. Lewis: Man & Writer; Essays and Reviews* (Belton, TX: The University of Mary Hardin-Baylor, 1994), 132.

126 "The reason for restricting moral judgements to a few v[ery] 'clear and trenchant' ones is humility and the wish not to mislead. We can say 'this book prompts to lechery' because we *know* that lechery is evil. To condemn because it 'implies the baroque standards which descend from North's Plutarch' (this is a purely imaginary, laboratory example) is dangerous because the standards mentioned are not *known* by you and me to be bad – at the most they are merely suspected." Lewis, *The Collected Letters of C. S. Lewis: Volume II*, 447 [October 12, 1940].

127 "I do not think we are entitled to assume that all who use this Name [the Holy Name] without reverential prefixes are making a 'careless' use of it; otherwise, we should have to say that the evangelists were often careless. I do not think we are entitled to assume that the use of the word *Blessed* when we speak of the Virgin Mary is 'necessary'; otherwise, we should have to condemn both the Nicene and the Apostles' Creed for omitting it. Should we not rather recognize that the presence or absence of such prefixes constitute a difference, not in faith or morals, but simply in style?" C. S. Lewis, "The Holy Name," *The Church Times* (August 10, 1951). Similarly, Lewis capitalized the names of God not so much out of reverence but out of convenience. Lewis, preface to *George MacDonald: An Anthology*, xxxv.

128 "The law must rise to our standards when we improve and sink to them when we decay. It is a lesser evil that the laws should sink than that all judicial procedure should become a travesty." Lewis, "Sex in Literature," 479.

129 C. S. Lewis, "Prudery and Philology," in *C. S. Lewis: Essay Collection & Other Short Pieces*, ed. Lesley Walmsley (1955 essay reprint; London: HarperCollins, 2000), 515-8. Cf. "We need most urgently to recover the lost poetic art of enriching a response without making it eccentric, and of being normal without being vulgar." Lewis, *A Preface to Paradise Lost*, 57.

130 "Since it is likely that [children] will meet cruel enemies, let them at least have heard of brave knights and heroic courage. Otherwise you are making their destiny not brighter but darker. Nor do most of us find that violence and bloodshed, in a story, produce any haunting dread in the minds of children. As far as that goes, I side impenitently with the human race against the modern reformer. Let there be wicked kings and beheadings, battles and dungeons, giants and dragons, and let villains be soundly killed at the end of the book. Nothing will persuade me that this causes an ordinary child any kind or degree of fear beyond what it wants, and needs, to feel." Lewis, "On Three Ways of

Writing for Children," 512. Cf. "Something *was* crawling. Worse still, something was coming out, Edmund or Lucy or you would have recognized it once, but Eustace had read none of the right books. . . . Most of us know what we should expect to find in a dragon's lair, but, as I said before, Eustace had read only the wrong books. They had a lot to say about exports and imports and governments and drains, but they were weak on dragons." Lewis, *The Voyage of the Dawn Treader*, 67, 70. For reasons like these, Peter Schakel believes that Lewis would have approved of children reading Harry Potter books. Schakel, *Imagination and the Arts in C. S. Lewis*, 187.

Conclusion

Behold there was a certain philosopher, and the philosopher knew himself, and he was one. And the word arising in the philosopher was one god. And the Word as the light of his philosophy. And the light shone in the philosophy, and the philosopher knew it not. It was in the philosopher and the philosopher was born of it and the philosopher did not know it. And indeed the philosopher denied that anyone could behold the light in any other way. And having beheld the light the philosopher said that its name was Lord. And philosophy bore witness about the light that it was the word and the life of men; and about the philosopher that he was not born of blood or of the will of the flesh, or the will of a man or through the order of a master, but from God and was the son of God. And the philosopher did not comprehend the testimony.[1]

Thus wrote Owen Barfield about C. S. Lewis shortly after Lewis's conversion to Christianity. And in a way, this reworking of John 1 suits Lewis well, for as we saw throughout the first five chapters of this book, Lewis was without a doubt a philosopher in the ancient sense of the word – that is, he was one who saw philosophy as a way of life – and his attraction to, and love of, Truth, Goodness and Myth ultimately culminated in his philosophical conversion to Christianity, wherein the mythical elements of Christianity revealed themselves to be the fulfillment of, rather than the opposition to, naturally-revealed Truth.

However, as we have seen throughout, Barfield was not alone in recognizing Lewis's philosophical abilities: Lewis's brother, Warnie, once said, "Being what [Lewis] is the study of philosophy was to him as inevitable

---

1   Owen Barfield, "C. S. L.: Biographia Theologica," in *C. S. Lewis, My Godfather: Letters, Photos and Recollections* by Laurence Harwood (Downers Grove, IL: IVP Books, 2008), 69-70.

as death will be,"[2] and even a hostile critic like John Beversluis admitted, "Although there have been Christian philosophers of far greater stature than Lewis, I know of no apologist in any age who has struggled with the intellectual difficulties involved in Christian belief in so grippingly visible way and at such personal cost."[3] Indeed, it was comments like these that first moved me to write this book not only to show, as I did in the first half, that Lewis ought to be considered a philosopher, but also, as I did the second half, what Lewis's philosophy was throughout his entire life and how it came be what it was. Such a study, I felt, was long overdue since even though there have been a few recent books about Lewis and philosophy – all of which are of a high quality, I feel I must add – none of them dealt with the history of Lewis's philosophical thoughts, and as a result, there was something missing.

And so, while better Lewis scholars and philosophers than I will no doubt find flaws with this book, my hope is that every reader will be stirred to further pursue the study of Lewis and philosophy, for if it is true that "[t]he worst philosophers are often the most jejune, and the worst poets the most unreasonable,"[4] then, while acknowledging some of Lewis's imprecision's as a philosopher and remembering his warning "never [to] pin your whole faith on any human being: not if he is the best and wisest in the whole world,"[5] I would not hesitate to call Lewis a noteworthy philosopher and one well-worth studying.

---

2   Warren Lewis, *Brothers and Friends*, 161 [November 12, 1934].
3   Beversluis, *C. S. Lewis and the Search for Rational Religion*, 165.
4   Lewis, *The Personal Heresy*, 111.
5   Lewis, *Mere Christianity*, 443.

Appendix
A Note in Lewis's Edition of Lucretius's *De Rerum Natura*

[This note is found in Book IV of Lewis's edition of Lucretius's *De Rervm Natvra*, ed. Cyrilvs Bailey (Oxonii: E Typographeo Clarendoniano, n.d.; The Rare Book Collection, The University of North Carolina at Chapel Hill). It is not clear who the author is, though it seems unlikely that it is Lewis himself due to differences in tone.]

Lucretius:

Although his poem contains no direct revelations concerning himself, there are few writers whose character lies more often to the reader than that of Lucretius. More than a philosophical system, more as picture of the world as conceived by Epicurus, the *Rerum Natura* is a poignant and often painful psychological document. The facts that are definitely known of the poet may be very briefly stated: born, as it would seem, in 95, and dying about 54, he had lived through a period of terror and bloodshed into one of comparative security. He was acquainted with Cicero: a tradition relates that he died by his own hand in madness.

Though it would be foolish to accept Jerome's statement as literal truth, yet here the mythopoeic faculty of ancient criticism has fabled not without discretion. The poem is the work of an unbalanced mind. No reader can have failed to mark the atmosphere of weirdness and terror which, while it does not prevent him from joining hands in one direction with Wordsworth and Milton, allies Lucretius in another with Edgar Allen Poe and Apuleuis. The gods are down: dreams, magic and potents have had their fangs drawn. But the old evil is not banished so far that it cannot continually disturb the peace of the saints. Lucretius must watch and pray lest he enters again into religion. Reason must fight a ceaseless, hardly triumphant battle against the old terrors. And even inside the garden of Epicurus we are not safe. How significant is his sudden parenthesis when in explaining world's mortality he suddenly turns aside with a hysterical prayer that the awful proof may not even then descend upon them. His account of love, again, is not that of a whole or happy mind: alternating between passages of rich sensuality and others of [. . .] and intolerable revulsion he reveals a mind torn with overwhelming passions and equally overwhelming disgust. One feels the presence of some great tragedy, some terrible disillusion. Here as elsewhere the *Rerum Natura* is a photograph of Hell.

It has always been difficult to account for the extraordinary violence of Lucretius's attack on the degrading terrors of religion. If his work had been lost we should have scarcely thought it possible that educated men in the Ciceronian age could entertain such feelings. Probably they did not. We may suppose that Plutarch's reply to the Epicureans gives a truer account of the universal feeling of Paganism. With Lucretius however to exaggerate the horrors of supernatural dogma and the relief of atheism was partly a tradition inherited from his master, partly a polemical device. But when we have made full allowance for both these reasons, there remains a passionate sincerity in his indictment which can be accounted for only by the sensitive melancholy of an abnormal mind to whom the cold safety of Epicureanism represented a very real and necessary salvation.

Yet Lucretius was not mad: the lucid disposition and sustained power of his work is sufficient proof to the contrary. His moments of noble calm and even of holy ecstasy are not less but more admirable because he has come through fire to find them. Yet even here the old spectres survive, transformed in the light of attainment

> *His ibe me rebus quaedam divinia voluptas*
>
> *Percipit atque horror*

[With me by a certain divine pleasure understands and fears]

His highest joy is an emotional thrill of awe that recalls the nightmare horror of an earlier state. He is still swayed by the majestic force of nature and prostrates himself before the "élan vital" the "*rerum natura cretix*" the "*hominom divemque voluptas,*" rising to his highest poetry while he sings of a life for which his mechanism really found no place. One sees that he was ill fitted to be an Epicurean: but the intensity of feeling which drove him for his very safety into the garden, preserved his poet's heart even within. As a man he represents a tortured and troubled spirit rising by sheer strength of will above persistent melancholia and fear: as a poet he is an artist who surmounts with all the success possible the difficulties of an abstract subject, a newly-tamed language and a scarcely naturalized metre. His character excites the strongest feelings of sympathy and admiration. None felt more keenly the burden of mortality, the old "*weltsmerz*"; yet he will seek no solace elsewhere. Annihilation is the cold Nirvana of his system. Hopelessly inadequate as the Epicurean doctrine was too great tho' sombre genius, it was a defence against worse evils: his first step out of the garden must be into terror, perhaps into madness. Clinging desperately to the one teacher who seemed to offer peace, he went no further and produced a poem where the earnest devotion of the poet almost ennobles the paltry creed upon which it was lavished.

Classical and Medieval Sources Cited

Aeschylus. *Agamemnon*
_____. *Prometheus Bound*
Albert the Great. *De Anima*
Anselm. *Proslogion*
Aristotle. *De Anima*
_____. *Ethics*
_____. *Metaphysics*
_____. *Poetics*
_____. *Politics*
Augustine. *The City of God*
_____. *Confessions*
_____. *The Trinity*
Basil. *Concerning the Holy Spirit*
Bernardus Silvestris. *Commentum Super Sex Libros Eneidos Virgilii*
_____. *Cosmographia*
Bible
Boethius. *The Consolation of Philosophy*
Cicero. *On Good and Bad Ends*
_____. *On the Nature of the Gods*
Diogenes Laertius. *Lives of the Philosophers*
Epicurus. *Letter to Menoecus*
Julian of Norwich. *Revelations of Divine Love*
Justin Martyr. *Apology*
Lucretius. *On the Nature of Things*
Marco Polo. *The Travels of Marco Polo*
Macrobius. *Commentary on the Dream of Scipio*
Martianus Capella. *The Marriage of Philology and Mercury*
Plato. *Gorgias*
_____. *The Laws*
_____. *Phaedo*
_____. *Phaedrus*
_____. *Philebus*
_____. *Republic*
_____. *Symposium*
_____. *Timaeus*
Plotinus. *Enneads*
Plutarch. *Moralia*
Porphyry. *Life of Plotnius*

Pseudo-Dionysius. *The Mystical Theology*
Seneca. *The Dialogues of Lucius Annaeus Seneca: Book II; To Serenus on the Firmness of the Wise Man*
_____. *Letters to Lucilius*
Sextus Empiricus. *Outlines of Pyrrhonism*
Snorri Sturluson. *Glyfaginning*
Theologica Germanica
Thomas Aquinas. *Summa Theologica*
Virgil. *The Aeneid*

Bibliography

Abraham, William. "C. S. Lewis and the Conversion of the West." In *Permanent Things: Toward the Recovery of a More Human Scale at the End of the Twentieth Century*, edited by Andrew Tadie and Michael Macdonald, 270-82. Grand Rapids, MI: Eerdmans, 1995.

Adams, Marilyn McCord. *William Ockham*. Vol. 1. 2nd revised ed. Notre Dame, IN: University of Notre Dame Press, 1989.

Addison, Paul. "Oxford and the Second World." In *The History of the University of Oxford: Volume VIII; The Twentieth Century*, edited by Brian Harrison, 167-88. Oxford: Oxford University Press, 1994.

Adey, Lionel. *C. S. Lewis's 'Great War' with Owen Barfield*. Victoria, BC: University of Victoria Press, 1978.

_____. *C. S. Lewis: Writer, Dreamer & Mentor*. Grand Rapids, MI: Eerdmans, 1998.

Adkin, Neil. "Pride or Envy?" *Augustiniana* 34 (1984): 340-60.

Adkison, Danny. "The Politics of C. S. Lewis Reconsidered." *CSL: The Bulletin of the New York C. S. Lewis Society* 15, no. 8 (June 1984): 4-6.

Aeschliman, Michael. *The Restitution of Man: C. S. Lewis and the Case Against Scientism*. Grand Rapids, MI: Eerdmans, 1983.

Ainslie, Douglas. Preface to *Philosophy of the Practical: Economic and Ethic*, by Benedetto Croce. London: MacMillian, 1913.

Alexander, Samuel. *Space, Time and Deity: The Gifford Lectures at Glasgow, 1916-1918*. 2 vols. New York: Dover Publications, 1966.

Allred, David. "The Platonic Foundation of the Great Divorce." http://cslewis.drzeus.net/papers/platonic.html (accessed on April 15, 2004).

Amis, Kingsley. *The Letters of Kingsley Amis*. Edited by Zachary Leader. London: HarperCollins, 2000.

Anderson, Greg. "A Most Potent Rhetoric: C. S. Lewis, 'Congenital Rhetorician.'" In *Scholar, Teacher, & Public Intellectual*. Vol. 4, *C. S. Lewis: Life, Works, and Legacy*, edited by Bruce Edwards, 195-228. Westport, CT: Praeger, 2007.

Angus, Katrelya. "C. S. Lewis: A Pioneer of Chivalry Today." *Chivalry Today*. http://www.chivalrytoday.com/Essays/Angus/Lewis-Chivalry.html (accessed on April 23, 2004): 1-2.

Anscombe, G. E. M. *Metaphysics and the Philosophy of Mind*. Vol. 2, *The Collected Papers of G. E. Anscombe*. Minneapolis: University of Minnesota Press, 1981.

Armitage, Christopher Mead. "Smartened Up By Lewis." In *C. S. Lewis: Remembered*, edited by Harry Lee Poe and Rebecca Whitten Poe, 159-60. Grand Rapids, MI: Zondervan, 2006.

Arnason, H. H. et al. *History of Modern Art*. 4th ed. Singapore: Prentice Hall, 1998.

Arnold, Bill T. and Bryan E. Beyer. *Encountering the Old Testament: A Christian Survey*. Grand Rapids, MI: Baker Books, 1999.

Aulén, Gustaf. *Christus Victor: An Historical Study of the Three Main Types of the Idea of Atonement*. Translated by A. G. Herbert. 1931. Reprint, Eugene, OR: Wipf & Stock, 2003.

Ayer, A. J. *Language, Truth and Logic*. 1936. Reprint, London: Penguin, 2001.

_____. *Part of My Life: The Memoirs of a Philosopher*. London: Harcourt Brace Jovanovich, 1977.

Babbage, Stuart Barton. "C. S. Lewis and the Humanitarian Theory of Punishment." *Christian Scholar's Review* 2, no. 3 (1972): 224-35.

Bailey, George. "In the University." In *C. S. Lewis: Speaker & Teacher*, edited by Carolyn Keefe, 105-22. Grand Rapids, MI: Zondervan, 1974.

Balfour, Arthur J. *Theism and Humanism*. Edited by Michael Perry. Seattle: Inkling Books, 2000.

Barfield, Owen. "C. S. L.: Biographia Theologica." In *C. S. Lewis, My Godfather: Letters, Photos and Recollections*, by Laurence Harwood. Downers Grove, IL: IVP Books, 2008.

_____. *Owen Barfield on C. S. Lewis*. Edited by G. B. Tennyson. Middletown, CT: Wesleyan University Press, 1989.

_____. *Poetic Diction: A Study in Meaning*. 1927. Reprint, London: Wesleyan University Press, 1984.

Barkman, Adam. "'All is Righteousness and there is no Equality': C. S. Lewis on Gender and Justice." *Christian Scholar's Review* 36, no. 4 (Summer 2007): 415-36.

_____. "Aristotelian Ethics in C. S. Lewis' Philosophy." *CSL: The Bulletin of the New York C. S. Lewis Society* 38, no. 2 (March-April 2007): 1-9.

_____. "Augustinian Will and Aristotelian *Phronesis* in C. S. Lewis' Theory of Moral Action." *Inklings-Jahrbuch für Literatur und Ästhetik* 24 (2006): 117-42.

_____. "Beyond Good? Beyond Evil? Beyond Your Wildest Imagination? in *Transformers and Philosophy*, ed. John Shook and Liz Stillwaggon, 165-175 (Chicago: Open Court, 2009).

_____. Review of *The Chronicles of Narnia and Philosophy: The Lion, the Witch and the Worldview*, edited by Gregory Bassham and Jerry L. Walls. *Christian Scholar's Review* 35, no. 4 (Summer 2006): 537-40.

_____. Review of *The Collected Letters of C. S. Lewis: Volume III; Narnia, Cambridge and Joy; 1950-1963*, by C. S. Lewis. Edited by Walter Hooper. *Christian Scholar's Review* 37, no. 1 (Fall 2007): 117-9.

_____. Review of *The Collected Letters of C. S. Lewis: Volume III; Narnia, Cambridge and Joy; 1950-196*, by C. S. Lewis. Edited by Walter Hooper. *Philosophia Christi* 10, \ no. 1 (2008): 262-5. N.B. This review, being more philosophically-orientated, is different than the one in *Christian Scholar's Review*.

_____. Review of *The Collected Letters of C. S. Lewis: Volume II; Books, Broadcasts and War; 1931-1949*, by C. S. Lewis. Edited by Walter Hooper. *Philosophia Christi* 7, no. 1 (2005): 227-31.

_____. "C. S. Lewis and Philosophy as a Way of Life: An Essay on Being and Becoming." *Lamp-Post: The Bulletin of the Southern-California C. S. Lewis Society* 29, no. 3 and 30, no. 4 (Fall and Winter 2005): 3-15.

_____. "C. S. Lewis and the Concept of an 'Old Western Man.'" *Inklings-Jahrbuch für Literatur und Ästhetik* 25 (2007): 253-68.

_____. "C. S. Lewis and the Enduring Relevance of Monarchy." *CSL: The Bulletin of the New York C. S. Lewis Society* 37, no. 4 (July-August 2006): 1-15.

_____. "C. S. Lewis: Sexist and Masculine Idolater?" *Inklings-Jahrbuch für Literatur und Ästhetik* (Forthcoming 2009).

_____. Review of *C. S. Lewis's Dangerous Idea: A Philosophical Defense of Lewis's Argument from Reason*, by Victor Reppert. *Pilgrimage* 12, no. 1 (January 2005): 8.

_____. "'First to Aslan and Truth': Images of Christ in *The Last Battle*." *Pilgrimage* 13, no. 3 (May 2006): 12-5.

_____. Review of *God and the Reach of Reason: C.S. Lewis, David Hume, and Bertrand Russell*, by Erik Wielenberg. *Christian Scholar's* 38, no. 1 (Fall 2008): 160-3.

_____. "'Made for Infinite Happiness': Boethian Happiness in C. S. Lewis." *Lamp-Post: The Bulletin of the Southern-California C. S. Lewis Society* (Forthcoming).

_____. "'The Shame of Glad Surrender Stood Confessed': C. S. Lewis and Confession." *CSL: The Bulletin of the New York C. S. Lewis Society* 36, no. 4 (July-August 2005): 1-15.

_____. "Some Ancient Philosophical Sources in C. S. Lewis' Practical Ethics." In *Surprised by Faith: Conversion and the Academy; A Collection of Papers Commemorating the 75th Anniversary of the Conversion of C. S. Lewis*, edited by Daryl McCarthy, Bob VanderVennen and Joy McBridge, 161-80. Cambridge: Cambridge Scholar's Press, 2007.

_____. "Some Comments about the Future of Lewis Scholarship." *Lamp-Post: The Bulletin of the Southern-California C. S. Lewis Society* 29, no. 3 (Fall 2005): 21-4.

_____. "'The Uncreative Spell': St. Augustine and C. S. Lewis on Pride." *CSL: The Bulletin of the New York C. S. Lewis Society* 39, no. 2 (March-April 2008): 1-16.

_____. "Was Epicurus a Buddhist? An Examination and Critique of the Theories of Negative Happiness in Buddha and Epicurus." *Ethica: An International Journal for Moral Philosophy* 7, no. 2 (December 2008): 287-94. http://www.cfh.ufsc.br/ethicA/et72art11Barkman.pdf

_____. "'We Must Go Back to Our Bibles': A Response to Mary Stewart Van Leeuwen." *Christian Scholar's Review* 36, no. 4 (Summer 2007): 445-54.

Bassham, Gregory and Jerry Walls, eds. *The Chronicles of Narnia and Philosophy: The Lion, the Witch, and the Wordview.* Chicago: Open Court, 2005.

Bayley, Peter. "From Master to Colleague." In *C. S. Lewis at the Breakfast Table and Other Reminiscences*, edited by James Como, 77-86. San Diego: Harcourt Brace & Company, 1992.

Beach, Charles. "C. S. Lewis vs. E. M. W. Tillyard: The Personal Heresy." *CSL: The Bulletin of the New York C. S. Lewis Society* 38, no. 1 (January-February 2007): 1-17.

Beer, John. "Basil Willey: 1897-1978." *Proceedings of the British Academy.* Vol. 66. London: Oxford University Press, 1982.

Bergson, Henry. *Creative Evolution.* Translated by Arthur Mitchell. 1911. Reprint, Lanham, MD: University Press of America, 1983.

Berkeley, George. *Principles of Human Knowledge.* In *Philosophical Works including the Works on Vision.* Edited by Michael Ayers. London: Everyman, 1996.

_____. *Three Dialogues between Hylas and Philonous.* In *Philosophical Works including the Works on Vision.* Edited by Michael Ayers. London: Everyman, 1975.

Berry, Patricia. "Part B: With Women at College." In *In Search of C. S. Lewis*, edited by Stephen Schofield, 67-70. South Plainfield, NJ: Bridge Publishing, 1983.

Betjeman, John. *John Betjeman's Oxford.* Oxford: Oxford University Press, 1990.

Bevan, Edwyn. *Symbolism and Belief.* 1938. Reprint, Boston: Beacon Press, 1957.

Beversluis, John. *C. S. Lewis and the Search for Rational Religion.* Grand Rapids, MI: Eerdmans, 1985.

Blake, Andrew. "Of More Than Academic Interest: C. S. Lewis and the Golden Age." In *Behind the Veil of Familiarity: C. S. Lewis (1898-1998)*, edited by Margarita Carretero González and Encarnación Hidalgo Tenorio, 47-60. Bern: Peter Lang, 2001.

Bleakley, David. *C. S. Lewis – at Home in Ireland.* Eason, Ireland: Strandtown Press, 1998.

Blumenthal, M. L. "William Morris, Heretic Among Socialists." Review of *William Morris and the Early Days of the Socialist Movement*, by J. Bruce Glasier. *The New York Times*, July 24, 1921.

Bosanquet, Bernard. *The Philosophical Theory of the State*. 1899. Reprint, London: MacMillian, n.d.

Boswell, James. *Life of Johnson*. London: Oxford University Press.

Bradley, F. H. *Appearance and Reality: A Metaphysical Essay*. N.p.: Elibron Classics, 2005.

_____. *Ethical Studies*. 2nd ed. Oxford: Oxford University Press, 1988.

_____. *The Principles of Logic*. Vol. 2. London: Oxford University Press, 1922.

Bradshaw, Norman. "Impressions of a Pupil." In *In Search of C. S. Lewis*, edited by Stephen Schofield, 17-27. South Plainfield, NJ: Bridge, 1983.

Bray, Suzanne. "C. S. Lewis and Politics." *VII: An Anglo-American Literary Review* 20 (2003): 13-32.

Brewer, Derek. "C. S. Lewis: Sixty Years On." In *C. S. Lewis: Remembered*, edited by Harry Lee Poe and Rebecca Whitten Poe, 55-71. Grand Rapids, MI: Zondervan, 2006.

_____. "The Tutor: A Portrait." In *C. S. Lewis at the Breakfast Table and Other Reminiscences*, edited by James Como, 41-67. San Diego: Harcourt Brace & Company, 1992.

Brown, Peter. *Augustine of Hippo: A Biography*. New ed. Berkeley: University of California Press, 2000.

Browne, Thomas. *Religio Medici*. In *The Harvard Classics*, edited by Charles W. Elliot, 249-332. New York: P. F. Collier & Sons, 1937.

Bundy, Murray Wright. *The Theory of Imagination in Classical and Medieval Thought*. Urbana, IL: The University of Illinois Press, 1927.

Buning, Marius. "*Perelandra* in the Light of Modern Allegorical Theory." In *Word and Story in C. S. Lewis*, edited by Peter Schakel and Charles Huttar, 277-98. Columbia, MO: University of Missouri Press, 1991.

Burke, Edmund. *On the Sublime and Beautiful*. 1756. Reprint, New York, P. F. Collier & Son, 1937.

Burson, Scott and Jerry Walls. *C. S. Lewis & Francis Schaeffer: Lessons for a New Century from the Most Influential Apologists of Our Time*. Downers Grove, IL: InterVarsity Press, 1998.

Carnell, Corbin Scott. *Bright Shadow of Reality: Spiritual Longing in C. S. Lewis*. Grand Rapids, MI: Eerdmans, 1999.

Carpenter, Humphrey. *The Inklings: C. S. Lewis, J. R. R. Tolkien, Charles Williams and Their Friends*. London: HarperCollins, 1997.

_____. *J. R. R. Tolkien: A Biography*. London: Unwin Paperbacks, 1978.

Carretero-González, Margarita. "Sons of Adam, Daughters of Eve, and Children of Aslan: An Environmentalist Perspective on *The Chronicles of Narnia*." In *Fantasist, Mythmaker, & Poet*. Vol. 2, *C. S. Lewis: Life, Works, and Legacy*, edited by Bruce Edwards, 93-114. Westport, CT: Praeger, 2007.

Carritt, E. F. *The Theory of Beauty*. 1914. Reprint, London: Methuen & Co., 1949.

Cavaliero, Glen. *Charles Williams: Poet of Theology*. Grand Rapids, MI: Eerdmans, 1983.

Chesterton, G. K. *The Everlasting Man*. 1925. Reprint, San Francisco: Ignatius Press, 1993.

Christensen, Michael. *C. S. Lewis on Scripture: His Thoughts on the Nature of Biblical Inspiration, the Role of Revelation and the Question of Inerrancy*. London: Hodder and Stoughton, 1979.

Christopher, Joe. "Gender Hierarchies and Lowerarchies: A Response to Mary Stewart Van Leeuwen and Adam Barkman." *Christian Scholar's Review* 36, no. 4 (Summer 2007): 461-8.

Clark, David. *C. S. Lewis: A Guide to His Theology*. Oxford: Blackwell, 2007.

Coleridge, Samuel Taylor. *Biographia Literaria; or, Biographical Sketches of My Literary Life and Opinions*. Vol. 7, *The Collected Works of Samuel Taylor Coleridge*. Edited by James Engell and W. Jackson Bate. Princeton: Princeton University Press, 1983.

Collingwood, R. G. *An Autobiography*. Oxford: Clarendon Press, 1939.

Collins, Francis. *The Language of God: A Scientist Presents Evidence for Belief*. New York: Free Press, 2007.

Como, James. *Branches to Heaven: The Geniuses of C. S. Lewis*. Dallas: Spense Publishing, 1998.

Cook, Edward. "Does Joy Lead to God? Lewis, Beversluis, and the Argument from Desire." http://homepage.mac.com/edcook/lewis-desire.html (accessed on February 12, 2005).

Copleston, Fredrick. *A History of Philosophy: Volume I; Greece and Rome*. New York: Doubleday, 1993.

Covington, Michael. "C. S. Lewis as a Semanticist." *CSL: The Bulletin of the New York C. S. Lewis Society* 13, no. 1 (November 1981): 1-6.

Cowan, Rosamund. "Part A: With Women at College." In *In Search of C. S. Lewis*, edited by Stephen Schofield, 61-6. South Plainfield, NJ: Bridge Publishing, 1983.

Cox, John. "Epistemological Release in *The Silver Chair*." In *The Longing for a Form: Essays on the Fiction of C. S. Lewis*, edited by Peter Schakel, 159-70. Grand Rapids, MI: Baker Book House, 1977.

Craighead, Houston. "C. S. Lewis' Teleological Argument." *Encounter* 57, no. 2 (Spring 1996): 171-85.

Croce, Benedetto. *The Essence of Aesthetic*. Translated by Douglas Ainslie. London: William Heinemann, 1921.

_____. *Philosophy of the Practical: Economic and Ethic*. Translated by Douglas Ainslie. London: MacMillian and Co., 1913.

Csapo, Eric. *Theories of Mythology*. Oxford: Blackwell, 2005.

Cunningham, Richard. *C. S. Lewis: Defender of the Faith*. Philadelphia: Westminster Press, 1967.

Cunningham, Valentine. "Literary Culture." In *The History of the University of Oxford: Volume VIII; The Twentieth Century*, edited by Brian Harrison, 413-50. Oxford: Clarendon Press, 1994.

Currie, Robert. "The Arts and Social Studies, 1914-1939." In *The History of the University of Oxford: Volume VIII; The Twentieth Century*, edited by Brian Harrison, 109-38. Oxford: Clarendon Press, 1994.

Daniel, Jerry. "The Taste of the Pineapple: A Basis for Literary Criticism." In *The Taste of the Pineapple: Essays on C. S. Lewis as Reader, Critic, and Imaginative Writer*, edited by Bruce Edwards, 9-27. Bowling Green, OH: Bowling Green State University Popular Press, 1988.

Dart, Ron. "C. S. Lewis and George Grant: A Tale of Two Anglican Tories." *Pilgrimage: The Toronto C. S. Lewis Society Bulletin* 9, no. 2 (April 2002): 1-11. Previously published in the final edition of *The Canadian C. S. Lewis Journal* (Autumn 2001).

_____. "C. S. Lewis: The Culture Wars." *Clarion: Journal of Spirituality and Justice*. http://www.clarion-journal.ca/article.php?story (accessed on December 3, 2004).

Davies, Robertson. "Letter: January 22, 1979." In *We Remember C. S. Lewis: Essays & Memories*, edited by David Graham, 149. Nashville: Broadman & Holman, 2001.

Dawkins, Richard. *The God Delusion*. New York: Houghton Mifflin, 2006.

Derrick, Christopher. *C. S. Lewis and the Church of Rome: A Study in Proto-Ecumenism*. San Francisco: Ignatius Press, 1981.

de Sales, Francis. *Philothea, or An Introduction to the Devout Life*. 1608. Reprint, Rockford, IL: Tan Books, 1994.

Descartes, René. *Discourse on Method*. Translated by Donald Cress. Indianapolis: Hackett Publishing, 1998.

_____. *Meditations on First Philosophy*. Vol. 2, *The Philosophical Writings of Descartes*. Translated by John Cottingham, Robert Stoothoff and Dugald Murdoch. Cambridge: Cambridge University Press, 1999.

Dorsett, Lyle. *And God Came In: The Extraordinary Story of Joy Davidman; Her Life and Marriage to C. S. Lewis*. New York: Ballantine, 1983.

_____. *Seeking the Secret Place: The Spiritual Formation of C. S. Lewis*. Grand Rapids, MI: BrazosPress, 2004.

Downing, David. *Into the Region of Awe: Mysticism in C. S. Lewis*. Downers Grove, IL: InterVarsity, 2005.

_____. *Into the Wardrobe: C. S. Lewis and the Narnia Chronicles*. San Francisco: Jossey-Bass, 2005.

_____. *The Most Reluctant Convert: C. S. Lewis's Journey to Faith*. Downer's Grove, IL: InterVarsity, 2002.

_____. *Planets in Peril: A Critical Study of C. S. Lewis's Ransom Trilogy*. Amherst, MA: The University of Massachusetts Press, 1992.

_____. "Rehabilitating H. G. Wells: C. S. Lewis's *Out of the Silent Planet*." In *Fantasist, Mythmaker, & Poet*. Vol. 2, *C. S. Lewis: Life, Works and Legacy*, edited by Bruce Edwards, 13-34. Westport, CT: Praeger, 2007.

Dronke, Peter. *Fabula: Explorations into the Uses of Myth in Medieval Platonism*. Leiden: E. J. Brill, 1974.

Dulles, Avery Cardinal. "C. S. Lewis: The Case for Apologetics." *CSL: The Bulletin of the New York C. S. Lewis Society* 36, no. 1 (January-February 2005): 1-9.

Dundas-Grant, James. "From an 'Outsider.'" In *C. S. Lewis at the Breakfast Table and Other Reminiscences*, edited by James Como, 229-33. San Diego: Harcourt Brace & Company, 1992.

Duriez, Colin. *The C. S. Lewis Chronicles: The Indispensible Biography of the Creator of Narnia Full of Little-Known Facts, Events and Miscellany*. New York: BlueBridge, 2005.

_____. "C. S. Lewis's Theology of Fantasy." In *Behind the Veil of Familiarity: C. S. Lewis (1898-1998)*, edited by Margarita Carretero González and Encarnación Hidalgo Tenorio, 301-26. Bern: Peter Lang, 2001.

Easterbrook, Gregg. "In Defense of C. S. Lewis." *The Atlantic Monthly* (October 2001).

Edmonds, E. L. "C. S. Lewis, the Teacher." In *In Search of C. S. Lewis*, edited by Stephen Schofield, 37-52. South Plainfield, NJ: Bridge, 1983.

Edwards, Bruce. "Literary Criticism." In *Reading the Classics with C. S. Lewis*, edited by Thomas Martin, 330-48. Grand Rapids, MI: Baker Academic, 2000.

Eggen, Paul and Don Kauchak. *Educational Psychology: Windows on Classrooms*. 7th ed. Upper Saddle River, NJ: Pearson, 2007.

Eliot, T. S. Review of *Ideas and Ideals*, by Hastings Rashdall. *Criterion* 8 (1928-1929).

Farrer, Austin. "The Christian Apologist." In *Light on C. S. Lewis*, edited by Jocelyn Gibb, 23-43. London: Geoffrey Bles, 1965.

Feinendegen, Norbert. "Contemplating C. S. Lewis's Epistemology: Reflections on C. S. Lewis's Argument with Owen Barfield about the Distinction between Enjoyment and Contemplation during the 'Great War.'" *VII: An Anglo-American Literary Review* 24 (2007): 29-52.

Fernandez, Iréne. *C. S. Lewis – Mythe, Raison Ardente: Imagination et Réalité Selon C. S. Lewis*. Geneva: Ad Solem, 2005.

Fitzgerald, Penelope. "Letter." In *We Remember C. S. Lewis: Essays & Memories*, edited by David Graham, 152-3. Nashville: Broadman & Holman, 2001.

Fitzpatrick, F. J. "Neoscholasticism." In *The Cambridge History of Later Medieval Philosophy: From the Rediscovery of Aristotle to the Disintegration of Scholasticism 1100-1600*, edited by Norman Kretzmann, Anthony Kenny and Jan Pinborg, 838-52. Cambridge: Cambridge University Press, 2003.

Flew, Antony and Gary Habermas. "From Atheism to Deism: A Conversation between Antony Flew and Gary Habermas." In *C. S. Lewis as Philosopher: Truth, Goodness, and Beauty*, edited by David Baggett, Gary Habermas and Jerry Walls, 37-52. Downers Grove, IL: InterVarsity Press, 2008.

_____. "My Pilgrimage from Atheism to Theism: A Discussion between Antony Flew and Gary Habermas." *Philosophia Christi* 6, no. 2 (2004): 197-211.

_____. *There is a God: How the World's Most Notorious Atheist Changed His Mind*. New York: HarperOne, 2007.

Foucault, Michel. "What Is an Author?" In *The Critical Tradition: Classic Texts and Contemporary Trends*, edited by David Richter, 889-99. Boston: Bedford/St Martin's, 1998.

Fowler, Alastair. "C. S. Lewis: Supervisor." In *C. S. Lewis Remembered*, edited by Harry Lee Poe and Rebecca Whitten Poe, 98-114. Grand Rapids, MI: Zondervan, 2006.

Fox, Adam. "At the Breakfast Table." In *C. S. Lewis at the Breakfast Table and Other Reminiscences*, edited by James Como, 89-95. San Diego: Harcourt Brace & Company, 1992.

Frazer, James. *The Golden Bough: A Study in Religion and Magic*. Abridged ed. Mineola, NY: Dover Publications, 2002.

Fredrick, Candice and Sam McBride. *Women Among the Inklings: Gender, C. S. Lewis, J. R. R. Tolkien, and Charles Williams*. London: Greenwood Press, 2001.

Freshwater, Mark. *C. S. Lewis and the Truth of Myth*. Lanham, MD: University Press of America, 1988.

Freud, Jill. "Part B: With Girls at Home." In *In Search of C. S. Lewis*, edited by Stephen Schofield, 55-60. South Plainfield, NJ: Bridge, 1983.

Freud, Sigmund. *Interpreting Dreams*. Translated by J. A. Underwood. 1899. Reprint, Toronto: Penguin, 2006.

_____. *Introductory Lectures on Psychoanalysis*. Translated by James Strachey. Edited by James Strachey and Angela Richards. 1917. Reprint, New York: Penguin, 1984.

Fry, Karin. "No Longer a Friend of Narnia: Gender in Narnia." In *The Chronicles of Narnia and Philosophy*, edited by Gregory Bassham and Jerry L. Walls, 155-66. Chicago: Open Court, 2005.

Fryer, W. R. "Disappointment at Cambridge?" In *In Search of C. S. Lewis*, edited by Stephen Schofield, 29-35. South Plainfield, NJ: Bridge, 1983.

Fukuyama, Francis. *The End of History and the Last Man*. Toronto: Free Press, 1992.

Garside, W. R. "Declining Advantage: the British Economy." In *The British Isles: 1901-1951*, edited by Keith Robbins, 163-96. Oxford: Oxford University Press, 2006.

Garth, John. *Tolkien and the Great War: The Threshold of Middle-Earth*. London: HarperCollins, 2003.

Gibbons, Stella. "Imaginative Writing." In *Light on C. S. Lewis*, edited by Jocelyn Gibb, 86-101. London: Geoffrey Bles, 1965.

Gilchrist, K. J. *A Morning After War: C. S. Lewis and WWI*. New York: Peter Lang, 2005.

Goleman, Daniel. *Emotional Intelligence*. 10th ed. New York: Bantam, 2006.

Gore, Charles. *The Philosophy of the Good Life*. London: J. M. Dent, 1954.

Grayling, A. C. "Berkeley's Argument for Immaterialism." In *The Cambridge Companion to Berkeley*, edited by Kenneth Winkler, 166-89. Cambridge: Cambridge University Press, 2005.

Green, Roger Lancelyn and Walter Hooper. *C. S. Lewis: A Biography*. Revised ed. London: HarperCollins, 2003.

Green, T. H. *Prolegomena to Ethics*. Edited by A. C. Bradley. 1834. Reprint, New York: Thomas Y. Crowell, 1969.

Green, William. *Initium Omnis Peccati Superbia: Augustine on Pride as the First Sin*. Berkeley, CA: University of California Press, 1949.

Gresham, Douglas. *Lenten Lands: My Childhood with Joy Davidman and C. S. Lewis*. San Francisco: HarperSanFrancisco, 1989.

Griffin, William. *C. S. Lewis: The Authentic Voice*. Trig: Lion Publishing, 1988.

Griffith, Gwilym. *Interpreters of Man: A Review of Secular and Religious Thought from Hegel to Barth*. London: Lutterworth Press, 1944.

Griffiths, Dom Bede. "The Adventure of Faith." In *C. S. Lewis at the Breakfast Table and Other Reminiscences*, edited by James Como, 11-30. San Diego: Harcourt Brace & Company, 1992.

_____. "Forty Years' Perspective." In *We Remember C. S. Lewis: Essays & Memories*, edited by David Graham, 32-5. Nashville: Broadman & Holman, 2001.

_____. *The Golden String: An Autobiography*. 1954. Reprint, London: Fount Paperbacks, 1979.

Hadot, Pierre. *Philosophy as a Way of Life: Spiritual Exercises from Socrates to Foucault*. Edited by Arnold I Davidson. Translated by Michael Chase. Oxford: Blackwell Publishing, 1995.

_____. *The Veil of Isis: An Essay on the History of the Idea of Nature*. Translated by Michael Chase. Cambridge, MA: Belknap Press, 2006.

_____. *What is Ancient Philosophy?* Translated by Michael Chase. Cambridge, MA: Belknap Press, 2004.

Hannay, Margaret Patterson. *C. S. Lewis*. New York: Frederick Ungar, 1981.

Harris, Jose. "The Arts and Social Sciences, 1939-1970." In *The History of the University of Oxford: Volume VIII; The Twentieth Century*, edited by Brian Harrison, 217-50. Oxford: Oxford University Press, 1994.

Harrison, Brian. "College Life, 1918-1939." In *The History of the University of Oxford: Volume VIII; The Twentieth Century*, edited by Brian Harrison, 81-108. Oxford: Oxford University Press, 1994.

Harrold, Philip. "Stealing Past the Watchful Dragons: C. S. Lewis's Incarnational Aesthetics and Today's Emerging Imagination." In *Apologist, Philosopher, & Theologian*. Vol. 3, *C. S. Lewis: Life, Works, and Legacy*, edited by Bruce Edwards, 183-208. Westport, CT: Praeger, 2007.

Hart, Dabney. *Through the Open Door: A New Look at C. S. Lewis*. N.p.: The University of Alabama Press, 1986.

Hartshorne, Charles. "Philosophy and Orthodoxy: Reflections upon C. S. Lewis' *The Problem of Pain* and *The Case of Christianity*." *Ethics* 54, no. 4 (July 1944): 295-8.

Harwood, Laurence. *C. S. Lewis, My Godfather: Letters, Photos and Recollections*. Downers Grove, IL: IVP Books, 2008.

Heck, Joel. *Irrigating Deserts: C. S. Lewis on Education*. Saint Louis: Concordia Academic Press, 2005.

____. "*Praeparatio Evangelica*." In *C. S. Lewis: Lightbearer in the Shadowlands; The Evangelistic Vision of C. S. Lewis*, edited by Angus Menuge, 235-58. Wheaton, IL: Crossway Books, 1997.

Heidelberger, Patricia. "Part A: With Girls at Home." In *In Search of C. S. Lewis*, edited by Stephen Schofield, 53-4. South Plainfield, NJ: Bridge, 1983.

Herbert, George. *The Temple*. In *The Works of George Herbert*. Hertfordshire: Wordsworth Editions, 1994.

Hiebert, Dennis. "Can We Talk? Achieving Dialogue between Sociology and Theology." *Christian Scholar's Review* 37, no. 2 (Winter 2008): 199-214.

Hobbes, Thomas. *Leviathan*. Edited by C. B. Macpherson. New York: Penguin, 1985.

Holbrook, David. *The Skeleton in the Wardrobe: C. S. Lewis's Fantasies; A Phenomenological Study*. Lewisburg: Bucknell University Press, 1991.

Holyer, Robert. "C. S. Lewis on the Epistemic Significance of the Imagination." *Soundings* 74, no. 1 and 2 (1991).

____. "C. S. Lewis – The Rationalist?" *Christian Scholar's Review* 18, no. 3 (Spring 1989): 148-67.

Hooper, Walter. "Biographical Appendix." In *All My Road Before: The Diary of C. S. Lewis; 1922-1927*, by C. S. Lewis. Edited by Walter Hooper. San Diego: Harcourt Brace & Company, 1991.

____. "C. S. Lewis and C. S. Lewises." In *G. K. Chesterton and C. S. Lewis: The Riddle of Joy*, edited by Michael Macdonald and Andrew Tadie, 33-52. Grand Rapids, MI: Eerdmans, 1989.

____. *C. S. Lewis: Companion & Guide*. San Francisco: HarperSanFrancisco, 1996.

____. "C. S. Lewis in Hertforshire's 'Belsen.'" *Hertfordshire Countryside* 37 (September 1982): 10, 18.

____. "C. S. Lewis: Oxford's Literary Chameleon of Letters." In *Behind the Veil of Familiarity: C. S. Lewis (1898-1998)*, edited by Margarita Carretero González and Encarnación Hidalgo Tenorio, 23-46. Bern: Peter Lang, 2001.

____. "Interview." *Crisis* (July-August 1994).

____. "The Lectures of C. S. Lewis at the Universities of Oxford and Cambridge." *Christian Scholar's Review* 27, no. 4 (Summer1998): 436-53.

____. Introduction to *The Letters of C. S. Lewis to Arthur Greeves (1914-1963)*, by C. S. Lewis. Edited by Walter Hooper. New York: Collier Books, 1979.

____. "Mary Neylan." In *The Collected Letters of C. S. Lewis: Volume II; Books, Broadcasts, and the War 1931-1949*. Edited by Walter Hooper, 1054-5. San Francisco: HarperSanFrancisco, 2004.

____. "Oxford's Bonny Fighter." In *C. S. Lewis at the Breakfast Table and Other Reminiscences*, edited by James Como, 137-85. San Diego: Harcourt Brace & Company, 1992.

____. *Past Watchful Dragons: The Narnian Chronicles of C. S. Lewis*. New York: Collier Books, 1979.

_____. "Private Letter to Adam Barkman: May 31, 2007."

_____. Preface to *Selected Literary Essays*, by C. S. Lewis. Edited by Walter Hooper, vii-xx. Cambridge: Cambridge University Press, 1969.

_____. Preface to *Spirits in Bondage: A Cycle of Lyrics*, by C. S. Lewis. Edited by Walter Hooper, xi-xl. San Diego: Harcourt Brace & Company, 1984.

_____. "Tolkien and C. S. Lewis: An Interview with Walter Hooper." In *Tolkein: A Celebration*, edited by Joseph Pearce, 190-8. San Francisco: Ignatius Press, 2001.

_____. "To the Martlets." In *C. S. Lewis: Speaker & Teacher*, edited by Carolyn Keefe, 47-84. Grand Rapids, MI: Zondervan, 1974.

Horner, David. "*Aut Deus Aut Malus Homo*: A Defense of C. S. Lewis's 'Shocking Alternative.'" In *C. S. Lewis as Philosopher: Truth, Goodness, and Beauty*, edited by David Baggett, Gary Habermas and Jerry Walls, 68-84. Downers Grove, IL: InterVarsity Press, 2008.

Howarth, Janet. "Women." In *The History of the University of Oxford: Volume VIII; The Twentieth Century*, edited by Brian Harrison, 345-76. Oxford: Oxford University Press, 1994.

Howell, Russell. "Lewis's *Miracles* and Mathematical Elegance." In *C. S. Lewis as Philosopher: Truth, Goodness and Beauty*, edited by David Baggett, Gary Habermas and Jerry Walls. Downers Grove, IL: InterVarsity Press, 2008.

Hume, David. *An Enquiry Concerning the Principles of Morals*. Edited by J. B. Schneewind. Indianapolis: Hackett Publishing, 1983.

_____. *A Treatise of Human Nature*. Edited by Ernest Mossner. New York: Penguin,1985.

"The 100 Best Books of the Century: Non-Fiction." *The National Review*. www.nationalreview.com/100best/100_books.html (accessed on October 5, 2003).

Hunt, David. "Observations of a Magdalen Don." In *In Search of C. S. Lewis*, edited by Stephen Schofield, 123-5. South Plainfield, NJ: Bridge, 1983.

Hunt, Patricia. "Awe and Delight." In *We Remember C. S. Lewis: Essays & Memoirs*, edited by David Graham, 56-8. Nashville: Broadman & Holman, 2001.

Hyatt, Douglas. "Joy, the Call of God in Man: A Critical Appraisal of Lewis's Argument from Desire." In *C. S. Lewis: Lightbearers in the Shadowlands; the Evangelistic Vision of C. S. Lewis*, edited by Angus Menuge, 305-28. Wheaton, IL: Crossway Books, 1997.

Jackson, Holbrook. *Dreamers of Dreams: The Rise and Fall of 19th Century Idealism*. New York: Farrar, Straus and Co., n.d.

Jacobs, Alan. *The Narnian: The Life and Imagination of C. S. Lewis*. San Francisco: HarperSanFrancisco, 2005.

Jaeger, Werner. *Paideia: The Ideals of Greek Culture*. Vol. 1. 2nd ed. Translated by Gilbert Highet. New York: Oxford University Press, 1963.

James, William. *The Varieties of Religious Experience: A Study in Human Nature*. Edited by Martin Marty. 1902. Reprint, Toronto: Penguin, 1982.

Jones, Murial. "Part C: With Women at College." In *In Search of C. S. Lewis*, edited by Stephen Schofield, 74-5. South Plainfield, NJ: Bridge Publishing, 1983.

Joseph, H. W. D. *An Introduction to Logic*. Oxford: Clarendon Press, 1916.

Jung, C. G. "The Role of the Unconscious [1918]." In *Civilization in Transition*. Vol. 10, *The Collected Works of C. G. Jung*. 2nd ed. Edited by H. Read et al., 3-28. Princeton, NJ: Princeton University Press, 1970.

Kahn, Charles H. "Discovering the Will: From *Aristotle* to *Augustine*." In *The Question of 'Eclecticism': Studies in Later Greek Philosophy*, edited by John M. Dillon and A. A. Long, 234-59. Berkeley: University of California Press, 1988.

Kant, Immanuel. *Critique of Judgement*. Translated by J. H. Bernard. 1790. Reprint, New York: Hafner, 1961.

_____. *Critique of Practical Reason*. In *The Cambridge Edition of the Works of Immanuel Kant: Practical Philosophy*. Translated and edited by Mary Gregor. Cambridge: Cambridge University Press, 1999.

_____. *Critique of Pure Reason*. Translated and edited by Paul Guyer and Allen Wood. Cambridge: Cambridge University Press, 2006.

_____. *The Metaphysics of Morals*. In *The Cambridge Edition of the Works of Immanuel Kant: Practical Philosophy*. Translated and edited by Mary Gregor. Cambridge: Cambridge University Press, 1999.

Karamanolis, George. *Plato and Aristotle in Agreement? Platonists on Aristotle from Antiochus to Porphyry*. Oxford: Oxford University Press, 2006.

Kent, Bonnie. "Augustine's Ethics." In *The Cambridge Companion to Augustine*, edited by Eleonore Stump and Norman Kretzmann, 205-33. Cambridge: Cambridge University Press, 2001.

King, Don. *C. S. Lewis, Poet: The Legacy of His Poetic Impulse*. Kent, OH: Kent State University Press, 2001.

Kinghorn, Kevin. "Virtue Epistemology: Why Uncle Andrew Couldn't Hear the Animals Speak." In *The Chronicles of Narnia and Philosophy: The Lion, the Witch, and the Worldview*, edited by Gregory Bassham and Jerry Walls, 15-26. Chicago: Open Court, 2005.

Kirkpatrick, W. T. "Letter: August 17, 1915." In *The Collected Letters of C. S. Lewis: Volume I*. Edited by Walter Hooper, 141. London: HarperCollins, 2000.

_____. "Letter: 1916." In *The Lewis Papers: Memoirs of the Lewis Family; 1850-1930*. Vol. 5. Edited by Warren Lewis. The Marion E. Wade Center, Wheaton College.

_____. "Letter: October 2, 1914." In the preface of *Spirits in Bondage: A Cycle of Lyrics*, by Walter Hooper. San Diego: Harcourt Brace & Company, 1984.

Knuuttila, Simo. *Emotions in Ancient and Medieval Philosophy*. Oxford: Oxford University Press, 2006.

Kohlberg, Lawrence. *Philosophy of Moral Development*. New York: Harper & Row, 1981.

Koonz, Mark. "George Sayer on C. S. Lewis' Definition of a Great Book." *CSL: The Bulletin of the New York C. S. Lewis Society* 37, no. 5 (September-October 2006): 1-7.

Kort, Wesley. *C. S. Lewis: Then and Now*. Oxford: Oxford University Press, 2001.

Kreeft, Peter. "C. S. Lewis' Argument from Desire." Appendix A in *Heaven: The Heart's Deepest Longing*. San Francisco: Ignatius Press, 1989.

_____. *C. S. Lewis for the Third Millennium: Six Essays on The Abolition of Man*. San Francisco: Ignatius Press, 1994.

_____. "Gender and the Will of God: The Issue of Priestesses is Ultimately an Issue of God." http://lrc.edu/rel/blosser/Kreeft_gender.htm (accessed on May 19, 2005).

_____. "Lewis's Philosophy of Truth, Goodness, and Beauty." In *C. S. Lewis as Philosopher: Truth, Goodness, and Beauty*, edited by David Baggett, Gary Habermas and Jerry Walls, 23-36. Downers Grove, IL: InterVarsity Press, 2008.

Ladborough, Richard. "In Cambridge." In *C. S. Lewis at the Breakfast Table and Other Reminiscences*, edited by James Como, 98-104. San Diego: Harcourt Brace & Company, 1992.

Lawlor, John. *C. S. Lewis: Memories and Reflections*. Dallas: Spence, 1998.

Lea, Kathleen. "Memories of Lewis as a Colleague." *Chesterton Review* 17, no. 3 and 4 (August and November 1991): 399-400.

Lewis, C. S. *The Abolition of Man; or, Reflections on Education with Special Reference to the Teaching of English in the Upper Forms of Schools.* In *C. S. Lewis: Selected Books* [Short Edition]. 1943. Reprint, London: HarperCollins, 2002.

_____. "Addison." In *Selected Literary Essays*, by C. S. Lewis. Edited by Walter Hooper. Cambridge: Cambridge University Press, 1969. This essay was originally published in *Essays on the Eighteenth Century Presented to David Nichol Smith* in 1945.

_____. "After Priggery – What?" In *C. S. Lewis: Essay Collection & Other Short Pieces.* Edited by Lesley Walmsley. London: HarperCollins, 2000. This essay was originally published in *The Spectator* 175 (December 7, 1945).

_____. "Ajax and Others." Review of *On Aristotle and Greek Tragedy*, by John Jones. *The Sunday Telegraphy* 98, no. 6 (December 16, 1962).

_____. *The Allegory of Love: A Study in the Medieval Tradition.* 1936. Reprint, Oxford: Oxford University Press, 1969.

_____. *All My Road Before Me: The Diary of C. S. Lewis; 1922-1927.* Edited by Walter Hooper. San Diego: Harcourt Brace & Company, 1991.

_____. "And After This They Sent Me." In "The Unpublished Short Poetry of C. S. Lewis," by Don King. *VII: An Anglo-American Literary Review* 15 (1998): 73-96.

_____. "And Less Greek." *Church Times* (July 20, 1962).

_____. Marginalia in his edition of *Annalivum*, by Cornelii Taciti. Edited by C. D. Fisher. Oxonii: E Typographeo Clarendoniano, n.d. The Rare Book Collection, The University of North Carolina at Chapel Hill.

_____. "Answers to Questions about Christianity." In *C. S. Lewis: Essay Collection & Other Short Pieces.* Edited Lesley Walmsley. London: HarperCollins, 2000. This essay was first published as a pamphlet by the Electrical and Musical Industries Christian Fellowship in 1944.

_____. "The Anthropological Approach." In *Selected Literary Essays*, by C. S. Lewis. Edited by Walter Hooper. Cambridge: Cambridge University Press, 1969), 301. This essay was originally published in *English and Medieval Studies Presented to J. R. R. Tolkien on the Occasion of His Seventieth Birthday*, edited by Norman Davis and C. L. Wreen (London: George Allen and Unwin, 1962).

_____. "The Anvil." In *Mere Christianity: Anniversary Edition*, by C. S. Lewis. Edited by Walter Hooper. New York: Macmillan, 1981. "The Anvil" was a regular programme broadcasted on the BBC, and the particular broadcasting I am here referring to was originally recorded on July 19, 1943.

_____. "Are Athletes Better Than Scholars?" In *Cherbourg School Magazine*, no. 2 (1913). Found in *The Lewis Papers: Memoirs of the Lewis Family; 1850-1930.* Vol. 3. Edited by Warren Lewis. The Marion E. Wade Center, Wheaton College.

_____. Marginalia in his edition of *Arthurian Romances: Lancelot*, by Chrétien de Troyes. Translated by W. WisterComfort. London: J. M. Dent, n.d. The Rare Book Collection, The University of North Carolina at Chapel Hill.

_____. *The Arthurian Torso: Containing the Posthumous Fragment of 'The Figure of Arthur' by Charles Williams and a Commentary on the Arthurian Poems of Charles Williams.* 1948. Reprint, London: Oxford University Press, 1952.

_____. "Autobiographical Note." Prepared by the Macmillian Company in 1946. The Marion E. Wade Center, Wheaton College.

_____. Underlining in his edition of *Autobiography*, by Charles Darwin. Edited by Francis Darwin. London: Watts and Co., 1929. The Marion E. Wade Center, Wheaton College.

_____. Marginalia in his edition of *Autobiography*, by John Stuart Mill. Oxford: Oxford University Press, 1958. The Marion E. Wade Center, Wheaton College.

_____. "Basic Fears." *The Times Literary Supplement* (December 2, 1944): 583.

_____. "Blimpophobia." In *C. S. Lewis: Essay Collection & Other Short Pieces*. Edited by Lesley Walmsley. London: HarperCollins, 2000. This essay was originally published in *Time and Tide* 25 (September 9, 1944).

_____. "Bluspels and Flalansferes." In *Selected Literary Essays*, by C. S. Lewis. Edited by Walter Hooper. Cambridge: Cambridge University Press, 1969.

_____. Review of *Boethius: Some Aspects of His Times and Works*, by Helen Barrett. *Medium Aevum* 10, no. 1 (February 1941): 29-34.

_____. Underlining in his edition of *The Book of the Courtier*. Edited by W. H. D. Ross. London: J. M. Dent & Sons, n.d. The Rare Book Collection, The University of North Carolina at Chapel Hill.

_____. *Boxen: The Imaginary World of the Young C. S. Lewis*. Edited by Walter Hooper. San Diego: Harcourt Brace Jovanovich, 1985.

_____. "Bulverism: Or the Foundation of Twentieth-Century Thought." In *C. S. Lewis: Essay Collection & Other Short Pieces*. Edited by Lesley Walmsley. London: HarperCollins, 2000. This essay was originally published as "Notes on the Way." *Time and Tide* 22 (March 29, 1941).

_____. "Christian Apologetics." In *C. S. Lewis: Essay Collection & Other Short Pieces*. London: HarperCollins, 2000. This paper was originally read to the Carmarthen Conference for Youth Leaders and Junior Clergy at Easter in 1945.

_____. "Christian Behaviour Outline." In *In Pursuit of C. S. Lewis: Adventures in Collecting His Works*, by Edwin Brown. Bloomington, IN: AuthorHouse, 2006.

_____. Underlining in his edition of *Christianity after Freud*, by B. G. Sanders. London: Geoffrey Bles, 1949. The Rare Book Collection, The University of North Carolina at Chapel Hill.

_____. "Christianity and Culture." In *C. S. Lewis: Essay Collection & Other Short Pieces*. Edited by Lesley Walmsley. London: HarperCollins, 2000. This essay was originally published in *Theology* 40 and 41 (March-December 1940).

_____. "Christianity and Literature." In *C. S. Lewis: Essay Collection & Other Short Pieces*. Edited by Lesley Walmsley. London: HarperCollins, 2000. This essay was originally read to a religious society sometime before 1939.

_____. "Christian Reunion: An Anglican Speaks to Roman Catholics." In *C. S. Lewis: Essay Collection & Other Short Pieces*. Edited by Lesley Walmsley. London: HarperCollins, 2000.

_____. *Clivi Hamiltonis Summae Metaphysices Contra Anthroposophos Libri II*. November 1928. Unpublished "Great War" document. The Marion E. Wade Center, Wheaton College.

_____. *The Collected Letters of C. S. Lewis: Volume I; Family Letters 1905-1931*. Edited by Walter Hooper. London: HarperCollins, 2000.

_____. *The Collected Letters of C. S. Lewis: Volume II; Books, Broadcasts, and the War 1931-1949*. Edited by Walter Hooper. San Francisco: HarperSanFrancisco, 2004.

_____. *The Collected Letters of C. S. Lewis: Volume III; Narnia, Cambridge, and Joy 1950-1963*. Edited by Walter Hooper. San Francisco: HarperSanFrancisco, 2007.

_____. *Commentarium in Tractatum De Toto et Parte*. 1929? Unpublished "Great War" document. The Marion E. Wade Center, Wheaton College.

_____. Underlining in his edition of "The Communings with himself of Marcus Aurelius Antoninus," by Marcus Aurelius. Translated by C. R. Haines. London: William Heinemann, 1930. The Rare Book Collection, The University of North Carolina at Chapel Hill.

_____. "The Conditions for a Just War." In *C. S. Lewis: Essay Collection & Other Short Pieces*. Edited by Lesley Walmsley. London: HarperCollins, 2000. This letter / essay was originally published in *Theology* (May 1939).

_____. Marginalia in his edition of *Confessions*, by Augustine. Translated by William Watts. 2 vols. London: William Heinemann, 1931. The Rare Book Collection, The University of North Carolina at Chapel Hill.

_____. "Correspondence." *Delta: The Cambridge Literary Magazine* no. 23 (February 1961): 4-7.

_____. Marginalia in his edition of *Critique of Practical Reason and Other Works on the Theory of Ethics*, by Immanuel Kant. Translated by Thomas Kingsmill Abbott. London: Longmans, Green & Co., 1923. The Marion E. Wade Center, Wheaton College.

_____. "Cross-Channel Ships." *The Times* (18 November 1938): 12.

_____. "Cross-Examination." In *C. S. Lewis: Essay Collection & Other Short Pieces*. Edited by Lesley Walmsley. London: HarperCollins, 2000. This interview originally appeared as "I was Decided Upon" and "Heaven, Earth and Outer Space" in *Decision* 2 (September and October 1963).

_____. "C. S. Lewis." *Encounter* (December 1962).

_____. "C. S. Lewis on Rationalism: (Unpublished Notes)." *VII: An Anglo-American Literary Review* 9 (1988): 87-9. These notes were written in the 1940s, when Lewis was a Christian.

_____. "*De Audiendis Poetis*." In *Studies in Medieval and Renaissance Literature*, by C. S. Lewis. Edited by Walter Hooper. 1966. Reprint, Cambridge: Cambridge University Press, 1998.

_____. *De Bono et Malo*. 1929? Unpublished "Great War" document. The Marion E. Wade Center, Wheaton College.

_____. Underlining in his edition of *De Civitate Dei*, by Sancti Aurelii Augustini. 2 vols. Lipsiae: in aedibus B. G. Teubneri, 1909. The Rare Book Collection, The University of North Carolina at Chapel Hill.

_____. "*De Descriptione Temporum*." In *Selected Literary Essays*, by C. S. Lewis. Edited by Walter Hooper. Cambridge: Cambridge University Press, 1969. This was Lewis's 1954 inaugural lecture as the Professor of Medieval and Renaissance Literature at the University of Cambridge.

_____. "De Descriptione Temporum." *Essays in Criticism* 6, no. 1 (January 1956), 247.

_____. "*De Futilitate*." In *C. S. Lewis: Essay Collection & Other Short Works*. Edited by Lesley Walmsley. London: HarperCollins, 2000. This essay was originally given as an address at Magdalen College, Oxford during WWII.

_____. Marginalia in his edition of *De Incarnatione*, by Athanasius. Edited by Frank Leslie Cross. London: T. and A. Constable, 1939. The Rare Book Collection, The University of North Carolina at Chapel Hill.

_____. "Delinquents in the Snow." In *C. S. Lewis: Essay Collection & Other Short Pieces*. Edited by Lesley Walmsley. London: HarperCollins, 2000. This essay was originally published in *Time and Tide* 38 (December 7, 1957).

_____. "Democratic Education." In *C. S. Lewis: Essay Collection & Other Short Pieces*. Edited by Lesley Walmsey. London: HarperCollins, 2000. This essay was originally published as "Notes on the Way." *Time and Tide* 25 (April 29, 1944).

_____. Marginalia in his edition of *De Monarchia*, by Dantis Alligherii. Edited by Carolum Witte. Vindobonae: Sumptibus Guilielmi Braumuller, 1874. The Rare Book Collection, The University of North Carolina at Chapel Hill.

_____. Marginalia in his edition of *De Re Publica*, by Aristotle. Edited by Immanuelis Bekkerr. Oxonii: E Typographeo Academico, 1837. The Rare Book Collection, The University of North Carolina at Chapel Hill.

_____. "A Difference of Outlook." *The Guardian* (June 27, 1947): 283.

_____. "Different Tastes in Literature." In *C. S. Lewis: Essay Collection & Other Short Pieces*. Edited by Lesley Walmsley. London: HarperCollins, 2000. This essay was originally published as "Notes on the Way." *Time and Tide* 27 (May 25, 1946 and June 1, 1946).

_____. *The Discarded Image: An Introduction to Medieval and Renaissance Literature.* 1964. Reprint, Cambridge: Cambridge University Press, 1998.

_____. *Dymer.* In *Narrative Poems*, by C. S. Lewis. Edited by Walter Hooper. London: HarperCollins, 1994. This poem was first published in 1926.

_____. "*Dymer* Rough Draft." In "Henry More and Dymer, MS-170." 1924? Unpublished draft. The Marion E. Wade Center, Wheaton College.

_____. Marginalia in his edition of *Ecce Homo*, by John Robert Seeley. London: J. M. Dent & Sons, 1932. The Rare Book Collection, The University of North Carolina at Chapel Hill.

_____. "Edmund Spenser 1552-99." In *Studies in Medieval and Renaissance Literature*, by C. S. Lewis. Edited by Walter Hooper. Cambridge: Cambridge University Press, 1998. This 1954 essay originally accompanied Lewis's selections from *The Faerie Queene* and *Epithalamion* in *Major British Writers*, vol. 1.

_____. "Equality." In *C. S. Lewis: Essay Collection & Other Short Pieces*. Edited by Lesley Walmsley. London: HarperCollins, 2000. This essay originally appeared in *The Spectator* 171 (August 17, 1943).

_____. "Eric Bentley: An Appreciation." In *The Play and Its Critic: Essays for Eric Bentley*, edited by Michael Bertin. New York: University of America Press, n.d.

_____. Marginalia in his edition of *Essays of Schopenhauer*, by Arthur Schopenhauer. Translated by Mrs. Rudolf Dircks. London: Walter Scott Publishing, 1908. The Rare Book Collection, The University of North Carolina at Chapel Hill.

_____. Marginalia in his edition of *Ethical Studies*, by F. H. Bradley. 2nd ed. London: Clarendon Press, 1927. The Marion E. Wade Center, Wheaton College.

_____. Marginalia in the back of his edition of *Ethica Nicomachea*, by Aristotelis. Edited by I. Bywater. Oxonii: E Claredoniano Typographeo, n.d. The Rare Book Collection, The University of North Carolina at Chapel Hill.

_____. Marginalia in his edition of *The Ethics of Aristotle*, by Aristotle. Edited by John Burnet. London: Methuen & Co., 1900. The Rare Book Collection, The University of North Carolina at Chapel Hill.

_____. *An Experiment in Criticism.* 1961. Reprint, Cambridge: Cambridge University Press, 1999.

_____. "First and Second Things." In *C. S. Lewis: Essay Collection & Other Short Pieces*. Edited by Lesley Walmsley. London: HarperCollins, 2000. This essay was first published as "Notes on the Way." *Time and Tide* 23 (June 27, 1942).

_____. "Foreword." In *Smoke on the Mountain: An Interpretation of the Ten Commandments*, by Joy Davidman. Philadelphia: Westminster Press, 1953.

_____. "The Founding of the Oxford Socratic Club." In *C. S. Lewis: Essay Collection & Other Short Pieces*. Edited by Lesley Walmsley. London: HarperCollins, 2000. This essay originally appeared as the preface to *The Socratic Digest*, no. 1 (1942-3).

_____. *The Four Loves.* In *C. S. Lewis: Selected Books* [Long Edition]. 1960. Reprint, London: HarperCollins, 1999.

_____. "From Johnson's *Life of Fox*." *The Oxford Magazine* 56 (June 9, 1938): 737-8.

_____. "The Funeral of a Great Myth." In *C. S. Lewis: Essay Collection & Other Short Pieces*. Edited by Lesley Walmsley. London: HarperCollins, 2000.

_____. "The Genesis of a Medieval Book." In *Studies in Medieval and Renaissance Literature*, by C. S. Lewis. Edited by Walter Hooper. 1966. Reprint, Cambridge: Cambridge University Press, 1998.

_____. "Genius and Genius." In *Studies in Medieval and Renaissance Literature*, by C. S. Lewis. Edited by Walter Hooper. Cambridge: Cambridge University Press, 1998. This essay was originally published in *The Review of English Studies* 12, no. 46 (1936).

_____, ed. *George MacDonald: An Anthology*. 1947. Reprint, London: Simon & Schuster, 1996.

_____. "God in the Dock." In *C. S. Lewis: Essay Collection & Other Short Pieces*. Edited by Lesley Walmsley. London: HarperCollins, 2000. This essay was originally published as "Difficulties in Presenting the Christian Faith to Modern Unbelievers." *Lumen Vitae* 3 (September 1948).

_____. Marginalia in his edition of *God the Known and God the Unknown*, by Samuel Butler. London: A. C. Fields, 1909. The Marion E. Wade Center, Wheaton College.

_____. "Good Work and Good Works." In *C. S. Lewis: Essay Collection & Other Short Pieces*. London: HarperCollins, 2000. This essay was first published in *The Catholic Art Quarterly* (1959).

_____. *The Great Divorce*. In *C. S. Lewis: Selected Books* [Long Edition]. 1946. Reprint, London: HarperCollins, 1999. This book originally appeared in serial form in 1945.

_____. *A Grief Observed*. 1961. Reprint, Toronto: Bantam Books, 1976.

_____. Marginalia in his edition of *Hamlet*, by William Shakespeare. In "C. S. Lewis's Annotations to His Shakespeare Volumes," by Lionel Adey. *CSL: The Bulletin of the New York C. S. Lewis Society* 8, no. 7 (May 1977): 1-8.

_____. "Hamlet: The Prince or the Poem?" In *Selected Literary Essays*, by C. S. Lewis. Edited by Walter Hooper. Cambridge: Cambridge University Press, 1969. This essay was originally read at the Annual Shakespeare Lecture of the British Academy in 1942.

_____. "Heart-Breaking School." In "The Unpublished Short Poetry of C. S. Lewis," by Don King. *VII: An Anglo-American Literary Review* 15 (1998): 73-96.

_____. "Hedonics." In *C. S. Lewis: Essay Collection & Other Short Pieces*. Edited by Lesley Walmsley. London: HarperCollins, 2000. This essay originally appeared in *Time and Tide* 26 (June 16, 1945).

_____. "Hegemony of Moral Value Outline." 1924. Unpublished notes. Marion E. Wade Center, Wheaton College. Wheaton College has confusingly labelled this document "Hegemony of Moral Virtue," MS-171.

_____. "Henry More." 1924. Unpublished notes. The Marion E. Wade Center, Wheaton College.

_____. "Hero and Leander." In *Selected Literary Essays*, by C. S. Lewis. Edited by Walter Hooper. Cambridge: Cambridge University Press, 1969. This essay was read to the British Academy in 1952 and was published in the *Proceedings of the British Academy* 38 (1952).

_____. "High and Low Brows." In *C. S. Lewis: Essay Collection & Other Short Pieces*. Edited by Lesley Walmsley. London: HarperCollins, 2000. This essay was originally published in *Rehabilitations: And Other Essays*, by C. S. Lewis. London: Oxford University Press, 1939.

_____. "Historicism." In *C. S. Lewis: Essay Collection & Other Short Pieces*. Edited by Lesley Walmsley. London: HarperCollins, 2000. This essay originally appeared in *The Month* 4 (October 1950).

_____. "The Holy Name." *The Church Times* (August 10, 1951).

_____. "Home Rule." In *The Lewis Papers: Memoirs of the Lewis Family; 1850-1930*. Vol. 5. Edited by Warren Lewis. The Marion E. Wade Center, Wheaton College. This essay was written in 1908.

_____. *The Horse and His Boy*. 1954. Reprint, London: Fontana, 1985.

_____. "The Humanitarian Theory of Punishment." In *C. S. Lewis: Essay Collection & Other Short Pieces*. Edited by Lesley Walmsley. London: HarperCollins, 2000. This essay was originally published in *20th Century: An Australian Quarterly Review* 3 (1949).

_____. "The Idea of an 'English School.'" In *Rehabilitations: And Other Essays*, by C. S. Lewis. London: Oxford University Press, 1939.

_____. Underlining in his edition of *The Idea of the Holy: An Inquiry in to the Non-Rational Factor in the Idea of the Divine and its Relation to the Rational*, by Rudolf Otto. Translated by John W. Harvey. Oxford: Oxford University Press, 1936. The Rare Book Collection, The University of North Carolina at Chapel Hill.

_____. "Imagination and Thought in the Middle Ages." In *Studies in Medieval and Renaissance Literature*, by C. S. Lewis. Edited by Walter Hooper. Cambridge: Cambridge University Press, 1998. This paper was originally given as a series of lectures in 1956.

_____. "The Inner Ring." In *C. S. Lewis: Essay Collection & Other Short Pieces*. Edited by Lesley Walmsley. London: HarperCollins, 2000. This essay was first delivered as a Memorial Oration at King's College, London in 1944.

_____. "Interim Report." In *C. S. Lewis: Essay Collection & Other Short Pieces*. Edited by Lesley Walmsley. London: HarperCollins, 2000. This report originally appeared in *The Cambridge Review* (April 21, 1956).

_____. Marginalia in his edition of *An Interpretation of Christian Ethics*, by Reinhold Niebuhr. London: Student Christian Movement Press, 1937. The Rare Book Collection, The University of North Carolina at Chapel Hill.

_____. "Interview." *Christian Century* 79 (June 6, 1962).

_____. Marginalia in his edition of *An Introduction to Logic*, by H. W. D. Joseph. Oxford: Clarendon Press, 1916. The Marion E. Wade Center, Wheaton College.

_____. "Is English Doomed?" In *C. S. Lewis: Essay Collection & Other Short Pieces*. Edited by Lesley Walmsley. London: HarperCollins, 2000.This essay was originally published in *The Spectator* 172 (February 11, 1944).

_____. "Is History Bunk?" In *C. S. Lewis: Essay Collection & Other Short Pieces*. Edited by Lesley Walmsley. London: HarperCollins, 2000. This essay was originally published in *The Cambridge Review* 78 (June 1, 1957).

_____. "Is Theism Important?" In *C. S. Lewis: Essay Collection & Other Short Pieces*. Edited by Lesley Walmsley. London: HarperCollins, 2000. This essay was originally published in *The Socratic Digest* 5 (1952).

_____. "Is Theology Poetry?" In *C. S. Lewis: Essay Collection & Other Short Pieces*. Edited by Lesley Walmsley. London: HarperCollins, 2000. This essay was originally published in *The Socratic Digest* 3 (1945).

_____. "It All Began with a Picture." In *C. S. Lewis: Essay Collection & Other Short Pieces*. Edited by Lesley Walmsley. London: HarperCollins, 2000. This essay was originally published in *The Radio Times, Junior Section* 148 (July 15, 1960).

_____. "Joy." *The Beacon* 3 (May 1924): 444-51.

_____. Marginalia in his edition of *King Alfred's Old English Version of Boethius' De Consolatione Philosophiae*, by Boethius. Translated by King Alfred. Edited by Walter John Sedgefield. Oxford: Clarendon Press, 1899. The Rare Book Collection, The University of North Carolina at Chapel Hill.

_____. "The Language of Religion." In *C. S. Lewis: Essay Collection & Other Short Pieces*. Edited by Lesley Walmsley. London: HarperCollins, 2000. This essay was \ prepared for the Twelfth Symposium of the Colston Research Society, held at the University of Bristol in March 1960.

_____. *The Last Battle*. 1956. Reprint, London: Fontana, 1985.

_____. "The Last Will of C. S. Lewis." http://www.discovery.org/cslewis/articles/writingsspblcdmn/will.php (accessed on February 8, 2005).

_____. Marginalia in his edition of *Leges*, by Plato. In *PLATONIS OPERA TOMVS V*. Edited by Ioannes Burnet. Oxonii: E Typograheo Clarendoniano, 1899. The Rare Book Collection, The University of North Carolina at Chapel Hill.

_____. "Learning in Wartime." In *C. S. Lewis: Essay Collection & Other Short Pieces*. Edited by Lesley Walmsley. London: HarperCollins, 2000. This sermon was originally preached in the Church of St. Mary the Virgin, Oxford, on December 22, 1939.

_____. *Letters of C. S. Lewis*. Edited by Warren Lewis and Walter Hooper. Revised. ed. San Diego: Harcourt Brace & Company, 1993.

_____. *Letters to Children*, by C. S. Lewis. Edited by Lyle W. Dorsett and Marjorie Lamp Mead. New York: Simon & Schuster, 1995.

_____. "Lilies That Fester." In *C. S. Lewis: Essay Collection & Other Short Pieces*. Edited by Lesley Walmsley. London: HarperCollins, 2000. This essay was originally published in *Twentieth Century* 157 (April 1955).

_____. *The Lion, the Witch and the Wardrobe*. 1950. Reprint, London: Fontana, 1985.

_____. "The Literary Impact of the Authorised Version." In *Selected Literary Essays*, by C. S. Lewis. Edited by Walter Hooper. Cambridge: Cambridge University Press, 1969. This essay was originally delivered as the Ethel M. Wood lecture at the University of London on March 20, 1950.

_____. Review of *Longius and English Criticism*, by T. R. Henn. *The Oxford Magazine* 53 (December 6, 1934): 264.

_____. *The Magician's Nephew*. 1955. Reprint, London: Fontana, 1985.

_____. "Man or Rabbit?" In *C. S. Lewis: Essay Collection & Other Short Pieces*. Edited by Lesley Walmsley. London: HarperCollins, 2000. This essay was originally published as a pamphlet by the Student Christian Movement in Schools in 1946.

_____. Marginalia in his edition of *The Medieval Contribution to Political Thought: Thomas Aquinas, Marsilius of Padua, Richard Hooker*, by A. P. D'Entreves. Oxford: Oxford University Press, 1939. The Marion E. Wade Center, Wheaton College.

_____. "Meditation in a Toolshed." In *C. S. Lewis: Essay Collection & Other Short Pieces*. Edited by Lesley Walmsley. London: HarperCollins, 2000. This essay was originally published in *The Coventry Evening Telegraph*, July 17, 1945.

_____. "Meditation on the Third Commandment." In *C. S. Lewis: Essay Collection & Other Short Pieces*. Edited by Lesley Walmsley. London: HarperCollins, 2000. This essay was originally published in *The Guardian*, January 10, 1941.

_____. "Membership." In *C. S. Lewis: Essay Collection & Other Short Pieces*. Edited by Lesley Walmsley. London: HarperCollins, 2000. This essay was originally published in *Sobornost* 31 (June 1945).

_____. *Mere Christianity*. In *C. S. Lewis: Selected Books* [Long Edition]. 1952. Reprint, London: HarperCollins, 1999. This book is a collection of broadcast talks that Lewis gave on the BBC from 1941-1944.

_____. Marginalia in his edition of *Metaphysics*, by Aristotle. Edited and translated by John Warrington. London: J. M. Dent and Sons, 1956. The Rare Book Collection, The University of North Carolina at Chapel Hill.

_____. Review of *The Mind of the Maker*, by Dorothy Sayers. *Theology* 43, no. 256 (October 1941): 248-9.

_____. "Miracles." In *C. S. Lewis: Essay Collection & Other Short Pieces*. Edited by Lesley Walmsley. London: HarperCollins, 2000. This essay was originally published in *The Guardian* (October 2, 1942).

_____. *Miracles*. In *C. S. Lewis: Selected Books* [Long Edition]. 1947. Reprint, London: HarperCollins, 1999.

_____. "Modern Man and His Categories of Thought." In *C. S. Lewis: Essay Collection & Other Short Pieces*. Edited by Lesley Walmsley. London: HarperCollins, 2000.

_____. "Modern Translations of the Bible." In *C. S. Lewis: Essay Collection & Other Short Pieces*. Edited by Lesley Walmsley. London: HarperCollins, 2000. This essay was originally published as the preface to J. B. Phillips's *Letters to Young Churches: A Translation of the New Testament Epistles* in 1947.

_____. "The Moral Good – Its Place Among the Values." 1924-1925. Lecture Notes. The Marion E. Wade Center, Wheaton College. It should be noted that while Wheaton has named this set of lecture notes (MS-76) "The Moral Good – Its Place Among the Values," they are almost certainly mislabelled, for as I have argued, the Wade Center's set of lecture notes are *actually* "The Good – Its Place Among the Values."

_____. "My First School." In *C. S. Lewis: Essay Collection & Other Short Pieces*. Edited by Lesley Walmsley. London: HarperCollins, 2000. This essay was originally published as "Notes on the Way." *Time and Tide* 24 (September 4, 1943).

_____. "Myth Became Fact." In *C. S. Lewis: Essay Collection & Other Short Pieces*. Edited by Lesley Walmsley. London: HarperCollins, 2000. This essay was originally published in *World Dominion* 22 (September-October 1944).

_____. Underlining in his edition of *Natural Law: An Introduction to Legal Philosophy*, by A. P. D'Entreves. London: Hutchinson House, 1951. The Marion E. Wade Center, Wheaton College.

_____. "The Necessity of Chivalry." In *C. S. Lewis: Essay Collection & Other Short Pieces*. Edited by Lesley Walmsley. London: HarperCollins, 2000. This essay was originally published as "Notes on the Way." *Time and Tide* 21 (August 17, 1940).

_____. "Neoplatonism in Spenser's Poetry." In *Studies in Medieval and Renaissance Literature*, by C. S. Lewis. Edited by Walter Hooper. Cambridge: Cambridge University Press, 1998. This essay was originally published in *Etudes Anglaises* 14, no. 2 (1961).

_____. Marginalia in his edition of *The New Testament: A New Translation*, by James Moffat. London: Hodder & Stoughton, 1926. The Rare Book Collection, The University of North Carolina at Chapel Hill.

_____. *Note on the Law of Contradiction*. 1929? Unpublished "Great War" document. The Marion E. Wade Center, Wheaton College.

_____. "The Novels of Charles Williams." In *C. S. Lewis: Essay Collection & Other Short Pieces*. Edited by Lesley Walmsley. London: HarperCollins, 2000. Lewis read this essay on the BBC's *Third Programme* on February 11, 1949.

_____. Marginalia in his edition of *Of the Laws of Ecclesiastical Polity*, by Richard Hooker. Vol. 1. London: J. M. Dent & Sons, 1925. The Rare Book Collection, The University of North Carolina at Chapel Hill.

____. "Old Kirk, Like Father Time Himself." In "The Unpublished Short Poetry of C. S. Lewis," by Don King. *VII: An Anglo-American Literary Review* 15 (1998): 73-96.

____. "On Bolshevism." In "The Moral Good – Its Place among the Values." Unpublished essay. The Marion E. Wade Center, Wheaton College. This essay, which the Wade Center did not separate from Lewis's 1924-1925 lecture notes, is difficult to date. It could have been written somewhere around 1924-1925 since that is when the other documents in the folio were composed. We know that as late as 1939 Lewis taught his political science students about Lenin, who this essay is about; however, internal evidence suggests that this essay was written by a neophyte, which, if this is the case, would mean that it was likely written by Lewis when he was a student in "Greats" – thus, somewhere between 1920-1922.

____. "On Criticism." In *C. S. Lewis: Essay Collection & Other Short Pieces.* Edited by Lesley Walmsley. London: HarperCollins, 2000.

____. "On Ethics." In *C. S. Lewis: Essay Collection & Other Short Pieces.* Edited by Lesley Walmsley. London: HarperCollins, 2000.

____. "On Juvenile Tastes." In *C. S. Lewis: Essay Collection & Other Short Pieces.* Edited by Lesley Walmsley. London: HarperCollins, 2000. This essay was originally published in *The Church Times, Children's Supplement* (November 28, 1958).

____. Marginalia in his edition of *On Liberty.* In *Utilitarianism, Liberty and Representative Government,* by John Stuart Mill. London: J. M. Dent & Sons, 1922. The Marion E. Wade Center, Wheaton College.

____. "On Living in an Atomic Age." In *C. S. Lewis: Essay Collection & Other Short Pieces.* Edited by Lesley Walmsley. London: HarperCollins, 2000. This essay was originally published in *Informed Reading* 6 (1948).

____. "On Obstinacy in Belief." In *C. S. Lewis: Essay Collection & Other Short Pieces.* Edited by Lesley Walmsley. London: HarperCollins, 2000. This essay was originally published in *The Sewanee Review* 66 (Autumn 1955).

____. "On Punishment: A Reply." In *C. S. Lewis: Essay Collection & Other Short Pieces.* Edited by Leslie Walmsley. London: HarperCollins, 2000. This reply was originally published in 1954.

____. "On Science Fiction." In *C. S. Lewis: Essay Collection & Other Short Pieces.* Edited by Lesley Walmsley. London: HarperCollins, 2000. This talk was originally given to the Cambridge University English Club on November 24, 1955.

____. "On Stories." In *C. S. Lewis: Essay Collection & Other Short Pieces.* Edited by Lesley Walmsley. London: HarperCollins, 2000. This essay was originally published in *Essays Presented to Charles Williams,* edited by C. S. Lewis. Oxford: Oxford University Press, 1947.

____. "On the Reading of Old Books." In *C. S. Lewis: Essay Collection & Other Short Pieces.* Edited by Lesley Walmsley. London: HarperCollins, 2000. This essay was originally published as the preface to St. Athanasius' *The Incarnation of the Word of God.* Translated by a Religious of CSMV. London: Geoffry Bles, 1944.

____. "On the Transmission of Christianity." In *C. S. Lewis: Essay Collection & Other Short Pieces.* Edited by Lesley Walmsley. London: HarperCollins, 2000. This essay was originally published as the preface to G. B. Sandhurst's *How Heathen Is Britain?* in 1946.

____. "On Three Ways of Writing for Children." In *C. S. Lewis: Essay Collection & Other Short Pieces.* Edited by Lesley Walmsley. London: HarperCollins, 2000. This essay was originally read to the Library Association at the Bournemouth Conference in 1952.

_____. "Open Letter." *The Christian News-Letter* 119 (February 4, 1942): 4.

_____. Review of *The Other World, According to Descriptions in Medieval Literature*, by Howard Rollin Patch. *Medium Aevum* 20 (1951): 93-4.

_____. "Our English Syllabus." In *Rehabilitations: And Other Essays*, by C. S. Lewis . London: Oxford University Press, 1939.

_____. *Out of the Silent Planet*. In *The Cosmic Trilogy*, by C. S. Lewis. 1938. Reprint, London: Pan Books, 1990.

_____. "A Panegyric for Dorothy L. Sayers." In *C. S. Lewis: Essay Collection & Other Short Pieces*. Edited by Lesley Walmsley. London: HarperCollins, 2000. This was written for Dorothy Sayers's memorial service, which was held on January 15, 1958.

_____. Review of *Paradise Lost in Our Time: Some Comments*, by Douglas Bush. *The Oxford Magazine* 65 (February 13, 1947): 215-7.

_____. "The Parthenon and the Optative." In *C. S. Lewis: Essay Collection & Other Short Pieces*. Edited by Lesley Walmsley. London: HarperCollins, 2000. This essay was originally published as "Notes on the Way." *Time and Tide* 25 (March 11, 1944).

_____. Review of both *Passion and Society*, by D. de Rougemont, and *The Bride of Christ*, by Claude Chavasse. *Theology* 40, no. 240 (June 1940): 459-61.

_____. *Perelandra*. In *The Cosmic Trilogy*, by C. S. Lewis. 1943. Reprint, London: Pan Books, 1990.

_____. The dust-jacket of *Perelandra*. N.p.: MacMillan, 1944.

_____. "Period Criticism." In *C. S. Lewis: Essay Collection & Other Short Pieces*. Edited by Lesley Walmsley. London: HarperCollins, 2000. This essay was originally published as "Notes on the Way." *Time and Tide* 27 (November 9, 1946).

_____ and E. M. W. Tillyard. *The Personal Heresy*. 1939. Reprint, London: Oxford University Press, 1965. The essays in this book were originally published in *Essays and Studies* (1934, 1935, 1936).

_____. Marginalia in his edition of *Phaedo*, by Plato. In *PLATONIS OPERA TOMVS I*. Edited by Ioannes Burnet. Oxonii: E Typograheo Clarendoniano, 1899. The Rare Book Collection, The University of North Carolina at Chapel Hill.

_____. Underlining in his edition of *The Philosophy of the Good Life*, by Charles Gore. London: J. M. Dent, 1938. The Marion E. Wade Center, Wheaton College.

_____. Marginalia in his edition of *Philosophy of the Practical: Economic and Ethic*, by Benedetto Croce. Translated by Douglas Ainslie. London: St. Martin's, 1913.

_____. *The Pilgrim's Regress*. In *C. S. Lewis: Selected Books* [Short Edition]. 1933. Reprint, London: HarperCollins, 2002.

_____. Marginalia in his edition of *Platonism and the Spiritual Life*, by George Santayana. London: Constable and Co., 1927. The Marion E. Wade Center, Wheaton \ College.

_____. *Poems*. Edited by Walter Hooper. San Diego: Harcourt Brace Jovanovich, 1964.

_____. "Poetry & Exegesis." Review of *The Visionary Company, a Reading of English Romantic Poetry*, by Harold Bloom. *Encounter* 22, no. 6 (June 1963), 74-5.

_____. *Poetry and Prose in the Sixteenth Century*. Vol. 4, *The Oxford History of English Literature*. 1954. Reprint, Oxford: Clarendon Press, 1997.

_____. "The Poison of Subjectivism." In *C. S. Lewis: Essay Collection & Other Short Pieces*. Edited by Lesley Walmsley. London: HarperCollins, 2000. This essay was originally published in *Religion in Life* 12 (September 1943).

_____. *Prayer: Letters to Malcolm*. In *C. S. Lewis: Selected Books* [Short Edition]. 1964. Reprint, London: HarperCollins, 2002.

____. Preface to *Essays Presented to Charles Williams*, edited by C. S. Lewis, v-xiv. London: Oxford University Press, 1947.

____. *A Preface to Paradise Lost.* 1942. Reprint, Oxford: Oxford University Press, 1969. This book was originally given as the Ballard Mathews Lectures in 1941.

____. "Priestesses in the Church?" In *C. S. Lewis: Essay Collection & Other Short Pieces.* Edited by Lesley Walmsley. London: HarperCollins, 2000. This essay was originally published as "Notes on the Way." *Time and Tide* 29 (August 14, 1948).

____. *Prince Caspian: The Return to Narnia.* 1951. Reprint, London: Fontana, 1984.

____. Marginalia in his edition of *The Principles of Logic*, by F. H. Bradley. Vol. 2. London: Oxford University Press, 1922. The Marion E. Wade Center, Wheaton College.

____. "Private Bates." In *C. S. Lewis: Essay Collection & Other Short Pieces.* Edited by Lesley Walmsley. London: HarperCollins, 2000. This essay was originally published in *The Spectator* 173 (December 29, 1944).

____. *The Problem of Pain.* In *C. S. Lewis: Selected Books* [Long Edition]. 1940. Reprint, London: HarperCollins, 1999.

____. Marginalia in his edition of *Prolegomena to Ethics*, by Thomas Hill Green. Edited by A. C. Bradley. 5th ed. Oxford: Clarendon Press, 1924. The Marion E. Wade Center, Wheaton College.

____. "Prudery and Philology." In *C. S. Lewis: Essay Collection & Other Short Pieces.* Edited by Lesley Walmsley. London: HarperCollins, 2000. This essay was originally published in *The Spectator* 119 (January 21, 1955).

____. "The Psalms." In *C. S. Lewis: Essay Collection & Other Short Pieces.* Edited by Lesley Walmsley. London: HarperCollins, 2000. This essay was originally published in two parts in *The Guardian*, March 19 and 26, 1943.

____. "Psycho-Analysis and Literary Criticism." In *Selected Literary Essays*, by C. S. Lewis. Edited by Walter Hooper. Cambridge: Cambridge University Press, 1969. This essay was originally published in *Essays and Studies* 27 (1942).

____. "Public Schools." *The Church Times* 130, no. 4 (October 3, 1947): 417.

____. *The Queen of Drum.* In *Narrative Poems*, by C. S. Lewis. Edited by Walter Hooper. London: HarperCollins, 1994.

____. *The Quest of Bleheris.* 1916? Unpublished novel. The Marion E. Wade Center, Wheaton College.

____. "Recommendation Letter for E. L. Edmonds." *The Canadian C. S. Lewis Journal* no. 59 (Summer 1987): 1.

____. "Recommendation Letter for Helen Tyrrell Wheeler." *The Canadian C. S. Lewis Journal* no. 67 (Summer 1989): 2.

____. "Recommendation Letter for N. Bradshaw." *The Canadian C. S. Lewis Journal* no. 7 (July 1979): 16.

____. *Reflections on the Psalms.* In *C. S. Lewis: Selected Books* [Short Edition].1958. Reprint, London: HarperCollins, 2002.

____. Marginalia in his edition of *The Reformation in England*, by F. M. Powicke. Oxford: Oxford University Press, 1941. The Rare Book Collection, The University of North Carolina at Chapel Hill.

____. "Rejoinder to Dr Pittenger." In *God in the Dock: Essays on Theology and Ethics*, by C. S. Lewis. Edited by Walter Hooper. Grand Rapids, MI: Eerdmans, 1970. This essay originally appeared in *The Christian Century* 75 (November 26, 1958): 1359-61.

____. "Religion and Rocketry." In *C. S. Lewis: Essay Collection & Other Short Pieces.* Edited by Lesley Walmsley. London: HarperCollins, 2000. This essay was originally published as "Will We Lose God in Outer Space?" *The Christian Herald* 81 (April 1958).

_____. "Religion: Reality or Substitute?" In *C. S. Lewis: Essay Collection & Other Short Pieces*. Edited by Lesley Walmsley. London: HarperCollins, 2000. This essay was originally published in *World Dominion* 19 (September-October 1943).

_____. "Religion without Dogma?" In *C. S. Lewis: Essay Collection & Other Short Pieces*. Edited by Lesley Walmsley. London: HarperCollins, 2000. This essay was originally read to the Socratic Club on May 20, 1946.

_____. *Replies to Objections in Detail*. 1929? Unpublished "Great War" document. The Marion E. Wade Center, Wheaton College.

_____. "A Reply to Professor Haldane." In *Of This and Other Worlds*, by C. S. Lewis. Edited by Walter Hooper. London: Fount, 2000. This essay was given as a rejoinder to J. B. S. Haldane in 1946.

_____. Marginalia in his edition of *RES PVBLICA*, by Plato. Edited by Ioannes Burnet. Oxonii: E Typographeo Clarendoniano, n.d. The Rare Book Collection, The University of North Carolina at Chapel Hill.

_____. "Revival or Decay?" In *C. S. Lewis: Essay Collection & Other Short Pieces*. Edited by Lesley Walmsley. London: HarperCollins, 2000. This essay was first published in *Punch* 235 (July 9, 1958).

_____. "Rhyme and Reason." Review of *The Poetry of Search and the Poetry of Statement*, by Dorothy Sayers. *Daily Telegraph* (December 1, 1963).

_____. "The Sagas and Modern Life: Morris, Mr Yeats and the Originals." A review of *The Works of Morris and of Yeats in Relation to Early Saga Literature*, by Dorothy M. Hoare. *The Times Literary Supplement* (May 29, 1937): 409.

_____. "Scraps." In *C. S. Lewis: Essay Collection & Other Short Pieces*. Edited by Lesley Walmsley. London: HarperCollins, 2000. This essay was originally published in *St. James' Magazine* (December 1945).

_____. *The Screwtape Letters*. In *C. S. Lewis: Selected Books* [Long Edition]. 1942. Reprint, London: HarperCollins, 1999. This book originally appeared in serial form in 1941.

_____. "Screwtape Proposes a Toast." In *C. S. Lewis: Essay Collection & Other Short Pieces*. Edited by Lesley Walmsley. London: HarperCollins, 2000. This essay originally appeared in *The Saturday Evening Post* 232 (December 19, 1959).

_____. "The 'Seat of the Soul' in [the] Brain – Alcmaeon of Croton." Unpublished notes. The Marion E. Wade Center, Wheaton College. It is impossible to date this piece; however, it was almost certainly written when Lewis was a Christian.

_____. "The Seeing Eye." In *C. S. Lewis: Essay Collection & Other Short Pieces*. Edited by Lesley Walmsley. London: HarperCollins, 2000. This essay was originally entitled "Onward, Christian Spacemen." *Show* 3 (February 1963).

_____. Underlining in his edition of *A Serious Call to a Devout Life*, by William Law. London: J. M. Dent & Sons, 1926. The Rare Book Collection, The University of North Carolina at Chapel Hill.

_____. "The Sermon and the Lunch." In *C. S. Lewis: Essay Collection & Other Short Pieces*. Edited by Lesley Walmsley. London: HarperCollins, 2000. This essay was originally published in *The Church of England Newspaper* (September 21, 1945).

_____. Underlining in his edition of *Sermons*, by Hugh Latimore. London: J. M. Dent & Sons, 1926. The Rare Book Collection, The University of North Carolina at Chapel Hill.

_____. "Sex in Literature." In *C. S. Lewis: Essay Collection & Other Short Pieces*. Edited by Lesley Walmsley. London: HarperCollins, 2000. This essay was originally published in *The Sunday Telegraph* 87 (September 30, 1962).

_____. "Shelley, Dryden and Mr. Eliot." In *Selected Literary Essays*, by C. S. Lewis. Edited by Walter Hooper. Cambridge: Cambridge University Press, 1969.

_____. Marginalia in his edition of *The Signature of all Things with other Writings*, by Jacob Boehme. London: J. M. Dent & Sons, 1926. The Rare Book Collection, The University of North Carolina at Chapel Hill.

_____. *The Silver Chair*. 1953. Reprint, London: Fontana, 1985.

_____. Review of *Sir Thomas Wyatt and Some Collected Studies*, by E. K. Chambers. *Medium Aevum* 3, no. 3 (October 1931): 237-40.

_____. "Sir Walter Scott." In *Selected Literary Essays*, by C. S. Lewis. Edited by Walter Hooper. Cambridge: Cambridge University Press, 1969. This essay was originally read to the Edinburgh Sir Walter Scott Club on March 2, 1956.

_____. Marginalia in his edition of *Some Thoughts Concerning Education*, by John Locke. Cambridge: Cambridge University Press, 1895. The Marion E. Wade Center, Wheaton College.

_____. "Sometimes Fairy Stories May Say Best What's To Be Said." In *C. S. Lewis: Essay Collection & Other Short Pieces*. Edited by Lesley Walmsley. London: HarperCollins, 2000. This essay was first published in *The New York Times Book Review, Children's Section*, November 18, 1956.

_____. "Spelling Reform." *The Times Educational Supplement* (Jan 1, 1960): 13.

_____. *Spenser's Images of Life*. Edited by Alastair Fowler. Cambridge: Cambridge University Press, 1967.

_____. *Spirits in Bondage: A Cycle of Lyrics*. Edited by Walter Hooper. 1919. Reprint, San Diego: Harcourt Brace & Company, 1984.

_____. Unpublished poem in his edition of *The Structure of Complex Words*, by William Empson. London: Chatto & Windus, 1951. The Rare Book Collection, The University of North Carolina at Chapel Hill.

_____. Underlining in his edition of *St. Thomas Aquinas*, by G. K. Chesterton. N.p.: n.p., 1933. The Marion E. Wade Center, Wheaton College.

_____. *Studies in Words*. 2nd ed. 1960. Reprint, Cambridge: Cambridge University Press, 1996.

_____. Underlining in his edition of *Studies of Political Thought from Gerson to Grotius 1414-1625*, by John Neville Figgis. Cambridge: Cambridge University Press, 1923. The Marion E. Wade Center, Wheaton College.

_____. *Surprised by Joy*. In *C. S. Lewis: Selected Books* [Long Edition]. 1955. Reprint, London: HarperCollins, 1999.

_____. Marginalia in his edition of *A System of Logic, Ratiocinative and Inductive*, by John Stuart Mill. Vol. 1. 3rd ed. London: John W. Parker, DCCCLI. The Marion E. Wade Center, Wheaton College.

_____. "Talking about Bicycles." In *C. S. Lewis: Essay Collection & Other Short Pieces*. Edited by Lesley Walmsley. London: HarperCollins, 2000. This essay was originally published in *Resistance* (October 1946).

_____. *That Hideous Strength*. In *The Cosmic Trilogy*, by C. S. Lewis. 1945. Reprint, London: Pan Books, 1990.

_____. Review of *The Three Estates in Medieval and Renaissance Literature*, by Ruth Mohl. *Medium Aevum* 3, no. 1 (February 1934): 68-70.

_____. "Three Kinds of Men." In *C. S. Lewis: Essay Collection & Other Short Pieces*. Edited by Lesley Walmsley. London: HarperCollins, 2000. This essay was originally published in *The Sunday Times*, March 21, 1943.

_____. *Till We Have Faces*. In *C. S. Lewis: Selected Books* [Long Edition]. 1956. Reprint, London: HarperCollins, 1999.

_____. Marginalia in his edition of *TIMAEVS*, by Plato. In *PLATONIS OPERA TOMVS IV*. Oxonii: E Typograheo Clarendoniano, 1899. The Rare Book Collection, The University of North Carolina at Chapel Hill.

_____. "Tolkien's *The Lord of the Rings*." In *C. S. Lewis: Essay Collection & Other Short Pieces*. Edited by Lesley Walmsley. London: HarperCollins, 2000. This essay originally appeared as two separate reviews of *The Lord of the Rings*, by J. R. R. Tolkien. *Time and Tide* (August 14, 1954 and October 22, 1955).

_____. "Tragic Ends." Review of *The Death of Tragedy*, by George Steiner. *Encounter* 18, no. 2 (February 1962): 97-101.

_____. "Transposition." In *C. S. Lewis: Essay Collection & Other Short Pieces*. Edited by Lesley Walmsley. London: HarperCollins, 2000. This sermon was originally preached in Mansfield College, Oxford, and later appeared in *Transposition and Other Addresses*, by C. S. Lewis. London: Geoffrey Bles, 1949.

_____. Marginalia in his edition of *A Treatise of Human Nature*, by David Hume. Vol. 2. London: J. M. Dent & Sons, 1911. The Marion E. Wade Center, Wheaton College.

_____. "The Trouble with 'X' . . ." In *C. S. Lewis: Essay Collection & Other Short Pieces*. Edited by Lesley Walmsley. London: HarperCollins, 2000. This essay was originally published in *The Bristol Diocesan Gazette* 27 (August 1948).

_____. "Two Lectures." In *C. S. Lewis: Essay Collection & Other Short Pieces*. Edited by Lesley Walmsley. London: HarperCollins, 2000. This essay was originally published as "Who Was Right – Dream Lecturer or Real Lecturer?" *The Coventry Evening Telegraph* (February 21, 1945).

_____. "Two Ways with the Self." In *C. S. Lewis: Essay Collection & Other Short Pieces*. Edited by Lesley Walmsley. London: HarperCollins, 2000. This essay originally appeared in *The Guardian* (May 3, 1940).

_____. "Unreal Estates." In *C. S. Lewis: Essay Collection & Other Short Pieces*. Edited by Lesley Walmsley. London: HarperCollins, 2000. This dialogue was originally recorded in 1962 and was published as "'The Establishment Must Die and Rot . . ,' C. S. Lewis Discusses Science Fiction with Kingsley Amis." *SF Horizons* no. 1 (Spring 1964).

_____. "The Vision of John Bunyan." In *Selected Literary Essays*, by C. S. Lewis. Edited by Walter Hooper. Cambridge: Cambridge University Press, 1969. This essay was first read over the BBC and then published in *The Listener* 68 (December 13, 1962).

_____. "Vivisection." In *C. S. Lewis: Essay Collection & Other Short Pieces*. Edited by Lesley Walmsley. London: HarperCollins, 2000. This essay originally appeared as a pamphlet from the New England Anti-Vivisection Society in 1947.

_____. *The Voyage of the Dawn Treader*. 1952. Reprint, London: Fontana, 1984.

_____. "We Have No 'Right to Happiness.'" In *C. S. Lewis: Essay Collection & Other Short Pieces*. Edited by Lesley Walmsley. London: HarperCollins, 2000. This essay first appeared in *The Saturday Evening Post* 236 (December 21-28, 1963).

_____. "The Weight of Glory." In *C. S. Lewis: Essay Collection & Other Short Pieces*. Edited by Lesley Walmsley. London: HarperCollins, 2000. This was originally given as a sermon in the Church of St. Mary the Virgin, Oxford in 1941.

_____. "What France Means to You." In *We Remember C. S. Lewis: Essays & Memoirs*, edited by David Graham, 1-5. Nashville: Broadman & Homan Publishers, 2001. This article was originally published in *La France Libre: Liberte, Egalite, Fraternite* (April 15, 1944).

_____. "Who Gaf Me Drink?" A review of *Romanticism Comes of Age*, by Owen Barfield. *Spectator* (March 9, 1945): 224.

_____. "The Whole." In "Henry More and Dymer, MS-170," 105-14. March 1924. Unpublished essay. The Marion E. Wade Center, Wheaton College. This essay is not listed on the Wade Center's online catalogue of unpublished works by Lewis that they have. The reason for this is that the Wade Center apparently thought that "The Whole" was merely a part of Lewis's notes on Henry More.

_____. "Why I Am Not a Pacifist." In *C. S. Lewis: Essay Collection & Other Short Pieces*. Edited by Lesley Walmsley. London: HarperCollins, 2000. This essay was originally read to a pacifist society in Oxford in 1940.

_____. "William Morris." In *Selected Literary Essays*, by C. S. Lewis. Edited by Walter Hooper. Cambridge: Cambridge University Press, 1969. This essay was originally presented to the Martlets on November 5, 1937.

_____. "Willing Slaves of the Welfare State." In *C. S. Lewis: Essay Collection & Other Short Pieces*. Edited by Lesley Walmsley. London: HarperCollins, 2000. This essay was originally published in *The Observer* (July 20, 1958).

Lewis, Warren. *Brothers and Friends: The Diaries of Major Warren Hamilton Lewis*. Edited by Clyde Kilby and Marjorie Lamp Mead. San Francisco: Harper & Row, 1982.

_____. "Memoirs of C. S. Lewis." In *Letters of C. S. Lewis*. Edited by Warren Lewis and Walter Hooper, 21-46. San Diego: Harvest, 1993.

Lindvall, Terry. *Surprised by Laughter: The Comic World of C. S. Lewis*. London: Thomas Nelson, 1996.

Lindskoog, Kathryn. *Finding the Landlord: A Guidebook to C. S. Lewis's Pilgrim's Regress*. Chicago: Cornerstone, 1995.

_____. *Sleuthing C. S. Lewis: More Light in the Shadowlands*. Macon, GA: Mercer University Press, 2001.

_____. "Women." In *The C. S. Lewis Readers' Encyclopedia*, edited by Jeffrey Schultz and John West Jr., 429-30. Grand Rapids, MI: Zondervan, 1998.

Lings, Martin. "A Debt Repaid." In *We Remember C. S. Lewis: Essays & Memories*, edited by David Graham, 53-5. Nashville: Broadman & Holman, 2001.

Lloyd, A. C. *The Anatomy of Neoplatonism*. Oxford: Clarendon Press, 2005.

_____. "Athenian and Alexandrian Neoplatonism." In *The Cambridge History of Later Greek and Early Medieval Philosophy*, edited by A. H. Armstrong, 302-25. Cambridge: Cambridge University Press, 2005.

_____. "The Later Neoplatonists." In *The Cambridge History of Later Greek and Early Medieval Philosophy*, edited by A. H. Armstrong, 272-322. Cambridge: Cambridge University Press, 2005.

Locke, John. *An Essay Concerning Human Understanding*. Edited by Roger Woolhouse. New York: Penguin, 1997.

_____. *Second Treatise of Government: An Essay Concerning the True Original, Extent and End of Civil Government*. Edited by Richard Cox. Wheeling, IL: Harlan Davidson, 1982.

Lovell, Steve. "C. S. Lewis and the Euthyphro Dilemma." http://www.theism.net/article/29 (accessed on March 18, 2005).

Lowe, Rodney. "Riches, Poverty, and Progress." In *The British Isles: 1901-1951*, edited by Keith Robbins, 197-228. Oxford: Oxford University Press, 2006.

Lucas, J. R. "The Restoration of Man." A Lecture Given in Durham on Thursday, October 22, 1992. http://users.ox.ac.uk/~jlucas/lewis.html.

Mabbott, John. *Oxford Memories*. Oxford: Thornton's, 1986.

Macaulay, Rose. *Letters to a Sister from Rose Macaulay*. Edited by Constance Babington Smith. London: Collins, 1964.

MacDonald, George. *Unspoken Sermons: Series I, II, III*. Boston, MA: IndyPublish, n.d.

Machin, G. I. T. *Churches and Social Issues in Twentieth-Century Britain*. Oxford: Clarendon Press, 2006.

Manzalaoui, M. A. "Narnia: The Domain of Lewis's Beliefs." In *We Remember C. S. Lewis: Essays & Memories*, edited by David Graham, 9-25. Nashville: Broadman & Holman, 2001.

Marenbon, John. *Later Medieval Philosophy (1150-1350)*. London: Routledge, 2003.

Markos, Louis. *Lewis Agonistes: How C. S. Lewis Can Train Us to Wrestle with the Modern and Postmodern World*. Nashville: Broadman & Holman, 2003.

Marwick, Arthur. *A History of the Modern British Isles, 1914-1999: Circumstances, Events and Outcomes*. Oxford: Blackwell, 2000.

Mastrolia, Arthur. *C. S. Lewis and the Blessed Virgin Mary: Uncovering a 'Marian Attitude.'* Lima, OH: Fairway, 2000.

Matthews, Gareth. *Socratic Perplexity and the Nature of Philosophy*. Oxford: Oxford University Press, 2006.

McLaughlin, Sara. "*The City of God* Revisited: C. S. Lewis's Debt to Saint Augustine." *CSL: The Bulletin of the New York C. S. Lewis Society* 23, no. 6 (April 1992): 1-9.

McSporran, Cathy. "Daughters of Lilith: Witches and Wicked Women in the Chronicles of Narnia." In *Revisiting Narnia: Fantasy, Myth and Religion in C. S. Lewis' Chronicles*, edited by Shanna Caughey, 191-204. Dallas: Benbella Books, 2005.

Médaille, John C. "Heaven as the Home of the Free: The Primacy of the Will in Duns Scotus." http://www.medaille.com/primacy.html (accessed February 2, 2005).

Meilaender, Gilbert. *The Taste for the Other: The Social and Ethical Thought of C. S. Lewis*. Grand Rapids, MI: Eerdmans, 1980.

Memory, J. D. "C. S. Lewis and the Mind-Body Identity Thesis." *CSL: The Bulletin of the New York C. S. Lewis Society* 5, no. 10 (August 1974): 17-8.

Meynell, Hugo. "An Attack on C. S. Lewis." *Faith and Philosophy* 8, no. 3 (July 1991): 305-15.

Micklem, Nathaniel. *The Box and the Puppets (1888-1953)*. London: Geoffrey Bles, 1957.

Mill, John Stuart. *The Subjection of Women*. Mineola, NY: Dover, 1997.

_____. *A System of Logic, Ratiocinative and Inductive*. Vol. 1. 3rd ed. London: John W. Parker, 1851.

_____. *Utilitarianism*. Edited by Geraint Williams. London: J. M. Dent, 1999.

Miller, Laura. "Return to Narnia." *The Los Angeles Times*, December 4, 2005.

Mills, David. "Rationality and Revelation: C. S. Lewis and Lambeth." *Mandate* (July / August 1998). http://theroadtoemmaus.org/RDLb/12The/SxTh/WmO/WmODMlls.htm (accessed on May 6, 2005).

Milward, Peter. *A Challenge to C. S. Lewis*. London: Associated University Presses, 1995.

Mitchell, Basil. "C. S. Lewis on *The Abolition of Man*." In *C. S. Lewis Remembered*, edited by Harry Lee Poe and Rebecca Whitten Poe, 174-83. Grand Rapids, MI: Zondervan, 2006.

Mitchell, Basil and Andrew Walker. "Reflections on C. S. Lewis, Apologetics, and the Moral Tradition: Basil Mitchell in Conversation with Andrew Walker." In *Rumours of Heaven: Essays in Celebration of C. S. Lewis*, edited by Andrew Walter and James Patrick, 7-26. London: Eagle, 1998.

Mitchell, Christopher W. "University Battles: C. S. Lewis and the Oxford University Socratic Club." In *C. S. Lewis: Lightbearer in the Shadowlands; The Evangelistic Vision of C. S. Lewis*, edited by Angus Menuge, 329-51. Wheaton, IL: Crossway Books, 1997.

Moore, G. E. *Philosophical Studies.* 1922. Reprint, London: Routledge, 2002.

Moorman, Charles. *The Precincts of Felicity: The Augustinian City of the Oxford Christians.* Gainesville, FL: University of Florida Press, 1966.

Moreland, J. P. *The Kingdom Triangle.* Grand Rapids, MI: Zondervan, 2007.

Morris, Tom. "Foreword." In *C. S. Lewis as Philosopher: Truth, Goodness, and Beauty,* edited by David Baggett, Gary Habermas and Jerry Walls, 9-10. Downers Grove, IL: InterVarsity Press, 2008.

Moynihan, Martin. "C. S. Lewis and T. D. Weldon." *VII: An Anglo-American Literary Review* 5 (1984): 101-5.

_____. "I Sleep but My Heart Watcheth." In *We Remember C. S. Lewis: Essays & Memories,* edited by David Graham, 36-40. Nashville: Broadman & Holman, 2001.

Mrs. B. "Rebellion and Feminism: My Story." http://www.ladiesagainstfeminism.org/artman/publish/article_1363.shtml (accessed on May 25, 2005).

Mueller, Steven. *Not a Tame God: Christ in the Writings of C. S. Lewis.* Saint Louis: Concordia Publishing House, 2002.

Musacchio, George. *C. S. Lewis: Man & Writer; Essays and Reviews.* Belton, TX: The University of Mary Hardin-Baylor, 1994.

Muth, Michael. "Beastly Metaphysics: The Beasts of Narnia and Lewis's Reclamation of Medieval Sacramental Metaphysics." In *C. S. Lewis as Philosopher: Truth, Goodness, and Beauty,* edited by David Baggett, Gary Habermas and Jerry Walls, 228-44. Downers Grove, IL: InterVarsity Press, 2008.

Myers, Doris. *C. S. Lewis in Context.* Kent, OH: Kent State University Press, 1994.

_____. "Lewis in Genderland," *Christian Scholar's Review* 36, no. 4 (Summer 2007): 455-60.

Nadeau, Maurice. *The History of Surrealism.* Cambridge, MA: Belknap Press, 1989.

Neuhaus, Richard John. "C. S. Lewis in the Public Square." *First Things* (December 1998).

Neuhouser, David. "Higher Dimensions: C. S. Lewis and Mathematics." *VII: An Anglo-American Literary Review* 13 (1996): 45-63.

Nicholas, Siân. "Being British: Creeds and Culture." In *The British Isles: 1901-1951,* edited by Keith Robbins, 103-36. Oxford: Oxford University Press, 2006.

Nicholi, Armand, Jr. *The Question of God: C. S. Lewis and Sigmund Freud Debate God, Love, Sex, and the Meaning of Life.* New York: The Free Press, 2002.

Novalis. *Heinrich von Ofterdingen.* In *The Collected Works of Novalis.* Vol. 1. Edited by Hans-Joachim Mähl, 237-413. Munich: Hanser, 1978.

Nussbaum, Martha. *The Therapy of Desire: Theory and Practice in Hellenistic Ethics.* Princeton: Princeton University Press, 1996.

O'Hare, Joan. "Intellectual Development." In *We Remember C. S. Lewis: Essays & Memoirs,* edited by David Graham, 41-5. Nashville: Broadman & Holman, 2001.

"One Year Ago in the Bulletin." *CSL: The Bulletin of the New York C. S. Lewis Society* 2, no. 10 (August 1971): 5.

Orwell, George. "As I Please." *Tribute,* October 27, 1944.

_____. "The Scientist Takes Over." Review of *That Hideous Strength,* by C. S. Lewis. *Manchester Evening News,* August 16, 1945.

Otto, Rudolf. *The Idea of the Holy: An Inquiry into the Non-rational Factor in the Idea of the Divine and its Relation to the Rational.* Translated by John W. Harvey. Oxford: Oxford University Press, 1958.

Owen, W. J. B. "Splendid Tutor." In *We Remember C. S. Lewis: Essays & Memories,* edited by David Graham, 59-60. Nashville: Broadman & Holman, 2001.

Packer, J. I. "What Lewis Was and Wasn't." In *We Remember C. S. Lewis: Essays & Memories*, edited by David Graham, 6-8. Nashville: Broadman & Holman, 2001.

Patrick, James. "C. S. Lewis and Idealism." In *Rumours of Heaven: Essays in Celebration of C. S. Lewis*, edited by Andrew Walker and James Patrick, 156-73. London: Eagle, 1998.

____. "The Heart's Desire and the Landlord's Rules: C. S. Lewis as a Moral Philosopher." In *The Pilgrim's Guide: C. S. Lewis and the Art of Witness*, edited by David Mills, 70-85. Grand Rapids, MI: William B. Eerdmans, 1998.

____. *The Magdalen Metaphysicals: Idealism and Orthodoxy at Oxford 1901-1945*. N.p.: Mercer University Press, 1985.

____. "Reason in Chesterton and Lewis." *Chesterton Review* 17, no. 3 and 4 (August and November 1991): 349-55.

Patterson, W. Brown. "C. S. Lewis: Personal Reflections." In *C. S. Lewis: Remembered*, edited by Harry Lee Poe and Rebecca Whitten Poe, 89-97. Grand Rapids, MI: Zondervan, 2006.

Pavlac Glyer, Diana. "'We are *All* Fallen Creatures and *All* Very Hard to Live With': Some Thoughts on Lewis and Gender." *Christian Scholar's Review* 36, no. 4 (Summer 2007): 477-83.

____ and Laura Simmons. "Dorothy L. Sayers and C. S. Lewis: Two Approaches to Creativity and Calling." In *VII: An Anglo-American Literary Review* 21 (2004): 31-46.

Payne, Leanne. *Real Presence: The Christian Worldview of C. S. Lewis as Incarnational Reality*. Westchester, IL: Crossway Books, 1988.

Peter, Thomas. *Simply C. S. Lewis: A Beginner's Guide to the Life of C. S. Lewis*. Wheaton, IL: Crossway Books, 1997.

Peterson, Michael et al. *Reason & Religious Belief*. 3rd ed. New York: Oxford University Press, 2003.

Petrik, James. "In Defense of C. S. Lewis's Analysis of God's Goodness." *International Journal for Philosophy of Religion* 36 (1994): 45-56.

Petty, Anne. *Tolkien in the Land of Heroes: Discovering the Human Spirit*. Cold Spring Harbor, NY: Cold Spring Press, 2003.

Philip, Peter. "South African View." In *In Search of C. S. Lewis*, edited by Stephen Schofield, 93-6. South Plainfield, NJ: Bridge, 1983.

Phillips, Justin. *C. S. Lewis at the BBC: Messages of Hope in the Darkness of War*. London: HarperCollins, 2002.

Piehler, Paul. "Encounters with Lewis: An Interim Report." In *C. S. Lewis: Remembered*, edited by Harry Lee Poe and Rebecca Whitten Poe, 115-58. Grand Rapids, MI: Zondervan, 2006.

____. "Visions and Revisions: C. S. Lewis's Contributions to the Theory of Allegory." In *The Taste of the Pineapple: Essays on C. S. Lewis as Reader, Critic, and Imaginative Writer*, edited by Bruce Edwards, 79-91. Bowling Green, OH: Bowling Green State University Popular Press, 1988.

Pierce, Joseph. *C. S. Lewis and the Church of Rome*. San Francisco: Ignatius Press, 2003.

Pile, Joan. "Part C: With Women at College." In *In Search of C. S. Lewis*, edited by Stephen Schofield, 71-3. South Plainfield, NJ: Bridge Publishing, 1983.

Pius IX. "Letter." *Acta Sanctae Sedis in Compendium Opportune Redacta* 12:97-115.

Plantinga, Alvin. "Ad Hick." *Faith and Philosophy* 14, no. 3 (July 1997): 295-8.

_____. "Two Dozen (or so) Theistic Arguments." In *Alvin Plantinga*. Edited by Deane-Peter Baker. Contemporary Philosophy in Focus. Cambridge: Cambridge University Press, 2007. These arguments were designed as lecture notes for a lecture given in 1986.

"'The Politics of C. S. Lewis': Report of the 140th Meeting." *CSL: The Bulletin of the New York C. S. Lewis Society* 12, no. 8 (June 1981): 3-5.

Poole, Roger. "Lewis Lecturing." In *We Remember C. S. Lewis: Essays & Memories*, edited by David Graham, 70-7. Nashville: Broadman & Holman, 2001.

Portman, Jamie. "Adamson's Work on Shrek Made Narnia His Next Cheque." *The National Post*, December 9, 2005 (PM6).

Pullman, Philip. Quoted in "Narnia Books Attacked as Racist and Sexist," by John Ezard. *Guardian*, June 3, 2002. http://www.guardian.co.uk/uk_news/story/0,3604,726739,00.html (accessed February 3, 2005).

Purtill, Richard. *C. S. Lewis's Case for the Christian Faith*. San Francisco, Harper & Row, 1985.

_____. "Did C. S. Lewis Lose His Faith?" In *Rumours of Heaven: Essays in Celebration of C. S. Lewis*, edited by Andrew Walker and James Patrick, 27-62. London: Eagle, 1998.

_____. *Lord of the Elves and Eldils: Fantasy and Philosophy in C. S. Lewis and J. R. R. Tolkien*. Grand Rapids, MI: Zondervan, 1974.

Ratzinger, Joseph. "Consumer Materialism and Christian Hope." http://www.catholic-ew.org.uk/resource/totf/ratzinger.html (accessed August 4, 2005).

Reilly, R. J. *Romantic Religion: A Study of Owen Barfield, C. S. Lewis, Charles Williams and J. R. R. Tolkien*. Great Barrington, MA: Lindisfarne Books, 2006.

"Report of the 138th Meeting: April 10, 1981." *CSL: The Bulletin of the New York C. S. Lewis Society* 12, no. 6 (April 1981): 5-6.

Reppert, Victor. *C. S. Lewis's Dangerous Idea: In Defense of the Argument from Reason*. Downers Grove, IL: InterVarsity Press, 2003.

_____. "Defending the Dangerous Idea: An Update on Lewis's Argument from Reason." In *C. S. Lewis as Philosopher: Truth, Goodness, and Beauty*, edited by David Baggett, Gary Habermas and Jerry Walls, 53-67. Downers Grove, IL: \ InterVarsity Press, 2008.

_____. "The Ecumenical Apologist: Understanding C. S. Lewis's Defense of Christianity." In *Apologist, Philosopher, & Theologian*. Vol. 3, *C. S. Lewis: Life, Works, & Legacy*, edited by Bruce Edwards, 1-28. Westport, CT: Praeger, 2007.

_____. "The Green Witch and the Great Debate: Freeing Narnia from the Spell of the Lewis-Anscombe Legend." In *The Chronicles of Narnia and Philosophy: The Lion, the Witch and the Wardrobe*, edited by Gregory Bassham and Jerry Walls, 260-72. Chicago: Open Court, 2005.

_____. "*Miracles*: C. S. Lewis's Critique of Naturalism." In *Apologist, Philosopher, & Theologian*. Vol. 3, *C. S. Lewis: Life, Works, and Legacy*, edited by Bruce Edwards, 153-82. Westport, CT: Praeger, 2007.

Richards, I. A. *Principles of Literary Criticism*. 1924. Reprint, London: Routledge, 2001.

Riga, Frank. "Augustinian Pride and the Work of C. S. Lewis." *Augustinian Studies* 16 (1984): 129-36.

_____. "Self-Love in Augustine and C. S. Lewis." *Cithara: Essays in the Judaeo-Christian Tradition* 26, no.2 (May 1987): 20-30.

Rigby, Luke. "A Solid Man," in *C. S. Lewis at the Breakfast Table and Other Reminiscences*, edited by James Como, 38-40. San Diego: Harcourt Brace & Company, 1992.

Rist, John. *Augustine: Ancient Thought Baptized*. Cambridge: Cambridge University Press, 2003.

Rogers, Katherine. "Augustinian Evil in C. S. Lewis's *Perelandra*." In *The Transcendent Adventure: Studies of Religion in Science Fiction/Fantasy*, edited by Robert Reilly, 83-99. Westport, CT: Greenwood Press, 1985.

Rook, Alan. "The Butcher." In *In Search of C. S. Lewis*, edited by Stephen Schofield, 11-5. South Plainfield, NJ: Bridge, 1983.

Root, Jerry. "C. S. Lewis and the Problem of Evil." In *Lightbearer in the Shadowlands: The Evangelistic Vision of C. S. Lewis*, edited by Angus Menuge, 353-66. Wheaton, IL: Crossway Books, 1997.

Rose, Mary Carman. "The Christian Platonism of C. S. Lewis, J. R. R. Tolkien, and Charles Williams." In *NeoPlatonism and Christian Thought*, edited by Dominic J. O'Meara, 203-12. Norfold, VA: International Society for NeoPlatonic Studies, 1982.

Ross, David. *Aristotle*. 1923. Reprint, London: Routledge, 1996.

Routley, Erik. "A Prophet." In *C. S. Lewis at the Breakfast Table and Other Reminiscences*, edited by James Como, 33-7. San Diego: Harcourt Brace & Company, 1992.

Rozema, David. "'Belief' in the Writings of C. S. Lewis." In *C. S. Lewis as Philosopher: Truth, Goodness, and Beauty*, edited by David Baggett, Gary Habermas and Jerry Walls, 144-58. Downers Grove, IL: InterVarsity Press, 2008.

Russell, Bertrand. "A Free Man's Worship." In *Why I Am Not a Christian and Other Essays on Religion and Related Subjects*. Edited by Paul Edwards. New York: A Touchstone Book, 1957.

Ryken, Leland and Marjorie Lamp Mead. *A Reader's Guide Through the Wardrobe: Exploring C. S. Lewis's Classic Story*. Downers Grove, IL: InterVarsity, 2005.

Ryle, Gilbert. *The Concept of Mind*. London: Hutchinson, 1949.

Santayana, George. *Reason in Art*. Vol. 4, *The Life of Reason*. 1905. Reprint, London: Dover, 1982.

Sartre, Jean-Paul. *Existentialism is a Humanism*. Translated by Carol Macomber. Edited by John Kulka. 1947. Reprint, New Haven: Yale University Press, 2007.

Sayer, George. *Jack: A Life o f C. S. Lewis*. Wheaton, IL: Crossway Books, 1988.

Sayers, Dorothy. *The Mind of the Maker*. 9th ed. 1941. Reprint, London: Methuen & Co., 1947.

Schakel, Peter. *Imagination and the Arts in C. S. Lewis: Journeying to Narnia and Other Worlds*. Columbia, MO: University of Missouri Press, 2002.

_____. *Is Your Lord Large Enough? How C. S. Lewis Expands Our View of God*. Downers Grove, IL: IVP, 2008.

_____. *Reason and Imagination in C. S. Lewis: A Study o f Till We Have Faces*. Grand Rapids, MI: 1984.

_____. "Seeing and Knowing: the Epistemology of C. S. Lewis's *Till We Have Faces*." *VII: An Anglo-American Literary Review* 4 (1983): 84-97.

Schiller, Fredrick von. *The Poems of Schiller*. New York: Dodo Press, 2007.

Schopenhauer, Arthur. "On Ethics." In *Essays and Aphorisms*. Translated by R. J. Hollingdale, 133-47. London: Penguin, 1970.

_____. "On the Vanity of Existence." In *Essays and Aphorisms*. Translated by R. J. Hollingdale, 51-4. London: Penguin, 1970.

Schroeder, Gerald. *The Hidden Face of God: Science Reveals the Ultimate Truth*. New York: Simon & Schuster, 2001.

Sibley, Brian. *C. S. Lewis Through the Shadowlands: The Story of His Life with Joy Davidman*. Grand Rapids, MI: Spire, 1999.

Sidney, Philip. *The Defence of Poesy*. In *Sir Philip Sidney*. Edited by Katherine Duncan-Jones. The Oxford Authors. Oxford: Oxford University Press, 1989.

Sinclair, Hugh. "Forgetful Rudeness." In *We Remember C. S. Lewis: Essays & Memories*, edited by David Graham, 115-8. Nashville: Broadman & Holman, 2001.

Skinner, B. F. *Beyond Freedom & Dignity*. 1971. Reprint, Cambridge: Hackett, 2002.

Skorupski, John. "Green and the Idealist Conception of a Person's Good." In *T. H. Green: Ethics, Metaphysics, and Political Philosophy*, edited by Maria Dimova-Cookson and W. J. Mander, 47-75. Oxford: Clarendon Press, 2006.

Slack, Michael. "Sehnsucht and the Platonic Eros in *Dymer*." *CSL: The Bulletin of the New York C. S. Lewis Society* 11 (August 1980): 3-7.

Smith, Huston. *The Religions of Man*. New York: Harper & Row, 1989.

Smith, Lyle Jr. "C. S. Lewis and the Making of Metaphor." In *Word and Story in C. S. Lewis*. Edited by Peter Schakel and Charles Huttar, 11-28. Columbia, MO: University of Missouri Press, 1991.

Smith, Richard. "Afterward: The Modern Relevance of Gnosticism." In *The Nag Hammdi Library*, edited by Richard Smith, 532-49. San Francisco: HarperSanFrancisco, 1990.

Smith, Robert Houston. *Patches of Godlight: The Pattern of Thought of C. S. Lewis*. Athens, GA: University of Georgia Press, 1981.

Spinoza, Baruch. *The Ethics*. Translated by Samuel Shirley. Edited by Seymour Feldman. Cambridge: Hackett, 1992.

Sturma, Dieter. "Politics and the New Mythology: the Turn to Late Romanticism." In *The Cambridge Companion to German Idealism*, edited by Karl Ameriks, 219-38. Cambridge: Cambridge University Press, 2006.

Talbott, Thomas. "C. S. Lewis and the Problem of Evil." *Christian Scholar's Review* 17, (1987): 36-51.

Taliaferro, Charles and Rachel Traughber. "The Atonement in Narnia." In *The Chronicles of Narnia and Philosophy: The Lion, the Witch and the Wardrobe*, edited by Gregory Bassham and Jerry L. Walls, 245-59. Chicago: Open Court, 2005.

Tallon, Philip. "Evil and the Cosmic Dance: C. S. Lewis and Beauty's Place in Theodicy." In *C. S. Lewis as Philosopher: Truth, Goodness, and Beauty*, edited by David Baggett, Gary Habermas and Jerry Walls, 195-210. Downers Grove, IL: InterVarsity Press, 2008.

Tanner, Duncan, "Electing the Governors / the Governance of the Elect." In *The British Isles: 1901-1951*, edited by Keith Robbins, 43-72. Oxford: Oxford University Press, 2006.

Taylor, A. J. P. "The Fun of the Thing." In *In Search of C. S. Lewis*, edited by Stephen Schofield, 117-22. South Plainfield, NJ: Bridge, 1983.

Thomas, Keith. "College Life, 1945-1970." In *The History of the University of Oxford: Volume VIII; The Twentieth Century*, edited by Brian Harrison, 189-216. Oxford: Oxford University Press, 1994.

Thorson, Stephen. "'Knowledge' in C. S. Lewis's Post-Conversion Thought: His Epistemological Method." *VII: An Anglo-American Literary Review* 9 (1988): 91-116.

Tolkien, J. R. R. *The Letters of J. R. R. Tolkien*. Edited by Humphrey Carpenter and Christopher Tolkien. London: HarperCollins, 1995.

_____. "On Fairy-Stories." In *The Tolkien Reader*. New York: Ballantine Books, 1975.

_____. *The Silmarillion*. Edited by Christopher Tolkien. London: Unwin Paperbacks, 1989.

Totaro, Rebecca. "Regaining Perception: The Ransom Trilogy as a Re-embodiment of the Neoplatonic Model." *CSL: The Bulletin of the New York C. S. Lewis Society* 22, no. 10 (August 1991): 1-11.

Travers, Michael. "The Letters of C. S. Lewis: C. S. Lewis as Correspondent." In *Scholar, Teacher, & Public Intellectual*. Vol. 4, *C. S. Lewis: Life, Works, and Legacy*, edited by Bruce Edwards, 19-48. Westport, CT: Praeger, 2007.

Trevor-Roper, Hugh. *Letters from Oxford: Hugh Trevor-Roper to Bernard Berenson*. Edited by Richard Davenport-Hines. London: Phoenix, 2007.

Trickett, Rachel. "Uncrowned King of Oxford." In *We Remember C. S. Lewis: Essays & Memoirs*, edited by David Graham, 61-4. Nashville: Broadman & Holman, 2001.

Traherne, Thomas. *Centuries of Meditation*. Edited by Bertram Dobell. London: Robert Stockwell, 1950.

Tynan, Kenneth. "Exhilaration." In *In Search of C. S. Lewis*, edited by Stephen Schofield, 3-9. South Plainfield, NJ: Bridge, 1983.

Unger, Walter. "C. S. Lewis at 100." *M. B. Herald* 37, no. 20.

Van Inwagen, Peter. "A Reply to Professor Hick." *Faith and Philosophy* 14, no. 3 (July 1997): 299-302.

Van Leeuwen, Mary Stewart. "A Sword Between the Sexes: C. S. Lewis's Long Journey to Gender Equality." *Christian Scholar's Review* 36, no. 4 (Summer 2007): 391-414. It should be noted that this essay was based on a 2004 lecture called "The Anti-Reductionist Reductionist: C. S. Lewis, Science, and Gender Relations," which Van Leeuwen gave at the University of Tennessee, Chattanooga.

Vaus, Will. *Mere Theology: A Guide to the Thought of C. S. Lewis*. Downers Grove, IL: InterVarsity Press, 2004.

Vidal, Jaime. "The Ubiquitous Center in Bonaventure and Lewis with Application to The Great Dance on Perelandra." *CSL: The Bulletin of the New York C. S. Lewis Society* 6, no. 5 (March 1975): 1-4.

Vincent, Andrew. "Metaphysics and Ethics in the Philosophy of T. H. Green." In *T. H. Green: Ethics, Metaphysics, and Political Philosophy*, edited by Maria Dimova-Cookson and W. J. Mander, 76-105. Oxford: Clarendon Press, 2006.

Vincent, Paul. "C. S. Lewis as Amateur Philosopher." *The New York C. S. Lewis Society Bulletin* no. 9 (July 1970): 1-3.

Volf, Miroslav. *Exclusion & Embrace: A Theological Exploration of Identity, Otherness, and Reconciliation*. Nashville: Abingdon, 1996.

von Hügel, Friedrich. *Essays and Addresses on the Philosophy of Religion*. 1921. Reprint, Eugene, OR: Wipf and Stock Publishers, 2001.

Wallsgrove, Pat. "Courtesy and Learning." In *We Remember C. S. Lewis: Essays & Memoirs*, edited by David Graham, 46-7. Nashville: Broadman & Holman, 2001.

Walsh, Chad. *The Literary Legacy of C. S. Lewis*. New York: Harcourt Brace Jovanovich, 1979.

Ward, Michael. *Planet Narnia: The Seven Heavens in the Imagination of C. S. Lewis*. Oxford: Oxford University Press, 2008.

Watson, George. "The Art of Disagreement: C. S. Lewis (1898-1963)." In *C. S. Lewis Remembered*, edited by Harry Lee Poe and Rebecca Whitten Poe, 77-88. Grand Rapids, MI: Zondervan, 2006.

Webster, Wendy. *Englishness and Empire: 1939-1965*. Oxford: Oxford University Press, 2007.

West, John G., Jr. "C. S. Lewis and Materialism." *Religion and Liberty* 6, no. 6 (November and December 1996): 1-6. http://www.acton.org/publicat/randl/article.php?id=211 (accessed February 3, 2005).

———. "Finding the Permanent in the Political: C. S. Lewis as a Political Thinker." In *Permanent Things: Towards the Recovery of a More Human Scale at the End of the Twentieth Century*, edited by Andrew Tadie and Michael Macdonald, 137-50. Grand Rapids, MI: Eerdmans, 1995.

———. "Politics from the Shadowlands: C. S. Lewis on Earthly Government." *Policy Review* (Spring 1994).

Wetherbee, Winthrop. *Platonism and Poetry in the Twelfth Century: The Literary Influence of the School of Chartres.* Princeton: Princeton University Press, 1972.

White, Michael. *C. S. Lewis: The Boy Who Chronicled Narnia.* London: Abacus, 2005.

White, William Luther. *The Image of Man in C. S. Lewis.* Nashville: Abingdon, 1969.

Wielenberg, Erik. *God and the Reach of Reason: C.S. Lewis, David Hume, and Bertrand Russell.* Cambridge: Cambridge University Press, 2008.

Willard, Dallas. "Truth in the Fire: C. S. Lewis and Pursuit of Truth Today." http://dwillard.org/articles/artview.asp?artID=68 (accessed October 13, 2003).

Williams, Charles. *He Came Down from Heaven.* London: Heinemann, 1938.

Willis, John Randolph. *Pleasures Forevermore: The Theology of C. S. Lewis.* Chicago: Loyola University Press, 1983.

Wilson, A. N. *C. S. Lewis: A Biography.* New York: W.W. Norton & Company, 1990.

Wolfe, Gregory. "Lewis on the Nature of Politics: A Reply to Danny Adkison." *CSL: The Bulletin of the New York C. S. Lewis Society* 16, no. 1 (November 1984): 6-7.

Wolheim, Richard. Introduction to *Ethical Studies*, by F. H. Bradley. 2nd ed. 1876. Reprint, Oxford: Oxford University Press, 1988.

Wordsworth, William. *The Prelude.* In *William Wordsworth: The Major Works.* Oxford: Oxford University Press, 2000.

———. "Preface to *Lyrical Ballads*." In *William Wordsworth: The Major Works.* Oxford: Oxford University Press, 2000.

Wrong, Charles. "A Chance Meeting." In *C. S. Lewis at the Breakfast Table and Other Reminiscences*, edited by James Como, 107-14. San Diego: Harcourt Brace & Company, 1992.

Yates, Courtney McKim. "The Girls of Narnia: Conflicts Between Religion and Gender in C. S. Lewis's Chronicles." http://www2.mcdaniel.edu/English/students/lit04/cyates.htm (accessed May 13, 2005).

General Index

Abbott, Thomas Kingsmill, 84n81, 552
Abortion, 363, 435, 435n107
Abraham, William, 302n143
Absolute, 23, 25n17, 42-43, 45-51, 48n145,
    49n147, 51n162, 54, 81n68, 84, 102,
    105n10, 116-117, 117n55, 121-122,
    128, 132, 150, 150n211, 174, 190,
    218n6, 220-221, 223n20, 224, 225n27,
    226-228, 227n31, 230, 232-233, 235,
    238-241, 243, 249, 256-258, 260, 262,
    264, 267, 275, 277, 283n67, 286, 294-
    296, 297n125, 300-301, 304, 314, 320,
    328, 333, 334n91, 335-337, 339n115,
    340-346, 340n119, 341n122, 343n132,
    348, 350, 351n159, 354, 364n203, 371,
    380, 385-386, 389, 396n332, 401, 403,
    411, 425, 446, 448, 471, 502
Absolute Idealism, 23, 46-48, 48n145, 49-51,
    51n162, 54, 102, 116, 121-122, 174,
    224, 226-228, 230, 232, 235, 239, 241,
    249, 257, 260, 262, 295-296, 337,
    339n115, 340n119, 341, 341n122,
    343n132, 344, 380, 385, 502
Abstract, 19, 32, 33n68, 44, 89, 95, 102, 117,
    117n55, 120n68, 122, 139, 142, 157n4,
    179n100, 189, 204n211, 225n27, 254,
    262-263, 266, 278n47, 281n59, 282,
    322, 334, 337, 340, 343n133, 383n271,
    429, 488n360, 518n88, 522
Academy, 13, 32, 311n2, 510n56
Actuality, 88, 88n96, 133, 152, 239, 242, 250,
    485n348
Adamson, Andrew, 419
Addison, Paul, 463n226
Adey, Lionel, 132, 270n19, 510n56
Adkin, Neil, 201n199
Adkison, Danny, 417n1
Adonis, 133-134
Adultery, 357n178, 436, 436n113, 460, 460n209
Aeschliman, Michael, 54n175
Aeschylus, 25n20, 105n12, 313n5, 384
Aesthetics, 8, 30, 33, 41, 76, 104, 168, 267, 320,
    495, 497, 499, 501, 503-505, 507, 509,
    511, 513, 515, 517, 519n95, 523, 525,
    527, 529
Aggiornamento, 184n127
Agnosticism / Agnostic, 25n17, 26, 36, 145, 475
Ainslie, Douglas, 113n38, 209, 319n33
Akrasia / Akratia / Akrates, 400, 401n340, 404
Alain de Lille, 131, 196n175
Alanus. *See* Alain de Lille
Albert the Great, 120n68, 269-270, 272

Alexander, Samuel, 41, 114-115, 114n44,
    115n47, 115n49, 122, 296, 349, 505,
    515
Alighieri, Dante, 51, 54-56, 150, 159n17,
    161-162, 183, 205, 297, 305, 376n240,
    403n355, 454n188, 510, 515n75, 526
Allegory / Allegorical, 17, 34n75, 50, 72, 102,
    128-132, 139-143, 143n173, 146n185,
    149n205, 159n17, 183n120, 187n138,
    205, 206n216, 284n68, 335, 359n183,
    403, 404n357, 407n373, 408, 503n23
Allenby, Edmund, 170
Allred, David, 235n60
Altar, 434n101
Amazon / Amazonian (Women), 431n88, 438
Ambrose, 199n180, 201n199
Ameriks, Karl, 250n131
Amis, Kingsley, 392n314
Analogy, 89, 93, 143, 164, 234, 236, 256, 262,
    335, 343, 376, 512
Ancient, 5, 11-13, 16-20, 23, 27, 29, 38, 54, 57,
    80, 86-87, 94, 104, 123-124, 128-131,
    141, 155-158, 160-162, 174-175, 182,
    212-213, 229, 249, 283, 284n70, 286,
    292, 302n143, 311, 327, 359, 404-405,
    426, 456, 468-469, 531, 533
Anderson, Greg, 522n104
Angel, 72, 74, 104, 198n184, 222, 229n41, 233-
    235, 237, 244-247, 278n44, 280n57,
    282, 290n93, 362n192, 376, 379n254,
    405, 406n367, 409, 523
Anglican, 2n6, 19, 63n225, 155, 166, 180,
    182n117, 185, 186n133, 187n138,
    195n172, 266, 302n143, 303n144, 305,
    308, 312, 356n176, 434n101, 436n113,
    452n176, 524n109
Anglo-Catholicism, 24-25, 57n191, 186n133
Angus, Katrelya, 462n219
Anscombe, G. E. M., 3n17, 4, 59-63, 59n201,
    60n203, 60n204, 60n208, 60n209,
    62n217, 160, 291, 298-299
Anselm, 87, 88n95, 144n176
Anthroposophy / Anthroposophist, 35, 39n97,
    48, 79, 114, 118-119, 137n144,
    140n159, 187, 199, 295, 328
Antiochus, 13, 16n24
Antiquity. *See* Ancient
Antisthenes, 14
Apologetics, 2n6, 4n21, 6n28, 60-62, 173n77,
    268, 311, 356n175, 423, 455n189, 479,
    512
Apologist, 3n14, 6n30, 60n208, 61, 62n217,

330n73, 332, 332n80, 332n81, 333n84,
334-339, 334n91, 336n99, 336n100,
341-350, 341n122, 342n128, 343n131,
344n134, 344n135, 351n160, 351n161,
352-354, 357, 357n178, 358n180, 359-
362, 360n185, 362n193, 362n195, 364,
364n203, 365n205, 366n209, 367n209,
367n210, 368n214, 368n215, 370-376,
370n226, 370n228, 370n228, 371n233,
372n234, 372n237, 373n237, 374n239,
377n246, 380-381, 380n257, 381n260,
381n262, 383-384, 383n270, 383n271,
384n271, 386, 388, 389n297, 390,
390n303, 391n309, 392n314, 393n321,
394-395, 394n323, 395n326, 395n327,
396n330, 396n332, 397-400, 397n335,
398n337, 402-405, 407n374, 408n374,
408n375, 409n376, 410, 412, 415n399,
421n32, 422-423, 427-428, 431n89,
435, 435n106, 438-439, 446, 448n155,
449n156, 449n158, 449n162, 450,
451n175, 452n175, 453-456, 454n186,
457n198, 461, 461n213, 463, 467-468,
468n254, 470n258, 473n282, 474-475,
476n294, 477n300, 480n310, 480n314,
481, 481n315, 481n317, 482n327,
485n346, 487n357, 488, 490n364,
491n368, 491n369, 492, 493n375, 494,
501-502, 503n24, 504n28, 504n29, 505,
509, 511, 513n70, 513n71, 515-516,
516n78, 518-523, 518n88, 520n95,
520n96, 523n105, 524n110, 525-526,
525n111, 526n120, 527n123, 531
Gore, Charles, 165n41, 175n81
Gospel, 172, 375, 511n62
Grace, 80, 85, 173, 205, 235, 244, 260, 265, 308,
345-346, 378, 403, 405, 410-411, 413,
413n392, 485, 511n62
Graham, David, 249n125, 422n37, 423n39,
423n41, 423n43, 482n328, 483n341,
483n342, 485n350, 486n352
Grammar, 95, 375-376, 488n360, 493, 493n376,
493n378, 505, 520n95
Grant, George, 2, 2n7, 356, 356n176, 452n176
Grant, Sheila, 356n176
Grayling, A. C., 300n137
Greece / Greek, 17n27, 18, 24n12, 29, 35,
63n222, 72, 80, 83-84, 97, 105, 119n66,
136, 144, 144n178, 159, 162n28,
175, 178n100, 181, 183, 184n126,
185, 196n531, 203n207, 228n37,
234, 236n61, 239, 255, 283, 286n79,
288n80, 288, 293n104, 313n9, 322,
333, 375, 398, 401n349, 413, 422n35,
428n73, 429n80, 437, 445, 456n197,

468, 480n310, 522n102, 526
Great Bookham, 27, 55, 474
Great Chain of Being, 17, 190, 228, 246
"Great War" (between C. S. Lewis and Owen
Barfield), 3, 3n15, 35n80, 36n82, 39-41
39n97, 42n115, 46, 46n134, 49n148,
81n68, 88, 88n97, 113-114, 114n45,
116-117, 117n55, 117n57, 120, 120n67,
120n69, 121n73, 122n77, 122n78,
122n80, 123n82, 124n85, 124n89,
126n94, 126n96, 128, 132, 132n125,
137, 173n74, 199n187, 223n23, 224,
239, 239n71, 256n161, 279, 282n64,
291, 293n103, 294, 295n113, 296n120,
301, 303, 320n35, 335, 340, 343n131,
385n281, 396n330, 400, 462n220, 501,
502n15, 508n46, 508n48
"Greats." *See Literae Humaniores*
Green, Roger Lancelyn, 45n130, 91n105,
273n32, 292n101
Green, T. H., 41n108, 42, 45n132, 46n139, 48,
277n41, 312, 333-337, 333n81, 333n83,
334n85, 340, 341n122, 385, 386n283,
406
Green, William, 201n199
Greeves, Arthur, 55, 105-106, 167, 317,
383n270, 383n271, 391n311, 414n396
Gregor, Mary, 84n80, 285n71
Gregory of Nazianzus, 196n531
Gresham, David, 177, 177n92
Gresham, Douglas, 431n88
Gresham, Joy. *See* Joy Lewis
Griffith, Gwilyn, 363n199
Griffiths, Dom Bede, 51-52, 52n165, 60,
60n204, 61n209, 157n3, 173-174, 180,
482, 482n328
Grotius, Hugo, 173n73, 348, 362n193
Guyer, Paul, 124n88

Habermas, Gary, 2n3, 3n10, 3n17, 6n28,
234n55, 298n132, 299n135, 353,
353n166, 477n300, 504n28, 504n29
Hades, 253n149. *Also see* Hell
Hadot, Pierre, 5n27, 6, 6n30, 10, 10n1, 10n2,
12, 13n13, 18, 18n36, 19n38, 130n111,
197n180
Haldane, J. B. S., 59, 202n203, 362n192, 363,
364n202, 447n150, 455n191, 458n199
Happiness, 13-17, 67, 69-71, 77, 79-85, 80n64,
82n73, 89, 90n102, 98-99, 190,
200n190, 228, 234, 245-246, 258-
259, 311-315, 311n2, 313n9, 316n20,
317, 319, 319n32, 321-322, 325-326,
326n56, 330-331, 333-335, 335n92,
339-341, 344, 346-347, 348n152,

340n119, 341, 341n122, 342n128, 343-
344, 347-348, 350, 372, 386-388, 391-
392, 396, 396n332, 401, 407-408, 425,
446-447, 501, 506-507, 509, 518
Ideas, 3n17, 5n28, 11-12, 14, 19, 22, 24, 24n9,
28, 29n23, 37n89, 40n105, 41, 47n140,
48n144, 59, 60n204, 68n5, 73, 73n30,
74n35, 74n37, 75, 75n40, 76n42,
76n43, 76n45, 77n47, 77n50, 87-89,
96, 98, 102-104, 102n6, 106, 108,
111, 114n46, 123, 126-127, 126n98,
130n111, 131, 133, 141n165, 141n166,
143, 144n176, 149, 152n215, 157n4,
163-164, 164n34, 165n39, 166, 172,
172n71, 174n79, 174n80, 178n99,
179n100, 180-181, 182n116, 183,
185n130, 187-188, 195n175, 196,
196n175, 208n225, 209n226, 210n234,
210n236, 211, 221-227, 229-231, 233,
237-238, 238n69, 239n71, 240-245,
248-249, 253-254, 253n149, 258n170,
260-262, 264, 267, 270, 272-275, 279-
281, 281n58, 284n70, 289, 290n93,
291n97, 297n125, 299n135, 303n147,
306, 306n167, 314-315, 321-322,
324n50, 329-331, 339n116, 350,
353n165, 355, 356n177, 360, 363, 368,
371n232, 372n234, 373n237, 374,
381n260, 386, 388, 396n332, 400, 403,
403n335, 409n379, 413n395, 423,
436n113, 448, 449n162, 463, 469,
472n273, 483, 489n362, 491n366,
492n370, 492n373, 493n376, 494n380,
493n381, 498, 500, 502n17, 502n18,
517n82, 518n88, 521
Ignorance, 44, 64, 128n103, 184, 188-189, 203,
288-289, 309, 311, 386-388, 390n303,
398, 398n336, 422n32, 445n142,
459n204, 491n366, 499, 506n35
Image, 55n181, 71n18, 82n71, 113n39, 120-
121, 120n68, 121n75, 124-126,
128n104, 129n110, 130n115, 136,
140n162, 142n171, 143, 145, 148,
152n217, 157, 157n5, 157n18, 178n98,
179n101, 189n147, 192, 196n175,
207n221, 229n39, 231n45, 234n56
237n65, 250n131, 253n145, 258-259,
262n187, 263n190, 268-270, 269n13,
270n21, 272, 272n29, 282n62, 284n70,
290n93, 292n100, 293n105, 296n122,
297n129, 302, 302n142, 305n160, 338,
382, 392n316, 395n327, 398, 398n339,
399n339, 408n374, 425, 428, 441-442,
441n133, 464, 472, 501, 501n10, 508,
511n63

Imagination, 3n13, 4-5, 4n719, 7, 39, 41, 48,
62n217, 78n52, 88, 103-104, 108-109,
111, 113-114, 117-127, 120n68, 130,
130n115, 132-133, 136-140, 137n144,
138n147, 139n152, 145, 146n184,
147-148, 150n210, 150n211, 151n213,
160, 160n21, 161n21, 162n28, 172,
205, 212, 222, 233, 242, 265, 270-
274, 270n20, 271n24, 272n30, 276,
281, 289-291, 291n97, 291n98, 301,
306n162, 318, 339, 339n115, 339n116,
359n183, 363n199, 382, 384n271, 392,
413n395, 501, 504n30, 512, 522n103,
524n110, 525n115, 529n130
Immanence, 187-188, 258, 260
Immaterial, 12, 12n8, 13n8, 31, 37, 124,
130n115, 271, 276, 290n93
Immortality / Immortal, 12-13, 39, 70, 72, 79,
90n102, 111, 120n66, 235, 248, 252,
255, 273, 322, 326-327, 326n56,
339n116, 344-345, 372n234, 395n327,
396n330, 428
Impassibility, 254, 261-263
Incarnation, 133, 143, 143n173, 147, 170,
207n221, 258, 472n273
Indeterminism, 334
Inferior, 114n46, 122, 139, 140n161, 190, 197,
228-229, 231, 234, 372, 393n321,
421n31, 429, 439, 468n254, 525n115
Injustice, 201n199, 358n178, 406-407, 430
Innate, 13, 69-70, 79, 92, 95, 273, 283, 304,
330-331, 355, 464n232
Instinct, 112, 138, 209, 271-272, 276, 364,
389n297, 427n72, 446
Integrity, 26-27, 39, 83, 176, 513n70
Intellect, 28, 48, 101, 108, 113, 117-118, 120,
120n68, 140, 148, 160, 173, 260,
265, 273-274, 276, 278n47, 281-282,
282n61, 285, 290-291, 303, 303n147,
307, 318, 360, 390, 393n321, 410n380,
468n254
Intention, 6, 37, 104, 168, 308, 316, 384, 398,
527
Interpretation / Interpret, 35, 57n191, 68n3,
131-132, 177n92, 223, 228n36, 253,
262, 270, 279, 297-298, 297n127, 306,
353, 356n174, 360n185, 380n258, 443
Introspection, 115n49, 174, 277, 279, 296,
297n125, 379n255
Intuition, 113, 113n39, 222, 273, 355
Ireland / Irish, 1, 52n167, 106, 107n17, 111,
155, 165-168, 167n46, 167n50, 167n51,
168n181, 201, 312, 419, 444-445, 448,
448n152, 474
Irrationality / Irrational, 17, 56, 59, 195, 212,

202, 204-206, 205n212, 205n214,
207n224, 219n8, 240, 240n74, 251,
264-267, 283n67, 285, 285n73, 292-
299, 293n104, 293n106, 293n107,
294n108, 294n109, 294n110, 294n111,
301, 303, 303n145, 303n147, 307, 309,
320n38, 341, 352n165, 327n237, 488,
493n377, 502, 511n62
Logical Positivism, 1, 204-206, 204n211,
205n214, 207n224, 208, 219n8, 265
Logos, 42, 102n6, 153, 267, 282, 520, 527n123
Loki, 25n20, 105-106, 106n13, 108, 313
Long, A. A., 287n80
Longaevi, 237, 237n66
Longfellow, Henry, 105
Longing, 3n16, 26, 69n8, 71-72, 72n25, 72n26,
79, 79n56, 81, 83, 90, 98, 116, 150,
265n1, 351n159, 375. *Also see* Heavenly
Desire
Love, 4n25, 5n28, 12, 15n22, 18, 27n31, 30,
32n66, 34n75, 41, 48n144, 50, 54-55,
54n177, 61, 63-64, 68n4, 69-71, 69n7,
69n8, 72n26, 77, 80, 80n64, 82n73,
86n85, 91n104, 103-104, 105n10,
107-108, 109n25, 110-112, 127-128,
129n110, 131-133, 131n117, 135,
140n161, 142n171, 146n185, 148,
155, 159n14, 159n17, 160n21, 161,
167, 170n58, 173, 175, 175n85, 181,
182n116, 183n120, 186n133, 187n138,
188, 196-197, 197n178, 201n199,
202, 205, 206n216, 207n222, 210,
211n237, 224, 229, 234n57, 235-236,
240, 241n78, 247, 250, 252n138,
254-255, 259n175, 260n179, 269n10,
274, 280n57, 283, 284n68, 292, 295-
297, 299, 302, 314-315, 325, 325n54,
326n56, 339, 341, 342n125, 345n136,
347, 349, 351n159, 357n178, 358n181,
359n183, 362n195, 370n230, 371n232,
374-377, 377n244, 378, 378n247,
378n249, 378n251, 378n252, 379n253,
380, 380n258, 380n259, 382n264,
383n271, 386-387, 390n303, 391n313,
392, 392n315, 394n323, 396n330, 401,
403, 404n357, 405n358, 405n360,
405n362, 406, 407n372, 407n373,
407n374, 408-410, 408n374, 410n380,
410n383, 413, 423, 424n53, 426n61,
428-429, 429n79, 430n84, 431n87,
438-440, 440n128, 440n130, 443,
446n147, 449n158, 474, 476, 497, 499,
499n7, 503n24, 511, 511n62, 516n78,
516n79, 518n86, 520n95, 521, 531
Lovell, Steve, 361n187

(Titus) Lucretius, Carus, 24-26, 25n16, 25n20,
28, 30, 68n5, 104, 106, 182, 284n70,
312-313, 313n7, 497, 497n2, 515n75,
526
Lucilius, Gaius, 16n23

Mabbott, John, 2n2, 47n140
Macaulay, Rose, 396n332
MacDonald, George, 63n225, 75, 78, 78n51,
108, 108n23, 118, 132, 141n168, 144,
144n175, 285, 285n72, 287, 315,
315n16, 350, 379n254, 388n295,
528n147
MacDonald, Michael, 302n143, 417n1, 418n4
Machin, G. I. T., 195n172
MacIntyre, Alasdair, 356, 356n175
Macpherson, C. B., 320n34
Macrobius, 129-132, 129n110, 130n112
Magdalen College, 2n8, 4n20, 42n115, 42n117,
44-45, 45n132, 48, 48n143, 48n144,
48n145, 50, 50n152, 60n208, 114n44,
158n7, 172n68, 320n36, 324n51,
385n279, 446n147, 478, 485-486,
485n347
Magdalene College, 193, 193n167, 512
Magic / Magical, 72, 81, 107, 107n17, 109n25,
112, 122n79, 144, 146-147, 177,
177n91, 200n191, 201-203, 201n197,
202n205, 237n65, 253n147, 264, 282,
283n66, 308n180, 309n184, 366n208,
369n215, 369n217, 383n270, 395n326,
396n329, 430n83, 449n163, 456n196,
457n197, 458n202, 464n231, 470n258,
473n280, 482, 492n371, 502, 502n17,
513n68, 526n117, 533
Magnanimity, 159, 408
Malory, Thomas, 32n66, 72, 315, 382, 407n374
Malvern College, 24, 24n12, 26, 172, 447n150,
474, 476, 505
Man, 1, 2n6, 3n16, 4n21, 13, 17, 19, 23, 26-28,
26n21, 31, 34, 36, 36n85, 36n86,
37n87, 38-39, 41, 44, 48n143, 49n150,
50-51, 51n163, 52n165, 52n167, 54,
54n175, 57, 57n191, 58n197, 61-62,
69-71, 69n7, 80n64, 84n76, 85, 86n85,
86n87, 92n109, 93-94, 93n114, 96-99,
97n132, 98n140, 101n2, 102, 108,
109n25, 118, 120n72, 126n98, 128,
131, 132n126, 134n131, 136, 137n144,
138-139, 141, 141n165, 148-149,
148n197, 150n212, 151-153, 155-157,
157n4, 157n6, 162, 162n28, 164-166,
164n33, 168, 171, 173-178, 173n74,
174n80, 181-182, 183n122, 184,
185n131, 186n136, 187-190, 189n144,

302, 308, 313, 315, 316n20, 316n22,
318n25, 322, 334, 336, 337n107, 338-
339, 339n116, 341, 347-348, 351n159,
351n161, 355, 357n178, 361, 363n198,
367, 369-370, 369n221, 370n229,
371n233, 371n234, 377n243, 379n252,
388-389, 389n297, 393n319, 395, 399,
400n342, 405n363, 409, 412, 419n21,
420n25, 423, 426n63, 427n72, 428,
428n74, 436n111, 437, 448, 449n158,
450n165, 451n173, 452n175, 453, 456,
458-459, 459n203, 460n207, 462n219,
463n226, 464, 469n256, 469n257, 472,
475, 486n352, 489, 491n368, 498, 501-
502, 501n12, 502n17, 507, 510n56,
511, 512n67, 516n78, 516n79, 521n98,
522n103, 523n105, 524, 532-533
Worldview, 3n11, 50, 51n163, 96, 120n68, 181,
225n27, 265n1, 301, 312n2
World Council of Churches, 185n129, 185n131
World War I / WWI, 30-31, 32n66, 32n67, 34,
109, 110n28, 166, 169n56, 197,
197n182, 210n235, 210n236, 315,
317n23, 384, 448, 462, 462n220, 475,
498
World War II / WWII, 191n155, 192n157, 201,
210, 366n209, 422n35, 424, 430n86,
448, 463, 484, 488
Worship, 36, 36n86, 107, 143, 145, 168,
207n221, 326n56, 328, 360-362,
362n193, 371n233, 379n253, 403n355,
405, 413, 413n395, 516n78
Wrong, Charles, 460n208, 483, 483n340
Wynyard School, 25, 313n10, 465n240, 474
Wyvern. *See* Malvern College

Yeats, William Butler, 32n66, 90n102, 106,
107n16, 107n17, 112, 177
Ymir, 110

Zeno of Citium, 15
Zeus, 105, 129n106, 255, 313, 313n5, 384

Other Zossima Press Titles

C. S. Lewis

C. S. Lewis: Views From Wake Forest
Michael Travers, editor

Contains sixteen scholarly presentations from the international C. S. Lewis convention in Wake Forest, NC. Walter Hooper shares his important essay "Editing C. S. Lewis," a chronicle of publishing decisions after Lewis' death in 1963. Other contributors include James Como and Sanford Schwartz.

"Scholars from a variety of disciplines address a wide range of issues. The happy result is a fresh and expansive view of an author who well deserves this kind of thoughtful attention." Diana Pavlac Glyer, author of *The Company They Keep: C. S. Lewis and J.R.R. Tolkien as Writers in Community.*

Why I Believe in Narnia:
33 Essays & Reviews on the Life & Work of C. S. Lewis
By James Como

Chapters range from reviews of critical books, documentaries and movies to evaluations of Lewis's books to biographical analysis. In addition to close-up looks, Como reflects on the "big picture" of the most important contributions Lewis has made, not just in literature, but as a social philosopher and reformer. An invaluable tool for appreciating the breadth and depth of Lewis' thinking.

"A valuable, wide-ranging collection of essays by one of the best informed and most astute commentators on Lewis' work and ideas." Peter Schakel, author *Imagination & the Arts in C. S. Lewis*

The Library Jack Built:
A Comprehensive Listing of C. S. Lewis' Personal Library
By Roger White *(January 2010 publication)*

This book traces the dispersal of C. S. Lewis' personal library following his death in 1963. The acquisition history is detailed and the books are listed. User-friendly bibliographic listing is coded by collection location and presented in two forms: first alphabetically by author and then grouped by subject. Two appendices are included that list books originally in, or believed to have been in, Lewis' library that are currently unaccounted for in terms of location, owner, or provenance. Devotees and scholars of Lewis will appreciate *The Library that Jack Built* for the insight it provides into the books that captured and shaped this much loved and influential man.

George MacDonald

Diary of an Old Soul & The White Page Poems
George MacDonald and Betty Aberlin

In 1880, George MacDonald, the Scottish poet, novelist and preacher, published *A Book of Strife in the Form of the Diary of an Old Soul*. The first edition of this book of daily poems included a blank page opposite each page of poems. Readers were invited to write their own reflections on the "white page." MacDonald wrote: "Let your white page be ground, my print be seed, growing to golden ears, that faith and hope may feed." Betty Aberlin responded to MacDonald's invitation with daily poems of her own.

Betty Aberlin's close readings of George MacDonald's verses and her thoughtful responses to them speak clearly of her poetic gifts and spiritual intelligence.   Luci Shaw, poet

George MacDonald: Literary Heritage and Heirs
Roderick McGillis

It has been 15 years since Roderick McGillis edited *For the Childlike*, a landmark collection of essays about George MacDonald's writings. This latest collection of 14 essays sets a new standard that will influence MacDonald studies for many more years. George MacDonald experts are increasingly evaluating his entire corpus within the nineteenth century context. This volume provides further evidence that MacDonald will eventually emerge from the restrictive and somewhat misleading reputation of being C. S. Lewis' spiritual "master."

This comprehensive collection represents the best of contemporary scholarship on George MacDonald.   Rolland Hein, author of *George MacDonald: Victorian Mythmaker*.

In the Near Loss of Everything: George MacDonald's Son in America
Dale Wayne Slusser

In the summer of 1887, George MacDonald's son Ronald, newly engaged to artist Louise Blandy, sailed from England to America to teach school. The next summer he returned to England to marry Louise and bring her back to America. On August 27, 1890, Louise died leaving him with an infant daughter. Ronald once described losing a beloved spouse as "the near loss of everything". Dale Wayne Slusser unfolds this poignant story with unpublished letters and photos that give readers a glimpse into the close-knit MacDonald family. Also included is Ronald's essay about his father, *George MacDonald: A Personal Note*, plus a selection from Ronald's 1922 fable, *The Laughing Elf*, about the necessity of both sorrow and joy in life.

Harry Potter

Harry Potter & Imagination:
The Way Between Two Worlds
Travis Prinzi

"What we achieve inwardly will change outer reality." Those words, written by Plutarch and quoted by J.K. Rowling her 2008 Harvard commencement speech, sum up both the importance of the *Harry Potter* series and the argument of Travis Prinzi's analysis of the best-selling books in *Harry Potter & Imagination: The Way Between Two Worlds*. Imaginative literature places a reader between two worlds: the story world and the world of daily life, and challenges this reader to imagine and to act for a better world. Starting with discussion of Harry Potter's more important themes, *Harry Potter & Imagination* takes readers on a journey through the transformative power of those themes for both the individual and for culture by placing Rowling's series in its literary, historical, and cultural contexts.

Deathly Hallows Lectures
John Granger

In *The Deathly Hallows Lectures*, John Granger reveals the finale's brilliant details, themes and meanings. Even the most ardent of *Harry Potter* fans will be surprised by and delighted with the Granger's explanations of the three dimensions of meaning in *Deathly Hallows*. Ms. Rowling has said that alchemy sets the "parameters of magic" in the series; after reading the chapter-length explanation of *Deathly Hallows* as the final stage of the alchemical Great Work, the serious reader will understand how important literary alchemy is in understanding Rowling's artistry and accomplishment.

Repotting Harry Potter:
A Professor's Book-by-Book Guide for the Serious Re-Reader
James Thomas

A professor of literature for over thirty years, Dr. James W. Thomas takes us on a tour through the *Potter* books in order to enjoy them in different ways upon subsequent readings. Re-readers will be pleasantly surprised at what they may have missed in the books and at what secrets Rowling has hidden for us to uncover as we revisit these stories. The professor's informal discussions focus on puns, humor, foreshadowing, literary allusions, narrative techniques, and other aspects of the *Potter* books that are hard-to-see on the hurried first or fifth reading. Dr. Thomas's light touch proves that a "serious" reading of literature can be fun.

Printed in the USA
CPSIA information can be obtained
at www.ICGtesting.com
LVHW091547181223
766789LV00003B/9

9 780972 322164